Latin America since Independence

What is Latin America, after all? While histories of the "other" Americas often link disparate histories through revolutionary or tragic narratives, *Latin America since Independence* begins with the assumption that our efforts to imagine a common past for nearly thirty countries are deeply problematic. Without losing sight of chronology or regional trends, this text offers glimpses of the Latin American past through carefully selected stories. Each chapter introduces students to a specific historical issue, which in turn raises questions about the history of the Americas as a whole. Key themes include:

- Race and Citizenship
- Inequality and Economic Development
- Politics and Rights
- Social and Cultural Movements
- Globalization
- Violence and Civil Society

The short, thematic chapters are bolstered by the inclusion of relevant primary documents—many translated for the first time—including advertisements and posters, song lyrics, political speeches, government documents, and more. Each chapter also includes timelines highlighting important dates and suggestions for further reading. Richly informative and highly readable, *Latin America since Independence* provides compelling accounts of this region's past and present.

This second edition brings the story up to the present, with revised chapters, new primary documents and images, and a new 'At A Glance' feature that uses a selection of maps and tables to illuminate key issues like the economy, the environment, and demographics.

For additional information and classroom resources please visit the *Latin America since Independence* companion website at **www.routledge.com/cw/dawson**.

Alexander Dawson is Professor of Latin American History at Simon Fraser University, in British Columbia, Canada. He is the author of *First World Dreams: Mexico since 1989* and *Indian and Nation in Revolutionary Mexico*.

Latin America since Independence

A History with Primary Sources

2nd Edition

ALEXANDER DAWSON

Routledge
Taylor & Francis Group

NEW YORK AND LONDON

Second edition published 2015
by Routledge
711 Third Avenue, New York, NY 10017

and by Routledge
2 Park Square, Milton Park, Abingdon, Oxon OX14 4RN

Routledge is an imprint of the Taylor & Francis Group, an informa business

© 2015 Taylor & Francis

The right of Alexander Dawson to be identified as author of this work has been asserted by him/her in accordance with sections 77 and 78 of the Copyright, Designs and Patents Act 1988.

First edition published in 2011 by Taylor and Francis

Library of Congress Cataloging-in-Publication Data

Dawson, Alexander S. (Alexander Scott), 1967–
    Latin America since independence : a history with primary sources / Alexander Dawson. — 2nd edition.
        pages cm
    Includes bibliographical references and index.
    1. Latin America—History—1830—Textbooks.   2. Latin America—History—1830—Sources.   I. Title.
    F1413.D39   2014
    980.03—dc23
    2014003909

ISBN: 978-0-415-85436-8 (hbk)
ISBN: 978-0-415-85437-5 (pbk)
ISBN: 978-0-203-74402-4 (ebk)

Typeset in Dante
by Apex CoVantage, LLC

Contents

Illustrations

Figures

Tables

At A Glance Illustrations

Acknowledgments

The ideas that ultimately became this book began percolating a very long time ago, when as a student of Latin American History, I had the good fortune to be taught by Christon Archer, Paul Gootenberg, Brooke Larson, Barbara Weinstein, Fred Weinstein, and Gene Lebovics, teachers who never failed to insist that however much I strived to understand this region, there was always more work to do. As a teacher of Latin America's past, I am similarly indebted to my students, who over the years collectively pushed me to provide them with access to the best that my field has to offer, and deliver that knowledge in a way that they find relevant and compelling. I have done my best here to meet all your expectations.

I received specific help in this project from Mónica Amaré, Santiago Anria, Dain Borges, Gaston Gordillo, José Gordillo, Adrian López Denis, Martín Monsalve, Timo Schaeffer, Richard Slatta, Perry Stein, Hannah Wittman, and Wendy Wolford. Even more critical was the patient and constant advice I received from Alejandra Bronfman and Jon Beasley-Murray, who suggested many of the documents and offered valuable critiques of every aspect of the book. Alejandra also read the entire manuscript, improving it considerably in the process. At Routledge, I have enjoyed the generous support of numerous individuals. Kimberly Guinta oversaw both the first and second editions. Nicole Solano and Angela Chnapko steered the book through the first production process, and Genevieve Aoki the second. Patricia Rosas, Diane Grosklaus Whitty, Robert A. Forstag, Laura F. Temes, Elizabeth Medina, and Marina Soldati provided excellent translations of several texts.

And of course, my warmest thanks are to Maia, Nina, and Alejandra, for giving me a reason to turn off the computer.

I would also like to thank the following academic reviewers whose anonymous suggestions during the reviewing process helped me greatly as I prepared the book:

Onur Bakiner, Simon Fraser University
Francisco Barbosa, University of Colorado Zach Brittsan, Texas Tech University
Marc Becker, Truman State University
Millagros Denis, Hunter College
John J. Dwyer, Duquesne University

Mary Karasch, Oakland University
Andrew Kirkendall, Texas A&M University
Peter Klaren, George Washington University
Richard Kotter, Northumbria University
Kris Lane, College of William & Mary
Mollie Lewis, University of South Alabama
Rosa Maria Pegueros-Lev, University of Rhode Island
Bryan McCann, Georgetown University
Jocelyn Olcott, Duke University
Charles F. Walker, University of California-Davis
Elliott Young, Lewis & Clark College

Abbreviations

ABI: Bolivian Information Agency (*Agencia Boliviana de Información*)—Bolivia

AJR: Association of Rebel Youth (*Asociación de Juventud Rebelde*)—Cuba

ALBA: Bolivarian Alternative for Latin America and the Caribbean (*Alternativa Bolivariana para America Latina y El Caribe*)

ANAP: National Small Farmers Association (*Asociación Nacional de Agricultores Pequeños*)—Cuba

APRA: American Popular Revolutionary Alliance (*Alianza Popular Revolucionaria Americana*)—Peru

CDR: Committees for the Defense of the Revolution (*Comités de Defensa de la Revolución*)—Cuba

CGT: General Confederation of Labor (*Confederación General del Trabajo*)—Argentina

CIA: Central Intelligence Agency—United States of America

CONADEP: National Commission on the Disappearance of Persons (*Comisión Nacional sobre la Desaparición de Personas*)—Argentina

CONAIE: Confederation of Indigenous Nationalities of Ecuador (*Confederación de Nacionalidades Indígenas del Ecuador*)

CPBs: Pro-Bolivia Councils (*Consejos Pro-Bolivianos*)—Bolivians residing in Europe

CSUTCB: Bolivian Confederation of Rural Workers (*Confederación Sindical Unica de Trabajadores Campesinos de Bolivia*)—Bolivia

CTC: Cuban Workers Confederation (*Central de Trabajadores de Cuba*)—Cuba

EZLN: Zapatista Army of National Liberation (*Ejercito Zapatista de Liberación Nacional*)—Mexico

FAO: Food and Agriculture Organization of the United Nations

FDR: Franklin Delano Roosevelt—thirty-second president of the United States of America

FEP: Eva Perón Foundation (*Fundación Eva Perón*)—Argentina

FMC: Cuban Federation of Women (*Federación de Mujeres Cubanas*)—Cuba

FORA: Argentine Regional Worker's Federation (*Federación Obrera Regional Argentina*)—Argentina

FTAA: Free Trade Area of the Americas

GDP: Gross Domestic Product
HDI: Human Development Index
IMF: International Monetary Fund
IRCA: International Railroads of Central America
ISI: Import Substitution Industrialization
MAS: Movement Towards Socialism (*Movimiento al Socialismo*)—Bolivia
MCAS: Consular Identification Cards (*Matriculas Consulares de Alta Seguridad*)—Mexico
MERCOSUR: Southern Common Market (*Mercado Común del Sur; Mercado Comum do Sul*)—
    Argentina, Brazil, Paraguay, Uruguay
MFI: Multilateral Financial Institution
MIR: Revolutionary Left Movement (*Movimiento de la Izquierda Revolucionaria*)—Bolivia
MNR: Nationalist Revolutionary Movement (*Movimiento Nacionalista Revolucionario*)—
    Bolivia
NAFTA: North American Free Trade Agreement—Canada, Mexico, United States
NGO: Non-Governmental Organization
NIC: Newly Industrialized Country
OAS: Organization of American States
PAN: National Action Party (*Partido de Acción Nacional*)—Mexico
PCS: Political Constitution of the State—Bolivia
PDVSA: *Petróleos de Venezuela*—Venezuela
PEMEX: *Petróleos Mexicanos*—Mexico
PIC: Independent Party of Color (*Partido Independiente de Color*)—Cuba
PRI: Institutional Revolutionary Party (*Partido Revolucionario Institucional*)—Mexico
SIN: National Intelligence Service (*Servicio Nacional de Inteligencia*)—Peru
UCR: Radical Civic Union (*Unión Cívica Radical*)—Argentina
UDP: Democratic and Popular Unity (*Unidad Democrática y Popular*)—Bolivia
UFCO: United Fruit Company—United States of America
UN: United Nations
USAID: United States Agency for International Development—United States of America

Introduction

Latin America's Useable Past

Strolling through Mexico City's Parque Lincoln on any given Sunday, it is easy to forget the world beyond this small bit of paradise. Motorized toy boats meander around the small pond. The water is clean and inviting. Children run around and laugh inside the high fences of a public playground that puts most North American parks to shame. The mouth-watering smells of Argentine and Italian bistros waft through the air, reminding you that you are in the heart of Polanco, one of the nicest neighborhoods in the city. Surrounding art deco apartment buildings provide a sense of safe and comfortable living, while the *belle époque* grandeur of the nearby Ford Foundation mansion evokes both a wealthy past and a beneficent present. People are out and about, seemingly unafraid. Bicycles abound, evidence that some of those eating lunch by the park took advantage of the relatively new practice of closing down the Paseo de la Reforma (this city's great nineteenth-century boulevard) on Sunday mornings so that people may ride, run, or walk from Chapultepec Park to the Zocalo.[1] No one here seems to mind that the greening of Sunday mornings has brought an end to the tradition of holding protest marches at this same time, along this same route.

Sundays tell a different story in Ecatepec, just a few short miles away. Many residents here are at work, in locations across the metropolis, selling in the informal and formal sector, driving busses and taxis, cleaning, working in shops, earning the few pesos upon which they depend for their survival. Open-air stalls sell tacos, *dulces* (sweets), and any number of treats, but the table-cloths are made of plastic, not linen. Children play in largely neglected parks, many of them decades old, where instead of falling to a rubberized mat the unlucky toddler hits the pavement with a thud when tumbling from a swing. Here and there one also sees the tragic signs of a discarded childhood, youths splayed out on cardboard mats, their minds lost in a haze produced by thinners or cement, homeless, desperate. The smell of diesel fuel is stronger here, the dust in the air more present, the result of untended roads, construction sites, and the paucity of trees and grass. Few people here rode bicycles on the Paseo de la Reforma this morning.

At times these two versions of Mexico City seem unknown to one other. This is a survival strategy on the part of both. While the crossings are continual (poor people sustain communities like Polanco through their labor and consumption, and the wages paid by

Polcano residents allow the poor in Ecatepec to survive), a certain amount of blindness allows residents of both communities some peace of mind. Poor people stay out of rich neighborhoods, for the most part, when they are not at work, as life is easier and the violence and powerlessness of everyday life less jarring when one stays closer to home or in more welcoming locales. They know their neighbors, often look out for one another, and feel somehow safer in their own community. The wealthy, for their part, are just as jarred by their adventures into the slums. They are not welcome there, and are more content when they can imagine that the world beyond their own neighborhoods does not really exist. One might describe this as a kind of fragmentary consciousness, in which residents of both Ecatepec and Polanco carefully shape their view of the world to make daily life in the city viable. Whenever possible, phenomena that are too difficult to confront must be made invisible.

The fragmentary nature of life in the metropolis reminds us that we need to go beyond the lines drawn on a map to understand the boundaries that we use to make sense of the world around us. In North America, we might call a person Mexican, perhaps Latin American, or even *Latino* or *Chicano*[2] if he or she comes from Mexico City, but do these designations really tell us much about a person or their place of origin? Do they even tell us if a person identifies with a shared community, or what that community might be? Residents of Polanco and Ecatepec may all be Mexicans to the wider world, and *chilangos*[3] in the eyes of other Mexicans, and may even be mutually dependent on one another, but it is not at all clear that they imagine themselves as residents of a common city or that they share common interests. It is equally difficult to weave them into a common history.

A Common Past

History found itself in the curriculum of public schools in the nineteenth century precisely because it seemed like an ideal tool for producing communities. Historians were charged with writing national histories, stories that explained who we are through reference to where we came from. Nationalist histories proliferated in the former colonies of the Americas during this era, as local intellectuals endeavored to give shape to their nations through reference to the ancient indigenous past, colonial society, and the glorious quest for independence. Often written by prominent politicians, these histories served as foundational narratives for the post-colonial states of the Americas, proof that they had every right to stand apart from their former rulers.

Latin America was invented in the process. The term was first proposed by the Colombian José María Caicedo in the mid-nineteenth century to describe former colonies in the Americas whose languages shared a common origin, grouping French-, Spanish-, and Portuguese-speaking regions in the hemisphere together.[4] Others adopted the term soon thereafter, sometimes in an effort to simplify a collection of nearly thirty countries for outsiders, and sometimes because the idea of Latin America offered a vision of strength through unity. Reformers and revolutionaries have long embraced the ideal of a united Latin America that could stand up to the power of both Europe and the United States. In order to make their case, they invariably turned to history, producing narratives that create a common Latin American past as precursor to a single future.

There is real power in the story. In crafting a Latin American past, we have the opportunity to justify or critique existing power structures, to offer a vision of greater or lesser
unity, and to help shape the region's relationship to the outside world. This indeed is the
reason that local elites began writing national and regional histories in the eighteenth century. The nations they described were then mostly an illusion, conjured up from the ancient
indigenous past and their own sense of personal injustice. Still, they offered a compelling
vision of a common past that could in turn presage a common future.

Today, the same impulse remains. Because we want to describe something we call Latin
America, we produce narratives that somehow connect vast and diverse peoples to a common community. We choose a specific place, incident, or person, and somehow describe
them in ways that suggest that they speak for some larger Latin American experience—a
part standing in for the whole. Alternately, we rely on other narrative devices, making sense
of Latin America through dramas about good versus evil, stories of backwardness and
progress or the primitive and the modern,[5] or equally odd narratives of cultural sameness
(they are really no different than us). Latin America thus becomes legible because we tell its
history through reference to other familiar stories.

We might, for instance, introduce the wealthy residents of Polanco as models of civilization or capitalist fat-cats. Residents of Ecatepec then become ignorant drug-abusers who re-
inscribe their own poverty through their lifestyles, or oppressed revolutionaries in waiting.
Linked to nationalist narratives, romantic or tragic stories about these individuals remind
us that all Mexicans, as Octavio Paz once suggested, are children of *la Malinche*.[6] And, if we
want to suggest even grander commonalities, we might mention the Dora and Spiderman
backpacks that one sees in both places in order to convince the reader that, as participants
in global mass cultural phenomena, children are the same, wherever you go. The narrative
is yours to choose, and reveals little more than your own ideological preferences.

History, as Michel-Rolph Trouillot reminds us, is not what happened, but is what is said
about what happened.[7] The stories we tell are invariably limited by the incompleteness of
the historical record, and its tendency to reflect the views of those whose power allows
them to leave traces of their lives in archives, libraries, and private collections. Out of these
materials historians of Latin America tend to produce two types of narratives. The first,
the grand story of change over time, endeavors to look at the way that phenomena like
colonialism, capitalism, demographic, and environmental change offer broad explanations
for why Latin America has taken a specific historical path.[8] Social history, economic history,
even political history tend to be rooted in these larger explanations, and at various points in
this text play an important role in considering the broad transformations Latin Americans
have experienced since Independence.

These powerful, broad explanations come at a price. In narratives that cover a century
or more, we lose the opportunity to consider the ways in which specific historical moments
are singular unto themselves and to understand the ways that large sweeping narratives
often speak as much to our desire to make sense of a past that may, in fact, be incoher-
ent. These narratives also sacrifice a close reading of the fragmentary historical record, a
reading that might shed important light on the ways that people lived within the political,
social and other forces that shaped their lives. These particular stories can offer insight into
the ways that power was arranged different places and times, insights about the values,
beliefs, and assumptions (things we often call culture) that animated daily life. What we

learn about ourselves from these moments is often as significant as what we learn in grand historical narratives.[9] We see, for instance, the ways that assumptions about race, class, and gender influenced the arrangement of power in discrete moments, the ways that inclusionary and exclusionary practices constituted specific social, economic, and political terrains. We are also confronted with the problems of agency in those moments.

Agency—that is, an individual's capacity to be an agent for change or stasis—is a key concern of both the grand and the particular narratives of the Latin American past.[10] Do broad historical forces (say, global capitalism) overwhelm individual agency, so that we are simply cogs in a machine whose gears cannot be stopped? Are we the subjects of systems of power so overwhelming and diffuse that we cannot change them?[11] Do visionary figures make history, bending events to their will (Fidel Castro?), or are they produced by the events that they seem to control? And what of contingency? Do unexpected political and social forces come together in unpredictable moments to change the course of history (the masses, or multitude[12]), prompted not by predictable motivations but by forces and habits[13] that by their very nature defy control and organization? Is history a straightforward and predictable unfolding of events, or is it a shambles, something that only has the order we impose on it?

These issues matter a great deal to historians of Latin America, in part because this region has long been the subject of a series of grand historical projects, suggesting that, at heart, Latin America is a problem in need of a solution. Simón Bolívar was one of the first to make this claim, insisting that the region needed to build a strong unified front lest it be swallowed by the emergent United States. The nineteenth and twentieth centuries saw countless others who, in one way or another, echoed his concerns. Latin America was too unequal, too poor, too "underdeveloped." At times these complaints took a darker turn, suggesting that Latin America had a cultural problem (too Catholic, too Spanish) or a racial problem (too African, too indigenous). These meta explanations approach the region based on broad assumptions that make Latin America a problem to be solved instead of a region whose multiple histories are not easily reducible to problems and solutions, and whose experience might inform the way we view our own past and present.

It may be that the very project of trying to tell the story of the Latin American past as a common history forces these types of short-hand, as efforts to keep this vast region in the frame seem to invariably require a series of intellectual tricks. This is why this book turns instead to the idea of the fragment as a means of exploring the Latin American past. This concept informs this text in two ways. We begin by acknowledging that lived experience in this part of the world is fragmentary. Proximity does not always mean that different communities and individuals in the region share a common sense of the past or the present, let alone the future. Second, the concept of the fragment informs the way we approach the past itself. In writing history, we take small bits and pieces of experience and transform them into a narrative. No history can be an exhaustive rendering of the past, so we must decide which fragments we will privilege and which story we will tell. In doing so we also reveal the extent to which history is a story about the past told in order to justify the present or make a claim on the future, and not simply a naïve arrangement of facts, an unvarnished truth.

Fragmentation does not speak to an absence of nations or nationalism. Latin Americans embrace their national soccer teams, join together in the veneration of national symbols, and celebrate national holidays. Yet these practices do not erase the deep divisions found here, divisions that are rooted in centuries of experience. When celebrating the victories of their national soccer teams, poor Latin Americans sometimes turn against their more wealthy compatriots. They might venerate some of the same heroes, but often do so in idiosyncratic ways. If we were to ask ten Venezuelans to describe Simón Bolívar's values, we might receive several radically different answers. The same would be true were we to ask ten Mexicans about their great national hero, Emiliano Zapata. Even Roman Catholicism, which was once thought to be the cultural practice that linked all people of the region, is practiced in highly particular ways from one community to the next. Every time we offer a single rendering of Catholicism, Zapata or Bolívar, we tell one version of the past as the Latin American past. In doing so we privilege one set of voices while silencing others.

This text seeks a way out of that dilemma by proposing a fragmentary history of Latin America. The following chapters do not purport to render a single Latin American past. They are instead offered merely as a collection of eleven stories from that past. While chronologically ordered, and chosen because they are among the stories that Latin American historians generally consider important, they were also selected because each story defies easy narration. The stories told here do not offer authoritative ways of understanding an episode from the Latin American past so much as they suggest that each story could be told in multiple ways. Neither do they connect seamlessly or easily into a single narrative about Latin America. It would seem that many of these accounts are connected. We leave it to the reader to decide the nature and significance of these links.

We begin our effort to consider Latin America as both a region embedded in long-term historical processes and a collection of fragmentary experiences by confronting the difficulties faced when we attempt to describe independence in the early nineteenth century (Chapter 1). This is in some ways an arbitrary choice, as independence was a political act that did not dramatically change the lives of most people in the region. It was however significant in the creation of an idea of Latin America, and its meanings and implications for the Latin American future remain the subject of debate today. Chapter 2 introduces the *caudillo*, a mythical military figure who is sometimes blamed for centuries of political strife in the region, but whom others have always seen as a complex, even heroic defender of common people. Even if we describe *caudillos* generally, they are best understood in very specific terms.

Chapter 3 begins with a general concern; it introduces us to the question of what individual freedom meant in societies that had long relied on the forced labor of slaves and indigenous peoples for their prosperity. Independence promised a series of freedoms, and, during the nineteenth century, those freedoms gradually expanded to include all male citizens across the region. Nonetheless, lingering colonial attitudes and scientific racism also conditioned the rights and privileges that non-whites enjoyed. We see here a variety of struggles, not the least of which were the efforts of the newly free to defend their citizenship rights.

Chapters 4 and 5 explore two ways of narrating a single period in the Latin American past. The export boom of the late nineteenth and early twentieth centuries saw similar efforts across the region to create communities predicated on common values, in this instance shared faith in the nineteenth-century version of progress. Electric trams, railways, and booming exports came to signify a modern Latin America, even as millions of rural and poor people experienced modernity as the violent loss of their freedom and well-being. Through these chapters we see the possibility of narrating this period simultaneously as triumph and tragedy.

Latin America's twentieth-century history was similarly framed by global phenomena that played out in distinctly local ways. The United States cast a long shadow on the internal affairs of many societies in the region during the past century, but in ways that defy easy characterization (Chapter 6). Some viewed the United States as an imperial hegemon, living off the blood and sweat of the Latin American poor. Others admired the United States for its technological innovations, economic progress, and capacity to trade globally. At various points, American-made products were eagerly consumed across the region, often desired both for their quality and for the ways they suggested good taste on the part of the consumer. Then as now, Latin Americans had an unsettled relationship with the United States. The United States is easily the most commonly mentioned enemy of the Latin American people. It is also the destination of choice for the vast majority of migrants who leave the region.

Other episodes from the twentieth-century history of Latin America consider the rise of mass politics and its relationship to Import Substitution Industrialization (ISI) in the 1930s and 1940s (Chapter 7), the Cuban revolution (Chapter 8), the Dirty Wars (Chapter 9), and the emergence of a new lexicon of rights with the end of the Dirty Wars and its connection to global technological changes since the 1970s (Chapter 10). Many of these phenomena were transnational. The rise of broadcast media, the intensification of cold-war hostilities after 1959, and the growing influence of rights-based non-governmental organizations (NGOs) beginning in the 1980s were all global phenomena. This might lead us to propose a common Latin American (or even larger) experience. And then again, it is also possible that the connections we see in these experiences are imposed from the outside, that it is more important that we understand the specific local ways that each of these developments played out in the latter half of the twentieth century.

We conclude with an eye to the future and the past in Chapter 11, which draws from Albert O. Hirschman's *Exit, Voice, and Loyalty* to consider the interlocked experiences of political and economic upheaval since the 1980s. Latin Americans, like people in much of the world, have gone through successive crises since the end of the era of ISI, sometimes rooted in economic challenges, but just as often tied to political, social, and even environmental issues. At the same time, those crises have been accompanied by other developments that suggest that in some ways, things have never been better for the people of Latin America. Extreme poverty across the region has fallen substantially since the 1980s, and, as a whole, the region has never been more democratic than it is today. Nonetheless, for reasons that remain the subject of debate, the capacity of Latin American states to command loyalty from their citizens may be weaker today than it has ever been. Multiple varieties of exit, coupled with a variety of iterations of voice, place Latin American at the forefront of the conflicts that confront our global community today.

It is easy to make sense of these conflicts by making them into stories of good versus evil. Today this is common, as opposing groups demonize one another in order to justify their demands for change or stasis. Interestingly, the power of their antipathies (if not their specific demands) resonates with the ways that residents of Polanco and Ecatepec often view one another (when they view one another at all), each with a hostility that imagines the other as the cause of their problems. At various points in the Latin American past, any number of individuals and communities have been subjected to this kind of scorn.

My hope is that the stories contained in this text make it more difficult to demonize the people lunching in Polanco, the marginalized poor of Ecatepec, or for that matter, anyone whose story is told here. The text aims to instead offer some insight into the complexities of daily life in this part of the world as we enter a challenging period in the early twenty-first century. Latin Americans live in a fragmentary present, which is a product of their fragmentary past.

The Documents: A User's Guide

The chapters in this book represent one type of story about the past. The documents that accompany these chapters are another. Traces of a specific moment in time, they offer readers the voices of witnesses to history, individuals who record their views because they want to shape the way we understand the past and the present.

The chapters and the documents are complementary, though imperfectly so. Both the documents and the essays provide information, though that is not their primary task. They are interpretations, and as such readers are encouraged to examine them critically. As much as possible, they are not excerpted (where they are, the entire text generally can be found on the book's website, www.routledge.com/cw/dawson). Excerpting is a form of editing, in which someone other than the creator of a text determines what is significant about that text before it reaches the reader. Access to the entire text, changed only by the act of trans-lation, offers readers the opportunity to develop their own interpretations, allowing them to more fully participate in the process of making history.

In some cases I provide preliminary questions that might be useful in reading the docu-ments (more questions can be found on the book's website), though, for the most part, the documents are introduced in a manner that is sufficiently open-ended to allow readers to approach them with their own interests and questions. My intention is to allow these, like all historical documents, to be read in multiple ways. They can be read simply as interest-ing commentaries, or they can be approached as lenses into specific times, places, and as opportunities to understand the worldviews and desires of their creators. We learn more by imagining the multiple ways that these texts can be read than we do by imagining that there is *one* correct reading. This will allow the reader to produce their own version of the past, to do their own historical thinking.

But what does historical thinking look like? This is a question that arises again and again in contemporary society. We justify so much of what we do through reference to the past (it was always this way, or historical precedent justifies present action), yet in many ways we live in historically illiterate times. These documents are meant to address historical literacy in certain ways. We begin by attempting to situate the documents in time, by endeavoring simply to understand how people in the past made sense of their worlds. After this, we must consider the question of change over time. How have things changed since then? What does it mean that they have changed? How can we situate our present beliefs and practices in historical context? Can we judge the past using the same values we invoke in judging the present? Can we understand the past in ways that do not simply justify our present views?

Some of the documents we use for this task are widely regarded as classics. José Martí's *Our America*, Emiliano Zapata's *Plan de Ayala*, and Augusto Sandino's *Political Manifesto* have been read by generations of students as important historical texts. Others are familiar mainly to specialists, though within the various sub fields of Latin American history they are generally perceived as significant texts. Drawn from letters, short stories, speeches, manifestos, personal memoirs, newspaper editorials, newsreels, and films, the documents introduce readers to a multitude of ways of understanding the past, a range of story-telling techniques, and a significant number of interpretive dilemmas. In the end, they remind readers that history is not simply culled from documents, but is an act of interpretation built upon an act of interpretation. For those who want to delve even further into these questions, the book's website includes links to and copies of other documents that might be of interest.

Some years ago, my students became increasingly interested in the concept of bias. Driven by a larger public debate on objectivity in journalism,[14] they came into the classroom with a desire to distinguish the unvarnished truth from that which was somehow tainted by the values and beliefs of the interlocutor. Many left my classroom disappointed when I agreed with them that historians were biased, though I disagreed with them when they asserted that the absence of bias (as they conceived it) was possible. I told them that these texts, like all texts, were written from a perspective, and that one of the things that historians do is examine the ways that our narratives are influenced by the perspectives we and our historical subjects bring to the text. I insisted that there were many potential truths to be found in the Latin America past, and not one unbiased truth waiting to be discovered. I then encouraged them to take this insight about the past and apply it to their understandings of the Latin American present. It is my hope that the present text contributes to that endeavor.

1717–1790s	1780–1781	1791–1804	1807–1808	April 19, 1810	May 1810
Bourbon reforms	Túpac Amaru rebellion in Andes	Haitian revolution	Napoleon invades Iberian Peninsula, installs his brother on Spanish throne	Cabildo of Caracas deposes Spanish governor, establishes Caracas Junta	Revolution in Argentina

August 24, 1821	September 7, 1822	August 6, 1825	1829–1830
Treaty of Córdoba recognizes Mexican independence	Pedro, son of Portuguese King, declares Brazilian independence and is Crowned emperor of Brazil in December	Bolivian independence	Dissolution of Gran Colombia

Independence Narratives, Past and Present

September 16, 1810	December 15, 1812	1815	July 9, 1816	February–July, 1819	July 28, 1821
Grito de Dolores by Father Miguel Hidalgo (Mexico)	Simón Bolívar announces support of independence in Cartagena Manifesto	Brazil made co-kingdom with Portugal	Congress of Tucumán declares Argentine independence	Congress of Angostura leads to creation of Gran Colombia	Peruvian Declaration of Independence. Struggles with royalist forces would continue until 1824

The Shot Heard Round the World
Was the Start of the Revolution
The Minutemen were Ready
On the Move[1]

In what seems like the stone age of television, millions of North American schoolchildren once spent their Saturday mornings watching *Schoolhouse Rock*, a series of public service announcements that occasionally interrupted their cartoons. They learned about grammar, math, civics, and science from the program. They were also subjected to a series of lessons about a seminal moment in the national past. The best among the history lessons, the "Shot Heard Round the World," was a delightfully entertaining rendering of Paul Revere's ride, in which children learned that "we" kicked out the British Redcoats in order to "let freedom reign." It was also a clever work of propaganda. Independence was narrated not as the birth of the United States (there was, after all, already a "we" and a "British," and a pre-existing history covered in another episode called "No More Kings"), but as a moment in which Americans acted out preexisting values through the violent expulsion of tyrants.

Schoolhouse Rock's rendering of U.S. independence works as history because in the aftermath of the war (a war which in some ways was many different wars, fought in several different colonies) those colonies created a common government, which in turn success-fully promoted the belief that North Americans shared a common national history. That national government also endeavored to promote a vision of independence that held that the war was right and just, that the English colonists living here were more American than European, that they were being oppressed by people with whom they shared few com-mon values, and that having escaped religious persecution in Europe more than a century before, it was their destiny to demand political freedom.

There were, of course, silences in this narrative. The "shot heard round the world" story ignores the fact that those who won their freedom were overwhelmingly white male property owners and that women did not gain the right to vote in most of the country until the twentieth century. It overlooks the fact that not all settlers came to the colonies because of religious discrimination, that many atrocities were committed in the name of independence, and that tens of thousands of people who were born in the colonies and no less American than those neighbors who lost their property and community standing after the war because they supported the losing side. It also, of course, ignores other significant silences, such as the role of indigenous peoples in the story, and the fact that the compro-mise that eventually produced a United States of America actively denied freedom for the majority of those of African origin; a compromise that in turn was partially responsible for a fratricidal conflict that seven decades later, would cost over 600,000 lives.

Those silences remain in the shadows when Americans today celebrate the Fourth of July, largely ignored in favor of the narrative reproduced in *Schoolhouse Rock*. For all its limi-tations, the nationalist narrative, reinforced by the state, its educational institutions, and generation after generation of repetitions in literature, art, music, and the movies (not to mention Saturday morning cartoons), continues to privilege the story of the heroic indi-viduals who fought for American freedom.

The power of the story is instructive of the challenge that confronts us when we try to produce a similarly straightforward understanding of independence in the Spanish, Por-tuguese, and French colonies that lay to the south of the thirteen British colonies that formed the United States of America. There was no "shot heard round the world" to signal a struggle for Latin American independence, in part because there was no single war for Latin American independence. It is difficult to narrate the history of the French, Spanish, English, Dutch, and Portuguese colonies that comprised this part of the world in a way that sets up independence as the logical or inevitable culmination of a national destiny—a story of freedom or otherwise. No single nation with the capacity to control the narrative emerged out of this region's battle for independence. The battles lasted longer, represented an even greater diversity of interests and claims, and yielded no consistent outcome. We must wonder then, could there be a *Schoolhouse Rock* version of Latin American indepen-dence? Where would it begin? What would be its lesson?

The Problem of Beginnings

The first problem we encounter in trying to narrate Latin American independence lies on the national level. Mexicans, Argentines, Brazilians, Chileans, and residents of other societies in the region all have their own national independence narratives, and they often differ a great deal, not just in the military heroes they venerate, but in the underlying values these stories inculcate. Mexicans for instance, lionize a liberal priest (Father Miguel Hidalgo). Brazilians claim a slave owning aristocrat (Dom Pedro I). Venezuelans, Colombians, and Peruvians credit an autocrat (Simón Bolívar) as the "Great Liberator," a reference to the fact that he led the military coalition that ultimately drove the Spanish out of their last footholds in South America. Some Bolivians (whose country is named for the Great Liberator) also celebrate Bolívar, but others in this country also venerate Túpac Katari, an Ayamara leader who died in a rebellion against the Spanish more than forty years before independence. Their divided loyalties offer different perspectives on where we should begin and end the story of this era.

As the Bolivian case suggests, the type of independence narrative we choose depends upon what sorts of actors we privilege. Told from the perspective of European descended elite males (*criollos*), independence was often a story of bravery and sacrifice in the name of ideals (national independence, freedom, self-determination). Told from the perspective of elite women, it was often a much more ambivalent story of frustrated ambitions (see the story of Manuela Sáenz, Bolívar's lover and savior, on this account[2]). Indigenous peoples often opposed these local leaders, fearing that self-determination for colonial elites would signal ruin for themselves, as those same colonial elites were their worst exploiters. African-descended slaves had similarly complex views, supporting a variety of sides in the conflicts depending on where individual and collective opportunities for emancipation seemed to lie.

These challenges might lead us to abandon both the idea of a common independence narrative and a sense that there can be a common story of Latin America. Yet if we do this, we risk losing sight of what seems to be a significant fact: between 1790 and 1830 almost every colony in the Americas (excepting Canada, Cuba, and a small number of other colonies in or bordering the Caribbean) violently dispossessed their European rulers. A shared history of colonial rule marked all of these societies and left common legacies and challenges for most. Moreover, the battles for independence connected societies across the region. News of rebellions in one colony spread to others, as did rebel and imperial armies. The fact that different parts of the region were under the control of different empires also facilitated the process, as rebel leaders could flee from their home to the colony of another European Empire (thus Bolívar's *Letter from Jamaica*, excerpted below), and could at times enlist the support of the European enemies of their colonial overlords. This, of course, was possible because during the late eighteenth and early nineteenth centuries Europe was consumed by the Napoleonic Wars, leaving the governments of the old world without the wherewithal to fully dominate their colonies.

These phenomena leave us with a series of uncomfortable choices. If we choose one independence narrative, we are given a chance to imagine a common Latin American past at the risk of silencing other, equally valid ways of understanding this history. If we choose too many narratives, we do greater justice to personal and local stories at the risk of losing a larger view of Latin America in the cacophony. My response to this dilemma is two-fold. Below I will tell three stories of independence instead of one. And rather than considering independence as a series of personages and events that need to be remembered and venerated, the sections that follow focus on the ways that independence is narrated—the morals and messages that are usually invoked through the story of Latin American independence.

Stories of Freedom

On November 4, 1780, in the Andean town of Tinta, Túpac Amaru II (José Gabriel Candorcanqui) seized the local Spanish Governor, Antonio de Arriaga, and ordered that he be put on trial. Executing de Arriaga a week later, he declared a rebellion against the Spanish Empire. His rebellion failed, leading to his death and the deaths of thousands of his compatriots. Though short lived, the cathartic (or alternately, frightening) power of his rebellion resonates in much of Latin America to this day. In part because he took his name from the last Inca ruler to be conquered by the Spaniards, and in part because his rebellion took as its goal the elimination of Spaniards from the Americas, the 1780 revolt has long stood for the complete rejection of the evils of the race-based oppression that colonialism and its aftermath entailed. It has been an inspiration to revolutionaries and those battling inequality across the hemisphere.

Colonial Latin Americans lived in unfree and unequal societies, and while most struggled against the injustices they faced in limited ways, stealing from landlords, occasionally poisoning their bosses, Europe's colonies in the Americas saw their share of spectacularly violent uprisings. Indigenous peoples (locked in a caste system that offered limited rights and made many demands) and slaves (who lacked legal personhood) were the most unfree, and led the most impressive struggles. The Caste War in the Yucatán in 1712, millenarian revolts in the Andes like the one sparked by Túpac Amaru II, and the vast communities of escaped slaves that flourished from Brazil to the Caribbean (the largest, Palmares, survived in Brazil from 1605 to 1694) acted as repeated reminders that those most oppressed by the colonial system were never all that far from responding the violence of the system with violence of their own. At their extreme, these movements envisioned a world without Spaniards, Portuguese, and other colonial overlords. They banished Europeans, their languages, and their food in their effort to return to a distant, utopian past. Nonetheless, as they were fighting against colonial states that were much stronger than them, most struggles for freedom in colonial Latin America were ultimately defeated; that is, until Haitian slaves took on the most powerful European nation of the day in 1791.

If we narrate independence as a story about freedom, Haiti (St. Domingue) is a good place to begin. During the 1780s, St. Domingue accounted for 40 percent of France's foreign trade, and was arguably the richest colony in Latin America, producing two-fifths of the world's sugar and half the world's coffee, virtually the entire volume of each produced by a slave population that reached a half million at its peak. A glimpse of the island in 1791 would reveal hundreds of thousands of recently enslaved Africans, persons who had been born free and longed for emancipation. One would also see a small but significant number of free people of color on the island, individuals who were increasingly important to the island's economy. Some owned slaves and supported slavery, though they chafed at the fact that the revolutionary Estates General of the French Revolution denied them political rights.

It was in this context that a slave revolt in 1791 metastasized into a civil war, and then a colonial war, leaving the island's white planters unable to defend their possessions. Slave emancipation came in 1793, when a French appointed governor (Léger-Félicité Sonthonax) used the promise of freedom for the slaves to recruit them into an army that could re-establish French control over the island. Eleven years later, after a decade more of civil strife, occupations by British, French, and Spanish armies, and numerous attempts to re-establish slavery on the island, Haitians won their independence. Theirs was the first republic in the Americas to ban slavery.

Events in St. Domingue had an impact elsewhere. Slave uprisings in the Spanish colonies (e.g., Coro, Venezuela, in 1795) followed news of St. Domingue. Planters around the Caribbean responded in kind, increasing discipline on their estates and mercilessly punishing even the hint of slave resistance. When war broke out in the Spanish colonies just a few years later, slavery was on many people's minds. Some slaves, like Juan Izaguirre in the Valle de Onato in Venezuela, appropriated the language of *criollo* liberators to claim their own freedom. Others opted for loyalty to Spain when this seemed a likelier route to freedom. Slaves defended Buenos Aires against the British Invasion in 1806–1807 and supported the royalist forces in large numbers in return for promises of rights and freedoms (commonly the right to be treated as a Spaniard). Not to be outdone, several rebel governments (*juntas*) outlawed the slave trade and passed (post-dated) free womb laws[3] (Santiago in 1811, Buenos Aires in April 1812, and Lima in 1821). The Venezuelan rebel Francisco Miranda, who was personally opposed to slavery, offered slaves freedom in return for ten years of military service. Bolívar, who followed Miranda as a leading figure in Venezuelan revolutionary circles (and who was a member of the group that arrested Miranda and turned him over to the Spanish), actively recruited slaves beginning in 1816, and would not have succeeded without drawing them away from the royalist cause.

Miranda, Bolívar, and the other rebel leaders who openly opposed slavery have come to be known as Latin America's early liberals. This term was bandied about constantly during the nineteenth century, used to describe any number of political movements that identified with progress and against tradition. Liberals called for greater freedom, sometimes individual freedom and equality before the law, sometimes the elimination of government imposed trade restrictions, and often an end to the power of the corporate entities that characterized colonial society—the Church, the nobility, the military, and the communal Indian village (the latter because liberals believed that communal land tenure restricted the free circulation of private property and thus limited economic growth).

Other stories of freedom in the region are similarly complex. In Mexico, Father Miguel Hidalgo's followers responded to his *Grito de Dolores* by raising a rag-tag army that swept through the Bajío in late 1810. Unlike earlier movements in the Andes, Hidalgo's armies were multiethnic, composed mainly of people who were already, to a certain extent free, but who, after years of drought and declining wages, viewed wealthy Spaniards (particularly grain merchants) as enemies. Some wanted independence, but many simply wanted the king to intercede in their favor. "Death to Spaniards"—the popular slogan they shouted as they marched—did not refer to the king, but his venal surrogates. More complex still, it appears that beyond economic concerns, many of their grievances were the product of eighteenth-century religious reforms, which undermined traditional religious practices in an attempt to enforce Catholic orthodoxy. They demanded a return to the colonial system as they had known it in the past, and restoration of the *old* Spanish King.

Freedom, then, was invoked to justify many different things. It could speak to a desire to escape human bondage, the demand that the avarice of your social betters be constrained, or even be framed as the right to worship according to the dictates of one's ancestors. And for the liberal merchants of cities like Buenos Aires, Caracas, or Mexico City, it might mean freedom to trade directly with their British partners, the manufacturers of Manchester and elsewhere who were forced to work through Spanish intermediaries to send their goods to the colonies. What is more, those urban liberals might view freedom in terms that were diametrically opposed to their rural counterparts. An indigenous peasant in Oaxaca might see freedom as freedom from the pressures of outsiders who wanted to appropriate his land, a freedom best defended through the intercession of the king. For the liberal elites, it could very well mean freedom from the laws and regulations that kept that land out of circulation, and thus made it impossible for them to freely acquire these properties.

Stories of Tradition

Most individuals in the contemporary world chafe at the idea of corporate privilege. We do not generally believe that members of the nobility, military, and clergy should enjoy special privileges, or that rights should be apportioned differently based on one's place of birth. We see those who might defend these privileges as backward at best, and antidemocratic at worst. We can easily understand villagers in the Mexican Bajío revolting because elites were treating them particularly harshly in the context of a famine (1808–1810). It is easy to imagine slaves demanding the right to be free. It makes less sense to us that indigenous people might in fact support colonial rule, defending a system of corporate privileges that seemed to place them at the bottom of the social hierarchy. Nonetheless, this too is an important story of independence.

Indigenous peoples (Indians in colonial parlance) owed service and tribute to the state. They also possessed rights to self-rule, to land, water, timber, and the practice of customary law. Though not always perfectly respected, these rights represented the most powerful currency that most indigenous peoples possessed within colonial society, claims that could be invoked in order to defend individual and community interests against more powerful outsiders, many of whom were politically connected *criollos*. A significant number of indigenous rebellions during the colonial period were efforts to preserve and expand these rights; rebellions in defense of village autonomy. In fact, the Andean rebellions of 1780 were not invariably tied to demands for freedom or equality. They were often the product of efforts to defend local village rights and ensure that royal officials respected local prerogatives. Moreover, it was not simply military repression that brought peace to the Andes in the aftermath of 1780. Long-term peace emerged from a concerted effort by the Spanish state to deal more effectively with local grievances. In part due to these efforts to forge a new colonial pact of domination, this region did not see much violence during the wars for independence. Liberal ideals generally fell on deaf ears here.

Tradition carried a great deal of weight elsewhere in Latin America. Honorable families could trace their propriety back generations. Access to political privilege was decided by lineage. The Catholic Church acted as the social glue, operating schools, hospitals, orphanages, charities, and cemeteries, and dominating social and ecclesiastical life through its calendar. Agents of the Spanish Inquisition policed spiritual life in the colony. If change was in the air—and it was, as more and more Latin Americans read enlightenment thinkers, called themselves liberals, and questioned tradition—the backlash against new ideas was just as strong.

In Mexico, struggles between liberals and traditionalists (conservatives) spawned a decade of civil war and then a compromise at independence. The royalist Agustín de Iturbide turned on his superiors and joined the struggle for independence in 1821 in a bargain that saw the primacy of the Catholic Church and the unity of the nation preserved. In the Andes, the pull of tradition (and a fear of the power of the masses) would keep many on the royalist side until the region was liberated from the outside in the 1820s.

More powerful still was the claim to tradition in the parts of Latin America where slavery remained a dominant mode of economic production. In order to function, slave societies relied on a series of myths about stability, the power and virtue of the planter, and the natural order of things. Cuban elites, their terror stoked by race war in Haiti, never seriously considered independence in the early nineteenth century. In Brazil, the weight of tradition and the power of aristocracy were critical to the illusion that slavery was anything but an abomination. The Portuguese emperor was a father to the people of Brazil in the same way that the planter was a father to the slave.

This logic explains Brazil's unusual path to independence. Like other regions in the Americas, Brazil experienced its share of late eighteenth-century rebellions (the most famous led by Tiradentes, in 1789), but by a particular turn of fate, these rebellions never became part of a national independence narrative in which Brazilians freed themselves from oppressive and distant colonial rulers. Instead, the distant colonial state came to Brazil and indirectly set off a series of events that would lead to independence. Fleeing the Napoleonic invasion of Portugal, Emperor João VI and 15,000 Portuguese relocated to Rio de Janeiro in 1808. The city quickly became the official center of the Empire, with concomitant increases in trade and investment. Brazil was even formally elevated to the status of co-kingdom in 1815. Still, this newfound prestige did not preclude mounting calls for independence. Rebellions in Pernambuco and elsewhere repeatedly threatened royal authority during these years.

It is difficult to underestimate the role slavery played in Brazilian independence, even if slavery was rarely discussed and never seriously contested. Free Brazilians understood that their society depended on slavery for its economic well-being. This severely limited the appeal of liberalism in Brazil, as a mutual dependence on slavery and a profound antipathy of anyone who might favor emancipation acted to unite Brazilian elites (and many in the middle sectors). For most Brazilians of European ancestry, independence did not seem inherently logical until 1820, when liberal army officers in Portugal rebelled, formed a *Cortes* (a legislature), and called the king home. The liberals in Lisbon then demanded that João bow down before their new constitution and that Brazil bow down before Portugal. They also seemed poised to abolish slavery. When the *Cortes* demanded that Pedro, the king's son and interim ruler in Brazil return home, Pedro refused. He instead declared Brazil independent on September 7, 1822. A series of military skirmishes followed, but Pedro rapidly established a constitutional monarchy under the banner of the Brazilian Empire. Slavery was saved.

Stories of Nationhood

When did Latin Americans begin to think of themselves as members of national communities, and not as colonial subjects? There are a number of interesting signs from this era. When they rallied behind the flag of rebellion, Mexicans followed the image of the Virgin of Guadalupe, a markedly local patron saint. Local publishing and literary communities flourished during the independence era, producing a sense of local specificity through the written word. Across the region, intellectuals actively condemned the evils of Spanish colonialism and celebrated incipient national cultures, defining themselves as fundamentally distinct from their colonial overlords. Some even excavated local Indian pasts in order to claim an ancient history for themselves that pre-dated the arrival of Europeans, and to argue that the presence of the Spanish crown in the Americas was pernicious, destructive; that they, like their fictive ancestors, were enslaved.

These rebels did feel connected to Europe. Europeans in the Americas remained powerfully linked to their origins. They returned to Spain or Portugal to be educated. They actively looked for opportunities to marry their daughters to recent arrivals. They followed the fashions and attitudes of the Iberian Peninsula. Nonetheless, by the early nineteenth century *criollo* elites increasingly saw themselves as rooted in the Americas. This sentiment—that they were Americans rather than Europeans—was both the product of their long history in the region and of recent developments, most notably a series of political and economic changes that historians have come to call the Bourbon Reforms. After the Bourbons ascended to the Spanish throne in the early eighteenth century, they gradually implemented new and often unwelcome policies in their American colonies. While local merchants benefited from some of the reforms (such as Bourbon efforts to create more legal avenues for trade), the new royal family collected taxes more aggressively and effectively, increasingly substituted peninsular Spanish officials for local ones, reserved many of the new economic opportunities in the colonies for Spaniards, and disrupted traditional governance in the colonies. *Criollo* grievances steadily accumulated through the century, erupting into rebellion as early as the 1740s.

It is not clear that these grievances were destined to lead to independence. Even if they were drawn to liberal values during this era, *criollos* remained deeply bound to the mother country. Latin American liberalism was hierarchical, favoring individual equality for males of Spanish descent. Few liberals imagined that these same rights ought to extend to the lower castes or women. Moreover, even in the 1810s there was very little of what one might call nationalist sentiment in the region, and elite *criollo* liberals shared little in common with the peasants, Indians, slaves, and *castas* (individuals of a variety of racial mixtures) who labored in the colonies.

Chance intervened in this story in the form of a diminutive Frenchman. Napoleon's invasion of Spain in 1808 threw the Iberian Peninsula into turmoil, and had the effect of bringing the distinction between *criollo* and peninsular Spaniard to the fore in several colonies. Spain did not formally relinquish control of her Latin American colonies, but when Charles IV (the Spanish King) was forced from the throne and replaced by Napoleon's brother Joseph, many in the colonies were not inclined to swear loyalty to the new Emperor. In capital cities across the region, local elites clashed with vice-regal authorities as a multitude of conspiracies flourished. When residents of Buenos Aires learned from sailors aboard a British frigate on May 13, 1810, that Iberia was almost entirely under French rule, they deposed the Spanish Viceroy and formed a *junta*, initiating La Plata's May Revolution. Though the *junta* leaders (among them, Argentine national heroes Cornelio Saavedra, Mariano Moreno, and Manuel Belgrano) declared their loyalty to the authentic Spanish King, they also demanded the right to choose their own Viceroy.

Although La Plata *criollos* clearly wanted to promote their own material interests (e.g., to trade more directly with England), their desires were not limited to financial matters. Members of the First *Junta* already felt an incipient sense of national belonging, which hardened into an unrelenting desire for freedom from Spain through the course of several brutal military campaigns. It was following these battles, and not before (as in the case of the United States) that the rebels made a formal Declaration of Independence from Spain on July 9, 1816. With independence won in the core of the old colony of La Plata, José de San Martín (their chief military leader) expanded his battle against Spanish forces across the continent, fighting into the 1820s.

The ease of initial victory was deceptive. As *criollo* nationalists would quickly discover, it was much easier to imagine a nation than it was to see it come into existence. Elite liberals often shared little more than a desire to be free of the constraints of colonial rule, and turned on one another in internal struggles that resulted in the dissolution of their new nations even as the wars for independence raged around them. Still more complex was their relationship to the popular groups that formed the core of their armies. We lack comprehensive understandings of why poor and marginalized people joined the independence armies, but what we know suggests that their understandings of the struggle and the nations that would come out of it often differed from the views held by elites. Efforts to knit together these disparate passions into unified nations would not yield rapid returns.

The Documents: Bolivarian Dreams

No single figure is more associated with independence in Latin America than Simón Bolívar. His statue can be found in any major city in the region, and his image is known to schoolchildren everywhere in Latin America. In part his fame is tied to his exploits, especially his role in leading victorious rebel armies across the Andes. His lasting fame however, more clearly derives from his visionary ideals, from his dream that Latin America should stand united against all enemies, his insistence that out of unity would come strength, prosperity, and freedom. Independence in Latin America left many dreams unfulfilled—dreams that in many ways have gone unfulfilled to this day—and Bolívar's dream has been a reference point for that sense of incompleteness for nearly two centuries.

Below are three examples of the Bolivarian dream, each composed roughly a century apart. Each evokes Bolívar's hopes for the region in its own particular way. Document 1.1, an excerpt from Bolívar's *Letter from Jamaica*,[4] offers us an opportunity to consider the Bolivarian dream in its original iteration. Written in the midst of the wars for independence, while Bolivar was briefly exiled in the British island colony, the letter reflects the effort of a leading liberal figure to explain both to his correspondent and to himself what was at stake in these conflicts, and to explain the struggle through reference to a common Latin American past and hoped-for future. Shortly after writing the letter, he returned to Caracas and gradually assumed leadership of the rebel cause.

Born into an aristocratic family in Caracas, Bolívar was simultaneously privileged and disadvantaged, a person of wealth and status and a second-class citizen next to the *peninsulares*. For these and other reasons Bolívar was drawn to both liberalism and to intellectual currents that envisioned Latin Americans as distinct from their Spanish rulers. He and his counterparts were Americans. Unsurprisingly then, Bolívar played an active part in the conspiracies that followed the Napoleonic invasion of Spain, leading several campaigns in Venezuela and Colombia, and establishing himself as an important intellectual author of independence through public speeches and his writings (see, for example, his Manifesto of Cartagena, in 1813, and his Address to the Congress of Angostura, in 1819, both on the book's website at www.routledge.com/cw/dawson).

Over time he refined his vision, which was always a complex combination of liberal republicanism and authoritarian values. Bolívar opposed slavery and proposed the distribution of land to those who fought for independence, but also favored heavy restrictions on suffrage and believed in a strong, almost dictatorial presidency. He attempted to fulfill this vision with the creation of Gran Colombia (modern Venezuela, Colombia, Panama, and Ecuador), over which he became president in September 1821. However, the country would dissolve even before his death in 1830, and Bolívar himself would die in disgrace, either the victim of his own ambitions or his follower's failures, depending on who told the tale. Whether or not these contradictions are tied to his enduring appeal, it is clear that his vision of a strong and united Latin America—an effective bulwark against an ascendant United States and imperial Europe—has always had the power to inspire political leaders in the region.

Our America, Document 1.2, is one of the most famous essays ever penned by a Latin American intellectual. Writing in 1891, three quarters of a century after the *Letter from Jamaica*, Martí confronts both the rise of the United States as the new imperial threat to Latin American sovereignty, and the fact that his own country (Cuba) remained a European colony. The essay introduces us to a particular tradition of Latin American essay writing in which the political and the poetic combine in a powerful mix to call readers to action. In part a contemplative piece of philosophy, and in part a direct call to political action, the essay argues both for Cuban independence and for a larger project of Latin American unity. In this sense, his essay is both about the crisis of a nation as yet chained to its colonial overlords and about the problem of forging a strong, united, and independent Latin America.

The final document in this chapter (1.3) is a speech delivered in 2004 by Venezuelan President Hugo Chávez (1954–2013). The speech invokes both Bolívar and the Chilean poet Pablo Neruda from the perspective of the early twenty-first century in ways that remind readers that while a great deal has in fact changed in two centuries (Chávez was, after all, the president of one of the wealthier countries in the region, capable of forging alliances with political leaders around the world, a spokesman for the "global south," all of which offered a stark contrasted to Martí and Bolívar, who both penned their tracts from exile), many of the basic, even visceral desires of Bolívar's original letter continued to resonate.

Elected president of Venezuela in 1998, Chávez actively laid claim to Bolívar's legacy, calling his movement a Bolivarian revolution. He renamed his country the *Bolivarian Republic of Venezuela*, and built an enormous 17-story mausoleum in Caracas to house the mortal remains of the Great Liberator (see Figure 1.1). His vision of the dream called for radical internal reforms (an egalitarian social project that distributes wealth to the poor) and an expansive geo-political project that would unite Latin America through military and economic alliances such as the *Alternativa Bolivariana para América Latina y El Caribe* (Bolivarian Alternative for Latin America and the Caribbean—ALBA). The project was complex, fueled by a mix of anti-imperial and socialist sentiments, along with a healthy dose of petro-dollar assistance from Venezuela. His political style, characterized by long, often rambling,

Figure 1.1   The Simon Bolivar Mausoleum in Caracas

Source: Reuters/Carlos Garcia Rawlins

speeches, crude references to foreign heads of state, and mesmerizing political theater, made him a singular figure during the first decade of the twenty-first century.

At the time of his death in 2013, Chávez was one of the most polarizing figures in Latin America. His enemies accused him of limiting press freedoms, of using the power of the state illegitimately against his rivals, of acting like an autocrat, and of failing to resolve Venezuela's deep social and economic problems. To his supporters however, he offered the hope of a better future through his twentieth-century version of socialism, which promised to redistribute Venezuela's natural wealth to those who deserved and needed it most. More broadly, he offered to restore Latin American sovereignty, to combat the power of imperial hegemons like the United States.

Many of Chávez' enemies celebrated his passing at an early age, dead of cancer at the age of 58. Chávez' re-election to the Venezuelan presidency in the fall of 2012 had been more narrow than his allies had hoped, and his chosen successor, Nicolas Madero, won election by only a 2 percent margin amid accusations of voter fraud. The thinness of the victory reminds us that Venezuela is a deeply divided society, where a certain iteration of the Bolivarian dream persists in spite of food and electricity shortages, inflation and other problems, and where opponents of that vision remain vocal, angry, and unbowed. These divisions also speak to the fact that the original promise of strength, unity, and prosperity uttered by Bolívar remains unfulfilled for tens of millions of Venezuelans. For similar reasons, the Bolivarian dream continues to resonate across Latin as an optimistic alternative to a dystopian present.

Whether viewed through Bolivar, Martí, Chávez, or others (e.g., Calle 13's "Latino-américa"[5]), the Bolivarian vision uses a story about the past, about how the nations define themselves, to call for a future that does justice to that past. One might suppose that in the face of so many discordant nationalisms—tensions between Argentines and Brazilians, El Salvadorans and Hondurans, Venezuelans and Colombians—the effort to invoke that common past and the fact that it has been done again and again over the course of two centuries is in itself worth noting. What the documents ask us to do however, is to look deeper, to ask what sorts of histories are privileged, what sorts of implications they have for the present and future, and perhaps most importantly, whose version of the past is privileged and whose is silenced?

Document 1.1 Simón Bolívar, the *Letter from Jamaica*: Kingston, Jamaica, September 6, 1815

Source: *Selected Writings of Bolívar*, translated by Lewis Bertrand. New York: The Colonial Press, 1951.

My Dear Sir:

With what a feeling of gratitude I read that passage in your letter in which you say to me: "I hope that the success which then followed Spanish arms may now turn in favor of their adversaries, the badly oppressed people of South America." I take this hope as a prediction, if it is justice that determines man's contests. Success will crown our efforts, because the destiny of America has been irrevocably decided; the tie that bound her to Spain has been severed. Only a concept maintained that tie and kept the parts of that immense monarchy together. That which formerly bound them now divides them. The hatred that the Peninsula has inspired in us is greater than the ocean between us. It would be easier to have the two continents meet than to reconcile the spirits of the two countries. The habit of obedience; a community of interest, of understanding, of religion; mutual goodwill; a tender regard for the birthplace and good name of our forefathers; in short, all that gave rise to our hopes, came to us from Spain. As a result there was born [the] principle of affinity that seemed eternal, notwithstanding the misbehavior of our rulers which weakened that sympathy, or, rather, that bond enforced by the domination of their rule. At present the contrary attitude persists: we are threatened with the fear of death, dishonor, and every harm; there is nothing we have not suffered at the hands of that unnatural stepmother—Spain. The veil has been torn asunder. We have already seen the light, and it is not our desire to be thrust back into darkness . . .

The role of the inhabitants of the American hemisphere has for centuries been purely passive. Politically they were nonexistent. We are still in a position lower than slavery, and therefore it is more difficult for us to rise to the enjoyment of freedom . . . States are slaves because of either the nature or the misuse of their constitutions; a people is therefore enslaved when the government, by its nature or its vices, infringes on and usurps the rights of the citizen or subject. Applying these principles, we find that America was denied not only its freedom but even an active and effective tyranny. Let me explain. Under absolutism there are no recognized limits to the exercise of governmental powers. The will of the great sultan, khan, bey, and other despotic rulers is the supreme law, carried out more or less arbitrarily by the lesser pashas, khans, and satraps of Turkey and Persia, who have an organized system of oppression in which inferiors participate according to the authority vested in them. To them is entrusted the administration of civil, military, political, religious, and tax matters. But, after all is said and done, the rulers of Isfahan are Persians; the viziers of the Grand Turk are Turks; and the sultans of Tartary are Tartars.

How different is our situation! We have been harassed by a conduct which has not only deprived us of our rights but has kept us in a sort of permanent infancy with regard to public affairs. If we could at least have managed our domestic affairs and our internal administration, we could have acquainted ourselves with the processes and mechanics of public affairs. We should also have enjoyed a personal consideration, thereby commanding a certain unconscious respect from the people, which is so necessary to preserve amidst revolutions. That is why I say we have even been deprived of an active tyranny, since we have not been permitted to exercise its functions.

Americans today, and perhaps to a greater extent than ever before, who live within the Spanish system occupy a position in society no better than that of serfs destined for labor, or at best they have no more status than that of mere consumers. Yet even this status is surrounded with galling restrictions, such as being forbidden to grow European crops, or to store products which are royal monopolies, or to establish factories of a type the Peninsula itself does not possess. To this add the exclusive trading privileges, even in articles of prime necessity, and the barriers between American provinces, designed to prevent all exchange of trade, traffic, and understanding. In short, do you wish to know what our future held?—simply the cultivation of the fields of indigo, grain, coffee, sugar cane, cacao, and cotton; cattle raising on the broad plains; hunting wild game in the jungles; digging in the earth to mine its gold—but even these limitations could never satisfy the greed of Spain.

So negative was our existence that I can find nothing comparable in any other civilized society, examine as I may the entire history of time and the politics of all nations. Is it not an outrage and a violation of human rights to expect a land so splendidly endowed, so vast, rich, and populous, to remain merely passive?

As I have just explained, we were cut off and, as it were, removed from the world in relation to the science of government and administration of the state. We were never viceroys or governors, save in the rarest of instances; seldom archbishops and bishops; diplomats never; as military men, only subordinates; as nobles, without royal privileges. In brief, we were neither magistrates nor financiers and seldom merchants—all in flagrant contradiction to our institutions.

It is harder, Montesquieu has written, to release a nation from servitude than to enslave a free nation. This truth is proven by the annals of all times, which reveal that most free nations have been put under the yoke, but very few enslaved nations have recovered their liberty. Despite the convictions of history, South Americans have made efforts to obtain liberal, even perfect, institutions, doubtless out of that instinct to aspire to the greatest possible happiness, which, common to all men, is bound to follow in civil societies founded on the principles of justice, liberty, and equality. But are we capable of maintaining in proper balance the difficult charge of a republic? Is it conceivable that a newly emancipated people can soar to the heights of liberty, and, unlike Icarus, neither have its wings melt nor fall into an abyss? Such a marvel is inconceivable and without precedent. There is no reasonable probability to bolster our hopes.

More than anyone, I desire to see America fashioned into the greatest nation in the world, greatest not so much by virtue of her area and wealth as by her freedom and glory. Although I seek perfection for the government of my country, I cannot persuade myself that the New World can, at the moment, be organized as a great republic. Since it is impossible, I dare not desire it; yet much less do I desire to have all America a monarchy because this plan is not only impracticable but also impossible. Wrongs now existing could not be righted, and our emancipation would be fruitless. The American states need the care of paternal governments to heal the sores and wounds of despotism and war . . .

From the foregoing, we can draw these conclusions: The American provinces are fighting for their freedom, and they will ultimately succeed. Some provinces as a matter of course will form federal and some central republics; the larger areas will inevitably establish monarchies, some of which will fare so badly that they will disintegrate in either present or future revolutions. To consolidate a great monarchy will be no easy task, but it will be utterly impossible to consolidate a great republic.

When success is not assured, when the state is weak, and when results are distantly seen, all men hesitate; opinion is divided, passions rage, and the enemy fans these passions in order to win an easy victory because of them. As soon as we are strong and under the guidance of a liberal nation which will lend us her protection, we will achieve accord in cultivating the virtues and talents that lead to glory. Then will we march majestically toward that great prosperity for which South America is destined.

I am, Sir, etc., etc.

Simón Bolívar

Document 1.2 José Martí, "Our America," from *La Revista Ilustrada*, New York, January 1, 1891

Source: "Our America" from *The America of José Martí*, translated by Juan de Onís. Translation copyright © 1954, renewed 1982 by Farrar, Straus, & Giroux, Inc.

The prideful villager thinks his hometown contains the whole world, and as long as he can stay on as mayor or humiliate the rival who stole his sweetheart or watch his nest egg accumulating in its strongbox he believes the universe to be in good order, unaware of the giants in seven-league boots who can crush him underfoot or the battling comets in the heavens that go through the air devouring the sleeping worlds. Whatever is left of that sleepy hometown in America must awaken. These are not times for going to bed in a sleeping cap, but rather, like Juan de Castellanos' men, with our weapons for a pillow, weapons of the mind, which vanquish all others. Trenches of ideas are worth more than trenches of stone.

A cloud of ideas is a thing no armored prow can smash through. A vital idea set ablaze before the world at the right moment can, like the mystic banner of the last judgment, stop a fleet of battleships. Hometowns that are still strangers to one another must hurry to become acquainted, like men who are about to do battle together. Those who shake their fists at each other like jealous brothers quarreling over a piece of land or the owner of a small house who envies the man with a better one must join hands and interlace them until their two hands are as one. Those who, shielded by a criminal tradition, mutilate, with swords smeared in the same blood that flows through their own veins, the land of a conquered brother whose punishment far exceeds his crimes, must return that land to their brother if they do not wish to be known as a nation of plunderers. The honorable man does not collect his debts of honor in money, at so much per slap. We can no longer be a nation of fluttering leaves, spending our lives in the air, our treetop crowned in flowers, humming or creaking, caressed by the caprices of sunlight or thrashed and felled by tempests. The trees must form ranks to block the seven-league giant! It is the hour of reckoning and of marching in unison, and we must move in lines as compact as the veins of silver that lie at the roots of the Andes.

Only runts whose growth was stunted will lack the necessary valor, for those who have no faith in their land are like men born prematurely. Having no valor themselves, they deny that other men do. Their puny arms, with bracelets and painted nails, the arms of Madrid or of Paris, cannot manage the lofty tree and so they say the tree cannot be climbed. We must load up the ships with these termites who gnaw away at the core of the patria that has nurtured them; if they are Parisians or Madrileños then let them stroll to the Prado by lamplight or go to Tortoni's for an ice. These sons of carpenters who are ashamed that their father was a carpenter! These men born in America who are ashamed of the mother that raised them because she wears an Indian apron, these delinquents who disown their sick mother and leave her alone in her sickbed! Which one is truly a man, he who stays with his mother to nurse her through her illness, or he who forces her to work somewhere out of sight, and lives off her sustenance in corrupted lands, with a worm for his insignia, cursing the bosom that bore him, sporting a sign that says "traitor" on the back of his paper dress-coat? These sons of our America, which must save herself through her Indians, and which is going from less to more, who desert her and take up arms in the armies of North America, which drowns its own Indians in blood and going from more to less! These delicate creatures who are men but do not want to do men's work! Did Washington, who made that land for them, go and live with the English during the years when he saw the English marching against his own land? These *incroyables* who drag their honor across foreign soil, like the *incroyables* of the French Revolution, dancing, smacking their lips, and deliberately slurring their words!

And in what patria can a man take greater pride than in our long-suffering republics of America, erected among mute masses of Indians upon the bloodied arms of no more than a hundred apostles, to the sound of the book doing battle against the monk's tall candle? Never before have such advanced and consolidated nations been created from such disparate factors in less historical time. The haughty man thinks that because he wields a quick pen or a vivid phrase the earth was made to be his pedestal, and accuses his nature republic or irredeemable incompetence because its virgin jungles do not continually provide him with the means of going about the world a famous plutocrat, driving Persian ponies and spilling champagne. The incapacity lies not in the emerging country, which demands forms that are appropriate to it and a grandeur that is useful, but in the leaders who try to rule unique nations of a singular and violent composition, with laws inherited from four centuries of free practice in the United States and nineteen centuries of monarchy in France. A gaucho's pony cannot be stopped in mid-bolt by one of Alexander Hamilton's laws. The sluggish blood of the Indian race cannot be quickened by a phrase from Sieyes. To govern well, one must attend closely to the reality of the place that is governed. In America, the good ruler does not need to know how the German or Frenchman is governed, but what elements his own country is composed of and how he can marshal them so as to reach, by means and institutions born from the country itself, the desirable state in which every man knows himself and is active, and all men enjoy the abundance that Nature, for the good of all, has bestowed on the country they make fruitful by their labor and defend with their lives. The government must be born from the country. The spirit of the government must be the spirit of the country. The form of the government must be in harmony with the country's natural constitution. The government is no more than an equilibrium among the country's natural elements.

In America the natural man has triumphed over the imported book. Natural men have triumphed over an artificial intelligentsia. The native mestizo has triumphed over the alien, pure-blooded *criollo*. The battle is not between civilization and barbarity, but between false erudition and nature. The natural man is good, and esteems and rewards a superior intelligence as long as that intelligence does not use his submission against him or offend him by ignoring him—for that the natural man deems unforgivable, and he is prepared to use force to regain the respect of anyone who wounds his sensibilities or harms his interests. The tyrants of America have come to power by acquiescing to these scorned natural elements and have fallen as soon as they betrayed them. The republics have purged the former tyrannies of their inability to know the true elements of the country, derive the form of government from them, and govern along with them. Governor, in a new country, means Creator.

In countries composed of educated and uneducated sectors, the uneducated will govern by their habit of attacking and resolving their doubts with their fists, unless the educated learn the art of governing. The uneducated masses are lazy and timid about matters of the intellect and want to be well-governed, but if the government injures them they shake it off and govern themselves. How can our governors emerge from the universities when there is not a university in America that teaches the most basic element of the art of governing, which is the analysis of all that is unique to the peoples of America? Our youth go out into the world wearing Yankee- or French-colored glasses and aspire to rule by guesswork a country they do not know. Those unacquainted with the rudiments of politics should not be allowed to embark on a career in politics. The literary prizes must not go to the best ode, but to the best study of the political factors in the student's country. In the newspapers, lecture halls, and academies, the study of the country's real factors must be carried forward. Simply knowing those factors without blindfolds or circumlocutions is enough—for anyone who deliberately or unknowingly sets aside a part of the truth will ultimately fail because of the truth he was lacking, which expands when neglected and brings down whatever is built without it. Solving the problem after knowing its elements is easier than solving it without knowing them. The natural man, strong and indignant, comes and overthrows the authority that is accumulated from books because it is not administered in keeping with the manifest needs of the country. To know is to solve. To know the country and govern it in accordance with that knowledge is the only way of freeing it from tyranny. The European university must yield to the American university. The history of America from the Incas to the present must be taught in its smallest detail, even if the Greek Archons go untaught. Our own Greece is preferable to the Greece that is not ours; we need it more. Statesmen who arise from the nation must replace statesmen who are alien to it. Let the world be grafted onto our republics, but we must be the trunk. And let the vanquished pedant hold his tongue, for there is no patria in which a man can take greater pride than in our long-suffering American republics.

Our feet upon a rosary, our heads white, and our bodies a motley of Indian and *criollo* we boldly entered the community of nations. Bearing the standard of the Virgin, we went out to conquer our liberty. A priest, a few lieutenants, and a woman built a republic in Mexico upon the shoulders of the Indians. A Spanish cleric, under cover of his priestly cape, taught French liberty to a handful of magnificent students who chose a Spanish general to lead central America against Spain. Still accustomed to monarchy, and with the sun on their chests, the Venezuelans in the north and the Argentines in the south set out to construct nations. When the two heroes clashed and their continent was about to be rocked, one of them, and not the lesser one, turned back. But heroism is less glorious in peacetime than in war, and thus rarer, and it is easier for a man to die with honor than to think in an orderly way. Exalted and unanimous sentiments are more readily governed than the diverging, arrogant, alien, and ambitious ideas that emerge when the battle is over. The powers that were swept up in the epic struggle, along with the feline wariness of the species and the sheer weight of reality, undermined the edifice that had raised the flags of nations sustained by wise governance in the continual practice of reason and freedom over the crude and singular regions of our mestizo America with its towns of bare legs and Parisian dress-coats. The colonial hierarchy resisted the republic's democracy, and the capital city, wearing its elegant cravat, left the countryside, in its horsehide boots, waiting at the door; the redeemers born from books did not understand that a revolution that had triumphed when the soul of the earth was unleashed by a savior's voice had to govern with the soul of the earth and not against or without it. And for all these reasons, America began enduring and still endures the weary task of reconciling the discordant and hostile elements it inherited from its perverse, despotic colonizer with the imported forms and ideas that have, in their lack of local reality, delayed the advent of a logical form of government. The continent, deformed by three centuries of a rule that denied man the right to exercise his reason, embarked—overlooking or refusing to listen to the ignorant masses that had helped it redeem itself—upon a government based on reason, the reason of all directed toward the things that are of concern to all, and not the university-taught reason of the few imposed upon the rustic reason of others. The problem of independence was not the change in form, but the change in spirit.

Common cause had to be made with the oppressed in order to consolidate a system that was opposed to the interests and governmental habits of the oppressors. The tiger, frightened away by the flash of gunfire, creeps back in the night to find his prey. He will die with flames shooting from his eyes, his claws unsheathed, but now his step is inaudible for he comes on velvet paws. When the prey awakens, the tiger is upon him. The colony lives on in the republic, but our America is saving itself from its grave blunders—the arrogance of the capital cities, the blind triumph of the scorned campesinos, the excessive importation of foreign ideas and formulas, the wicked and impolitic disdain for the native race—through the superior virtue, confirmed by necessary bloodshed, of the republic that struggles against the colony. The tiger waits behind every tree, crouches in every corner. He will die, his claws unsheathed, flames shooting from his eyes.

But "these countries will be saved," in the words of the Argentine Rivadavia, who erred on the side of urbanity during crude times; the machete is ill-suited to a silken scabbard, nor can the spear be abandoned in a country won by the spear, for it becomes enraged and stands in the doorway of Iturbide's Congress demanding that "the fair- skinned man be made emperor." These countries will be saved because, with the genius of moderation that now seems, by nature's serene harmony, to prevail in the continent of light, and the influence of the critical reading that has, in Europe, replaced the fumbling ideas about phalansteries in which the previous generation was steeped, the real man is being born to America, in these real times.

What a vision we were: the chest of an athlete, the hands of a dandy, and the forehead of a child. We were a whole fancy dress ball, in English trousers, a Parisian waistcoat, a North American overcoat, and a Spanish bullfighter's hat. The Indian circled about us, mute, and went to the mountaintop to christen his children. The black, pursued from afar, alone and unknown, sang his heart's music in the night, between waves and wild beasts. The campesinos, the men of the land, the creators, rose up in blind indignation against the disdainful city, their own creation. We wore epaulets and judge's robes, in countries that came into the world wearing rope sandals and Indian headbands. The wise thing would have been to pair, with charitable hearts and the audacity of our founders, the Indian headband and the judicial robe, to undam the Indian, make a place for the able black, and tailor liberty to the bodies of those who rose up and triumphed in its name. What we had was the judge, the general, the man of letters, and the cleric. Our angelic youth, as if struggling from the arms of an octopus, cast their heads into the heavens and fell back with sterile glory, crowned with clouds. The natural people, driven by instinct, blind with triumph, overwhelmed their gilded rulers. No Yankee or European book could furnish the key to the Hispanoamerican enigma. So the people tried hatred instead, and our countries amounted to less and less each year. Weary of useless hatred, of the struggle of book against sword, reason against the monk's taper, city against countryside, the impossible empire of the quarreling urban castes against the tempestuous or inert natural nation, we are beginning, almost unknowingly, to try love. The nations arise and salute one another.

"What are we like?" they ask, and begin telling each other what they are like. When a problem arises in Cojimar they no longer seek the solution in Danzig. The frock-coats are still French, but the thinking begins to be American. The young men of America are rolling up their sleeves and plunging their hands into the dough, and making it rise with the leavening of their sweat. They understand that there is too much imitation, and that salvation lies in creating. Create is this generation's password. Make wine from plantains; it may be sour, but it is our wine! It is now understood that a country's form of government must adapt to its natural elements, that absolute ideas, in order not to collapse over an error of form, must be expressed in relative forms; that liberty, in order to be viable, must be sincere and full, that if the republic does not open its arms to all and include all in its progress, it dies. The tiger inside came in through the gap, and so will the tiger outside. The general holds the cavalry's speed to the pace of the infantry, for if he leaves the infantry far behind, the enemy will surround the cavalry. Politics is strategy. Nations must continually criticize themselves, for criticism is health, but with a single heart and a single mind. Lower yourselves to the unfortunate and raise them up in your arms! Let the heart's fires unfreeze all that is motionless in America, and let the country's natural blood surge and throb through its veins! Standing tall, the workmen's eyes full of joy, the new men of America are saluting each other from one country to another. Natural statesmen are emerging from the direct study of nature; they read in order to apply what they read, not copy it. Economists are studying problems at their origins. Orators are becoming more temperate. Dramatists are putting native characters onstage. Academies are discussing practical subjects. Poetry is snipping off its wild, Zorilla-esque mane and hanging up its gaudy waistcoat on the glorious tree. Prose, polished and gleaming, is replete with ideas. The rulers of Indian republics are learning Indian languages.

America is saving herself from all her dangers. Over some republics the octopus sleeps still, but by the law of equilibrium, other republics are running into the sea to recover the lost centuries with mad and sublime swiftness. Others, forgetting that Juárez traveled in a coach drawn by mules, hitch their coach to the wind and take a soap bubble for coachman—and poisonous luxury, enemy of liberty, corrupts the frivolous and opens the door to foreigners. The virile character of others is being perfected by the epic spirit of a threatened independence. And others, in rapacious wars against their neighbors, are nurturing an unruly soldier caste that may devour them. But our America may also face another danger, which comes not from within but from the differing origins, methods, and interests of the containment's two factions. The hour is near when she will be approached by an enterprising and forceful nation that will demand intimate relations with her, though it does not know her and disdains her. And virile nations self-made by the rifle and the law love other virile nations, and love only them. The hour of unbridled passion and ambition from which North America may escape by the ascendancy of the purest element in its blood—or into which its vengeful and sordid masses, its tradition of conquest, and the self-interest of a cunning leader could plunge it—is not yet so close, even to the most apprehensive eye, that there is no time for it to be confronted and averted by the manifestation of a discreet and unswerving pride, for its dignity as a republic, in the eyes of the watchful nations of the Universe, places upon North America a brake that our America must not remove by puerile provocation, ostentatious arrogance, or patricidal discord. Therefore the urgent duty of our America is to show herself as she is, one in soul and intent, rapidly overcoming the crushing weight of her past and stained only by the fertile blood shed by hands that do battle against ruins and by veins that were punctured by our former masters. The disdain of the formidable neighbor who does not know her is our America's greatest danger, and it is urgent—for the day of the visit is near—that her neighbor come to know her, and quickly, so that he will not disdain her. Out of ignorance, he may perhaps begin to covet her. But when he knows her, he will remove his hands from her in respect. One must have faith in the best in man and distrust the worst. One must give the best every opportunity, so that the worst will be laid bare and overcome. If not, the worst will prevail. Nations should have one special pillory for those who incite them to futile hatreds, and another for those who do not tell them the truth until it is too late.

There is no racial hatred, because there are no races. Sickly, lamp-lit minds string together and rewarm the library-shelf races that the honest traveler and the cordial observer seek in vain in the justice of nature, where the universal identity of man leaps forth in victorious love and turbulent appetite. The soul, equal and eternal, emanates from bodies that are diverse in form and color. Anyone who promotes and disseminates opposition or hatred among races is committing a sin against humanity. But within that jumble of peoples which lives in close proximity to our peoples, certain peculiar and dynamic characteristics are condensed—ideas and habits of expansion, acquisition, vanity, and greed—that could, in a period of internal disorder or precipitation of a people's cumulative character, cease to be latent national preoccupations and become a serious threat to the neighboring, isolated and weak lands that the strong country declares to be perishable and inferior. To think is to serve. We must not, out of a villager's antipathy, impute some lethal congenital wickedness to the continent's light-skinned nation simply because it does not speak our language or share our view of what home life should be or resemble us in its political failings, which are different from ours, or because it does not think highly of quick-tempered, swarthy men or look with charity, from its still uncertain eminence, upon those less favored by history who, in heroic stages, are climbing the road that republics travel. But neither should we seek to conceal the obvious facts of the problem, which can, for the peace of the centuries, be resolved by timely study and the urgent, wordless union of the continental soul. For the unanimous hymn is already ringing forth, and the present generation is bearing industrious America along the road sanctioned by our sublime forefathers. From the Rio Bravo to the Straits of Magellan, the Great Cemi, seated on a condor's back, has scattered the seeds of the new America across the romantic nations of the continent and the suffering islands of the sea!

Document 1.3 Speech by President Hugo Chávez at the opening of XII G-15 Summit, Monday, March 1, 2004

. . . Ladies and Gentlemen.

Welcome to this land washed by the waters of the Atlantic Ocean and the Caribbean Sea, crossed by the magnificent Orinoco River. A land crowned by the perpetual snow of the Andean mountains . . .!

A land overwhelmed by the never-ending magic of the Amazon forest and its millenary chants . . .!

Welcome to Venezuela, the land where a patriotic people has again taken over the banners of Simón Bolívar, its Liberator, whose name is well known beyond these frontiers!

As Pablo Neruda said in his "Chant to Bolívar":
Our Father thou art in Heaven,
in water, in air
in all our silent and broad latitude
everything bears your name, Father in our dwelling:
your name raises sweetness in sugar cane
Bolívar tin has a Bolívar gleam
the Bolívar bird flies over the Bolívar volcano the potato, the saltpeter, the special
shadows, the brooks, the phosphorous stone veins everything comes from your
extinguished life your legacy was rivers, plains, bell towers
your legacy is our daily bread, oh Father.

Yes, ladies and gentlemen: Bolívar, another "Quixote but not mad" (as Napoleon Bonaparte had already called Francisco de Miranda, the universal man from Caracas), who on this very same South American soil tried to unite the emerging republics into a single, strong and free republic.

In his letter from Jamaica in 1815, Bolívar spoke of convening an Amphictyonic Congress in the Isthmus of Panama:

"I wish one day we would have the opportunity to install there an august congress with the representatives of the Republics, Kingdoms and Empires to debate and discuss the highest interests of Peace and War with the countries of the other three parts of the world."

Bolívar reveals himself as an anti-imperialist leader, sharing the same ideals that materialized in the Bandung Conference in April 1955, 140 years after that insightful letter from Kingston. Inspired by Nehru, Tito, and Nasser, a group of important leaders gathered at this conference to confront their great challenges, and expressed their desire to not be involved in the East-West Conflict, but rather to work together toward national development. This was the first key milestone: It was the first Afro-Asian conference, the immediate precedent of the Non-Aligned Countries, which gathered 29 Heads of State and gave birth to the "Conscience of the South."

Two events of great political significance occurred in the 60s: the creation of the Non-Aligned Movement in Belgrade in 1961 and the Group of the 77 in 1964: Two milestones and a clear historic trend: the need of the South to be self-aware and to act in concert in a world characterized by imbalance and unequal exchange.

In the 70s a proposal from the IV Summit of Heads of State of the Non-Aligned Countries in Algiers in 1973 becomes important: the need to create a new international economic order. In 1974 the UN Assembly ratified this proposal, and while it remains in effect to this day, it has ended up becoming a mere historical footnote.

Two events that were very important for the struggles in the South occurred during the 80s: the creation of the Commission of the South in Kuala Lumpur in 1987 under the leadership of Julius Nyerere, the unforgettable fighter of Tanzania and the world.

Two years later, in September 1989, the Group of the 15 is created out of a meeting of the Non-Aligned Countries, with the purpose of strengthening South-South cooperation.

In 1990, the South-Commission submitted its strategic proposal: "A Challenge for the South." And later on . . . later on came the flood that followed the fall of the Berlin Wall and the implosion of the Soviet Union. As Joseph Stiglitz said, this brought unipolarity and the arrival of the "happy 90s."

All those struggles, ideas and proposals sank in the neo-liberal flood. The world experienced the so-called end of History, accompanied by the triumphant chant of (those who advocated) neo-liberal globalization, which today, besides being an objective reality, is a weapon they use to manipulate us into passivity in the face of an economic world order that excludes our countries of the South and condemns us to perpetually play the role of producers of wealth and recipients of leftovers.

Never before had the world such tremendous scientific-technical potential, such a capacity to generate wealth and well-being. Authentic technological wonders that have eliminated the distances between places. Still, (these innovations) have helped only a very few people, the 15 percent of the global population that lives in the countries of the North.

Globalization has not brought so-called interdependence, but an increase in dependency. Instead of wealth being globalized, it is poverty that is increasingly widespread. We have not seen general or shared development. Instead, the abyss between the North and South is so enormous that it is obviously unsustainable—those who try and justify their opulence and waste are simply blind.

The faces of the neo-liberal world economic order are not only the Internet, virtual reality, or the exploration of outer-space, but they can also be seen—and more dramatically—in the countries of the South, where 790 million people are starving, where 800 million adults are illiterate, and where 654 million human beings alive today will not grow older than 40 years of age. This is the harsh and hard face of a world economic order dominated by neo-liberalism, and it is seen every year in the South, where every year 11 million boys and girls below 5 years of age die as a result of illnesses that are practically always preventable and curable. They die at the appalling rate of over 30 thousand every day, 21 every minute, 10 each 30 seconds. In the South, the proportion of children suffering from malnutrition reaches 50 percent in quite a few countries, while according to the FAO (Food and Agriculture Organization of the United Nations), a child who lives in the First World will consume the equivalent of what 50 children consume in an underdeveloped country during his or her life time.

The great hope that a globalization based in solidarity and true cooperation would bring scientific-technical wonders to all people in the world has been reduced to this grotesque caricature, full of exploitation and social injustice, by the neo-liberal model.

Our countries of the South were told a thousand times that the only and true "science" capable of ensuring development and well-being for everybody dictated that we let the markets operate without regulation, privatize everything, create the conditions for transnational capital investment, and ban the State from intervening the economy.

Almost the magical and wonderful philosopher's stone!!

Neo-liberal thought and politics were created in the North to serve their interests, but it should be highlighted that they have never been truly applied there. They have instead been spread throughout the South in the past two decades and have now come to be become the only acceptable way of thinking, with disastrous results.

As a result of the application of (neo-liberal) thinking, the world economy as a whole has grown less than in the three decades between 1945 and 1975, when the Keynesian theories, which promoted market regulation through State intervention, were applied. The gap separating the North and the South continued to grow, not only in terms of economic indicators, but also with regards to access to knowledge, the strategic sector that creates the fundamental possibility of integral development in our times.

With only 15 percent of the world population, the countries of the North count over 85 percent of Internet users and control 97 percent of the patents. These countries have an average of over 10 years of schooling, while in the countries of the South schooling barely reaches 3.7 years and in many countries it is even lower. The tragedy of under-development and poverty in Africa, with its historic roots in colonialism and the enslavement of millions of its children, is now reinforced by neo-liberalism imposed from the North. In this region, the rate of infant mortality in children under 1 year of age is 107 per each thousand children born alive, while in developed countries this rate is 6 per each thousand children born alive. Also, life expectancy is 48 years, 30 years less than in the countries of the North.

In Asia, economic growth in some countries has been remarkable, but the region as a whole is still lagging behind the North in basic economic and social development indicators.

We are, dear friends, in Latin America, the favorite testing-ground of the neo-liberal model in the recent decades. Here, neo-liberalism reached the status of a dogma and was applied with greatest severity. Its catastrophic results can be easily seen, and explain the growing and uncontrollable social protests unleashed by the poor and excluded people of Latin America for some years now, and which every day grow stronger. They claim their right to life, to education, to health, to culture, to a decent living as human beings.

Dear friends:

I witnessed this with my own eyes, on a day like today but exactly 15 years ago, the 27th of February 1989, an intense day of protest that erupted on the streets of Caracas against the neo-liberal reforms of the International Monetary Fund and ended in a very real massacre known as "The Caracazo."

The neo-liberal model promised Latin Americans greater economic growth, but during the neo-liberal years growth has not even reached half the rate achieved in the 1945–1975 period under different policies.

The model recommended the most strict financial and trade liberalization in order to achieve a greater influx of foreign capital and greater stability. But during the neo-liberal years the financial crises have been more intense and frequent than ever before. The external regional debt was non-existent at the end of the Second World War, and today amounts to 750 billion dollars, the per capita highest debt in the world and in several countries equal to more than half the GDP. Between 1990 and the year 2002 alone, Latin America made external debt payments amounting to 1 trillion 528 billion dollars, which is twice the amount of the current debt and represented an annual average payment of 118 billion. That is, we pay the debt every 6.3 years, but this evil burden continues to be there, unchanging and inextinguishable.

¡¡It is a never-ending debt!!

Obviously, this debt has exceeded the normal and reasonable payment commitments of any debtor and has turned into an instrument to undercapitalize our countries. It has additionally forced the imposition of socially adverse measures that in turn politically destabilize those governments that implement them. We were asked to be ultraliberal, to lift all trade barriers to imports coming from the North, but those oral champions of trade have in practice been champions of protectionism. The North spends 1 billion dollars per day practicing what it has banned us from doing, that is, subsidizing inefficient products. I want to tell you—and this is true and verifiable—that each cow grazing in the European Union receives in its four stomachs 2.20 dollars a day in subsidies, thus having a better situation than the 2.5 billion poor people in the South who barely survive on incomes of less than 2 dollars a day.

With the FTAA (Free Trade Agreement of the Americas), the government of the United States wants us to reduce our tariffs to zero for their benefit and wants us to give away our markets, our oil, our water resources and biodiversity, in addition to our sovereignty, whereas walls of subsidies for agriculture keep access closed to that country's market. It seems a peculiar way to reduce the huge commercial deficit of the United States; to do exactly the opposite of what they claim is a sacred principle in economic policy.

Neo-liberalism promised Latin Americans that if they accepted the demands of multinational capital, investments would flood the region. Indeed, the in-flow of capital increased. Some portion (came) to buy state-owned companies, sometimes at bargain prices, another portion was speculative capital that seized opportunities arising from financial liberalization.

The neo-liberal model promised that after the painful adjustment period, which was necessary to deprive the State of its regulatory power over the economy and liberalize trade and finance, wealth would spread across Latin America and the region's long history of poverty and underdevelopment would be left in the past. But the painful and temporary adjustment became permanent and appears to be becoming everlasting. The results cannot be concealed.

If we look at 1980, the year we conventionally denote as the start of the neo-liberal cycle, we see that at that time around 35 percent of Latin Americans were poor. Two decades later, 44 percent of Latin American men and women are poor. Poverty is particularly cruel to children. It is a sad reality that in Latin America most of the poor people are children and most children are poor. In the late 90s, the Economic Commission for Latin America reported that 58 percent of children under 5 were poor, along with 57 percent of children between 6 and 12. Poverty among children and teenagers tends to reinforce and perpetuate unequal access to education, as was shown by a 15 country survey conducted by the Inter-American Development Bank. Among households in the 10 percent of the population with the highest income average schooling was 11 years, whereas among households in the bottom 30 percent of income the average was 4 years.

Neo-liberalism promised wealth. And poverty has spread, thus making Latin America the most unequal region in the world in terms of income distribution. The wealthiest 10 percent of the population in the region—those who are satisfied with neo-liberalism and feel enthusiastic about the FTAA—receive nearly 50 percent of the total income, while the poorest 10 percent—those who never appear in the society pages of the oligarchic mass media—barely receive 1.5 percent of total income.

This model based on exploitation has turned Latin America and the Caribbean into a social time-bomb; ready to explode, should anti-development, unemployment and poverty keep increasing.

Even though the social struggles are growing sharp and even some governments have been overthrown in uprisings, we are told by the North that neo-liberal reforms have not yielded good results because they have not been implemented in full. So, they now intend to recommend a formula for suicide. But we know, brothers and sisters, that countries do not commit suicide. The people of our countries will awaken, stand up and fight!

As a conclusion, Your Excellencies, (I say that) because of its injustice and inequality, the economic and social order of neo-liberal globalization appears to be a dead-end street for the South.

Therefore, the Heads of State and governments who are responsible for the well-being of our peoples cannot passively accept the exclusionary rules imposed by this economic and social order.

The history of our countries tells us that without doubt, passivity and grieving are useless. Instead, the only conduct that will enable the South to raise itself from its miserable role as backwards, exploited, and humiliated is concerted and firm action.

Thanks to the heroic struggle against colonialism, the developing countries destroyed an economic and social order that condemned them to the status of exploited colonies. Colonialism was not defeated by the accumulation of tears of sorrow, or by the repentance of colonialists, but by centuries of heroic battles for independence and sovereignty in which the resistance, tenacity and sacrifices of our peoples worked wonders.

Here in South America, we commemorate this very year the 180th anniversary of the Battle of Ayacucho, where people united in a liberating army after almost 20 years of revolutionary wars under the inspired leadership of José de San Martín, Bernardo O'Higgins, José Inacio de Abreu e Lima, Simón Bolívar and Antonio José de Sucre, expelling a Spanish empire that had hitherto extended from the warm beaches of the Caribbean to the cold lands of Patagonia, and thus ending 300 years of colonialism.

Today, in the face of the obvious failure of neo-liberalism and the great threat that the international economic order represents for our countries, it is necessary to reclaim the Spirit of the South.

That is where this Summit in Caracas is heading.

I propose to re-launch the G-15 as a South Integration Movement rather than a group. A movement for the promotion of all possible trends, to work with the Non-aligned Movement, the Group of 77, China . . . The entire South!!

I propose that we reiterate the proposals of the 1990 South Commission:

Why not focus our attention and political actions to the proposal that we offer several thousand "Grants of the South" per year to students from under-developed countries so that they can continue their studies in the South; or (the proposal that we) dramatically increase our cooperation in health in order to decrease infant mortality, provide basic medical care, fight AIDS?

We must develop these and many other programs with solidarity in order to ease the deep suffering that characterizes the South, and confront the costly and ineffective results of our dependence on the North.

Why not create the Debtor's Fund as an elemental defense tool? It could have consultations and coordinate collective action policies to confront the ways creditor's forum protect their interests.

Why not transform our symbolic system of trade preferences among developing countries into something more advanced, that can counteract the protectionism of the North, which excludes our countries from their markets?

Why not promote trade and investment flows within the South instead of competing in a suicidal fashion to offer concessions to the multinationals of the North?

Why not establish the University of the South? Why not create the Bank of the South?

These and other proposals will retain their value. They await our political will to turn them into reality.

But finally, dear friends, I would like to mention a particular proposal, which, in my opinion, has great significance:

In the South we are victims of the media monopoly of the North, which acts as a power system that disseminates in our countries and plants in the minds of our citizens information, values and consumption patterns that are basically alien to our realities and that have become the most powerful and effective tools of domination. Never is domination more perfect than when the dominated people think like the dominators do.

To face and begin to change this reality, I dare to propose the creation of a TV channel that could be seen throughout the world, showing information and pictures from the South. This would be the first and fundamental step in crushing the media monopoly.

In a very short time this TV channel of the South could broadcast our values and our roots throughout the world. It could tell the people in the world, in the words of the great poet Mario Benedetti, a man from the deep South, Uruguay, where the La Plata River opens so much that it looks like a silver sea, and washes my dear Buenos Aires and bluish Montevideo:

"The South Also Exists"
With its French horn
and its Swedish academy its American sauce
and its English wrenches with all its missiles
and its encyclopedias its star wars
and its opulent viciousness with all its laurels
the North commands,
but down here, down close to the roots
is where memory no memory omits and there are those who defy death for
and die for

and thus together achieve what was impossible
that the whole world would know
that the South,
that the South also exists

Ladies and Gentlemen, thank you very much

For Further Reading

Blanchard, Peter. "The Language of Liberation: Slave Voices in the Wars of Independence," *Hispanic American Historical Review* 82:3, 499–523.

Bolívar, Simón. *El Libertador: Writings of Simón Bolívar*. Oxford: Oxford University Press, 2007.

Brading, David. *The First America: The Spanish Monarchy, Creole Patriots and the Liberal State 1492–1867*. Cambridge: Cambridge University Press, 1993.

Canizares-Esguerra, Jorge. *How to Write the History of the New World: Histories, Epistemologies, and Identities in the Eighteenth-Century Atlantic World*. Palo Alto: Stanford University Press, 2001.

Earle, Rebecca. *The Return of the Native: Indians and Myth-Making in Spanish America, 1810–1930*. Durham, NC: Duke University Press, 2008.

Fernandez De Lizardi, and Jose Joaquin. *The Mangy Parrot: The Life and Times of Periquillo Sarniento Written by Himself for His Children*. Cambridge, MA: Hackett, 2005.

James, C. L. R. *Black Jacobins: Toussaint L'Ouverture and the San Domingo Revolutions*. New York: Vintage, 1989.

Lynch, John. *Simón Bolívar: A Life*. New Haven: Yale University Press, 2007.

Rama, Angel. *The Lettered City*. Durham, NC: Duke University Press, 1996.

Scott, David. *Conscripts of Modernity: The Tragedy of Colonial Enlightenment*. Durham, NC: Duke University Press, 2004.

Stein, Stanley J., and Barbara H. Stein. *The Colonial Heritage of Latin America: Essays on Economic Dependence in Perspective*. Oxford: Oxford University Press, 1970.

Trouillot, Michel-Rolph. *Silencing the Past: Power and the Production of History*. Boston: Beacon, 1997.

Van Young, Eric. *The Other Rebellion: Popular Violence, Ideology, and the Mexican Struggle for Independence, 1810–1821*. Palo Alto: Stanford University Press, 2001.

Walker, Charles F. *Smoldering Ashes: Cuzco and the Creation of Republican Peru, 1780–1840*. Durham, NC: Duke University Press, 1999.

White, Hayden. *Metahistory: The Historical Imagination in Nineteenth-Century Europe*. Baltimore: Johns Hopkins University Press, 1975.

At A Glance: Political Divisions

L atin America's political boundaries were transformed at independence, as a system of Vice-Royalties, along with several Captaincies General, became sovereign nations (**Figure A.1**). While in the United States thirteen colonies yielded one federally organized state, the Spanish colonies fragmented into a multitude of countries between 1810 and 1850. In the Caribbean, the changes were even more complex. Some colonies won independence, while others remained within a variety of European imperial systems (some remain de-facto colonies to this day).

By the mid-nineteenth century, Latin America's colonial divisions had largely given way to the nations that exist today (**Figure A.2**), although a series of wars would redraw the national boundaries of several nations into the twentieth century. Among the countries that lost the most territory was Mexico, which lost Central America, Texas, half of the remaining national territory in the Mexican-American War, and later a sliver of the northern border region in the Gadsden Purchase (**Figure A.3**). Bolivia and Paraguay also lost significant portions of their national territory in nineteenth-century wars. Bolivia would also lose more territory during the twentieth century (see Figure 2.3 in Chapter 2).

Latin America's contemporary territorial boundaries were mostly settled by the mid-twentieth century (**Figure A.4**). Most of the remaining conflicts concerned small portions of land along international frontiers. Today, the most significant boundary questions that confront the region are internal secessionist movements and movements that claim indigenous autonomy.

Figure A.1   Colonial Latin America

Figure A.2 Mid-nineteenth-century Latin America

Source: *First Lessons in Geography, or, Introduction to "Youth's Manual of Geography"* by James Monteith (1856). The Baldwin Library of Historical Literature, George A. Smathers Libraries, University of Florida.

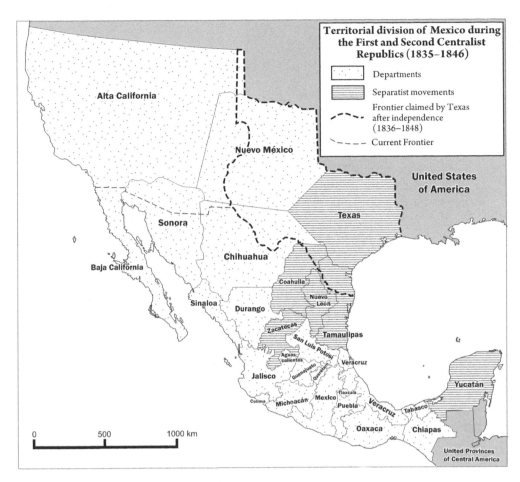

Figure A.3   Mexico's Loss of Territory, 1835–1846

Figure A.4 Contemporary Latin America

July 1, 1823	1829–1852	1833–1855	1835–1836	1839–1865
Central American Independence (from Mexico)	Juan Manuel de Rosas is de facto ruler of Argentina	Antonio López de Santa Anna rules Mexico on eleven different occasions	War for Texas independence	Rafael Carrera is de facto ruler of Guatemala

Caudillos Versus the Nation State

2

For the rare visitor who wanders through the Museum of the Illinois National Guard in Springfield, the oddest part of the adventure comes when they encounter the regiment's most famous trophy, a wooden leg encased in glass, which once belonged to General Antonio López de Santa Anna (Figure 2.1). It seems that in 1847 a group of Illinois National Guardsmen took it from the eleven-time Mexican president as he was eating his lunch during a lull in the fighting of what Mexicans refer to as the North American Invasion. Santa Anna removed the leg (his left) so he could eat comfortably, unaware of the Illinoisans lurking in the nearby bushes. Seizing the moment, they pounced and made off with the leg. As far as macabre symbolism goes, it ranks pretty high. American soldiers steal the prosthesis of a Mexican general, making his disability their booty.

Strange though it may seem, this is but one episode from the story of Santa Anna and his leg. This sometime president and sometime rebel marked the history of post-independence Mexico more than any other public figure. He was a hero of independence and the civil strife that followed, and first elected president in 1833 (see Figure 2.2). He lost his actual leg in the Pastry War (so named because one of the grievances that prompted the war was a demand for reparations from a French baker whose shop had been destroyed in a riot) with France in 1838. Initially, the leg was buried on his estate at Manga de Clavo in Veracruz. It was disinterred and given a state funeral in Mexico City in 1842, when Santa Anna was

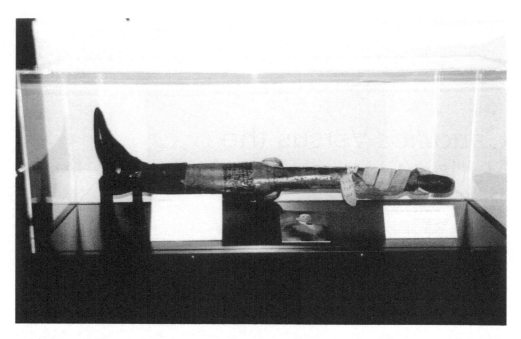

Figure 2.1 Picture of wooden leg belonging to the Mexican President, General Antonio López de Santa Anna

Source: Reprinted with permission from Dr. Antonio de la Cova

again president. Some years later his political enemies removed the leg from its tomb and dragged it through the streets of the city until it disintegrated.

Told as a sort of tragic comedy, this story often stands in for the larger history of Latin America in the half century after independence. Santa Anna assumed the Mexican presidency eleven times, often for short periods, and typically left office in disgrace. Mexicans nonetheless turned to him time and time again to defend their country or take on its internal enemies, and each time he willingly assumed the role of national savior. He oversaw many national disasters, the loss of Texas (1836), the loss of the Mexican–American War (1846–1848), and ultimately the Gadsden Purchase (1853), when he sold a sliver of Northern Mexico to the United States for $10 million (a map of these losses can be found in At a Glance: Political Divisions, on p. 41). This signaled the end for Santa Anna. Driven into exile in 1855, he did not return to Mexico until 1874. He died two years later in relative obscurity.

To the contemporary reader the story of Santa Anna's leg seems macabre, and slightly disconcerting. It reminds us that, as the novelist Leslie Poles Hartley famously noted, "the past is a foreign country,"[1] that the ways that people made sense of the world in the past were often profoundly different from the way we make sense of the world today, so different as to seem bizarre. To get beyond the farce we need signposts, an explanatory framework that will allow us to make sense of the way that people lived in the past, so that we might treat them as more than simple caricatures. We explain Santa Anna and his leg by reminding ourselves of the deeply Catholic quality of Mexican society during this era. Relics—sometimes simply the hair of a saint, or a drop of Jesus' blood—played an important

Figure 2.2 Antonio López de Santa Anna

Source: Southern Methodist University, Central University Libraries, DeGolyer Library

role in Mexican Catholicism. Many people invested the relic with a special kind of power, mixing their reverence for the relic with the sense that it (in this case, Santa Anna's leg) embodied the properties of the thing it represented. A cultural practice rooted both in Mexico's pre-Colombian past and to the folk cultures of medieval Europe, this had the capacity to transform Santa Anna's leg into a sacred object, first to be worshiped and then despised.

North of the border, visitors to the Illinois National Guard Museum have the opportunity to see Santa Anna's leg, much like Latin America (and in particular Mexico's North), as a prize, won through American ingenuity. Taken to its extreme, North Americans use the leg to symbolize a region that lacks a capacity to control itself and its own destiny (after all, the Mexican president was too fuzzy-headed to pay attention to his own wooden leg). Mexicans, on the other hand, can view the display as representative of both a national tragedy and a reminder of the cruelty of their northern neighbours.

In a global sense, the leg and the man who lost it have the capacity to stand in for something even larger. The fact that he became president so many times, that his leg was bound up in a story that mixed personal charisma with Catholic iconography in what seems like a peculiarly Latin American fashion, and that he oversaw such a series of national disasters, have transformed Santa Anna into an icon of the turmoil that engulfed Latin America during the nineteenth century, a period sometimes referred to as the *caudillo* age.

The *Caudillo*

How was it that Santa Anna ruled Mexico eleven times? His story can seem idiosyn-cratic, about Mexico at a certain time and place, except for the fact that the term we use to describe him—*caudillo*—links him to the type of political leader who dominated the nineteenth-century history of Latin America. *Caudillos* were critical figures in societies torn by conflict, nations where citizens could not turn to civic institutions or processes to defend their interests. They were strongmen, literally, charismatic figures who could defend their interests and the interests of their supporters by unleashing a torrent of violence against their enemies. Inasmuch as *caudillos* oversaw their share of national disasters, they were also formed by those disasters. They were figures who entered the vacuum of power left by the collapse of the Spanish colonial state and who offered hope for stability through the force of their will and their capacity to vanquish their enemies.

Independence in the Americas left the new nations of the region with numerous chal-lenges. Many members of the old political and cultural elites were suddenly unwelcome, viewed as foreigners loyal to an imagined enemy who had not quite given up the dream of re-colonizing their nations. The Catholic Church too was suspect. Long a servant of the colonial state and a possessor of great wealth, it promised stability to some and offered the threat of a return of the Spanish crown to others. More than this, the elites who remained in the former colonies generally took a dim view of the populace, which was generally poor, uneducated, and either indigenous, African, or of mixed racial origin. While Europe-ans increasingly viewed their nations as folk cultures, united through language, tradition, and blood, Latin American elites did not tend to view their societies in this fashion. In the Americas the ethnic and cultural divides were too vast.

Just as daunting was the task of physically controlling national territories. England, then the emerging great power of Europe, was a tiny country. France was not much larger, and Spain was a country in name only. The United States of America were substantial, but mostly comprised of settlements along the eastern seaboard, easily traversed and relatively unobstructed by geography. Latin Americans faced an entirely different set of challenges. Most Latin American nations were, when first imagined, vast territories. In comparison to their Anglo-American cousins, the colonies had been far flung, often characterized by long distances between mining centers, administrative and commercial capitals, and the ports, all of which were linked by narrow and sometimes impassable trails. Consider a coun-try like Mexico, which spanned from contemporary Oregon to Costa Rica, or the United Provinces of La Plata (modern Argentina), which spanned from the Tierra del Fuego to contemporary Bolivia. Even when these countries were sparsely populated, vast distances and geography put the lie to all illusions of central control.

These territories were linked more loosely under colonial rule than the map of the colonial world suggested. Brazil's vast Amazonian interior remained largely outside the purview of the state. In many regions, colonial officials lived exclusively in cities, towns, and mining camps, relying on a network of indigenous and mixed-raced intermediar-ies to maintain the façade of colonial rule beyond these locales. In the countryside the colonial state was a shadowy presence, and the illusion of centralized authority collapsed quickly when local interests were threatened. The long history of rebellions in the colo-nies, in which not just the poor, but sometimes even colonial elites used violence to defend their autonomy, revealed a state that was weak, and relied more on negotiation than coercion to rule.

The size of the territories and the physical obstacles to travel (mountain ranges, gorges, nearly impassable jungles) produced the logic by which the colonial state functioned. The same would be true for independent nations. Local officials acted mostly autonomously, only loosely controlled from the outside. To this, however, was added a new problem. With the collapse of colonial rule the citizens of the new republics had few compelling reasons to maintain the types of erstwhile loyalty to central government that had informed three centuries of colonial rule. Cities and institutions that had once embodied royal authority now symbolized a recently vanquished oppressor, and regional elites did not need to bow down to the centralized authority of the capital. With neither king nor church to justify their position in the nation, the capital cities risked becoming shadows of their former selves.

This again, takes us back to one of the important features of colonial life. The emperor and the Catholic Church played powerful symbolic roles as the social glue of colonial society. The Spanish king did not represent the imposition of foreign authority, but was a paternal mediator who sometimes intervened against a venal local aristocracy. Church and state were consciously positioned this way in the colonies, defending local peoples against their enemies, who were often installed in colonial capitals. The king might intervene in local land or political disputes, might remove corrupt officials, or confer a pardon for crimes committed. Likewise the church played a critical role in ministering to the poor and shaping ceremonial life across the colonies. With these two institutions gone or severely weakened, only the long-standing enemies of local interests were left in their place in the capital cities. The *caudillo* emerged in the midst of this divide.

In some ways *caudillos* provided a link to the colonial past. The types of loyalty they commanded were reminiscent of the devotion once paid to the Spanish crown. *Caudillos* were physically strong, and carried an air of invincibility. They were closely connected to their followers, intervening on their behalf to settle grievances, defending them (as the king had once done) against pernicious outsiders. But the fact that *caudillos* generally relied on narrow regional power-bases also reminds us of the extent to which post-colonial societies were fractured. Regional, class, and ethnic cleavages meant that *caudillos* had to rule through a number of distinct mechanisms. The first was the force of arms, their armies being largely local and tied together by personal connections and fictive kinship. The second was through the creation of informal patronage networks that promoted stability beyond the local level.

These networks functioned through a constant process of negotiation between different regional strongmen, which when successful produced a minimum level of political peace and the appearance of functioning states. Rooted in convenience and personal relationships instead of common ideological commitments, these pacts were always in danger of collapsing as new internal and external threats emerged. These were therefore governments characterized by the absence of powerful or relatively autonomous bureaucracies, of regularly occurring elections, or of the markers of a robust civil society (independent newspapers, political parties, and the like). Perhaps best described as weak states, the governments ensconced in the capital cities lacked the power to enforce laws, collect taxes, or impose their will outside of regions militarily controlled by the ruling *caudillo*.

The Mexican case is poignant, as a nation in turmoil lost half its territory to the ascendant United States, and at other times saw secession in the south (Central America in 1823, which in turn dissolved in 1838), but perhaps the most powerful example of the dissolution produced through *caudillismo* comes from the Andes. At independence, Chile was a relatively peripheral nation in the region, while Peru and Bolivia represented two of the crown jewels of the Spanish Empire. Nonetheless, in the aftermath of independence Chilean elites bound themselves together to produce a stable oligarchy[2] empowered by revenues from mining exports, a formidable merchant marine, and a state that was capable of investing in economic development. Though Chile was hardly democratic (civil society was dominated by the church and military, and most land in the country remained locked in a semi-feudal system characterized by huge agricultural estates known as *latifundio*), the Chilean state had the resources to invest in education, a modern military, and public services.

Chile was well situated to gain control of the nitrate deposits of the northern Atacama Desert, which became increasingly valuable as fertilizer by the 1870s. Though many of the deposits were on Bolivian soil, Chilean and British companies were better situated to exploit them than the Bolivians, and gained concessions to work these deposits in the 1870s. When the Bolivian government decided to raise the taxes charged in these concessions in 1878, Chilean merchants protested that these increases were illegal, and the conflict quickly spiraled into a much more serious dispute over the border. Bolivia declared war on Chile in February 1879, pulling Peru into the conflict because of a secret treaty between the two countries. In the war a relatively small and previously poor country took on two much larger neighbors, and defeated both conclusively.

The figure of the *caudillo* looms large over both Bolivia's and Peru's disasters in the war. Bolivian elites did not manage to consolidate under a stable national state after independence. Over time, peace between the cities and the countryside was maintained only through the Andean Pact, in which indigenous *ayllus* (clans) essentially acted as independent states, paying tribute to the Bolivian government in return for autonomy. This left a series of *caudillos* in control of an extremely weak central state, unable to build a modern infrastructure, develop the national economy, or create a modern military. Peru's story was even more desultory. After banning Indian tribute in the country's first constitution, Peruvian elites rapidly retreated from their image of a modern nation. An impoverished Peruvian state reinstated tribute as early as 1826, and even when the country experienced a boom in *guano* (bird or bat droppings, used to make fertilizer) exports in the 1840s, most of the revenues from *guano* were lost to ill-considered development efforts, civil war, and graft. In spite of his country's export boom, Peru's dominant *caudillo* of the era, Ramón Castilla, who ruled 1845–1851 and 1855–1862, left behind an empty treasury and growing foreign debt. When Chile invaded, Peruvians had little capacity to mount a spirited resistance, a problem made worse by the fact that Andean elites refused to arm Andean peasants, for fear that the arms might be ultimately turned on them. Peru lost territory and the lingering traces of parochial pride that came from its place in history. Bolivia lost its only access to the sea, a blow that is a source of bitterness to this day. What is more, the weakness of the Bolivian state would lead to further territorial losses in conflicts with Brazil and Paraguay in the decades to follow. By the mid-twentieth century *caudillo* politics ultimately resulted in the loss of half of the national territory (see Figure 2.3).

Figure 2.3 Bolivia's territorial losses, 1867–1938

The Cause of All National Disasters?

It is difficult to tell these histories without rendering the *caudillo* age as a story of national disasters. The internal violence, economic catastrophes, and territorial losses seem to bear this view out. Were these not somehow terror states, where people lived in fear of the dictator and civil rights were non-existent? Did this era not also signal an exodus of foreign and domestic capital from the region, and little economic growth or development, because investors avoided putting their money into zones characterized by civil war? There are reasons to answer all these questions in the affirmative, especially if we take Santa Anna and Castilla as the archetypal *caudillo*. It becomes more difficult to do this confidently if we look at others who just as easily lay claim to the moniker, or look more deeply into the larger social phenomena that characterized the *caudillo* age, and the ways that the emergence of *caudillos* spoke to the nature of daily life in the early nineteenth century.

We might begin to understand the *caudillo*'s capacity to command loyalty by imagining the sorts of social and political attachments that characterized Latin American societies in this era. People in the region tended to organize their lives around enduring familial, religious, and political loyalties, and though these loyalties often seemed to link one community to the next through ritual, practice, and shared symbols, for the most part those loyalties were in fact intensely local. While it is true that colonial elites imagined attachments that transcended the colonies, connecting them to Europe and the Spanish Empire more generally, and even the lower castes revered the king, in practice most people in the region tended to be deeply parochial, to cultivate loyalties first and foremost to their home community and real or fictive kin. In the colonial system the town council (*cabildo*) was one of the few political bodies that could represent local people against the state and more powerful economic interests, and as such was one of the most important components of associational life. What is more, local networks were incredibly effective at limiting the power of the central state, as the bosses (sometimes called *caciques*) simply refused to implement the rulings of their colonial overlords when they determined that it was importune to do so (thus, the famous colonial idiom, "I obey, but do not comply").

Local attachments were not simply a matter of taste. For residents of poor communities and local elites alike, unity on the local level had always been a strong bulwark against sinister external forces. Indigenous peoples in particular were given a great deal of power at the local level under the colonial system, an autonomy that was mostly exercised through the privileges assigned to local indigenous authorities by the colonial state. Village autonomy was often justified as a defense of *usos y costumbres* (customary law), a concept that suggested that indigenous villages represented cultures that were distinct from the societies around them, a Republic of Indians distinct from the Republic of Spaniards.

Indigenous in this usage was more of a spatial than a racial moniker. By the nineteenth century most of the people with indigenous ancestry in Latin America did not live as Indians per se, but as miners, porters, muleteers, agricultural workers, and as part of vast and growing urban underclasses. They spoke Spanish and wore clothing that gave no sign of their ethnic origins. They did not generally think of themselves as Indians, but as Mexicans, Peruvians, Chileans, etc. They also had relatively little invested in the struggles of their rural brethren to defend the spaces—the communities, their adjacent land, timber, and water— that made one Indian. "Indian," in this sense, was not a broad category, easily mobilized in the way that "Catholic," or "Mexican" might be. It spoke to a very specific place, a history in that place, and a series of linguistic, religious, political, and social practices that rooted given individuals in those places, and that local elites carefully reproduced in order to maintain a clear sense of "us" and "them." The leaders of indigenous communities (which in turn, were not generally identified as Indian, but by the specific ethnic group to which members of a community belonged) were inclined to make alliances with outsiders mainly based on their sense that those alliances would work in defense of their communities.

The same could be said more broadly for peasant communities across Latin America, where the defense of local customs and life-ways had long been bound up with other strategies for personal and community survival. Former slaves in Surinam (the Saramakas), Spanish-speaking, Catholic peasants in the Andes, cowboys in Argentina (*gauchos*), and *mestizo*[3] ranchers in Mexico (*rancheros*) all sought to defend their communities from the depredations of outsiders during the years following independence. All defined themselves as not quite white, not quite European, and believed that the things that made them particular were also qualities that they had a right to defend, by force of arms if necessary.

Peasants and Indians depended on powerful interlocutors (first the king, later the *caudillo*) to defend their interests in the face of attacks on village autonomy and communal land-holding even in the late colonial period. Committed to a variety of forms of modernization, the emerging liberal[4] elites in the region viewed peasant communal lands and autonomy as the essence of backwardness, signs of nations that lacked a coherent form, and of property regimes that stifled productivity because communal villagers could not profit individually from their toil. Villagers, on the other hand, believed that these traditions were essential to their survival. They acted as barriers to *hacendados*[5] and others who coveted their lands by making those lands inalienable and by establishing mechanisms whereby the poor could demand more land. They depended on the practices whereby the colonial state and later the *caudillos* periodically granted lands to the rural poor as a reward for military service, or in response to claims that a village's current boundaries could not support its population.

Independence disrupted the political and social order, and the civil wars that followed devastated the export sectors that had prospered under colonial rule. In much of the region the mines and plantations went into prolonged declines, impoverishing some elites and making it more difficult for them to maintain the labor regimes of the past. In this context poor rural people often found that they were able to live and work under conditions that were more equitable than in the past. Peasants across the region faced less pressure from expanding commercial agriculture. Demands for forced labor declined because of the shuttering of mines and plantations. And states that were weaker than ever before were less able to tax and draft their citizens into service. As in the past, economic decline on the macro level left many poor people with more control over their own destinies, better able to use their own labor power for themselves, and more likely to be able to negotiate the terms of their participation in political and military movements. Strong liberal states might have appropriated peasant and indigenous resources in order to promote national economic growth and development. In the absence of such states, many rural communities flourished, promising their loyalty to individuals who promised to defend them against their liberal enemies in the capital cities.

It was this milieu that produced the *caudillo*. Drawing their power from shifting personal networks, and needing to attend to the demands of these clients, *caudillos* were anathema to the project of the modern state, which seeks to create systems, institutions and practices that exist independent of the individuals who operate the levers of power. Unlike a strong central state, which might draw on the resources of the entire nation (or colony) to make demands of poor peasant villagers, a *caudillo* could only command loyalty from his soldiers if he delivered the goods. This was a tragedy to those liberals who saw in Latin America a series of unrealized potentials, the urban and economic elites who wanted to harness the productive capacity of the mines and plantations for national progress and their own benefit, and a respite for those who felt in the pressures of modernity something that would destroy their way of life.

Rafael Carrera, the nineteenth-century Guatemalan *caudillo* who was widely hated by Central American elites, was extremely popular among indigenous peoples precisely because he stood between Guatemala's liberal elites and the rural poor, stifling the growth of the central state and defending rural autonomy. It should be unsurprising that he drew most of his soldiers from the rural poor. In this he was similar to José María Urvina (president of Ecuador from 1851 to 1859), who leveraged the deep inequalities in Ecuador to his advantage. Both leaders acted as interlocutors between marginalized peoples and more powerful groups (often the state, foreign interests, or national elites). Their power came both from their ability to oversee large-scale patronage systems, distributing political spoils to their supporters (this is often called clientelism), and from their ability to cultivate a sense of closeness, of fictive kinship (known here as *compadrazgo*) in their followers because of their brotherly or fatherly concern for them. They did so by conjuring the same sentiments that had long kept the Spanish king relevant in the colonies. He was the ultimate defender of the rights and interests of the poor, and especially Indians. This pact was in part acted out through elaborate symbolic acts, but it was also acted out through concrete acts, land grants, intercessions between local elites and indigenous peoples, and acts of clemency for crimes committed against the state. In societies characterized by deep inequalities, rigid hierarchies, and enormous antipathies, the king, and later the *caudillo*, acted as a mediator.

Caudillos occupied contradictory roles in this conflict. Urvina, for example, won indigenous allies by attacking their traditional exploiters, the Catholic Church and the landlords of the highlands (on whose estates Indians lived in semi-serfdom). He eliminated the tribute that Indians had been forced to pay and banned the widely-despised Indian Protectorate.[6] As a liberal however, Urvina supported the parcelization of indigenous lands, a reform that would cause indigenous villages to lose much of their land. On top of this, his efforts to undermine the power of highland landlords had the effect of freeing up Indian laborers for service on the cacao estates on the coast (which suffered severe labor shortages). Former serfs from the highlands often found themselves toiling in conditions on the coast that were even worse than what they had experienced previously.

Perhaps no one better exemplified these sorts of compromises between defending a constituency and supporting economic development than the Argentine *caudillo* Juan Manuel de Rosas (see Figure 2.4). The model for the barbaric *caudillo* in Domingo Faustino Sarmiento's classic *Facundo: Civilization and Barbarism*,[7] Rosas was in many ways an archetypical *caudillo*. Born to a wealthy landowning family, he made his name as a military man in the wars of independence. He became governor of the Province of Buenos Aires in 1829, a position he would hold with only brief absences until he was overthrown in 1852. As governor he positioned himself as the defender of order, a warrior for traditional values, and nurtured a personality cult around his Holy Federation that placed him at the symbolic center of the nation in ways that were not unlike the role assigned to the Spanish king in earlier times. Followers assiduously placed his portrait in their homes, and wore the red of the Holy Federation as much to deny disloyalty as to prove loyalty. In return for giving up any pretense to civil rights, they received the economic spoils and personal security gained from order; an order which was situated as the antidote to the violence and dislocation produced in the wars of independence.

Rosas' reign was brutal. Enemies were shown no mercy, and his opponents lived in fear of his personal army, the *mazorca*. Like other *caudillos*, when he assumed the governorship he confiscated the property of his enemies and used it to pay his soldiers and provide recompense to the poor peons who had suffered losses in earlier conflicts. Rosas paid particular attention to Afro-Argentines, as they represented around 30 percent of the population of Buenos Aires and formed much of his political base. His *Gaceta Mercantil* called them "valiant defenders of liberty," and declared that "General Rosas so appreciates the mulattos and *morenos* that he has no objection to seating them at his table and eating with

Figure 2.4   Juan Manuel de Rosas

Source: Portrait by Cayetano Descalzi, Museo histórico nacional, Buenos Aires, Argentina

them."[8] Rosas' enemies among the Unitarians (including Esteban Echeverría) recoiled at these images, as they represented a direct repudiation of the deeply racist values that predominated among elites of the day. His supporters however, reveled in these performances of loyalty to his followers.

Traditional assessments of Rosas held that the terror of these years somehow precluded the creation of a nation. These judgments were originally penned by Argentines themselves, most notably Sarmiento. Rosas came to represent a kind of rural backwardness, whether cultural or racial, a kind of degeneration that prevented the advance of civilization. However, in recent decades a more complex narrative has emerged. Revisionist histories begin by acknowledging that in the aftermath of Argentine independence, the odds were stacked against anyone who might aspire to rule this vast region through a strong centralized state. In the 1820s Bernardino Rivadavia tried to expand federal control and create a balanced economy with a powerful centralized and efficient state, but his efforts were undermined by recurring civil war. Not only were distances great and hard to travel, the regional strongmen who emerged during the wars for independence possessed their own armies, and were unlikely to cede authority to Buenos Aires. At this moment the complete dissolution of Argentina was possible, as Bolivia's, Paraguay's, and Uruguay's secessions revealed. Facing these facts on the ground, Rosas wove together a loose coalition of *caudillos*. Each *caudillo* was essentially autonomous, but all were expected to swear loyalty to the Holy Federation. In return for their autonomy, they recognized Buenos Aires' right to control foreign policy and ceded any interest in foreign trade to *porteño*[9] merchants. Rosas' position in turn allowed him to use the National Customs House to raise revenue.

Starting from this position of relative weakness, Rosas used customs revenues to gradually expand the authority of Buenos Aires across the national territory, bringing the other *caudillos* increasingly under the central state's authority. He never produced the strong centralized state that Unitarians wanted, but the alliances and agreements he oversaw maintained the peace and allowed the early development of Argentina's agricultural export economy, especially beef and hides (with some wheat). Under Rosas, the patterns of land tenure and oligarchical rule that would later characterize the country's export boom were established. The state and private interests built roads, transportation and communications networks, and the transformation of the pampas from free range into private property gradually proceeded. Domination of the export sector also allowed Buenos Aires merchants to make vast fortunes by exporting salted beef to feed slaves in Brazil and Cuba. Without Rosas' particular style of rule, much of this may have been impossible. Whether that is a good thing or a bad thing depends on one's perspective.

Over time, Rosas' enemies grew in number, but until the very end Rosas had considerable support from *estancieros*[10] in Buenos Aires, the Catholic Church, and the poor. In part this support was strategic, followers followed because it was the safest thing to do, but his broad appeal should not be underestimated. He defended religious tradition and placed Catholicism at the center of his symbolic repertoire, which stood in stark contrast to his liberal enemies. He spoke a language that resonated with the rural and urban poor, showing them that he was one of them. And he always divvyed up the spoils of power among his followers. The combination of these factors allowed him to be one of the most important *caudillos* in the history of Latin America.

Ending the *Caudillo* Age?

Did Argentina's *caudillo* age end with the overthrow of Rosas in 1852 and the gradual creation of a more republican system of government? Did Mexico's end with the exile of Santa Anna? These questions are extremely difficult to answer, as the political style of *caudillismo*, of strong charismatic leaders with military backgrounds, would persist long after the fratricidal violence and instability of the mid-century receded. Rosas' successors focused on building formal institutions of government, on creating national economic and educational policies, on creating a state that ruled as much through a judicial and political system as it did through the force of arms. And yet the threat of violence (along with actual violence) remained a necessary part of Argentine statecraft long after Rosas was cold in his grave. Across the region it would be very difficult to effectively separate the state from the ruler, to produce societies in which government was a series of institutions that in some ways operated autonomously from the person who, at any given moment, occupied the presidential chair.

We see this challenge quite starkly in Mexico's *Reforma*, a period that lasted roughly from 1854 until 1876. The collapse of Santa Anna's last regime emboldened a generation of young liberals, led by the likes of Benito Juárez and the Lerdo de Tejada brothers (Miguel and Sebastián), many of them young lawyers with a radically liberal democratic bent. These reformers rapidly pushed through a series of major legal reforms that they then enshrined in the 1857 Constitution. Among the most controversial reforms were those that eliminated the corporate rights and privileges (*fueros*) of the military, the church, economic guilds, and Indian communities. Liberals viewed these as vestiges of colonial rule that undermined the capacity of the state to collect taxes and retarded economic growth (as only a small amount of land circulated in the market, leaving much of the country tied up in what they viewed as unproductive estates). The church was predictably opposed, as were those elites who had enjoyed these privileges. The opposition also included the residents of many indigenous communities (*ejidos*), who could no longer hold land collectively and who feared that privatization of their lands (the requirement that land be held by private individuals) would inevitably mean that poor indigenous peasants would lose their land to rich outsiders.

Mexican conservatives went to war against the new order in 1857, recruiting many of their foot soldiers from within indigenous communities on the promise that they would restore the colonial order. Conservatives also promised to implement a head tax (*capacitación*) that would provide exemptions from military service and sales taxes for residents of indigenous communities. Nonetheless, even with these commitments, not all indigenous communities supported the conservatives. Mid-century Mexican liberalism found adherents among some indigenous Mexicans, particularly because of it inclusivity (its promise to offer equal rights to all Mexicans) and its promise of democratic freedoms, which in many cases was taken to mean the right of indigenous communities to establish their own rules and practices, an interpretation that Mexican liberals were in no condition to contest at this point.[11] Mexican liberalism in its most radical forms called for the devolution of political authority to the local level, a promise that was likewise appealing in indigenous communities. Furthermore, when Mexican conservatives, having lost the battle on the ground, went so far as to invite a foreign despot to rule Mexico in 1861 (the Austrian Prince Maximilian), significant numbers of indigenous Mexicans lined up to defend the patria against a foreign invader.

That indigenous Mexicans lined up behind conservative and liberal causes, and sometimes both in short order, reminds us that this was an era in which popular sectors had a great deal of room to maneuver when it came to their relationships with elites. Residents of indigenous communities might support a conservative leader because of their promise to defend communal rights, or a liberal leader because of their appeal to democratic rights and defense of the nation; what mattered most of all was the content of the shifting bargains through which indigenous communities endeavored to defend a series of interests against outsiders—some national, some foreign. These arrangements were invariably informed by a sense of urgency. Liberal and conservative elites relied on militias drawn from the rural poor to fight their battles, and indigenous communities needed relationships with powerful outsiders in order to reduce their vulnerability. The *caudillo* age was thus a moment in which a variety of popular and elite projects could intersect, a time when marginalized groups found opportunities to negotiate the terms of their inclusion in the national project through military service.

This did not mean that peasant and indigenous groups could invariably or permanently leverage their military capacities into partnerships with elites. It was, in fact, the potential power of these subaltern groups that prompted Peruvian elites to spurn their assistance during the Chilean invasion in 1881, fearful as they were of the capacity of Andean peasants to threaten their own power (they preferred Chilean overlords to the specter of Túpac Amaru). And in Mexico, as central state authority expanded under Porfirio Díaz after 1876, the alliances that had made Díaz a powerful *caudillo* during and after the French Intervention were no longer necessary, as indigenous and peasant supporters were supplanted by a modern army, a modern state, and technologies (railroads, telegraphs, machine guns) that facilitated the concentration of power. No longer needing the support of his indigenous allies as Mexico left the *caudillo* era behind, in the 1870s and 1880s Díaz passed a series of laws that designated indigenous lands as *terrenos baldios* (vacant lands), facilitating their transfer to private ownership. The government allowed private land survey companies to establish the physical coordinates of these lands in return for the right to keep one-third of the land surveyed. Indian communities were in theory entitled to turn their *ejidos* into private property, but many resisted and had their lands expropriated by the stroke of a pen. Others found that the interlocutors with whom they worked misrepresented the deeds and other papers that community leaders signed, resulting in significant losses. Within a half century nearly 90 percent of the land in the country fell into the hands of less than 1 percent of the population.

Díaz the *caudillo* was a far better ally to these communities than Díaz the victorious liberal. In his former self he depended on the military capacity of these communities because of his relative weakness, and tended to reward their loyalty with his. As a *caudillo* Díaz was less concerned with ideology than cultivating a network that could place him in the presidential palace, and correspondingly less concerned with extending the power of the government into peasant communities in the interest of national integration and development. The appeal of *caudillos* like Díaz to these communities was inextricably tied up with this fact, that in return for loyalty he respected village autonomy (at least he did so early on). And that respect was not simply evidenced through a tendency not to meddle, it was demonstrated in the respect that the most successful *caudillos* showed to the poor, indigenous, and *casta*[12] followers who made up their armies. With the emergence of a stronger state, comprised of armies and institutions that could effectively extend the power of that state throughout the national territory, that bond was broken.

The Document: Literature as History

When Latin Americans looked for a language to describe the anxieties they felt about their societies during the nineteenth century, the images they turned to were often rooted in a very specific binary—the struggle between barbarism and civilization. One was rooted in the past, the other oriented to the future. One held the promise of modern nationhood, the other poverty and dependence. Race, class, gender, and culture were all described through these lenses, producing clear visions of who promised to be enlightened citizens, and who were drags on progress. At their most extreme, the modernizers sought to remake their societies into American copies of Europe, transforming their cities to mimic the latest European architectural styles, importing fashions and trends from the old world, and sending their children to European finishing schools so that they might be even more civilized than the civilized.

Not everyone agreed that this was the best course for the future. Just as the rural and urban poor often carried on their own traditions alongside the elites, sometimes expressing their opposition to elite domination through popular culture, there were many in the intelligentsia who recoiled at the idea of Latin America as a European copy. Many nationalists saw in the region's popular cultures the traditions that gave the Latin America its form and specificity, even if they also wanted to embed those practices within modern nations. They did not want civilization to flatten out those things that made one an Argentine, a Brazilian, a Mexican, a Chilean.

Over many decades literature became one of the critical forums in which this interplay of local and universal values was dissected. Below (Document 2.1) we present one of the brilliant early examples of this tradition. *The Slaughterhouse* (*El Matadero*), written by the Argentine Esteban Echeverría in 1838, is not a screed against either the traditional or the modern, but is instead a deeply ambivalent story of change. Like other notable writers of his day, Echeverría imagined himself as a nationalist and a political activist. He was a prominent member of several political clubs founded to oppose Rosas in the 1830s, including the *Associación de Mayo*, named for Argentina's independence heroes. He used fiction to articulate a vision of the nation as it was and how it should be, and in many ways lived the tragedies he described through the experience of forced exile. It was in exile in Uruguay that he wrote this powerful indictment of Rosas, and where he died while Rosas was still in power. *The Slaughterhouse* would not be published until 1871.

Echeverría's anxieties about barbarism were also evident in his other work, especially *la insurrección del sur* and *la cautiva*, his epic poem about a European woman kidnapped by Mapuche Indians. In this, he was very much like other liberal intellectuals of his day. Strong opponents of dictatorship and *caudillismo*, these figures are in some ways sympathetic, yet they situate their opposition to dictatorship in ways that remind us of the elitism of the era. Theirs was an urbane intellectual liberalism, with little sympathy for the sensibilities and capacities of the rural folk who formed the backbone of the Rosas regime. And in the end, their admiration of civilization would have its genocidal variant, as the logics of modernity under-girded decisions to eliminate those who were unwilling or unable to embrace modern liberal sensibilities.

Other important texts in this literary cannon include *Facundo, Martín Fierro, Rebellion in the Backlands, Don Diego Sombra*, and *Birds Without a Nest*. Some of these are more sympathetic to the backwards folk than others, situating them as the true nationalists in contrast to the morally bankrupt city-folk. Others see rural backwardness as both the characteristic that gives the nation its form and the nation's undoing. All agree however, that the great struggle that confronts Latin America is the battle between civilization (read Europe) and backwardness (read the dark skinned people of countryside). Almost invariably cast in racial terms, this precluded any possibility that the new republics would embrace horizontal, fraternal forms of citizenship.

Document 2.1 Esteban Echeverría, *The Slaughterhouse* (*El Matadero*)

Source: Trans. Elizabeth Medina, with assistance from Marina Soldati; http://www. biblioteca.clarin.com/pbda/cuentos/matadero/matadero.htm.

Even though what I am about to tell is essentially history, I will not begin with Noah's Ark and his ancestors' genealogy, as the early Spanish chroniclers of the New World were wont to do and whose example we should emulate. I have many reasons for not follow-ing their example, reasons I will not elaborate on in order to avoid long-windedness. I will merely say that the events in my narration took place in the 1830s of the Chris-tian era. It was, moreover, during Lent, a time of year when meat is scarce in Buenos Aires because the Church, in deference to Epictetus's precept of *sustine et abstine*—to bear and forbear—ordains that vigil and abstinence be imposed on the stomachs of the faithful as the flesh is sinful, and thus, as the proverb says: *flesh seeks flesh*. And since the Church, *ab initio* and by direct authorization from God Himself, holds material power over the consciences and stomachs that do not, in any way whatsoever, belong to the individual, then nothing more is fair or rational than for it to forbid what is evil.

The purveyors of meat, on the other hand—good Federalists all, and therefore good Catholics—knowing full well that the people of Buenos Aires possess the pre-cious quality of an extraordinary docility for bowing to any kind of command, bring only the number of steers strictly necessary during the Lenten season to feed the children and the sick—who are excused from the abstinence mandated by the Papal Bull—and without any intention of letting a few intractable heretics stuff their gullets. For there is never any lack of such people, ever prepared to transgress the Church's meat commandments and spread the contagion of their bad example to society.

Thus, it happened that in those days, there was a very heavy rainfall. Roads were flooded. Marshes became lakes, and the streets that led into and out of the city over-flowed with slushy mud. A huge torrent suddenly cascaded down Barracas Creek and majestically spread its murky waters until they reached the gully beds of Alto. The Río de la Plata swelled fiercely, propelling the turgid waters that were searching for a channel, making them rush over fields, embankments, groves, and hamlets, until they spread out like a vast lake across all the lowlands. Ringed from north to west by a swath of water and mud, and south by a whitish ocean on whose surface a number of small boats bobbed precariously about, and chimneys and treetops marked with black smudges, the city gazed at the horizon in astonishment from its towers and its ravines, as though imploring for protection from the Most High. The rain seemed to portend another Great Flood. Pious men and women wailed as they prayed novenas and recited endless litanies. Preachers stormed the churches and made the pulpits creak under their hammering fists. "This is Judgment Day," they said. "The end of the world is near. God's wrath is overflowing and spilling forth as floodwaters. Woe unto you, sinners! Woe unto you, wicked Unitarians[13] who mock the Church and its wise men, and fail to listen reverentially to the word of the Lord's anointed! Woe unto you who do not beg for God's mercy before the altars! The terrible hour approaches of use-less gnashing of teeth and feverish cursing. Your wickedness, heresies, blasphemies, your horrendous crimes have caused the plagues of the Lord to veer towards our land. The Lord of the Federation's just hand will damn you."

The wretched women streamed out of the churches, overwhelmed and gasping for air, blaming the calamity, as was to be expected, on the Unitarians.

Still the heavy rains continued falling relentlessly and the flooding worsened, as if to confirm the preachers' predictions. Church bells began tolling, invoking divine aid, on the orders of the very Catholic and universalist Restorer,[14] who it seemed was rather worried. The libertines, the unbelievers—that is to say, the Unitarians—grew fearful at the sight of so many remorseful faces and at the sound of such a bedlam of profanity. There was already talk, as though the matter had been decided, of a procession that all the people would be obliged to attend, unshod and bareheaded, accompanying the Sacred Host to be carried by the Bishop beneath a canopy, to Balcarce Gully. There, thousands of voices would have to implore for divine mercy, exorcising the cause of the flood—the Unitarian devil.

Happily—or better said, unfortunately, for it would have been a sight to behold—the ceremony was not performed because as the Río de la Plata's floodwaters abated, the immense flood bed gradually drained away without any need of exorcism or supplications.

Now the most relevant circumstance for my story is that as a result of the flood, the Convalescencia Slaughter Yard saw not a single head of cattle for fifteen days, and in one or two days all of the farmers' and water sellers' oxen had been consumed in order to supply the city with beef. The poor children and the sick were fed on eggs and chicken, and the gringos[15] and renegade heretics bellowed for beefsteak and roast. Abstinence from meat was widespread among the common folk, who were blessed as never before by the Church, and thus millions upon millions of plenary indulgencies showered down on them. The price of a hen rose to six pesos while eggs went for four *reales* each, and fish was exorbitantly expensive. In those Lenten days, people did not consume fish and red meat in the same meal, nor indulge in gluttonous excess; but, on the other hand, innumerable souls rose straight to heaven and events took place that seemed the stuff of dreams.

Not a single live mouse was left in the slaughter yard, out of the thousands that had found shelter there before. They all died, either from starvation or from drowning in their burrows because of the incessant rain.

Swarms of black women, scavenging in the manner of *caranchos*[16] for viscera to steal, spread throughout the city like mythical harpies, ready to devour anything edible they could find. Their inseparable rivals in the slaughter yard, the seagulls and the dogs, migrated elsewhere in search of animal feed. A number of ailing elderly people contracted consumption for lack of nutritious broth. But the most striking event of all was the near-sudden death of some gringo heretics, who committed the transgression of gorging on Extremadura sausages, ham, and cod, and departed for the afterlife to atone for such an abominable sin as to partake of meat and fish in the same meal.

Some physicians expressed their opinion that if the scarcity of meat continued, then half of the population would suffer from fainting spells because their stomachs were so habituated to the fortifying juices of meat. One could not help noticing the stark contrast between these dire scientific predictions and the condemnations hurled down by the reverend fathers from the pulpits, against all carniferous nutriments and the combined consumption of meat and fish during those days, set aside by the Church for fasting and penance. This set off a kind of internecine warring between stomachs and consciences, stoked on one hand by unrelenting appetite, and on the other by the priests' no-less-implacable vociferations, duty bound as they are to brook no vice that might lead to a relaxing of Catholic customs. On top of this, there was the inhabitants' condition of intestinal flatulence from eating fish and beans and other somewhat indigestible fare.

This war was manifested by the jarring sobs and cries that were heard as the priests delivered their sermons, and in the rumblings and sudden explosive noises coming from the city's houses and streets, or wherever people gathered together. The Restorer's government—as paternal as it was far-sighted—grew rather alarmed. Believing that these instances of unrest were instigated by revolutionaries, and attributing them to the savage Unitarians themselves (whose wickedness, said the Federalist preachers, had brought down the flood of God's wrath upon the nation), the government took active measures. It sent out its spies among the populace, and finally, well apprized, issued a decree that was soothing for consciences as well as for stomachs, with a most wise and pious declaration, so that—at all costs and charging across high water if need be—cattle should be brought to the corrals.

And indeed, on the sixteenth day of the scarcity, on the eve of the Day of Sorrows,[17] a troop of fifty fattened steers waded across Paso de Burgos and entered the Alto Slaughter Yard. This number, incidentally, was a mere trifle, given that the population was accustomed to consuming 250 to 300 steers a day and at least a third of the inhabitants were under a special dispensation from the Church allowing them to eat meat. How strange that there should be stomachs subject to inviolable laws and that the Church holds the key to all stomachs!

But there really isn't anything strange about it at all, since the Devil customarily enters the body through the flesh, and the Church has the power to cast him out. It is a matter of reducing man to a machine, whose driving force is not his own will but that of the Church and the government. A time may come when it will be forbidden to breathe fresh air, take a walk, or even to have a conversation with a friend, without first obtaining permission from the competent authorities. This was how it was, more or less, in the happy times of our pious grandparents, which the May Revolution unfortunately disrupted.

In any event, upon the announcement of the government decree, the corrals of Alto filled up—despite all the mud—with butchers, scavengers for viscera, and curious onlookers, all of whom welcomed the fifty steers headed for the slaughter yard with boisterous shouts and applause.

"Smallish, but fat!" they exclaimed. "Long Live the Federation! Long Live the Restorer!"

My readers surely must know that in those days, the Federation was everywhere—even amidst the filth of the slaughterhouse—and just as there could be no sermon without St. Augustine, there was no festival without the Restorer. It is said that when they heard the wild shouting, the last of the rats that were starving to death in their rat holes sprang back to life and began madly scurrying about, for they realized that the familiar merriment and uproar were announcing the return of abundance.

The first steer butchered was gifted whole to the Restorer, who was known for his penchant for grilled meat. A committee of butchers marched off to deliver it in the name of the Federalists of the Alto Slaughter Yard, and they personally expressed their gratitude for the government's wise providence, their unlimited support for the Restorer, and their deep hatred of the enemies of God and man—the Unitarian savages. The Restorer responded to their harangue in the same vein, and the ceremony ended with the appropriate cheers and vociferations from spectators and actors. One must assume that the Bishop had granted the Restorer a special dispensation to eat meat, since being such a strict observer of the laws, such a good Catholic, and such a staunch defender of the faith, he would have set a bad example by accepting such a gift on a holy day.

The slaughter proceeded, and in one hour, forty-nine steers had been laid out in the slaughter yard, some skinned and others about to be. It was a lively and picturesque scene, though one that brought together the most hideous, filthy, malodorous, and deformed elements of the small proletarian class typical of the Río de la Plata. However, to enable the reader to readily picture the scene, a sketch of the venue is required.

The Convalescencia or Alto Slaughter Yard is a parcel of land near the country estates south of Buenos Aires. The large rectangular lot lies at the end of two streets, one of which stops there, while the other continues eastward. This south-sloping lot is divided by a rain-carved channel lined with innumerable rat holes, with the channel bed in the rainy season collecting all of the blood, both dry and fresh, from the slaughter yard. At the right-angle junction, to the west, stands what is known as the *casilla* or judge's quarters, a low building consisting of three small, sloping-roofed rooms, with a porch along its front that faces the street and a hitching post for horses. To the rear of the building are several corrals of *ñandubay* wood, with heavy gates for securing the cattle.

In the winter these corrals are veritable quagmires. The animals crowd together, buried up to the tops of their legs in the mud, stuck together, as it were, and nearly motionless. Corral duties and fines for violations of the regulations are collected in the *casilla*, where the slaughter yard judge holds court—an important personage, the *caudillo* of the butchers, who wields supreme power over this small republic by delegation of the Restorer. It isn't hard to imagine the kind of man required to perform such an office. As for the *casilla*, it is such a small and shabby building that no one in the corrals would give it any importance but for the association of its name with that of the feared judge and the garish red signs painted on its white walls: "Long Live the Federation"; "Long Live the Restorer and the Heroic Doña Encarnación Ezcurra"; "Death to the Unitarian Savages." They are signs fraught with meaning, symbolic of the political and religious faith of the slaughter yard's people. But some readers will likely be unaware that the aforementioned "heroine" is the Restorer's late wife, the butchers' beloved patroness, venerated by them after her death for her Christian virtues and Federalist heroism during the revolution against Balcarce.[18] It so happened that during an anniversary of that memorable feat by the *Mazorca*, the butchers celebrated with a splendid banquet in the heroine's *casilla*, which she attended with her daughter and other Federalist ladies. There, before a great crowd, she offered her Federalist patronage to the gentlemen butchers in a solemn toast, whereupon they enthusiastically proclaimed her patroness of the slaughter yard, inscribing her name on the walls of the *casilla*, where it will remain until it is erased by the hand of time.

From a distance, the slaughter yard was a grotesque, bustling sight. Forty-nine cattle were laid out on their skins, and nearly two hundred people trudged around in the sloughy ground that was drenched with the blood from the animals' arteries. A group of people of different races and complexions gathered around each steer. The most prominent figure in each group was a butcher with knife in hand, his arms and chest bare, hair long and tangled, his shirt, *chiripá*,[19] and face smeared with blood. Behind him, following his every move, was a band of swarming, capering boys and black and mulatto women, these last scavengers for chitterlings, as ugly as the viragos of legend. Intermingled among them were some huge hounds that sniffed, growled, or snapped at each other as they wrangled over a prize piece of offal. Forty-some carts covered with blackened, worn hides were ranged unevenly along the entire length of the lot. A few men on horseback, wearing ponchos and with lassoes lightly and expertly held in one hand, rode their mounts at a brisk stride amid the crowds, while others slouched over their horses' necks, training an indolent eye on one of the lively groups. Meanwhile, above them, a swarm of blue-and-white gulls, drawn back to the slaughterhouse by the smell of flesh, fluttered in the air, blanketing the slaughter yard's din and babble with dissonant squawks and casting a shadow over the field of gruesome carnage. Such was the scene at the start of the butchering.

However, as the slaughter continued, the scene began to change. The groups broke apart and new ones formed, which took on assorted attitudes, and then the people scattered at a run, as though a stray bullet had hit where they stood or the jaws of a rabid mastiff had burst into their midst. In one group, a butcher hacked at a slaughtered animal's flesh; in a second, another butcher hung up the quartered sections on wagon hooks. One skinned a carcass here, another trimmed off the fat there. And from time to time, from among the ranks of the mob that eyed and waited for a piece of offal, a grimy hand holding a knife would dart out to slice a piece of fat or meat from a steer's quarters. This would set off the butcher's shouts and explosions of anger, the renewed swarming of the groups, and the young boys' jeers and jarring shouts.

"Hey, over there! That woman is slipping fat into her bosoms!" one of them shouted. "That man stuffed it in his pants flap," retorted the black woman.

"Hey you, black witch, get out of here before I cut you open!" exclaimed the butcher.

"What have I done to you, ño Juan? Don't be mean—all I want is the belly and the guts."

"They're for that there witch—goddamn it!"

"Get the witch! Get the witch!" the young boys chanted. "She's taking the kidney fat and the liver!" And two chunks of clotted blood and some enormous mud balls began raining on her head.

In another part of the yard, two African women half-carried, half-dragged an animal's entrails. Over in another area, a mulatto woman was walking off with a ball of viscera when she suddenly slipped in a puddle of blood and fell flat on her backside, shielding her precious booty with her body. Farther away, huddled together in rows, four hundred black woman unwound a tangle of intestines in their laps. One by one, they picked off the last bits of fat that the butcher's miserly knife had left on the entrails. Meanwhile, others emptied out stomachs and bladders and filled them with air from their own lungs so that they could deposit offal inside them once they were dry.

Youths, gamboling about on foot and on horseback, smacked each other with inflated bladders or lobbed rolled pieces of meat at one another, scattering with the exploding balls of meat and their boisterous antics a cloud of seagulls that balanced in the air, celebrating the slaughter with their raucous screeching. Despite the Restorer's prohibition against swearing and the holiness of the day, profanities and obscenities were often to be heard, vociferations laden with the bestial cynicism that is so typical of the riffraff in our slaughter yards, and which I am disinclined to share with my readers.

Without warning a bloody lung would fall over someone's head, which was then passed on to someone else's, until some deformed hound grabbed it firmly, only to be accosted by a pack of other dogs that tried to wrest a piece of it away in a horrific melee of snarls and savage bites. An old woman set off in angry pursuit behind a young man who had smeared her face with blood. His friends, responding to the troublemaker's yelling and cursing, surrounded and harassed her the way dogs will badger a bull. She was pelted with pieces of meat and balls of dung, as well as with guffaws and repetitive shouts, until the judge commanded that order be restored and the field cleared.

To one side, two boys practiced handling their knives by throwing horrendous slashes and blows at each other. In another spot, four already-adolescent boys flicked knives at each other for the right to a thick length of intestine and a piece of tripe filched from a butcher. And not far from them, some dogs, gaunt from forced absti-nence, employed the same means to see which one would carry away a mud-slathered liver. It was all a simulacrum in miniature of the barbaric ways in which individual and social issues and rights are resolved in our country. All told, the scenes unfolding in the slaughter yard were for seeing—not for consigning to paper.

One animal, with a short, thick neck and a fierce look, had been left behind in the pens. Opinions were divided regarding its genitals, because they seemed to be similar to both a bull's and a steer's. The animal's hour arrived. Two lassoers on horseback entered the corral, now surrounded by crowds milling about, some on foot, others mounted, and still others straddling the corral's gnarled timbers. The most grotesque, conspicuous group of all was standing by the gate: several expert lassoers on foot, their arms bare, each one armed with an unerring noose, bright red kerchiefs tied around their heads, wearing vests and red *chiripás*. Behind them were several riders and expectant onlookers, intently observing the scene.

The animal, a slipknot already around its horns, bellowed wildly, spraying foam from its mouth. But the devil himself could not get it to emerge from the thick slime that like glue mired down the beast and made it impossible to lasso its legs. The boys perched on the corral fence shouted at and heckled the animal, waving their ponchos and kerchiefs to no avail. The cacophony of whistles, clapping, high-pitched and guttural voices blaring from that extraordinary orchestra was something to hear.

The boorish comments and shouts of raillery and obscenities rolled from mouth to mouth, each one there making a spontaneous show of their cleverness and wit, excited by the scene or prompted by someone else's sallies.

"Son of a bitch, that bull."

"To hell with those castrated bulls from Azul."[20] "Damned cheating driver passed a bull off for a steer." "I'm telling you it's a steer—that's no bull!"

"Can't you see it's an old bull?"

"The hell it is—show me its balls if you're so sure, damn it!"

"There they are—he's got them between his legs. Can't you see, my friend? They're bigger than your chestnut horse's head. Or did you go blind on the way here?"

"Your mother would be the blind one, if she gave birth to a son like you. Can't you see that lump's nothing but mud?"

"You're as stubborn and ornery as a Unitarian . . ."

At the sound of the magic word they all shouted, "Death to the Unitarian savages!" "Send the sons of bitches to One-Eye."

"Yes, to One-Eye—he's got the balls for fighting Unitarians. Flank steak[21] for Matasiete, executioner of Unitarians! Long Live Matasiete!" "The flank steak to Matasiete!"

"There he goes!" shouted a man with a guttural voice, cutting short the bluster of cowardly bullies. "There goes the bull!"

"Watch out! Look sharp you, by the gate! He's headed there, mad as a devil!" Indeed the animal—harassed by the shouting and, most of all, by two sharp cattle prods spurring his hindquarters—sensing that the noose had loosened, rushed the gate with a powerful snort, hurling fiery looks from side to side with its reddened eyes. The lassoer yanked the lariat and dislodged the noose on the bull's horn, making his horse fall back on its haunches. A sharp hiss flayed the air and, from atop a fence fork, a boy's head was seen to roll down, as though severed from the base of the neck by a hatchet blow, his motionless trunk still sitting astride its wooden horse and shooting out from every artery a long torrent of blood.

"The rope was cut!" some shouted. "There goes the bull!"

But others, bewildered and stunned, were silent, because everything had happened as quickly as though a lightning bolt had struck.

The group that was by the gate began to break up. Some crowded around the head and still-quivering body of the boy decapitated by the lasso, expressing horror at the final look of shock on its face. The others, horsemen who had not witnessed the tragedy, fanned out in different directions in pursuit of the bull, yelling and screaming, "There he goes!" "Intercept him!" "Watch out!" "Rope him, Sietepelos!" "Get away from him, Botija!" "He's furious, stay out of his way!" "Head him off, head him off, Morado!" "Spur that lazy horse!" "The bull's on Sola Street!" "The devil stop that bull!"

The riders' mad rush and the shouting were infernal. When they caught wind of the tumult, a handful of black women who had scavenged chitterlings and sat in a row along the water channel's edge curled up and crouched over the stomachs and entrails that they had been unraveling and rolling up with the patience of Penelope. This action surely saved them, because when the animal caught sight of them, it gave a terrifying snort, jumped sideways, then continued running straight ahead, the riders in hot pursuit. They say that one of the women soiled herself, another prayed ten Hail Marys in two minutes, and two promised San Benito[22] never to return to those accursed corrals and to abandon the occupation of collecting entrails. It is not known whether they made good on their promise.

Meanwhile, the bull entered the city through a long, narrow street that originates from the sharpest angle of the rectangle we had described before, a street enclosed by a water canal and a living fence of prickly pear. It was called "Sola" because it had no more than two adjacent houses on it. In its flooded center was a deep mud pool that covered the road's entire width, between one canal and the other. At that moment, an Englishman returning from his saltworks on a somewhat intractable horse was slowly wading across the bog and no doubt he was so absorbed in his mental calculations that he heard the bedlam of the onrushing riders with their infernal shouting only when the bull had already rushed into the pool of mud. Without warning, his horse spooked, bolted sideways, then broke into a gallop, leaving the poor man submerged in two feet of mud. The accident, however, neither stopped nor slowed down the headlong race of the bull's pursuers. On the contrary, they exclaimed, amid sarcastic guffaws, "The gringo screwed up!—back on your feet, gringo!" And as they crossed the morass, the mud churned up by their horses' hooves kneaded the man's miserable body. The gringo extricated himself as best he could, reaching the edge of the bog looking more like a devil browned by the fires of hell than a blond-haired white man. Farther ahead, four black women collectors of chitterlings who were heading home with their loot, upon hearing the shouts of "After the bull!" dove into the canal full of water, the only refuge left to them.

In the meantime, after having run some twenty blocks in various directions and frightening every living creature with its presence, the animal went through the palisade gate of a country home, where it met its doom. Though tired, it still showed vigor and a fierce mien. But it was surrounded by a deep canal and a thick fence of agaves, and there was no escape. Its persecutors had dispersed, but soon they banded together again and decided to use a team of oxen as a decoy and lead the bull back, to atone for its crime on the very spot where it had committed it.

One hour after its escape, the bull was back in the slaughter yard, where the few riffraff who had stayed around spoke of nothing but its misdeeds. The gringo's adventure in the mud hole aroused mainly derisive laughter and sarcasm. Of the boy decapitated by the lasso nothing remained, except for a puddle of blood—his body was in the cemetery.

Very quickly, they roped the animal's horns as it bucked, pawed its hooves, and bellowed with rage. They threw one, two, three lassoes at it to no avail, but the fourth snared a leg. The bull's vigor and fury redoubled—its tongue stretched out convulsively, froth spewed from its mouth, smoke from its nostrils. Its eyes blazed.

"Hamstring that animal!" a commanding voice exclaimed. Matasiete jumped off his horse, slashed the bull's hock in one swing, then, dancing around it, enormous dagger in hand, buried the blade up to the hilt in the animal's neck and showed the steaming red gash to the crowd. A torrent spurted from the wound, the bull exhaled one or two hoarse bellows. Then the proud animal collapsed, amid the mob's shouts, proclaiming Matasiete's prize of a flank steak. For the second time, Matasiete proudly stretched out his arm and the bloodstained knife, then bent down to skin the animal with his comrades.

The question of the dead animal's genitals still had to be settled, though it was provisionally classified as a bull because of its indomitable ferocity. However, everyone was so exhausted from the long exertion that the matter was momentarily forgotten. But just then, a rough voice exclaimed: "Here are the balls!" Extricating two enormous testicles from the animal's belly, the man displayed them—the unmistakable marker of the animal's dignity as a bull—to the bystanders. His words were met with uproarious laughter and loud chatter—all of the lamentable incidents were now easily explained. It was an extreme rarity for a bull to turn up in the slaughter yard. It was even forbidden. The rules of proper social practice dictated that the animal be thrown to the dogs; but there was such a lack of meat, and so many inhabitants were going hungry, that His Honor the Judge was forced to turn a blind eye.

In a flash the wretched bull was skinned, quartered, and hung on the wagon. Matasiete slid the flank steak under his saddle blanket and prepared to set off. The butchering had ended at noon, and the few stragglers who had been there until the end were now leaving in groups, on foot and on horseback, or using their cinch straps to haul carts loaded with meat.

But, suddenly, a butcher shouted in a gravelly voice:

"Here comes a Unitarian!" And at the sound of the fraught word, the entire rabble stopped dead in its tracks, as though stunned.

"Can't you see his U-shaped side whiskers? He doesn't have a ribbon on his tail coat or a mourning band on his hat."

"Unitarian dog." "He's a dandy."

"He rides English saddle, like the gringos." "Give him the corncob."

"The shears!"

"He needs a whipping."

"He's got a pistol case on his saddle to look smart." "All those Unitarian dandies are a bunch of show-offs." "Bet you aren't up to it—eh, Matasiete?"

"Bet you he isn't." "Bet you he is."

Matasiete was a man of few words and much action. When it came to violence, agility, skill with the hatchet, the knife, or the horse, he was closemouthed and acted swiftly. They had piqued him: he roweled his horse and galloped, loose reined, toward the Unitarian.

The man in question was young, aged 25, elegantly dressed and good-looking. He was heading for Barracas at a trot, unaware of any impending danger, at the same time that the mob was shouting out the exclamations just heard at the tops of their lungs. He then realized that the pack of slaughter-yard guard dogs was staring ominously at him, and his right hand automatically reached for the holsters on his English saddle. That was when the sideways blow from the chest of Matasiete's horse threw him backwards over his mount's haunches, landing him on his back some distance away, where he lay quite still.

"Cheers for Matasiete!" the rabble exclaimed in unison, madly rushing at the victim like rapacious caranchos alighting on the bones of a tiger-ravaged ox.

Still dazed, the young man got up, and hurling a fiery look at the ferocious men, began walking toward his horse, which stood motionless a short distance away, intent on getting vengeance and justice with his pistols. Matasiete leapt down from his horse, and blocking him, grabbed him by the cravat and threw him to the ground, at the same time drawing his dagger from his waist and pressing it against the young man's throat.

An explosion of laughter was followed by yet another resounding "Hurrah!" that rose in the air in praise of Matasiete.

What noble souls, what courage, that of the Federalists! Always in gangs and swooping down on their defenseless victims like vultures!

"Cut his throat, Matasiete; he was going for his pistols. Slit his throat like you did the bull's."

"Mischievous Unitarian. We need to cut off his sideburns." "He's got a nice neck for the violin."

"Better to slit his throat."

"We'll give it a try," said Matasiete. He started smiling as he slid the dagger's blade across the fallen man's throat, as he pressed down on his chest with his left knee, and held his head rigid by grabbing his hair with his left hand.

"No, no—don't slit his throat," the slaughter-yard judge shouted in his imposing voice, as he approached from a distance on his horse.

"To the *casilla* with him. Prepare the corncob and the shears. Death to the Unitarian savages! Long Live the Restorer of Laws!"

"Long Live Matasiete!"

"Death!" "Long Live!" the spectators echoed in a chorus. And tying up his elbows, between blows and shoves, shouts and insults, like Christ's executioners they dragged the wretched youth to the torture bench.

In the middle of the receiving room in the *casilla*, there stood a large, massive table that was never cleared of glasses of drink and playing cards except when it was used for executions and torture by the slaughter yard's Federalist executioners. Also visible in one corner was another, smaller table with writing materials and a notebook, and a number of chairs, among which stood out the arm chair used by the judge. A man, apparently a soldier, was seated on one of the chairs, singing a *resbalosa* tune to the melody of a guitar. The song, about torturing Unitarians, was extremely popular among the Federalists. Just then, the gang reached the *casilla's* front porch and shoved the young Unitarian toward the center of the room.

"It's your turn for the *resbalosa*," one of the men shouted at him. "Commend your soul to the devil."

"He's as furious as a wild bull."

"The stick will tame you soon enough." "He needs a whipping."

"For now, the pizzle[23] and shears." "Otherwise, the candle."

"Better the corncob."

"Silence, and sit down!" exclaimed the judge, as he sank down on an armchair. Everyone obeyed, while the young man, who was standing, confronted the judge and exclaimed in a voice full of indignation.

"Miserable killers! What do you intend to do to me?"

"Calm down!" the judge said, smiling. "No reason to lose your temper. You'll find out in time."

The young man was, in fact, beside himself with rage. His entire body seemed to be in the throes of a seizure. His pallid, bruised face, his voice, his trembling lip showed the alteration of his heart, the agitation of his nerves. His burning eyes seemed about to burst out of their sockets, his lanky black hair bristled. The veins on his bare neck throbbed visibly and his chest heaved violently beneath his shirtfront.

"Are you trembling?" the judge said to him.

"With rage, because I can't strangle you with my bare hands." "Would you have the strength and the courage for it?"

"More than enough will and courage for you, you snake."

"Let's see, bring the shears for trimming my horse's mane. Give him a trim, Federalist style."

Two men grabbed him, one by the rope binding his arms, the other by his head, and in a minute one of his side whiskers, that continued all the way down to his beard, had been sheared off. The audience exploded with laughter.

"Let's see," said the judge, "a glass of water to refresh him." "I'd make you drink a glass of gall, you scum."

A diminutive black soon stood before him with a glass of water in his hand. The young man kicked his arm, sending the glass flying and crashing against the ceiling, spattering the spectators' astonished faces.

"This one's impossible."

"We'll break him soon enough."

"Silence," said the judge. "You've already gotten a Federalist shearing. All you need is a moustache. Don't forget to grow one. Now let's get down to business. Why aren't you wearing an insignia?"

"Because I don't want to."

"Don't you know that the Restorer orders it?" "Livery is for you slaves, not for free men."

"The free men are made to wear one by force."

"Yes—force and bestial violence—those are your weapons, despicable wretches. Wolves, tigers, panthers are also strong like you; you ought to walk on all fours like them."

"Aren't you afraid that the tiger will tear you to pieces?"

"I prefer it to you tying me up and plucking out my entrails one by one, like a crow." "Why don't you have a mourning sash on your hat in memory of the Heroine?"

"Because I wear one in my heart, in memory of the country you've murdered, you villains."

"Don't you know that the Restorer has decreed it?"

"You are the ones who've decreed it, you slaves, to flatter your master's pride and render him your disgraceful vassalage."

"Impudent fool! You've got your gorge up all right, but say another word and I'll have your tongue cut off. Pull the pants off this stupid dandy and give him the pizzle on his bare ass; tie him down tightly to the table."

Immediately the judge spoke, four blood-bespattered ruffians lifted the young man and stretched him out on top of the table, pressing down on his arms and legs.

"You'll have to cut my throat before I'll let you strip me, you bastard."

They gagged him and began to pull off his clothes. The young man curled up, kicked, clenched and grinded his teeth. Now his limbs became as pliant as a reed, now they were as hard as iron, and his spine was twisting, snake-like. Drops of sweat slid down his face, as large as pearls; his pupils flashed with anger, his mouth foamed and the veins beneath his pale skin were dark, as though turgid with blood.

"Tie him up first!" the judge shouted.

"He's roaring with rage," said one of the thugs.

Moments later they tied his legs at an angle to the table's four legs, turning his body face down. The same thing had to be done to do the same with his hands, and to do it they loosened the rope that had tied his hands behind his back. The young man felt that his hands were free, and in a violently abrupt movement that seemed to drain him of all his strength and vitality, he raised himself, first on his arms, next on his knees, then he collapsed on the table and murmured, "You'll slit my throat first before you'll strip me, filthy scum." His strength was gone.

They immediately tied him down in a crucified position and began the work of pull-ing off his clothes. That was when the blood gushed out, bubbling out of the young man's mouth and nose, then trickling down both sides of the table. The thugs stood motionless; the onlookers were dumbfounded.

"The savage Unitarian burst with rage," said one.

"He had a river of blood in his veins," muttered another.

"Poor devil, all we wanted was to have a bit of fun with him, and he took things too seriously," the judge declared, his tiger's brow contracted in a frown. "A report must be filed. Untie him, and let's go."

The order was carried out, they locked the door, and the mob soon trailed behind the judge as he rode his horse, head bowed, and silent.

The Federalists had concluded one of their innumerable achievements.

In those days, the slaughter yard's butchers-cum-executioners were the apostles who by dagger and fist spread the gospel of the Holy Federation, and it is easy to imag-ine what sort of federation would emerge from their heads and knives. In keeping with the jargon invented by the Restorer, the patron of their brotherhood, they labeled a "savage Unitarian" anyone who was not an executioner, a butcher, a barbarian, or a thief; any man who was decent and whose heart was in the right place; any patriot with an education who was a friend of enlightenment and freedom. The events described above may allow us to see, in all clarity, that the center of the Federation was the slaughter yard.

For Further Reading

Chasteen, John Charles. *Heroes on Horseback: A Life and Times of the Last Gaucho Caudillos.* Albuquerque: University of New Mexico Press, 1995.

De la Fuente, Ariel. *Children of Facundo: Caudillo and Gaucho Insurgency during the Argentine State-Formation Process (La Rioja, 1853–1870).* Durham, NC: Duke University Press, 2000.

Gootenberg, Paul. *Between Silver and Guano: Commercial Policy and the State in Postindependence Peru.* Princeton: Princeton University Press, 1991.

Guardino, Peter. *Peasants, Politics, and the Formation of Mexico's National State: Guerrero, 1800–1857.* Palo Alto: Stanford University Press, 2000.

Johnson, Lyman (ed.). *Death, Dismemberment, and Memory: Body Politics in Latin America.* Albuquerque: University of New Mexico Press, 2004.

López-Alves, Fernando. *State Formation and Democracy in Latin America, 1810–1900.* Durham, NC: Duke University Press, 2000.

Lynch, John. *Argentine Caudillo: Juan Manuel de Rosas.* Wilmington: Scholarly Resources, 2001.

Mallon, Florencia. *Peasant and Nation: The Making of Postcolonial Mexico and Peru.* Berkeley: University of California Press, 1995.

Méndez, Cecilia. *The Plebeian Republic: The Huanta Rebellion and the Making of the Peruvian State, 1820–1850.* Durham, NC: Duke University Press, 2005.

Sanders, James. *Contentious Republicans: Popular Politics, Race, and Class in Nineteenth-Century Colombia.* Durham, NC: Duke University Press, 2004.

Sarmiento, Domingo Faustino. *Facundo: Civilization and Barbarism.* New York: Penguin, 1998.

Shumway, Nicholas. *The Invention of Argentina.* Berkeley: University of California Press, 1993.

Thurner, Mark. *From Two Republics to One Divided: Contradictions of Postcolonial Nationmaking in Andean Peru.* Durham, NC: Duke University Press, 1997.

August 29, 1793	1820	1825	1838	1851	1854
Slave emancipation in Haiti	British Navy begins to suppress slave trade	Bolivar decrees an end to Indian tribute in Bolivia	Slavery abolished in British colonies	Slave trade to Brazil ends	Ramón Castilla abolishes Indian tribute and slavery in Peru

May 13, 1888	November 15, 1889	August 7, 1908	May 1912
Full abolition in Brazil	Fall of Brazilian Empire	Founding of Partido Independiente de Color (Cuba)	Cuban race war

Citizenship and Rights in the New Republics

3

1861–1865	1862	September 22, 1862	1868–1878	1879–1880	October 7, 1886
Civil War in United States	Slave trade to Cuba ends	President Lincoln issues Emancipation Proclamation in United States	Ten Year War (Cuba)	Julio Roca's Conquest of the desert in Argentina	Full abolition in Cuba

When the delegates to the French National Constituent Assembly issued the *Declaration of the Rights of Man and Citizen* in August 1789, many believed that they sat at a crossroads in human history. Best summed up with the phrase that declared that all "men are born and remain free and equal in rights," the declaration signaled the convergence of revolutionary fervor and the ideals of perhaps the most important intellectual of the eighteenth century, Jean Jacques Rousseau. Repudiating a history in which rights had been apportioned according to lineage and special status (i.e., membership in a religious order), this document, for the first time, made the citizen the only legitimate possessor of rights. To be sure, the declaration did not include women, and made no mention of freedom for slaves, but it was a hopeful beginning that would animate much of nineteenth- and twentieth-century global history. Since that time, one of the critical stories of humankind has been the struggle to become more free, to extend more rights to more people, and to establish universal standards and practices of justice. Latin America occupies an important place in that story.

In theory, freedom and equality before the law are universal values; ideals that remain valid no matter what the context. In practice, freedom and equality have always been the product of local circumstances. They are rights granted to citizens, who are individuals designated as members of a national community. What is more, while the rights might be universal, the category of "citizen" is invariably particular. Citizenship is extended only to those who qualify, and denied on the basis of class (property as a precondition of citizenship), gender, age, national origin, and race. In much of Europe during the nineteenth century, one could not be a citizen if one did not belong to the national folk—through language, religion, or customs. In the United States, already an ethnically diverse society, only property-owning white men could become citizens.

Even more, the very question of what set of practices constituted citizenship rights would be the subject of repeated struggles during the course of the century. Political rights—the right to vote, to stand for office, to choose one's rulers counted among many types of contested rights, including the right to free speech, to freedom of religion, to freedom of assembly, to equality before the law, and so on. Added to this were other claims to rights, not always framed according to universal liberal values. Emancipated slaves sometimes demanded the right to recompense for their suffering (perhaps a plot of land, maybe more). Peasants might insist on their right to village autonomy, to the land, timber and water rights they had enjoyed under colonial rule. This expectation, once guaranteed to them as vassals of the king, would be recast as a citizenship claim made by villages that called themselves *comunidades ex-indios* (ex-Indian communities).

Latin Americans faced innumerable obstacles in defining suitable qualities of citizenship in their newly independent republics. Independence represented a kind of freedom—freedom from colonial rule—but in societies with no tradition of liberal rights and such a long history of legally enshrined religious, social, and racial hierarchies, the question of how freedom from colonial rule translated into citizenship rights was daunting. Would slaves be emancipated, granted rights equal to those of educated urban elites? Would the indigenous populations of the Andean and Mexican countrysides, upon whom rural elites depended for labor, be granted freedom from the tributes that had kept the colonial economy afloat? Would those who did not even speak Spanish or Portuguese, but instead spoke Aymara, Quechua, Nahuatl, or one of over a hundred other indigenous languages, be expected to learn Spanish in order to become a citizen? What too, of the plebian multitudes, working in the mines, plantations, and cities of the formal colonies. Often illiterate and invariably unruly (at least in the eyes of elites), were these people ready to be responsible citizens, to vote wisely?

More vexing still was the question of how women fit into the picture. Women played active roles in the independence wars and years that followed—sometimes as actual combatants, and at others as co-conspirators, merchants, teachers, nurses, artisans, financiers and defenders of social and cultural institutions. It remained to be seen whether this might translate into any sort of acknowledgement of their right to citizenship, especially because the male-dominated political assemblies that wrote the constitutions and passed the laws also invariably assumed that the role of proper women was in the home, fulfilling the private function of family reproduction while their men dominated the public sphere.

Caste Systems

While Latin Americans would for the most part defer struggles over gender rights until well into the twentieth century, race and caste were critical categories in the citizenship debates of the early republican period. Colonial society was predicated on caste hierarchies (in late colonial Mexico there were at least eighteen caste categories) that determined where one lived, which occupations were available, and one's opportunities for marriage, political, and social advancement. Whites were at the top of those hierarchies, though the *criollos* (Europeans born in the Americas) who took power in the new republics were not always supporters of these forms of distinction, as they often felt the sting of standing second to peninsular Spaniards. In the immediate aftermath of independence, utopian liberals in various parts of the region tried to strike down all barriers (again, except those that excluded women), pushing through emancipation declarations, prohibitions of the caste system, and constitutions that granted nearly universal citizenship rights to adult males.

These were, however, idealistic moments. The law in Latin America has a long history of acting as a projection of how society might function, and not so much as a prescription for how it will function, and these laws were no exception. The urban, educated, middle-class and elite liberals who wrote these constitutions could not, for the most part, imagine people of the lower castes as their equals, and with independence formal discrimination would gradually be replaced by unofficial practices that accomplished the same ends. In some cases (in Peru in 1826, for example), old systems of tribute and forced labor would be reintroduced by states in need of resources, and in others informal exclusionary practices would simply supersede formal ones.

As ideas emanating from Europe and North America about the biological differences between the races gained purchase in Latin America, the old systems of hierarchy were gradually remade into new systems of direct exclusion based on categories created by scientific racism. European theorists argued variously that the different races descended from different origins (i.e., Samuel Von Sommering), that different groups had innately different abilities (i.e., Johann Blumenbach), that the mixing of races led to the degeneration of the species (i.e., Arthur de Gobineau), and that society was responsible for maintaining and improving the gene pool (i.c., Francis Galton). These ideas were adopted unevenly in Latin America, particularly by those who hoped to redeem the indigenous, black, and mixed majorities in most societies in the region, but the influences of new sciences like eugenics, phrenology, and craniometry were unmistakable during the nineteenth century. Scientific racism allowed a colonial system favoring cleanliness of the blood (*limpieza de sangre*—a hierarchical system based on one's ability to claim blood untainted by the infidels) to give way to a modern system in which whiteness was a scientific virtue. Whites were smarter, more rational, more fit to govern, and more fit to be citizens of any society. For those most in the thrall of these ideas, Blacks, Indians, Asians, and those of mixed racial origins were a burden at best and a threat to civilization at worst.

The rise of racial thinking in much of the region had the effect of naturalizing past hierarchies in novel ways, substituting the power of modern science for what was once a religiously justified system of social differentiation (old Christians, those who could trace their lineage entirely to Spain, being closer to God). Drawing on the ways in which Western culture has long naturalized presumed differences between men and women—men as aggressive, sexual, public beings and women as passive, chaste, and private—the racial hierarchies of the nineteenth century reinvigorated caste distinctions to justify a civic culture dominated by white, elite males. And just as these gendered practices pathologized women who entered the public sphere as dishonorable (all work in some way being tantamount to prostitution, justifying the assumption that, unless she was a widow, the woman undertaking this work had loose sexual morals) these hierarchies justified the active exclusion from public life of all those deemed racially unworthy. Unless they could prove their virtue (a virtue that was presumed for most whites) the *mestizo* peddler, worker, or merchant, was not to be trusted, suspected of being a scoundrel, and certainly not suitable for public office.

In practice, this meant that the elite males who dominated public life tended to assume that the mixed race and indigenous women who worked for them, as servants, raising their children as nannies, laboring in their workshops and fields, were invariably open to their sexual advances, not sufficiently chaste in any event that their sexual depredations counted for much. They assumed something similar for the formerly *casta* males who made life in the new republics possible through their work, though in this case assumptions about loose morals were made into assumptions that they should be treated with suspicion. Ironically, even tragically, those very same males tended to reproduce these sensibilities when they did manage to ascend the class hierarchy. One of the greatest prizes a *mestizo* male could gain was a wife who was whiter than himself, the surest guarantee of both her virtue and a better future for his children.

Troubled by the prospects for their nations to become civilized because of the racial makeup of their societies, Latin American elites undertook any number of projects to improve the race. Where possible, they gradually erased the stain of blackness or Indianness through intermarriage or reclassification. As late as 1838, Afro-Argentines represented 25 percent of the population of Buenos Aires, but by 1887 they were counted as only 2 percent of the city's residents. Many were reclassified as *trigueño*, or "wheat colored." Others hoped for redemption through education, modernization, hygiene, nutrition, healthy motherhood, and any number of other improvements, believing that if they could elevate the poor, racially compromised masses out of their civilizational slumber, their societies might prosper. Their vision was not so much egalitarian as it was rooted in a history of Catholic paternalism, of helping defenseless and pathetic vassals.

Others took a darker view of the racial divide. Nationalists in Peru drew on the Inca past for their symbols even as they actively despised living Indians. In the minds of *Limeños* (and for that matter highlanders), the regional geography of the country was also indelibly racial—a white/*mestizo* city and coast confronted the Indian highlands and countryside. This deep fragmentation would ultimately harden into the system Peruvians called *gamonalismo*, in which the landlords and merchants who controlled the highlands like feudal kingdoms were tolerated both because they delivered loyalty to the national government, and because *Limeños* had little faith in the capacity of Andean peoples for citizenship.

The racial geographies of places like Mexico and Argentina were less well defined, as most of rural Mexico and the pampas had indeterminate racial origins. Where, however, race could be clearly linked to a region's identity, it was sometimes turned to genocidal ends. In Chiapas, the Indian highlanders who were forced into *enganche* (forced contract) labor on the coastal coffee plantations earned little sympathy from outsiders. In Mexico's North, the government of Porfirio Díaz forcibly moved approximately 15,000 Yaquis from their homes in Sonora and condemned them to labor on henequen plantations in the Yucatán following their military defeat at the hands of the army in the early 1900s. Julio Roca's Conquest of the Desert in Argentina (1879–1880) was informed by similar attitudes towards race, and left over 1,300 indigenous dead. In these cases, the clearing of indigenous lands left new territory open for white speculators and settlers to turn to "productive" ends.

Indigenous peoples were left in a series of binds by these conflicts. Though some tried to appropriate the language of liberalism, demanding their rights as citizens, fighting in national wars (as mentioned in Chapter 2, thousands of indigenous Mexicans fought in Benito Juárez' liberal armies against the French invasion of Mexico, 1861–1867), they were hamstrung in a variety of ways. Liberal elites were not inclined to recognize the participation of racial others in their great national struggles. They erased them from their historical memory once they consolidated power. Neither were popular groups served well by their own versions of liberal rights. When peasant or indigenous villagers came to the liberal cause, they generally interpreted the right to freedom to mean village autonomy. Individual rights were transformed into the right of local communities to set their own laws, to live free of interference from the outside world. Just as importantly, indigenous peoples were as likely to be tied up in fratricidal struggles with neighboring communities as they were national or international elites. The net result was that indigenous peoples were increasingly excluded from national politics, which was instead dominated by those who saw the Indian, the *mestizo*, the peasant, as little more than fodder for their own dreams.

The break-up of communal peasant villages, accomplished mainly by liberal states which had relied on these same peasants to consolidate their hold on power, would be one of the great tragedies of the nineteenth century and a source of enduring grievances into the twentieth. Across the region land surveyors, speculators, and investors took advantage of liberal legislation to gobble up a great deal of land that was deemed vacant, largely because it was occupied by indigenous peoples. Former peasants were increasingly thrust onto the labor market, forced to work in export agriculture as debt peons[1] or day laborers. This in turn is part of the reason why village autonomy would remain a critical peasant demand across the region for generations to come (including in violent conflicts in Mexico in 1910, Bolivia in 1952, Peru in 1968, and arguably in Mexico in 1994).

The emerging *mestizo* majorities in many parts of the region fared somewhat differently under these circumstances, though not always markedly better. Most could distance themselves from their indigenous ancestry, and early republican constitutions in much of the region were sufficiently radical in their democratic vision to call for their participation as equals with their former social betters. Nonetheless, over time elite interests favored a hardening of social hierarchies in ways that made it difficult for people of plebian origin to rise, especially once the military conflicts of the mid-century (which created opportunities for the ambitious to rise both through military service and because of instability within the elites) gave way to stable elites who reproduced themselves through nepotism and increasingly narrow political networks. Should a poor *mestizo* or mulatto[2] succeed in business or school (or even a poor indigenous peasant, for that matter), they might be accepted within polite society (this distinguishing Latin America from the US), but the odds of success were invariably low, and lower still as the free-for-all of the *caudillo* era retreated into the distant past.

The Stain

Slaves created the first republic in the Caribbean. Just fifty miles away, emancipation would take nearly an entire century longer. This contrast reminds us that the story of freedom and citizenship is a varied one across the Americas, invariably rooted in local histories, cultures, and circumstances. Those places where slavery was not a centrally important institution generally produced different kinds of histories than those where it was.

Slaves could be found in most parts of the region at the beginning of the nineteenth century. On the eve of independence, there were 30,000 slaves in La Plata, 78,000 in New Granada, 64,500 in Venezuela, and 89,000 in Peru. They worked on Peruvian sugar plantations and wineries, on cacao and sugar estates in Venezuela, in Colombian gold mines, and on ranches in Argentina. They were also common in urban areas, toiling as servants, and skilled and unskilled workers. In most places they were important, but not critical sources of labor, often working alongside free laborers. By contrast, plantation agriculture in the Caribbean and Brazil relied on slavery for its very existence. In Brazil, slaves were also critical to gold and diamond mining in Minas Gerais, and to an emerging coffee economy in and around São Paulo.

It is not really sufficient to describe societies in the region as characterized by the presence or absence of slaves. Across the Americas there were too many distinctions even within slavery to do this. Take the United States, for instance. In the nineteenth century, the United States had a slave population that was unlike any other. Whereas in most of Latin America a considerable percentage of slaves were of African origin, in the United States the vast majority of slaves were native born. Perhaps because of the historical cost of importing slaves and the relative poverty of U.S. plantation societies, North America had only a marginal presence in the history of the slave trade, importing something like 500,000 slaves over several centuries (4.4 percent of the total, as compared to the 4 million imported to Brazil, which represented 35 percent of the total).

The slave population of the United States was among the largest in the Americas in the early nineteenth century, but that population was the product of natural increase and extremely low levels of manumission. Because so few slaves were ever freed, to be black in the United States (and particularly the South) was almost certainly to be a slave. Miscegenation produced more blacks, more slaves. The fact that many slaves had some European ancestry was simply ignored. Furthermore, those who were free were generally treated almost as badly as slaves (except, to some extent, in Louisiana). Among other prohibitions, many Southern states forbade free persons of color from becoming preachers, selling certain goods, tending bars, staying out past a certain time of night, or owning dogs.

Just a few hundred miles away, Haiti's history of slavery was quite different. A marginal colony until the end of the seventeenth century, during the eighteenth century St. Domingue emerged as one of the richest colonies in the world, due to a booming sugar plantation complex and the importation of 790,000 slaves. The story of Haitian independence was told in Chapter 1, but it is worth recalling that unlike in the United States, slavery and race were not entirely contiguous in Haiti. In fact, much of the wealth in the colony was in the hands of free people of color. Their role in independence was ambiguous. Free blacks first struggled for rights for themselves. As slave-owners, they were not universally in favor of emancipation. Over time some free blacks came to embrace emancipation, either because they genuinely believed in the cause, or because the offer of freedom could be used to recruit slaves to their side in the civil war that engulfed Haiti during the 1790s.

Across a narrow strait, slavery remained essential to a colonial Cuban economy well into the nineteenth century. With the demise of the sugar industry in Haiti, Cuban planters grew more cane, and imported more slaves. Still, while slavery played a critical role in maintaining Cuba's colonial status early in the century, the logics that underpinned this option gradually grew less compelling after the 1820s. North American investment began to supplant the power of Spanish capital, and the Cuban population grew more diverse (in part due to European immigration, which government officials promoted in an effort to dilute the African blood of the island's population). As the British government intensified its pressure on the slave trade, Cuban planters began to look elsewhere for labor. By mid-century the planters in Santa Clara and Matanzas (the most prosperous sugar zones) were importing indentured Chinese laborers in significant numbers. Even so, Cuban planters imported 400,000 slaves between 1835 and 1864.[3]

Cuba's booming economy enriched a growing number of free blacks. Black professionals and petty merchants with middle-class aspirations shaped the face of a changing Havana, and like elsewhere, offered models of upward mobility for other free but poor blacks. This caused alarm in some quarters, and colonial officials ultimately tightened caste restrictions, making it harder for blacks to move up the social ladder and also restricting the movement of people of color onto and off of the island. Fearing that Cuban and foreign blacks were fomenting rebellion among the slaves, royal officials launched a major campaign against free blacks in 1844 (the *escalera*), in which they arrested two thousand and exiled several hundred. The *escalera* set the tone for at least one aspect of emancipation in Cuba: free people of color were increasingly made into objects of fear and the targets of official discrimination as slavery came to an end.

In Brazil, government officials did the opposite, loosening colonial era restrictions that limited the upward mobility of free people of color in response to an upwardly mobile Afro-Brazilian population. By the mid-nineteenth century, *libertos* (former slaves) even enjoyed the right to vote as long as they met property qualifications. Non-whites could be found across the professions, in government, and among the nation's most important writers and intellectuals by the 1870s, and faced no formal social prohibitions. To be sure, mulattos generally fared better in society than blacks, but by this time most discrimination in Brazil was informal, outside of the law.

As international pressure brought the slave trade to an end, the patterns of slavery across the hemisphere changed. Slavery became more rural, more closely tied to the most profitable export commodities (cotton in the United States, coffee in Brazil, sugar in Cuba), more absent from daily life in the cities and rare in less prosperous regions. Cuba was an increasingly divided place, as some regions depended even more on slavery than they had in the past, and others increasingly did not rely on slavery at all. Complicating this situation further, a growing number of Cubans openly argued for both freedom from Spain and freedom from slavery, identifying both as a kind of bonded servitude that crippled the nation. The racist elements of this sentiment were sometimes explicit. Many whites believed that the continued presence of large numbers of black slaves represented a barrier to Cuba becoming a modern nation.

Slaves and former slaves were active participants in this struggle. Runaway slaves and slave revolts in Cuba and elsewhere in the Caribbean reminded Cuban whites of the injustices of the institution. *Cofradias* (fraternal societies organized by slaves and former slaves) kept pressure on the system by raising funds to purchase freedom and agitating for rights. Whenever laws were passed to ameliorate the harshest conditions of slavery in Cuba, slaves used their extensive oral networks to pass the news. Once armed with this knowledge, slaves actively challenged their overseers and claimed whatever rights they believed they had. The refusal of overseers to respect those rights (which in some cases may be as simple as the right to talk back) could at times ignite a volatile situation. Moreover, planters could be put at a severe disadvantage by these information networks. Rumor and speculation could transform relatively minor reforms into something much more significant. Whispers of imminent emancipation (and the belief that planters were defying orders from above) helped launch the Haitian revolution, revolts in Barbados (1816), Demerara (1823; now part of Guyana), and Jamaica (1831).[4]

The issue of slavery came to a head during Cuba's independence wars, beginning with the Ten Years War (1868–1878). The war took place largely in Oriente, a relatively poor and remote region of the island at the time. Perhaps because Oriente had relatively few *ingenios* (sugar mills), and thus relatively few slaves, both the rebels and Spanish promised freedom to Afro-Cubans who fought on their side. Neither side imagined extensive emancipation, but slaves actively joined both in significant numbers. Fearing that the rebels in the Oriente were going to emancipate all the slaves, the wealthy sugar planters in Santa Clara and Matanzas remained resolutely in the royalist camp during the war.

Even though limited to eastern Cuba, the war did initiate the process of emancipation, and once it began it was hard to reverse. The international slave trade had ended. Along with Brazil, Cuba was one of only two places in the Americas where slavery remained legal. Furthermore, low reproduction rates on the island meant that the competition for slaves would only become more fierce. Those with sufficient resources turned to other (principally Chinese) forms of labor servitude. For their part, former slaves pressed the system with increasing confidence, pooling their resources to purchase the freedom of friends and relatives, and pressuring the judicial authorities whenever they could to limit abuses and punish masters who broke the law. Slavery was becoming unworkable.

During the war (in 1870), the Spanish *Cortes* passed the Moret Law, which declared that all individuals born on the island henceforth would be born free, though the law required a twenty-two-year apprenticeship for children born to slave mothers. Under increasing pressure from abolitionists, including former slaves, ten years later the Spanish *Cortes* passed a law calling for gradual abolition, which included an eight-year period of indentured servitude for the former slaves (this was called the *patronato*). Increasingly unwilling to allow any limits to their freedom, slaves challenged the *patronato* with such effectiveness that it was abolished two years early on October 7, 1886. Slavery in Cuba had come to its end (see Table 3.1).

The active role that slaves played in their own emancipation in Cuba is striking, in part because Cuba seems to stand out from societies like the United States and Brazil. This is, however, probably more a result of the stories we privilege than it is a sign that emancipation in Cuba was unique. In all cases in the Americas, emancipation was a complex story of pressures from the outside world, internal elite conflicts, and pressure from slaves themselves. In Cuba, as in Haiti, slaves took hold of their freedom in the context of civil wars. In the United States, cross-class unity among whites limited the ways blacks could participate in the Civil War, but pressure from former slaves helped to mobilize northern whites against the abomination of slavery.

In Brazil, the story of emancipation is similarly complex. The first real pressures on Brazilian slavery came from abroad. As early as 1815, the Portuguese crown submitted to British

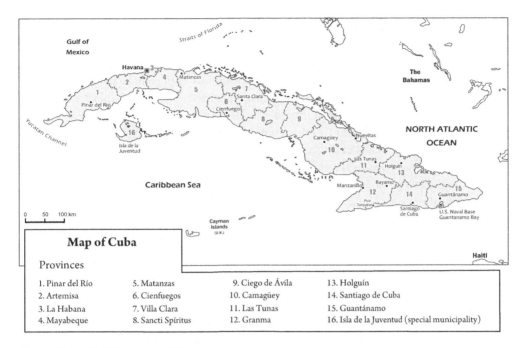

Figure 3.1 Political map of Cuba

Table 3.1 Emancipation in the Americas

Country	Dates
Haiti	1793
Argentina	1813 (free womb), 1851 (full)
Chile	1823
Mexico	1829
Venezuela	1830 (children), 1854 (full)
Bolivia	1831
British colonies	1833
Uruguay	1842
Danish colonies	1847
French colonies	1848
Colombia	1851
Peru	1854
Ecuador	1854
Dutch colonies	1863
United States	1865
Cuba	1870 (free womb), 1886 (full)
Brazil	1871 (free womb), 1888 (full)
Puerto Rico	1873

pressure to limit the Atlantic slave trade, and in the 1830s the Imperial state formally agreed to a process that would gradually end the trade. Still, until the British pressured Brazil into abolishing the legal slave trade in 1851, Brazilian slave imports remained robust. During the nineteenth century, Brazil imported 1.3 million slaves, including 371,000 in the ten years prior to the end of the trade. The United States, by contrast, imported just 51,000 slaves during the nineteenth century. Brazil suffered some spectacular slave rebellions during these years (especially in 1835, in Bahia), and public sentiment gradually turned against slavery. Brazilian liberals also believed the country's failings in their war with Paraguay during the 1860s were a result of slavery. Nonetheless, slavery remained sufficiently important to the economies of the northeast, south, and southwest of the country that abolition seemed unlikely.

Around this time, changing patterns in the global economy—namely, the end of a global market for slaves—began to undermine the economics of slavery in Brazil. After 1851 the percentage of slaves in the labor force and their importance as a source of capital began to decline. As access to slaves became more limited, they were increasingly concentrated around a few commodities. Slaves were transferred from declining regions (like the northeast) to the more robust coffee and mining regions (particularly Rio de Janeiro and Minas Gerais). Although São Paulo had one of the most robust coffee economies in the country, planters there increasingly recruited European and Asian migrants, relying less on slaves (coffee exports would surpass sugar by the 1850s). São Paulo was soon followed by other regions, as a growing number of planters and miners sought to reduce their reliance on slavery, not because it was unprofitable, but because most believed that their long-term survival depended on finding new sources of labor. By 1884 slaves accounted for more than 10 percent of the population in less than half of Brazil's provinces, and in the northeast slave populations were comparable to what they were in the United States North around the time of abolition (5 percent of the total). As these shifts became more pronounced, the moral arguments against slavery gradually gained more adherents.

After a series of failed efforts, the Brazilian Parliament eventually passed a free womb law (the Rio Branco Law) in 1871. The law established a fund to purchase the freedom of slaves, though it required the "free" children of slaves to work for their masters to the age of twenty-one, and compensated slave-owners for their losses. Inadequate though it was, it did signal the eventual end of slavery. Wealthy planters redoubled their efforts to find alternative labor sources, and opponents resolved to put more pressure on the system. Over the course of the next fifteen years, slaves and former slaves protested, marched, and pressured the Imperial government to end slavery, forming the backbone of a popular abolitionist movement. Black and mulatto intellectuals wrote extensive tracts decrying the evils of slavery. Free black dockworkers and others struck or otherwise mobilized against slavery. In response, local governments in several regions passed acts of emancipation, declaring slavery-free zones. Ceará declared itself a free state in 1884, followed by Amazonas in 1885. In the South, a November 1886 strike by free workers forced the city of Santos to declare itself free. By the end of the year, the city housed 10,000 runaway slaves (see Figure 3.2).

White liberals also participated, writing letters to the newspapers, traveling to slave plantations to monitor the conditions of slaves and report abuses, and as a result of these combined pressures, slavery became increasingly untenable—a system that was driving the country towards chaos. Attempting to stave off this threat, the Brazilian Parliament passed a law freeing all slaves over sixty-five in 1885, and then its Golden Law—emancipation without recompense to the owners for Brazil's 723,000 remaining slaves—in 1888. By this time three-quarters of Brazil's slaves toiled in the three major coffee provinces of São Paulo, Minas Gerais, and Rio de Janeiro.

Figure 3.2   Territorial boundaries and major cities of Brazil

Different Paths

Critics of slavery in the nineteenth century described this institution as not simply a stain on humankind, but as hopelessly antiquated and ultimately unproductive. The historical record from Cuba and elsewhere, however, suggests something to the contrary. Here, as in Brazil, slaves worked alongside free laborers, in skilled and unskilled positions, and often in industries that produced immense profits. Cultural attachments to systems of forced labor aside, the capital slave owners had tied up in slaves was extremely productive. The problems they faced came from an increasingly fragile supply chain and an increasingly powerful opposition. Where the rate of natural increase in the slave population could replace existing labors, slavery could have continued indefinitely. Where the slave trade was critical to maintaining the labor force, slavery's days were numbered.

Why did Cuban and Brazilian planters rely so heavily on the slave trade to replenish their supply of slaves? In part it was simply because the trade had always been more developed in these areas, bringing in more slaves. In part it was because the life span of slaves on plantations in these regions was shorter than in the United States. More than half of Brazilian slaves died within the first three years of arriving. Life expectancies for slaves were two-thirds that of whites (in the United States it was 90 percent of whites). This would seem to suggest a more benign slavery in North America, but such comparisons can be deceiving.

Because slaves were more costly the further one got from West African slave markets, planters in the United States had more incentive to see that their slaves lived long lives. Likewise, slaves in the United States tended to work on smaller plantations and in smaller numbers than elsewhere, meaning that each slave's value to their owner as a percentage of their overall capital tended to be greater. This also meant that a North American planter had more economic incentive than a Brazilian planter to see a son born of a slave as a unit of production. A Brazilian slave-owner may have been less concerned about the health of an easily replaced slave than his North American counterpart, but they were also more willing to consider manumission. Legally enforceable contracts in which slaves and their masters agreed to a price for freedom were relatively common in Brazil. They had no history in the United States. Furthermore, in both contexts slaves who worked as household servants, or on small estates where they enjoyed face-to-face relationships with their owners, would have experienced slavery far differently than those who worked on large commercial estates.

One of the rather significant differences among these societies—and one that would have important implications for the rights blacks acquired after slavery—lay in the ways that race and slavery were linked. Unlike in the United States, in Brazil and Cuba slavery and race were never coterminous. In Cuba, the population of free blacks during the nineteenth century amounted to 39 percent of the people of African origin on the island. In Brazil it was more than 75 percent. The urban working class of cities like Rio de Janeiro included significant numbers of free blacks. Free people of color also worked in agriculture, owned land, even owned slaves. In Bahia, Afro-Brazilians owned both sugar plantations and slaves in significant numbers.

In Brazil the black population as a whole was never isolated within a single social system (Table 3.2). In the United States the opposite happened. North American planters used the fear that emancipation stirred among southern whites to build a regional coalition with poor whites (almost none of whom owned slaves) in defense of slavery, playing on the theme of a unified white southern culture threatened by black savagery. In Brazil (particularly in Rio and São Paulo, where most slave holding was concentrated) slave owners did not try to produce these regional cross-class coalitions opposing abolition. Brazilian elites feared the racially heterogeneous masses that characterized their countryside and cities, and preferred to keep them out of the political battles of the day as much as possible. These differences were played out in the different sorts of processes that unfolded around emancipation. For example, the anxieties that led whites in the state of Delaware to vote against compensated emancipation in 1861—in spite of the fact that there were only 2,000 slaves in

Table 3.2 The eve of emancipation: United States, Cuba, Haiti, Brazil

Country	Total Population	Free People of Color	Slaves
Haiti (1789)	523,000	28,000	465,000
USA (1860)	31,443,321	488,070	3,953,760
Cuba (1862)	1,396,530	232,433	370,533
Brazil (1872)	9,930,000	4,250,000	1,510,00

the state—did not emerge in Brazil, where emancipation became a multilayered negotiation. Here, representatives from the states of Pernambuco and Bahia (where between 12 and 20 percent of the population were slaves) supported the Rio Branco law because it seemed like a reasonable strategy for maintaining elite control while managing what seemed like an inevitable change. Limited concessions to the poor would reduce the likelihood of conflicts that might overturn the entire social structure.

Rights and the Color Line

The history of the denial of rights to people of color in the United States is well known. After a brief period during which blacks in the defeated South embraced the franchise and a radical Republican Congress tried to punish a recalcitrant South by letting former slaves, carpetbaggers, and scalawags take the reins of government, northern reformers gradually retreated and southern whites created local political systems characterized by the Black Codes, Jim Crow Laws, the Ku Klux Klan, and a landscape where the threat of lynching was ever present. The cross-class alliance that defined the secessionist movement evolved into a political alliance rooted in anti-black hysteria. American historians generally agree that all but the most enlightened of thinkers never really believed African Americans deserved equal citizenship rights, and that in the North as well as the South blacks had few opportunities to press for their legal rights during the ensuing century. Equally important, in the United States the "one drop rule," was enforced rigorously across the country, eliminating the possibility that miscegenation might entail a proliferation of categories. If you had a black ancestor, you were black.

Latin American societies did not generally see a legal codification of discrimination based on race, a fact that many Latin American nationalists have long used to argue that their nations are more enlightened when it comes to matters of race. Some have even taken this as evidence that Latin Americans are not really racists (the Brazilian Gilberto Freyre and Mexican Manuel Gamio are famous examples). Early in the twentieth century, North American blacks who visited Brazil described their experiences there as a welcome relief from what they experienced at home. Still, the absence of violent codified discrimination did not exactly translate into the existence of enforceable rights, in Brazil, Cuba, or anywhere else. Former slaves across the Americas confronted a great deal of prejudice, lived in an era of virulent scientific racism, and, at the very least, faced the prospects of being very poor in poor countries; nations without the means to ameliorate their poverty even had they possessed the will.

Because the states that governed post-emancipation societies were weak, local power brokers determined the terms and nature of labor arrangements. Coercive but somewhat flexible labor systems like debt peonage, share cropping, and contract labor prevailed in many areas, and the political connections between landowners and political elites undermined most efforts to enforce existing labor laws or the civil rights of newly emancipated citizens. Planters in Cuba, Mexico, Jamaica, Brazil, and elsewhere also turned to migrant labor to meet their needs. As a result, some former slaves were left without any form of work.

The experience of former slaves in Brazil differed a great deal depending on where they lived. In São Paulo, slaves tended to move away from their former masters. The *libertos* (former slaves) in this part of Brazil often demanded respect, an end to corporal punishment, appreciation for their family units, and wages that planters would not offer. In response, local planters created a series of obstacles that blocked their efforts to enter the growing urban and agricultural workforce. Planters and the state worked together to flood the São Paulo labor market with subsidized immigrants, hoping that they could avoid employing what they viewed as uppity former slaves. Nonetheless, the system of subsidized immigration was phased out in a few years, and the new immigrants found their footing and moved into better jobs, leaving former slaves with a multitude of opportunities to join São Paulo's agricultural and emerging industrial workforce.

Elsewhere in Brazil, former slaves were left to the mercy of changing economic conditions, finding employment and a measure of autonomy in regions where dynamic economic growth offered new opportunities, and finding themselves as vulnerable as ever in regions where economic decline meant that jobs were scarce. In Bahia, by the late nineteenth century one of Brazil's poorest regions, former slaves often remained tied to their former owners, working on their estates as agricultural laborers, only migrating away from estates that suffered economic catastrophes in the aftermath of emancipation.

These distinct experiences helped produce a series of new images of Brazil that would supplant older ones. The northeast (poor, black, remote from the capital, tropical) came to be understood as a backwards region, filled with people not exactly ready for citizenship. Rio de Janeiro (the capital, the intellectual and cultural center) and São Paulo (the engine of economic growth and industry) came to be imagined as both less black and more modern than the rest of the country. It did not make sense for Brazilians to create formal systems of racial discrimination, as the northeast–southwest distinction did not align perfectly with racial classifications, and the centuries-old free-black community in Brazil had both intermarried with Europeans and produced its own share of wealthy, prestigious families. Instead, what Brazilians saw was the emergence of a series of softer designations that could maintain the hierarchies that existed under slavery. These soft gradations also allowed Brazilians to embrace the image of Brazil as a racially mixed society. Somewhere between the rich white *paulista*[5] and poor black *nordestina*[6] was a mulatto, sometimes rich, sometimes poor, and sometimes a little of both.

On the national level, many former slaves supported the monarchy as a potential ally in the fight against discrimination and for voting and other rights, largely because the monarchy had been behind many anti-slavery measures over the years. This alliance was short lived, however, because elites in Rio de Janeiro, along with *paulista* planters, conspired to overthrow the crown and create a republic in 1889. Power in the new republic was highly decentralized, and while the only restrictions on male suffrage were literacy, politics increasingly became an entirely elite affair, with very little popular participation. Brazilians of color first tried to defend their old allies through a series of black guards, and later tried to organize independently in defense of their rights in newly formed clubs and militias, but the new elites aggressively put down all forms of popular mobilization. The new planter state, in effect, eliminated the one element of the government to which Brazilian blacks had looked for support. Moreover, because people of African ancestry could hope to move up the social hierarchy by acquiring wealth, prestige, and power, after 1889 a confrontational struggle for civil rights gave way to more individualized strategies of advancement. If you followed the rules of the system, you might get ahead. If you protested, you were certain to be left behind.

Such was not the case in Cuba. Former slaves in Cuba did what slaves did elsewhere. They focused on creating stable families and communities in the aftermath of an experience that had denied them both, and often left political organizing for individual rights for later. Many moved eastward to Oriente in search of a better life, away from the sugar zones of Santa Clara and Matanzas. Still, when Cuba's final war for independence broke out in 1895, thousands of free blacks joined in. Their participation reminds us that the meaning of freedom to slaves was neither universal nor simply tied to bondage. Veterans of those battles would repeatedly insist that, having spilt blood for Cuban independence, they were entitled to the full rights of citizenship, along with specific privileges as a reward for their sacrifices.

Cuba's 1902 Constitution granted all adult males the right to vote, regardless of color, but when Afro-Cuban veterans insisted that this right and their service be respected in meaningful ways, white Cubans responded by trying to erase those contributions, and by increasingly defining blackness as a threat to the nation. The Cubans of color who demanded their rights as citizens, who demanded a share of positions in the bureaucracy, representation among elected officials, and the elimination of discrimination against blacks, were increasingly cast as dangerous primitives, threats to national progress.

Cuba was thus like Brazil in that Cuban whites did not formally exclude all blacks from positions of privilege based on the qualities of their blood. They instead focused on a series of practices, specifically Afro-Cuban religious traditions, arguing that significant numbers of former slaves were unfit for civilization. As in Brazil, where *capoeira*[7] was criminalized during the nineteenth century, Afro-Cuban religious traditions became a particular target. Images of the black Cuban as non-Christian, as a practitioner of witchcraft, of animal and human sacrifices, and particularly of the kidnapping of white children for the purposes of ritual sacrifice, filled Cuban newspapers in the early years after independence (Figure 3.3). Police, scientists, criminologists, and elected officials railed against a perceived epidemic of savagery, and in the process laid the groundwork for recasting thousands of patriotic veterans (and citizens) as threats to the nation. The two processes were intertwined; the more Afro-Cubans demanded rights, the more Cubans were subjected to stories of strange rituals and the kidnapping of white children.

Unbowed by the racist attacks, Afro-Cubans continued to organize for civil rights, rights built around a complex mix of universal values and rights won through the struggle. In 1908 Evaristo Estenoz, Pedro Ivonet, Gregorio Surín and several others founded the *Partido Independiente de Color* (Independent Party of Color, PIC), which was mainly made up of veterans of the wars for independence. The PIC was the first race-based political party in the Americas, and was banned by the Cuban Congress shortly after it was founded (incidentally,

I-a Política Cómica

La justicia del pueblo

CASTIGANDO EL CRIMEN

Figure 3.3 "Justice by the people: punishing the crime" political cartoon
Source: Courtesy of Alejandra Bronfman

the Morúa Amendment, the law that made the PIC illegal by banning parties based on race or class, was proposed by an Afro-Cuban). PIC supporters did not back down, continuing to protest for rights after the Morúa Law was passed. Their opponents were similarly resolute, describing the PIC as seditious, barbaric, and suggesting that its members represented threats to the virtue of white women. The conflict came to a head after a series of protests in May 1912, which were reported in the press as the opening salvos of a race war that would imperil the nation. In the following weeks some party supporters and poor peasants did engage in violent protests, but the response by the Cuban army was swift and decisive. Perhaps as many as 6,000 PIC supporters were massacred, and the party was wiped out.

The Documents: Limiting Citizenship

What was to happen after emancipation? Post-emancipation societies were simultaneously driven by nineteenth-century liberalism, the claim that all men should be free and equal before the law, and nineteenth-century scientific racism, the insistence that some men were destined to rule, and others be ruled. This was the world in which all former slaves negotiated not just their freedom, but the rights that derived from their erstwhile status as citizens within free republics. People of color were not denied a voice in this process, as they might have been under slavery, in part because by the time emancipation came in Latin America's two most significant slave-holding societies, both countries also housed a significant population of literate, free people of color who made the most of these developments, whether by taking advantage of their new rights to pursue their own interests, or by organizing for an expanding series of rights.

It is no coincidence that the new freedoms granted Afro-Latin Americans were accompanied by a powerful conservative response designed to create new bases for limiting the opportunities emancipated slaves enjoyed. One of the significant early examples of this came in the form of *The Fetishist Animism of the Bahian Blacks,* a book written by Raimundo Nina Rodrigues (Document 3.1). Nina Rodrigues (1862–1906) was one of Brazil's most important social scientists, psychiatrists, and interpreters of race during the emancipation era. His work is notable for his darkly negative view of blacks and somewhat kinder rendering of mulattos, a tendency that some scholars explain as due to the fact that Nina Rodrigues was a mulatto. It may be that he was, and it may also be the case that his enemies called him a mulatto in order to discredit his work. We do not know with any certainty.

Nina Rodrigues distinguished himself from his colleagues in the United States by taking a positive view of mulattos. He saw them as backwards, but redeemable, whereas North American intellectuals generally viewed mulattos as racially degenerate, criminal, and lazy, and thus immune to improvement. Though strongly influenced by the Italian criminologist Césare Lombroso in the ways he linked race, culture, and crime, Nina Rodrigues also believed that Brazilian blacks might become civilized through the intervention of the state. Race in his work is something more fluid, less essential, than it was in the work of North Americans. It created challenges and obstacles that needed to be overcome, but race was not destiny.

Nina Rodrigues' work, widely read in Latin America, was particularly influential on the Cuban criminologist Fernando Ortiz. Working within a milieu in which North American ideas of racial separation and Afro-Cuban demands for rights came into constant conflict, Ortiz' scholarly writings and work as a public official helped to shift the terrain on which Cubans struggled for their rights. Rather than denying rights based upon race, Ortiz, with the collaboration of a series of newspapers and other public officials, highlighted the dangers that Afro-Cuban religions represented to civilization. Drawing from a series of grotesque images, Ortiz' work created the impression that Afro-Cubans were not Christian, were cannibalistic and dangerous, and needed to be controlled. The resulting stigmatization of blackness created immense problems for Afro-Cuban activists and veterans. When they organized for civil rights based on the fact that they faced discrimination for being black (see Document 3.2), they wound up highlighting their blackness, and fomented further white hysteria over the black threat.

It is within this context that Document 3.3 must be read. It was written in the aftermath of the massacre of 1912, when it became impossible to organize a party around blackness. Some Afro-Cubans responded to these events by asserting that they were, indeed, civilized. Some eschewed separatist politics (Nicolás Guillén, senator and father of the poet, for example), insisting that there was no real racism in Cuba and that they were happy to work within the system. Others denied the claim that all Afro-Cubans practiced *brujeria* (witchcraft), using Nina Rodrigues' own logic to argue that they had erased their racial origins, and deserved to be treated as honorable and civilized. Fernando Guerra, however, was one of many who openly defended Afro-Cuban religious forms. Guerra represents a particularly interesting case, because he was in fact in close contact with Fernando Ortiz and eventually invited Ortiz to Lucumí ceremonies and initiated him into the religion. Having seen these eloquent defenses and participated in the rituals, Ortiz later muted his criticisms of Lucumí.

Documents 3.4 and 3.5 take us back in time and to the issue of citizenship rights as they pertained to women. They come from a public exchange between two prominent Argentine women, Maria Eugenia Echenique and Josefina Pelliza de Sagasta, which took place in May and June 1876. The exchange began with a brief essay Echenique published in *La Ondina del Plata*, a Buenos Aires women's magazine, in which she lamented the fact that women lacked political rights and access to education, the two things they needed in order to be self-sufficient. Pelliza de Sagasta responded with a sharp rebuke of Echenique's feminist sensibilities, invoking widely held beliefs about women's natural subservience to men.

The exchange between Echenique and Pelliza de Sagasta, a portion of which is presented below[8] reminds us that essentialist arguments about the natural inclinations of a given identity in this era invariably linked a series of overlapping assumptions about both the gender and race of the subject. What was more, the power of these assumptions lay in their capacity to invoke a belief that difference was natural, an argument that was made both by women and men. And yet, the very fact of this exchange should also alert us to the fact that Latin American feminists consistently struggled throughout the nineteenth century and well into twentieth century for their citizenship rights. Their struggles were not entirely distinct from the struggles for racial equality, and the price paid for their activism was often high. As late as 1924, María Jesús Alvarado Rivera would be exiled from Peru for actively campaigning for women's equality. While it is true that most of the women's political parties and feminine congresses that took place during these decades were middle-class affairs that offered little for poor, working-class women (indeed, middle-class women often viewed poor women with the same sense of superiority and distaste as their male counterparts), they nonetheless represent an important reminder of the struggles Latin Americans from a variety of backgrounds have undertaken to establish their rights as citizens.

Together, the documents offer a limited view of the complex terrain upon which individuals demanded and were denied rights in late nineteenth- and early twentieth-century Latin America. In terms of race, we see notable differences from the United States here, as well as some marked similarities. Race would invariably be used in an effort to limit the rights of non-whites, and yet the indeterminacy of Nina Rodrigues' work—the fact that mulattos could be redeemed—and the continued and active demand for rights on the part of Afro-Cuban veterans remind us that race relations in these societies were in some ways constituted on different grounds than in the United States. Race would never be as universally used as a basis for exclusion in Latin America as it was in the United States, where a certain version of whiteness allowed for no African stain. This in turn produced some phenomena that would have been inconceivable in the United States, including a leading scientist whose racial identity was never clear, and a criminologist who, after visiting the Lucumí ceremonies of an Afro-Cuban friend, decided that blackness was not such a threat, after all.

The same could not be said when it came to gender. Though Cuba was an early adopter of women's rights, granting them control of their property in 1917, and the right to a no-fault divorce in 1918, Latin America lagged behind the United States in granting suffrage to women by several decades. Whether this meant that North American feminism was more dynamic than its Latin American cousin is a matter of some dispute. At the very least, it does seem that the relative size of the middle classes in Latin America and their greater capacity to police certain forms of conservative gender conformity limited the appeal of the radical forms of feminism Echenique advocated until much later in the twentieth century.

Document 3.1 Raimundo (Raymundo) Nina Rodrigues, *The Fetishist Animism of the Bahian Blacks* (*O Animismo Fetischistados Negros Bahianos*) (Excerpt)

Source: Excerpt from Raimundo (Raymundo) Nina Rodrigues, *O Animismo Fetischistados Negros Bahianos* (*The Fetishist Animism of the Bahian Blacks*, published 1896–1900). Translated by Diane Grosklaus Whitty.

The Fetishist Animism of Bahian Negroes

Only official science, because of the superficial, dogmatic nature of teaching, could insist in asserting even today that the population of Bahia is by and large a monotheistic Christian one. This assertion must reflect either a systematic disregard for calculating the two-thirds African negroes and mixed-race mestizos that make up the great majority of the population, or a naïveté born of brute ignorance that blindly yields to outward appearances that will prove illusory and misleading upon the most superficial examination.

The prediction that this is not how it should be follows both from an understanding of the mental conditions prerequisite to the adoption of any religious belief and from these inferior races' psychic unfitness for the elevated abstractions of monotheism. But in the case at hand, citing this deduction as proof would of course be to commit a gross *petitio principii*, for here the opposite assertion is intended to do no less than stand as a tacit, formal disapprobation of the inductive conclusion reached by ethnographic researches. And only documented observation as thorough and rigorous as that exacted by the delicate nature of this subject matter should, in the final analysis, speak for or against the soundness and applicability of this principle, or for or against its repudiation.

More than once during my exercise of the teaching profession, the demands of psychological analysis in the field of forensic psychiatry have brought me practical experience with the problems raised by this controversy, where the facts always reveal themselves to be in formal contradiction with the ungrounded assertions of official science. Thus engaged in accurately ascertaining the nature and form of the religious feeling of Bahian negroes, I have endeavored to study the facts with the utmost neutrality and impartiality and have devoted nearly five years of time and effort to attentive observations. Considering the strictly scientific spirit in which these painstaking investigations were conceived in my quest to solve a serious issue in practical ethology, any preliminary declaration that they neither had nor have anything in common with controversies that debate "the metaphysics of matter and of the spirit" is hardly warranted.

Within the realm of that which is knowable, religious feeling is a positive psychological condition, which in no way presumes the animosities manifested between deists and atheists.

The persistence of African fetishism as an expression of the religious feeling of Bahian negroes and mixed-race mestizos is a fact that has not been disguised by the outward appearances of their apparently adopted Catholic worship, belied in the form of widespread hybrid associations between this worship and fetishism and also in the genuine practice of African sorcery, which thrives exuberantly and heartily alongside Christian worship there. In Bahia there exist deep-rooted fetishist beliefs and practices, established as ordinarily as those in Africa, neither hidden nor disguised but present in the full light of day; there exists a life that evinces its licitness in the police licenses granted for large annual festivals or *candomblés* and that enjoys the tolerance of public opinion, as reflected in how matter-of-factly the daily press reports on these gatherings, as if they were just another facet of our normal life; there exist practices whose activities reach into far broader realms than those in which they originated, and beliefs that are adopted and followed by the soi-disant civilized classes, in virtue of alliances formed with Catholic worship and the union forged with spiritual practices—that these manifold experiences exist lies within the spirit of the public and is fully known to all.

But observations that aspire to be scientific in nature and in value demand a rigor and precision that precludes simply using as references information which can be greatly adulterated or enlarged upon, even if only unconsciously. This subject does not require only authenticity and precision; it also calls for objective references to specific facts that are at any moment liable to verification and examination by those desiring to challenge them. Without a doubt, there arise all sorts of obstacles and stumbling blocks to a fair and just interpretation of facts of this nature, here more than anywhere. "Even dedicating much time and care to it," says Tylor (E. B. Tylor, *La civilisation primitive*, trans. Mme. Pauline Brunet, Paris, 1876, vol. 1, p. 489).

"It is not always easy to elicit from savages information on their theology. They customarily try to hide from the prying and contemptuous foreigner the details of their worship and all knowledge of their gods, who seem to tremble, like their worshippers, before the white man and his mightier Deity." As to not knowing their language, slavery must exacerbate in the African negro the savage's natural tendency to hide his beliefs.

The conviction that religious conversion is a simple matter of willingness and that nothing could be easier than annulling the negro's beliefs through punishment, to then replace these with the white man's, was shaped so as to satisfy the master's interests and thereby justify, as a veritable meritorious deed, all the violence employed to convert them to the Christian faith. However, the deeper reasons that incited the violence of masters and their agents against the fetishist practices of the negro slave were quite other than catechistic zeal.

In the first place, we have a fear that sorcery would be used in retaliation for the mistreatment and punishment inflicted on the slaves and a superstitious dread of cabbalistic practices of a mysterious, unknown nature; secondly, the indeed well-founded apprehension that religious practices and festivals would come to hinder the regular course of work and justify idleness; thirdly, the despotic deterrent power wielded by the master, who could not admit that the negro might have any will other than his own—these were the true reasons why *candomblés* were continually disbanded through violence, sanctuaries violated, and fetishes destroyed, even when licenses were granted to negroes so that they might amuse themselves to the monotonous sound of the drumbeat. Even freed, the negro could find no protection or aid from the law so that he might freely express his beliefs during the regime of slavery, because then the mission of the law was to preserve this regime. Under the pretext that *candomblés* were a steady source of conflict and affrays and the site of unbridled debauchery and licentiousness, the police would harshly suppress them and at times would hunt them out in the cities, where, considering their nature and location, they should be more protected from the direct action of slave masters than on sugar plantations.

As an overall consequence, since these negroes have been forced their whole lives to disguise and hide their faith and religious practices, the remembrance of persecutions suffered for their beliefs still persists today and will long persist in their memory, closely tied within their spirits to a fear of confessing and explaining these beliefs. As the elimination of slavery is still quite recent, the greatest part of fetishist priests are old Africans who were all slaves. In addition to these motives, a no less powerful reason for the negro's reserve and mystery is the sorcerer's interest in the enhanced prestige he derives from this secrecy. The faith of believers and the credulity of the superstitious are crudely and gainfully exploited by these sorcerers: divulging their practices would divest them of the prestige of the unknown and would seriously damage the influence they exercise.

Along with these multiple causes contributing to our problem of understanding, we find others involving the problem of interpreting the meaning and form of fetishist practices that have been greatly modified by their environment. Transported to American soil and supplanted by an officially taught Catholicism imposed through the violence of slavery, the African element has been diluted in a large heterogeneous social environment, and the purity of African practices and rituals has necessarily and inevitably vanished, replaced by mongrel practices and beliefs. The only whole, pure thing we should expect to find is the feeling that animates their beliefs, as fetishist when the objects of this belief are rocks, trees, or shells from the seashore as when they are the many Catholic saints.

In examining and analyzing this feeling as it presents itself and lives on in the negroes who have become part of the Brazilian population and as it broadly manifests itself in all aspects of our private and public lives, we have set ourselves the task of this study, which intends to deduce therefrom sociological laws and principles that generally go unnoticed or ignored. The Portuguese language that everyone speaks today and the medical profession that I practice have been of equal assistance to me in the accomplishment of this task. The latter has served me twofold, inspiring and strengthening my innermost confidence as a general practitioner, affording a multitude of observations, and creating opportunities to examine these freely.

This is my objective, less than uncovering the African phylogenesis of our negro fetishism and asking how purely these imported religious practices and beliefs have been preserved.

In the descriptions that follow—which are the premises grounding my final conclusions—an obligation to show that African fetishism prevails in Bahia, that it is the authentic manifestation of the religious feeling of the negroes and vast majority of mestizos here, and that it is not just some chance occurrence coming from this or that sporadic society of superstitious negroes or impostors obliges me to delve into minute details and particulars that under other circumstances could very well be omitted for the sake of clarity and succinctness.

Document 3.2 Political Program of the *Partido Independiente de Color*, 1908

Source: Aviva Chomsky, translator, "The Independent Party of Color, El Partido Independiente de Color," in *The Cuba Reader: History, Culture, Politics*, eds. Aviva Chomsky, Barry Carr, and Pamela Smorkaloff, pp. 163–164. © 2003 Duke University Press. Republished by permission of the copyright holder.

The "Independent Association of Color" hereby constitutes itself as a national organization in the entire territory of the Republic. We seek to maintain a balance among all Cuban interests, spread love for the Fatherland, develop cordial relations and interest everybody in the conservation of Cuban nationality, allowing everybody born in this land to participate equally in public administration.

Our motto is an egalitarian, sovereign, and independent republic, without racial divisions or social antagonisms. All Cubans who are worthy should be able to be named to the diplomatic corps, and, as a matter of important and urgent necessity, citizens of the race of color should be named, so that the republic can be represented in all its hues.

We believe that all court trials that take place in the Republic should be trials by jury, and that the duty of serving on the jury should be mandatory and free.

We call for

The abolition of the death penalty, and for the creation of penitentiaries that fulfill the needs of modern civilization.

The creation of correctional School-ships (Barcos-escuelas) for youthful offenders who, according to the law, cannot suffer greater penalties.

Free and compulsory education for children from ages six to fourteen.

The creation of polytechnic (vocational) schools in each of the six provinces, free and compulsory for adults, to be considered as the second stage of compulsory education, and consisting Arts and Trades.

Official, national, and free university education available to all.

The regulation of private and official education, under the auspices of the state, so that the education of all Cubans will be uniform.

The creation of a Naval and Military Academy.

Free and faithful (leal) admission into military, administrative, government, and judicial services of citizens of color, so that all of the races can be represented in the service of the state.

Immigration should be free for all races, without giving preference to any. The free entrance of all individuals who, within sanitary prescriptions, come in good faith to contribute to the development of the public good.

The repatriation, at public expense, of all Cubans from foreign shores who want to return to their native land but lack the necessary resources.

The creation of a Law to guarantee that in employment in all public enterprises, in Cuba and abroad, Cubans will be given preference to foreigners, until the latter are naturalized, and preventing new enterprises from being established in other countries.

We will work to make the eight-hour day the norm in all of the territory of the republic. The creation of a Labor Tribunal to regulate any differences that arise between capital and labor.

The promulgation of a law prohibiting the immigration of minors, and of women, except when they are accompanied by their families.

The distribution of plots of land from State reserves, or from lands acquired by the state for this purpose, among veterans of the War of Independence who lack resources and who wish to devote themselves to agriculture, giving preference to those who are not suited for public office.

Document 3.3 *Manifiesto, "Santa Rita de Casia," y "San Lázaro," Sociedad de Protección Mutua, Canto y Baile*

Source: Instituto de Literatura y Linguística, Havana, Cuba. Translated by Patricia Rosas.

We Are Religious People, Not Atheists

This manifesto is directed to the people who upon the death of our Director, señor Silvestre Erise, knew how to fulfill like true Christians the high mission of respect and consideration for the dead, as the lifeless material must not be profaned by anyone, much less by people educated and intellectual in matters of human understanding.

To all those who felt in their hearts the nostalgia of others' grief in the sad moments experienced by the family, friends, and members of the Society, the Board of Directors wishes to thank them. Together we felt the death of our Director of the "Santa Rita de Casia" and "San Lázaro" Society, the man who founded it in 1902 in the Barrio del Cerro.

We Christians who belong to the aforementioned society pray to the Supreme Being for the happiness and consolation of those people who, in the columns of certain newspapers, like La Marina, profaned the name of the person who in life was called SILVESTRE ERISE and who, we have heard, on various occasions donated 300 pesos to help build the Reina Mercedes Hospital and 500 more for a Cuban who is living in Spain.

As mourners and aggrieved friends, who loved the person who is gone, we would like to say something to those people who, despite their culture and social contacts, lack respect for those who mourn the death of a beloved person. If we say nothing, it is to show that the sentiments of our unwarranted enemies are not equal to those of the mourners and friends of the deceased.

We say this because, as true Christians, we beseech in our prayers to Providence for all kinds of happiness and comforts for those whose bodies, like that of Señor Erice [sic], will always have to cover the earth with its mantle of rocks and multi-colored roots. Like the social laws of nature, this makes us all equals.

We all know that to be born means to die and that we must comply with the immutable laws of Nature. For this reason, despite the human species feeling the great weight of death, the end and the beginning of social life in Nature teaches us to know what we are and for what purpose we serve here on earth: to be born, to die, and to die to be born.

All human beings, given that they are born, must necessarily take care of themselves, and for that, it is clear, one must assimilate whatever is appropriate for life and for the development of a person's being, whatever is befitting for the self-same transmission of life. This is necessary so that the species can reproduce with all of the conditions of a healthy and strong constitution, so that development may be what it ought to be, within biological laws.

Death is Nature's justice. Before it, we are all equals: scholar, philosopher, oppressor, tyrant, the proud, the haughty, the humble, rich and poor, the ignorant, ruler and the ruled, oppressor and the oppressed, the fulfilled person and the beggar, the civilized and the uncivilized, all on the earth who hate each other because of our human preoccupations. As death is Nature's justice, thus all we are is dust, smoke, and ashes here on this earth.

After all that has come before, we move on to the duty that our Director left us before his passing, as well as encountering impassioned love for our fellow men, the bond felt by those who loved him. Thus, through the unity of those who profess the Lucumí religious doctrine, and with the justice of the Republic's laws, we shall be able to maintain the prestige and equilibrium of the Society, the object of his desires, sacrifices, and sorrows until the last moments of his Christian life, as a man faithful to God and fulfilling his duties as head of the family.

Nothing is so Christian, noble, and sacred in the conscience of social beings as fulfilling the request of a person on his deathbed. For this reason, we are inviting those people who are known in the province of Havana and who wish to formally join this Society for Mutual Protection, Song, and Dance.

We let it be known that the fee for joining is one peso; 20 centavos, weekly and 80 centavos, monthly. The allowance for ill members who are bedridden is one official peso coin. In the case of death, to defray the costs of the burial, 25 pesos in the same coin will be delivered to the family member closest to the deceased who had helped that person until the final moments of life.

The "Santa Rita de Casia" and "San Lázaro" Society does not require a member to have a medical certificate, since the person covered by the treasury must present himself in good health before the President, Secretary, Treasurer, and Director.

We also wish to announce that the Reformed Regulation of the aforementioned Society does not recognize chronic illnesses because it is a society of a distinct nature from the Socorros Mutuos (Mutual Aid Societies), which requires a medical certificate because members declared as suffering from a chronic disease are separated from other members. For that reason, we call attention to those of us who profess the African religion Lucumí, and to whom we are able to say that with the succor they give us during Sunday services, it is possible to pay the rental of a house and other expenses of the Society.

We also let it be known that the weekly and monthly membership fee is destined for cases of members' illnesses or death. For that reason, the Treasurer cannot hold an amount greater than 20 pesos, and the remainder of the money with the President's help will be deposited in his bank in the capital.

Now, since those of us who profess the African religious doctrine of Lucumí have clearly taken into account what is mutual protection for the cases of illness and death, we are certain that we have complied with these words of Jesus: "love one another"—and to that we add—for our Father who art in Heaven, that he protect the collective unit of the oppressed and the abused, for those who as human beings are like us, of flesh and blood.

After all that has been explained in this manifesto, as religious people and not atheists, it remains for us to say to the members and protectors of the Society that on Sunday, October 17, we will begin our Sunday services with the recognition of the municipal mayor and the chief of police, señor Placido Hernandez, who respectful of the laws of the Republic faithfully fulfills what his superiors order him to do. And as the chief of police is the guarantor of public order in the Barrio del Cerro, the board of directors of the aforementioned Society respectfully salute him, señor Placido Hernandez, the officials, and other subordinates from the 11th police station.

For the Board of Directors, Fernando Guerra, President

Havana, September 30, 1915

Document 3.4 Maria Eugenia Echenique, "Brushstrokes," May 7, 1876

Source: Translated by the Palouse Translation Project. "The Emancipation of Women: Argentina 1876." *Journal of Women's History* 7:3 (Fall 1995), 103–104. © 1995 *Journal of Women's History*. Reprinted with permission of Johns Hopkins University Press.

I have held my pen in hand for five minutes, and I still do not know what I am going to write about. There are so many ideas and feelings overwhelming me at this moment that I remain in doubt about the choice of a specific point to serve as the topic for an article.

I could easily allow myself a pleasant moment of innocent entertainment that still would have a certain utility—surrendering to purely imaginative games, tracing with my pen beautiful images capable of stirring sweet emotions in the heart without compromising men's morality or dignity, writing a dream, a meditation, or a fantasy drawing all the soul's sensations into a world of poetry—that would satisfy the need that my spirit feels to communicate and open the gate to vast fields of thought.

But to write a fantasy when the women of this century have need of our meager education and of resources useful to them in the difficult circumstances through which they are passing; when they have need of the cooperation of Argentine women writers in the great work of their regeneration, begun recently in this part of America, that brings to each of us serious obligations to fulfill in the social and moral order; to waste time in futile games when the majority of our sex cries forgotten on the path of ignorance, being toys of charlatanism, waiting for a protecting hand to come take them out of inaction and put them in their rightful position—that would be an unpardonable failure that would injure the delicate susceptibility of our sensitive and thoughtful women.

Our heart rebels against the ideas of spirituality, sensibility, and poetry that, as cultivated by women, have callously contributed until now to women's delay on the road of progress and the improvement of their condition. That remains from those ancient times when women were slaves under the power of absolute masters, subject to the whims and rule of the "heads" of families or of tyrannical husbands, when women had no aspirations nor anything to think about, when they felt a profound emptiness in their hearts that they needed to fill with beautiful daydreams and gilded illusions; the reduced sphere of action to which they had been relegated and the absolute ostracism which surrounded them wherever they were, developed their melancholy feelings to a high degree, making it necessary for them to seek solace for their moments of bitterness and disillusionment.

The ideas of freedom born in this century, by extending the circle of women's prerogatives, have infused them with new aspirations and unveiled great things to think about and occupy themselves with. The women of today are not the women of the past. The change that has taken place within them in these recent times is profound. Instead of poetry, today they need philosophy, practical philosophy that better idealizes life when it saves women from the critical circumstances of a dark and difficult existence, responding to the great interests of humanity.

How do women look when they spend days and years crying at the least disappointments and deceptions of life, exaggerating to themselves the pain of their existence, forging a world of sadness, at each step finding ominous specters in everything, living solely on illusions, feigning lovely ideals that vanish like smoke, in contrast with men who laugh at everything, who make a joke of themselves, who only think of filling their pockets and satisfying their own desires, who if they encounter an obstacle to the pursuit of any goal they set, become angry and trample over everything, men who live impatient to climb mountains of glory in the progress of science in all its manifestations?

In the materialistic century in which we live, it is necessary to make women a bit philosophical if we do not want them to become lost in their endeavors. Less sensibility and more reflection! With sentimentalism, women will not satisfy their needs in a century in which gold and the prosaic shine of possessions are king.

In the press, our mission is as interpreters of their affections and aspirations, a sacred mission from which we cannot exempt ourselves without compromising our own interests. To smooth the road of civilization and of culture, removing the barriers that oppose the achievement of the great thoughts and generous desires that stir women's hearts in the present century, contributing with our pen to the realization of their most beautiful hopes; to teach them to overcome the prejudices that diminish their rights, opposing the torrent of disorderly passions that destroy them; to show them the path that leads to happiness in the attainment of sacred duties and the cultivation of elevated passions, infusing in them love of the arts and sciences, of reading and working; in short, to teach them the way to take care of their physical needs more skillfully according to their social standing—such is the vast circle of obligations that our position as writers undertakes in a country where the regeneration of women has begun in such a splendid and brilliant way.

Document 3.5 Judith [Josefina Pelliza de Sagasta], "Women: Dedicated to Miss Maria Eugenia Echenique," June 4, 1876

Source: Translated by the Palouse Translation Project. "The Emancipation of Women: Argentina 1876." *Journal of Women's History* 7:3 (Fall 1995), 105–107. © 1995 *Journal of Women's History*. Reprinted with permission of Johns Hopkins University Press.

You discuss improving the present condition of women, but in this question of such interest and such serious consequences for South American women, we encounter very grave drawbacks. The emancipation of women, treated with enthusiasm by Argentine and even Peruvian authors, is an unattainable feat in our humble opinion and, moreover, harmful if it were to be attained. Entirely free women, with as much independence as men, would lose their greatest charms and the poetic prestige of their weakness: the prestige which forms the most noble attribute of their sex, the prestige that later, when women are mothers, doubly beautifies them and places them on the sacred throne of the home, where women best belong.

Women, in our opinion, should never even in thought surpass the limits that God when making them—their souls with the softest breaths of divine light and their bodies with the purest of His celestial conceptions—gave them as their path on earth: He pointed out their mission, and gave them a physical and moral constitution different from men and in accordance with the sorrows and sufferings of their destiny as daughters, wives, and mothers. Woman, one celebrated writer has said, "is the poetry of God, and man is His prose." There only remains to admire women's delicate shapes (with some exceptions), their souls susceptible to tender emotions, always gentle and loving, their thoughts, in short their physical beauty, in order to exclaim: the destiny of women is not, as has mistakenly been said, equal to the destiny of men, because the former are weak and tender in their spirit and their bodies cannot endure the difficult hardships to which men are subjected; their dignity would be diminished if they were to attempt to liberate themselves from those sweet attributes of their nature, from those bonds that the propagandist writers of emancipation have been calling guardianship, without realizing that it is precisely that guardianship which makes women more beautiful, that elevates them to their true pedestal without aspirations of glory or applause, that binds them to their husbands, that binds them to the home, and that makes them into the guardian angel of the family. She is a slave! you emancipated women will exclaim—and I in turn will reply to you: not a slave but a companion, man's other half, slave perhaps to her children, but how seductive and poetic is her beautiful sacrifice. Blessed be the woman who is a mother!

Woman is born to love, to be protected by the generous heart of man, guided by him and embodied in that powerful and noble soul like the purest breath of celestial tight; sheltered by man, defended by him, always joined to him, and supported by him like the tender shoots that cling to the shade and protection of the stake that sustains them if they waver, that helps and reinforces them if they wilt, and that always defends them with solicitous care.

But let us hear the authoritative word of the sublime Spanish author Maria del Pilar Sinués de Marco. She says: "There will never be a husband for an emancipated woman, whether her emancipation be a dream of sick fantasies or whether it be imposed upon society as law! What man would want to see his daughters educated to be teachers and his sons for uselessness? What man would thus decline the sacred rights of his nature? What honorable occupation would remain to men in their homes, if the wives managed the businesses and disposed of the assets? Bah! Bah! Is this nothing more than abolishing marriage? Thus emancipation is a monstrosity which few women would be party to; homes would remain without warmth and without light because there would be no wives nor mothers.

"Love would remain for women. Horror! What is love when it is not restrained and beautified by duty? To pretend that men only speak to the senses and never to the heart?

"No, no, God made man the natural head of the family. Work! He said to Adam. Love, He said to women in general through Eve. Console man! Make my punishment more bearable! Follow him wherever he goes! With science the heart petrifies and one lives without love! . . . Without love! the redemption, consolation, strength, and heaven on earth for women!"

So says the inspired author of Angel of the House. We will add: good women are virtuous, talented, with legitimate aspirations, with freedom of beliefs, educated, with mutual rights between them and their companions for life, energetic, capable of sacrifice, capable of the martyrdom of heroism, well-read, a writer, progressive, an initiator— in short everything but emancipated, less free in independence and rights than men.

Women should be educated; give them a solid education, based on wholesome principles, cemented with moral and sensible beliefs; they should have a general knowledge of everything that awakens ingenuity and determines ideas, but not for them are the calculation and egotism with which they instruct English women, not for them the ridiculous ideas of North American women who pretend in their pride to be equal to men, to be legislators and obtain a seat in Congress or be university professors, as if it were not enough to be a mother, a wife, a housewife, as if her rights as a woman were not enough to be happy and to make others happy, as if it were not enough to carry out her sacred mission on earth: educating her family, cultivating the tender hearts of her children making them useful citizens, laborers of intelligence and progress, with her words and acts; cultivating love in her children and the sentiments that most enhance women: virtue, modesty and humility. Girls, women someday, be tender and loving wives, able to work for the happiness of your life's partner instead of bringing about his disgrace with dreams and aspirations beyond your sphere. We concede to women, if their ability is sufficient, that they be well-read; the woman who writes, when that woman is virtuous, is always useful to society; there are women, wives and mothers, who without forgetting their responsibilities are writers and are the glory of their sex. One only has to look to Europe to see distinguished against a backdrop of light the most passionate and gentle of the poetesses of our era and the most tender and kind of wives—the beautiful Staël, the divine author of Uncle Tom's Cabin, Harriet Beecher Stowe, Madame Gay, her daughter Emilia de Girardin.

I will conclude this already too-long article, beseeching Argentine women writers, and those who are not, to look over the pages of Severo Catalina's *Woman* and Marco's *Angel of the House*, and we are sure that your ideas will take another turn. Above all else, read *Love* by Mr. de Michelet. Ah! Then see if you have adopted with your thought and with your pen the emancipation of women; there woman as a divine work of idealism and perfection is lover and beloved, esteemed by men and respected by them, in short she is the woman of our dreams—pure, delicate, modest woman; the woman that only the great French writer's pen dipped in glory could draw with tight and beauty, with tints and perfumes of inexpressible color and perfect naturalness; look there, in that chaste and sublime poem of Love for the real and most beautiful type of women, true daughters, wives, and mothers, and you will find them profiled with fragrance, with a magnetic attraction that will make you exclaim—blessed be the woman under the guardianship of man. And in concluding my article I will say to you: love women in their true form, exalted in their homes, absolute queens of the hearts of men, exercising their unequaled mastery, on their immovable diamond thrones, strong, colossal in the midst of their weakness.

For Further Reading

Andrews, George Reid. *Blacks and Whites in Sao Paulo, Brazil, 1888–1988* Madison: University of Wisconsin Press, 1993.

Andrews, George Reid. *Afro-Latin America, 1800–2000.* Oxford: Oxford University Press, 2004.

Borges, Dain. "'Puffy, Ugly, Slothful, and Inert': Degeneration in Brazilian Social Thought, 1880–1930," *Journal of Latin American Studies* 25:2 (1993), 235–256.

Bronfman, Alejandra. *Measures of Equality: Social Science, Citizenship, and Race in Cuba, 1902–1940.* Chapel Hill: University of North Carolina Press, 2004.

Butler, Kim D. *Freedoms Given, Freedoms Won: Afro-Brazilians in Post-Abolition Sao Paulo and Salvador.* New Brunswick: Rutgers University Press, 1998.

Ferrer, Ada. *Insurgent Cuba: Race, Nation, and Revolution, 1868–1898.* Chapel Hill, University of North Carolina Press, 1999.

Gotkowitz, Laura. *A Revolution for Our Rights: Indigenous Struggles for Land and Justice in Bolivia, 1880–1952.* Durham, NC: Duke University Press, 2007.

Graham, Sandra Lauderdale. *Caetana Says No: Women's Stories from a Brazilian Slave Society.* Cambridge: Cambridge University Press, 2002.

Grandin, Greg. *The Blood of Guatemala: A History of Race and Nation.* Durham, NC: Duke University Press, 2000.

Helg, Aline. *Our Rightful Share: The Afro-Cuban Struggle for Equality, 1886–1912.* Chapel Hill: University of North Carolina Press, 1995.

Helg, Aline. "Race and Black Mobilization in Colonial and Early Independent Cuba: A Comparative Perspective," *Ethnohistory* 44:1 (1997), 53–74.

Larson, Brooke. *Trials of Nation Making: Liberalism, Race, and Ethnicity in the Andes, 1810–1910*. Cambridge: Cambridge University Press, 2004.

Lasso, Marixa. *Myths of Harmony: Race and Republicanism during the Age of Revolution, Colombia, 1795–1831*. Pittsburgh: University of Pittsburgh Press, 2007.

Reis, João José. *Slave Rebellion in Brazil: The Muslim Uprising of 1835 in Bahia*. Baltimore: Johns Hopkins University Press, 1995.

Scott, Rebecca. *Slave Emancipation in Cuba: The Transition to Free Labor, 1860–1899*. Pittsburgh: University of Pittsburgh Press, 2000.

Scott, Rebecca, *Degrees of Freedom: Louisiana and Cuba after Slavery*. Cambridge, MA: Belknap Press, 2008.

Stepans, Nancy. *The Hour of Eugenics: Race, Gender, and Nation in Latin America*. Ithaca: Cornell University Press, 1993.

Viotti Da Costa, *Emilia. The Brazilian Empire: Myths and Histories*. Chapel Hill: University of North Carolina Press, 2000.

Williams, Derek. "Popular Liberalism and Indian Servitude: The Making and Unmaking of Ecuador's Antilandlord State, 1845–1868," *Hispanic American Historical Review* 83:4, 697–734.

At A Glance: People

Below we consider several of the important demographic trends that have shaped Latin America since the early nineteenth century. We begin with three figures that are rooted in the colonial past. **Figure B.1** measures the indigenous population of the region from the sixteenth to the twentieth centuries. **Figure B.2** considers the impact of the importation of eleven million African slaves on Latin America. **Table B.3** surveys the complex ethnic mix that characterized the colonies at Independence, and represents an effort to consider miscegenation over time. Obsessed with racial difference, the Spanish colonial state separated the casta (mixed race) population into more than fifteen different categories. This obsession took a different form in Latin America than in Anglo America. Whereas in the North mixed origins were rarely acknowledged (consider the "One Drop Rule" in the U.S.), in Latin America and the Caribbean hybridity was generally recognized, and later celebrated in anti-imperial nationalist discourses during the twentieth century.

Figure B.4 measures population growth in Latin America since 1750. One can see that the rate of population growth increased dramatically during the twentieth century, a rate likely attributable to better nutrition and health care. This rate has slowed considerably in recent years, and is expected to be modest during the first half of the twenty-first century.

The following figures delve deeper into these numbers, examining the contemporary ethnic breakdown of the region and the different experiences of men and women. **Table B.5** is the result of research that endeavors to use recent census data to track the indigenous and African origin populations of Latin America. In one example of the diversity of racial typologies in the region, the researchers used a variety of labels to assess the Afro-descended population, including black, mulatto, garifuna, criollo, indio (in the case of the Dominican Republic), and moreno. In sum, these figures show the complex ways that indigenous and Afro-descended populations are spread across the region, with little presence in some countries and constituting majorities in others.

Table B.6 considers life expectancies, separated out by men and women, between 1950 and 2004. During this period the mean life expectancy for men in the region rose by twenty years and for women it rose by twenty-two years. Latin America today exceeds global averages in this measure, but still lags behind the wealthiest nations. Coupled with falling fertility rates, these figures demonstrate the importance of improved social and health services across the region during the latter half of the twentieth century, along with general improvements in the standard of living. What they do not allow us to see is the way that growing inequality figures into these statistics. Although the average figures are quite impressive, they hide the fact that some are doing far better than the average, and that a significant number are lagging quite a bit behind.

Figure B.7 offers an opportunity to break down these numbers according to percentage of women in any given country who have completed a primary education. This measure tends to be a fairly robust indicator of social and economic well-being, as well as a strong indicator of the state of gender relations in any given setting. This graph shows unprecedented growth in educational levels for women in Latin America since the start of the twentieth century. Women still lag behind men in several countries, but elsewhere seem to have caught up. In Argentina and Uruguay, where educational levels were higher than in much of the region at the beginning of the century, nearly all women now receive a primary education. Most Central American countries have seen steady gains, but still lag behind other countries. Others, like Mexico and Peru, have outperformed the region as a whole relative to where they began.

Figure B.8 is a map of poverty in contemporary Latin America. This graphic offers us an opportunity to interrogate the previous measures of social well-being. Poverty has been declining in aggregate terms across the region in recent years, although the picture gets more complex when broken down by country. And as is the case in Mexico, even within individual countries we see regions with very low incidences of poverty, and other regions where poverty rates remain quite high. If mapped onto these indicators of poverty, the statistics presented in Figures B.6 and B.7 would look somewhat different. The measures of education, gender equality, and life expectancy in more prosperous regions would approximate what we find in the Global North, whereas in regions characterized by extreme poverty and inequality the results would be quite different.

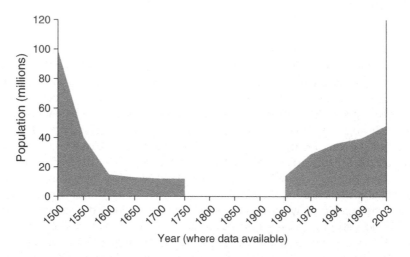

Figure B.1   Graph: The Indigenous Population of the Americas, 1500–2003

Source: Reprinted from Raul A. Montenegro and Carolyn Stephens, "Indigenous health in Latin America and the Caribbean," *The Lancet*, Volume 367, Issue 9525, Pages 1859–1869, with permission from Elsevier.

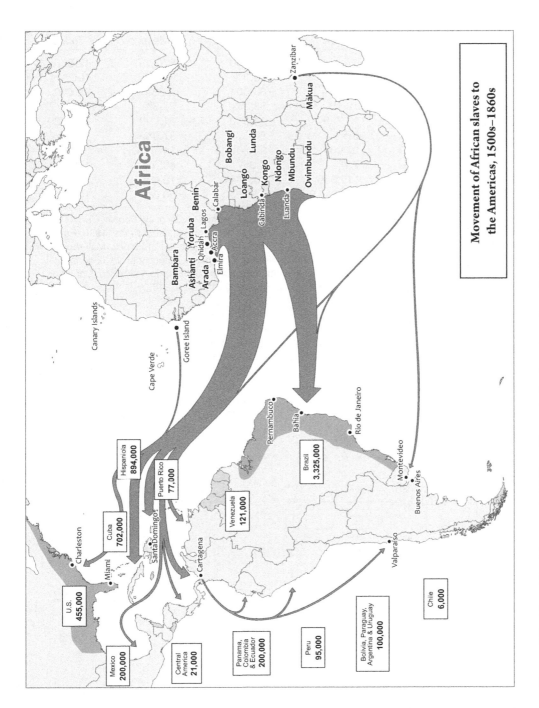

Figure B.2 Map: The Movement of African Slaves to the Americas, from the 1400s to the 1860s

Table B.3   Breakdown of the Population of Latin America by the Categories White, Black/Mulatto, Amerindian, and Mestizo, from the eighteenth to the twentieth centuries in hundreds of thousands

Year	White	Black	Amerindian	Mestizo	Total
1650	138	67	12,000	670	12,875
Percentages	1.1%	0.5%	93.2%	5.2%	100%
1825	4,350	4,100	8,000	6,200	22,650
Percentages	19.2%	18.1%	35.3%	27.3%	100%
1950	72,000	13,729	14,000	61,000	160,729
Percentages	44.8%	8.5%	8.7%	37.9%	100%
1980	150,000	27,000	30,000	140,000	347,000
Percentages	43.2%	7.7%	8.6%	40.3%	100%
2000	181,296	119,055	46,434	152,380	502,784
Percentages	36.1%	23.6%	9.2%	30.3%	100%

Source: http://en.wikipedia.org/wiki/White_Latin_American; taken from *The Cry of My People. Out of Captivity in Latin America*, written by Esther and Mortimer Arias. New York: Friendship Press, 1980. Pages 17 and 18. Data belonging to the year 2000 are taken from Francisco Lizcano Fernández (May–August 2005). "Composición Étnica de las Tres Áreas Culturales del Continente Americano al Comienzo del Siglo XXI". *Convergencia* (in Spanish) (Mexico: Universidad Autónoma del Estado de México, Centro de Investigación en Ciencias Sociales y Humanidades) 38: 185–232; table on p. 218.

1750	16,000,000
1800	24,000,000
1850	38,000,000
1900	74,000,000
1950	160,729,000
2000	502,784,000
2050	750,956,000

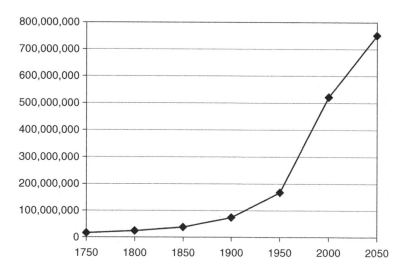

Figure B.4   Table and Graph: Population Growth in Latin America Since 1750

Table B.5   Afrodescendent and Indigenous Population (in Thousands) and Percentages in Contemporary Latin America by Country, Using Most Recent Census Data When Available (PERLA Countries in Bold)

Countries	Year	Afrodescendant Population	Percentage	Year	Indigenous Population	Percentage	Total National Population
Argentina[1]	2010	150	0.4	2010	955	2.4	40,117
Bolivia[2]	2012	24	0.2	2012	4,068	40.6	10,027
Brazil[3]	**2010**	**97,083**	**50.9**	**2010**	**897**	**0.5**	**190,733**
Chile[4]	2012	97	0.6[5]	2012	1,700	10.2	16,636
Colombia[6]	**2005**	**4,274**	**10.3**	**2005**	**1,393**	**3.4**	**41,468**
Costa Rica[7]	2011	334	7.8	2011	104	2.4	4,302
Cuba[8]	2012	3,885	34.8[9]	2012	–	–	11,163
Dominican Republic[10]	2010	A) 2,267 B) 8,406	A) 24.0 B) 89.0[11]	2010	–	–	9,445
Ecuador[12]	2010	1,043	7.2	2010	1,014	7.0	14,484
El Salvador[13]	2007	7	0.1	2007	13	0.2	5,744
Guatemala[14]	2011	5	0.0	2011	4,428[15]	30.1	14,713
Honduras[16]	2011	59	0.7	2001	428	5.1	8,448
Mexico[17]	**2010**	**2,366**	**2.1**[18]	**2010**	**15,700**	**15.9**	**112,337**
Nicaragua[19]	2005	23	0.4	2005	444	8.6	5,142
Panama[20]	2010	313	9.1	2010	418	12.1	3,454
Paraguay[21]	2012	234	3.5[22]	2012	116	1.7	6,673
Peru[23]	**2007**	**411**	**1.5**[24]	**2007**	**7,600**	**27.0**[25]	**28,221**
Uruguay[26]	2011	255	7.8	2011	159	4.8	3,286
Venezuela[27]	2011	A) 953 B) 14,534	A) 3.5 B) 53.4[28]	2011	953[29]	3.5	27,228
TOTAL		A) 113,783 B) 136,723	A) 20.6 B) 24.7		40,390	7.3	553,621

Source: Edward Telles, *Pigmentocracies: Ethnicity, Race, and Color in Latin America* (Chapel Hill: University of North Carolina Press, 2014). Reprinted by permission of the publisher. www.uncpress.unc.edu.

Notes:

[1] Argentine Census 2010, INDEC, http://www.censo2010.indec.gov.ar/archivos/censo2010_tomo1.pdf.

[2] Bolivian census 2012, INE, http://www.ine.gob.bo:8081/censo2012/default.aspx. The Bolivian census counts only those 15 and older for indigenous and Afrodescendant affiliation. As such, the projected total number of indigenous and Afro-Colombians was calculated by multiplying the percentage of 15+ year olds by the total number of Bolivians.

[3] Brazilian Census 2010, IBGE.

[4] "Chile's "Official" Indigenous Population More than Doubles with New Census Results," Indigenous News, http://indigenousnews.org/2013/04/08/chiles-official-indigenous-population-more-than-doubles-with-new-census-results/. Upon time of research, the census data was undergoing an internal audit, and as such, was unavailable to corroborate the report of this news source.

[5] 2010 America's Barometer (LAPOP)

[6] *La visibilización estadística de los grupos étnicos colombianos* (2005), DANE, http://www.dane.gov.co/files/censo2005/etnia/sys/visibilidad_estadistica_etnicos.pdf.

[7] Costa Rican Census 2011, INEC, http://www.inec.go.cr/Web/Home/GeneradorPagina.aspx;2010 America's Barometer (LAPOP). Figure includes those who reported as "Indio."

[8] Cuban Census 2012, ONE, http://www.one.cu/cifraspreliminares2012.htm.

[9] Ibid., http://www.one.cu/publicaciones/08informacion/panorama2012/10%20Demograficos.pdf; the 2012 census showed that 10.4% of Cubans reported as "negro" and 24.8% reported as "mulatto."

[10] Dominican Census 2010, ONE, http://censo2010.one.gob.do/index.php.

[11] 2010 America's Barometer (LAPOP). Estimate A includes only persons identifying as negro, mulatto or Afro-Dominican. Estimate B also includes persons identifying as Indio.

[12] Ecuadorian Census 2010, INEC, http://www.elcomercio.com/sociedad/resultados-censo-Censo_de_ Poblacion_y_Vivienda-INEC_ECMFIL20110905_0005.pdf.

[13] Salvadoran Census 2007, DIGESTYC, http://www.digestyc.gob.sv/servers/redatam/htdocs/CPV2007S/ index.html.

[14] Guatemalan Census 2011, INE, http://www.ine.gob.gt/np/poblacion/index.htm.

[15] Includes Maya and Xinka.

[16] Honduran census bureau site (http://www.ine.gob.hn/drupal/)

[17] Basesdedatospormunicipio2010,CDI(Comisiónnacionalparaeldesarrollodelospueblosindígenas),http:// www.cdi.gob.mx/index.php?option=com_content&view=article&id=1327:cedulas-de-informacionbasica- de-los-pueblos-indigenas-de-mexico-&catid=38:indicadores-y-estadisticas&Itemid=54.

[18] 2010 America's Barometer (LAPOP).

[19] Census 2005, INIDE, http://www.inide.gob.ni/censos2005/ResumenCensal/Resumen2.pdf.

[20] Panamanian Census 2010, http://estadisticas.contraloria.gob.pa/Resultados2010/.

[21] Paraguayan Census 2012, DGEEC, http://www.dgeec.gov.py/index.php.

[22] Inter-American Development Bank projection, http://www.iadb.org/en/topics/gender-indigenous-peoples- and-african-descendants/percentage-of-afro-descendants-in-latin-america,6446.html.

[23] Peruvian Census 2007, INEI, http://www.inei.gob.pe/.

[24] ENCO 2006, INEI.

[25] ibid.

[26] Uruguayan Census 2011, INE, http://www.ine.gub.uy/censos2011/index.html.

[27] Venezuelan Census 2011, INE, http://www.redatam.ine.gob.ve/redatam/index.html. Estimate A includes only persons identifying as negro, mulatto, or Afro-Venezuelan. Estimate B also includes per- sons identifying as moreno.

[28] The figure counts those who self-identified as "negro," "afrodescendiente," as well as those who iden- tify as "moreno."

[29] Primeros Resultados Censo Nacional 2011: Población Indígena De Venezuela, Ine, http://www.ine.gov. ve/documentos/Demografia/CensodePoblacionyVivienda/pdf/PrimerosResultadosIndigena.pdf.

Table B.6   Male Vs. Female Lifespans by Country, 1950–2004

Countries	Men		Women		Total		Gains between 1950–1954 and 2000–2004		
	1950–1954	2000–2004	1950–1954	2000–2004	1950–1954	2000–2004	Men	Women	Total
Mesoamerica	47.8	71.3	51.0	76.5	49.3	73.8	23.5	25.5	24.5
Costa Rica	56.0	75.8	58.6	80.6	57.3	78.1	19.8	22.0	20.9
Guatemala	41.8	65.5	42.3	72.5	42.0	68.9	23.7	30.2	26.9
Honduras	40.5	68.6	43.2	73.4	41.8	71.0	28.1	30.2	29.2
Mexico	48.9	72.4	52.5	77.4	50.7	74.8	23.5	24.8	24.1
Nicaragua	40.9	67.2	43.7	71.9	42.3	69.5	26.3	28.2	27.2
Panama	54.4	72.3	56.2	77.4	55.3	74.7	17.9	21.1	19.5
El Salvador	44.1	67.7	46.5	73.7	45.3	70.6	23.6	27.3	25.4
Caribbean	51.8	68.3	54.8	72.8	53.3	70.5	16.5	18.0	17.2
Netherlands Antilles	59.1	73.3	61.6	79.2	60.5	76.3	14.2	17.6	15.9
Bahamas	58.3	63.9	61.2	70.3	59.8	67.1	5.6	9.1	7.3
Barbados	55.0	74.5	59.5	79.5	57.2	77.2	19.5	20.0	20.0
Belize	57.1	69.9	58.3	73.0	57.7	71.4	12.9	14.7	13.7
Cuba	57.8	75.3	61.3	79.1	59.5	77.1	17.5	17.8	17.7
Dominica	–	–	–	–	–	–	–	–	–
Grenada	–	–	–	–	–	–	–	–	–
Guadeloupe	55.0	74.8	58.1	81.7	56.5	78.3	19.8	23.6	21.8
Guyana	50.8	60.1	53.9	66.3	52.3	63.2	9.3	12.4	10.9
French Guiana	50.3	72.5	56.9	78.3	53.3	75.1	22.2	21.4	21.9
Haiti	36.3	57.8	38.9	60.7	37.6	59.2	21.5	21.9	21.7
Jamaica	56.9	73.7	60.2	77.8	58.5	75.7	16.8	17.6	17.2
Martinique	55.0	75.8	58.1	82.3	56.6	79.1	20.8	24.2	22.6
Puerto Rico	62.7	71.2	66.0	80.1	64.3	75.6	8.5	14.1	11.3
Dominican Rep.	44.7	67.8	47.3	72.4	46.0	70.1	23.1	25.1	24.1
Saint Lucia	52.7	70.8	55.3	74.1	54.1	72.5	18.1	18.8	18.4
Suriname	54.4	68.5	57.7	73.7	56.0	71.1	14 1	16.0	15.1
Trinidad and Tobago	58.2	68.5	59.9	74.4	59.1	71.3	10.2	14.5	12.2
Andean Countries	47.2	68.6	50.2	74.3	48.7	71.4	21.4	24.1	22.7
Bolivia	38.5	61.8	42.5	66.0	40.4	63.8	23.3	23.5	23.4
Colombia	49.0	69.2	52.3	75.3	50.6	72.2	20.2	23.0	21.6
Ecuador	47.1	71.3	49.6	77.2	48.4	74.2	24.2	27.6	25.8
Peru	42.9	67.3	45.0	72.4	43.9	69.8	24.5	27.4	25.9
Venezuela	53.8	69.9	56.6	75.8	55.2	72.8	16.1	19.2	17.6
Southern Cone and Brazil	52.5	68.4	56.3	75.8	54.3	72.0	15.9	19.5	17.7
Argentina	60.4	70.6	65.1	78.1	62.7	74.3	10.2	13.0	11.6
Brazil	49.3	67.3	52.8	74.9	51.0	71.0	18.0	22.2	20.0
Chile	52.9	74.8	56.8	80.8	54.8	77.7	21.9	24.0	22.9
Paraguay	60.7	68.6	64.7	73.1	62.6	70.8	7.9	8.5	8.2
Uruguay	63.3	71.6	69.4	78.9	66.3	75.2	8.3	9.5	8.9
Total	49.7	68.3	53.1	74.9	51.4	71.5	18.6	21.8	20.1

Sources: estimates by CELADE (http://www.eclac.cl/celade/proyecciones/basedatos_BD.htm);
United Nations (2005) for data on English-speaking Caribbean countries

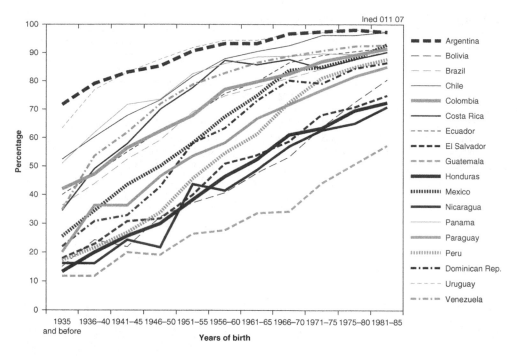

Figure B.7   Graph: Proportion of Women Who Completed Their Primary Schooling, by Cohort Group (19 countries)

Source: José Miguel Guzman et al., "The Demography of Latin America and the Caribbean since 1950." Population vol. 61, no. 5/6 (2006), Figure 18 (data in table A.33). Reprinted courtesy of I.N.E.D. (Institut national d'études démographiques), Paris.

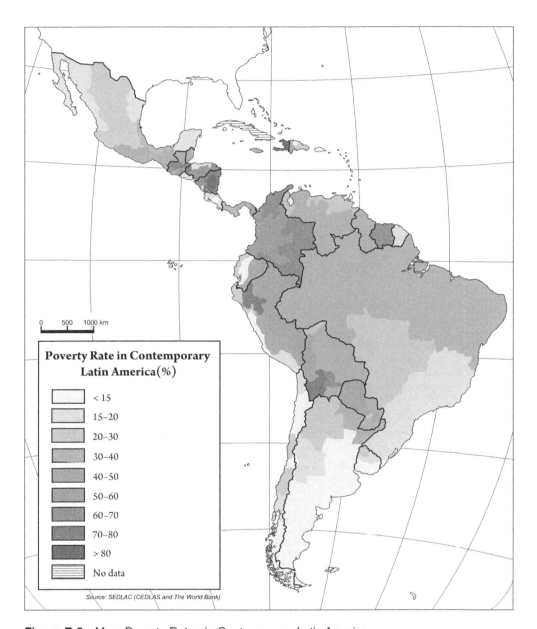

Figure B.8   Map: Poverty Rates in Contemporary Latin America

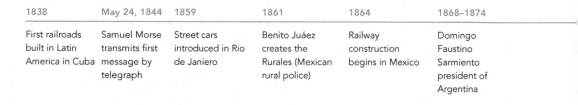

1838	May 24, 1844	1859	1861	1864	1868–1874
First railroads built in Latin America in Cuba	Samuel Morse transmits first message by telegraph	Street cars introduced in Rio de Janiero	Benito Juáez creates the Rurales (Mexican rural police)	Railway construction begins in Mexico	Domingo Faustino Sarmiento president of Argentina

The Export Boom as Modernity

4

1882	1885	1879–1880	1904–1907	April 23, 1906	September 1910
Electric lighting introduced in Santiago, Chile	Electricity introduced in Buenos Aires	War of the Desert in Argentina removes indigenous peoples from Pampas	Expulsion of Yaquis from Sonora to Yucatán (Mexico)	Brazilian Alberto Santos Dumont becomes first person to fly an airplane in Europe	Mexico celebrates Independence Centenary

In September 1910, with Mexico's tumultuous first century of independence coming to its conclusion President Porfirio Díaz decided to throw a party. There was a great deal to celebrate. He had ruled Mexico for thirty-four years, and had just been re-elected to another six-year term. Mexico's government was more stable, the treasury healthier, and its infrastructure more developed than at any time since independence. New public works were evident everywhere. A new opera house was under construction in Mexico City, government office buildings were going up throughout the downtown core, and electric lights and automobiles were everywhere on the city's streets. Mexicans could also celebrate the success of massive engineering projects, including a drainage tunnel that emptied the waters of the Valley of Mexico, ending the threat of malaria in the capital city. Though it had slowed in recent years, Mexico's economy had been growing spectacularly since the 1880s, bringing along with it new agricultural wealth, new mines, and even an emerging industrial sector, and the celebration showcased these developments. Diaz covered the city in lights, announced new public works projects, and held parades celebrating the long and now glorious history of the nation. He treated partygoers to a breathtaking catalogue of achievements, all of them signs that Mexico had finally arrived to the modern age. Foreign dignitaries marveled at it all, seemingly unaware that the political opposition was in exile, plotting revolution, that peasants in several regions were on the verge of open rebellion, and that the economy as a whole was in a tailspin.

Throughout Latin America, the late nineteenth century witnessed a very particular form of modernity. With the independence wars and fratricidal struggles of earlier decades in the past, and with slavery and other caste systems firmly abolished, Latin America was well situated to become an important participant in that era's boom in global trade. The industrial economies of the North needed a variety of inputs—copper, nitrates, silver, oil, iron, rubber, coffee, sugar, tobacco, and others—that could be found in abundance in Latin America. In return they promised a range of highly desired manufactures, including steam engines, barbed wire, shoes, machine guns, cameras, medicines, and later, refrigerators, radios, telephones, and automobiles. All these goods circulated on global transportation networks at reduced costs, with a speed and in volumes never seen before. Ideas, fashions, and various cultural forms also entered global networks in new ways in the late nineteenth century. Steamships, railways, photographs, telegraphs, and recorded sound changed the ways that people around the world understood distance and their connections to others.

Sometimes called the golden age of the export oligarchy (an oligarchy, because both the political and economic realms were controlled by a small elite), this period can seem like Milton Friedman's idea of the Latin American Dream.[1] As efficient exporters of raw materials, Latin American countries prospered because they could cheaply produce certain valuable commodities that were then in demand in the industrial north. Northern economies were sufficiently prosperous to invest the capital that Latin Americans needed in order to exploit those commodities, a phenomenon most powerfully symbolized through railroad development. Latin Americans lacked the resources needed to build railroads, but needed them to unleash the region's economic potential. Railroads could open otherwise isolated regions to export agricultural and mineral commodities. They could move people into and around their nations. This was an added bonus in countries where there were few navigable rivers, like Mexico, Colombia, Peru, and Chile. Railroads could also ensure central government control, and, along with barbed wire (patented in the United States by Joseph Glidden in 1874) and machine guns (the Gatling Gun was patented in 1861), they facilitated the concentration of governmental power in ways that earlier technologies could not. Foreign investors could thus provide the tools to allow Latin Americans to become consumers in the global industrial economy, to make their countries more stable and modern, and to restore something of the wealth and elegance that was lost during decades of internecine conflict.

But wait: This is not the only way to begin this story. Milton Friedman is not terribly popular these days, and his critics prefer to invoke a tragic tone when introducing the export boom. They see it as a sad tale of economic dependency, as a time when powerful foreign interests and a small elite found new ways to monopolize Latin America's wealth, while the vast majority remained poor. They would remind us that this was an era in which rich nations gained the economic upper hand because of the asymmetries produced by an arrangement in which Latin America exported raw materials and imported manufactured goods. As a result, the gulf between the rich and poor nations grew larger, reinforced as always through the use of violence.

The differences between these views are in part ideological (left vs. right) and in part professional (economic vs. social historians). They also say a great deal about the types of stories we like to tell when we narrate the past. The export boom can be told as a tragedy in which inequalities deepened and were further entrenched, where certain forms of violence intensified, and the victimization of the region at the hands of the outside world was re-inscribed through an unequal global system. It can also be told as a kind of epic, where Latin Americans of a variety of classes struggled to make themselves and their societies more prosperous, more modern. Some tell it as a comedy, an era when foolish prognosticators imagined that Latin America had solved all its problems. Even more, this era can be told as a romance, a time when Latin Americans embraced a series of innovative phenomena—new ideas, commodities, and practices—because of what they promised for themselves personally and for their societies in general. The appeal of the telephone, the horseless carriage, the streetlight, and the modern sewer is difficult to explain to those for whom these are now century-old relics. And even if these things transformed people's lives in uneven ways, they were nonetheless among the most significant measures of Latin America's first modern age.

Order, Then Progress

Order and Progress. The phrase is so critical to the story of the late nineteenth century in Latin America that it is emblazoned on the Brazilian flag. Unlike the liberal democracies of that era, most Latin American elites believed that their societies would never prosper, would never become modern, if order was not first established. They believed that democracy, a messy process everywhere, brought only chaos to regions like Latin America, because the people there were not civilized enough to exercise their democratic rights responsibly. Indeed, neither conservatives nor liberals had much faith in the capacity of their societies to be orderly absent the threat of punitive violence. Rosas' *Mazorca*, like Juárez' *Rurales* (Mexico's rural police, founded 1861) of a later generation were charged with preserving the order by force of arms. Both forces were informed by the assumption that Latin America had to be made safe by an iron hand before it could enter the modern world.

Latin America urgently needed to become more modern, at least this is what the region's elites believed by the middle of the nineteenth century. They sensed that this region, once home of the richest colonies on the planet, was falling behind, and increasingly backwards not just in the eyes of Europeans, but of their North American cousins. Elites in the region did not just want an order that would save them from chaos (like that theorized by Thomas Hobbes in *Leviathan*), they wanted an order that produced modernization, progress. Order however, is not as straightforward a concept as it might seem. While its advocates generally imagine order and stability as an intrinsic good, political stability is almost always stability in someone's interest. Instability at the national level during the nineteenth century was accompanied by a great deal of stability at the local level in some regions, because small communities had the power to live as they saw fit, controlling their lands, water, timber, and setting their own political agendas. Stability at the national level gave the state the power to reach into local affairs, especially when the resources to build railroads, telegraphs, roads, and national armies accompanied political stability. The central government could change the rules of land-ownership, it could influence local political arrangements, and force their citizens to sell their goods and perhaps their labor in an expanding national and international economy. Stability, in this sense, meant stability in the interest of those who would direct the project of modernization. Water once reserved for local use would become a commodity, valuable to the export economy and diverted to those with the means to build irrigation systems. Lands once used for subsistence farming would become potential sources of cash crops for export. Marginalized peoples who had often lived far from the purview of the state would either become compliant workers or potential threats to the rule of law. Thus were the implications of order and progress, the mantra of the export boom.

This is a complex story, told time and again as Latin Americans wondered why certain forms of state sanctioned violence persisted in their societies. When modern states were created in Latin America, those states lacked the democratic processes or civil rights regimes that characterized the states that were then emerging, if haltingly, in western Europe and North America. Over the decades, historians have offered many explanations for this divergence. Some attribute it to the authoritarianism of the colonial past, or blame outsiders, who favored repressive regimes that privileged their interests over unpredictable democratic processes. Latin American countries desperately needed people willing to invest capital in their economies because of what had been lost in a half century of conflict, and capital would not come without stability. Goods would not get to market without safe effective means of transport. Nothing would be built if the builders could not expect their factories, railroads, and port facilities to stand.

Others blame the cultures of the region for how order and progress played out, suggesting that there was something intrinsic to the ways people in the region saw the world that favored dictatorships. Authoritarian states were paired with authoritarian educational systems, an authoritarian Catholic Church, and even highly authoritarian family structures during the nineteenth century (it was a time when the male father figure was widely believed to be the natural and absolute ruler of his family). Beyond this, the anti-democratic practices of these states had a racial cast. People of African and indigenous origins were most often the victims of Latin American modernization.

Where these cultural explanations break down is when we examine other regions in the Americas that did not share common cultural values with Latin America and yet produced similarly authoritarian practices. Leaving aside the fact that Latin Americans themselves did not share a common culture, when we look at the U.S. South during this era we see a region that was hardly more democratic in its practices than Latin America. While it is true that property-holding white males enjoyed rights, women, indigenous peoples, and people of African ancestry were vigorously and often violently denied rights. We are thus left with the possibility that it was the post-colonial condition, especially in societies that, under colonial rule, had been characterized by systems of caste-based forced labor, which impeded the creation of democratic polities. Canadians did not admit Asians or indigenous peoples to their democracy (Indians did not become Canadian citizens until 1969). The United States actively excluded slaves and the descendants of slaves through systems of discrimination that were codified in law until the 1960s. Latin Americans similarly struggled where humans, who had been the objects of colonial control (i.e., Indians and slaves), became potential citizens.

Latin American elites turned to the antidemocratic Enlightenment tradition of positivism to rationalize their exclusionary proclivities. Drawing from the writings of Herbert Spencer and Auguste Comte, positivists rejected liberal democratic values (the idea that the best society maximizes individual freedom) in favor of a political and social philosophy that called for society to be organized along scientific lines, an order that would allow them to find rational/scientific solutions to their problems. Government should be managed according to scientific principles, economies made to run as efficiently as possible, and the fuzzy-headed, mystical, and backwards practices of the national folk should be eradicated. The people should be taught to be patriotic, dress in modern (read European) style clothes, embrace modern medicine (which at that point was about as likely to kill its patients as cure them), and eat more meat.[2] Globally these were the early days of sciences like anthropology, criminology, phrenology, and any number of organizing practices designed to make modern nations out of the detritus of independence. It would be an order imposed from above, as the masses could not expect to understand their own interests. Where it succeeded, the new order promised a better life for all.

And so, with the help of modern technology and the incentives provided by a booming global economy, Latin American nations gradually became more orderly after the 1850s. In part that order was illusory, the result of careful public relations, but the region as a whole did exhibit enough signs of stability that foreign investors began to return. Investments became railroads, barbed wire, telegraphs, and modern weaponry for Latin American armies, which in turn wrought more order, and then progress. We see a powerful example of how this process took place in the ranching sector, which flourished across Latin America after 1850. Lands where thousands of cattle once roamed, the common property of herdsmen, became ranches. The cattle became the property of the landowner, and the herdsmen became employees. Old cattle breeds were then eliminated (a process made possible by enclosure) and new scientific breeds were introduced, generating more wealth for ranchers, their employees, and the national treasury. Order had made progress, easily measured in exports, employment, income, and customs revenues.

Measuring a Golden Age

Statistics can be deceiving, especially when we choose a few select measures to represent the experience of dozens of countries over several decades. The export boom did not begin in all of Latin America at once. In some parts it dated to the 1830s (mining in Chile, and a decade later guano in Peru), and was not beginning elsewhere until the 1890s. That said, between 1870 and 1930 (when the Great Depression began) most countries in the region enjoyed a sustained period of economic growth by following economic strategies that privileged the export sector and encouraged foreign investment (Table 4.1). These observations, however, leave critical questions unanswered. For example, did this growth benefit Latin America as a whole, or did it re-inscribe a relationship between Latin America and the outside world that enriched the North at the South's expense?

Looking at lists not unlike Table 4.1, the Argentine economist Raúl Prebisch once lamented that Latin America was on the wrong side of the international division of labor. Prebisch influenced generations of dependency theorists, who argued that Latin America simply replaced one colonial master with others (principally England and the United States) at independence. This resulted in economies characterized by perpetually worsening terms of trade,[3] export enclaves that did not benefit larger national economies, monocrop dependence (in almost all countries one or two commodities made up more than 50 percent

Table 4.1 Principal exports in Latin America, 1870–1930

Argentina	Corn, wheat, livestock
Bolivia	Tin, silver
Brazil	Coffee, rubber
Chile	Nitrates, copper
Colombia	Coffee, gold
Costa Rica	Coffee, bananas
Cuba	Sugar, tobacco
Dominican Republic	Cacao, sugar
Ecuador	Cacao, coffee
El Salvador	Coffee, precious metals
Guatemala	Coffee, bananas
Haiti	Coffee, cacao
Honduras	Bananas, precious metals
Mexico	Silver, copper, zinc, lead, oil, henequen, sugar
Nicaragua	Coffee, precious metals
Puerto Rico	Sugar, coffee
Paraguay	Yerba mate, tobacco
Peru	Copper, sugar, nitrates, cotton
Venezuela	Coffee, cacao
Uruguay	Beef, wool

Source: Courtesy of Victor Bulmer Thomas, *The Economic History of Latin America since Independence*, Cambridge: Cambridge University Press, 1994, p. 59.

of exports, which meant that falling prices for a single commodity could have devastating repercussions throughout the economy), and extreme vulnerability to international economic cycles, especially given the fact that in some countries as much as 50 percent of capital was in foreign hands. Particularly popular on the political left during the 1960s and 1970s, this school of thought sometimes came to explain the tragedies that characterized Latin American society almost exclusively through reference to the global economic system.

Today, economic historians are not so sure about these explanations. They point out that some export-based economies have managed over the generations to be quite prosperous, and that these countries succeed because they used revenues from the export sector to promote economic diversification (Asia's newly industrialized countries, or NICs, are the most prominent example). Contemporary economic historians also point out that many of the specific claims dependency theorists make about terms of trade, enclaves, and monocrops do not withstand the close scrutiny of actual case studies. What contemporary economists offer instead is a complex rendering of a region that, lacking capital and domestic markets, relied on the export sector during the latter half of the nineteenth century to generate wealth that could not be created through any other means. Foreign capital paid for railroads, dock facilities, and communications infrastructures. Revenues collected at customs houses provided income for states in need of revenue to govern, police, and invest in their countries. In Chile, for example, the export tax on nitrates provided 50 percent of government revenue during the years 1890 to 1914. Across the region finance ministries used these monies to pay off foreign debts, balance their budgets, and build a great deal of infrastructure; remarkable feats given the decades of chaos that followed independence.

Recent studies of the nineteenth century suggest that while the impacts of foreign investments were uneven, the ancillary benefits and linkages created by foreign investment in countries like Mexico, Argentina, Venezuela, Brazil, and elsewhere, were considerable. After having had almost no railroads fifty years earlier (Cubans built the first railway in Latin America in 1838), by the eve of the First World War Argentina had 31,859 km of railroads, Mexico 25,600 km, Brazil 24,737 km, Chile 8,069 km, and Colombia 1,061 km. Even if the results were ambiguous, without these railroads economic growth would have been impossible. Furthermore, along with these railroads these countries saw a considerable expansion of the middle class, along with the emergence of a waged working class, which worked in industries processing goods for export. In several countries local governments used revenues from export and import duties, along with the manipulation of tariff rates, to promote local industrial development.

Medellín, Buenos Aires, São Paulo, Mexico City, Monterrey, Santiago, and other cities across the region industrialized during this era by relying on profits from the export sector. Industrial workers often found themselves able to take advantage of their new settings (concentrated in cities) to successfully agitate for better wages and living conditions, and they clearly had a higher standard of living than their rural counterparts. Members of the urban working and middle classes became part of a small but growing community of consumers, purchasing goods made locally and imported from abroad, and contributing in dynamic ways to the growth of industries devoted to food processing, beverages, cigarettes, clothing and textiles, construction materials, and other goods. Though small relative to Europe and North America, in at least five countries (Mexico, Argentina, Peru, Brazil, and Chile) domestic manufacturing provided most of the local market's needs for manufactured consumer goods by the eve of the First World War.

The new industrial economies had significant impacts on the rhythms of everyday life in Latin America. The export and industrial economy produced new classes of middle level managers, lawyers, government bureaucrats, and small businessmen. Though more dependent on a small number of business enterprises and activities for its prosperity than middle sectors in the northern countries, and perhaps somewhat more conservative than their northern counterparts, these emerging sectors often stood at the forefront of significant social change. Their prosperity put them into a position to remake Latin American landscapes, as they increasingly favored single-family houses and the privatization of family life, the sequestration of gardens behind high walls in increasingly suburbanized cities characterized by the growing importance of private transport. They insisted that children remain longer in school, that good housewives carefully manage the family unit, and that the material arrangements of middle-class life—a lawn, a car, modern conveniences, and later, golf club memberships—be acquired. These accouterments were essential to affirming the class status of the holders.

For middle-class women, the onset of export-based prosperity also created new constraints. Many small-scale family enterprises gave way to large firms that employed their male partners, leaving women who had once had a hand in managing family businesses relegated to the domestic sphere, with little option to escape. Increasingly literate, some would begin agitating for women's rights and suffrage even in the 1870s (see Documents 3.4 and 3.5 in Chapter 3). Latin American feminism emerged from this milieu, along with a steady stream of demands by women for greater personal, professional, and sexual freedom. These demands were, of course, matched by an equally fervent insistence that women's liberation would destroy families, the social order, and society more generally.

Working-class women saw their lives similarly transformed by the advent of the industrial age. As factories opened in cities like Medellín, São Paulo, Buenos Aires, Santiago, and Lima, new mining camps sprang up and port cities grew to accommodate the growth in exports, migrants flocked to these boomtowns. Just as male workers found opportunities, so too did migrant women, in some cases as entrepreneurs, laundresses, seamstresses, cooks, and maids for the rising middle class. In other cases, women worked as prostitutes near the mines, plantations, ports, and anywhere large groups of single male migrants congregated. These women lived vulnerable lives, often harassed by police and considered undesirable by local elites. Excluded from proper society, they responded by making their own support networks, which in turn served as autonomous spaces for working-class female sociability.

Women were also an essential component of the industrial workforce in Latin America. Later social reformers and efficiency experts from the United States would decry the presence of women in factories, and endeavor to enforce the normative idea of an all-male factory work force, but in the fluid social settings of the late nineteenth and early twentieth century, women worked in large numbers at factories in many parts of the region. Young women had a complex relationship to this type of work, moving in and out of the factory as their and their families needs' dictated, and almost invariably expressing a preference for married family life over work in the factory, yet many had long careers in the industrial workforce, employment that provided a limited degree of financial and personal independence.

Conservative Catholics feared that these vulnerable young women might have their virtue compromised in these settings. Factory owners often imagined themselves as benevolent father figures to their employees, sometimes acting as if their own honor was tied up in the honor of their employees. In part this was an inheritance from a past in which the rich and powerful imagined themselves as benevolent dictators to a dependent workforce, and in part it was a strategy to fend off unions. This explains their efforts to protect the virtue of their female employees. Factory owners were reluctant to employ married women, or women with children, and at times used virginity tests to ensure the virtue of their workers. They also tried to segregate workforces as much as possible so as to reduce the women's exposure to men, and provided cultural activities and "education" that emphasized the importance of chastity. In some contexts these programs also offered loans that helped female (and male) workers purchase their own homes in model communities, carefully engineered spaces in which male workers could produce households modeled on the bourgeois ideal, and women workers (when they were tolerated) could protect their virtuousness. In return, women workers were expected to reject labor unions, behave at work, maintain their virtue in public, and most of all, constitute a passive and compliant workforce (a workforce incidentally paid less than their male counterparts, who were assumed to be breadwinners).

Some complied, and some did not. Just as male workers in the mining, agricultural, and industrial sectors agitated for better pay, shorter hours, and better working conditions, so too did women workers. As Ann Farnsworth-Alvear notes, talking, flirting, and fighting on the factory floor were common practices that women workers used to remake spaces otherwise characterized by male control, and those same workers were adverse neither to manipulating the system to maximize their benefits (hiding pregnancies, collecting extra benefits, and the like) nor going on strike when it seemed like a viable means to improve their conditions.[4]

The frequency of strikes in cities like Buenos Aires, Medellín, and mining camps like Cananea, Mexico, remind us that the benefits of the boom were distributed unevenly. At the same time, workers flocked to factories because of the opportunities they afforded. Workers did in fact see significant increases in their standards of living during the export boom, and created dynamic working-class cultures in cities across the Americas. These developments remind us that the benefits of the boom were not entirely monopolized by the owners of capital. Indeed, in some instances the strikes that took place during these years actually reflected an empowered working class that was well positioned to make demands on their employers, and which won repeated concessions, not just on the wage front, but in terms of workplace conditions and safety. Female workers in Medellín, for instance, were able to reduce the amount of sexual harassment they faced in the factories both through regular complaints and through strikes.

These improvements were made possible by a fifty-year period during which exports and industrial production steadily grew. Workers, managers, and owners with connections to these dynamic sectors gained a great deal from that growth. However, given the levels of poverty in Latin America, the region as a whole needed exceptionally high rates of growth in gross domestic product (GDP)[5] if the benefits of the export boom were to be widely shared. By most measures manufacturing was a poor option for generating that growth. In most countries the manufacturing sector had no hope of producing goods that could compete on the global market. Industrialists lacked the capital, the expertize, and the technologies they needed to produce goods suitable for export, so they instead produced for a fairly small domestic market, limiting their overall contribution to GDP. Because of this, manufacturing was highly dependent on the state for support and unable to lift wages in other sectors. Factories in Latin America were unlikely to demand so much labor that employers in other sectors would need to increase the wages they paid in order to keep their workers.

Given these weaknesses in the industrial economy, export growth was the only viable strategy for generating substantial economic growth. In order to produce per capita GDP growth that was comparable to that in the United States and Europe, Latin American economies needed annual per capita GDP growth of 1.5 percent (this would double per capita GDP in fifty years). Region-wide, export growth needed to average 4.5 percent in order to produce that level of per capita growth in the GDP, yet this level of growth was extremely difficult to achieve (see Table 4.2). Only two countries (Chile and Argentina) saw this rate of growth during this period.[6]

Some scholars dispute these figures, arguing that changing local conditions in several countries did produce significant growth.[7] However, even if we agree that this is too conservative an approach, what does it mean to say that per capita income doubled in extremely unequal societies? In every country in the region except Argentina and Uruguay agricultural wages fell even as per capita GDP rose during these years, increasing inequality. The privatization of landholdings in Mexico may have increased exports and GDP, but by 1910 more than half the land in the country was in the hands of one percent of the population, and 97 percent of Mexicans were landless. Small-scale peasants could rarely produce documents that proved they owned the land they worked, and even if they did, they confronted recalcitrant government officials and corrupt powerbrokers who preferred to place land in

Table 4.2 Annual percentage rates of export growth, 1850–1912

Bolivia	2.5
Brazil	3.7
Chile	4.3
Colombia	3.5
Costa Rica	3.5
Cuba	2.9
Ecuador	3.5
El Salvador	3.5
Guatemala	3.6
Mexico	3.0
Nicaragua	2.9
Paraguay	3.9
Peru	2.9
Uruguay	3.4
Venezuela	2.7

Source: Courtesy of Victor Bulmer Thomas, *The Economic History of Latin America since Independence*, Cambridge: Cambridge University Press, 1994, p. 63.

the hands of investors who promised to grow cash crops. And since land ownership was so critical to prosperity, the concentration of landholdings was closely linked to increasing inequality. Workers on large estates producing commodity crops (sugar, cacao, tobacco, coffee, henequen, etc.) sometimes toiled in conditions that approximated slavery.

Signs of Civilization

In the early twentieth century, Argentines could proudly claim that theirs was one of the ten richest countries in the world. Buenos Aires, like a number of Latin American cities, was a modern showpiece with a population of 1.5 million people, complete with new mansions, electric lights, department stores, and trolleys. Porteños could also point to the immense population growth of their nation since the 1880s, fueled by almost five million European immigrants. These new Argentines were not just engines of economic progress, they had also helped to erase the country's muddy racial origins, making Argentina a white nation. Brazilians likewise successfully turned to European migration (attracting 1.6 million) to whiten their country, though the regional impacts of migration were quite distinct as Europeans tended to settle in the southwest. Successive waves of Asian migration were viewed less favorably, though Asians were still preferable to the degraded racial stock of Africans and indigenous peoples.

Latin Americans recorded their progress in a number of ways. Statistics were critical, telling the story of railroads, canals, and roads constructed, public works completed, economies that were growing, budgets that were balanced. Populations were increasingly measured, though many of the measures that would characterize the twentieth century (literacy and education, crime statistics, health, wages, working conditions, voter turnouts, and hygiene) would not appear until some time later. Beyond statistical representations, modernity was also a visceral experience, felt in particular ways. As latecomers to modernity, Latin Americans modeled their idea of progress on trends and technologies acquired from abroad, on their capacity to both emulate and equal the societies everyone knew were the most modern of places. *Tropicalista* doctors in Salvador dedicated themselves to operating at the cutting edge of tropical medicine, and Brazilians claimed that one of their own, Alberto Santos-Dumont, was the first to fly an airplane unassisted in 1906. Many Mexicans marveled when their president installed an elevator in Chapultepec Castle.

There may have been no more powerful symbol of this transformation than the photograph. Photography and modernity are powerfully linked. The photographic medium was invented in the nineteenth century, one of the first representational practices that was itself produced through technological innovation. Photographs offered a powerful means with which to capture reality, distinct from other forms that seemed more deeply mediated by the hand of the artist. They could document Latin America for outsiders, render Indians, slaves, and the geographies of the region as curiosities, phenomena in some cases on the verge of disappearing. The subjects of the photos often had little choice, as their photographers used them to show racial types, criminal types, and a variety of forms of rural and urban poverty.

One of the popular early forms of photography in Latin America was the type photograph, which became common in the 1860s. These photographs introduced viewers to the Indian, the peasant, the agricultural laborer, the *cargador*, and others (see Figure 4.1).

Figure 4.1 Photograph of two young indigenous men

Source: Library of Congress, Prints and Photographs Division (LC-USZ62-78963)

Collected and used by the state to document its population, they were also turned into postcards, mementos of sojourns that circulated among wealthy *aficionados* in the urban centers of Latin America and elsewhere. As Deborah Poole argues, these photos could fix the racial identity of their subject in ways that were often more powerful than any other means. The types that emerged from them were defined not just by phenotype and shape, but through dress, background, and accessories, all of which gave the subject in the photo a racial identity.

Over time, many of the photographers who initially made their living with these photos established portrait studios and took on clients who wanted to have their pictures taken. These portraits revealed a great deal about the complex ways in which modernity was experienced during this period, the ways in which individuals of both European and non-European ancestry aspired to define themselves as both modern and traditional through dress, grooming, and the poses they assumed in these photographs. In sitting for a family portrait, the subjects could choose Western attire (i.e., suits) or traditional dress, could look squarely into the camera or avert its gaze, each gesture indicating something about the subject's engagement with modernity. These portraits also spoke to gender norms, as one could regularly find the males and females wearing different kinds of dress—typically, the males a more modern style and the females a more traditional—indicating who in the photo was focused on the future and who was focused on the past.[8] Upwardly mobile individuals with indigenous and African ancestries regularly used these portraits to situate themselves as different from the racial types who populated photographs of peasants and slaves. Consider the following image of Benito Juárez, the Mexican President, in 1861. Though of Zapotec origin, Juárez erased his indigenous past through dress, manner, and profession, all aptly summed up in Figure 4.2.

Figure 4.2 Benito Juárez
Source: Time & Life Pictures/Getty Images

Figure 4.3
Peruvian soldier and
his wife

Source: Library of Congress,
Prints and Photographs
Division (LC-USZ62-53038)

More complicated still are those photographs where the meanings are oblique. In Figure 4.3 (which dates to 1868) it is not clear that the subjects, a Peruvian soldier and his wife, asked to be photographed or simply consented. A complex mix of the modern and traditional can be seen in this photo, as the wife retains Andean dress, a long braid, and a somewhat frayed version of European bowler that marked Andean female identity in this era (the hat was worn by female Andean merchants). It is unclear whether the husband chose a military uniform to signal his participation in the modern project of Peruvian nationhood, or was marked as disciplined into the modern nation by the photographer's choice to place him in uniform. During this and later eras, white elites across the Americas sought to impose order on unruly indigenous masses through military discipline, and some Andean peoples sought upward mobility through service in the armed forces. We can see a story of modernity told through this photograph, we just cannot know which story it is.

Figure 4.4 Image of an early tram system, Belem, early twentieth century
Source: Courtesy of tram website photo: http://www.tramz.com/br/be/be.html

Photographs were also critical to documenting the material signs of progress. Construction projects, new buildings, national festivals, electrical lights, paved roads—all were frequently photographed during the export boom. Some of these photos simply documented new things (Figure 4.4), a trolley, a train, a tram, a road excavated in order to build a modern sewage system. Others mixed new aesthetic sensibilities with a desire to represent modernity as more than just something that derived from Europe. Latin Americans wanted to prove that their countries were as capable as any other of participating in the endless cycles of innovation—artistic and scientific—that characterized modernity. Images like the one in Figure 4.5, of the Retiro train station in Buenos Aires in 1915, remind us of this desire. Modernity, represented in this building and the photo that captures it, is a deeply aesthetic experience. Modern nations were prosperous, they were rational, they were scientific, and they were sites of innovation and creativity.

Figure 4.5 Estación Retiro del Ferrocarril, Central Argentino

Source: Margarita Gutman (editora) *Buenos Aires 1910: Memoria del Porvenir*, Buenos Aires: Gobierno de la Ciudad de Buenos Aires, Facultad de Arquitectura Diseño y Ubranismo de la Universidad de Buenos Aires, Instituto Internacional de Medio Ambiente y Desarrollo IIED-America Latina, 1999

One final photograph completes this section. Figure 4.6 embodies all the qualities of the previous four. It is a photo of indigenous subjects in modern dress. It is not clear that the students were coerced into being subjects in this photo. On the other hand, it would be silly to conclude that their presence here was entirely voluntary (such a conclusion is not warranted given what we know about the coercive nature of education, especially indigenous education, in this era). They are students in Mexico City's *Casa del Estudiante Indígena* (House of the Indian Student) and part of a group of indigenous students who were often forcibly recruited to this school. Once in the school however, most remained there voluntarily and refused to leave Mexico City once their studies were complete.[9] This photo then, reveals a very interesting play on the type photograph, which was still common in Mexico in the 1920s. These were Indians, who just two years earlier might have been photographed to establish their racial alterity, now participating in a photograph that showed their capacity to be modern subjects. Modernity here is a series of qualities—the substitution of modern dress for peasant clothes, the presence of the automobile workshop and the auto in the photo, and the fact that these students were being trained as mechanics. That this photo was in fact taken after Mexico underwent a massive social revolution reminds us that the logics that underpinned the export boom would remain powerful even after its end.

Figure 4.6   La Casa del Estudiante Indigena: male students working in the auto shop
Source: Courtesy of SEP, La Casa del Estudiante Indigena

The Document: On the Eve of Revolution

During the first decade of the twentieth century, Mexico was awash with writings about its past, present, and future. Many described conditions in the country in optimistic terms, while some described social conditions in Mexico largely negatively. Given that we know what happened next, it is tempting to pit the two trends against one another in what could be an elaborate game of historical gotcha. Critics like the Flores Magón brothers and Andrés Molina Enríquez become prescient observers of their country's problems, while those who marveled at the achievements of the Díaz regime are revealed to be naïve at best, and capitalist lackeys at worst.

This practice is both unsatisfying and misleading. Yes, some Mexicans suggested that their country had serious problems in the years before the collapse of Porfirio Díaz' dictatorship, but their descriptions of the nation's ills were not always particularly accurate or influential. The Flores Magón brothers' newspaper *Regeneración* (see the book's website at www.routledge.com/cw/dawson), while now an important historical artifact, was not widely read in Mexico. Their anarchism never found much purchase among Mexican workers, and, for the most part, appealed to a small group of dissident intellectuals. Andrés Molina Enríquez' 1909 indictment of the regime, *los grandes problemas nacionales* (the great national problems—sections of this too can be found on the book's website) offered its own particular view of the national problems. As a prescription for what ailed Mexico in 1910 however, it is highly problematic. Molina Enríquez found fault not in the process of development per se, but in the ways that development had undermined the Indian pueblo as a social and juridical institution, thus undermining the natural evolution of Indian communities (in this, he was deeply positivist). While sympathetic to Indians, he saw them as fundamentally backwards. Even the manifesto published by Francisco Madero, Díaz' opponent in the 1910 elections (*la succession presidencial en 1910*), offered little that would help explain much of what would follow.

This then, is one of the challenges we face when reading documents that precede momentous events. We have the benefit of hindsight, and tend to impose *ex post facto* meanings and importance on these texts, looking for a writer's capacity to predict the future rather than situating the text carefully in its present. Inasmuch as any document captures a moment in time, the effort of its creator (or creators) to make sense of a complex world, to put together a series of "facts" into a meaningful narrative, we get the most out of these texts by reading them closely, unpacking the arguments, looking for assumptions and silences, and by carefully interrogating the logics that inform the text. Only then might we use this fragment from the past to gain some insight into the text and the context in which it was produced.

The document provided below (Document 4.1), an interview between the American journalist James Creelman and Porfirio Díaz from 1908, offers readers an opportunity to do just this. Díaz, the seventy-eight-year-old dictator, uses the interview to reflect on what he has made of his country after thirty-two years in power, and what it might become. Creelman, the forty-nine-year-old yellow journalist, famous for taking up arms against the Spanish even as he reported on the Spanish–American War for the *New York World*, reveals his own sensibilities when he describes what is modern in Mexico. In part it is from his distinctly North American view of the world that Díaz emerges as the "Hero of the Americas." That said, Creelman's view of Díaz was not so alien to Mexicans that it went un-noticed south of the border. It was reproduced in several Mexican newspapers, including *El Imparcial* and *El Tiempo*.

Document 4.1 James Creelman, "Porfirio Díaz, Hero of the Americas" (Excerpts)

Source: *Pearson's Magazine*, March, 1908.

From the heights of Chapultepec Castle President Díaz looked down upon the venerable capital of his country, spread out on a vast plain, with a ring of mountains flung up grandly about it, and I, who had come nearly four thousand miles from New York to see the master and hero of modern Mexico—the inscrutable leader in whose veins is blended the blood of the primitive Mixtecs with that of the invading Spaniards— watched the slender, erect form, the strong, soldierly head and commanding, but sensitive, countenance with an interest beyond words to express.

A high, wide forehead that slopes up to crisp white hair and over hangs deep-set, dark brown eyes that search your soul, soften into inexpressible kindliness and then dart quick side looks—terrible eyes, threatening eyes, loving, confiding, humorous eyes—a straight, powerful, broad and somewhat fleshy nose, whose curved nostrils lift and dilate with every emotion; huge, virile jaws that sweep from large, flat, fine ears, set close to the head, to the tremendous, square, fighting chin; a wide, firm mouth shaded by a white mustache; a full, short, muscular neck; wide shoulders, deep chest; a curiously tense and rigid carriage that gives great distinction to a personality suggestive of singular power and dignity—that is Porfirio Díaz in his seventy-eighth year, as I saw him a few weeks ago on the spot where, forty years before, he stood—with his besieging army surrounding the City of Mexico, and the young Emperor Maximilian being shot to death in Queretaro, beyond those blue mountains to the north—waiting grimly for the thrilling end of the last interference of European monarchy with the republics of America.

It is the intense, magnetic something in the wide-open, fearless, dark eyes and the sense of nervous challenge in the sensitive, spread nostrils, that seem to connect the man with the immensity of the landscape, as some elemental force.

There is not a more romantic or heroic figure in all the world, nor one more intensely watched by both the friends and foes of democracy, than the soldier-statesman, whose adventurous youth pales the pages of Dumas, and whose iron rule has converted the warring, ignorant, superstitious and impoverished masses of Mexico, oppressed by centuries of Spanish cruelty and greed, into a strong, steady, peaceful, debt-paying and progressive nation.

For twenty-seven years he has governed the Mexican Republic with such power that national elections have become mere formalities. He might easily have set a crown upon his head.

Yet to-day, in the supremacy of his career, this astonishing man—foremost figure of the American hemisphere and unreadable mystery to students of human government— announces that he will insist on retiring from the Presidency at the end of his present term, so that he may see his successor peacefully established and that, with his assistance, the people of the Mexican Republic may show the world that they have entered serenely and preparedly upon the last complete phase of their liberties, that the nation is emerging from ignorance and revolutionary passion, and that it can choose and change presidents without weakness or war.

It is something to come from the money-mad gambling congeries of Wall Street and in the same week to stand on the rock of Chapultepec, in surroundings of almost unreal grandeur and loveliness, beside one who is said to have transformed a republic into an autocracy by the absolute compulsion of courage and character, and to hear him speak of democracy as the hope of mankind.

This, too, at a time when the American soul shudders at the mere thought of a third term for any President.

The President surveyed the majestic, sunlit scene below the ancient castle and turned away with a smile, brushing a curtain of scarlet trumpet-flowers and vine-like pink geraniums as he moved along the terrace toward the inner garden, where a fountain set among palms and flowers sparkled with water from the spring at which Montezuma used to drink, under the mighty cypresses that still rear their branches about the rock on which we stood.

"It is a mistake to suppose that the future of democracy in Mexico has been endangered by the long continuance in office of one President," he said quietly. "I can say sincerely that office has not corrupted my political ideals and that I believe democracy to be the one true, just principle of government, although in practice it is possible only to highly developed peoples."

For a moment the straight figure paused and the brown eyes looked over the great valley to where snow-covered Popocatapetl lifted its volcanic peak nearly eighteen thousand feet among the clouds beside the snowy craters of Ixtaccihuatl—a land of dead volcanoes, human and otherwise.

"I can lay down the Presidency of Mexico without a pang of regret, but I cannot cease to serve this country while I live," he added.

The sun shone full in the President's face but his eyes did not shrink from the ordeal. The green landscape, the smoking city, the blue tumult of mountains, the thin, exhilarating, scented air, seemed to stir him, and the color came to his cheeks as he clasped his hands behind him and threw his head backward. His nostrils opened wide.

"You know that in the United States we are troubled about the question of electing a President for three terms?"

He smiled and then looked grave, nodding his head gently and pursing his lips. It is hard to describe the look of concentrated interest that suddenly came into his strong, intelligent countenance.

"Yes, yes, I know," he replied. "It is a natural sentiment of democratic peoples that their officials should be often changed. I agree with that sentiment."

It seemed hard to realize that I was listening to a soldier who had ruled a republic continuously for more than a quarter of a century with a personal authority unknown to most kings. Yet he spoke with a simple and convincing manner, as one whose place was great and secure beyond the need of hypocrisy.

"It is quite true that when a man has occupied a powerful office for a very long time he is likely to begin to look upon it as his personal property, and it is well that a free people should guard themselves against the tendencies of individual ambition.

"Yet the abstract theories of democracy and the practical, effective application of them are often necessarily different—that is when you are seeking for the substance rather than the mere form.

"I can see no good reason why President Roosevelt should not be elected again if a majority of the American people desire to have him continue in office. I believe that he has thought more of his country than of himself. He has done and is doing a great work for the United States, a work that will cause him, whether he serves again or not, to be remembered in history as one of the great Presidents. I look upon the trusts as a great and real power in the United States, and President Roosevelt has had the patriotism and courage to defy them. Mankind understands the meaning of his attitude and its bearing upon the future. He stands before the world as a states-man whose victories have been moral victories.

"In my judgment the fight to restrain the power of the trusts and keep them from oppressing the people of the United States marks one of the most important and significant periods in your history. Mr. Roosevelt has faced the crisis like a great man.

"There can be no doubt that Mr. Roosevelt is a strong, pure man, a patriot who understands his country and loves it well. The American fear of a third term seems to me to be without any just reason. There can be no question of principle in the matter if a majority of people in the United States approve his policies and want him to continue his work. That is the real, the vital thing—whether a majority of people need him and desire him to go on.

"Here in Mexico we have had different conditions. I received this Government from the hands of a victorious army at a time when the people were divided and unprepared for the exercise of the extreme principles of democratic government. To have thrown upon the masses the whole responsibility of government at once would have produced conditions that might have discredited the cause of free government.

"Yet, although I got power at first from the army, an election was held as soon as possible and then my authority came from the people. I have tried to leave the Presidency several times, but it has been pressed upon me and I remained in office for the sake of the nation which trusted me. The fact that the price of Mexican securities dropped eleven points when I was ill at Cuernavaca indicates the kind of evidence that persuaded me to overcome my personal inclination to retire to private life.

"We preserved the republican and democratic form of government. We defended the theory and kept it intact. Yet we adopted a patriarchal policy in the actual administration of the nation's affairs, guiding and restraining popular tendencies, with full faith that an enforced peace would allow education, industry and commerce to develop elements of stability and unity in a naturally intelligent, gentle and affectionate people.

"I have waited patiently for the day when the people of the Mexican Republic would be prepared to choose and change their government at every election without danger of armed revolutions and without injury to the national credit or interference with national progress. I believe that day has come."

Again, the soldierly figure turned toward the glorious scene lying between the mountains. It was plain to see that the President was deeply moved. The strong face was as sensitive as a child's. The dark eyes were moist.

And what an unforgettable vision of color, movement and romance it was!

Beneath the giant trees still surrounding the rock of Chapultepec—the only rise in the flat valley—Montezuma, the Aztec monarch, used to walk in his hours of ease before Cortés and Alvarado came with the cross of Christ and the pitiless sword of Spain, to be followed by three hundred terrible years in which the country writhed and wept under sixty-two Spanish viceroys and five governors, to be succeeded by a ridiculous native emperor and a succession of dictators and presidents, with the Emperor Maximilian's invasion between, until Díaz, the hero of fifty battles, decided that Mexico should cease to fight, and learn to work and pay her debts . . .

As we paced the castle terrace we could see long processions of Mexican Indians, accompanied by their wives and children, with monstrous hats, bright colored blankets and bare or sandaled feet, moving continuously from all parts of the valley and from the mountain passes toward Guadalupe; and two days later I was to see a hundred thousand aboriginal Americans gather about that holiest of American shrines, where, under a crown of emeralds, rubies, diamonds, and sapphires that cost thirty thousand dollars merely to fashion, and before a multitude of blanketed Indians, kneeling with their wives and babies, holding lighted candles and flowers, and worshiping with a devotion that smote the most cynical spectator into reverence, the resplendent Archbishop of Mexico celebrated mass before the altar-enclosed blanket of the pious Indian, Juan Diego, upon whose woven surface the image of the Virgin Guadalupe appeared in 1531 . . .

"It is commonly held that true democratic institutions are impossible in a country which has no middle class," I suggested.

President Díaz turned, with a keen look, and nodded his head.

"It is true," he said. "Mexico has a middle class now; but she had none before. The middle class is the active element of society, here as elsewhere.

"The rich are too much preoccupied in their riches and in their dignities to be of much use in advancing the general welfare. Their children do not try very hard to improve their education and their character.

"On the other hand, the poor are usually too ignorant to have power.

"It is upon the middle class, drawn largely from the poor, but somewhat from the rich, the active, hard-working, self-improving middle class, that a democracy must depend for its development. It is the middle class that concerns itself with politics and the general progress.

"In the old days we had no middle class in Mexico because the minds of the people and their energies were wholly absorbed in politics and war. Spanish tyranny and misgovernment had disorganized society. The productive activities of the nation were abandoned in successive struggles. There was general confusion. Neither life nor property was safe. A middle class could not appear under such conditions."

"General Díaz," I interrupted, "you have had an unprecedented experience in the history of republics. For thirty years the destinies of this nation have been in your hands, to mold them as you will; but men die, while nations must continue to live. Do you believe that Mexico can continue to exist in peace as a republic? Are you satisfied that its future is assured under free institutions?"

It was worthwhile to have come from New York to Chapultepec Castle to see the hero's face at that moment. Strength, patriotism, warriorship, prophethood seemed suddenly to shine in his brown eyes.

"The future of Mexico is assured," he said in a clear voice. "The principles of democracy have not been planted very deep in our people, I fear. But the nation has grown and it loves liberty. Our difficulty has been that the people do not concern themselves enough about public matters for a democracy. The individual Mexican as a rule thinks much about his own rights and is always ready to assert them. But he does not think so much about the rights of others. He thinks of his privileges, but not of his duties. Capacity for self-restraint is the basis of democratic government, and self-restraint is possible only to those who recognize the rights of their neighbors.

"The Indians, who are more than half of our population, care little for politics. They are accustomed to look to those in authority for leadership instead of thinking for themselves. That is a tendency they inherited from the Spaniards, who taught them to refrain from meddling in public affairs and rely on the Government for guidance.

"Yet I firmly believe that the principles of democracy have grown and will grow in Mexico."

"But you have no opposition party in the Republic, Mr. President. How can free institutions flourish when there is no opposition to keep the majority, or governing party, in check?"

"It is true there is no opposition party. I have so many friends in the republic that my enemies seem unwilling to identify themselves with so small a minority. I appreciate the kindness of my friends and the confidence of my country; but such absolute confidence imposes responsibilities and duties that tire me more and more.

"No matter what my friends and supporters say, I retire when my present term of office ends, and I shall not serve again. I shall be eighty years old then.

"My country has relied on me and it has been kind to me. My friends have praised my merits and overlooked my faults. But they may not be willing to deal so generously with my successor and he may need my advice and support; therefore I desire to be alive when he assumes office so that I may help him."

He folded his arms over his deep chest and spoke with great emphasis.

"I welcome an opposition party in the Mexican Republic," he said. "If it appears, I will regard it as a blessing, not as an evil. And if it can develop power, not to exploit but to govern, I will stand by it, support it, advise it and forget myself in the successful inauguration of complete democratic government in the country.

"It is enough for me that I have seen Mexico rise among the peaceful and useful nations. I have no desire to continue in the Presidency. This nation is ready for her ultimate life of freedom. At the age of seventy-seven years I am satisfied with robust health. That is one thing which neither law nor force can create. I would not exchange it for all the millions of your American oil king."

His ruddy skin, sparkling eyes and light, elastic step went well with his words. For one who has endured the privations of war and imprisonment, and who to-day rises at six o'clock in the morning, working until late at night at the full of his powers, the physical condition of President Díaz, who is even now a notable hunter and who usually ascends the palace stairway two steps at a time is almost unbelievable.

"The railway has played a great part in the peace of Mexico," he continued. "When I became President at first there were only two small lines, one connecting the capital with Vera Cruz, the other connecting it with Queretaro. Now we have more than nineteen thousand miles of railways. Then we had a slow and costly mail service, carried on by stage coaches, and the mail coach between the capital and Puebla would be stopped by highwaymen two or three times in a trip, the last robbers to attack it generally finding nothing left to steal. Now we have a cheap, safe and fairly rapid mail service throughout the country with more than twenty-two hundred post-offices. Telegraphing was a difficult thing in those times. Today we have more than forty-five thousand miles of telegraph wires in operation.

"We began by making robbery punishable by death and compelling the execution of offenders within a few hours after they were caught and condemned. We ordered that wherever telegraph wires were cut and the chief officer of the district did not catch the criminal, he should himself suffer; and in case the cutting occurred on a plantation the proprietor who failed to prevent it should be hanged to the nearest telegraph pole. These were military orders, remember.

"We were harsh. Sometimes we were harsh to the point of cruelty. But it was all necessary then to the life and progress of the nation. If there was cruelty, results have justified it."

The nostrils dilated and quivered. The mouth was a straight line.

"It was better that a little blood should be shed that much blood should be saved. The blood that was shed was bad blood; the blood that was saved was good blood.

"Peace was necessary, even an enforced peace, that the nation might have time to think and work. Education and industry have carried on the task begun by the army."

. . .

"And which do you regard as the greatest force for peace, the army or the schoolhouse?" I asked.

The soldier's face flushed slightly and the splendid white head was held a little higher. "You speak of the present time?"

"Yes."

"The schoolhouse. There can be no doubt of that. I want to see education throughout the Republic carried on by the national Government. I hope to see it before I die. It is important that all citizens of a republic should receive the same training, so that their ideals and methods may be harmonized and the national unity intensified. When men read alike and think alike they are more likely to act alike."

"And you believe that the vast Indian population of Mexico is capable of high development?"

"I do. The Indians are gentle and they are grateful, all except the Yaquis and some of the Mayas. They have the traditions of an ancient civilization of their own. They are to be found among the lawyers, engineers, physicians, army officers and other professional men."

Over the city drifted the smoke of many factories. "It is better than cannon smoke," I said.

"Yes," he replied, "and yet there are times when cannon smoke is not such a bad thing. The toiling poor of my country have risen up to support me, but I cannot forget what my comrades in arms and their children have been to me in my severest ordeals."

There were actually tears in the veteran's eyes . . .

Throughout the valley moves a wondrous system of electric cars, for even the crumbling house of Cortés is lit by electricity, and an electric elevator runs through the shaft of Chapultepec hill by which the Montezumas used the escape from their enemies.

It is hard to remember that this wonderful plain was once a lake and that the Aztecs built their great city on piles, with causeways to the mainland. President Díaz bored a tunnel through the eastern mountains and the Valley of Mexico is now drained to the sea by a system of canals and sewers that cost more than twelve million dollars . . .

"In my youth I had a stern experience that taught me many things (said Díaz). When I commanded two companies of soldiers there was a time when for six months I had neither advice, instructions nor support from my government. I had to think for myself. I had to be the government myself. I found men to be the same then as I have found them since. I believed in democratic principles then and I believe in them yet, although conditions have compelled stern measures to secure peace and the development which must precede absolutely free government. Mere political theories will not create a free nation . . ."

(Díaz) was the son of an inn-keeper. An institution of learning now stands memorially on the site of his birth. Three years after he was born his father died of cholera and his Spanish–Mixtec mother was left alone to support her six children.

When the grown boy wanted shoes, he watched a shoemaker, borrowed tools, and made them himself. When he wanted a gun he took a rusty musket-barrel and the lock of a pistol, and constructed a reliable weapon with his own hands. So, too, he learned to make furniture for his mother's house.

He made things then, as he afterward made the Mexican nation, by the sheer force of moral initiative, self-reliance and practical industry. He asked no-one for anything that he could get for himself.

Go from one end to the other of Mexico's 767,005 square miles, on which no more than 15,000,000 persons live to-day, and you will see everywhere evidence of this masterful genius. You turn from battlefields to schools to railways, factories, mines and banks, and the wonder is that one man can mean so much to any nation, and that nation an American republic next in importance to the United States and its nearest neighbor.

He found Mexico bankrupt, divided, infested with bandits, a prey to a thousand forms of bribery. To-day life and property are safe from frontier to frontier of the republic.

After spending scores of millions of dollars on harbor improvements, drainage works and other vast engineering projects, and paying off portions of the public debt—to say nothing of putting the national finances on a gold basis—the nation has a surplus of $72,000,000 in its treasury—this, in spite of the immense government subsidies which have directly produced 19,000 miles of railways.

When he became President, Mexico's yearly foreign trade amounted to $36,111,600 in all. To-day her commerce with other nations reaches the enormous sum of $481,363,388, with a balance of trade in her favor of $14,636,612.

There were only three banks in the country when President Díaz first assumed power, and they had a small capital, loaning at enormous and constantly changing rates.

To-day, there are thirty-four chartered banks alone, whose total assets amount to nearly $700,000,000, with a combined capital stock of $158,100,000.

He has changed the irregular and ineffective pretense of public instruction, which had 4,850 schools and about 163,000 pupils, into a splendid system of compulsory education, which already has more than 12,000 schools, with an attendance of perhaps a million pupils; schools that not only train the children of the Republic, but reach into the prisons, military barracks and charitable institutions . . .

There are nineteen thousand miles of railways operated in Mexico, nearly all with American managers, engineers and conductors, and one has only to ride on the Mexican Central system or to enjoy the trains de luxe of the National Line to realize the high transportation standards of the country.

So determined is President Díaz to prevent his country from falling into the hands of the trusts that the Government is taking over and merging in one corporation, with the majority stock in the Nation's hands, the Mexican Central, National and Inter-oceanic lines so that, with this mighty trunk system of transportation beyond the reach of private control, industry, agriculture, commerce and passenger traffic will be safe from oppression.

This merger of ten thousand miles of railways into a single company, with $113,000,000 of the stock, a clear majority, in the Government's hands, is the answer of President Díaz and his brilliant Secretary of Finances to the prediction that Mexico may some day find herself helplessly in the grip of a railway trust.

Curiously enough, the leading American railway officials representing the lines which are to be merged and controlled by the Government spoke to me with great enthusiasm of the plan as a distinct forward step, desirable alike for shippers and passengers and for private investors in the roads.

Two-thirds of the railways of Mexico are owned by Americans, who have invested about $300,000,000 in them profitably.

As it is, freight and passenger rates are fixed by the Government, and not a time table can be made or changed without official approval.

It may surprise a few Americans to know that the first-class passenger rate in Mexico is only two and two-fifths cents a mile, while the second-class rate, which covers at least one-half of the whole passenger traffic of the country, is only one cent and one-fifth a mile—these figures being in terms of gold, to afford a comparison with American rates.

I have been privately assured by the principal American officers and investors of the larger lines that railway enterprises in Mexico are encouraged, dealt with on their merits and are wholly free from blackmail, direct or indirect . . .

More than $1,200,000,000 of foreign capital has been invested in Mexico since President Díaz put system and stability into the nation. Capital for railways, mines, factories and plantations has been pouring in at the rate of $200,000,000 a year. In six months the Government sold more than a million acres of land.

In spite of what has already been done, there is still room for the investment of billions of dollars in the mines and industries of the Republic.

Americans and other foreigners interested in mines, real estate, factories, railways and other enterprises have privately assured me, not once, but many times, that, under Díaz, conditions for investment in Mexico are fairer and quite as reliable as in the most highly developed European countries. The President declares that these conditions will continue after his death or retirement.

Since Díaz assumed power, the revenues of the Government have increased from about $15,000,000 to more than $115,000,000, and yet taxes have been steadily reduced.

When the price of silver was cut in two, President Díaz was advised that his country could never pay its national debt, which was doubled by the change in values. He was urged to repudiate a part of the debt. The President denounced the advice as foolishness as well as dishonesty, and it is a fact that some of the greatest officers of the government went for years without their salaries that Mexico might be able to meet her financial obligations dollar for dollar.

The cities shine with electric lights and are noisy with electric trolley cars; English is taught in the public schools of the great Federal District; the public treasury is full and overflowing and the national debt decreasing; there are nearly seventy thousand foreigners living contentedly and prosperously in the Republic—more Americans than Spaniards; Mexico has three times as large a population to the square mile as Canada; public affairs have developed strong men like Jose Yves Limantour, the great Secretary of Finances, one of the most distinguished of living financiers; Vice-president Corral, who is also Secretary of the Interior; Ignacio Mariscal, the Minister of Foreign Affairs, and Enrique Creel, the brilliant Ambassador at Washington.

And it is a land of beauty beyond compare. Its mountains and valleys, its great plateaus, its indescribably rich and varied foliage, its ever blooming and abundant flowers, its fruits, its skies, its marvelous climate, its old villages, cathedrals, churches, convents—there is nothing quite like Mexico in the world for variety and loveliness. But it is the gentle, trustful, grateful Indian, with his unbelievable hat and many-colored blanket, the eldest child of America, that wins the heart out of you. After traveling all over the world, the American who visits Mexico for the first time wonders how it happened that he never understood what a fascinating country of romance he left at his own door.

It is the hour of growth, strength and peace which convinces Porfirio Díaz that he has almost finished his task on the American continent.

Yet you see no man in a priest's attire in this Catholic country. You see no religious processions. The Church is silent save within her own walls. This is a land where I have seen the most profound religious emotion, the most solemn religious spectacles— from the blanketed peons kneeling for hours in cathedrals, the men carrying their household goods, the women suckling their babies, to that indescribable host of Indians on their knees at the shrine of the Virgin of Guadalupe.

I asked President Díaz about it while we paced the terrace of Chapultepec Castle. He bowed his white head for a moment and then lifted it high, his dark eyes looking straight into mine.

"We allow no priest to vote, we allow no priest to hold public office, we allow no priest to wear a distinctive dress in public, we allow no religious processions in the streets," he said. "When we made those laws we were not fighting against religion, but against idolatry. We intend that the humblest Mexican shall be so far freed from the past that he can stand upright and unafraid in the presence of any human being. I have no hostility to religion; on the contrary, in spite of all past experience, I firmly believe that there can be no true national progress in any country or any time without real religion."

Such is Porfirio Díaz, the foremost man of the American hemisphere. What he has done, almost alone and in such a few years, for a people disorganized and degraded by war, lawlessness and comic opera polities, is the great inspiration of Pan-Americanism, the hope of the Latin-American republics.

Whether you see him at Chapultepec Castle, or in his office in the National Palace, or in the exquisite drawing-room of his modest home in the city, with his young, beautiful wife and his children and grandchildren by his first wife about him, or surrounded by troops, his breast covered with decorations conferred by great nations, he is always the same—simple, direct and full of the dignity of conscious power.

In spite of the iron government he has given to Mexico, in spite of a continuance in office that has caused men to say that he has converted a republic into an autocracy, it is impossible to look into his face when he speaks of the principle of popular sovereignty without believing that even now he would take up arms and shed his blood in defense of it.

Only a few weeks ago Secretary of State Root summed up President Díaz when he said:

"It has seemed to me that of all the men now living, General Porfirio Díaz, of Mexico, was best worth seeing. Whether one considers the adventurous, daring, chivalric incidents of his early career; whether one considers the vast work of government which his wisdom and courage and commanding character accomplished; whether one considers his singularly attractive personality, no one lives to-day that I would rather see than President Díaz. If I were a poet I would write poetic eulogies. If I were a musician I would compose triumphal marches. If I were a Mexican I should feel that the steadfast loyalty of a lifetime could not be too much in return for the blessings that he had brought to my country. As I am neither poet, musician nor Mexican, but only an American who loves justice and liberty and hopes to see their reign among mankind progress and strengthen and become perpetual, I look to Porfirio Díaz, the President of Mexico, as one of the great men to be held up for the hero-worship of mankind."

For Further Reading

Bulmer Thomas, Victor. *The Economic History of Latin America Since Independence*. Cambridge: Cambridge University Press, 1994.

Coatsworth, John. *Growth against Development*. Dekalb: Northern Illinois University Press, 1981.

Farnsworth-Alvear, Ann. *Dulcinea in the Factory: Myths, Morals, Men, and Women in Colombia's Industrial Experiment, 1905–1960*. Durham, NC: Duke University Press, 2000.

French, John D., and Daniel James, eds. *The Gendered Worlds of Latin American Women Workers: From Household and Factory to the Union Hall and Ballot Box*. Durham, NC: Duke University Press, 1998.

Haber, Stephen. *Industry and Underdevelopment: The Industrialization of Mexico, 1890–1940*. Palo Alto: Stanford University Press, 1995.

Haber, Stephen. *How Latin America Fell Behind: Essays on the Economic Histories of Brazil and Mexico*. Palo Alto: Stanford University Press, 1997.

Hutchison, Elizabeth Quay. *Labors Appropriate to Their Sex: Gender, Labor, and Politics in Urban Chile, 1900–1930*. Durham, NC: Duke University Press Books, 2001.

Kouri, Emilio. "Interpreting the Expropriation of Indian Pueblo Lands in Porfirian Mexico: The Unexamined Legacies of Andrés Molina Enríquez," *Hispanic American Historical Review*, 82:1 (2002), 69–118.

Peard, Julyan. *Race, Place, and Medicine: The Idea of the Tropics in Nineteenth-Century Brazil*. Durham, NC: Duke University Press, 2000.

Poole, Deborah. *Vision, Race, and Modernity: A Visual Economy of the Andean World*. Princeton: Princeton University Press, 1997.

"Special Issue: Can the Subaltern See? Photographs As History," *Hispanic American Historical Review*, 84:1 (2004).

Tenorio-Trillo, Mauricio. *Mexico at the World's Fairs: Crafting a Modern Nation*. Berkeley: University of California Press, 1996.

1895	1895–1898	1907	1910	November 25, 1911
José Martí returns to Cuba, is quickly killed in action	Cuban War of Independence	Global Depression results in repatriation of thousands of Mexican migrant workers in the United States	Francisco I Madero issues the Plan de San Luis Potosi, calling for an uprising in Mexico against Porfirio Díaz, to begin November 20, 1910	Peasants in Morelos, led by Emiliano Zapata, issue the Plan de Ayala, beginning a rebellion against the government of Francisco Madero

Signs of Crisis in a Gilded Age

5

November 1914	April 10, 1919	January 1919	1919	July 20, 1923	1924
Zapatistas and Villistas converge on Mexico City	Emiliano Zapata ambushed by government forces during negotiations for a truce	Tragic Week in Buenos Aires during general strike	Argentine Patriotic League founded	Pancho Villa killed	APRA (Alianza Popular Revolucionaria Americana) founded by Peruvian Víctor Raíl Haya de la Torre

The challenges we encounter in attempting to render the histories of a region as diverse as Latin America become immediately apparent with one simple question: When did the golden age of the export oligarchy end? Was it 1907 (with the onset of a global recession), 1910 (with the beginning of the Mexican Revolution), 1914 (with the beginning of the First World War), 1919 (with the economic crisis at the end of the war), 1929 (with the onset of the Great Depression), or perhaps some other date? The question becomes still more vexing when we attempt to characterize the export boom as a whole. If we focus on economic growth and modernity, it is possible to lose sight of the fact that many people never enjoyed the benefits of economic growth, that for millions of Latin Americans this period was characterized by a loss of rights, lands, and autonomy. Moreover, the threats posed by imperialism, instability, and violence were never far from people's minds throughout this golden age. In short, Latin Americans lived in a fragmentary world; one person's boom was always another's crisis.

It would be misleading to represent this as a period of perpetually looming crisis. At any given time it is always possible to find contradictory signs pointing to multiple futures. James Creelman may have been wrong to think that Porfirio Díaz would be remembered as the "hero of the Americas," but his legacy has not simply been that of a villain. Mexican high school textbooks these days portray him as an ambiguous figure, a dictator who introduced lasting and largely positive changes to the national economy even as he stifled the development of civil society. Instead of reading his critics as valiant sages, we tend to view them as dissidents whose views tell us a great deal about the values and assumptions that informed their worlds. This offers a larger model for how we ought to read the voices raised in protest as the golden age drew towards its end. Progress came at a great cost—with increasing inequality, greater dependence on the global economy (and the United States in particular), and economic and political instability. It entailed the forced elimination of certain ways of life, sometimes with great violence. And on some level, the process was never entirely complete. Latin Americans today continue to live in multiple worlds, at the same time ultramodern and deeply traditional. Néstor García Canclini calls the cultures of this region hybrid, a concept he uses to suggest the simultaneity of two different worldviews, often in the same person.[1]

It may be telling that even as some writers celebrated Latin America's great leaps forward, others lamented imperialist and other threats. José Martí's 1891 essay *Our America* (included in Chapter 1) immediately alerts its readers to a series of crises, of the need for Latin Americans to find their common voice in order to strengthen the region in the face of North American expansion. From his exile in New York, Martí wrote of a crisis in nationhood that in some ways links him more closely to José Hernández (whose *gaucho* Martín Fierro was a national hero quite opposed to the modern world Domingo Faustino Sarmiento wanted to create) than to many of the liberal social critics of his day. Like these critics, Martí was raised to believe in the possibilities of progress. Unlike them, he sees the price of progress as a new era of outside domination (which, in the case of Cuba, was coming even before the previous imperial era ended), and an obliteration of what was virtuous and original in his America. Months after publishing the essay he would found the *Partido Revolucionario de Cuba* (the Cuban Revolutionary Party), which aimed to bring Cuban exiles in the United States together to advance the struggle for independence and against U.S. annexation (the alternative favored by many in Washington at that time). He would return to Cuba to lead the struggle in 1895, only to be killed in battle with the Spanish a short time later.

Our America circulated widely across the region precisely because it gave voice to the fear that the boom and its version of modernity were coming at too high a price. Others followed. José Enrique Rodó's "Ariel" (1900), and Rubén Dario's "To Roosevelt" (written in 1904, included as Document 5.1) were complex meditations on the threat that the United States represented to Latin American sovereignty. In subsequent years an entire generation of intellectuals would take up where they left off, celebrating a Latin American folk rooted in the indigenous and African cultures of the region. For some, like José Vasconcelos, the folk became an aesthetic ideal, Latin American beauty as an antidote to North American cold rationality. Others, like José Mariátegui, saw in the indigenous peasantries of the region a revolutionary force that, if unleashed, could pave the way for a socialist utopia.

Crises in the Countryside

José Martí did not need to tell the rural poor that the export boom had come with a great cost. In Mexico, almost every mile of railway construction was accompanied by some minor conflict. Rural groups were neither as compliant nor as easily controlled as Porfirio Díaz had hoped. Araucanians in Argentina and Mapuches in Chile could only be displaced through military campaigns. Brazil had its own rebellions, the most famous being the millennial movement led by Antônio Conselhiero at Canudos in the 1890s.[2]

As widespread political chaos faded at the national level during the boom, other forms of violence intensified in the countryside. Local and national elites used the police and the military to ensure order. Political thugs "recruited" labor, "bought" land from unwilling peasants, and ensured that they had a monopoly on legitimate violence. Political parties played a fixed game, controlled by a small oligarchy who perpetually deferred the promise that once order and progress were assured, democracy would follow.

Those rural peoples excluded from the game had few options. They could migrate to more marginal regions, other countries, or the cities. They could remain behind and become workers on estates growing commodities for export. Or they could fight. Historically, this last option was risky, though not necessarily fatal. The threat of rebellion had always been a part of the peasant's political repertoire, used quite effectively in negotiations with more powerful groups. However, by the late nineteenth century this option was increasingly closed off. In part this was due to the fact that modern technologies (railroads, telegraphs, machine guns) made it easier to repress rural protest, yet during this period the nature of the protest itself began to change. Acts of violence that had once played a role in shaping the nature of elite domination (violence that might limit the demands made on a community or restore lost lands) increasingly seemed to be aimed against the project of modernization itself. Railroads, barbed wire, and telegraphs were destined to transform social relations in the countryside, facilitating the concentration of power, linking previously remote regions to national and global markets, and facilitating what is sometimes described as "capitalist penetration" into regions previously governed by different logics.[3] The losers in these transformations could not easily negotiate the terms of their subordination into systems that discarded older social and cultural patterns and elevated market relations, leaving some to reject these transformations in their entirety.

Their responses did not always seem like negotiations over a new "pact of domination"[4] that would govern future social relations. The new order created by economic modernization seemed to obliterate the old logics of peasant–state relations. Peasants increasingly longed for a lost world, and in some cases opted to escape from a project that seemed to be destroying their ways of life. For their part, central government authorities also made sense of rural protest differently than they had in the past. Rendering rebellion as the sobs of primitive, inferior people, they concluded that rural protest was best dealt with through a type of repressive violence that would clear the way for more civilized people. Unrest in the countryside thus became an excuse for the nineteenth-century equivalent of "shock and awe," used to clear the land for more productive purposes.

The growing intensity of the violence mobilized against peasants did not mute their grievances. It simply made the stakes of the struggle much higher. At times, they steeled themselves for wars to the end of the world (e.g., Canudos 1897, Tomochic, Mexico, 1892). At others, they compensated for the losses they suffered through surreptitious means, stealing cattle and food, sabotaging the property of their overlords. At still others, they waited quietly for an opportunity to strike back against their oppressors. Elite conflicts, larger social or economic crises, wars and disasters of all kinds could fracture the ruling classes. If the collapse was sufficient, the rural poor might have an opportunity to step in and reshape the order of things, to negotiate a new ruling pact at a time when their superiors were at their most weak and divided. In Mexico, 1910 provided such an opportunity.

Porfirio Díaz made one substantial blunder in his interview with James Creelman (see Document 4.1). He implied that he was not going to run for re-election in 1910, declaring that the country was ready for democracy. His promise unleashed a wave of political activity. Millions of middle-class Mexicans tried to take advantage of the first political opening in the country in more than three decades. For the most part, they supported the opposition candidate Francisco Madero, a prosperous northern *hacendado* who promised to modernize the political system. Madero famously misread the political situation in 1910, aligning himself to a middle-class desire for greater political power while largely ignoring the larger social crises that were brewing, though the simple promise of change was enough to energize tens of thousands of supporters leading up to the election. Most predictions had him winning the election handily against the man Díaz seemed likely to choose as his successor, Bernardo Reyes.

When Díaz changed his mind about retiring, and won an obviously fixed election (notable for the fact that Madero was jailed before election and then exiled), middle-class optimism turned to rage. Madero called for Mexicans to overthrow the regime by the force of arms in a rebellion that began in November 1910 (see his *Plan de San Luis Potosí* on the book's website at www.routledge.com/cw/dawson). The rebellion began slowly at first, but within months the country had become ungovernable. Madero forced Díaz to flee the country in May 1911 and then proposed new elections, which he won the following November. The political transition complete, and the democratic process guaranteed, Madero and his many middle-class, liberal followers believed these elections marked the successful conclusion of the 1910 Mexican Revolution.

They were wrong. The collapse of the regime unleashed waves of violence that would not be easily contained. Madero fell quickly, as did his successors, and by 1913 the country was mired in a series of civil wars with no end in sight. Pictures of peasant armies, of poor indigenous soldiers and their female companions (some camp followers, some soldiers themselves) circulated broadly in Mexico and elsewhere, serving as stark reminders that those groups that elites had hoped would disappear under the mantle of progress were very much present, and entirely capable of disrupting "civilized" politics. At no point was that more obvious than in December 1914, when the peasant armies of Francisco (Pancho) Villa and Emiliano Zapata converged on Mexico City, turning Mexico's most modern city into the site of a stunning social inversion. Among the most famous records produced during the occupation of the city was a photo of two Zapatista soldiers, faces creased by age and hands calloused by years of agricultural labor, sitting at the lunch counter in Sanborns, one of the most exclusive restaurants in Mexico City, drinking chocolate and eating rolls (Figure 5.1). The photo taken of this moment is today one of the most easily recognized images of the Revolution.

Costing over a million lives and lasting a decade, Mexico's Revolution was in fact several revolutions. Some revolutionaries demanded land and liberty, others had specific grievances against local landlords and government officials. Some were committed to democracy, the rule of law, or social reforms that would ameliorate inequality. Others were simply carried by the wind. Nonetheless, like all momentous experiences, the Revolution was ultimately distilled into a series of iconic moments or representations that could stand for the experience as a whole.[5] More than any other image, those created during the occupation of Mexico City are used to represent this ten-year civil war. The photos are iconic in part because they capture the meeting of two of the most important revolutionary leaders (see Figure 5.2). More broadly, this moment stands for the whole because of the ways that the invasion of the hyper-modern national capital by rural, unwashed, and impoverished masses captures both the threat and promise of the Revolution.

To contemporary eyes, the moments captured in Figures 5.1 and 5.2 evoke the carnivalesque. Mexico City was a profoundly segregated space, where class, culture, and ethnicity produced impermeable boundaries; boundaries that everyone understood and no one transgressed. Indigenous peasants knew better than to even look a white, middle-class Mexicans in the eye, or to speak to them without due reverence. To occupy the physical spaces monopolized by members of polite society was beyond the pale. And here they were, a northern cattle rustler (Villa) and a Nahuatl-speaking peasant (Zapata), sitting on the thrones of Maximilian and Carlotta, while their armies ruled the streets and ate in fancy restaurants.

One reading then, was that the country had conquered the city. Another reading is that the peasants were merely temporary guests, that the way they occupied the city actually served as a reminder that they did not belong there. If one looks closely, is there not just a hint of discomfort in Zapata's eyes as he sits on the throne? Don't the Zapatistas drinking

Figure 5.1 Two Zapatistas eating at Sanborns

Figure 5.2 Villa and Zapata in Mexico City
Source: Underwood Photo Archives/SuperStock

chocolate seem nervous, like they don't quite belong? In the end, they were not driven out of the city, they left of their own accord. They were not city folk. Their revolution was about regaining lands and liberties taken from them by Porfirio Díaz. To be sure, by occupying the city in December 1914 they established that they were a force to be reckoned with, and that they could claim both their lands and the spaces of the rich and powerful through their military capabilities. Beyond proving this, an extended stay in Mexico City did nothing to further their goals. In fact, extended absences from their home communities imperiled hard won local victories.

Indigenous communities across Mexico participated in revolutionary movements on these ambiguous terms, their decisions invariably informed by a desire to preserve local forms of autonomy. Porfirio Díaz did indeed represent a threat to village autonomy, but so too did any national government committed to the project of economic moderniza-tion and the creation of a stronger state. Some indigenous peasantries in western Mexico would support the Cristero Revolt, a Catholic counter-revolution during the 1920s that also grew in response to efforts by the revolutionary state to meddle in local affairs (though in this case it was more focused on religious customs than land-holding). Indigenous peas-antries were likewise ever wary that some of their greatest threats came not from distant authorities, but from local strongmen and their neighbors, who might take advantage of the absences caused by men fighting in the Revolution to appropriate local lands. The safest way to avoid these losses was to remain close to home, where you could protect those things that really mattered.

Villistas had an even more complicated agenda. Inasmuch as the Zapatistas had a declaration that identified their goals (the *Plan de Ayala*, Document 5.2), Villistas formed a cross-class alliance held together mostly by their northern frontier traditions. Alan Knight describes them as *serrano* revolutionaries, products of independent traditions who chafed at the ways that economic development and political centralization had undermined their autonomy. The *serrano* revolutionary harkened back to a romantic past, a time when their physical movement was not impeded by barbed wire and railroads, when land was plentiful and cheap, when people had the ability to work for themselves rather than as employees in some larger enterprise, and when the corrupt government officials who now imposed their will so capriciously lacked the ability to enforce rules drafted in Mexico City.

The Villistas, not unlike the Zapatistas, spoke of a society that had disappeared during the export boom. Both wanted freedoms and rights, along with material possessions that they no longer had. Their visual appearance, the Indian peasant and the gun-toting frontiersman, spoke of a past that urbane Mexicans wanted to leave behind, which is why middle-class, urban Mexicans responded to their invasion of Mexico City with horror; a response that would in many ways seal the fate of these revolutionaries. Zapatistas became backwards Indians. Villistas became bandits. And the Constitutionalists, a diverse collection of liberals, intellectuals, modernizers, and even former supporters of the old regime, became the men who would save the nation from chaos.

Perhaps the aftermath is just as important. Zapata and his followers retreated to Morelos. Villa returned to the north. Neither seemed capable of creating a ruling coalition in partnership with the other. Instead it was their enemies, the Constitutionalists, who emerged from this convergence re-energized. Using the new military technologies that were then being tested on the battlefields of Europe, Constitutionalist armies routed Villa at Celaya in April 1915, and then set out to establish a new state. In 1917 they passed a constitution, which while promising to return land to the victims of Porfirio Díaz's dictatorship, to educate the masses, and protect workers, was for the most part not all that different from the Constitution that an earlier generation of liberals had written in 1857. The new regime would prioritize political stability over social reform, and would defer most reforms, preferring to exercise its power by silencing their enemies. Zapata was assassinated as he attempted to negotiate a truce with the government in April 1919. Villa, ever a threat even after he retired from the field, was murdered in July 1923.

To the Barricades

By their nature, peasants face limits to their ability to affect national politics. Their politics begin and end with local grievances, and this tends to restrict their interest in sustained participation in national movements. States have historically responded to their grievances by mixing local concessions with local repression, cleaving off one peasant group from another by dealing directly with each. Rural rebellions may be difficult to defeat, but as long as rebels remain isolated in small groups, they rarely have the ability to threaten the survival of the state.

Urban populations present an entirely different kind of challenge to the state. City dwellers can disrupt national-level politics in ways that rural people cannot, because their proximity to power and their capacity to act in a concerted manner makes it easier for them to directly attack the institutions that constitute the state. Because their subsistence depends on national and international networks, city dwellers of all classes also have interests that extend beyond their neighborhoods. Urban rebellion in modern cities can thus produce a multiplier effect that rural revolt often cannot, creating a particularly thorny set of problems for the state. Simply put, modern states are rooted in urban settings, and should those settings become ungovernable, those states are likely to fail. These problems grew even more serious towards the end of the nineteenth century, when urban proletariats emerged across Latin America.

Industrial growth in Latin America was accompanied by the development of an industrial working class. Most lived in expanding cities like Monterrey, Mexico City, Havana, Medellín, São Paulo, Buenos Aires, and Santiago, where the processing of goods for export and domestic manufacturing were concentrated.[6] Some were the descendants of longtime city dwellers. Others were recent migrants from the countryside, some of them former slaves. Still others came from the waves of European and Asian migration that arrived in Latin America in the late nineteenth century. Walking into their factories, workers entered a fluid setting; a place where grievances over wages and working conditions were sometimes resolved peacefully, and sometimes turned into violent confrontations with lasting repercussions. They were also sites where workers' and employers' attitudes towards one another were shaped by more opaque concepts like respect and propriety, the proper (and sometimes beloved) boss, and the honorable worker.

Believing themselves to be good Catholic patrons, factory bosses loathed anything that disrupted the orderly functioning of their factories. They could stomach certain types of grievances, as they understood that by resolving complaints about workplace order and safety they could build a stronger bond of loyalty with their workers. On the other hand, strikes, protests, and other forms of "immoral" behavior undermined their sense of order, and threatened their power. The bosses did all they could to discourage unionization efforts and anything else that came between the benevolent patron and the employee.

Workers had quite a different view of unions. Unionization created opportunities to break free of a patronage system that denied them rights outside of the dependent relationship they had with their bosses, but it also created new risks for workers in societies where the state tended to support the bosses. Workers put their own lives at risk by walking off the job collectively. The larger the strike was, the greater the risk it posed. And should that strike become political, and escalate into a general strike, the bosses and the state were likely to consider it a declaration of war.

This is precisely what happened in Buenos Aires, in January 1919. Once a relatively sleepy capital, dependent mainly on the collection of taxes on wheat and hide exports and European imports, the export boom transformed Buenos Aires into one of the largest cities in the Americas. The city attracted 800,000 immigrants, growing to over 1.6 million. International migrants formed a considerable part of the working classes in a number of Latin American cities, including Havana, São Paulo, Rio, and Caracas, but Buenos Aires was singular in the size of its foreign born population, which came to make up half of the city by 1910. By 1914 the foreign born represented two-thirds of skilled and white-collar workers in the capital, and 80 percent of unskilled labor in the city.[7]

The foreign born could not vote and lacked political rights. Politics in Argentina was a tightly controlled affair, and even at the end of the nineteenth century the political system remained entirely in the control of the oligarchy. It was not until 1891 that the opposition *Unión Cívica Radical* (the Radical Party, UCR) was founded, and it was not until the 1912 Sáenz-Peña electoral law that all native born and naturalized males were granted the vote. This gave middle-class Argentines a political voice in the form of the Radical Party (the Radical Hipólito Yrigoyen was elected president in 1916), but left millions of immigrants, most of whom had never become citizens, with no voice at all. Drawn mostly from the middle class, Radical Party members sympathized with the economic interests of the oligarchs, as their own prosperity was derived from the same export economy that made the rich, rich, and left the poor, poor.

Middle-class Radicals, like members of the oligarchy, did not trust immigrants. For all their racial virtue, they spoke foreign tongues, ate alien foods, did not celebrate the national traditions or owe any loyalty to Argentina. Some also brought with them objectionable ideas about workers rights, anarchism, and democracy. Moreover, because of immigration Buenos Aires was a city beset by a series of social crises. Sex ratios were skewed, single-motherhood was widespread (20 percent of children were born to single mothers), and the sex trades were more prominent here than in all but a few other cities in the Americas. The oligarchs shared with most middle-class Radicals a deep anxiety about slums, anarchism, strikes, loose morals, family decay, and crime in the immigrant neighborhoods. They also feared that "true" Argentines were in danger of being swamped by the foreign (often represented as Jewish[8]) element. When workers protested or struck, their actions were construed as the work of foreign agitators, not the product of legitimate grievances.

It is unsurprising that these conflicts came to a head in 1919. World War One, known in various parts of Latin America as the *Dance of the Millions*, brought high commodity prices and immense wealth for the oligarchy. For workers it brought rising prices and stagnating wages. During the war the cost of living in Buenos Aires climbed 60 percent, while wages fell by 16 percent. Workers responded by striking in increasing numbers. Elsewhere in Latin America (Cuba, the Amazon, Chile), the end of the war also saw widespread labor unrest and economic crisis, but few places were as volatile as Buenos Aires at the time. Living in crowded tenements with a growing array of grievances, and cognizant of the recent successes of the Bolshevik revolution in Russia, Argentine workers were ready for a confrontation. Many simply wanted to win better wages and working conditions. Others, including supporters of anarchist and socialist unions, or the Socialist Party, saw this as a revolutionary moment, a chance to participate in a movement that they believed was coalescing around the western world. Their weapon: the general strike.

Workers struck the Vasena Metallurgical workshop on January 7, 1919. They demanded a reduction in the workday from eleven to eight hours, better working conditions, Sundays off, better wages, and the reinstatement of fired union delegates. The company responded by hiring strike-breakers and non-union workers, and in the ensuing conflict the police were brought in and fired on workers. Four workers were killed, and more than thirty wounded. The story of the strike—which to this point was fairly typical of strikes during this era and might have ended unremarkably as just another violent confrontation between workers and bosses—took an unusual turn when police again opened fire on the workers who gathered to care for the dead and take them to the Chacarita Cemetery. The following day *La Prensa* reported eight had been killed. Strikers claimed the death toll was more than fifty. In the ensuing hours, as stories circulated about the conflict, a growing number of *porteño* workers agitated for some sort of significant response from working people. Leaders of the 20,000 member *Federación Obrera Regional Argentina* (Argentine Regional Worker's Federation—FORA), which had organized the strike, seized the moment. They launched a general strike on January 9. The strike rapidly spread to the provinces.

It would be a gross understatement to say that the FORA overestimated their strength. General strikes are dangerous things, perhaps successful when a regime is so discredited and weak that a widespread civic disturbance can topple the government. Should they fail to gain traction, they leave unarmed workers facing a militarized regime; a regime that can win the battle for popular support by casting the strikers as seditious terrorists. However real their grievances, and however thrilling the first turn at the barricades was, strikers had to confront both Yrigoyen's Radical government and those Argentines who for years had been nursing an increasingly hysterical fear of immigrant workers. This sector of society, comprised of many in the middle class, the elites, and even some working-class nationalists, would support extreme measures to rein the strikers in.

Almost immediately after the 9th of January, a militia made up of middle-class and wealthy young men joined with the military and police in responding to the strike. They targeted striking workers, immigrants, and members of the political left with breathtaking violence. This *semana trágica* (tragic week) of the general strike left 1,000 dead, 4,000 injured, and around 50,000 imprisoned. Foreshadowing the extreme (and extremely xenophobic) measures that conservatives would use against their foes at various points during the twentieth century, reactionaries also used the pretext of the general strike to target Jewish neighborhoods in an effort to dismantle a supposed "Argentine Soviet" that did not in fact exist. Yrigoyen repudiated the violence, but did little to punish those who were responsible, driving workers away from the Radical Party for decades to come and indirectly enhancing the power of the oligarchy (which could count on antipathies between the middle and working classes to limit the political strength of both). For their part, workers were reminded that they had no rightful place in the system.

The most significant political movement to emerge out of the *semana trágica* was the *Liga Patriótica Argentina* (Argentine Patriotic League). The league was an extreme right-wing organization that was formed from the militias that terrorized workers and immigrants during the general strike. Given aid and training by the Argentine Army, the Catholic Church, and the wealthy, it was xenophobic, anti-communist, and anti-Semitic. By the early 1920s, it had about 300,000 members in over 600 brigades, who participated in any number of violent campaigns in defense of "Fatherland and Order." Catholic workers who committed themselves to capitalism and self-improvement were welcomed in the League, as long as they eschewed any interest in principles like equality. League members believed egalitarian values were utopian and dangerous, that society was naturally hierarchical and should remain so.

The Documents: Questioning a Golden Age

In some senses, Document 4.1 and those included below have a great deal in common. All were penned during the export boom. All try and make sense of that boom in ways that draw moral conclusions about the kinds of economic and political transformations the region had seen in the recent past. Each however, offers a different account of what has happened, and what is happening. In Creelman (Document 4.1), we saw optimism about the future. In the four that follow we see angst, anger, and a demand for change. The documents take a variety of approaches to making their points. One is a poem, another a manifesto, the third a philosophical treatise, and the final one written as history. As twenty-first-century readers of these texts, we have the opportunity to read them closely for what is fact and what is fiction. We also have the opportunity to read them as powerful expressions of the moment in which they were created, expressions that would in turn help shape the worlds Latin Americans made during the twentieth century.

Document 5.1 is the poem "To Roosevelt," written by the Nicaraguan poet, diplomat, and intellectual Rubén Darío. As the founding figure of Latin American modernism, Darío was one of the most cosmopolitan men of letters of his day, travelling across the region and living frequently in Europe during his short life. He was not invariably given to harsh critiques of the ultra-modern United States, but was driven to pen this poem in 1904, after the United States intervened in Panama to secure that country's independence and obtain concessions to build a U.S. dominated Panama Canal. Like José Martí had done in *Our America*, he used this poem to upend North American assumptions about their own superiority. In "To Roosevelt" it is the Latin Americans who possess virtue, spirit, and a glorious civilization, and the ascendant United States, with its threat to their sovereignty, which is furthest from god.

Document 5.2 introduces a different kind of threat. It is the *Plan de Ayala*, penned by Emiliano Zapata and a group of Nahuatl speaking villagers in the highlands of Morelos in 1911. Their plan amounted to a declaration of war against Francisco Madero, whom they supported in the overthrow of Porfirio Díaz. Some of their grievances were quite specific, quasi-legal explanations and justifications for their own perilous act of rebellion. And yet, the *Plan de Ayala* was much more than a simple catalogue of complaints. Embedded within the document are a series of assumptions and claims about the rights of villagers, and how the violation of those rights justifies rebellion. Though much more practical than Darío, their larger insights were no less profound.

The United States did not figure into the grievances aired by the villagers of Morelos. The sugar from the new plantations in the region probably remained in Mexico. The owners of the estates that had taken their land were in many cases Mexican, and rarely from the United States. The role that the United States had played in the changes that had affected their lives (providing capital to stimulate economic growth and offering markets for Mexican exports) was, for the most part, a distant abstraction. This in part explains why, during a decade of revolution in Mexico, foreign owners and foreign capital were not targeted with any greater frequency than Mexican owners and their estates. Later ideologues would cast the Revolution as an anti-imperial, nationalist movement to restore Mexican sovereignty, and for some it clearly was. For the Zapatistas however, the nationality of the men who took their land was of little importance.

Our penultimate document (5.3), an excerpt from *The Cosmic Race (la raza cosmica)*, by José Vasconcelos, was written in the aftermath of that conflict. If the Zapatistas were driven by a grievance, Vasconcelos was driven by a desire to reconstitute and celebrate a country torn apart by years of fratricidal violence. Vasconcelos was an active participant in the process of reconstruction, serving as rector of the National University, and then as the country's first Minister of Public Education between 1920 and 1924. In 1929 he ran for president, and some believe only lost because of electoral fraud. For all these accomplishments, *The Cosmic Race*, published shortly after he resigned as Minister of Public Education, represents his most lasting contribution to Mexican life. In the essay Vasconcelos dismisses the racism and sensibilities of the North (in particular the United States) as old fashioned, as doomed. He celebrates Latin America's embrace of racial hybridity (*mestizaje*) as mankind's best hope. He sees in *mestizaje* a process in which all the best qualities of all the races will be saved, and all the worst discarded.

Vasconcelos, like Darío, reminds us of the increasingly important role the specter of the United States played in the unfolding crises of the early twentieth century. At the turn of the century, the United States was the ascendant power in the Americas. In the Caribbean, Central America, and Mexico especially, U.S. investors had supplanted their European competitors, and owned an increasingly large portion of the region's productive capacity (on the eve of World War One, U.S. investments in the region had reached $1.6 billion, up from $300 million twenty years earlier[9]). Exports to the United States had become critical to the survival of the export oligarchy, and thus critical to social stability in general. And yet these things came at a cost, both in terms of the loss of sovereignty, a feeling that one colonial overlord was being supplanted by another, and in terms of the psychic cost of facing the racist and otherwise superior attitudes of North American sojourners. In the eyes of North American investors, this was not a relationship of equals. They were the hand of civilization reaching out to lift their lesser cousins. It was a degrading experience, to say the least.

Degrading, in part, because Vasconcelos and Darío, like José Marti, Enrique Rodo and countless others, actually admired the United States. They admired the wealth, the progress, and the modernity they saw there, and adhered to many of the same values that their North American counterparts embraced. For instance, Vasconcelos adopted North American racist stereotypes in describing his country even as he tried to upend them in an argument that Mexico was actually more progressive than the United States. Vasconcelos' contradictions speak to simultaneous desires; a desire to be more like the ascendant United States, and a desire to reject North American racism. In this sense Vasconcelos was very different from Zapata. He was a philosopher deeply steeped in the Western canon, an educator who as Minister of Public Education in Mexico insisted that indigenous Mexicans read Homer and Aristotle so that they might be properly educated. These strains run through his references to Comte and others in *The Cosmic Race*, demonstrating his belief in modernization as something that somehow originates in Europe and the United States. And yet, his nationalist desires, his need to distinguish Latin America from the coldly rational North, leads him to propose that the very thing North Americans see as irredeemable in the region will be the source of its greatness.

The starkly racist language in Vasconcelos must alert us to the fact that he is of a particular time and a particular place, even if in place of biological determinism he offers aesthetic determinism (the ugly will ultimately die out, as they will not procreate). Some readers will find it difficult to read these words without getting caught up in these references. This then, becomes the challenge for the historian. How do we place Vasconcelos in context? How do we understand him as a product of his own time and gain greater insights into the political and intellectual struggles of this period, in particular the desire by Latin Americans to imagine a sovereign future, one free of imperial entanglements, when, given contemporary sensibilities, certain words and phrases seem to jump off the page?

A different set of challenges confront us with Document 5.4, which is excerpted from the book *Seven Interpretive Essays on Peruvian Reality*, written by the Peruvian intellectual José Carlos Mariátegui in 1928. An avowed Marxist, he combined the political ideology of those who advocated the 1919 general strike in Buenos Aires with a focus on the rural problems that shaped the Peruvian left (Mariátegui was an advocate of workers rights, and supported Peru's 1919 strikes). Mariátegui was an early supporter of Raúl Haya de la Torre's *Alianza Popular Revolucionaria Americana* (American Popular Revolutionary Alliance, APRA), though he left the party just prior to the publication of *Seven Essays* to establish his own Socialist Party.

What makes this essay particularly important is that it represents a form of Marxism that instead of focusing on an emergent (often immigrant) working class, looks to Peru's indigenous peoples as the source of an organic Peruvian form of communism. It draws on the specific histories of the Andes, where Indian–white relations were more openly contentious than elsewhere, where the possibility of pan-Indian movements seemed more likely, and where movements that invoked a utopian Inca past had long flourished. Moreover, unlike "To Roosevelt" and the *Plan de Ayala*, *Seven Essays* was penned at a time when the left was ascendant. Buoyed by Russia's 1917 revolution, leftists truly believed in the global socialist revolution. Mariátegui brought to this struggle a particularly Peruvian viewpoint. It was not the modern proletariat who would defeat capitalism in Peru, but the communist Indian.

Document 5.1 Rubén Darío, "To Roosevelt," 1904

Source: From *Selected Poems of Rubén Darío*, translated by Lysander Kemp, © 1965, renewed 1993. Reprinted by permission of the University of Texas Press.

To Roosevelt

The voice that would reach you, Hunter, must speak
in Biblical tones, or in the poetry of Walt Whitman.
You are primitive and modern, simple and complex;
you are one part George Washington and one part Nimrod.
You are the United States,
future invader of our naive America
with its Indian blood, an America
that still prays to Christ and still speaks Spanish.
You are strong, proud model of your race;
you are cultured and able; you oppose Tolstoy.
You are an Alexander-Nebuchadnezzar,
breaking horses and murdering tigers.
(You are a Professor of Energy,
as current lunatics say).

You think that life is a fire,
that progress is an eruption,

that the future is wherever
your bullet strikes.
No.

The United States is grand and powerful.
Whenever it trembles, a profound shudder
runs down the enormous backbone of the Andes.
If it shouts, the sound is like the roar of a lion.
And Hugo said to Grant: "The stars are yours."
(The dawning sun of the Argentine barely shines;
the star of Chile is rising.) A wealthy country,
joining the cult of Mammon to the cult of Hercules;
while Liberty, lighting the path
to easy conquest, raises her torch in New York.
But our own America, which has had poets
since the ancient times of Nezahualcóyolt;
which preserved the footprint of great Bacchus,
and learned the Panic alphabet once,
and consulted the stars; which also knew Atlantic
(whose name comes ringing down to us in Plato)
and has lived, since the earliest moments of its life,
in light, in fire, in fragrance, and in love—
the America of Moctezuma and Atahualpa,
the aromatic America of Columbus,
Catholic America, Spanish America,
the America where noble Cuauthémoc said:
"I am not in a bed of roses"—our America,
trembling with hurricanes, trembling with Love:
O men with Saxon eyes and barbarous souls,
our America lives. And dreams. And loves.
And it is the daughter of the Sun. Be careful.
Long live Spanish America!
A thousand cubs of the Spanish lion are roaming free.
Roosevelt, you must become, by God's own will,
the deadly Rifleman and the dreadful Hunter
before you can clutch us in your iron claws.
And though you have everything, you are lacking one thing:
God!

Document 5.2 Emiliano Zapata, *The Plan de Ayala*, 1911

Liberating Plan of the sons of the State of Morelos, affiliated with the Insurgent Army which defends the fulfillment of the Plan of San Luis, with the reforms which it has believed proper to add in benefit of the Mexican Fatherland.

We who undersign, constituted in a revolutionary junta to sustain and carry out the promises which the revolution of November 20, 1910 just past, made to the country, declare solemnly before the face of the civilized world which judges us and before the nation to which we belong and which we call [*sic, llamamos*, misprint for *amamos*, love], propositions which we have formulated to end the tyranny which oppresses us and redeem the fatherland from the dictatorships which are imposed on us, which [propositions] are determined in the following plan:

1.   Taking into consideration that the Mexican people led by Don Francisco I. Madero went to shed their blood to reconquer liberties and recover their rights which had been trampled on, and not for a man to take possession of power, violating the sacred principles which he took an oath to defend under the slogan "Effective Suffrage and No Reelection," outraging thus the faith, the cause, the justice, and the liberties of the people: taking into consideration that that man to whom we refer is Don Francisco I. Madero, the same who initiated the above-cited revolution, who imposed his will and influence as a governing norm on the Provisional Government of the ex-President of the Republic Attorney Francisco L. de Barra [*sic*], causing with this deed repeated sheddings of blood and multiplicate misfortunes for the fatherland in a manner deceitful and ridiculous, having no intentions other than satisfying his personal ambitions, his boundless instincts as a tyrant, and his profound disrespect for the fulfillment of the preexisting laws emanating from the immortal code of '57, written with the revolutionary blood of Ayutla;

      Taking into account that the so-called Chief of the Liberating Revolution of Mexico, Don Francisco I. Madero, through lack of integrity and the highest weakness, did not carry to a happy end the revolution which gloriously he initiated with the help of God and the people, since he left standing most of the governing powers and corrupted elements of oppression of the dictatorial government of Porfirio Díaz, which are not nor can in any way be the representation of National Sovereignty, and which, for being most bitter adversaries of ours and of the principles which even now we defend, are provoking the discomfort of the country and opening new wounds in the bosom of the fatherland, to give it its own blood to drink; taking also into account that the aforementioned Sr. Francisco I. Madero, present President of the Republic, tries to avoid the fulfillment of the promises which he made to the Nation in the Plan of San Luis Potosí, being [*sic, siendo*, misprint for *ciñendo*, restricting] the above-cited promises to the agreements of Ciudad Juárez, by means of false promises and numerous intrigues against the Nation nullifying, pursuing, jailing, or killing revolutionary elements who helped him to occupy the high post of President of the Republic;

      Taking into consideration that the so-often-repeated Francisco I. Madero has tried with the brute force of bayonets to shut up and to drown in blood the pueblos who ask, solicit, or demand from him the fulfillment of the promises of the revolution, calling them bandits and rebels, condemning them to a war of extermination without conceding or granting a single one of the guarantees which reason, justice, and the law prescribe; taking equally into consideration that the President of the Republic Francisco I. Madero has made of Effective Suffrage a bloody trick on the people, already against the will of the same people imposing Attorney José M. Pino Suárez in the Vice-Presidency of the Republic, or [imposing as] Governors of the States [men] designated by him, like the so-called General Ambrosio Figueroa, scourge and tyrant of the people of Morelos, or entering into scandalous cooperation with the científico party, feudal landlords, and oppressive bosses, enemies of the revolution proclaimed by him, so as to forge new chains and follow the pattern of a new dictatorship more shameful and more terrible than that of Porfirio Díaz, for it has been clear and patent that he has outraged the sovereignty of the States, trampling on the laws without any respect for lives or interests, as has happened in the State of Morelos, and others, leading them to the most horrendous anarchy which contemporary history registers.

For these considerations we declare the aforementioned Francisco I. Madero inept at realizing the promises of the revolution of which he was the author, because he has betrayed the principles with which he tricked the will of the people and was able to get into power: incapable of governing, because he has no respect for the law and justice of the pueblos, and a traitor to the fatherland, because he is humiliating in blood and fire Mexicans who want liberties, so as to please the científicos, landlords, and bosses who enslave us, and from today on we begin to continue the revolution begun by him, until we achieve the overthrow of the dictatorial powers which exist.

2. Recognition is withdrawn from Sr. Francisco I. Madero as Chief of the Revolution and as President of the Republic, for the reasons which before were expressed, it being attempted to overthrow this official.

3. Recognized as Chief of the Liberating Revolution is the illustrious General Pascual Orozco, the second of the Leader Don Francisco I. Madero, and in case he does not accept this delicate post, recognition as Chief of the Revolution will go to General Don Emiliano Zapata.

4. The Revolutionary Junta of the State of Morelos manifests to the Nation under formal oath: that it makes its own the plan of San Luis Potosí, with the additions which are expressed below in benefit of the oppressed pueblos, and it will make itself the defender of the principles it defends until victory or death.

5. The Revolutionary Junta of the State of Morelos will admit no transactions or compromises until it achieves the overthrow of the dictatorial elements of Porfirio Díaz and Francisco I. Madero, for the nation is tired of false men and traitors who make promises like liberators and who on arriving in power forget them and constitute themselves as tyrants.

6. As an additional part of the plan we invoke, we give notice: that [regarding] the fields, timber, and water which the landlords, científicos, or bosses have usurped, the pueblos or citizens who have the titles corresponding to those properties will immediately enter into possession of that real estate of which they have been despoiled by the bad faith of our oppressors, maintaining at any cost with arms

in hand the mentioned possession; and the usurpers who consider themselves with a right to them [those properties] will deduce it before the special tribunals which will be established on the triumph of the revolution.

7. In virtue of the fact that the immense majority of Mexican pueblos and citizens are owners of no more than the land they walk on, suffering the horrors of poverty without being able to improve their social condition in any way or to dedicate themselves to Industry or Agriculture, because lands, timber, and water are monopolized in a few hands, for this cause there will be expropriated the third part of those monopolies from the powerful proprietors of them, with prior indemnization, in order that the pueblos and citizens of Mexico may obtain ejidos, colonies, and foundations for pueblos, or fields for sowing or laboring, and the Mexicans' lack of prosperity and wellbeing may improve in all and for all.

8. [Regarding] The landlords, científicos, or bosses who oppose the present plan directly or indirectly, their goods will be nationalized and the two third parts which [otherwise would] belong to them will go for indemnizations of war, pensions for widows and orphans of the victims who succumb in the struggle for the present plan.

9. In order to execute the procedures regarding the properties aforementioned, the laws of disamortization and nationalization will be applied as they fit, for serving us as norm and example can be those laws put in force by the immortal Juárez on ecclesiastical properties, which punished the despots and conservatives who in every time have tried to impose on us the ignominious yoke of oppression and backwardness.

10. The insurgent military chiefs of the Republic who rose up with arms in hand at the voice of Don Francisco I. Madero to defend the plan of San Luis Potosí, and who oppose with armed force the present plan, will be judged traitors to the cause which they defended and to the fatherland, since at present many of them, to humor the tyrants, for a fistful of coins, or for bribes or connivance, are shedding the blood of their brothers who claim the fulfillment of the promises which Don Francisco I. Madero made to the nation.

11. The expenses of war will be taken in conformity with Article II of the Plan of San Luis Potosí, and all procedures employed in the revolution we undertake will be in conformity with the same instructions which the said plan determines.

12. Once triumphant the revolution which we carry into the path of reality, a Junta of the principal revolutionary chiefs from the different States will name or designate an interim President of the Republic, who will convoke elections for the organization of the federal powers.

13. The principal revolutionary chiefs of each State will designate in Junta the Governor of the State to which they belong, and this appointed official will convoke elections for the due organization of the public powers, the object being to avoid compulsory appointments which work the misfortune of the pueblos, like the so-well-known appointment of Ambrosio Figueroa in the State of Morelos and others who drive us to the precipice of bloody conflicts, sustained by the caprice of the dictator Madero and the circle of científicos and landlords who have influenced him.

14. If President Madero and other dictatorial elements of the present and former regime want to avoid the immense misfortunes which afflict the fatherland, and [if they] possess true sentiments of love for it, let them make immediate renunciation of the posts they occupy and with that they will with something staunch the grave wounds which they have opened in the bosom of the fatherland, since, if they do not do so, on their heads will fall the blood and the anathema of our brothers.

15. Mexicans: consider that the cunning and bad faith of one man is shedding blood in a scandalous manner, because he is incapable of governing; consider that his system of government is choking the fatherland and trampling with the brute force of bayonets on our institutions; and thus, as we raised up our weapons to elevate him to power, we again raise them up against him for defaulting on his promises to the Mexican people and for having betrayed the revolution initiated by him, we are not personalists, we are partisans of principles and not of men!

Mexican People, support this plan with arms in hand and you will make the prosperity and well-being of the fatherland.

Ayala, November 25, 1911
Liberty, Justice, and Law

Document 5.3 José Vasconcelos, Excerpt from *La raza cosmica* (1925).

José Vasconcelos, *The Cosmic Race/La raza cosmica: A Bilingual Edition,* translated and annotated by Didier T. Jaén, pp. 28–40. © 1979 California State University, Los Angeles (English Edition) Afterword © 1997 Johns Hopkins University Press. Reprinted with permission of Johns Hopkins University Press.

On several occasions, I have proposed this law of personal taste as the basis of all human relationships under the name of the law of the three social stages. This is not to be taken in the Comtian sense, so but much more comprehensively. The three stages indicated by this law are: The material or warlike, the intellectual or political, and the spiritual or aesthetic. They represent a process that is gradually liberating us from the domination of necessity and, step by step, is submitting all life to the superior norms of feeling and fantasy. In the first stage, only matter rules. Social groups confronting each other either fight or join one another following no other law but violence and relative power. Sometimes, they exterminate each other, or else, they celebrate agreements according to convenience or necessity. This is the way of life typical of the hordes or tribes of all races. In such a situation, the mixing of bloods has also been imposed by material power, which is the only element of cohesion in the group. There can be no selection where the strong take or reject, according to their fancy, the vanquished female.

Of course, even in this period, the instinct of sympathy beats at the core of human relationships, attracting or repelling according to that mystery we call taste, that mystery which is the secret reason for all aesthetics. However, the influence of taste does not constitute the predominant motivation in the first period, nor in the second, which is subjected to the inflexible norms of reason. Reason is also present in the first period as the origin of conduct and human actions, but it is weak, like the suppressed taste. It is not reason that decides but power, and judgment is submitted to that, usually brutal, force, and made into a slave of primitive will. Judgment, thus corrupted into cunning, debases itself in order to serve injustice. In the first period, it is not possible to work towards the cordial fusion of the races. On the one hand, because the law of violence itself, to which this period submits, excludes possibilities of spontaneous cohesion; on the other, because even geographical conditions themselves do not permit the constant communication between all peoples of the earth.

In the second period, reason tends to prevail, artfully making use of the advantages conquered by force and correcting the latter's mistakes. Boundaries are defined by treaties, and customs are organized according to laws derived from reciprocal convenience and logical thinking. Romanism is the most complete model of this rational social system, although it actually started before Rome, and still continues in this time of nationalities. In this system, racial mixing partially obeys the fancy of free instinct, exercised beneath the rigors of the social norm, but more strongly it obeys the ethical and political conveniences of the moment. In the name of morality, for instance, matrimonial ties, difficult to break, are imposed between persons who do not love each other. In the name of politics, internal and external liberties are restricted. In the name of religion, which should be sublime inspiration, dogmas and tyrannies are imposed. Each case is, however, justified with the dictates of reason, recognized as supreme in human affairs. Those who condemn racial mixture in the name of a scientific eugenics which, based on incomplete and false data, has not been able to produce valid results, also proceed according to superficial logic and questionable knowledge. The main characteristic of this second period is faith in the formula. For that reason, in every respect, this period does nothing but give norms to intelligence, limits to action, boundaries to the nation, and reins to the emotions. Rule, norm and tyranny—such is the law of the second period in which we are imprisoned and from which it is necessary to escape.

In the third period, whose approach is already announced in a thousand ways, the orientation of conduct will not be sought in pitiful reason that explains but does not discover. It will rather be sought in creative feeling and convincing beauty. Norms will be given by fantasy, the supreme faculty. That is to say, life will be without norms, in a state in which everything that is born from feeling will be right: Instead of rules, constant inspiration. The merit of an action will not be sought in the immediate and tangible results, as in the first period; nor will it be required to adapt itself to predetermined rules of pure reason. The ethical imperative itself will be surpassed. Beyond good and evil, in a world of aesthetic *pathos*, the only thing that will matter will be that the act, being beautiful, shall produce joy. To do our whim, not our duty; to follow the path of taste, not of appetite or syllogism; to live joy grounded on love—such is the third stage.

Unfortunately, we are so imperfect, that in order to attain such a godly life, it will be necessary that we previously pass through all the paths. First, the path of duty, where the lower appetites are purified and surpassed; then, the path of illusion, that stimulates the highest aspirations. Passion, which redeems lower sensuality, will come immediately afterwards. To live in *pathos*, to feel towards the world an emotion so intense that the movement of things adopts rhythms of joy is a feature of the third period. We arrive at it by letting loose the divine desire, so that it may reach, without moral and logical bridges, in one nimble leap, the realms of revelation. Such immediate intuition that jumps over the chain of sorites is an artistic gift and, being passion, goes beyond duty from the very beginning, and replaces it with exalted love. Duty and logic, it is clear, are the scaffold and the mechanics of building, but the soul of architecture is rhythm, which transcends mechanics and knows no other law but the mystery of divine beauty.

What role is played in this process by the will, that nerve of human destinies that the fourth race even deified in the intoxicating instant of its triumph? Will is power, blind power running after ambiguous ends. In the first period, it is directed by appetite which uses it for all its whims. Then, reason shines her light, the will is refrained by duty and takes shape into logical thinking. In the third period, the will is liberated, it surpasses the finite and explodes and becomes infused with a sort of infinite reality. It fills with rumors and remote purposes. Logic does not suffice and the will takes on the wings of fantasy. It sinks into the deepest and descries the highest. It expands into harmony and ascends into the creative mystery of melody. It satisfies itself and dissolves into emotion, fusing itself with the joy of the universe: It becomes passion of beauty.

If we acknowledge that Humanity is gradually approaching the third period of its destiny, we shall see that the work of racial fusion is going to take place in the Ibero-American continent according to a law derived from the fruition of the highest faculties. The laws of emotion, beauty, and happiness will determine the selection of a mate with infinitely superior results than that of a eugenics grounded on scientific reason, which never sees beyond the less important portion of the love act. Above scientific eugenics, the mysterious eugenics of aesthetic taste will prevail. Where enlightened passion rules, no correctives are necessary. The very ugly will not procreate, they will have no desire to procreate. What does it matter, then, that all the races mix with each other if ugliness will find no cradle? Poverty, defective education, the scarcity of beautiful types, the misery that makes people ugly, all those calamities will disappear from the future social stage. The fact, common today, of a mediocre couple feeling proud of having multiplied misery will seem repugnant then, it will seem a crime. Marriage will cease to be a consolation for misfortunes that need not be perpetuated, and it will become a work of art.

As soon as education and comfort become widespread, there will be no danger in the mixture of the most divergent types. Unions will be effected according to the singular law of the third period, the law of sympathy, refined by the sense of beauty; a true sympathy and not the false one that, today, necessity and ignorance impose upon us. Sincerely passionate unions, easily undone in case of error, will produce bright and handsome offspring. The entire species will change its physical makeup and temperament. Superior instincts will prevail and, in a happy synthesis, the elements of beauty apportioned today among different races will endure.

At present, partly because of hypocrisy, and partly because unions are made between miserable persons in an unfortunate state, we see with profound horror the marriage of a black woman and a white man. We would feel no repugnance at all if it were the union of a black Apollo and a blond Venus, which goes to prove that everything is sanctified by beauty. On the other hand, it is repugnant to see those married couples that come out of the judge's office or the temples. They are ugly in a proportion of, more or less, ninety percent of the cases. The world is thus full of ugliness because of our vices, our prejudices, and our misery. Procreation by love is already a good antecedent for a healthy progeny, but it is necessary that love itself be a work of art, and not the last resort of desperate people. If what is going to be transmitted is stupidity, then the ties between the parents is not love, but opprobrious and base instinct.

A mixture of races accomplished according to the laws of social well-being, sympathy, and beauty, will lead to the creation of a type infinitely superior to all that have previously existed. The crossing of opposites, according to Mendel's laws of heredity, will produce discontinuous and quite complex variations, as multiple and diverse as are the elements of human interbreeding. For this reason, such crossing is a guarantee of the limitless possibilities that a well oriented instinct offers for the gradual perfection of the species. If, until now, the human species has not improved greatly, it is because it has lived in conditions of agglomeration and misery which have made impossible the free function of the instinct of beauty. Reproduction has been accomplished in the manner of beasts, with no limit in quantity and no aspiration for improvement. The spirit has not taken part in it, but the appetite that satisfies itself whichever way it can. Thus, we are not in the position even to imagine the modalities and the effects of a series of truly inspired crossings. Unions based on the capability and beauty of the types would have to produce a great number of individuals gifted with the predominant qualities. As a result of choosing quickly, not with reflective thinking but with taste, the qualities we wish to make predominant, the selective types will gradually multiply, while the recessive types will tend to disappear. Recessive offspring would no longer unite among themselves, but in turn would go in search of quick improvement, or would voluntarily extinguish all desire of physical reproduction. The awareness of the species itself would gradually develop an astute Mendelianism, as soon as it sees itself free from physical pressure, ignorance and misery. In this way, in a very few generations, monstrosities will disappear; what today is normal will come to seem abominable. The lower types of the species will be absorbed by the superior type. In this manner, for example, the Black could be redeemed, and step by step, by voluntary extinction, the uglier stocks will give way to the more handsome. Inferior races, upon being educated, would become less prolific, and the better specimens would go on ascending a scale of ethnic improvement, whose maximum type is not precisely the White, but that new race to which the White himself will have to aspire with the object of conquering the synthesis. The Indian, by grafting onto the related race, would take the jump of millions of years that separate Atlantis from our times, and in a few decades of aesthetic eugenics, the Black may disappear, together with the types that a free instinct of beauty may go on signaling as fundamentally recessive and undeserving, for that reason, of perpetuation. In this manner, a selection of taste would take effect, much more efficiently than the brutal Darwinist selection, which is valid, if at all, only for the inferior species, but no longer for man.

No contemporary race can present itself alone as the finished model that all the others should imitate. The mestizo, the Indian, and even the Black are superior to the White in a countless number of properly spiritual capacities. Neither in antiquity, nor in the present, have we a race capable of forging civilization by itself. The most illustrious epochs of humanity have been, precisely, those in which several different peoples have come into contact and mixed with each other. India, Greece, Alexandria, Rome are but examples that only a geographic and ethnic universality is capable of giving the fruits of civilization. In the contemporary period, while the pride of the present masters of the world asserts through the mouth of their scientists the ethnic and mental superiority of the Whites from the north, any teacher can corroborate that the children and youths descendant from Scandinavians, Dutch, and English found in North American universities, are much slower, and almost dull, compared with the mestizo children and youths from the south. Perhaps this advantage is explained as the result of a beneficial spiritual Mendelianism, caused by a combination of contrary elements. The truth is that vigor is renewed with graftings, and that the soul itself looks for diversity in order to enrich the monotony of its own contents. Only a long lasting experience will be able to show the results of a mixture no longer accomplished by violence, nor by reason of necessity, but by the selection founded on the dazzling produced by beauty and confirmed by the *pathos* of love.

In the first and second periods in which we live, because of isolation and war, the human species lives to a certain extent according to Darwinist laws. The English, who see only the present in the external world, did not hesitate to apply zoological theories to the field of human sociology. If the false translation of physiological law to the realm of the spirit were acceptable, then to speak of the ethnic incorporation of the Black would be tantamount to defending retrogression. The English theory supposes, implicitly or frankly, that the Black is a sort of link nearer the monkey than the blond man. There is no other recourse, for that reason, but to make him disappear. On the other hand, the White, particularly the English-speaking White, is presented as the sublime culmination of human evolution; to cross him with another race would be equivalent to muddling his stock. Such a way of seeing things is nothing but the illusion of each fortunate people during the period of their power. Throughout history, every great nation has thought of itself as the final and chosen one. When these childish presumptions are compared with each other, one can see that the mission each nation attributes to itself is, at the bottom, nothing else but its eagerness for booty and the desire to exterminate the rival power. The official science itself is, in each period, a reflection of the pride of the dominant race. Hebrews grounded the belief in their superiority upon divine oracles and promises. The English base theirs on observations relative to domestic animals. From observations about the crossing and hereditary varieties of such animals, Darwinism gradually emerged, first as a modest zoological theory, and later as a social biology that granted the English definitive preponderance over all the other races. Every imperialistic policy needs a philosophy to justify itself. The Roman Empire proclaimed order, that is, hierarchy: First came the Roman, then his allies, and then the Barbarian under slavery. The British preach natural selection, with the tacit conclusion that world domination belongs by natural and divine right to the dolichocephalic man from the Isles and his descendants. But this science, which invaded us together with the artifacts of conquering commerce, is fought as all imperialism is fought, by confronting it with a superior science, and with a broader and more vigorous civilization. The truth is that no race suffices by itself and that humanity would stand to lose; it loses each time a race disappears by violent means. It is well and good for each race to transform itself according to its own design, but within its own vision of beauty, and without breaking the harmonious development of human elements.

Each ascending race needs to constitute its own philosophy, the *deux ex machina* of its own success. We have been educated under the humiliating influence of a philosophy conceived by our enemies, perhaps innocently if you will, but with the purpose of exalting their own goals and annulling ours. In this manner, even we have come to believe in the inferiority of the mestizo, in the unredemption of the Indian, in the damnation and the irreparable decadence of the Black. Armed rebellion was not followed by a rebellion of the consciences. We rebelled against the political power of Spain and yet did not realize that, together with Spain, we fell under the economic and moral domination of a race that has been mistress of the world since the demise of Spanish greatness. We shook off one yoke to fall under a new one. This displacement to which we fell victims could not have been avoided, even if we had been aware of it sooner. There is a certain fatefulness in the destiny of nations, as well as in the destiny of individuals, but now that a new phase of history has been initiated, it becomes necessary to reconstruct our ideology and organize our continental life according to a new ethnic doctrine. Let us begin, then, by making a new life and a new science. If we do not first liberate the spirit, we shall never be able to redeem matter.

* * *

We have the duty to formulate the basis of a new civilization, and for that very reason, it is necessary that we keep in mind the fact that civilizations cannot be repeated, neither in form nor in content. The theory of ethnic superiority has been simply a means of combat, common to all fighting peoples, but the battle that we must wage is so important that it does not admit any false trickery. We do not claim that we are, nor that we shall become, the first race of the world or the most illustrious, the strongest and the most handsome. Our purpose is even higher and more difficult to attain than temporary selection. Our values are still potential to such an extent that we are nothing yet. However, the Hebrew race was, for the arrogant Egyptians, nothing more than a miserable caste of slaves. Yet, from that race was born Jesus Christ, who announced the love of all men and initiated the greatest movement in history. This love shall be one of the fundamental dogmas of the fifth race that will be produced in America. Christianity frees and engenders life, because it contains universal, not national, revelation. For that reason, it had to be rejected by the Jews themselves, who could not decide to commune with gentiles. But America is the fatherland of gentility, the true Christian promised land. If our race shows itself unworthy of this consecrated land, if it lacks in love, it will be replaced by peoples more capable of accomplishing the fateful mission of those lands, the mission of serving as the seat for a humanity fashioned out of all the nations and all the racial stocks. The bionomy imposed by world progress on the America of Hispanic origin is not a rival creed that confronts the adversary saying: "I surpass you," or "I am self-sufficient." Instead, it is an infinite longing for integration and totality that, for the same reason, invokes the universe. The infinitude of her longing insures her strength to combat the exclusivist creed of the enemy faction and grants her confidence in victory, which always corresponds to the gentiles. The danger is rather that it may happen to us as it happened to the majority of the Hebrews, who, not wanting to become gentiles, lost the grace that originated in their midst. This may happen, if we do not learn how to offer a home and fraternity to all men. Then another people will serve as the axis, another tongue will be the vehicle, but no one can detain any longer the fusion of the races, the emergence of the fifth era of the world, the era of universality and cosmic sentiment.

The doctrine of sociological and biological formation we propose in these pages is not a simple ideological effort to raise the spirits of a depressed race by offering it a thesis that contradicts the doctrine with which its rivals wanted to condemn it. What happens is that, as we discover the falsity of the scientific premise upon which the domination of contemporary power rests, we also foresee, in experimental science itself, orientations that point the way, no longer for the triumph of a single race, but for the redemption of all men. It is as if the palingenesis announced by Christianity with an anticipation of thousands of years, would be confirmed at present by the different branches of scientific knowledge. Christianity preached love as the basis of human relations, and now it begins to be clear that only love is capable of producing a lofty humanity. The official policy and the Positivists' science, which was directly influenced by that policy, said that the law was not love but antagonism, fight, and the triumph of the fittest. However, they established no other criterion to judge fitness, but the curious begging of the question contained in that thesis itself, since the fittest is the one that triumphs, and only the fittest triumph. Thus, we can reduce to verbal formulas of this kind all the small wisdom that wanted to disassociate itself from the genial revelations, in order to substitute them with generalizations founded on the mere sum of details.

* * *

The discredit of such doctrines is aggravated by discoveries and observations that are revolutionizing the sciences today. It was not possible to combat the theory of History as a process of frivolities when it was thought that also individual life was deprived of a metaphysical end and a providential plan. But now mathematics wavers and modifies its conclusions in order to give us the concept of a moveable world, whose mystery changes according to our relative position and the nature of our concepts. Physics and chemistry no longer dare to affirm that the functions of the atom involve nothing else but the action of masses and forces. Biology also states in its new hypotheses, for example, with Uexküll, that in the course of life "cells behave as if they worked within a complete organism whose organs are harmonized according to a plan and work in conjunction, that is, they possess a functional plan . . . there being an interlocking of vital factors in the physico-chemical motor wheel"—a notion which contradicts Darwinism, at least in its interpretation by Darwinists who deny that nature obeys a plan. Mendelianism also demonstrates, according to Uexküll, that the protoplasm is a mixture of substances from which everything, more or less, can be made. Faced with all these changes in the concepts of science, it is necessary to recognize that the theoretical edifice for the domination by a single race has collapsed. This, in turn, is a forewarning that the material power of those who have produced all that false science of circumstance and conquest will not be long in falling.

Mendel's law, particularly when it confirms "the intervention of vital factors in the physico-chemical wheel," must be part of our new patriotism, because from it we can draw the conclusion that the different faculties of the spirit take part in the processes of destiny.

What does it matter if Spencerian materialism had us condemned, when today it turns out that we can see ourselves as a sort of reserve for humanity, as the promise for a future that will surpass all previous times? We find ourselves, then, in one of those epochs of palingenesis, and in the center of the universal maelstrom. It is urgent to bring to our consciousness all of our faculties in order that, alert and active, they begin to intervene right away in the process of collective redemption. This is the splendid dawn of a peerless age. One could say that it is Christianism that is going to be consummated, now not only in the souls, but at the root of beings. As an instrument for this transcendental transformation, a race has been developing in the Iberian continent; a race full of vices and defects, but gifted with malleability, rapid comprehension, and easy emotion, fruitful elements for the seminal plasma of the future species. The biological materials have already been gathered in abundance: the predispositions, the characters, the genes of which Mendelians speak. Only the organizing impulse, the plan for the formation of the species has been lacking. What should be the traits of this creative drive?

If we were to proceed according to the law of pure confused energy of the first period, according to primitive biological Darwinism, then blind force, by almost mechanical imposition of the most vigorous elements, would make the decision in a simple and brutal manner, exterminating the weak, or, properly speaking, those who do not fit into the plan of the new race. But in the new order, by its own law, the permanent elements will not support themselves on violence but on taste, and, for that reason, the selection will be spontaneous, as it is done by the artist when, from all the colors, he takes only those that are convenient to his work.

If in order to constitute the fifth race we should proceed according to the law of the second period, then a contest of craftiness would ensue, in which the astute ones and those lacking in scruples would win the game over the dreamers and the kind at heart. Probably, then, the new humanity would be predominantly Malaysian, for it is said that no one surpasses them in caution and ability, and even, if necessary, in perfidy. By the road of intelligence, one could even arrive, if you wish, at a humanity of stoics that would take duty as the supreme norm. The world would become like a vast nation of Quakers, where the plan of the spirit would end up strangled and deformed by the rule. Because reason, pure reason, may be home to all and needs all of them. Finally, in the center, a monument should have been raised that in some way would symbolize the law of the three states: The material, the intellectual and the aesthetic. All this was to indicate that through the exercise of the triple law, we in America shall arrive, before any other part of the world, at the creation of a new race fashioned out of the treasures of all the previous ones: The final race, the cosmic race.

Document 5.4   José Carlos Mariátegui, "The Problem of the Indian," from *Seven Interpretive Essays on Peruvian Reality*, 1928

Source: From *Seven Interpretive Essays on Peruvian Reality* by José Carlos Mariátegui, translated by Marjory Urquidi, copyright © 1971. By permission of the University of Texas Press.

A New Approach

Any treatment of the problem of the Indian—written or verbal—that fails or refuses to recognize it as a socioeconomic problem is but a sterile, theoretical exercise destined to be completely discredited. Good faith is no justification. Almost all such treatments have served merely to mask or distort the reality of the problem. The socialist critic exposes and defines the problem because he looks for its causes in the country's economy and not in its administrative, legal, or ecclesiastic machinery, its racial dualism or pluralism, or its cultural or moral conditions. The problem of the Indian is rooted in the land tenure system of our economy. Any attempt to solve it with administrative or police measures, through education or by a road building program, is superficial and secondary as long as the feudalism of the gamonales continues to exist.

Gamonalismo necessarily invalidates any law or regulation for the protection of the Indian. The hacienda owner, the latifundista, is a feudal lord. The written law is powerless against his authority, which is supported by custom and habit. Unpaid labor is illegal, yet unpaid and even forced labor survive in the latifundium. The judge, the subprefect, the commissary, the teacher, the tax collector, all are in bondage to the landed estate. The law cannot prevail against the gamonales. Any official who insisted on applying it would be abandoned and sacrificed by the central government; here, the influences of Gamonalismo are all-powerful, acting directly or through parliament with equal effectiveness.

A fresh approach to the problem of the Indian, therefore, ought to be much more concerned with the consequences of the land tenure system than with drawing up protective legislation. The new trend was started in 1918 by Dr. José A. Encinas in his *Contribución a una legislación tutelar indígena*, and it has steadily gained strength. But by the very nature of his study, Dr. Encinas could not frame a socio-economic program. Since his proposals were designed to protect Indian property, they had to be limited to legal objectives. Outlining an indigenous homestead act, Dr. Encinas recommended the distribution of state and church lands. Although he did not mention expropriating the land of the latifundium gamonales, he repeatedly and conclusively denounced the effects of the latifundium system and thereby to some extent ushered in the present socio-economic approach to the Indian question.

This approach rejects and disqualifies any thesis that confines the question to one or another of the following unilateral criteria: administrative, legal, ethnic, moral, educational, ecclesiastic.

The oldest and most obvious mistake is, unquestionably, that of reducing the protection of the Indian to an ordinary administrative matter. From the days of Spanish colonial legislation, wise and detailed ordinances, worked out after conscientious study, have been quite useless. The republic, since independence, has been prodigious in its decrees, laws, and provisions intended to protect the Indian against exaction and abuse. The gamonal of today, like the encomendero of yesterday, however, has little to fear from administrative theory; he knows that its practice is altogether different.

The individualistic character of the republic's legislation has favored the absorption of Indian property by the latifundium system. The situation of the Indian, in this respect, was viewed more realistically by Spanish legislation. But legal reform has no more practical value than administrative reform when confronted by feudalism intact within the economic structure. The appropriation of most communal and individual Indian property is an accomplished fact. The experience of all countries that have evolved from their feudal stage shows us, on the other hand, that liberal rights have not been able to operate without the dissolution of feudalism.

The assumption that the Indian problem is ethnic is sustained by the most outmoded repertory of imperialist ideas. The concept of inferior races was useful to the white man's West for purposes of expansion and conquest. To expect that the Indian will be emancipated through a steady crossing of the aboriginal race with white immigrants is an anti-sociological naiveté that could only occur to the primitive mentality of an importer of merino sheep. The people of Asia, who are in no way superior to the Indians, have not needed any transfusion of European blood in order to assimilate the most dynamic and creative aspects of Western culture. The degeneration of the Peruvian Indian is a cheap invention of sophists who serve feudal interests.

The tendency to consider the Indian problem as a moral one embodies a liberal, humanitarian, enlightened nineteenth-century attitude that in the political sphere of the Western world inspires and motivates the "leagues of human rights." The antislavery conferences and societies in Europe that have denounced more or less futilely the crimes of the colonizing nations are born of this tendency, which always has trusted too much in its appeals to the conscience of civilization. González Prada was not immune to this hope when he wrote that "the condition of the Indian can improve in two ways: either the heart of the oppressor will be moved to take pity and recognize the rights of the oppressed or the spirit of the oppressed will find the valor needed to turn on the oppressors." The Pro-Indian Association (1900–1917) represented the same hope, although it owed its real effectiveness to the concrete and immediate measures taken by its directors in defense of the Indian. This policy was due in large measure to the practical, typically Saxon idealism of Dora Mayer, and the work of the Association became well known in Peru and the rest of the world. Humanitarian teachings have not halted or hampered European imperialism, nor have they reformed its methods. The struggle against imperialism now relies only on the solidarity and strength of the liberation movement of the colonial masses. This concept governs anti-imperialist action in contemporary Europe, action that is supported by liberals like Albert Einstein and Romain Rolland and, therefore, cannot be considered exclusively Socialist.

On a moral and intellectual plane, the church took a more energetic or at least a more authoritative stand centuries ago. This crusade, however, achieved only very wise laws and provisions. The lot of the Indian remained substantially the same. González Prada, whose point of view, as we know, was not strictly Socialist, looked for the explanation of its failure in the economic essentials: "It could not have happened otherwise; exploitation was the official order; it was pretended that evils were humanely perpetrated and injustices committed equitably. To wipe out abuses, it would have been necessary to abolish land appropriation and forced labor, in brief, to change the entire colonial regime. Without the toil of the American Indian, the coffers of the Spanish treasury would have been emptied." In any event, religious tenets were more likely to succeed than liberal tenets. The former appealed to a noble and active Spanish Catholicism, whereas the latter tried to make itself heard by a weak and formalist criollo liberalism.

But today a religious solution is unquestionably the most outdated and antihistoric of all. Its representatives—unlike their distant, how very distant, teachers—are not concerned with obtaining a new declaration of the rights of Indians, with adequate authority and ordinances; the missionary is merely assigned the role of mediator between the Indian and the gamonal. If the church could not accomplish its task in a medieval era, when its spiritual and intellectual capacity could be measured by friars like Las Casas, how can it succeed with the elements it commands today? The Seventh-Day Adventists, in that respect, have taken the lead from the Catholic clergy, whose cloisters attract fewer and fewer evangelists.

The belief that the Indian problem is one of education does not seem to be supported by even a strictly and independently pedagogical criterion. Education is now more than ever aware of social and economic factors. The modern pedagogue knows perfectly well that education is not just a question of school and teaching methods. Economic and social circumstances necessarily condition the work of the teacher. Gamonalismo is fundamentally opposed to the education of the Indian; it has the same interest in keeping the Indian ignorant as it has in encouraging him to depend on alcohol. The modern school—assuming that in the present situation it could be multiplied at the same rate as the rural school-age population—is incompatible with the feudal latifundium. The mechanics of the Indian's servitude would altogether cancel the action of the school if the latter, by a miracle that is inconceivable within social reality, should manage to preserve its pedagogical mission under a feudal regime. The most efficient and grandiose teaching system could not perform these prodigies. School and teacher are doomed to be debased under the pressure of the feudal regime, which cannot be reconciled with the most elementary concept of progress and evolution. When this truth becomes partially understood, the saving formula is thought to be discovered in boarding schools for Indians. But the glaring inadequacy of this formula is self-evident in view of the tiny percentage of the indigenous school population that can be boarded in these schools.

The pedagogical solution, advocated by many in good faith, has been discarded officially. Educators, I repeat, can least afford to ignore economic and social reality. At present, it only exists as a vague and formless suggestion which no body or doctrine wants to adopt.

The new approach locates the problem of the Indian in the land tenure system . . . Those of us who approach and define the Indian problem from a Socialist point of view must start out by declaring the complete obsolescence of the humanitarian and philanthropic points of view which, like a prolongation of the apostolic battle of Las

Casas, continued to motivate the old pro-Indian campaign. We shall try to establish the basically economic character of the problem. First, we protest against the instinctive attempt of the criollo or mestizo to reduce it to an exclusively administrative, pedagogical, ethnic, or moral problem in order to avoid at all cost recognizing its economic aspect. Therefore, it would be absurd to accuse us of being romantic or literary. By identifying it as primarily a socio-economic problem, we are taking the least romantic and literary position possible. We are not satisfied to assert the Indian's right to education, culture, progress, love, and heaven. We begin by categorically asserting his right to land. This thoroughly materialistic claim should suffice to distinguish us from the heirs or imitators of the evangelical fervor of the great Spanish Friar, whom, on the other hand, our materialism does not prevent us from admiring and esteeming.

The problem of land is obviously too bound up with the Indian problem as to be conveniently mitigated or diminished. Quite the contrary. As for myself, I shall try to present it in unmistakable and clearcut terms.

The agrarian problem is first and foremost the problem of eliminating feudalism in Peru, which should have been done by the democratic-bourgeois regime that followed the War of Independence. But in its one hundred years as a republic, Peru has not had a genuine bourgeois class, a true capitalist class. The old feudal class—camouflaged or disguised as a republican bourgeois—has kept its position. The policy of disentailment, initiated by the War of Independence as the logical consequence of its ideology, did not lead to the development of small property. The old landholding class lost its supremacy. The survival of latifundistas, in practice, preserved the latifundium. Disentailment struck at the Indian community. During a century of Republican rule, great agricultural property actually has grown stronger and expanded, despite the theoretical liberalism of our constitution and the practical necessities of the development of our capitalist economy.

There are two expressions of feudalism that survive: the latifundium and servitude. Inseparable and of the same substance, their analysis leads us to the conclusion that the servitude oppressing the indigenous race cannot be abolished unless the latifundium is abolished.

When the agrarian problem is presented in these terms, it cannot be easily distorted. It appears in all its magnitude as a socio-economic, and therefore a political, problem, to be dealt with by men who move in this sphere of acts and ideas. And it is useless to convert it, for example, into a technical-agricultural problem for agronomists.

Everyone must know that according to individualist ideology, the liberal solution to this problem would be the breaking up of the latifundium to create small property. But there is so much ignorance of the elementary principles of socialism that it is worthwhile repeating that this formula—the breaking up of the latifundium in the favor of small property—is neither utopian, nor heretical, nor revolutionary, nor Bolshevik, nor avant-garde, but orthodox, constitutional, democratic, capitalist, and bourgeois. It is based on the same liberal body of ideas that produced the constitutional laws of all democratic-bourgeois states. In the countries of Central and Eastern Europe—Czechoslovakia, Rumania, Poland, Bulgaria, et cetera—agrarian laws have been passed limiting land ownership, in principle, to a maximum of five hundred hectares. Here, the Great War razed the last ramparts of feudalism with the sanction of the capitalist West, which since then has used precisely this bloc of anti-Bolshevik countries as a bulwark against Russia.

In keeping with my ideological position, I believe that the moment for attempting the liberal, individualist method in Peru has already passed. Aside from reasons of doctrine, I consider that our agrarian problem has a special character due to an indisputable and concrete factor: the survival of the Indian "community" and of elements of practical socialism in indigenous agriculture and life.

If those who hold a democratic-liberal doctrine are truly seeking a solution to the problem of the Indian that, above all, will free him from servitude, they can turn to the Czechoslovakian or Rumanian experience rather than the Mexican example, which they may find dangerous given its inspiration and process. For them it is still time to advocate a liberal formula. They would at least ensure that discussion of the agrarian problem by the new generation would not altogether lack the liberal philosophy that, according to written history, has governed the life of Peru since the foundation of the republic.

Colonialism-Feudalism

The problem of land sheds light on the socialist or vanguardist attitude toward the remains of the vice-royalty. Literary *perricholismo* does not interest us except as an indication or reflection of economic colonialism. The colonial heritage that we want to do away with is not really the one of romantic damsels screened from sight behind shawls or shutters, but the one of a feudal system with its gamonalismo, latifundium, and servitude. Colonial literature—nostalgic evocation of the viceroyalty and its pomp—is for me only the mediocre product of a spirit engendered and nourished by that regime. The viceroyalty does not survive in the *perricholismo* of troubadours and storytellers. It survives in a feudalism that contains the germs of an undeclared capitalism. We decry not only our Spanish but our feudal legacy.

Spain brought us the middle ages: The Inquisition, feudalism, et cetera. Later it brought us the Counter Reformation: a reactionary spirit, a Jesuit method, a scholastic casuistry. We have painfully rid ourselves of most of these afflictions by assimilating Western culture, sometimes obtained through Spain itself. But we are still burdened with their economic foundations embedded in the interests of a class whose hegemony was not destroyed by the War of Independence. The roots of feudalism are intact and they are responsible for the lag in our capitalist development.

The land tenure system determines the political and administrative system of the nation. The agrarian problem, which the republic has yet to solve, dominates all other problems. Democratic and liberal institutions cannot flourish or operate in a semi-feudal economy.

The subordination of the Indian problem to the problem of land is even more absolute, for special reasons. The Indigenous race is a race of farmers. The Inca people were peasants, normally engaged in agriculture and shepherding. The industries and arts were typically domestic and rural. The principle that life springs from the soil was truer in the Peru of the Incas than in any other country. The most notable public works and collective enterprises of Tawantinsuyo were for military, religious, or agricultural purposes. The irrigation canals of the sierra and the coast and the agricultural terraces of the Andes remain the best evidence of the degree of economic organization reached by Inca Peru. Its civilization was agrarian in all its important aspects. Valcárcel, in his study of the economic life of Tawantinsuyo, writes that "the land, in native tradition, is the common mother, from her womb come not only food but man himself. Land provides all wealth. The cult of Mama Pacha is in a part with the worship of the sun and, like the sun, Mother Earth represents no one in particular. Joined in the aboriginal ideology, these two concepts gave birth to agrarianism, which combines communal ownership of land and the universal religion of the sun."

Inca communism, which cannot be negated or disparaged for having developed under the autocratic regime of the Incas, is therefore designated as agrarian communism. The essential traits of the Inca economy, according to the careful definition of our historical process by César Ugarte, were the following:

Collective ownership of farmland by the ayllu or groups of related families, although the property was divided into individual and non-transferable lots; collective worship of waters, pasture, and woodlands by the marca or tribe, or the federation of ayllus settled around a village; cooperative labor; individual allotment of harvests and produce.

Colonization unquestionably must bear the responsibility for the disappearance of this economy, together with the culture it nourished, not because it destroyed autochthonous forms but because it brought no superior substitutes. The colonial regime disrupted and demolished the Inca agrarian economy without replacing it with an economy of higher yields. Under the indigenous aristocracy, the natives made up a nation of ten million men, with an integrated government that efficiently ruled all its territory; under a foreign aristocracy, the natives became a scattered and anarchic mass of a million men reduced to servitude and peonage.

In this respect, demographic data are the most convincing and decisive. Although the Inca regime may be censured in the name of modern liberal concepts of liberty and justice, the positive and material historical fact is that it assured the subsistence and growth of a population that came to ten million when the conquistadors arrived in Peru, and that this population after three centuries of Spanish domination had fallen to one million. Colonization stands condemned not from any abstract, theoretical, or moral standpoint of justice, but from the practical, concrete, and material standpoint of utility.

Colonization, failing to organize even a feudal economy in Peru, introduced elements of a slave economy.

For Further Reading

Belknap, Jeffrey, and Raúl Fernández (eds.). *José Martí's "Our America": From National to Hemispheric Cultural Studies.* Durham, NC: Duke University Press, 1998.

Deutsch, Sandra McGee. *Counterrevolution in Argentina, 1900–1932: The Argentine Patriotic League.* Lincoln: University of Nebraska Press, 1986.

Deutsch, Sandra McGee, and Ronald H. Dolkart (eds.). *The Argentine Right: Its History and Intellectual Origins, 1910 to the Present.* Wilmington: Scholarly Resources, 1993.

Farnsworth-Alvear, Ann. *Dulcinea in the Factory: Myths, Morals, Men, and Women in Colombia's Industrial Experiment, 1905–1960.* Durham, NC: Duke University Press, 2000.

Frías, Heriberto. *The Battle of Tomochic: Memoirs of a Second Lieutenant*. Oxford: Oxford University Press, 2006.

García Canclini, Néstor. *Hybrid Cultures: Strategies for Entering and Leaving Modernity*. Minneapolis: University of Minnesota Press, 1995.

Guy, Donna. *Sex and Danger in Buenos Aires: Prostitution, Family, and Nation in Argentina*. Lincoln: University of Nebraska Press, 1991.

Katz, Friedrich. *The Life and Times of Pancho Villa*. Palo Alto: Stanford University Press, 1998.

Klubock, Thomas. *Contested Communities: Class, Gender, and Politics in Chile's El Teniente Copper Mine, 1904–1951*. Durham, NC: Duke University Press, 1998.

Knight, Alan. *The Mexican Revolution* (2 vols.). Cambridge: Cambridge University Press, 1986.

Levine, Robert M. *Vale of Tears: Revisiting the Canudos Massacre in Northeastern Brazil, 1893–1897*. Berkeley: University of California Press, 1995.

Martí, José. *Selected Writings*. New York: Penguin Classics, 2002.

Piccato, Pablo. *City of Suspects: Crime in Mexico City, 1900–1931*. Durham, NC: Duke University Press, 2001.

Rock, David. *Authoritarian Argentina: The Nationalist Movement, Its History and Its Impact*. Berkeley: University of California Press, 1995.

Rodó, José Enrique. *Ariel*. Teddington, England: Echo Library, 2008.

Sabato, Hilda. *The Many and the Few: Political Participation in Republican Buenos Aires*. Palo Alto: Stanford University Press, 2001.

Vargas Llosa, Mario. *The War to the End of the World*. New York: Picador, 2008.

Womack, John. *Zapata and the Mexican Revolution*. New York: Vintage, 1970.

At A Glance: Economy

Economics is known as the "dismal science" largely because the measures used to evaluate economic performance are subject to a great deal of debate. Measures of economic activity are invariably imprecise, and the measures economists choose to privilege play a significant role in determining the picture that is presented (Does a soaring stock market amidst persistently high unemployment indicate a prosperous economy or a poor one?), and economies are generally so complex that economists face a great deal of difficulty in attempting to determine cause and effect. Nonetheless, certain broad measures over time do offer significant insights into the changing nature of economic activity.

We see this dilemma in **Figure C.1** and **Table C.2**. The first represents economic growth in Latin America since 1800 through a graph and offers a powerful visual impression of an economy that expanded very slowly for nearly a century, and then dramatically after 1950. Table C.2 illustrates the same figures, extended back in time to the early colonial period. As an aggregate measure, it offers little indication about how individual parts of the region performed over time, but it does offer a clearer sense of specific eras of economic growth and contraction. We see an economy that contracted in the century after the Conquest, and then doubled twice during the subsequent centuries. One of the most dramatic periods of growth actually comes between 1870 and 1913, and after 1973. Incidentally, both of those periods were characterized by increased integration in the global economy and growing inequality across the region.

Figure C.3 endeavors to complicate our understanding of the Latin American economy by exploring economic trends in the region following the first great boom of the Independence era, the Golden Age of the Export Oligarchy. It considers changes in GDP per capita comparatively from 1870 to 1940, revealing that while Latin American nations remained consistently behind the most prosperous countries of the day, they performed, on average, much like the Mediterranean countries of Europe during these years. Per capita GDP tends to be one of the best measures we have of general prosperity, because rather than measuring the economy as a whole, it takes into account both the overall population and population changes over time. While it cannot account for the distribution of the benefits of GDP (in highly unequal societies the value per capita measures are limited by vast income inequality, which does not show up in this figure), it does offer a broad measure of productivity and national wealth, and societies with high GDP per capita tend to be more prosperous as a whole.

We have here, then, a clear indicator that Latin America was not especially impoverished relative to all of Europe during this period, but also an indicator that dramatic economic growth in the region did not close the gap between Latin America and the industrialized countries of northern Europe (Britain, France, and Germany). What this means is open to speculation, but it does suggest that the industrialized countries of the North may have benefited just as much from Latin American exports as did Latin Americans.

Table C.4 adds to this with a comparative approach to GDP per capita in Latin America and elsewhere between 1900 and 1987 as it shows the vast differences in economic performance across the region over time, and how Latin American countries and the region as a whole have fared against other parts of the world, particularly Asia, the Newly Industrialized Countries (NICs) of South Korea and Taiwan, and the wealthy members of the Organization for Economic Co-operation and Development (OECD).[1] We see that on average Latin American GDP per capita increased fourfold during the twentieth century, while in the OECD countries it increased 5.6 times. The NICs saw a nine-fold increase. That said, the specific numbers show that Mexico, Brazil, and Chile vastly outperformed Argentina (which had the highest per capita income in Latin America in 1900) during the twentieth century.

Figure C.5 breaks down the contemporary economic performance of each country in the region by GDP per capita and shows the rate at which GDP per capita grew during the first decade of the twenty-first century. It also indicates regional GDP per capita growth since the 1960s and includes an indicator of the inflation rates since that time. This allows us to get somewhat closer to the way that economic growth has affected everyday life in the region in a way that is more precise than simple indicators of growth, as the impacts of growth are invariably different depending on population changes and changes in consumer prices. The impact of rapid growth can easily be nullified by a high rate of inflation or a high rate of population growth. What we see here once again is the significant variety of experiences in the region during the past decades. Interestingly, there seems to be no easy correlation between the overt ideologies of a given regime and the rate of growth.

Figure C.6 offers a final snapshot of the contemporary Latin American economy, breaking down economic activities by region. The region's economy remains diverse, ranging from mining, agriculture, and forestry, to manufacturing, tourism, and the service industry. No one economic sector seems likely to dominate the region as a whole in the twenty-first century, though extractive industries, particularly in the energy sector and mining, have clearly been the engines of economic growth in the early years of the century.

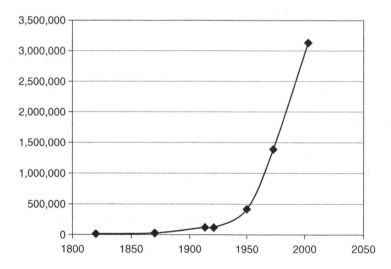

Figure C.1 GDP Growth in Latin America Since 1800 (in millions of 1990 US dollars)

Table C.2   GDP (PPP) in Millions Since 1500 (1990 dollars)

1500	7,288
1600	3,763
1700	6,346
1820	14,921
1870	27,311
1913	120,796
1921	116,277
1950	415,328
1973	1,389,460
2003	3,132,145

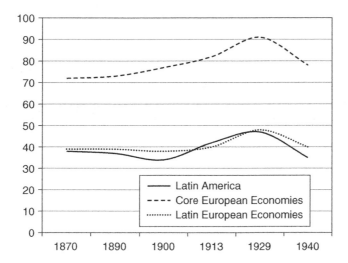

Figure C.3   Figure C.3 is a measure of GDP per capita in Latin America from 1870 to 1940. Great Britain represents 100, and are all expressed as a percentage of Britain. The solid line represents Latin America, the dashed line represents the Core European Economies (Britain, France, and Germany.), and the dotted line represents the Latin European Economies (Italy, Portugal, and Spain).

Source: Luis Bértola and Jeffrey G. Williamson, "Globalization in Latin America Before 1940," in *The Cambridge Economic History of Latin America*, Victor Bulmer-Thomas, John Coatsworth, and Roberto Cortés Conde, eds, (Cambridge: Cambridge University Press, 2006).

Table C.4   Income Per Capita, 1900–1990 (GDP per capita in 1980 international dollars)

	1900	*1913*	*1929*	*1950*	*1973*	*1987*
Argentina	1,284	1,770	2,036	2,324	3,713	3,302
Brazil	436	521	654	1,073	2,504	3,417
Chile	956	1,255	1,928	2,350	3,309	3,393
Colombia	610	801	975	1,395	2,318	3,027
Mexico	649	822	835	1,169	2,349	2,667
Peru	624	819	890	1,349	2,357	2,380
Latin American Average	760	998	1,220	1,610	2,758	3,031
Asian Average	485	539	601	505	2,061	1,952
NICs Average	492	532	690	545	1,939	4,444
OECD Average	1,817	2,224	2,727	3,553	7,852	10,205

Source: Alan M. Taylor, "Latin America and Foreign Capital in the Twentieth Century: Economics, Politics, and Institutional Change," Working Papers in Economics E-98-1, Hoover Institution, April 1998.

Note: NICs refers to Newly Industrialized Countries; in Maddison's database Taiwan and South Korea. Maddison, A. 1989. *The World Economy in the 20th Century*. Paris: OECD, cited in Taylor (1998).

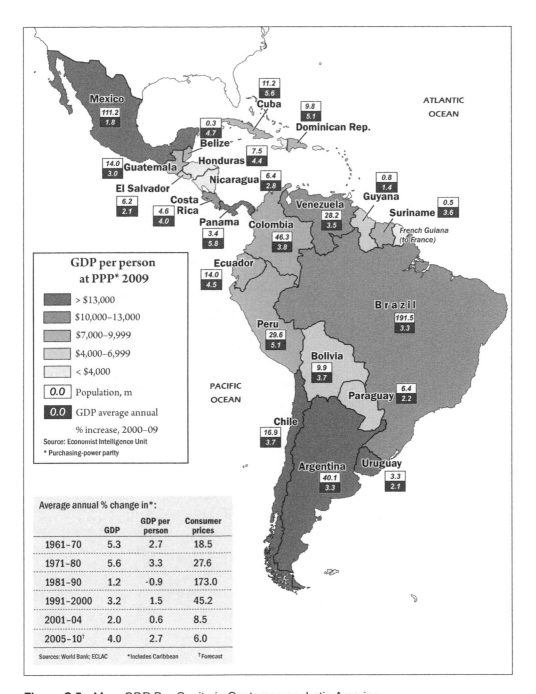

Figure C.5 Map: GDP Per Capita in Contemporary Latin America

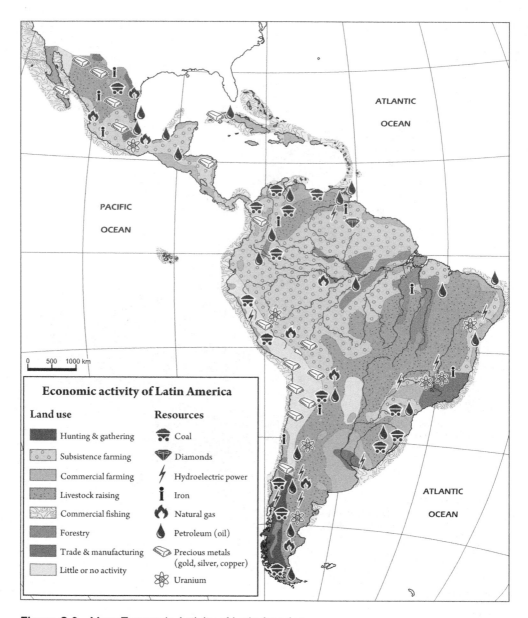

Figure C.6   Map: Economic Activity of Latin America

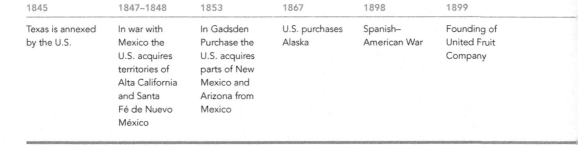

1845	1847–1848	1853	1867	1898	1899
Texas is annexed by the U.S.	In war with Mexico the U.S. acquires territories of Alta California and Santa Fé de Nuevo México	In Gadsden Purchase the U.S. acquires parts of New Mexico and Arizona from Mexico	U.S. purchases Alaska	Spanish–American War	Founding of United Fruit Company

1927	1934	1950	1954
Augusto Sandino releases his *Political Manifesto*	Sandino is killed by elements of the Nicaraguan National Guard, led by Anastasio Somoza García	Jacobo Arbenz elected president of Guatemala	Guatemalan exiles overthrow Arbenz with CIA aid

Commerce, Coercion, and America's Empire

6

1900–1901	1902	1903	1907–1909	1914	1917
Walter Reed publicizes work on Yellow Fever	Cuba adopts the Platt Amendment	U.S. government engineers Panamanian Independence	The Great White Fleet of the U.S. Navy circumnavigates the globe	Completion of Panama Canal	Puerto Ricans become U.S. citizens

"It's down that way, by the white man, who make the chicken."

While getting directions on a Kingston street one May afternoon, I was reminded of just how difficult it is to encapsulate history of United States–Latin American relations. The white man, it turned out, was Colonel Sanders, so ubiquitous in North America that today he registers simply as the cartoon icon of a fast food empire, neither "white," nor a "man." In a brief exchange, where I was asking a local man for directions, Colonel Sanders was rendered as both of those things, with a slight twist. He was not so much the unmistakable symbol of an American fast-food empire (and thus symbol of U.S. dominated global capitalism more generally) as he was a curiosity, odd enough that amidst all the landmarks on a busy street, his face stood out. Who ever heard of a white man who cooked chicken?

To be sure, we cannot be entirely certain as to why Colonel Sanders was rendered simply as the "white man, who make the chicken." The comment may have referred to his skin, his hair, his clothes, or all three, and this indeterminacy is exactly the point. The American[1] presence in Latin America is often represented in simple terms, as a violent oppressor or noble savior. These images serve immediate political interests but offer little access to larger truths. The United States has been a violent and often unwelcome presence in Latin America. The United States has also been a source of aid and investment, and the source of many of the mass cultural phenomena that shaped the region during the course of the twentieth century. Unlike the European empires of a bygone era, which were formal administrative systems founded on political, economic, and social control, the American Empire was in some ways a voluntary association, rooted in a burgeoning international mass market. The United States provided desirable objects (comestibles, modern conveniences, music, films, and television), and though they often came with asymmetrical power arrangements attached, the bargain inherent in U.S. global domination was not one sided. Recalling Colonel Sanders, we could say that just as the United States consumed the region, gobbling up its resources, land, and even its people, so too did Latin Americans consume the United States. This was the driving logic of what historians came to call the "American Century."

Here we will focus principally on American influence in Latin America in the decades prior to 1959, leaving later U.S. engagements in the region for other chapters. The temporal choice is an obvious one, bounded by the beginning of U.S. military interventions in the region and the fairly sudden change in U.S. attitudes towards Latin America that came with the Cuban Revolution. Before Fidel Castro, North Americans often saw threats coming from the south, but American hegemony (i.e., the domination of one place by another) was a more nuanced phenomenon, driven more by commercial interests than anti-communist hysteria. These were the halcyon days of American imperialism, a time when one could imagine that U.S. hegemony as not simply Great White Fleets and U.S. Marines, but as Coca Cola, jazz, baseball, and movie stars, as the things that people all over the world desired.

Empire?

We encounter our first problem with the term itself. American statesmen at the turn of the twentieth century insisted that European countries made empires, and that the United States was at its core an anti-imperialist nation. Empires were systems that linked ideological domination (often through Christian evangelism), physical domination (the mighty European military machines of the sixteenth to twentieth centuries), and economic control in formal imperial systems, governed from European capitals. Whether seen as the product of intrinsic European superiority or the outcome of brutal systems of exploitation that enriched Europeans at the expense of slaves and indigenous peoples,[2] empire was a concept that evoked Europe. By contrast the U.S. was a nation forged through anti-imperial struggle, a nation dedicated to the principles of freedom and self-determination.

As political rhetoric designed to stir patriotic feelings and win elections, the anti-imperial claim has long served its purpose within the United States As a description of actual practice, it has long been wanting. Since the very beginning, the United States has been an expansionist nation. At times, the federal government negotiated territorial acquisitions. At others, the government used American military and economic power to defend U.S. interests. Following their own historical precedents, in the early years of the nineteenth century settlers from the eastern seaboard gradually encroached on both indigenous lands and regions claimed by other European empires, moving into the Ohio Valley and Mississippi Basin, Florida, Louisiana, and other regions to the west. During the first half of the century, the United States was a generally prosperous, stable society, with an expanding population. Farm-children from the East needed land to work, and it made some sense that American expansion either came at the expense of increasingly weak European empires or nation states that were in the midst of fratricidal struggles and economic decline. North Americans fought two separate wars with Mexico, the first over Texas in 1836 (which was not technically a war with the United States) and the Mexican–American War in 1847–1848. Several years later, U.S. President Franklin Pierce bought a slice of territory from Mexican President Antonio López de Santa Anna (the Gadsden Purchase), bringing an end to the latter's iconic career. Alaska was purchased from Russia in 1867.

Viewed from the South, these wars looked like acts of imperial aggression. North Americans viewed them differently, as acts of manifest destiny, material reminders that God had given the responsibility of ruling the Americas to the United States. Moreover, these conquered territories did not become colonies. They were gradually incorporated into the United States, their residents newly minted as U.S. citizens (with all the racial and gendered caveats of the day).

These acts stand in stark contrast to American expansion elsewhere, where the racial makeup of extant populations caused American expansionists to demur on the issue of annexation. The American West, imagined as empty land, was incorporated into the political territory of the United States as a land that would, when peopled, be white. Americans viewed other regions—Mexico, Central America, and the Caribbean in particular—more skeptically, as poor racial candidates for incorporation into the United States. In a country whose self-image was anti-imperialist, there was not enough political will to colonize these places, yet the United States did need to dominate these regions if it was to become a global power. Though suspect in human terms, these countries had the raw materials American factories needed, were ideal markets for American exports, and were ideal jumping off points for American aspirations to global military power.

Two military conflicts at the turn of the twentieth century signaled the moment when U.S. military power and colonial aspirations coincided. The first was the Spanish–American War. The pretexts for the war (the protection of American lives, retaliation for the sinking of the *Maine*) were quickly overshadowed when, in the aftermath of a quick defeat of Spanish forces in Cuba, Puerto Rico, and the Philippines, the U.S. government demanded the transfer of the remaining fragments of the Spanish Empire to American control. In the Philippines this meant the United States would be the military overlord, reserving the right to dominate politically and economically. In Puerto Rico it meant a quasi-colonial status under which islanders would eventually receive U.S. citizenship in 1917. In Cuba, it meant the Platt Amendment, which gave the United States the right to meddle in the internal affairs of the island, to control its foreign policy, and the right to maintain a military base on the island (Guantánamo Bay). American forces did not depart the island until the Platt Amendment was incorporated into the 1902 Cuban constitution, and it remained the law of the land until it was abrogated in 1934 (see the Platt Amendment on the book's website: www.routledge.com/textbooks/dawson).

The second military conflict that signaled U.S. ascendance was the War for Panamanian Independence in 1903. After the acquisition of California in 1848, American businessmen and filibusterers spent decades embroiled in the internal affairs of several Central American countries (particularly Nicaragua) as they tried to secure the construction of a canal across the isthmus. Panama was not a viable option because the French Panama Canal Company already had a contract with the Colombian government to construct a canal in the region. Only in 1893, after the French Company ran out of money and abandoned the project, did the U.S. government and U.S. investors turn their sights on what seemed the most viable spot for constructing a canal. When the U.S. government offered to take over the project and Bogotá refused to agree to the terms offered, President Roosevelt threw his support behind a group of conservative landowners who had long favored Panamanian independence from Colombia. After a short conflict, Panamanian independence was won.

Roosevelt then undertook negotiations for the construction of a canal with the Panamanian Ambassador to the United States, the French engineer and canal booster, Phillipe-Jean Bunau Varilla. In return for an initial payment of $10 million and annual rent of $250,000 the resulting agreement (the Hay-Bunau Varilla Treaty) gave the United States rights to a Canal Zone that extended five miles on either side of the proposed canal in perpetuity. Work was resumed on the canal in 1904, and the 48-mile-long canal was completed in 1914.

The cost of the project was enormous, measured both in dollars and human lives. The U.S. government spent a total of $375 million to build the canal, and at times employed nearly 50,000 workers in the construction process. More than 27,500 people died during construction, though only 5,609 of them died in the ten-year period during which the United States government oversaw construction.

The fact that the United States saw many fewer deaths than the French even as they undertook the bulk of the work in constructing the canal speaks to the complex ways in which modernization and American power were linked. Most of those who died as the canal was built were victims either of yellow fever or malaria. These diseases had long been endemic to the Caribbean, taking thousands of lives annually. They limited the ability of European powers to rule outside of temperate zones, killing soldiers and administrators indiscriminately, and crippling colonial armies (the French faced enormous challenges in trying to control Mexico during the 1860s in part because of their high casualty rate due to yellow fever). Locals who survived their bouts with yellow fever emerged with some immunity. Malaria could strike the same person repeatedly. Not knowing the exact causes of these illnesses, most doctors simply tried to isolate patients in hospitals.

In 1881 a Cuban doctor and etymologist named Carlos Finley discovered that the vector for yellow fever was the Stegomyia Fasciata mosquito, an insect that could be found abundantly in the cisterns, sewage canals, cesspools, and other sources of open water that surrounded urban areas. His discovery gained little international attention until U.S. soldiers stationed in Cuba after the Spanish–American war began to suffer high casualty rates from yellow fever. Major Walter Reed, a doctor in the U.S. army, was sent to Cuba to investigate the epidemic, and after coming across Finlay's findings and testing them, he concluded that mosquitoes were indeed the cause of the malady. Reed recommended a series of measures that were carried out immediately in Havana. The incidence of yellow fever in the city fell from 1,400 in 1900 to 37 in 1901.

The new measures to combat yellow fever, which included putting screens on dwellings, fumigating houses, providing running water, building sewer systems, and putting oil or kerosene in all sources of standing water, had a dramatic impact on the canal project. The last case of yellow fever in Panama was reported in 1905. Malaria rates also fell after officials cut back the vegetation near work areas and housing, drained swamps, built ditches, and introduced larvae-eating minnows into the water supply.

The lives that were saved by these innovations were critical to American hegemony in the Americas, first in the form of the workers who constructed the infrastructures that allowed the United States to extend its military and commercial reach (the Panama Canal, after all, allowed both the U.S. Navy and U.S. merchant shipping newfound mobility), and later as workers in American-owned firms and consumers of U.S. exports. The value of American investment in the region, which jumped from around $308 million in the 1897 to $2 billion by 1929, spoke to that reach. Those investments needed to be safeguarded, making it likely that U.S. military capabilities would be brought to bear to defend U.S. interests in the region with some frequency.[3]

Table 6.1 offers a stark example of the implications of U.S. hegemony for Latin America. While for the most part the U.S. did not create formal apparatuses of imperialism (with the notable exceptions of Puerto Rico, Guantánamo Bay, and Panama), U.S. forces intervened in Latin America on dozens of occasions in the years after the Spanish–American War. These interventions created a permanent U.S. military presence in the region, either through ongoing occupations or through the threat of future invasions. Unlike formal empires, American officials foresaw an end to each occupation, and were invariably committed to training U.S.-friendly security forces that would permit their withdrawal. Like formal empires, U.S. occupations sometimes lasted for decades, creating a sense of their own permanence.

The sheer number of interventions suggests an American military with vast reach and aspirations. Close scrutiny reveals something else. For the most part United States interventions in Latin America were limited to the relatively small nations of the Caribbean. When the United States took on larger nations, the results were not always favorable. General John Pershing's "Punitive Expedition" in Mexico (March 1916 to February 1917) was a case in point. Sent across the border to capture Pancho Villa, who had the temerity to attack Columbus, New Mexico, the expedition returned home demoralized, its objectives unmet.

Pershing's failures revealed the limits of U.S. military capabilities. Mexico proved too great a challenge for a state that was not prepared to embrace total war. It was instead in the smaller countries of the Caribbean and Central America where American officials could flex their military muscles in the support of U.S. foreign policy without putting the country as a whole on a war footing. American investors in these countries often looked to the United States when their interests were threatened, but so too did many in the struggling middle classes and landed elites. American military power was a useful tool in their struggles against workers, peasants, and the political left, and they regularly aligned themselves with foreign investors in demanding U.S. intervention in the name of protecting lives, property, and order.

In the short run, these interventions had the effect of ensuring U.S. domination and protecting foreign economic interests. In the long run, they produced a series of distortions that have had lasting impacts on both the United States and the countries where U.S.

Table 6.1   U.S. military interventions in Latin America, 1898–1959

Country	Date
Cuba	1898–1902
Puerto Rico	1898–
Nicaragua	1898
Nicaragua	1899
Honduras	1903
Dominican Republic	1903–1904
Cuba	1906–1909
Nicaragua	1907
Honduras	1907
Panama	1908
Nicaragua	1910
Honduras	1911
Cuba	1912
Panama	1912
Honduras	1912
Nicaragua	1912–1933
Mexico	1913
Dominican Republic	1914
Mexico	1914–1918
Haiti	1914–1934
Dominican Republic	1916–1924
Cuba	1917–1933
Panama	1918–1920
Honduras	1919
Guatemala	1920
Costa Rica	1921
Panama	1925
El Salvador	1932
Uruguay	1947
Puerto Rico	1950
Guatemala	1954
Panama	1958

Source: Marc Becker, www2.truman.edu/~marc/resources/interventions.html

forces intervened. The figures propped up by American interventions, including the Somo-zas in Nicaragua, the Duvaliers in Haiti, and Fulgencio Batista in Cuba, could stand as the ultimate rogue's gallery of twentieth-century autocrats, violent men who depended on U.S. backing to defend elite interests and allow them to strip their countries of billions in wealth. Their foes, including Augusto Sandino, Fidel Castro, and Jean-Bertand Aristide either led or inspired movements that caused enough trouble for the U.S. to make one won-der if the costs of supporting the dictators might have outstripped the benefits. Even more, in the case of people like Castro, one could easily argue that the cost was not only paid by U.S. interests in Latin America; it was also borne by a political system that to this day suffers from a series of distortions that can be traced back to U.S. support for Batista (namely, the outsized role that Cuba plays in U.S. elections). Thus is the convoluted tale of a century of U.S. intervention in Latin America.

Bananas Are Our Business

There are very few commodities that explain American interests in Central America and the Caribbean as powerfully as the banana, a fruit that is infertile, highly vulnerable to disease, and delicious. North American consumers were first introduced to bananas in 1870, and quickly developed a strong attachment to them. By 1914 almost every American household could afford bananas, at least once in a while, and consumers in the United States purchased 45 million bunches per year. Though they would not grow in the United States, bananas were easily cultivated in Central America. This attracted even more North American capital to a region already coveted for its sugar, coffee, and potential for a canal.

Looking to dominate this emerging business, a group of North American plantation and railroad entrepreneurs created the United Fruit Company (UFCO) in 1899. At its founding the UFCO immediately became the largest banana company in the world, with plantations in Colombia, Costa Rica, Cuba, Jamaica, Nicaragua, Panama, and the Dominican Republic. The company had a fleet of ships (forty-one by 1912) that handled a booming two-way trade. Bananas came north, and construction materials and merchandise traveled south. The UFCO also controlled hundreds of miles of railroad in the Caribbean, employed tens of thousands of workers, and operated stores, schools, hospitals, radio stations, breweries, banks, and hotels.

United Fruit was a model for the modern, vertically integrated corporation. Bananas grown on UFCO plantations were transported on roadways and railroads the company built and owned to its own ports (UFCO essentially owned Puerto Barrios in Guatemala). The UFCO's Great White Fleet would then transport the bananas to the United States, where they would ripen artificially in UFCO-owned warehouses before distribution to wholesalers and supermarkets. This system gave the UFCO a degree of market domination that, over time, allowed the company to eliminate smaller producers in most places, and act as the principal employer in large parts of Central America, the Caribbean, and Colombia. While most scholars today reject the idea that the UFCO controlled enclaves (geographically, economically, and socially cut off from other parts of the country), its presence in some regions was overwhelming.

The unique characteristics of the banana facilitated this type of integration. Bananas are descended from a plant that grew wild many thousands of years ago in Oceania, spreading slowly across Asia and into Africa by the beginning of the Common Era (AD). Over many generations, banana growers tinkered with the plant's characteristics, turning a rather bitter fruit that was difficult to eat into the commodity we know today. Genetic modifications ultimately produced a fruit with a tough exterior that protects the inner fruit, and which needs to be cultivated because it cannot regenerate naturally. Modern bananas do not ripen on the branch. They require human intervention in order to be palatable.

The Gros Michel, the most important banana of the early twentieth century, could withstand schooner travel because it grew in very large bunches that did not protrude outwards, and ripened very slowly, allowing significant quantities of product to be transported to North American markets without spoiling. The Gros Michel's principal drawback was that it was susceptible to Panama disease, which could easily wipe out entire plantations (a problem that became more acute after most production was turned over to this variety). Because of this, the UFCO and its competitors claimed that they needed to keep millions of acres of potential plantation tracts in reserve. These lands could be colonized in the event of blight at existing plantations.[4]

Work in the banana business was arduous, a never ending process of cultivating existing plants and clearing land for new plantings, invariably done within a malarial environment. Cultivation, processing, and harvesting required a constant influx of migrant labor, workers who moved along labor circuits in the Caribbean by the tens of thousands. Living in company housing, workers earned meager wages, were away from their families for months or years at a time, and often found themselves in communities where they did not speak the local language. The standard dilemmas faced of these types of communities— alcohol abuse, prostitution, and violence—were common to banana zones.

These conditions lent themselves to charges that the UFCO was an agent of imperialism, especially in the case of Guatemala. Thanks to a close relationship between oligarchical interests in Guatemala and the UFCO, the company developed a dominant position in the country shortly after it was incorporated. In 1901 Guatemalan President Manuel Estrada Cabrera gave the UFCO a monopoly over the country's banana business, and promised the company veto power over legislation that might affect it adversely. In return the UFCO promised to turn hitherto unproductive lands (at least in the eyes of the state, if not those of the peasants who occupied those lands) into sources of national wealth, enriching its Guatemalan partners and the politicians who defended the company's interests.

Guatemalans responded to the pact between local elites and the UFCO in a variety of ways. Workers sometimes chafed at their conditions and pay, but were often cognizant that the opportunities afforded by the UFCO were better than those from any other employer. For some in the middle class and elites, the benefits bestowed on the country by its association with the UFCO seemed substantial enough to outweigh the costs. Material wealth, public services and infrastructure spawned by the UFCO seemed to promise a future that was better than the past.

Others took a more cynical view of the UFCO, concluding that even if the company acted only in its own interests, the individual benefits gained by playing along with the company outweighed the risks of resistance. Still others however, viewed the total domination of Guatemalan society by a single foreign company and industry with distaste, chafing at the loss of national sovereignty and deep inequalities that characterized their country under the UFCO. The Guatemalan government, like other Caribbean banana republics, was repressive, undemocratic, and beholden to the company. Here as elsewhere, guerrillas, political activists, and intellectuals called for an end to UFCO domination as early as the 1920s.[5]

The first serious signs of trouble for the banana pact came in 1944 when a military conspiracy led by Juan José Arévalo overthrew the government of Jorge Ubico. The junior officers who organized the coup did not simply seize power for themselves. They had visions of transforming Guatemala into a more democratic and equal society, a society less dominated by the logics of the banana republic. Looking on their country, the revolutionaries of 1944 saw a profoundly unequal society. Two percent of the population owned 72 percent of agricultural land. Rural poverty was extreme, and getting worse as coffee and banana cultivation spread. The political system they inherited was a simple appendage to the inequalities in the land tenure system, and lacked anything that resembled democratic practice.

Arévalo distinguished himself from previous politicians by insisting that the coup be followed by a democratic election, which he won in December 1944. He took office in 1945 for a five-year term. While in office Arévalo passed some minor reforms, but was reluctant to directly confront the power of the UFCO. The same could not be said for Jacobo Arbenz Guzmán, who was elected in 1950 to succeed Arévalo with 65 percent of the national vote. Though Arbenz was a committed anti-communist, he believed that some of Guatemala's wealth had to be redistributed if the country was to escape its desperate poverty and inequality. As the largest landowner in the country, the UFCO would need to make some sacrifices.

Arbenz faced a difficult task in his effort to push back against the UFCO and its local allies. The company was implacably hostile to all reform efforts, and would do almost anything to protect its interests. And by any measure, these interests were vast. The company owned 42 percent of the land in Guatemala. It owned the nation's railroad system, along with the utility that provided electricity to the Guatemala City (the capital). Even though it was the largest business in the country, the UFCO paid almost no taxes or duties to the government. If its capacity to paralyze the national economy, transportation, and power grids was not enough to ward off any threats, it could also count on the support of the U.S. government in battling its enemies.

Between 1944 and 1950 Arévalo maintained cordial, if strained, relations with the United States. Arbenz however, immediately drew the ire of the U.S. upon taking office. Within months of assuming the presidency he legalized the Communist Party, and threatened to expropriate the UFCO's railroads (International Railroads of Central America—IRCA). In response, the U.S. government announced a plan to implement trade sanctions and launched a propaganda war depicting Arbenz as threat to American national security. The U.S. government likely assumed that even the threat of sanctions would force Arbenz to backtrack, because at the time 85 percent of Guatemala's foreign trade was with the United States. Sanctions could rapidly cripple the country.

The threat did not work. To the contrary, in 1952 Arbenz undertook his most radical steps, introducing an Agrarian Reform Law called "Plan 900." The law allowed the government to expropriate unused land from large estates and redistribute it to peasants. Landowners would be compensated with twenty-five-year bonds that paid 3 percent interest, and compensation would be based on the value of the land as assessed in 1952 tax declarations.[6] It was a bold maneuver, aimed at creating a new political constituency for the regime. If it worked, it would also shift some production away from export commodities and towards staple crops.

The UFCO, which in 1952 cultivated only 139,000 acres of its 3 million acres of property in the country, lost 234,000 acres as a result of the law. Worse still for the company, the government offered only $1 million in compensation for the confiscated lands, basing the offer on the company's own tax filings, which were widely known to significantly undervalue their land.

The UFCO adopted multiple strategies to fight expropriation. First, they insisted that if they were to lose the land they should receive at least $16 million, as that was the fair value of the land. They also argued that the nature of banana cultivation should leave them exempt from seizure, because the threat of Panama disease meant that they might have to abandon their current plantations at any time. Without their reserves, they could be forced out of business, and this would be disastrous for everyone.

The company also launched a propaganda campaign against the government. Company spokesmen in the United States warned the American public of the threat emerging in Guatemala. Working in concert with their supporters in the Eisenhower administration, company officials called Arbenz a communist, evoking images of the Soviet Union gaining a foothold in America's backyard. For a country in the midst of the McCarthy-era Red Scare, the potential threat emerging in Guatemala seemed very real. Americans feared nuclear war (Stalin exploded an atom bomb in 1949), the Maoist revolution in China, and the ever present threat of a fifth column inside the United States, and the image of a communist Central American dictator threatening American freedom played very well at home. It was still early in the cold war, and millions of Americans genuinely believed that the dominoes were falling in their direction.[7] Naturally, it did not hurt that two key administration figures, Secretary of State John Foster Dulles and CIA director Allen Dulles, had close ties to the UFCO.[8]

U.S. officials began plotting the overthrow of Arbenz as early as 1952. The CIA played a particularly important role in the plans, establishing training camps for a rebel invasion on UFCO-owned lands in Honduras. When, U.S. officials learned that Arbenz had begun to import weapons from the Soviet bloc in May 1954, the CIA sprang into action with Operation PBSUCCESS. On June 17 a small rebel force under the command of Colonel Carlos Castillo Armas invaded the country, relying on arms, intelligence, aircraft, and an information blitz (radio broadcasts, overstating the size and power of the rebels, phone calls threatening enemies with death, etc.) provided by the CIA. On June 25 the army abandoned Arbenz without having suffered a major defeat. He resigned and fled to Mexico two days later.[9]

If ever there was a case for arguing that a specific result was over-determined, Arbenz' fall offers such an opportunity. Close business ties between UFCO and the administration, CIA fears of growing Soviet influence, anxiety about the potential success of socialist reforms, and the U.S. government's inability to distinguish nationalism from communism all worked against Arbenz. He was popular, to be sure, but this alone could not guarantee his survival.

Arbenz may have mistaken popular support for strength. In Latin America political leaders with strong regional bases, support from the military, and connections to allies outside their country have historically been better positioned than those who are simply popular in the broad sense. This is especially true for reformist regimes, and in particular those that position themselves as representatives of marginalized groups. Arbenz was a well-loved president, but he faced powerful enemies in the UFCO and its supporters (middle level managers, businessmen who profited from their connections to the company, anti-communists, and large portions of the military). Any democratic reformer would be hard pressed to prevail against such an array of adversaries.

Cultures of Consumption

It is difficult to misinterpret the meaning of a soldier pointing a rifle at your head, a foreign warship commanding your harbor, or bombs raining from the sky above you. U.S. military interventions are typically explained to North American audiences as exercises in the spread of democracy, but to the victims of those interventions American militarism means the naked use of violence in the defense of U.S. interests. The UFCO, working with the CIA, orchestrated the overthrow of Jacobo Arbenz and the installment of a friendly government in June 1954. These are facts that describe a series of events that took place over several days. In very short order, they left an indelible impression across the region. Outright opposition to U.S. interests means war; a war that democratic regimes like Guatemala's could not expect to win. Those committed to a radical path would need to adopt other means to resist U.S. military power.

Because they are so cataclysmic, so powerfully divisive, we might be inclined to see the totality of the U.S. role in Latin America through these military interventions. To do so however, is to miss out on the myriad other ways that the United States factored into everyday life in this region during the twentieth century. As the United States gradually supplanted Great Britain as the most important investor and trading partner in Latin America, American capital, innovations, and popular culture gradually became ubiquitous presences. Every day millions of people went to work for companies that were based in or did business with the United States. Millions more purchased products, heard sounds, saw images, or felt desires that linked them to their northern neighbor.

For the remainder of this chapter, we set aside the story of military domination and explore the more ambiguous story of the cultural flows that shaped both Latin America and the United States during the twentieth century. In the South the United States generated contradictory feelings and sensibilities. It was the home of the tourists who came to your cities, ruins, and beaches; tourists who often acted in boorish and disrespectful ways. It was the country of cold Anglo-Saxons, hard-hearted, rational people who had become rich because they lacked the passions and *joie de vivre* of their southern neighbors. It was a land of little culture, a land where diversity (indigenous peoples, Africans) was crushed instead of embraced. And still, it was the land of the future, of new things, of freshly unwrapped cellophane. It was a land of industrial invention, the best, largest, and fastest cars, trains, airplanes, and ships. It was the land of unimagined scientific innovation, of great cities, of foods and drinks that possessed properties never before imagined. And it was the land of glamorous movie stars, people so beautiful and wealthy that it was difficult to watch them without feeling a desire to be them, to be like them, or be with them.

During the twentieth century, American products and the aura of progress and wealth that they embodied circulated throughout Latin America. Jazz, baseball, Coca-Cola, and movie stars were among the early American icons in the region,[10] to be later supplemented by radio, television, and fast-food. Though objects of mass production and intended for a mass market, they were anything but one-size-fits-all impositions on a foreign consumer. American products found markets by marrying what was appealing in the foreign (its newness, its association with wealth and modernity) to what was appealing in the local (specific and often long-standing tastes and desires).

This goal was accomplished by making American products through local partnerships, and modifying them slightly to suit local tastes. Brands as varied as Budweiser, Coca-Cola, and Elvis Presley were recast to represent amalgams of North American modernity and specific Latin American sensibilities. In each instance American firms needed to find the right mixture, which they often did by manufacturing products locally and linking them to distinct regional symbols, while retaining the qualities that made their products more desirable, more modern. Take the advertisement reproduced as Figure 6.1, selling cigarettes made by the British American Tobacco Company, which was one of a series of ads that appeared in the Mexico City newspaper *El Universal* in late December 1949.[11]

Figure 6.1   Belmont Cigarettes magazine ad

Source: *El Universal*, December 22, 1949

The advertisement links a number of powerful images: the cigarette with the foreign name, the ubiquitous *Hecho en Mexico* symbol, the chocolate of the ancient Aztecs, and industrialization. It is accompanied by the following text:

> As an authentically Mexican product, our original "chocotl-atl" has been a globally important source of nutrition for centuries. And when it comes to satisfying the intelligent smoker, Belmont does the same for cigarettes. That is why, just as with the sweet smelling tablet of exquisite chocolate, we take great pride and satisfaction in our right to imprint the unmistakable red BELMONT package with the "Made in Mexico" seal.

We see here the complex alchemy of the foreign and the national that informed the new American empires. A British–American cigarette was appealing in part because it was a foreign cigarette. People who smoked Belmonts demonstrated that they could afford something more expensive, more classy than a local brand. Beyond this, tobacco evoked a combination of a particular national past and the universal industrial present, much in the way that chocolate also spoke to a mixture of the local and the universal. And like other advertisements in the series, which linked Belmont to the Mexican film industry, Mexican ceramics, and the revolutionary muralists, the advertisement ties Belmont to the industrial workers who produced chocolate, cigarettes, and revolutionary culture. If the people who produced the national treasures smoked Belmonts, why wouldn't you?

Cartoon Figures

Such were the complexities of the cultural flows that characterized the early decades of the "American Century." Objects—a cigarette, a drink, a movie star—acquired complex meanings within a series of asymmetrical exchanges. And interestingly, no object was more ambiguously woven into these exchanges than the banana, the commodity with which we began this story. For more than a century, bananas have signaled the tropical essence of their place of origin. Even today, when we peel the label off our Chiquita banana (for the record, it is now a Cavendish and not a Gros Michel), we come face to face with the image of Carmen Miranda. In our memory she is a sultry Latin belle, sexually inviting, colorfully dressed, her head adorned with tropical fruit (Figure 6.2).

Stereotypes are funny things. They can silence and marginalize individuals and groups, but they can also be quite useful, even for those who are stereotyped. For groups, stereotypes provide symbols that members may rally around in order to feel a sense of belonging. They can be comical signs of that group identity, points of departure for laughter as the collective chortles, "oh, that is us." Bananas and banana culture formed a part of this for tropical Latin Americans. The banana was a symbol (however skewed) of a tropical culture that stood as an alternative to the alienated industrial lifestyles of the North. Banana cultures were typified by sensuous women, men who played romantic tunes on their guitars, people who drank strong drink on their verandas, overlooking verdant palm forests, white-sand beaches, and clear blue waters. This was the image that Miranda parleyed into global fame. Truly an amalgam, this Portuguese-born woman gained fame as a samba star, capitalizing on a genre that appropriated the dress and music of the Afro-Brazilian *favela* (slum).

Figure 6.2 Carmen Miranda
Source: © Hulton-Deutsch Collection/CORBIS

Miranda first gained national attention in Brazil in the documentary film *A Voz Do Carnaval* in 1933. This led to the feature film *Alo, Alo, Brazil* in 1935, which made her into one of the biggest stars in the country. By the late 1930s, she was also garnering attention outside of Brazil. Miranda was cast in several Hollywood pictures, including *Down Argentine Way* (1940), *That Night in Rio* (1941), and *The Gang's All Here* (1943). By then Miranda had made it in Hollywood, and for much of the rest of her career she would pay relatively little attention to the Brazilian music and film industry.

Like artists all over the world who have moved to centers of creative energy and financial power, Miranda chose Hollywood over Rio. And like partners and friends left behind by their former collaborators all over the world in these moments, Miranda's former colleagues viewed her choice with a mixture of pride and resentment. That she made it at all spoke volumes to the quality of the cultural scene she left behind. That she left them behind was a reminder that the United States had the capacity to lure away Brazil's most powerful stars, to in effect consume both Brazilian music and its producers. It is a reminder that individually Brazilians are as good as anyone, but that collectively they are second class. Tellingly, the more Miranda became an international star, the more she faced scorn in her own country as a sell-out.

Local bitterness over her international stardom was complicated by the fact that others in Brazil continued to benefit from her fame even after she left. Brazilian musicians and singers developed international audiences. The samba grew more popular as a national art form in Brazil. American tourists were drawn both to Rio de Janeiro and to other tropical paradises in search of the sensual mystique she embodied. Carmen Miranda, Dolores Del Rio (who in fact played a Brazilian in Thornton Freelan's 1933 film *Flying Down to Rio*), and a host of other beautiful Latin American women profited from these exchanges, along with the hotel operators, musicians, vendors, and others who earned livings from the monetization of a stereotype. What is not certain is whether or not the benefits invariably outweighed the costs.

One of the most obvious costs came in the ways that particular cultures and individuals were flattened into a single image of Latin American sensuality for a global audience. That Dolores Del Rio (a legendary Mexican actress) could play a Brazilian quite seamlessly in an American movie represented an odd sort of affront to both Brazilians and Mexicans. It was the 1930s version of the Italian American actor Al Pacino playing a Cuban mobster in 1983's *Scarface* (his accent almost as dreadful as Marlon Brando's in *Mutiny on the Bounty*), a film that trafficked in disturbing stereotypes about Cuba. Yet if Pacino's Tony Montana was an anti-hero, Dolores del Rio and Carmen Miranda served more as objects of desire, place holders for North American fantasies and easily exchanged. Indeed, interchangeability has played significant part in the memories that North American audiences have of Carmen Miranda. When asked, many Americans of a certain age remember incorrectly that Miranda starred in a Disney cartoon, *The Three Caballeros*, released during 1945.[12] It was in fact her sister Aurora who starred in the film that introduced a generation of American children to the global South.

It may be somehow fitting that one of the most enduring symbols we have of the United States presence in Latin America during the first half of the twentieth century is a Disney cartoon. Perhaps more than any other company, Disney created products that were both globally popular, and indisputably associated with the United States (even if some Disney images were German before they were American). *The Three Caballeros*, along with 1943's *Saludos Amigos*,[13] captured a great deal of what was at stake in the emergence of the United States as a global power during the twentieth century. Walt Disney made the films at the conclusion of a goodwill tour of Latin America, which he took at the request of the Coordinator of Inter-American Affairs at the U.S. State Department. The trip was part of a larger effort by the U.S. government and American business interests to build friendly and supportive relationships with their Latin American neighbors; relationships that would favor both commerce and security. In the resulting films, we see Disney animators and their creations traveling to Latin America and becoming entranced by the cultures, geography, and mysteries of the region.

Reading these films is not as easy as it may seem. The cultural critic could easily jump on the gendered and racializing practices in the texts. Donald Duck, the American tourist, is taken on a wild ride through an exotic and titillating world by the gun-toting Mexican Panchito Pistoles and the sophisticated but androgynous Carioca Joe. Donald falls head over heels for Aurora Miranda. He is induced into a hallucinogenic stupor by her beauty (or perhaps, somebody put something in his drink?). Elsewhere in these films Goofy (at the very least a figure who evokes a racial stereotype in the U.S.) is made into an Argentine gaucho, his performance suggesting a degree of rusticity that would have made Sarmiento proud. The Andes are rendered as a terrifying, mystical place, cut off from Western civilization, and best avoided through the modern wonder of the airplane (Disney's little Pedro).

American audiences have loved these films for generations. They no doubt enjoy the humor, the music, the aesthetically pleasing quality of the cartoons, and probably the stereotypes (is Goofy not like some version of the Appalachian hick, or the southern sharecropper?). Interestingly, it appears that Latin American audiences have also long loved these movies as well. Both movies were quite successful in Latin America, and even debuted in Latin America before being released in the United States. Both have also had a long afterlife in the region.

How do we explain this? We might begin by remembering that different audiences often view the same film in distinct ways. Would Latin Americans have laughed at the bumbling fool Donald, easily tricked by his Latin American hosts, always lost, never quite at ease in a foreign land? Would they have been comforted by the fact that Joe and Panchito were much more in charge, much more in command of their faculties, than Donald? Would they have enjoyed the pleasing quality of the cartoons, and laughed at the stereotypes of themselves in the films because, after all, a cartoon by its very nature is a caricature, and these ones were funny? Given their own tendency to view the countryside as racially inferior, would urban Argentines have recognized their own stereotypes of the gaucho in Goofy? Would they have been happy to see beautiful images of their modern cities in the films, images that contrasted with the ways Americans often represented their countries? Did they like the films simply because Donald was already a huge draw for Latin American audiences? We do not know.

What we do know is that these films, like Carmen Miranda, like the banana, constituted part of the terrain on which United States–Latin American relations were negotiated during the twentieth century. Even after U.S. attitudes hardened during the cold war (and especially after the 1959 Cuban Revolution), the American presence in Latin America and the Latin American presence in the United States were framed as much by the market—each consuming the other—as they were by the simple imperatives of military might. We ought not lose sight of the significance of this fact in the face of otherwise overwhelming images of violent acts carried out in the name of U.S. domination, because the market gave the United States a far greater reach than its military ever could.

The Documents: Contesting Hegemony

No single text can convey the complexity of the American presence in Latin America. Because of that, below we have a selection of four different documents. Each tells a small part of that history. Our first is a fairly traditional text, the manifesto composed by the guerrilla leader Augusto Sandino (1895–1934) in 1927 as he confronted the Marines, the most visible sign of U.S. hegemony. Political strife was commonplace in Nicaragua at the time. Groups denoted by the labels "Liberal" and "Conservative" continually clashed under the watchful eye of the U.S. government, which in turn used these conflicts to press its own advantage. In part because of his experiences in exile between 1921 and 1926, Sandino took an unusual view of these struggles. He was less concerned with the parochial battles between Liberals and Conservatives than he was about the larger influence of the U.S. in Nicaragua. When the Liberals and Conservatives agreed to a U.S.-brokered truce in 1927, Sandino rejected the accord, and released the manifesto included below (Document 6.1).

One of the first Latin American guerrillas to specifically go to war against the United States, Sandino calls to mind Simón Bolívar's dream of a Latin America united against imperialism.[14] Still, the manifesto is not simply a transparent call for the Nicaraguan people to unite in defense of their sovereignty. Sandino's war mixed battles over long-standing and often personal local grievances (class, ethnic, and kinship conflicts in the Segovias region of Nicaragua) with opposition to the United States presence in the country, conflating local enemies with the imperial power. At the same time, by positioning his fight as an anti-imperial struggle, he could claim to represent all true Nicaraguans. His skill as an ideologue lay in his ability to conflate these various foes into one enemy. In light of this, Sandino's manifesto needs to be understood as a text that in some sense produces the enemy it describes.[15]

Document 6.2 shifts our attention away from the anti-imperial project and towards a more benevolent version of United States–Latin American relations. As U.S. president between 1932 and 1945, Franklin Roosevelt favored what he called the "Good Neighbor Policy," which funneled U.S. aid and investment into friendly countries, positioning that aid as the most effective means of promoting economic progress and modernization. Supplemented at the end of the Second World War with the World Bank, the International Monetary Fund, and later USAID, the Peace Corps, and John F. Kennedy's Alliance for Progress, these types of initiatives sought to help Latin Americans by paying for doctors and vaccines, teachers, agronomists, and engineers, and investing millions of dollars to build schools, homes, hospitals, electrical grids, dams, and improve infrastructure more generally. The U.S. government also hoped that the aid would thwart American enemies in Latin America by revealing the ways that capitalism could alleviate hunger and end poverty.

Our text, the documentary film *Silent War*, highlights a variety of these efforts. Like others of its day (notably *Good Neighbor Family* and *Roads South*), the film suggests that the United States can use its position on the cutting edge of all things modern to help Latin America. The progress described in the film (in this case, a yellow fever vaccine) serves U.S. strategic interests and saves the lives of the villagers in Popoyán; the kind of benefit that a contemporary management consultant might call synergy, and which was not unlike earlier efforts to reduce the impact of mosquito-borne illnesses, undertaken during construction of the Panama Canal. This was what made the logics of American influence in

Latin America so compelling. American officials, along with many Latin Americans, often believed that they were doing good deeds.

Idealism is not so easily evident in Document 6.3, the nakedly propagandistic film *Journey to Banana Land*. This film is said to have premiered on board the *S.S. Talamanca* of United Fruit Company's Great White Fleet in 1950, a setting somehow apt for a complete whitewash of the UFCO's business dealings in Guatemala. Under pressure in Guatemala because of its vast landholdings, the company used this film to show a North American audience the positive impact the company had on this country. Viewers witness the country's relative modernity and the ways in which banana production was benefiting everyone, worker and consumer alike. The film also represents a powerful source for interrogating a series of other assumptions about class, gender, and ethnicity (in both Guatemala and the United States).

Document 6.4 returns us to where we began, with a slight shift. Ariel Dorfman's critique of U.S. imperialism during the 1960s begins by arguing that we must understand a set of assumptions about the modern and the primitive in order to understand American imperial practices. Written during the United States' war in Vietnam, in the aftermath of both the overthrow of Arbenz and the Cuban Revolution, Dorfman's text describes a nakedly imperialist United States. His evidence for this: Donald Duck cartoons, icons of popular culture read across the hemisphere.

Dorfman's critique is powerful and illuminating, and provides a clear reading of cartoons that today seem quite troubling (indeed, far more troubling than *The Three Caballeros*, given their content). Still, we are left wondering whether his critique of Pato Donald and Huey, Lewey, and Dewey tells us more about the assumptions of the cartoon's creators than it does about Donald's readers. *Journey to Banana Land*, Donald Duck, *Silent War*, and other texts may have been created to serve as instruments of imperialism, but it seems unlikely that the audiences who consumed these texts were entirely naïve. North American school children may have thought the family in *Journey* silly, boring, or sufficiently unlike their own family as to be unrecognizable. Did they throw spitballs at the screen, go to sleep at their desks, or cut class? Latin American audiences may have laughed at *The Three Caballeros* because Donald was such a buffoon, a reminder of how unsophisticated North American tourists were. And that man on the street may have thought it odd, inexplicable, that the white man made the chicken. We will never know, and that is part of the magic of the mass consumption that accompanied the "American Century." Just as long as you bought a ticket, you could make the meanings your own.

Document 6.1 Augusto Sandino, *Political Manifesto*, Nicaragua, July 1927

Source: Bruce, Marcus (Ed). *Nicaragua: Sandinista Peoples' Revolution Speeches by Sandinista Leaders*. United Kingdom, Pathfinder Press, 1985, First Trade.

A man who does not ask his homeland for even a handful of earth for his grave deserves to be heard, and not only heard, but believed.

I am Nicaraguan and I am proud that in my veins flows, more than any other, the blood of the American Indian, whose regeneration contains the secret of being a loyal and sincere patriot. The bonds of nationality give me the right to assume responsibility for my actions on matters of Nicaragua and, therefore, of Central America and the entire continent that speaks our language, without concerning myself over what the pessimistic and cowardly eunuchs may call me.

I am a city worker, an artisan as they say in my country, but my ideals are broadly internationalistic in nature and entail the right to be free and demand justice, although to achieve this state of perfection it may be necessary to shed my own blood and that of others.

The oligarchs, who act like geese in a quagmire, will say I am plebeian. It doesn't matter. My greatest honor is to have emerged from the bosom of the oppressed, who are the soul and nerves of the race, who have lived put off and at the mercy of the shameless assassins who helped incubate the crime of high treason: the Nicaraguan Conservatives who wounded the free heart of the homeland and who pursued us ferociously as though we were not children of the same nation.

Sixteen years ago Adolfo Díaz and Emiliano Chamorro ceased being Nicaraguans, because their greed destroyed their right to claim that nationality, as they tore from its staff the flag that flew over all Nicaraguans. Today that flag hangs idle and humiliated by the ingratitude and indifference of its sons who don't make the superhuman effort to free it from the claws of the monstrous eagle with the curved beak that feeds on the blood of this people while the flag that represents the assassination of defenseless peoples and the enmity of our race flies in Managua's Mars Field.

Who are those who tie my homeland to the post of ignominy? Díaz and Chamorro and their bootlickers who still want the right to govern this hapless land, supported by the invaders' bayonets and Springfield rifles. No! A thousand times no!

The Liberal revolution is on the march. There are those who haven't betrayed, who haven't halted, who haven't sold their rifles to satisfy Moncada's greed. It is on the march and today stronger than ever, because the only ones who remain are the brave and the selfless.

The traitor Moncada naturally failed in his duties as a soldier and a patriot. Those who followed him weren't illiterate and neither was he an emperor, to have imposed such greedy ambition upon us. I place before his contemporaries and before history this deserter Moncada, who went over to the foreign enemy with his cartridge pouch and all. An unpardonable crime that demands vindication!

The big men will say that I am very little to have undertaken such a task; but my insignificance is surmounted by the loftiness of my patriotic heart, and so I pledge before my country and history that my sword will defend the national honor and will be the redemption of the oppressed.

I accept the invitation to the struggle and I myself will provoke it, and to the challenge of the cowardly invader and the traitors to my country I answer with my battle cry. My chest and that of my soldiers will form walls that the legions of Nicaragua's enemies will crash upon. The last of my soldiers who are soldiers for Nicaragua's freedom, might die, but first, more than a battalion of you, blond invader, will have bitten the dust of my rustic mountains.

I will not be Magdalena, begging on bent knee for the pardon of my enemies—who are the enemies of Nicaragua—because I believe that nobody on earth has the right to be a demigod. I want to convince the cold-hearted Nicaraguans, the indifferent Central Americans, and the Indo-Hispanic race, that in the spur of the Andean mountains there is a group of patriots who know how to fight and die like men.

Come, you gang of morphine addicts; come murder us in our own land, I am awaiting you, standing upright before my patriotic soldiers, not caring how many you may be. But bear in mind that when this occurs, the destruction of your grandeur will shake the Capitol in Washington, reddening with your blood the white sphere that crowns your famous White House, the den where you concoct your crimes.

I want to advise the governments of Central America, especially that of Honduras, that you need not fear that, because I have more than enough troops, I will militarily invade your territory in an attempt to overthrow it. No. I am not a mercenary, but a patriot who will not permit an offense against our sovereignty.

I wish that, since nature has given our country enviable riches and has put us at the crossroads of the world, and since that natural privilege is what has led others to covet us to the point of wanting to enslave us, for that same reason I wish to break the bonds that the disgraceful policies of Chamorro have bound us with.

Our young country, that tropical brown-skinned woman, should be the one to wear on her head the Phrygian cap with the beautiful slogan that symbolizes our "red and black" emblem, and not that country raped by Yankee morphine addicts brought here by four serpents who claim to have been born here in my country.

The world will be imbalanced if the United States of North America is allowed to be the sole owner of our canal, because that would put us at the mercy of the decisions of the colossus of the North—to whom we would have to pay tribute—those practitioners of bad faith, who with no justification whatsoever seek to become its owners.

Civilization demands that a canal be opened in Nicaragua, but it should be one with capital from the whole world, and not just U.S. capital. At least half the costs of construction should be paid with capital from Latin America and the other half from the rest of the countries of the world that want to hold stock in such a company, and the United States of North America could have only the three million that they gave to the traitors Chamorro, Díaz, and Cuadra Pasos; and Nicaragua, my homeland, will receive the tariffs that by right and justice belong to it, with which we will have sufficient income to build railroads across our territory and educate our people in a real environment of effective democracy, and at the same time we will be respected and not looked upon with the bloody contempt that we suffer today.

Brothers and sisters of my people: having expressed my most ardent desires for the defense of our homeland, I welcome you in my ranks regardless of political affiliation, as long as you come with good intentions, remembering that you can fool all of the people some of the time, but you can't fool all of the people all the time.

Document 6.2 *Silent War* (Film)

To view this film, please visit the book's companion website at www.routledge.com/cw/dawson.

Document 6.3 *Journey to Banana Land* (Film)

To view this film, please visit the book's companion website at www.routledge.com/cw/dawson.

Document 6.4 Ariel Dorfman and Armand Mattelart, "From the Noble Savage to the Third World," 1970

Source: From *How to Read Donald Duck* by Ariel Dorfman. Copyright © 1984 by Ariel Dorfman, reprinted with permission of The Wylie Agency LLC.

> Donald (talking to a witch doctor in Africa): "I see you're an up to date nation! Have you got telephones?"
> Witch doctor: "Have we gottee telephones! . . . All colors, all shapes . . . only trouble is only one has wires. It's a hot line to the world loan bank." (TR 106, US 9/64)

Where is Aztecland? Where is Inca-Blinca? Where is Unsteadystan?

There can be no doubt that Aztecland is Mexico, embracing as it does all the prototypes of the picture-postcard Mexico: mules, siestas, volcanoes, cactuses, huge sombreros, ponchos, serenades, machismo, and Indians from ancient civilizations. The country is defined primarily in terms of this grotesque folklorism. Petrified in an archetypical embryo, exploited for all the superficial and stereotyped prejudices which surround it, "Aztecland," under its pseudo-imaginary name becomes that much easier to Disnify. This is Mexico recognizable by its commonplace exotic identity labels, not the real Mexico with all its problems.

Walt took virgin territories of the United States and built upon them his Disneyland palaces, his magic kingdoms. His view of the world at large is framed by the same perspective; it is a world already colonized, with phantom inhabitants who have to conform to Disney's notions of it. Each foreign country is used as a kind of model within the process of invasion by Disney-nature. And even if some foreign country like Cuba or Vietnam should dare to enter into open conflict with the United States, the Disney Comics brand-mark is immediately stamped upon it, in order to make the revolutionary struggle appear banal. While the Marines make revolutionaries run the gauntlet of bullets, Disney makes them run a gauntlet of magazines. There are two forms of killing: by machine guns and saccharine.

Disney did not, of course, invent the inhabitants of these lands; he merely forced them into the proper mold. Casting them as stars in his hit-parade, he made them into decals and puppets for his fantasy palaces, good and inoffensive savages unto eternity.

According to Disney, underdeveloped peoples are like children, to be treated as such, and if they don't accept this definition of themselves, they should have their pants taken down and be given a good spanking. That'll teach them! When something is said about the child/noble savage, it is really the Third World one is thinking about.

The hegemony which we have detected between the child-adults who arrive with their civilization and technology, and the child-noble savages who accept this alien authority and surrender their riches, stands revealed as an exact replica of the relations between metropolis and satellite, between empire and colony, between master and slave. Thus we find the metropolitans not only searching for treasures, but also selling the natives comics (like those of Disney), to teach them the role assigned to them by the dominant urban press. Under the suggestive title "Better Guile Than Force," Donald departs for a Pacific atoll in order to try to survive for a month, and returns loaded with dollars, like a modern business tycoon. The entrepreneur can do better than the missionary or the army. The world of the Disney comic is self-publicizing, ensuring a process of enthusiastic buying and selling even within its very pages.

Enough of generalities. Examples and proofs. Among all the child-noble savages, none is more exaggerated in his infantilism than Gu, the Abominable Snow Man (TR 113, US 6–8/56, "The Lost Crown of Genghis Khan"): a brainless, feeble-minded Mongolian type (living by a strange coincidence, in the Himalayan Hindu Kush mountains among yellow peoples). He is treated like a child. He is an "abominable housekeeper," living in a messy cave, "the worst of taste," littered with "cheap trinkets and waste." Hats etc., lying around which he has no use for. Vulgar, uncivilized, he speaks in a babble of inarticulate baby-noises: "Gu." But he is also witless, having stolen the golden jeweled crown of Genghis Khan (which belongs to Scrooge by virtue of certain secret operations of his agents), without having any idea of its value. He has tossed the crown in a corner like a coal bucket, and prefers Uncle Scrooge's watch: value, one dollar ("It is his favorite toy"). Never mind, for "his stupidity makes it easy for us to get away!" Uncle Scrooge does indeed manage, magically, to exchange the cheap artifact of civilization which goes tick-tock, for the crown. Obstacles are overcome once Gu (innocent child-monstrous animal—underdeveloped Third Worldling) realizes that they only want to take something that is of no use to him, and that in exchange he will be given a fantastic and mysterious piece of technology (a watch) which he can use as a plaything. What is extracted is gold, a raw material; he who surrenders it is mentally underdeveloped and physically overdeveloped. The gigantic physique of Gu, and of all the other marginal savages, is the model of a physical strength suited only for physical labor.

Such an episode reflects the barter relationship established with the natives by the first conquistadors and colonizers (in Africa, Asia, America and Oceania): some trinket, the product of technological superiority (European or North American) is exchanged for gold (spices, ivory, tea, etc.). The native is relieved of something he would never have thought of using for himself or as a means of exchange. This is an extreme and almost anecdotic example. The common stuff of other types of comic book (e.g. in the internationally famous Tintin in Tibet by the Belgian Hergé) leaves the abominable creature in his bestial condition, and thus unable to enter into any kind of economy.

But this particular victim of infantile regression stands at the borderline of Disney's noble savage cliché. Beyond it lies the foetus-savage, which for reasons of sexual prudery Disney cannot use.

Lest the reader feel that we are spinning too fine a thread in establishing a parallel between someone who carries off gold in exchange for a mechanical trinket, and imperialism extracting raw material from a mono-productive country, or between typical dominators and dominated, let us now adduce a more explicit example of Disney's strategy in respect to the countries he caricatures as "backward" (needless to say, he never hints at the causes of their backwardness).

The following dialogue (taken from the same comic which provided the quotation at the beginning of this chapter) is a typical example of Disney's colonial attitudes, in this case directed against the African independence movements. Donald has parachuted into a country in the African jungle. "Where am I," he cries. A witch doctor (with spectacles perched over his gigantic primitive mask) replies: "In the new nation of Kooko Coco, fly boy. This is our capital city." It consists of three straw huts and some moving haystacks. When Donald enquires after this strange phenomenon, the witch doctor explains: "Wigs! This be hairy idea our ambassador bring back from United Nations." When a pig pursuing Donald lands and has the wigs removed disclosing the whereabouts of the enemy ducks, the following dialogue ensues:

> Pig: "Hear ye! hear ye! I'll pay you kooks some hairy prices for your wigs! Sell me all you have!"
> Native: "Whee! Rich trader buyee our old head hangers!"
> Another native: "He payee me six trading stamps for my beehive hairdo!"
> Third native (overjoyed): "He payee me two Chicago streetcar tokens for my Beatle job."

To effect his escape, the pig decides to scatter a few coins as a decoy. The natives are happy to stop, crouch and cravenly gather up the money. Elsewhere, when the Beagle Boys dress up as Polynesian natives to deceive Donald, they mimic the same kind of behavior: "You save our lives . . .We be your servants for ever." And as they prostrate themselves, Donald observes: "They are natives too. But a little more civilized."

Another example (Special Number D 423): Donald leaves for "Outer Congolia," because Scrooge's business there has been doing badly. The reason is "the King ordered his subjects not to give Christmas presents this year. He wants everyone to hand over this money to him." Donald comments: "What selfishness!" And so to work. Donald makes himself king, being taken for a great magician who flies through the skies. The old monarch is dethroned because "he is not a wise man like you [Donald]. He does not permit us to buy presents." Donald accepts the crown, intending to decamp as soon as the stock is sold out: "My first command as king is . . . buy presents for your families and don't give your king a cent!" The old king had wanted the money to leave the country and eat what he fancied, instead of the fish heads which were traditionally his sole diet. Repentant, he promises that given another chance, he will govern better, "and I will find a way somehow to avoid eating that ghastly stew."

> Donald (to the people): "And I assure you that I leave the throne in good hands. Your old king is a good king . . .and wiser than before."
> The people: "Hurray! Long Live the King!"

The king has learned that he must ally himself with foreigners if he wishes to stay in power, and that he cannot even impose taxes on the people, because this wealth must pass wholly out of the country to Duckburg through the agent of McDuck. Furthermore, the strangers find a solution to the problem of the king's boredom. To alleviate his sense of alienation within his own country, and his consequent desire to travel to the metropolis, they arrange for the massive importation of consumer goods: "Don't worry about that food," says Donald, "I will send you some sauces which will make even fish heads palatable." The king stamps gleefully up and down.

The same formula is repeated over and over again. Scrooge exchanges with the Canadian Indians gates of rustless steel for gates of pure gold (TR 117). Moby Duck and Donald (D 453), captured by the Aridians (Arabs), start to blow soap bubbles, with which the natives are enchanted. "Ha, ha. They break when you catch them. Hee, hee." Ali-Ben-Goli, the chief, says, "it's real magic. My people are laughing like children. They cannot imagine how it works." "It's only a secret passed from generation to generation," says Moby, "I will reveal it if you give us our freedom." (Civilization is presented as something incomprehensible, to be administered by foreigners.) The chief, in amazement, exclaims "Freedom? That's not all I'll give you. Gold, jewels. My treasure is yours, if you reveal the secret." The Arabs consent to their own despoliation. "We have jewels, but they are of no use to us. They don't make you laugh like magic bubbles." While Donald sneers "poor simpleton," Moby hands over the Flip Flop detergent. "You are right, my friend. Whenever you want a little pleasure, just pour out some magic powder and recite the magic words." The story ends on the note that it is not necessary for Donald to excavate the Pyramids (or earth) personally, because, as Donald says, "What do we need a pyramid for, having Ali-Ben-Goli?"

Each time this situation recurs, the natives' joy increases. As each object of their own manufacture is taken away from them, their satisfaction grows. As each artifact from civilization is given to them, and interpreted by them as a manifestation of magic rather than technology, they are filled with delight. Even our fiercest enemies could hardly justify the inequity of such an exchange; how can a fistful of jewels be regarded as equivalent to a box of soap, or a golden crown equal to a cheap watch? Some will object that this kind of barter is all imaginary, but it is unfortunate that these laws of the imagination are tilted unilaterally in favor of those who come from outside, and those who write and publish the magazines.

But how can this flagrant despoliation pass unperceived, or in other words, how can this inequity be disguised as equity? Why is it that imperialist plunder and colonial subjection, to call them by their proper names, do not appear as such?

"We have jewels, but they are of no use to us."

There they are in their desert tents, their caves, their once flourishing cities, their lonely islands, their forbidden fortresses, and they can never leave them. Congealed in their past-historic, their needs defined in function of this past, these underdeveloped peoples are denied the right to build their own future. Their crowns, their raw materials, their soil, their energy, their jade elephants, their fruit, but above all, their gold, can never be turned to any use. For them the progress which comes from abroad in the form of multiplicity of technological artifacts, is a mere toy. It will never penetrate the crystallized defense of the noble savage, who is forbidden to become civilized. He will never be able to join the Club of the Producers, because he does not even understand that these objects have been produced. He sees them as magic elements, arising from the foreigner's mind, from his word, his magic wand.

For Further Reading

Briggs, Laura. *Reproducing Empire: Race, Sex, Science, and U.S. Imperialism in Puerto Rico*. Berkeley: University of California Press, 2003.

Burton, Julianne. "Don (Juanito) Duck and the Imperial-Patriarchal Unconscious: Disney Studios, the Good Neighbor Policy and Packaging of Latin America," in Andrew Parker, Mary Russo, Doris Sommer, and Patricia Yaeger (eds.), *Nationalism and Sexualities*. New York: Routledge, 1992, pp. 21–41.

Cullather, Nick. *Secret History: The CIA's Classified Account of Its Operations in Guatemala, 1952–1954*. Stanford: Stanford University Press, 1999.

Dosal, Paul J. *Doing Business with the Dictators: A Political History of United Fruit in Guatemala 1899–1944*. Wilmington: Scholarly Resources, 1993.

Gilbert, Joseph M., Catherine LeGrand, and Ricardo Salvatore (eds.). *Close Encounters of Empire: Writing the Cultural History of U.S.–Latin American Relations*. Durham, NC: Duke University Press, 1998.

Gleijeses, Piero. *Shattered Hope*. Princeton: Princeton University Press, 1992.

Lafeber Walter. *Inevitable Revolutions: The United States in Central America*. New York: Norton, 1993.

McGuinness, Aims. *Path of Empire: Panama and the California Gold Rush*. Ithaca: Cornell University Press, 2007.

Mendible, Myra. *From Bananas to Buttocks: The Latina Body in Popular Film and Culture*. Austin: University of Texas Press, 2007.

Moreno, Julio. *Yankee Don't Go Home: Mexican Nationalism, American Business Culture, and the Shaping of Modern Mexico, 1920–1950*. Chapel Hill: University of North Carolina Press, 2003.

Pastor, Robert A. *Exiting the Whirlpool: U.S. foreign policy toward Latin America and the Caribbean*. Boulder: Westview, 2001.

Pérez, Louis Jr. *Cuba and the United States: Ties of Singular Intimacy*. Athens, GA: University of Georgia Press, 2003.

Pérez, Louis Jr. *On Becoming Cuban: Identity, Nationality, and Culture*. Chapel Hill, University of North Carolina Press, 2007.

Putnam, Lara. *The Company They Kept: Migrants and the Politics of Gender in Caribbean Costa Rica, 1870–1960*. Chapel Hill: University of North Carolina Press, 2001.

Schlesinger, Stephen, and Stephen Kinzer. *Bitter Fruit: The Story of the American Coup in Guatemala*. Cambridge, MA: David Rockefeller Center for Latin American Studies; rev. exp. ed., 2005.

Smith, Peter H. *Talons of the Eagle: Dynamics of U.S.–Latin American Relations*. Oxford: Oxford University Press, 2007.

Soluri, John. "Accounting For Taste: Export Bananas, Mass Markets, and Panama Disease," *Environmental History* 7 (2002), 386–410.

Soluri, John. *Banana Cultures: Agriculture, Consumption, and Environmental Change in Honduras and the United States*. Austin: University of Texas Press, 2006.

Zolov, Eric. *Refried Elvis: The Rise of the Mexican Counterculture*. Berkeley: University of California Press, 1999.

1929	1930	1930	1934	1937	1943
Collapse of U.S. Stock Exchange signals beginning of global economic crisis	Vargas takes power in Brazil	Military coup begins the decada infama (Infamous Decade) in Argentina	Lázaro Cárdenas elected president of Mexico	Vargas announces Estado Novo (New State)	Junior Officers Coup in Argentina

July 26, 1952	1955	June 1973	July 1, 1974	March 24, 1976
Evita dies	Perón is overthrown, goes into exil	Perón returns from exile, is re-elected president in September	Perón dies, leaving Isabel, his third wife, president	Isabel Perón is overthrown, military begins the Process of National Re-organization (Dirty War)

Power to the People

7

Heard on the radio, or viewed on a newsreel, the spectacle could be overwhelming. Here she was, the wildly popular wife of the Argentine president, addressing tens of thousands of crazed followers in the streets below. Her steady voice, simultaneously seductive, motherly, and commanding, was constantly interrupted by their chants; declarations that they were on her side and demands that she carry on as their leader. Evita had nothing of that apolitical, retiring sweetness that Latin Americans generally expected in prominent women. She attacked her enemies without mercy, and was loved and despised for it.

María Eva Duarte de Perón has long been categorized as a populist, a term that over time has been used so ubiquitously that it is difficult to ascertain exactly what it means. Historians use it much like they use the term *caudillo*, to identify a vast array of politicians who cannot be easily classified according to the matrices of left versus right. Populists were charismatic, nationalist, and good at mobilizing industrial workers. Into this category we can place Víctor Raúl Haya de la Torre (Peru), Getúlio Vargas (Brazil), Carlos Ibañez (Chile), Jorge Eliéser Gaitán (Colombia), Juan and Eva Perón (Argentina), Lázaro Cárdenas (Mexico), and perhaps even Fulgencio Batista (Cuba), Anastasio Somoza (Nicaragua), and Rafael Trujillo (Dominican Republic). This list goes on in a deeply unsatisfying way, because almost every popular Latin American leader of the mid-twentieth century could be called a populist. The debate over who was and who was not a populist winds up becoming a little like an argument about how many angels can fit on the head of a pin.

Our dilemma may lie in where we focus our attention. Populists were not just defined by a political style; they came of age in an era of significant social and technological change. We know Evita was a powerful speaker largely because she found her voice in the era of amplified, broadcast, and recorded sound (audio examples of her speeches can be found on the book's website, www.routledge.com/cw/dawson). Through these mediums she could expand the reach of her voice from a crowd of people within listening distance to tens of thousands, even an entire nation. Many of our most important traces of Evita include images of her speaking into a microphone, electronically enlarging her voice and mobilizing audiences far larger than politicians of an earlier era could have imagined. Her skills were honed over the years as a *radionovela* (radio soap opera) star; a genre that required that her to cultivate a powerfully melodramatic voice. This cadence would in turn serve her well when she addressed her beloved *descamisados* (shirtless ones) in later years. This was also the dawn of a visual age, for which she was well suited, but the dominant medium of her day was broadcast sound, the loudspeaker, the microphone, and the radio. These technological innovations transformed what it was to be a politician, and what it was to be a member of the crowd.

Gathered in a public square, on a street, or in a private dwelling, individuals in the crowd were transformed through the experience of listening together. Even when they listened by themselves, they could understand that it was the voice of their leader they heard, and that millions of others were doing the same thing at the same time. Listening was a sentient experience that had implied intimacy in the past; to hear the voice of a leader was to see them face to face, and to somehow be connected to power in that moment. In the radio age the act of listening to the leader still connected the listener to power, but instead of something that was individually empowering, it made the crowd into the people (Figure 7.1).

Figure 7.1 Evita at a microphone

The Crowd

A century and a half before Evita addressed the crowd, individuals like Father Miguel Hidalgo used similarly celebrated oratorical skills to stir his followers to action. Earlier leaders however, addressed a different kind of crowd. The groups were smaller. They were residents of a single town and its environs, and they were often intensely parochial in their worldviews. Hidalgo did not appeal to the crowd's Mexicanness. He addressed a much more local sense of self and very specific grievances. The crowd's political ties linked them to a distant king whose will was being subverted by venal officials, and not to a horizontal national community of "Mexicans." Indeed, the localistic sense of belonging that united those amassed in the town square in Dolores in 1810 was both a strength and a weakness for the popular movements that participated in nineteenth-century conflicts. Dispersed, and often divided by mutual feelings of hostility, Latin America's nineteenth-century crowds were threatening, but most often unable to sustain movements that went much further than the village boundary for any length of time.

The twentieth century transformed the cognitive capacities of the crowd. Cities grew larger, producing urban working classes that often had a much greater sense of their shared interests and cultures. Living and working together, developing common grievances, urban workers had a capacity to disrupt the system that their rural brethren lacked. It was however, not simply size and physical proximity that enlarged the political capacities of the urban masses. As the face-to-face culture and politics of the countryside were supplanted by interactions mediated through the radio, loudspeakers, and the photographic image, working people found new means to mobilize and insert themselves into politics. An image of a brutalized worker, reproduced thousands of times, has the capacity to stir outrage in ways that word of mouth reports never could. A radio broadcast could act in similar ways, whether it was of a song that everyone loved and knew, reminding them of their place in a national community, or was an overt act of propaganda designed to mobilize listeners in defense of a cause. This is why governments across Latin America did everything they could to control the medium in the early days of radio, and why radio stations were repeatedly the targets of attack (physical attacks, that is, on the stations) by individuals and groups that wanted to get their message out. There was great power in this new, urban crowd, and the radio seemed to be the pipeline to that power.

In part this was because, through the medium of the radio, the notion of simultaneous time, which produces a sense of community among people who otherwise do not know one another (i.e., a community of newspaper readers who count themselves members of the national community because they all read the same news at virtually the same time), was no longer reserved for the literate upper classes. With the introduction of the radio broadcast, sound came to be the force that constituted the national community, opening membership in that world to anyone within earshot. They could experience the feeling of fictive kinship by listening simultaneously to the same broadcasts. They could attend rallies that were larger, more disruptive, and more coherent than ever before. They could listen in the plazas, the schools, and their homes while national broadcasting companies (many government owned) aired the local and national news, and gave voice to a new generation of leaders. Politicians who were adept at using the new media found new, larger audiences in these contexts, and listeners constituted themselves as citizens, as members of the national community, simply by listening to these broadcasts.

Music played a defining role in this process. Through recorded and amplified sound, local songs increasingly became part of national repertoires. A song played again and again, heard in different places, reminded listeners that as they moved through space they remained rooted in a sentimental community comprised of millions of people whom they had never met. Popular music also contributed to the emergence of a novel kind of popular culture. Popular culture was no longer simply local practices that stood in opposition to elites, but it was also mass culture; *radionovelas*, movies, *historietas* (comic books), songs, and other mass phenomena. It was something that poor people shared, that gave them a sense of connectedness and of their own place in a modern world. Popular culture also sometimes blurred the boundaries between the classes. Middle-class children might read the same comic books and go to the same movies as the poor. Elite nationalists could often belt out the same ballad as the shopkeeper, each with as much conviction as the other. Their shared enthusiasms remind us that the common tastes developed and cultivated in these settings produced new forms of nationalist sentiment across Latin America.

The *Hora do Brazil*

Any close observer of Latin American society who utters the phrase "national culture" takes an enormous risk. Profoundly divided societies cannot generally be described as having national cultures. Yet if we discard the concept, we risk abandoning all efforts to understand how technology, style, and a sense of belonging came together to produce the phenomena that characterized Latin American politics in these years before the cold war imposed a very different dynamic on the political life of the region. Few politicians better understood this convergence than Getúlio Vargas, who claimed the Brazilian presidency in a military coup in 1930. In some ways, Vargas was an unremarkable authoritarian ruler. Like many others, he promised a great deal and delivered relatively little. What marked this era as different from others were his (and his opponents') efforts to use the radio to a means to create a national body politic.

Radio first arrived in Brazil in 1922, and was immediately popular, especially in urban areas. By the early 1930s, there were twenty stations in the country. Two decades later there were over one hundred. By the mid-1930s, 85 percent of households in the country's two most populous cities (São Paulo and Rio de Janeiro) owned radios. Most early broadcasting was commercial, but the power of the new medium was not lost on Vargas and his appointees in the Departamento de Imprensa e Propaganda (Department of Press and Propaganda). Several government radio stations were founded in the early 1930s, charged with the twin responsibilities of publicizing the good works of the government (social and educational programs, labor laws, the passage of a minimum wage) and turning Brazilian listeners into a reliable political constituency.

Like bureaucrats everywhere, Vargas and his appointees were not always adept at using the medium. The managers of the three stations run by the government favored didactic programming, speeches by government officials and classical music. Listeners rarely tuned into these programs, favoring the musical selections of commercial radio instead. If they wanted an audience, the regime needed to use the power of the decree. Under Vargas, all stations in the country were required to broadcast the *Hora do Brazil* (Brazil Hour) every evening at eight p.m. Filled with speeches, public announcements, and cultural forms that spoke more to elite sensibilities than popular tastes (marching music was more commonly played than samba), the *Hora* was widely ridiculed and ignored by radio listeners. Some stations simply refused to broadcast it, claiming they could not find the signal. It was popularly known as the *"hora fala sozinho"* or *"*hour that talks to itself.*"*[1]

Vargas recognized that popular music was a powerful unifying force, and did attempt to co-opt art forms like the samba and link them to his *Estado Novo* (the New State, based in a variant of fascism, which he inaugurated in 1937). He supported samba schools and Carnival parades, and samba music was regularly broadcast on Rádio Nacional, a government owned station.[2] Still, it is one thing to attempt to use national art forms to promote fraternal feelings between a listening public and the state. It is quite another thing to succeed at this endeavor. Federal officials tried to simultaneously appropriate the samba for nationalist purposes and define acceptable limits to its subject matter. They promoted patriotic content and tried to censor anti-authoritarian, outlaw images (e.g., the *malandro*, a popular outlaw figure) in samba music. Fans responded by rejecting the official samba, turning off the government sponsored broadcasts and seeking forums where they could listen to their preferred artists and songs.

In the end, there were too many samba artists, too many mediums through which it could be heard, and a fan base that was too vast and heterogeneous to ever allow the art form to be simply tamed, either by the state or the market. That was part of the magic of popular art forms in this era. Because they resisted both definition and control, they could be instruments in any number of cultural or political projects. Indeed, many of the most popular sambas of the era operated a nebulous world in between the licit and the illicit precisely because they were highly critical of the state. They produced a sense of national belonging even as they made Vargas the object of disdain.

Poor Brazilians had more power as consumers of popular music than they did as workers or as citizens. They could listen to what they liked, and reject what they did not, and in the process reveal what record companies have long known: it is harder to shape the tastes of consumers than it seems. Yet they also had the power to actually shape the art form. Fans wrote samba lyrics and submitted them to artists and producers, and sometimes saw their songs recorded. They went to radio shows and applauded their favorite acts, helping to determine which songs became hits and which did not. They distinguished good samba from bad, and Brazilian from foreign. It was they (and not the state) who made the samba so ubiquitous that it became synonymous with the nation, something elites had to embrace if they wished to be perceived as Brazilian. And if the state wanted to ride the samba to legitimacy, it would need to follow their tastes.

Vargas could not control the samba, and in the end neither could he control the radio. Commercial broadcasters understood the medium better than he did, and he lacked the types of charisma that mattered most in the new electronic age. We see this dramatically when we turn to the Brazilian who did use the radio extremely effectively during this era, Vargas' bitter rival Carlos Lacerda. Like most successful politicians in the age of mass communications, Lacerda openly courted workers with his ardent nationalism and willingness to support a limited array of workers' rights. Nonetheless, his core political constituency was middle class and conservative. He was pro-traditional family, vigorously attacked corruption, and recited regular moral diatribes on the air. Most of all, he was a riveting presence on the radio.

Much of the media in Brazil remained beyond government control during the Vargas regime, and in the early 1950s his enemies put Lacerda on the air on *Rádio Globo* and *TV Tupi*, the country's first television network. After struggling to find an audience with programming based on music and *radionovelas*, *Globo* hired Lacerda in 1953 as a talk show host. Lacerda found his niche by repeatedly attacking the government in his shows, much to the delight of his listening audience. He ran an improvisational and lengthy call-in program that used new tactics like media ambushes to produce electrifying radio. Though lambasted in the traditional media, the show was an immediate hit, turning *Globo* into the third most popular station in Rio by August 1954. As a radio and later television star, Lacerda continually demonstrated that elusive ability to turn listeners on, to draw them to his program, and keep them from changing the dial or turning off the set. This was a skill that became absolutely critical with the dawn of the radio and television age. Listeners suddenly had numerous options, and could not be compelled to pay attention.

Lacerda was so successful at attacking Vargas that someone close to the president (if not the president himself) concluded that he needed to be eliminated. Armed assailants tried to kill Lacerda outside his Copacabana apartment on August 5, 1954. He survived, but his bodyguard, an Air Force officer, died. Lacerda and the slain bodyguard were cast as heroes, and Vargas, who was widely viewed as the intellectual author of a botched murder, suddenly faced a united opposition openly talking about violent resistance to the regime. Vargas could still take to the airways to defend his positions and argue against his enemies, but at this point fewer and fewer Brazilians were listening.

Vargas did manage to dominate the airwaves one last time. On August 24, 1954, Brazilians listened with rapt attention as his suicide note was read on national radio just hours after his death (the note had actually been typed several days earlier). In part the note defended his specific policies. It reminded listeners of his attempts to create national oil and electricity monopolies in order to promote industrialization, of the national coffee department he hoped would maintain stable global coffee prices. It was also a dark attack on his enemies.

> Once more the forces and interests against the people are newly coordinated and raised against me. They do not accuse me, they insult me; they do not fight me, they slander me and refuse to give me the right of defense. They seek to drown my voice and halt my actions so that I no longer continue to defend, as I have always defended, the people and principally the humble . . . I have fought month after month, day after day, hour after hour, resisting constant, incessant pressures, unceasingly bearing it all in silence, forgetting everything and giving myself in order to defend the people that now fall abandoned. I cannot give you more than my blood. If the birds of prey wish the blood of anybody, they wish to continue to suck the blood of the Brazilian people. I offer my life in the holocaust. I choose this means to be with you always. When they humiliate you, you will feel my soul suffering at your side. When hunger knocks at your door, you will feel within you the energy to fight for yourselves and for your children. When you are scorned, my memory will give you the strength to react.[3]

Written as troops were preparing to overthrow the regime, the note exemplifies the novel ways in which radio contributed to that sense of belonging that is critical to popular nationalism. It did not matter whether or not Vargas actually wrote the note. Broadcast nationally on the radio, it had the capacity to draw hundreds of thousands of people into the streets, their anger and grief no doubt stoked by the simultaneity of their powerful emotions. Among other things, the crowds took out their anger on two radio stations that had been critical of the president in the weeks leading up to his death.

These outbursts do not tell us that poor Brazilians were ceaselessly loyal to Vargas. His regime never had the unquestioned support of working people, in part because working people in Brazil, as elsewhere, have always had a healthy skepticism for regimes that promise a great deal and deliver something less. Still, while their love was conditional, their grief at his loss was genuine and powerful. Poor Brazilians knew that they were better off with Vargas' unrealized promises than they had ever been in the past. Coming on the heels of the oligarchic republic, where the chasm between the *gente decente* (rich) and the *povo* (poor) was one of both wealth and dignity, Vargas spoke a language that resonated. He claimed to represent the poor, and actually passed laws in their favor.

Few Brazilians believed that these laws would be consistently enforced. When has that ever been the case in Brazil? Rather, these laws were tools that poor people used in their daily struggles to make ends meet. Some schools and hospitals were built, some roads completed, and wages for industrial workers in some sectors improved. And even if not always honored, the minimum wage (introduced in 1940) did impact the lives of millions of workers. Decades later, poor supporters would sum up their love of Vargas with the simple phrase "the president always remembered us."[4] It was a powerful statement about how they were treated by the regimes that preceded and followed his.

Tata Lázaro

Poor Mexicans felt similarly about their favorite president, Lázaro Cárdenas. Hailing from a lower middle-class background in the western state of Michoacán, Cárdenas gained national attention after serving as governor of his home state between 1928 and 1932. During this time, he helped contain the Cristero Revolt,[5] the most important challenge the federal government faced after the end of the revolution, by mixing repression and social reform, rewarding peasants and workers who supported the state with land and other concessions while jailing or killing the most recalcitrant. The country as a whole seemed on the verge of renewed unrest in 1934, prompting Plutarco Elías Calles (Mexico's most powerful figure) to tap Cárdenas as the presidential candidate of the government's political party. During the campaign, Cárdenas distinguished himself from his predecessors, travelling by car, plane, horse, and train around the country. He logged more than 27,000 km in the campaign, and visited every one of the country's twenty-eight states and territories. He even swam to one isolated indigenous community in the Gulf of California during the campaign, leaping from the presidential yacht in order to reach a village that had no road access.

Once in office, the highly symbolic actions continued. Cárdenas refused to move into the presidential palace, preferring to convert Chapultepec Castle into the National Museum of History. He immediately cut his salary in half. Legendary is the story that he would cancel cabinet meetings in favor of visiting poor peasants who had lost their cattle to disease. Other steps were more concrete. He distributed forty-five million acres of land to peasants, so that by 1940 nearly one third of Mexicans had received land via reform. Urban workers were allowed to unionize more easily and granted wage increases. The railways were nationalized and put under worker administration. Across the country he built roads, irrigation systems, schools, and hospitals. He doubled the budget allotted to rural education. He invited Leon Trotsky to live in exile in Mexico (where he was ultimately assassinated by a North American Stalinist). He fought corruption in the labor unions by supplanting the Confederación Regional Obrera Mexicana (the Regional Confederation of Mexican Workers, CROM) with the *Confederación de Trabajadores de Mexico* (Mexican Labor Confederation, CTM). He invited thousands of refugees of the Spanish Civil War to resettle in Mexico. He even remade the official party of the Revolution into a corporatist political party that tied peasants, workers, indigenous peoples, and professional and middle-class organizations to the state, allowing it to remain in power until the year 2000.

These efforts were not simply acts of beneficence. Cárdenas gave to the peasant, the Indian, the worker, and the middle-class professional, and expected that they in turn would contribute to a larger modernizing project. Peasants who received land were expected to produce for the market, participate in government agricultural programs, and be compliant and subservient partners with the state. Indigenous Mexicans, whom he treated with greater respect than any president ever had, were expected to abandon their rustic ways and attend schools, learn Spanish, adopt modern hygienic practices, and become productive farmers. At the First Interamerican Indigenous Congress, held at Pátzcuaro in 1940, he famously declared that his goal was "not to Indianize Mexico, but to Mexicanize the Indian."

Figure 7.2, which is a mural painted in his hometown of Jiquilpán in 1937, evokes much of what he hoped to accomplish with land reform and his particular brand of incorporationist *Indigenismo* (this being the term adopted to describe those who celebrated and sought to assist Mexico's indigenous peoples during this era). The president is surrounded by indigenous figures, dressed in their traditional costume. They are hard-working and deserving peasants, and his proximity to them, unmediated by guards or interlocutors, conveys his comfort and respect. Still, that respect does not extend to emulation. Cárdenas does not wear a peasant costume or indigenous mask, or dance in a fiesta. He sits there in a suit, poring over carefully drawn and thoroughly modern maps, the instruments that the revolutionary state will use to assign land-ownership. We see this in a similar way in Figure 7.3, a photograph taken in 1937. In it he is poised to step onto a *Mexicana* Aviation flight, traversing the nation in double-breasted suit and fedora. The image evokes a man who, like those before him and after him, aspired for a thoroughly modern nation, a man who had left behind the military regalia of his life as a general and was instead signaling Mexico's industrial aspirations as he boarded what was then the most modern form of transport.

Like other so-called populists, Cárdenas never quite managed to enact the lasting transformations he desired. Right-wing sinarquists and Catholics opposed him from the start, and managed to beat back the reformist impulse. Most reform efforts stalled by 1938. In 1940 a more conservative Manuel Ávila Camacho took the presidency, and gradually began to roll back many of Cárdenas' initiatives. Much of the land he put into peasant hands was lost in one form or another within a few decades, after government aid for small farmers

Figure 7.2 Mural depicting Lázaro Cárdenas approving the agrarian reform in his home town of Jiquilpán, Michoacán, painted in 1938

dried up, and large landowners found the means to get around government restrictions by making informal arrangements to take over *ejidal* lands. Many of those displaced peasants migrated to Mexican cities, where they became workers in a burgeoning industrial sector (this may have been a desired result, as Cárdenas favored industrial growth and high rates of productivity in the rural sector). Moreover, while fostering the participation of subaltern groups, Cardenismo was not exactly a liberal democratic ethos. Political bosses, known as caciques, dominated the organizations of the revolutionary state and Cárdenas' Party of the Democratic Revolution (later the Party of the Institutionalized Revolution, or PRI), doling out favors to those who went along or supported them, and taking violent retribution against those who did not.

If these outcomes represented failures in the democratic project, they did not necessarily signal problems for the nationalist agenda. His administration represented a defining moment for both the Mexican revolutionary state and for millions of Mexicans who participated in or supported revolutionary movements. In part this was because he responded to very specific demands, in particular the demand for land, for the tools to work that land, for schools, and for healthcare. More than this however, he celebrated an inclusive nationalism that venerated the *mestizo* as the national type, and Mexican folk music, crafts, and art as

Figure 7.3 Lázaro Cárdenas in 1937

truly original expressions of the people. He was not the first to do this. Mexican muralists including Diego Rivera, José Clemente Orozco, and David Siquieros had been painting nationalist scenes since the 1920s, and the music of Tata Nacho and others was widely played in Mexico during these years. His originality lay in the ways that he turned the presidency into a platform for fomenting popular (as opposed to elite) nationalism.

Cárdenas could never have visited every rural community in Mexico, nor talked to every peasant. He could however, give that impression by communing with the rural poor in very public ways. Newspapers offered some opportunity for the government to publicize his exploits, though only a limited one. Mexicans largely distrusted newspapers, which often acted as simple mouthpieces for the government, and few people read them outside of the literate middle classes of the capital. Cárdenas understood that if he wanted to reach a significant audience, the poor rural and urban folk whom he saw as his critical constituency, he needed the radio. He had a radio train follow him on the campaign trail, broadcasting speeches in the most remote regions of the country to national audiences. And every time he had the opportunity to visit the poor, through the many congresses he organized for workers, indigenous peoples, and women, to epic international moments like the Interamerican Congress at Pátzcuaro, he was careful to ensure that he spoke before a radio microphone.[6]

Radio was already an important medium in Mexico when Cárdenas came to power. Commercial radio had been around since the early 1920s, after Luis and Raul Azcárraga launched Mexico's first station. Mexico's most important commercial station, XEC, which broadcast at 50,000 watts and could be heard as far away as New York City, was founded by their brother Emilio Azcárraga in 1930.[7] By the time Cárdenas assumed office, the country had more than twenty radio stations, broadcasting to more than 100,000 radio sets. By 1940 there were forty stations broadcasting to 450,000 sets. Given the cost of radio sets, most listeners lived in urban areas and were middle class. Most also lived in the Valley of Mexico and in and around Mexico City, where nearly half of the national population resided. Rural people generally gained their limited access to radio through gifts provided by the *Secretaría de Educación Pública* (Ministry of Public Education, SEP), which installed radios in rural schools during the 1930s. Unlike urban middle-class neighborhoods, where radio listening quickly became a private affair, radio listening in small towns was a social event, gathering crowds in and around the schools to hear the news, listen to music and comedy, and follow the latest *radionovela*.

The Mexican government tried to get in on the radio vogue through a variety of means. Early on the government wrote licensing laws that made it illegal for commercial radio stations to criticize the state. The government also founded stations of their own, creating the SEP's XFX in 1924. Broadcasting at a mere 500 watts however, XFX produced a signal that could be heard only in the Valley of Mexico, and weakly at that. XFX did not even fill the broadcast day until 1933, when then Minister of Public Education Narciso Bassols decided that the radio station was an ideal means for promoting Socialist Education.[8] Bassols also tried to ensure that rural Mexicans would be forced to listen to XFX by distributing radios whose dials were glued to the SEP station. This effort flopped, as residents in virtually every community that received a radio freed the dials so that they could listen to more popular stations like XEW.[9] This then, was the dilemma that Lázaro Cárdenas faced as president. He now had the means of spreading a message across the country instantly. He simply needed to find a way to get people to listen.

In part he tried to solve this problem by significantly ramping up the state's use of radio. Aside from bringing radio broadcasting equipment along whenever he had an important public event, he created a new *Departamento Autónomo de Prensa y Publicidad* (Department of Press and Publicity, DAPP), specifically charged with promoting the Cárdenas brand. As Vargas did in Brazil, Cárdenas also created mandatory programming for commercial stations. Starting on January 1, 1935, Cárdenas broadcast a New Year's address that was carried on most stations in the country. In 1936 he increased the amount of obligatory government programming on commercial stations to thirty minutes per day (it had been ten). In July 1937 he created the *Hora Nacional* (National Hour), a program that all radio stations in the country were required to carry every Sunday night at 8 p.m. Though many may have turned off their radios when the program began, this gave him the opportunity to get his message out in an unmediated fashion once per week.

Cárdenas announced his most important and most controversial act as president through the radio, telling a national and international audience that he was expropriating the holdings of foreign companies that controlled Mexico's oil industry on March 18, 1938. Expropriation followed a series of labor disputes in which the companies refused to abide by the rulings of the Mexican courts, and held great significance for Mexicans, as it indicated that Mexico's most valuable national patrimony would no longer be in foreign hands. Oil would now not only profit the Mexican state (which for decades would use oil revenues to subsidize public spending), it could also be used to promote industrialization, providing subsidized fuel and lubricants to Mexican factory owners in return for their promise to invest in Mexico. He announced it on the radio even before he announced it to his cabinet.[10]

Nationalization of the oil industry was a risky move. Cárdenas would face hostility from foreign companies, their governments, the Mexican business community, and the far right. This is why he needed a strong showing of popular support, an outcome he guaranteed through an emotional radio address that highlighted both the mendacity of the oil companies and the urgent national interest that was served by his actions. In response, thousands of Mexicans flooded his office with telegrams expressing support. Days later over 100,000 attended demonstrations in Mexico City celebrating the expropriation. On April 12, thousands of women gathered at the *Palacio de Bellas Artes* to donate goods to remunerate the oil companies for their lost property. It seemed that everyone, from residents of the smallest indigenous communities, to members of the large industrial unions, united in support of the president in the aftermath of the broadcast. And it was largely because of this support that Cárdenas won his battle with the foreign oil companies.

Un Día Peronista[11]

Vargas and Cárdenas proved capable of using new mediums to enhance their power, though the results for both were uneven. Latching onto the radio, they tried to use it didactically, often producing propaganda that fell on deaf ears. Vargas in particular was often wooden in the way he courted the audience on the radio, and was ultimately less successful than the opposition in turning broadcast media into public spectacle. This in turn has become a part of how Vargas is remembered. He is invoked much more for his politics and policies than for his style. For his part, Cárdenas did manage to capture the medium at certain critical junctures, but was mostly several steps behind the commercial stations, who proved just as adept at stirring nationalist impulses in order to market their musical talent and sell commercial time as he was adept at turning those impulses into social and economic reform. The same cannot be said for Juan Domingo Perón and his wife Eva Duarte, whose particular political style and capacity to command the rapt attention of millions of Argentines can stir up visceral feelings to this day. The Peróns mastered the radio more effectively than any other politician of their day.

The best place to begin the story of Peronism in Argentina is in the 1930s, a period that workers in that country called the *Decada Infama* (Infamous Decade). During the same years that Getúlio Vargas was courting support from Brazilian workers and Cárdenas was distributing millions of acres of land, Argentine workers suffered a series of frustrating and humiliating setbacks. As a whole the decade was characterized by deeply cynical politics, punctuated by right-wing military coups. The military took power at the behest of the oligarchy in 1930, and unleashed a wave of repression against organized labor. Two years later the military, conservatives, and the Radical Party formed a *concordancia* (accord) in which they agreed to share power, implement a series of oligarchy-friendly policies, and freeze workers out of the government entirely, all the while maintaining the appearance of democratic practice through electoral fraud and repression. Matters were made much worse by the fact that workers endured a disproportionate share of the economic pain suffered during these years.

There can be little doubt that the xenophobic nationalism of the *Liga Patriotica Argentina*[12] underpinned the *concordancia*, bringing middle-class and elite Argentines together in a shared anxiety over the threat of a workers' revolt. Across Latin America, left-leaning regimes were courting support from workers, but in Argentina, where workers dominated the social terrain of the country's capital and were more essential to the economy than elsewhere, the antipathies between worker and oligarch were simply too deep, with too much history behind them, to be breached.

To be a worker in Argentina during the 1930s was to be in constant danger of arrest or assault from those who monopolized power, and to lack legitimate means of protesting your lot. This did not mean however, that workers remained quiet about their fate. They simply looked to other means, forums in which protest could be masked as something else. One could release frustration physically, through sport, manual labor, interpersonal violence, or heavy drinking. Just as importantly, one could turn on the radio, listen to a tango, and perhaps sing along. During these terrible years, the tango became the quintessential medium through which workers could voice their grievances. Consider the lyrics to *Cambalache*, written by Enrique Santos Discépolo in 1935.

> That the world was and it will be a pigsty
> I know . . . In the year 510 and in 2000 too
> There always have been thieves, hustlers, and fools
> The happy and bitter, idealists and frauds
> But, that the twentieth century is a display of insolent evil no-one can deny
> We live wallowing in the mess.
> And we are all covered by the same filth . . .
>
> Today it doesn't matter
> Whether you are decent or a traitor
> Whether you are ignorant, a genius, a pickpocket
> Generous or crooked
> All is the same, none better than the other
> The donkey is the same
> As the great professor!
> No one fails, no one has merit
> The immoral have reached our level

If one man lives as an imposter
And the other steals for ambition's sake
It doesn't matter if it is a priest
A mattress-maker, the king of clubs
Huckster or tramp

There is no respect, no reason
Anyone is a gentleman, anyone a thief
Stavinsku, Don Bosco, and La Mignon
Don Chicho and Napoleon
Carnera and San Martin, all mixed together

Like in the jumbled window of the bazaars
Life is mixed up
And wounded by a sword without rivets
You can see a crying Bible
Beside a water heater

Twentieth century bazaar
Bizarre and fevered
If you don't cry, mama won't feed you
And if you don't steal you're a fool
Go ahead, Keep it up
We'll meet again
In Hell
No need to think
Just move out of the way.
No-one cares
if you were born honorable.
He who works
Day and night like a mule
Is no different than the one who lives off of others
No different than he who kills or heals
No different than an outlaw.[13]

Like the samba in Brazil, the tango was a popular art form, played on the radio, filled with *lunfardo* (profane slang) expressions, and beloved by the country's working classes. Stories of love betrayed, lives empty of meaning, of violence and social discord gave listeners the smallest of opportunities to describe the world they lived in after the *Semana Trágica* in January 1919. It should come as no surprise then that the tango dismayed elites and was periodically censored by the Argentine state.

Not only did Juan Perón liberate the tango from censorship, he could speak the same language as the great tango singers. Their expressions, like their rage, were his as well. In this, he was unlike any other Argentine political leader in recent memory. Of relatively humble origins himself (he was after all, born to unwed parents), Perón was a self-made man whose relationship to the oligarchy was always uneasy. In particular, he was impressed by the social compacts between workers, industrialists, and the state that he witnessed while he was posted in Europe during the 1930s. He drew on them to imagine a new Argentina, no longer beholden to what was for all purposes a landed gentry. His Argentina would instead be industrialized, broadly prosperous, and modern.

Motivated by a desire to break the stranglehold that the oligarchy had on the system and to forge a new society (one where social peace would be forged not by simply repressing workers), a group of relatively junior officers overthrew the government in 1943. Among those officers, Perón stood out for his desire to change the face of Argentine politics. Put in charge of the Department of Labor (which he remade into the Department of Labor and Supply), he immediately began to construct a power base for himself.

His timing was serendipitous. Workers may have been marginalized politically, but in the decade before the Junior Officers Coup the industrial workforce had been rapidly expanding. Global trade was severely disrupted during the 1930s, and Argentines suddenly found themselves unable to import many of the manufactured goods that had become commonplace in their country since the turn of the century. Responding to demands for these goods, local manufacturers increased domestic industrial production, often building branch-plants of larger European and American conglomerates, importing technology and machinery, and then manufacturing locally (this was known as Import Substitution Industrialization, or ISI). Between 1935 and 1946 the number of industrial workers in Argentina grew from 435,816 to 1,056,673. Over the same period the number of factories in Argentina doubled, from 38,456 to 86,400.

Perón's challenge lay first in capturing the political loyalty of these new (and old) workers, and then turning their energies towards even more rapid industrialization. From his position as a government minister he was able to purchase some of the necessary loyalty by building clientelist networks[14] that could offer specific material benefits to his supporters. Drawing from a long tradition of Radical Party politics, the networks he cultivated were dominated by local bosses who used their connection to Perón to deliver jobs, fix problems, provide public services, favors, money, food, and aid in emergencies. In return for these benefits, members had to come out in support of the leader when needed, and vote for him on election day.

These networks were useful, but if Perón was to really transform Argentina he needed something more. He needed to update and enlarge the clientelist tradition by building a vast patronage network of government-affiliated unions that could ensure the broad labor peace that he believed was necessary for industrialization. To these ends he courted the large unions and promoted new unions among unskilled laborers. He attacked leftist unions and demanded that all workers, along with businessmen and industrialists, cooperate with the military to promote national development. Workers would be guaranteed wage increases (wages jumped 20 percent between 1943 and 1945), social security benefits, housing, education, and union representation (as long as they belonged to government unions). Industrialists would be granted government support through subsidies, preferential taxes, and a compliant workforce. Together with the state, these groups would work to make Argentina less reliant on foreign markets for its economic well-being. It would become a truly independent, industrialized nation.

This was a program that was destined to find adherents, and Perón's particular style represented an ideal vehicle for delivering this message. His use of *lunfardo* expressions, the way he mixed tango lyrics into his speeches, the fact that he actually delivered the goods, and his simple charisma—that nebulous capacity to connect to those with whom you speak, to make them feel connected to you—turned an otherwise technocratic project into a defining nationalist moment. He spoke to workers not as atomized individuals, but as powerful social actors, as Argentines, due the respect of anyone else. Peronism recast citizenship to include a claim to social justice and pride in working people. Because of this, by 1945 Perón had become the most powerful political figure in the country, much to the chagrin of his fellow junta[15] members. That is why they jailed him on October 9, a move that Perón believed signaled the end of his political career.

Like the officers who arrested him, he was wrong to imagine that the workers would stand for this turn of events. While he sat in a military prison cell, his supporters brought the country to a standstill. Unwilling to wait even for a protest planned by the *Confederación General del Trabajo* (General Confederation of Labor, CGT), on October 17 rank and file union members from all over the capital region converged on Buenos Aires, marched to the city's Plaza de Mayo, and demanded Perón's release. Workers remained in the public spaces they had occupied throughout the day and night, dancing and drinking, literally taking over the city from the wealthy. Fearing escalating chaos, the regime released Perón that evening, and asked him to find a way to convince the 250,000 people gathered in the Plaza de Mayo to disperse peacefully. Though the mainstream press had called them drunken rioters, Perón calmed the crowd, addressing them as the true "Argentine People." Elections were called for 1946, and Perón won the presidency handily.

It was a fantastical moment, marked by the sudden power that working people seemed to possess, which enhanced Peróns almost mythical stature. The moment was in turn amplified by Argentina's post-war economic boom. Europe was devastated and hungry, and with the U.S. government poised to rebuild the continent, Argentina entered a period in which demand for its exports and the price for those exports would be unusually high for the foreseeable future. The boom provided so much revenue to the state that the Argentine government paid off its foreign debt in 1947, and then nationalized British-owned railroads, French-owned docks, and U.S.-owned telecommunications. The government also assumed control of the agency that marketed beef exports. All the while Perón was able to reward workers for their support with repeated wage increases. Revenues were so strong that all of this was undertaken at little cost to the export sector, leaving the oligarchy unscathed. Rising incomes alone led to a further jump in consumption, benefiting local industries. High tariffs also helped these industries, though the key to everything Perón accomplished with the economy was a post-war export boom that made it possible to support workers and industry without demanding sacrifices from anyone. It was the end of the boom and new waves of inflation after 1949 that revealed the real cost of these reforms. After the economy encountered severe difficulties in the early 1950s, the Peronist project would quickly falter.

Santa Evita

If the story of economic booms and political networks was all there was to Perón, his decade in office (1946–1955) would be remembered much like that of many other industrializing mass politicians. Whether thought of fondly or with disdain, figures like Getúlio Vargas and Lázaro Cárdenas for the most part lost their capacity to stir up extreme emotions long ago. Such is not the case with Perón, a man who could still produce riots in the streets as late as 2006, when his body was moved from his family crypt in Buenos Aires to a mausoleum at his country estate. In order to understand the continued capacity of Perón to evoke such passions, we shift our focus to the story of his second wife, Evita.

Perón was always a polarizing figure, a reformer who insisted on reconfiguring political power in Argentina. Nonetheless, he possessed certain forms of social capital that gave him access to elite society. He was a military man (later referred to as the General), strong, a son of the countryside. He was a product of good military schools, a loyal (to a point) soldier, and never one to over-turn social hierarchies entirely. Indeed, it seems that when he was jailed in October 1945 he resigned himself to the end of his political career because he never imagined that the crowd would both liberate him and put him in the presidency. We might imagine that this was because however great his skill at addressing the crowd, he remained a military man, his gaze fixed more on his place in the ranks than on the masses.

Evita's role in freeing him from jail remains shrouded in myth. In popular memory she was the one who unleashed the transformative powers of the crowd in her efforts to free Perón. Conservatives prefer to downplay her role, claiming that she was swept along like everyone else. What is clear is that she had a relationship to the masses that set her apart from elite Argentines. Both her origins and her professional career gave her a unique perspective on Argentina, and she used those assets to make herself into one of the most powerful people in the country.

Born in Junín in 1919 to parents who never married because her father already had a family, Eva Duarte grew up in a working-class household, and moved to Buenos Aires as a young woman to pursue a career in the theater. She won minor parts in radio dramas during the 1930s, and by the early 1940s she had become something of a star through her leading role in a drama on *Radio El Mundo*, the most popular station in the country. She met Perón at a charity event for the victims of the San Juan earthquake in 1944.[16] She immediately became his mistress, causing something of a scandal. She would marry him in October 1945, the day after his release from prison.

In the curious alchemy that is attraction, Eva and Perón seem to have been drawn to one another for a multitude of reasons, both personal and political. Aside from the obvious, Perón found in Eva someone who could act as a conduit to the constituencies he needed in order to amass power. She was someone who could enhance his own populist charisma with her similarly powerful ability to draw people in. For her part, in linking her star to Perón, Eva had an opportunity to turn her popularity into something more substantial. Within weeks of meeting Perón, she was actively using her status as a radio star to advocate for Peronism. Within months, she was producing radio soap operas that dramatized Perón's accomplishments, and broadcasting recordings of his speeches over the air. She then dedicated an entire *radionovela* to his life story. Later, she used her radio program to promote his 1946 presidential campaign, and made weekly radio addresses as Argentina's First Lady once he was elected.

As popular as she was with the working classes, Eva Perón's turn as First Lady caused great deal of consternation in polite society. She had far too powerful a sexual presence than conservatives could stomach, and in part because of this she was regularly accused of sleeping her way to the top. Though these accusations did little to hurt her career in the less than proper world of radio entertainers, they were fatal to any aspirations she might have had to be accepted by the Argentine elite. Among the political classes, who tended to have extraordinarily narrow ideas about proper female behavior, her alleged sexual indiscretions and general comportment were viewed with horror. Her humble origins, her ways of speaking, and ultimately her place at Perón's side represented a complete affront to the *gente decente*. That she did these things while openly courting the admiration of working people further infuriated Argentine elites. In part because of this, rumor and innuendo would follow her incessantly. Dismissing Eva as little more than a prostitute, her enemies saw avarice and cruelty in her every act.

It is not clear that these attacks hurt her stature at all with those whose approval she really seems to have courted. Indeed, the more the oligarchy (and middling sectors) hated her, the more she showed her contempt for them, the more working people found her utterly adorable. She stood in for them, was glamorous and defiant, and openly courted their support in a way that re-inscribed their mutual antipathy for the oligarchy. Moreover, as she evolved from beautiful vamp to elegant benefactor of the poor (symbolized, literally, through an evolution in her wardrobe and hairstyle), she was able to cast herself in an increasingly defiant and self-sacrificing role—mother, sister, and lover of the people. Eva Duarte became simply Evita.

In Evita's rhetoric it was not the rich, but the *descamisados* who could claim to represent all that was worthy in the nation. She spoke to their sense of grievance, the feeling that they had been victimized for decades. Evita and Perón were simply their surrogates in a war against the nation's enemies, a revolution that required total loyalty to the cause. Whether railing against imperialist enemies, the Jockey Club, the oligarchy, the left, or liberal intellectuals, she was even more effective than Perón at moving the crowd.

Evita did deliver the goods, at least for a while (see Figure 7.4). After being spurned by the proper ladies of the *Sociedad de Beneficencia de la Capital* (Benevolent Society of the Capital), she managed to have their charitable foundation shuttered, and, in 1948 established her own, the *Fundación Eva Perón* (Eva Perón Foundation, FEP). Begun with a donation of 12,000 pesos from Evita herself, the FEP accumulated assets of over $200 million (U.S.) and employed 14,000 workers. It purchased 400,000 pairs of shoes, 500,000 sewing machines, and 200,000 pots for distribution annually.[17] The FEP also established the Eva Perón School of Nursing (which by 1951 had graduated more than 5,000 nurses), built 12 hospitals, 1,000 schools, and supported the construction of affordable housing across the country. With resources from donated union dues, government grants, lotteries, and taxes, the FEP was the most important social agency in Argentina during Perón's presidency. These were remarkable developments in a country that until 1943 lacked a formal system of social service and aid.

Perón and Evita left ambiguous legacies. Dying young at age thirty-three in 1952 (before everything went sideways for the General), she quickly became one of Argentina's enduring myths. Obviously frail in her last two years, she literally seemed to sacrifice her life for her husband and her *descamisados*. When she died, on July 26, the business of the nation came to a stop while millions grieved. In a tradition that reminds us of Santa Anna's leg, her body was embalmed, and kept in CGT headquarters until Perón was overthrown. She was then clandestinely moved around Buenos Aires for more than a year, and then spirited out of the country by the government. She was secretly buried under the name Maria Maggi de Magistris (an Italian-born émigré to Argentina), in a small cemetery in Milan, in 1956.

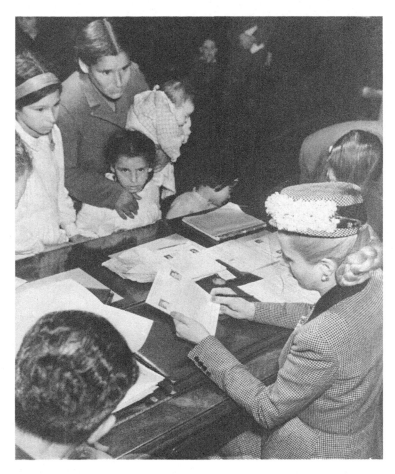

Figure 7.4   Evita administering her charitable works

Source: AFP / Getty Images

This was still not the end for Evita, She was dug up and returned to Perón in Madrid in 1971, where the body could occasionally be seen on his dining room table. Perón's third wife, Isabel, repatriated the remains in 1974. At this point the body was given to her family, and she was placed in a high-security compartment in her family's crypt in the Recoleta Cemetery. To this day the tomb receives a steady stream of visitors.

Overthrown in 1955 in the midst of an economic crisis, Perón left behind a national system of Peronist unions that would remain a focal point for political conflict in Argentine society for decades. Many of his efforts to centralize and coordinate education, healthcare, pensions, and welfare failed in the face of opposition from entrenched interests (sometimes undone by the very unions that served as his power bases). The centralized state Perón imagined, where industrial capital and workers cooperated under the authority of the state, never materialized.

In exile however, Peronism seemed to thrive. Though Peronist images were banned after 1955, the symbolic power of Peronism as a form of opposition to oligarchical interests remained powerful in Argentina. Tough economic times and the fact that Argentines were not allowed to even utter his name only increased Perón's mystique. Peronism ceased to be any sort of discrete ideology, and instead became a romantic longing for better times, expressed by a desire for the General's return.

That day came in 1973, when Perón was allowed to come home from Madrid. He was again elected president, but by this time he was an old man, and his political movement was so fragmented that it offered Argentines little more than violent acts perpetrated against its perceived enemies. Perón died the following year, succeeded in office by his third wife, Isabel. Under her the country veered out of control, rocked both by economic crisis and waves of political violence. She was overthrown in March 1976, succeeded by one of the bloodiest dictatorships in the history of the region. Peronists were again made into targets of repression by the ruling junta, which hoped to wipe them from the face of the nation once and for all.

They would not succeed. Memories of Juan, of Evita, and what they once promised persist to this day. In part this is due to the fuzzy ideological content of Peronism. In its current form, it remains nationalist, impassioned, and rooted in simple concepts like the appeal to social justice. In a world where poor people continue to face repeated humiliations at the hands of the powerful, Peronism remains a vivid symbol.

The Documents: Evita Speaks

On the evening of August 22, 1951, a visibly frail, almost translucent Eva Perón gave one of the most memorable performances of her life. Facing over a million people on the Avenida Nueve de Julio at the Cabildo Abierto (Open Meeting) of the CGT, she discovered the full power of the crowd. Attempting again and again to decline the honor of being nominated for vice-president in the upcoming elections, she encountered an audience that would not accept her decision. They howled in protest, they refused to go home. At nightfall, they rolled newspapers into torches, lit them on fire, and waited for the answer they demanded.

Eva Perón was not a retiring figure. In spite of her failing health, she was the head of the nation's largest social services organization, the head of the Peronist Women's Party (women, having received the vote in 1947, were critical to the Peronist strategy in the November 11, 1951, elections), and she was adored by the people she addressed. Nonetheless, in this moment she was forced to come to terms with the fact that, even when they come together in support of a speaker, a million people have a kind of power all their own. Gathered from across the country largely due to Eva's largesse (the FEP paid train and bus fares, and fed the crowds), they were there to accomplish one thing: to pressure Perón into including Eva on the ticket for the 1951 elections. When things did not appear to be going as they hoped, neither Perón, nor the union bosses, nor even Eva could calm the crowd. They interrupted her speech continually, refused to let others speak, and even seemed about to launch a spontaneous general strike. While the reasons they ultimately backed down are a little unclear, it seems likely that they only dispersed once she promised to do their bidding.

This was in many ways the apogee of Eva's political life, and the way it is remembered has long been a central part of her legend. The speech began as a stage-managed moment, but relatively quickly became an improvisation, a dialogue between Eva and the *descamisados*. We know this because the memories of the participants and newsreel footage show us a spectacle on the verge of turning into a revolt. Unfortunately though, when we endeavor to find out what really happened, we confront the fact that memories are faulty and the footage fragmentary.

The story of the *renunciamiento* (renouncement) has the power to make Eva Perón into an ambitious politician (she stoked the crowd to pressure Perón), a servant of the masses (she agreed to do as they wished), or a fool (she had no idea that events would get out of control). It also has the capacity to make the crowd into a powerful and disruptive political force (they do not leave until she agrees to their wishes), a mass that simply cannot sustain itself (they disperse because their energy dissipates, they may not even be able to hear what she says), or political dupes (they are fooled by Eva into dispersing). There are still other readings, which can render the moment variously as hopeful or sinister.

Presented below are several different renderings of the *renunciamiento*, each with its own truth claims. Document 7.1 is the newspaper article from the *New York Times* reporting the event. The *Times* reported a great deal from Argentina that year, relishing in tales of Peronist corruption, repression, and fakery. Other reports around that time informed readers that the Peróns were repressing striking rail workers, refusing to let the opposition parties have access to government radio, fomenting virulent anti-Americanism, and spending lavishly on new luxury cars while the country suffered. Critics have long accused the *Times* of selectively reporting Latin American events, and describing American foes in the most negative terms. One wonders if these factors are at work in this story, and just how much the event is being reported, as opposed to imagined, in the *Times'* reportage.

Document 7.2 comes from the Peronist Party of Buenos Aires' account of the *renunciamiento*. Proffered as her speech, with no other explanation, the text is notable both for the fact that the most important part of the event, the dialogue with the crowd, is missing, and for the fact that the words included in the text do not appear to be what she actually said. Were these the prepared remarks written for Eva but never delivered? One wonders. If they were, they provide an excellent opportunity for us to understand how speakers deliver the texts prepared for them by speechwriters. It also reminds us of just how perilous it is to rely on written texts from archives in order to reconstruct a past that did not take place through the medium of the written word.

Document 7.3 offers readers our best approximation of what was actually said on August 22. It is from a transcript prepared by the Argentine scholar Mónica Amaré, who assembled the dialogue from the bits and pieces of newsreel she acquired. Readers might also encounter heavily edited bits of those newsreels by searching for video of the *renunciamiento* on the web, or opt for a literary rendering of these clips in Tomás Eloy Martínez' *Santa Evita*. Nonetheless, while each of these texts offers a glimpse of the moment, they are partial; fragments that reveal as much about the method of representation and the persons representing the event as they do about the event itself.

For what it is worth, we know that Document 7.4 is an accurate rendering of what she said on the radio nine days later on August 31, when she announced that she would not run. We have the complete recording of the radio transmission, and it is word for word what we have here. Did she stick to her script in the absence of over a million screaming *descamisados*? It would seem so.

Document 7.1 Foster Hailey, "Peronists Will Head Argentine Ticket," *New York Times*, August 23, 1951

BUENOS AIRES, Aug. 22—Standing on a floodlit platform in Plaza Moreno before a crowd estimated all the way from 250,000 to 1,000,000 persons gathered from all over the nation, President Juan Perón and Señora Perón tonight accepted, in effect, a demand of the peronista party that they run for President and Vice President of Argentina.

The President's acceptance was unqualified. There was some doubt about his wife's decision, but it seemed to some listeners as unqualified as that of her husband.

"We subject ourselves to the decision of the people," said General Perón.

After first having asked for four days to make up her mind, then twenty-four hours, then two hours, Señora Perón's last words as she turned from the microphone were, "as General Perón says, we will do what the people want."

The Superior Council, meeting immediately after the rally disbanded, announced that its ticket for the November elections would be headed by the Peróns. It will officially convey this announcement to the President and his wife Friday.

Señora Perón did not make her promised appearance on the radio, apparently convinced that her silence would indicate consent.

The rally, which was not called by the official peronista party but by the General Confederation of Labor, was the culmination of months of organized supplications to President Perón to allow himself to be re-elected President for another six years. Nearly every day delegations have been presenting themselves at Casa Rosada pleading with the general to answer the demand of the people. Three weeks ago, the labor confederation entered Señora Peron in the list as its Vice Presidential choice.

An interesting feature of the speeches of both Peróns was that each recognized the opposition to her appearance on the ticket. Much of this opposition to her, Señora Perón said, might be that the opposition knew it could not attack General Perón directly because of the people's support of him, but felt it could attack him through her.

It has been no secret that there has been a serious split within the peronista party over her candidacy. Two members of the council were forced out a few days ago for having advocated the placing of Col. Domingo Mercante, Governor of Buenos Aires Province, in second place on the ticket. Colonel Mercante started an official trip through the province on Monday that would keep him out of the city through today. There was a report tonight that a delegation of 2,000 peronistas had come from La Plata with Mercante signs and been prevented from taking part in the rally.

Document 7.2 The Peronist Version of the Speech

Source: www.pjbonaerense.org.ar/peronismo/discursos_eva/discursos_eva.htm. Translated by Laura F. Temes and Patricia Rosas.

Your Excellency, Mr. President; my dear descamisados (shirtless ones) of our Nation:

It is a thrill for me to see the descamisados again, just as on October 17, and on all other dates when the people were present. Today, my General, at this Justicialist town hall meeting, the people who in 1810 gathered to ask what it all meant are gathered again to declare that they want General Perón to continue guiding the destiny of our Fatherland. It is the people, it is the women, the children, the elderly, and the workers who are here today because they have taken the future into their own hands, and they know that they will only find justice and freedom with General Perón at the helm of the Nation.

My General, your glorious vanguard of descamisados is present here today, as they were yesterday, and as they always will be, willing to give their lives for Perón. They fully understand that prior to the arrival of General Perón, they lived in slavery, and above all, they had lost all hope for a better future. They know it was General Perón who gave them social, moral, and spiritual dignity. They also know that the oligarchy, the mediocre, and the traitors of the Nation are not yet defeated, and that from their lairs, they undermine the people and the nation. But our oligarchy, who always sold itself for a pittance, does not expect the people to stand up this time nor does it realize that the Argentine nation is comprised of honorable men and women who are willing to die to finish off, once and for all, the traitors and the sellouts.

They will never forgive General Perón for improving conditions for the workers, creating Justicialismo, or establishing that dignity in our Fatherland is reserved only for those who work. They will never forgive General Perón for lifting up everyone they despise: the workers—whom they forgot—the children and the elderly and the women—whom they relegated to second place.

Those who made the country suffer an endless night will never forgive General Perón for raising the three flags that they should have raised over a century ago: social justice, economic independence, and the sovereignty of our Fatherland.

But today the people are sovereign, not only civically but also morally and spiritually. My General, we the people, your vanguard of descamisados, are willing to finish off, once and for all, the intrigue, the slander, the defamation, and the merchants who sell out their people and their country. The people want Perón not just because of the material gains—this Nation, my General, never thought of that. Instead, it thought of our country—the material, spiritual and moral greatness of our Fatherland. Because the Argentine people have a big heart, and they believe in values other than the material ones. For this reason, my General, they are here today, traveling the roads, and with thousands of sacrifices, taking shortcuts to come here to tell us that they want to be able to declare "Present!" at this Justicialist town hall meeting.

The Fatherland heeded the call of our compañeros from the General Labor Confederation to tell the Leader that a people stand behind him and that he should continue as he is doing now, fighting against those who are not patriots, against corrupt politicians, and against imperialism from the left and the right.

As for me, in General Perón, I always found a teacher and a friend, and he always stood as an example of unblemished loyalty to the workers. All these years of my life, I have devoted my nights and days to helping the humble people of our Fatherland, without consideration for the days or the nights or the sacrifices.

While by night the sellouts, the mediocre, and the cowardly plotted the next day's intrigues and infamy, I, a humble woman, only thought of the pain I had to alleviate and the people I had to comfort on your behalf, my General. For I know the deep affection you have for the descamisados and because I carry a debt of gratitude in my heart to them, the people who, on October 17, 1945, gave me back my life, my light, my soul, and my heart by bringing Perón back to me.

I am but a woman of the people, a descamisada of our Fatherland, a descamisada to the core. For I always wanted to rub shoulders with the workers, the elderly, the children, and those who suffer, working side by side and heart to heart with them to ensure that they love Perón even more, and to serve as a bridge of peace between Perón and the descamisados of our Fatherland.

My General, at this stunning sight, we witness once again the miracle that took place two thousand years ago. For it was not the wise, nor the wealthy, nor the powerful who believed, but rather the humble. The souls of the rich and the powerful are shut out from all the greed and the selfishness, but the humble, as they live and sleep out of doors, have the windows of their souls open to extraordinary things. My General, it is the descamisados who see you with the eyes of the soul, and that is why they understand you and follow you. That is why they only want one man and no other: Perón and no one else.

I take this opportunity to ask God to enlighten the mediocre, so they can see Perón and understand him. And also so that future generations will not point their fingers at us should they find out that there were Argentines who were such scoundrels that they made alliances with foreign interests to fight against a man like General Perón, who dedicated his entire life to trying to achieve greatness and happiness for our Fatherland.

I was never interested in deceit or slander when they unleashed their tongues against a frail Argentine woman. On the contrary, I felt happy inside, my General, because I wanted my bosom to shield any attacks directed at you, so they would hit me instead of you. But I was never fooled. Those who attack me do so not because of me, my General, but because of you. They are such traitors, such cowards that they do not want to say they do not love Perón. It is not Eva Perón they attack, it is Perón.

They are upset that Eva Perón has devoted herself to the Argentine people. They are upset that instead of devoting herself to the oligarchs' parties, she has devoted her hours, her nights and her days, to alleviating sorrows and healing wounds.

My General, before you stand the people, and I want to take the opportunity to thank all those who are humble, all the workers, all the women, children, and men of our Fatherland, who in their heart of hearts have praised a woman's name. I am a humble woman who loves them deeply and who doesn't mind devoting her life to them if it means bringing a little bit of happiness to one household in her Nation. I will always do what the people ask of me, but I say to my fellow workers, just as I told them five years ago, that I would rather be Evita than the President's wife if that Evita were uttered to soothe the pain in some household in our Fatherland. Today, I say to you that I prefer to be Evita, because in being Evita, I know that you will always carry me deep inside your heart. What glory! What honor! What more could a citizen aspire to than the love of the Argentine people!

I am so deeply moved. My humble person does not deserve the deep affection of all the workers of our Fatherland. You are placing a huge burden on the weak back of an Argentine woman. I do not know how to repay the affection and trust that the people have placed on me. I pay it back with love, by loving Perón and by loving all of you, which is like loving the Fatherland itself.

Compañeros, I want all of you, those in the provinces, those in metropolitan Buenos Aires, those in the capital, in short, people from all corners of the country, to tell the descamisados that all that I am, all that I have, all that I do, all that I will do, all that I think, and all that I possess, none of it is mine. It belongs to Perón because he gave me everything. By lowering himself to the level of a humble woman of the Fatherland, he raised her high up and placed her in the hearts of the Argentine people.

My General, if I could reserve any satisfaction for myself, it would be that of interpreting your dreams as a patriot, your concerns, and to have worked humbly, but steadfastly, to heal the wounds of the poor people of our Fatherland, to make hopes become reality and to alleviate sorrows, according to your wishes and your orders.

I have done nothing; everything is Perón. Perón is the Fatherland, Perón is everything, and we are all light-years distant from the Leader of the Nation. My General, before the people go to vote for you on November 11, with the full spiritual powers conferred upon me by the descamisados of our Fatherland, I proclaim you President of all Argentines. The Fatherland is saved because it is in the hands of General Perón.

To all of you, to my Fatherland's descamisados, and to all those who are listening, I hold you symbolically very, very, close to my heart.

Document 7.3 The Renunciamiento as Compiled from Newsreel and Archival Footage

Source: Compiled by Mónica Amaré. Translated by Laura F. Temes and Patricia Rosas.

[The event was scheduled to begin at 2:30 p.m. People, especially women, had camped out days in advance in the area surrounding the presidential balcony. Around 5:00 p.m., Perón arrived with his Ministers. The crowd gave him an ovation and immediately shouted out for Eva, who entered the balcony crying. José Espejo, Secretary General of the General Labor Confederation (CGT), spoke first. He ended his speech by proclaiming the Perón-Perón ticket for the following term. Next, Perón expressed his gratitude and promised to continue his government project. The crowd started chanting, "Perón with Evita!" Eva Perón began her speech.]

Your Excellency, Mr. President, dear descamisados of our Fatherland,

It is a thrill for me to see the descamisados again, just as on October 17, and on all other dates when the people were present. Today, my General, at this Justicialist town hall meeting, just as in 1810, the people ask, "what does it all mean?" Now, they know what it means, and they want General Perón to continue leading the destiny of our Nation.

With Evita! With Evita!

It is the people, it is the women, the children, the elderly, and the workers who are here today because they have taken the future into their own hands, and they know that they will only find justice and freedom with General Perón at the helm of the Nation.

My General, your glorious vanguard of descamisados is present here today, as they were yesterday, and as they always will be, willing to give their lives for Perón. They fully understand that prior to the arrival of General Perón, they lived in slavery, and above all, they had lost all hope for a better future.

Evita with Perón! Evita with Perón!

It was General Perón who gave them social, moral, and spiritual dignity. They also know that the oligarchy, the mediocre, and the traitors of the Nation are not yet defeated, and that from their filthy lairs, they undermine liberty and the people. But our oligarchy, who always sold itself for a pittance, does not expect the people to stand up this time nor does it realize that the Argentine nation is comprised of honorable men and women who are willing to die to finish off, once and for all, the traitors and the sellouts.

Fuel! Fuel! Fuel to the fire!

They will never forgive General Perón for lifting up everyone they despise: the workers— whom they forgot—the children and the elderly and the women—whom they relegated to second place. But today the people are sovereign, not only civically but also morally and spiritually. My General, we the people, your vanguard of descamisados, are willing to finish off, once and for all, the intrigue, the slander, the defamation, and the merchants who sell out their people and their country. The people want Perón not just because of the material gains—this Nation, my General, never thought of that. Instead, it thought of our country—the material, spiritual and moral greatness of our Fatherland. Because the Argentine people have a big heart, and they believe in values other than the material ones. For this reason, my General, they are here today, traveling the roads, and with thousands of sacrifices, taking shortcuts to come here to tell us that they want to be counted at this Justicialist town hall meeting.

The Fatherland heeded the call of our compañeros from the General Labor Confederation to tell the Leader that a People stand behind him and that he should continue as he is doing now, fighting against those who are not patriots.

As for me, in General Perón, I always found a teacher and a friend, and he always stood as an example of unblemished loyalty to the workers. All these years of my life,

I have devoted my nights and days to helping the humble people of our Fatherland, without consideration for the days or the nights or the sacrifices.

While by night the sellouts, the mediocre, and the cowardly plotted the next day's intrigues and infamy, I, a humble woman, only thought of the pain I had to alleviate and the people I had to comfort on your behalf, my General. For I know the deep affection you have for the descamisados and because I carry a debt of gratitude in my heart to them, the people who, on October 17, 1945, gave me back my life, my light, my soul, and my heart by bringing the General back to me.

Evita with Perón! Evita with Perón!

I am but a woman of the people, one of the descamisadas of our Fatherland, a descamisada to the core. For I always wanted to rub shoulders with the workers, the elderly, the children, and those who suffer, working side by side and heart to heart with them to ensure that they love Perón even more, and to serve as a bridge of peace between Perón and the descamisados of our Fatherland.

[A paragraph is missing on which there is no agreement in the records.]

I was never interested in deceit or slander when they unleashed their tongues against a frail Argentine woman. On the contrary, it made me happy inside, because I served my people and my General. [Applause.]

But I was never fooled. Those who attack me do so not because of me, my General, but because of you. They are such traitors, such cowards that they do not want to say they do not love Perón. It is not Eva Perón they attack, it is Perón.

They are upset that Eva Perón has devoted herself to the Argentine people; they are upset that instead of devoting herself to the oligarchs' parties, she has devoted her hours, her nights and her days, to alleviating sorrows and healing wounds.

My General, before you stand the people, and I want to take the opportunity to thank all those who are humble, all the workers, all the women, children, and men of our Fatherland, who in their heart of hearts have praised a woman's name. I am a humble woman who loves them deeply and who doesn't mind devoting her life to them if it means bringing a little bit of happiness to one household in her Nation. I will always do what the people ask of me, [applause] . . . but I say to my fellow workers, just as I told them five years ago, that I would rather be Evita than the President's wife if that Evita were uttered to soothe the pain in some household in our Fatherland. Today, I say to you that I prefer to be Evita, because in being Evita, I know that you will always carry me deep inside your heart. What glory! What honor! What more could a citizen aspire to than the love of the Argentine people!

I am so deeply moved. My humble person does not deserve the deep affection of all the workers of our country. You are placing a huge burden on the weak back of an Argentine woman. I do not know how to repay the affection and trust that the people have placed on me. I pay it back with love, by loving Perón and by loving all of you, which is like loving the Fatherland itself.

Compañeros, I want all of you, those in the provinces, those in metropolitan Buenos Aires, those in the capital, in short, people from all corners of the country, to tell the descamisados that all that I am, all that I have, all that I do, all that I will do, all that I think, and all that I possess, none of it is mine. It belongs to Perón because he gave me everything. By lowering himself to the level of a humble woman of the Fatherland, he raised her high up and placed her in the hearts of the Argentine people.

My General, if I could reserve any satisfaction for myself, it would be that of interpreting your dreams as a patriot, your concerns, and to have worked humbly, but steadfastly, to heal the wounds of the poor people of our Fatherland, to make hopes become reality and to alleviate sorrows, according to your wishes and your orders.

I have done nothing; everything is Perón. Perón is the Fatherland, Perón is everything, and we are all light-years distant from the Leader of the Nation. My General, before the people go to vote for you on November 11, with the full spiritual powers conferred upon me by the descamisados of our Fatherland, I proclaim you President of all Argentines. The Fatherland is saved because General Perón governs it.

To all of you, to my Fatherland's descamisados, and to all those who are listening, I hold you symbolically very, very, close to my heart.

[Perón is the next to speak. The event would have ended after he finished speaking. However, the crowd clamors for Evita. Espejo approaches her and says, "Madam, the People are asking you to accept your post . . ."]

[Eva returns to the microphones]

I ask the General Labor Confederation and I ask you, given the affection that binds us, that for such a momentous decision in the life of this humble woman, you give me at least four days.

No! No! With Evita!

Compañeros . . . Compañeros, I don't want any workers from our Fatherland to wake up tomorrow and have no arguments to counter the resentful and the mediocre who did not or do not understand me, thinking that everything I do, I do on behalf of petty interests . . .

No! No! With Evita!

Compañeros, due to the affection that binds us, I ask you please, do not make me do what I do not want to do.

With Evita! With Evita!

[Eva asks for silence with her hands.]

When has Evita let you down? When has Evita not done what you want? Don't you realize that this moment is very important, for a woman just as for any other citizen, and that she needs at least a few hours, only that?

No! Strike! Strike! General strike!

[Crying] Compañeros, don't you think that if my taking on the responsibility of vice president was a solution that I would have answered "yes"? I do not relinquish my post in the struggle; I relinquish the honors.

No! No!

With General Perón in government, the post of vice president is nothing but an honor, and I aspire to nothing else but the honor of the affection of the humble people of my Fatherland.

Compañeros, compañeros. The General is asking me to tell you that if tomorrow I were to . . .

[The crowd again interrupts her.]

Compañeros, I ask you as a friend, as a comrade, to disperse, to . . .

No! Answer! Answer!

[José Espejo speaks: "Compañeros, compañera Evita has requested two hours. We will remain here. We will not budge until she gives us an affirmative response."]

I am surprised . . . Never in my heart as a humble Argentine woman did I think I could accept that post . . .

(Note: while Amaré does not include it in her compilation, several versions of the dialogue between Evita and the crowd include the further phrase, placed at various points in the dialogue.)

In the end, I will do as the people decide . . .

Thunderous Applause

Document 7.4 Eva Perón's Final Response Broadcast over the Airwaves at 8.30 p.m. on August 31, 1951

Source: http://www.lafogata.org/evita/evita2.htm. Translated by Laura F. Temes and Patricia Rosas.

Compañeros,

I want to inform the Argentine people of my final and irrevocable decision to relinquish the honor that the workers and the people of this Fatherland wanted to bestow on me at the historic town hall meeting of August 22. That same marvelous afternoon that my eyes and heart will never forget, I realized that I should not trade my post in the Peronist movement's struggle for some other post. From that moment on, after conferring with my heart and with the people, I thought about this in the solitude of my own conscience, and I reflected on it with a cool head. I have reached my final and irrevocable decision and have presented it to the Supreme Council of the Peronist Party, before our supreme commander, General Perón. Now, I want the Argentine people to hear the reasons for my unwavering resignation directly from me. First, speaking as a proud Argentine woman and a Peronista, one who loves the cause of Perón, of my

Fatherland, and of my people, I hereby state that this decision arises from the very core of my conscience, and thus, it is utterly free and carries the full force of my definitive will.

On October 17, I made a lasting vow in the presence of my own conscience to focus my efforts entirely on serving the descamisados, who are the humble people and the workers. I had an infinite debt to settle with them. I think I did everything in my power to keep my promise and pay my debt. Then as now, I have but one ambition, a single, great personal ambition: in the marvelous chapter that History will doubtlessly devote to Perón, may it say that next to Perón stood a woman who devoted her life to bringing the hopes of the people before the President, and that the people affectionately called this woman "Evita." That is who I want to be.

For Further Reading

Anderson, Benedict. *Reflections on the Origin and Spread of Nationalism.* London: Verso, 1983.

Auyero, Javier. *Poor People's Politics: Peronist Survival Networks and the Legacy of Evita.* Durham, NC: Duke University Press, 2000.

Becker, Marjorie. *Setting the Virgin on Fire: Lázaro Cárdenas, Michoacán Peasants and the Redemption of the Mexican Revolution.* Berkeley: University of California Press, 1996.

Boyer, Christopher. *Becoming Campesinos: Politics, Identity, and Agrarian Struggle in Postrevolutionary Michoacan, 1920–1935.* Stanford: Stanford University Press, 2003.

Elena, Eduardo. *Dignifying Argentina: Peronism, Citizenship, and Mass Consumption.* Pittsburgh: University of Pittsburgh Press, 2011.

Farnsworth-Alvear, Ann. *Dulcinea in the Factory: Myths, Morals, Men, and Women in Colombia's Industrial Experiment, 1905–1960.* Durham, NC: Duke University Press, 2000.

Fraser, Nicholas, and Marysa Navarro. *Evita: The Real Life of Eva Peron.* New York: Norton, 1996.

Guillermoprieto, Alma. *Samba.* New York: Vintage, 1990.

Hayes, Joy Elizabeth. *Radio Nation: Communication, Popular Culture, and Nationalism in Mexico, 1920–1950.* Tucson: University of Arizona Press, 2000.

James, Daniel. *Resistance and Integration: Peronism and the Argentine Working Class, 1946–1976.* Cambridge: Cambridge University Press, 1988.

James, Daniel. *Doña María's Story: Life History, Memory, and Political Identity.* Durham, NC: Duke University Press, 2000.

Knight, Alan. "Populism and Neo-populism in Latin America, especially Mexico," *Journal of Latin American Studies* 30:2 (1998), 223–248.

Levine, Robert M. *Father of the Poor: Vargas and His Era.* Cambridge: Cambridge University Press, 1998.

Martínez, Tomás Eloy. *Santa Evita.* New York: Vintage, 1996.

McCann, Bryan. "Carlos Lacerda: The Rise and Fall of a Middle-Class Populist in 1950s Brazil," *Hispanic American Historical Review* 83:4 (2003), 661–696.

McCann, Bryan. *Hello, Hello Brazil: Popular Music in the Making of Modern Brazil.* Durham, NC: Duke University Press, 2004.

Purnell, Jennie. *Popular Movements and State Formation in Revolutionary Mexico: The Agraristas and Cristeros of Michoacán.* Durham, NC: Duke University Press, 1999.

Taylor, Julie M. *Eva Peron: The Myths of a Woman.* Chicago: University of Chicago Press, 1979.

Vianna, Hermano. *The Mystery of Samba: Popular Music and National Identity in Brazil.* Chapel Hill: University of North Carolina Press, 1999.

Whitney, Robert. *State and Revolution in Cuba: Mass Mobilization and Political Change, 1920–1940.* Chapel Hill: University of North Carolina Press, 2000.

Williams, Daryle. *Culture Wars in Brazil: The First Vargas Regime, 1930–1945.* Durham, NC: Duke University Press, 2001.

At A Glance: Urbanization

Since the 1950s, one of the most pronounced demographic trends in Latin America has been urbanization. Some of those who moved to the cities were displaced from their lands by armed conflicts, others in search of economic opportunities or to escape rural poverty; poverty that was often exacerbated by government policies designed to help export agriculture and maintain low staple prices for the burgeoning urban population of the region.

Table D.1 shows the growth of Latin America's most significant urban areas since 1950. Latin America today has at least nine cities with more than five million inhabitants (the number is likely larger, depending on how populations are counted). This represents a sharp transformation since 1950, when the region only had one city of this size. Buenos Aires, which was then the largest city in the region, is today third, far behind São Paulo and Mexico City. These urban populations offer one of the great challenges for twenty-first-century states, as they struggle to provide jobs, infrastructure, social services, food, and water to their sprawling suburbs, many of which are comprised mainly of the working poor. This in turn places new pressures on rural areas, which not only cannot easily produce enough food to feed the urban populations, but also must compete with the cities for dwindling water and other resources.

Figure D.2 illustrates the gradual growth of urban residents as a portion of the population of the region between 1950 and 2030. This graph reinforces the shift from an overwhelmingly rural population to an urban one in a relatively short period, and suggests the challenges that these transformations have posed for both rural and urban populations. It also speaks to the transformations in the rural and urban economy that this has entailed—the shift from employment in agriculture to manufacturing, services, and the informal economy, and changes in the nature of both of those economies, such as the industrialization of rural production.

Figure D.3 supplements this graph with a map indicating the most significant areas of population density across the region. We see here that it is not just the largest cities, but surrounding regions that have seen significant urbanization in recent decades. Latin American populations are not evenly divided across the region, but concentrated along the coasts, the major river systems, and in the highland plateaus of Mexico and Central America.

Figure D.4 considers a further aspect of migration in contemporary Latin America. In the early twenty-first century, around forty million people of Latin American origin live in the United States. Some of those lack documents (most guess this number is somewhere between seven and twenty million). Migrants with authorization from the U.S. government however, also represent a significant portion of this figure. This map shows legal migration from Mexico, Central America, and the Caribbean, between 1980 and 2010.

Although distinct from migration from the countryside to urban areas, emmigration (i.e., moving to a foreign country) is often rooted in similar motivations. Poor rural migrants, unable to find opportunities in their home countries and sometimes under threat from various agents, migrate from Bolivia and Paraguay to Argentina and Brazil, from Guatemala to Mexico, from Haiti to the Dominican Republic, and from across the region to the United States. Most initially maintain the hope that they will one day return to their place of origin. Most also maintain close connections to their home communities, regularly sending economic aid in the form of remittances (e.g., Mexicans send billions of dollars in remittances home from the United States every year). A significant number will ultimately remain in their new home societies, often deeply ambivalent about what they have gained, and what they have lost.

Table D.1   Urban Agglomerations with Five Million or More Inhabitants, 1950–2015 (population in thousands)

	1950	1975	2000	2015
Buenos Aires	5,042	7,963	12,024	13,185
Mexico City		10,691	18,066	20,434
São Paulo		10,333	17,962	21,229
Rio de Janeiro		9,144	10,652	11,543
Lima			7,443	9,388
Bogotá			6,771	8,970
Santiago			5,467	6,495
Belo Horizonte				5,395
Guatemala City				5,268
Total	5,042	**38,131**	78,385	101,907

Source: Jorge A. Brea, "Population Dynamics in Latin America," in *Population Bulletin* March 2003, Vol. 58, No.1. (www.un.org/esa/population/publications/wup2001/wup2001dh.pdf)

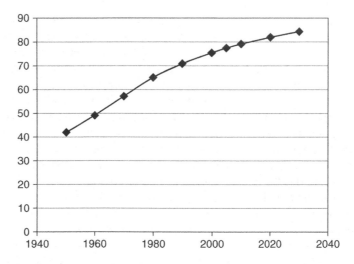

Figure D.2   Graph: Urbanization in Latin America (percent of total population)

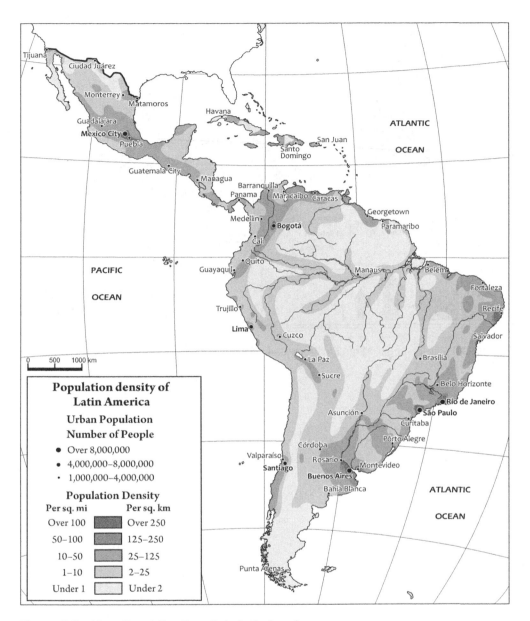

Figure D.3   Map: Population Density in Latin America

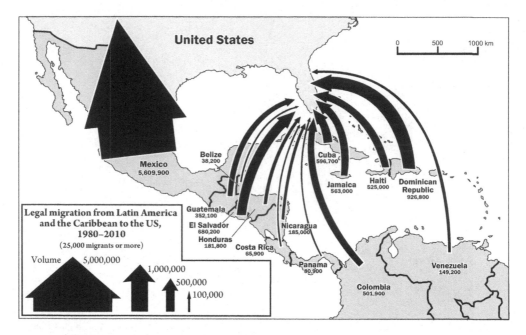

Figure D.4   Map: Legal Migration from Latin America and the Caribbean to the United States, 1980–2010

July 26, 1953	October 16, 1953	May 1955	November 26, 1956	December 31, 1958	January 1, 1959
Castro leads assault on Moncada Barracks	Castro, on trial, delivers "History Will Absolve Me" speech	Castro released from prison in general amnesty, moves to Mexico, where he meets Che Guevara	Castro, Guevara, and eighty others leave Mexico for Cuba on the yacht *Granma*	Batista flees	The revolution is in power

September 28, 1960	October 1960	April 1961	May 1, 1961	1965	1965–1967	1970
Committees for the Defense of the Revolution (CDRs) created	U.S. government declares partial embargo, increased to full embargo in February 1962	U.S. backed invasion takes place at Playa Girón (Bay of Pigs)	Castro declares Cuba a socialist nation	Che Guevara leaves Cuba to promote global revolution. He dies in Bolivia in 1967	Campaign against bureaucracy	Ten million ton sugar harvest fails

A Decade of Revolution in Cuba

8

April 1959	May 17, 1959	1960–1962	June 1960	July 6, 1960	August 23, 1960
Castro visits United Nations in New York	Agrarian reform law introduced	14,000 Cuban children are sent without parents to the United States in Operation Pedro Pan	U.S. oil refineries refuse to refine Soviet crude, resulting in nationalization; more nationalizations follow	United States cuts Cuban sugar quota by 700,000 tons	Cuban Federation of Women (FMC) founded

Some fifty years on, the Cuban Revolution remains a powerfully polarizing symbol.[1] Ideologues on both the left and the right still invoke the Cuban Revolution as a story of good versus evil, as something that is vibrant or nearly dead, and seem largely incapable of imagining it in historical (as something that changes over time) or ambiguous terms. Fidel Castro and Che Guevara are Third World heroes, standing up to U.S. imperialism on behalf of the poor. They represent an evil form of authoritarianism, and drove almost 10 percent of the island's population into exile. The Revolution taught the illiterate to read, provided healthcare to the poor, and reshaped the Cuban economy in spite of a crippling blockade. The revolutionaries were bumbling bureaucrats, relied on Soviet subsidies for decades, and ultimately made the island (once again) a haven for sex tourism in their effort to save themselves. Che was a model for the best kinds of youthful idealism and rebellion. Che was an incompetent ideologue who led a generation of naïve youths to their deaths.

Viewed together, these competing narratives provide a baffling portrait of revolutionary Cuba. When we add to that our current tendency to fetishize and massify star power, stories of the Revolution veer into the absurd. As Figure 8.1 attests, the complex ways in which ideology, youthful rebellion, and mass marketing have become embedded in narratives of the

Figure 8.1 Iconic Che cartoon

Source: Cartoon by Matthew Diffee. The New Yorker Collection / Cartoon Bank.

Revolution can leave us shaking our heads. The Revolution becomes an empty signifier—it can represent just about anything you might desire.

Then again, Bart Simpson on a t-shirt worn by Che Guevara, in a cartoon in the *New Yorker*, actually makes some sense. We understand how all these images are linked together because the Cuban government has taken a defiant attitude towards an imperial power through both its symbolic repertoire and its material acts for more than fifty years. Bart may be no revolutionary, but we can understand his resistance to unjust authority (Principal Seymour Skinner, Homer Simpson, and Nelson Muntz). Bart also shares a certain charisma with the icons of the Revolution. Like Castro and Che, he is quick-witted, intelligent, and a born leader for the weak, willing to stand up to bullies at risk to his own life.

Bart, of course, is a cartoon. Che and Fidel were idealistic revolutionaries, men willing to use violence in order to reshape Cuba in their image. Given this rather significant distinction, the fact that we can relate to Che and Fidel through Bart Simpson ought to give us pause. It tells us something about how North Americans have made meaning of the events in Cuba since the 1950s, how they have made the Revolution into a legend that serves their narrative needs (a need, for example, for youthful rebel heroes or despotic villains). It tells us very little about Cuba.

If we are to move beyond this problem, we must seek to understand the Cuban Revolution, along with Che and Fidel, as phenomena in time. Unlike cartoon figures, the Revolution and its leaders lived through specific historical moments, and changed along with global historical events. Even if part of Che's appeal was that he died young in a failed Bolivian Revolution (1967), he did leave a complex imprint on the historical record, and was fundamentally a man of the 1960s. Bart Simpson, on the other hand, will forever be ten years old, and seems to live out of time. He is a simple and enduring symbol of the youthful rebel spirit, leaving no actual victims in his wake and is as relevant today as he was when he was created in 1987. Real people don't enjoy that luxury. They impact other's lives in substantive ways, and they either change with the times or get left behind, dead or forgotten.

If we are thinking about change over time, we might begin by asking a simple question: when was the Cuban Revolution? A literal answer would focus on the violent conflict during 1957 and 1958, when a guerrilla movement led by Fidel Castro, his brother Raúl, Camilo Cienfuegos, Che Guevara, and others, fought Fulgencio Batista's regime to a standstill, helped discredit the government in the eyes of the United States (so that military support was cut off), and took their time while a broad opposition coalition came together to force Batista out of power. The Revolution, in this sense, was over on January 1, 1959, when rebels marched gloriously through the streets of Cuban cities.

With Batista gone, it was unclear what would happen next. The rebels were a loose coalition of different opposition groups, not a single army. The fluidity of the moment represented an opportunity for whoever might assert their control over the situation, and it was then that Fidel Castro's political and rhetorical skills became fully evident. In the weeks following January first, Castro made dozens of speeches and public appearances, declaring over and over again both the end of tyranny and the beginning of some as yet unspecified process. He mostly avoided talking about agendas, and focused his energies on transforming himself into the undisputed savior of the nation.

This helps to explain a photo taken while Castro spoke at Camp Colombia, an old army barracks, on January 8, 1959, which became one of the most powerful images we have of these early days. It records a speech that was not unlike many he gave during his victorious descent on Havana, full of exhortations to unity, promises of real change, and vague threats to his enemies. At some point during the speech, doves were released in the crowd (rumors always had them descending from the sky). They flew through the air and settled on the podium. One even sat on Castro's shoulders (Figure 8.2). Critics claim the fix was in, that Castro had seed for the birds or that the spotlight trained on Castro attracted them to him. It did not matter. The doves, read popularly both as a sign of peace and of divine approval of Castro's role as *El Comandante* (the Commander), sealed some unspoken deal. Castro, as the Revolution, would save the Cuban people.[2]

Castro's words and deeds signaled the next phase of the revolutionary process, which linked consolidation of the new regime to the transformation of Cuban society. The cross-class alliances that overthrew Batista rapidly disintegrated as Fidel asserted power within the new coalition and implemented a radical egalitarian transformation. He announced

Figure 8.2 Fidel Castro and the doves

land reforms, the nationalization of foreign property, and decided to build closer ties to the Soviet Union. He drove thousands of opponents into exile. At once radical and authoritarian, his government was simultaneously a revolution and a socialist regime intent on concentrating power.

The distinction between a regime and a revolution is not simply academic. The very term *revolution* implies a transformation, and has been used again and again across Latin America to denote moments in which the social and political order was overturned. The 1910 Mexican Revolution, the 1952 Bolivian Revolution, and the 1979 Nicaraguan Revolution saw old systems collapse and new political actors create more inclusive political orders. At some point each of these new regimes also seemed less like radical transformative governments and more like entrenched power blocs defending their own interests. The "Revolution" in each of these cases then became an argument. If you could claim to represent the Revolution, you were the legitimate heirs of the last popular upheaval, and thus the true representatives of the people. Mexico's *Partido Revolucionario Institucional* (Institutional Revolutionary Party, PRI), for example, ruled the country as the heirs of Pancho Villa and Emiliano Zapata for seventy-one years. This claim suggested that the Mexican Revolution had never ended, and that the best way poor people could see their interests served was to work with, and not against the state.

A similar, but even more powerful sentiment has long been attached to the Cuban Revolution. Even in 1959 Fidel insisted that the Revolution was not an event, but a process. Over time, the long-standing antipathy of the United States and the sense of incompleteness that has plagued the island have reinforced this claim. If you take the regime's rhetoric at face value, the Revolution is still not over, the battle is still being fought, and Cubans must remain loyal, forever, until victory.[3]

For more than half a century, this merging of Revolution–nation–regime has dominated everyday life in Cuba. It has shaped politics, social life, and even private affairs, leaving what was once one of the most dynamic and open societies in Latin America closed to most forms of political expression. Near constant surveillance, or at least a fear of surveillance, has produced a society where distrust is ever-present, where acts of criticism are carefully framed to avoid detection, and where individuals are acutely aware of their powerlessness.

As masters of political management, the regime has spent decades perfecting the craft of responding to growing disaffection by making limited concessions, and then rescinding those concessions just as quickly. Stressful moments may bring new busses or increased rations, restrictions on the entry into hotels might be lifted, or dollars (and even cell phones) legalized. These privileges may also be taken away in an instant. As long as the United States remains the enemy, Cubans must live in the Revolution, which links Cuban nationalism and Socialist revolution so seamlessly that to critique the Revolution is to be a traitor to the Cuban nation. And to do that is to opt for social and economic marginalization, the possibility of jail, and perhaps exile.

The threat may be constant, but the regime is not. There is little in the experience since the 1950s that suggests that the Revolution can be understood as a stable or singular phenomenon. Rather, the regime has taken a heterodox approach to changing Cuban society, keeping itself in power, coping with changing international circumstances, and dealing with their own successes and failures. Even Castro narrated different phases of the Revolution—the Push towards Communism during the 1960s (discussed below), the Retreat to Socialism of the 1970s (promoting soviet-style planning, material incentives, and limited private enterprise), the Rectification of the 1980s (when limited private enterprise was eliminated), and since 1989 the Special Period in a Time of Peace (the name seems fittingly empty of content). The only constant in Cuba's recent past has been the U.S. embargo, and the possibility of blaming all failures on the unflagging hostility of the U.S. government. One need not be too cynical to imagine that at critical moments of potential thawing in United States–Cuban relations, Castro actively sought to renew this enmity, as without it he would have no one to blame for Cuba's problems. How many of us recall that in February 1996 Castro shot down the Miami-based planes flown by *Brothers to the Rescue* (an anti-Castro group that was dropping pamphlets on the island) at the very moment when the Clinton administration seemed to be on the verge of changing U.S. policy towards Cuba?

Making a Revolution

With an annual per capita income of $353 in 1959, Cuba was hardly a poor country by Latin American standards. Cuba was, however, a highly unequal society, one of the most unequal in the Americas. Rural workers earned only about $91 annually, leaving the country with a Gini coefficient of around 0.57.[4] The economic instability of the sugar industry (almost one-quarter of the workforce was employed in sugar, leaving them idle four months per year) and foreign domination of the economy (among other things, 75 percent of arable land was foreign owned) exacerbated these inequalities, generating twin sets of grievances for ordinary Cubans. Though they relied on sugar and the United States for their livelihoods, both were also a source of misery.

The appropriate means to liberate the country from these dependencies were far from clear. While the M-26-7 (named for the origins of their movement in the failed July 26, 1953 attack on the Moncada Barracks in Santiago de Cuba) under Fidel Castro grabbed most headlines and clearly led the opposition, Batista fell because of a concerted effort that included rural guerrillas, an urban underground, and striking workers. His fate was sealed when the police and military refused to support the regime in late 1958. A small minority believed that all the opposition needed to do was topple the dictator, and that further reform was unnecessary. Many more believed that they needed to establish stable democratic institutions, like those imagined in earlier political struggles (as recently as 1940). Most Cubans agreed that their political parties were hopelessly rotten, and needed to be remade with entirely new faces. There was likewise considerable popular support for limited economic and social reforms, especially those that would put foreign owned assets into the hands of Cubans.

The differing agendas proposed in 1959 were not easily reconciled, and any faction that managed to consolidate their hold on power would have to do so in a perilous setting. Too much change would alienate the United States and powerful economic interests. In the past the enemies of reform had been quite capable of scuttling even minor efforts (notably during the regime of Ramón Grau San Martín in 1933). Yet many revolutionaries were unwilling to settle for meager results, and could defend their interests with weapons. Eastern peasants demanded immediate land reform. Urban workers demanded immediate 20 percent wage increases, better working conditions, and more control of the shop floor. Others demanded rent freezes, housing, education reform, women's rights, and the removal of Batista era government officials.

Castro proved to be an extraordinarily savvy politician as he dealt successfully with these various demands. He found ways to isolate (or execute) his rivals, to build a tight-knit and loyal following, to ensure his own survival, and concentrate power in his own hands. All of this he accomplished while also enacting concrete measures that responded to popular demands. The March 1959 Urban Reform Law mandated substantial rent reductions (50 percent for rent under $100). Telephone and utility rates were reduced, wages increased, and the property of high government officials seized. The Agrarian Law of May 1959 restricted landholdings to 1,000 acres, with limited exceptions. Together, these reforms dramatically reduced poverty in the early years of the Castro regime. By 1963 Cuba's Gini coefficient had fallen to 0.28.

Reform meant confrontation with the United States, and here Castro again proved adept at turning circumstances to his favor. As it became clearer during 1959–60 that radical reform meant a violent clash with the United States, the country grew increasingly polarized. Though much of the opposition was Cuban in origin, Castro managed to cast acts of sabotage, attempted assassinations, and any number of protests as the work of the CIA (in part, because sometimes they were). Cubans, he argued, must unify to confront Cuba's internal and external enemies. He also increasingly argued that the only way to do this was through an embrace of communism. As he convinced more and more Cubans that a liberated Cuba depended on his communist Revolution, he was also able to convince many that opposition amounted to treason.

With every successful confrontation with the United States, Cubans saw a leader who could defend their nation as no other ever had. He bravely went to New York and Washington, taking the rhetorical battle directly to the enemy. He survived their assassination attempts unscathed. And after the failed invasion at the *Playa Girón* (Bay of Pigs) on April 17, 1961, he could rightly claim to have repelled an American invasion. In the face of such a compelling heroic narrative, moderates who called for elections could be dismissed as bourgeois dupes, traitors to the Revolution who would allow an intractable enemy to weaken the nation by fomenting electoral discord. Dissent became criminal (100,000 suspected dissidents were in jail by the end of April 1961).

Radical economic policies had a similar effect on Castro's hold on power. By the end of 1961, Castro had nationalized 85 percent of Cuban industry. As more and more of the economy wound up in the hands of the state, the regime eliminated certain professions (including insurance, real estate, and law), and many of Castro's enemies and rivals lost their livelihoods. Without opportunities in Cuba, these potential opponents of the regime were increasingly inclined to consider exile. The pull to leave was exacerbated by the Kennedy administration's offer of asylum on exceptionally easy terms to Cubans, a policy designed to isolate the regime but which in fact made it easier for Castro to eliminate the opposition.[5] With the opposition increasingly ensconced in Miami, revolutionary militants took over virtually all facets of the island's economic and political life.

Had the Castro regime been simply a run-of-the-mill authoritarian government, its success in consolidating its hold on the state and isolating or eliminating the opposition might have been viewed as an end in and of itself, or at the very least a propitious moment to begin stripping the country of its assets and opening off-shore bank accounts. This was not however, a regime like those that then ruled Nicaragua, Haiti, the Dominican Republic, and elsewhere. Castro wanted control, but he wanted to use that power to bring Cubans together to collectively remake, defend, and police their nation.

Democratic processes could have linked the masses to the state, but would also create opportunities for the opposition to upend the revolutionary process. Castro then needed structures that would empower the masses, but would do so in ways that limited the autonomy individual actors enjoyed in liberal democracies. He needed to control the process even as he created a system that allowed popular groups to participate. The way he did this was by creating a series of mass organizations whose members had access to the state to make their demands and participate in the political life of the nation, but required that they swear complete loyalty to the state as a precondition for participating. The first of these organizations, *Asocicación de Juventud Rebelde* (Association of Rebel Youth, AJR), was created in March 1960. On the advice of Vilma Espín, a fellow M-26-7 fighter and then Castro's sister in law, the regime founded the *Federación de Mujeres Cubanas* (Cuban Federation of

Women, FMC) in August 1960. In September 1960, after a public rebuke from the Organization of American States (OAS), the *Comités de Defensa de la Revolución* (Committees for the Defense of the Revolution, CDRs) were convened. The *Asociación Nacional de Agricultores Pequeños* (National Small Farmers Association, ANAP) and *Central de Trabajadores de Cuba* (Cuban Workers Confederation, CTC) were likewise turned into mass organizations around this time.

In the heady days of the early 1960s, these associations offered Cubans an opportunity to participate in a process that promised to liberate Cuba from its imperial past, and they attracted tens of thousands of members, who in turn provided critical support for the regime. By the end of 1961, there were 300,000 members in popular militias, and 800,000 in the CDRs. Explicitly charged with physically defending the country from invasion, these groups did much more. Together with other mass organizations they served as pressure groups, demanding any number of benefits from the state, and taking credit for revolutionary programs. They were also instruments for the dissemination of revolutionary fervor, charged with raising consciousness, administering healthcare, encouraging students to go to school and workers to go to work, and as always, ferreting out enemies of the Cuban people.

When the labor ministry introduced new laws mandating secure and safe environments for women, the FMC used these laws to attract new members and new support for the regime. By 1962 the FMC had 376,000 members, many of whom could directly attribute significant life changes to the Revolution. In 1959 one quarter of the women in the workforce were domestic servants, a category that ceased to exist after the Revolution. During the early 1960s FMC efforts helped 19,000 former household servants attend special schools and find new jobs. Tens of thousands were given scholarships, materials, and training to study for new professions, and over a thousand entered the revolutionary vanguard in public administration.

Utopias

Although often undertaken as practical efforts to shore up support for the regime, we should not underestimate the ways early revolutionary projects were linked to a utopian vision of what Cuba could become. Articulated most clearly by Che Guevara, the Revolution was a movement against history, an effort to remake the world. This made particular sense given the challenges the new regime faced. Utopian thinking seemed in some ways the only means to get out of the very real conundrums that Cuba faced as a monoculture society ninety miles away from a hostile super power. At first, the utopian thinking came in a plan to shift the country away from its dependence on sugar exports, to diversify and industrialize Cuba in order to ensure its independence. As Minister of Industry and a principal architect of the land reform, Che directed this transformation.

Either out of pure naiveté or simple desperation, Guevara chose to forgo the socialist phase of revolutionary reform and push Cuba directly into communism. With an eye towards the end of money, Che worked to eliminate cash transactions for food, transportation, and rent. Rejecting the suggestion that he keep market mechanisms in place in order to ensure productivity, Che insisted that Cubans could do away with the law of value, which allocated resources where they were productive instead of where they were most needed. His was a program of centralized planning, a program in which the state would directly intervene in all aspects of the economy to ensure "balanced" development. He would rely mostly on the willingness of people to sacrifice for the common good in order to make this happen.

Under Che's economic model, businesses would not be supported because of their viability or efficiency or their capacity to generate enough revenues to cover their costs. They would be supported because they were deemed intrinsically good. Centralized budgeting would allow the government to allocate funds based on ideological rather than economistic (read bourgeois) reasons. Wage scales would be eliminated because all workers deserved the same income. Bonuses and overtime would similarly be banned. Even though material incentives were common in the Eastern Bloc, Che argued that they encouraged individualism and undermined the revolutionary project of creating "new men," with new forms of consciousness. Hard work would instead be recognized with moral rewards—banners, flags, pins, and plaques rewarding the contribution of workers to the Revolution. These would in turn help foment widespread revolutionary consciousness, which Che understood as an essential ingredient in the battle against Cuba's powerful enemies.

The gendered quality of this project was inescapable. Guevara's new man was just that. For all its pretenses to feminism and nods to Vilma Espín and the FMC, the leadership of the M-26-7 viewed males, females, and their sexuality in extraordinarily conservative ways. As images of Castro in the fields cutting sugar cane attested, the Revolution was the work of strong-backed men—men who enjoyed a cigar, a strong drink, and took pleasure in the sensuality of revolutionary women (Figure 8.3). This image linked Castro's physical strength to the survival of the Revolution against its enemies.

Figure 8.3 Castro cutting cane as a part of the 1970 Cuban sugar harvest
Source: Photo by Gilberto Ante/Roger Viollet/Getty Images

We see this both in the ways that Castro's heterosexual masculinity was fetishized, and in the fact that homosexuals were actively persecuted by the regime into the 1990s. In the *machista* culture of the Revolution, their attraction to males was linked to national weakness, decadence, and U.S. imperialism. The New Man could not tolerate homosexuals, narcissists who were supposedly obsessed with self-satisfying pleasure and debauchery; the essence of the counter-revolution.

Prostitutes likewise drew special ire from the regime. The sex trades were banned in the early revolutionary period, and former prostitutes were sometimes given opportunities to train for a new career. Like homosexuality, prostitution was linked to carnal pleasure, decadence, and U.S. imperialism (after all, North Americans were frequent sex-tourists in Cuba before 1959). The prohibition produced at least one memorable tale of a drug-dependent prostitute who turned her life around and received a university education as a result of the Revolution,[6] but one supposes that not all prostitutes viewed the regime's efforts to outlaw their profession favorably. The sex trades had always been one of the few ways that poor, uneducated women could earn a decent living, and quickly returned to prominence in the 1990s when Castro embraced tourism as a means to earn foreign revenues.

These experiences remind us of the difference between imagining and actually creating a new man, or new society. The new Cuba was the vision of a revolutionary vanguard, and in creating the new society the regime invariably attempted to impose a series of practices on Cubans, some of which were unwelcome. The Revolution promised to liberate women, but drove millions (if you include domestic workers) out of work. Indeed, the end of domestic service, prostitution, and the flight of many middle-class women to the United States actually caused a reduction in the number of women in the workforce during the 1960s.

Later the Revolution would promise domestic equality under the Family Code (1975), which required Cuban males to do an equal share of the housework. Like the ban on prostitution and domestic service, it was a utopian idea, dreamed up by the vanguard, and its affect on actual Cuban women was quite uneven. Yet even if we mock these top-down reforms for their idealism we should not forget the substantive changes Cuban women saw in their lives during these years. In part because of the exodus after 1959, in part because the Cuban state did open educational and professional opportunities for women, and in part due to the efforts of the FMC, by the end of the 1960s Cuban women found it easier to pursue a career, to get a divorce, and to make their own reproductive decisions than women anywhere else in Latin America. All could visit a doctor if they were sick, and virtually none faced the kind of desperate hunger that had affected millions before 1959, and still affected millions in other parts of the region.

Dystopias

There is no question that some aspects of Cuba's experience during the 1960s are best read as comedies. It seems quaint to think that anyone ever believed that moral incentives—asking workers to be more productive because it is good, rather than because they would personally benefit—would ever work. Few people today believe that the state has the capacity to transform consciousness in even small ways, let alone direct the massive transformation from individualistic thinking and towards the communist consciousness that Che envisioned. Our own awareness of corruption, nepotism, and cronyism in Eastern Bloc countries (and Cuba) long ago put the lie to that promise.

We need only examine the rate of absenteeism in Cuba during these years to see the problems in Che's theories. By 1967 the daily absentee rate at work was about 20 percent across the country, and 50 percent in some regions, including Oriente (the heartland of the Revolution). In part these rates were due to low morale, and in part they were due to the fact that mismanagement elsewhere left workers standing in long lines for food, provisions, and buses instead of working. Even accounting for these factors however, we are left with the clear impression that Cubans effectively went on strike to protest moral rewards.

It was not simply moral incentives that failed. Economic diversification failed. Industrialization failed. Centralized budgeting failed spectacularly. The government confronted food shortages as early as 1962, when it began rationing food, clothing and consumer items. By 1963 production volumes of any number of staple crops had plummeted and production across the economy had declined. The sugar harvest also fell, from 6.7 million tons in 1961 to 3.8 million in 1963. Facing pressure from the Soviets and an economy in chaos, Castro then turned his attention to increasing sugar exports in order to improve Cuba's balance of payments.

Even this was something of a disaster. As a part of a lurching series of policy shifts during the 1960s, Castro abandoned Che's management strategies in 1964 (Che himself went off to promote worldwide revolution), and committed most of the country's productive capacity to producing a ten million ton sugar harvest by 1970. Cuba had never had a harvest this large, and if successful, it would be an enormous victory for the Revolution. Road construction, manufacturing, port facilities, and agriculture were all refocused to serve sugar. Most other economic activities were neglected.

It may have made sense to prop up Cuban exports by reinvesting in the neglected sugar sector, but beyond emphasizing sugar, Castro also punished those sectors that might have dynamically supplemented sugar exports by selling to local markets. Renewed land reform in 1963 concentrated land in large state run export facilities (in sharp contrast to first land reform in 1959, which put land into the hands of peasants). Working under the logic that, if peasants possessed land, they would work on it to the detriment of the state farm, the state increasing denied small-scale farmers access to land of their own. Those most negatively affected by this decision were some of the Revolution's most ardent supporters, peasants who had been providing a wide range of fruits and vegetables to a shortage plagued domestic market since 1959.[7]

Fearing that small businessmen also represented a threat to the regime, Castro nationalized 57,000 small businesses in 1968. These were not pre-revolutionary holdouts. Most had been established since 1959. Among the prohibited businesses were street vendors who provided essential services, including sellers of fruit, bread, coffee, eggs, sandwiches, and other goods. These small businessmen and women worked in the space between the informal and formal economy, selling some goods they got from official sources and others they purchased on the black market; commodities grown on small farms and sent to market without the permission of the state. As such they also filled a critical need for Cuban consumers, because state cafeterias and stores could not meet the needs of the people. And with the formal sector unable to fill the void left by the absence of the informal economy, shortages became worse after the street vendors were banned. Spare parts for cars, fresh fruit, and even coffee were increasingly available only through the underground economy. Minor protests flared here and there, and graffiti attacking the regime began to show up on walls in Havana.

Even the mass organizations that earlier helped legitimize the revolutionary state were failing by the mid-1960s, their initial promise having faded into bureaucratic intransigence, nepotism, and a tendency to abuse their power and spy on ordinary Cubans. Castro responded with new efforts to win popular support, including a much ballyhooed program called Local Power, and the comical sounding Campaign against the Bureaucracy (parodied in Tómas Gutiérrez Alea's film, *The Death of a Bureaucrat*). Local Power was (as most Cubans knew) mostly an illusion. By the mid-1960s the mechanisms that had once promised power to the people were chained to the state.

Workers, for instance, saw their unions wither away during these years. They lost the right to strike, and thus to demand higher wages. The grievance commissions that the government put in place to arbitrate work-place conflicts were abandoned in 1964, jettisoned because they sided with workers too often. They were replaced with work councils, which were indirectly charged with enforcing the will of the state and labor discipline. Workers were invited to work cooperatively with management in the councils, where their demands were set aside in favor of efforts to increase productivity, save materials, reduce absenteeism, promote voluntary labor, prevent accidents, and of course, cultivate a revolutionary consciousness. There would be no more bonuses, guaranteed sick days, or strikes.

In a tragically absurd combination of these initiatives, the very mechanisms created to improve the lives of Cubans sometimes did the opposite. During the late 1960s planning was impossible, as the principal planning agencies, JUCEPLAN[8] and the National Bank, lost 1,500 positions in the Campaign Against Bureaucracy, and could not function because receipts, taxes, cost accounting, and interest were all abolished. The budget itself ceased to exist between 1967 and 1970, replaced by a series of *fidelista* mini-plans. Political control fell to an ever more vanguardist Cuban Communist Party (Fidel's version was founded in 1965), which spent most of its energies demanding revolutionary consciousness and self-sacrifice from Cubans. By 1970 the GDP was barely higher than it had been in 1965, and in per capita terms it was lower.

To be sure, more than mere incompetence hurt the Cubans. They faced the loss of professional technical expertise, and were not always up to the difficult task of reorienting Cuban trade away from the U.S. market and towards the Soviet bloc. The larger freighters that took Cuban sugar to Russian ports needed deeper harbors, more port facilities and warehouses. Inventory needed to be stored, and orders were not quickly filled. Cubans also had to deal with the challenges caused by bad Soviet parts and general shortages of spare parts for their U.S.-made cars, trucks, appliances, and more. Still, in simple terms, Cubans were worse off in 1970 than they had been in 1959. When it became clear that on top of all of this, the sugar harvest was going to fail to reach its goal (in the end it was 8.5 million tons), Castro appeared before an enormous crowd in the Plaza de la Revolucíon on July 26 to offer his resignation.

Cubans refused his offer, resoundingly. The question is: why? We might start with Castro's charisma. It is difficult to divorce the simple power of Castro's magnetism from his actual policies in the early years of his regime. He was rare among politicians for his ability to stir the crowd. Cubans also responded to his common touch, his willingness to get down from his jeep and cut cane with the workers, his capacity to appear anywhere and everywhere, his tirelessness, and his simple ability to stir up feelings of fraternal (and later paternal) love. These qualities made certain failings worthy of forgiveness. Nonetheless, while Castro's appeal ought to inform our interpretation of these events, it does not fully explain why the crowd refused his resignation.

It may be that the crowd's response was some sort of common emotional catharsis, the expression of the sense that his failure was everyone's failure. While not exactly a democratic mandate for thirty-eight more years in office, we could interpret this as a sign of just how successful Castro had been in identifying himself and his revolutionary struggle as synonymous with the Cuban people. Still, even this is not enough to understand the enduring popularity of Fidel Castro in 1970 in spite of the repeated failures of the 1960s. To understand this we need to come to terms with the fact that millions of Cubans shared Castro's utopian dreams, his belief that Cubans had to remain ever vigilant in defending their nation against the United States, and his sense that many of these crises were the fault of sinister foreign elements.

We see this in more than just the crowd's response. Moral incentives, for example, produced high rates of absenteeism. They also inspired millions of Cubans to sacrifice for their country/revolution. Volunteer work, begun in October 1959 to prepare the Havana waterfront for a convention of travel agents, drew many millions of participants during the 1960s. Two hundred thousand Cubans volunteered for a teachers' brigade committed to reducing illiteracy during the 1960s, which reduced the adult illiteracy rate from 21 percent in 1959 to 13 percent by 1970. In 1970 alone 1.2 million Cubans left their jobs and worked in the sugar harvest.

Moral incentives may have been a planning disaster, but in many ways they were an ideological success. They highlighted the need for sacrifice, and acted as a means of linking the people's sacrifice to a national revolutionary project that would not otherwise succeed. When Cubans suffered some form of deprivation, they were doing the work of the Revolution. One could be proud, and ought not complain. Moreover, Cubans did believe that they were a poor people living on a rich island. Who could challenge the argument that, absent the negative impact of neo-colonialism and capitalism, Cubans would be prosperous, even as prosperous as the North Americans? And who could argue with the material benefits many poor people gained under Castro?

Their idealism spoke of a generational moment, framed both by the cold war and Cubans' long history of fighting imperial rule. Twenty years later their willingness to contribute to voluntary labor was not nearly as strong as it was early on, and Cubans would increasingly be noted more for their cynicism than their idealism. These however, were heady times. Most Cubans were willing to suffer, and suffer a great deal, if it would lead to a better world.

The Documents: Over Time

Knowing what would become of Cuba's revolution in the 1970s and beyond, it might be tempting to dismiss those cane-cutting revolutionaries as naïve. Like North American anti-war protestors, Mexican students who marched before the 1968 Olympics demanding greater democracy, and the jubilant Czechoslovakians who celebrated the Prague Spring before the Soviet tanks rolled in, today the Cubans who sacrificed themselves in pursuit of becoming new men seem so very young, and so very distant. It is good to have this perspective, because it reminds us that the 1960s were a specific historical era in Cuba and elsewhere. This perspective also reminds us that the era was short lived. Cuba was not alone in growing increasingly conservative and authoritarian after 1970.

It is this shift that compels us to consider time very closely when we imagine the Cuban Revolution. Neither the Cuban state nor its enemies prefers this approach. The Cuban state represents the Revolution as timeless, as a single phenomenon that connects the M-26-7 Movement, the Bay of Pigs, and the idealism of the 1960s to the less than ideal present, holding that all the ideals of the era could have been accomplished if not for the implacable hostility of the United States. Its enemies prefer a stripped down and simplistic version of an unchanging evil, a totalitarian threat that is embodied by an unchanging Castro regime (even if Raúl has replaced Fidel). These images serve certain political ends very well. A dysfunctional relationship with the United States has reinforced the power of the regime for half a century (the 1996 Helms-Burton Act in the United States, for instance, strengthened the regime by mandating that U.S. relations with Cuba would not be normalized until all those who had lost property in the Revolution received full restitution). It has also provided a flash point for U.S. politics, creating opportunities for U.S. politicians to win votes in South Florida. What these images don't do is tell us much about what has changed over half a century. And they tell us almost nothing about how Cubans' perspective on their government has changed over time.

In order to attempt to capture some of this change, below we present five documents. The first comes from 1965, the second 1990, and the third, fourth, and fifth from the very recent past. The first is an iconic example of the optimism of the 1960s. The second, written in the immediate aftermath of the collapse of the Soviet Union, offers a perspective on the dashed hopes and dreams of that era through a meditation on the tensions between Cuba's New Man and the Cuba that has been lost through the exile of so many people. The final documents consider just what is left of the revolutionary dream after all these decades, and offer a perspective on the corrosive effects that five decades of authoritarian rule have had on life on the island.

Each document is in its own way a commentary on the tensions between idealist reform and authoritarian rule that first surfaced during the 1960s, and each is informed by a loyalty to something (Cuba, the Revolution) that over time became increasingly difficult to disentangle from the deleterious effects of one party rule. The author of the first document is no longer alive, but the authors of the other texts remained in Cuba, choosing their love of the patria and lingering attachment to the ideals of the 1960s over the freedom and prosperity of exile. That in and of itself should remind us that this era continues to offer a promise that we are well advised to take seriously.

Document 8.1 is a letter that Che Guevara wrote to Carlos Quijano, editor of the Montevideo weekly magazine *Marcha*, in March 1965. The letter represents one of Che's signature intellectual accomplishments, written while on a tour of Asia, Africa, and Europe. While it seems clear in retrospect that the tour represented an effort by Castro to move Che out of the administrative responsibilities he had assumed in Cuba, at the time it also made a great deal of sense to promote Che as the face of the utopian project. This essay contributed in considerable ways to building the legend of Che the visionary revolutionary, as it contains his clearest description of the New Man, the figure who promised to realize the revolutionary project. Because of this, this essay has long been read in contradictory ways; as an ideal to live up to, and as an impossibly naïve work of propaganda.

By the time Che wrote the New Man essay, a clear majority of those who remained on the island supported the regime, especially because of its success in defending the country from what Cubans understood as a foreign invasion. Those who spoke critically of the Revolution often found themselves in prison or forced out of the country, often the former leading to the latter. Once in exile in Miami, New York, or Madrid, their writing came to be characterized by bitter feelings of loss and a clear and unremitting hatred of Castro. Even if they had once been somewhat sympathetic to the reform agenda, in their stories the regime was violent, arbitrary, cynical, the worst kind of dictatorship.[9]

On the island these writers were often called *gusanos* (worms), an insult that suggested treason on their part. In the 1960s it was relatively easy to dismiss critics in this way, in part because the Revolution had such an array of genuine boosters who had remained in Cuba, including a new generation of artists, filmmakers, poets and writers who were producing brilliant and innovative work in support of the regime. These artists were not simple stooges for the regime. Much of their work was mildly critical of the government, mocking bureaucrats and demanding the best from the Revolution. They were tolerated because they were producing brilliant work, work that found an audience around the world, work that signaled the openness of the Cuban Revolution to self-criticism.

This happy state of affairs came to an abrupt end with the arrest of the poet Herberto Padilla in 1971. Imprisoned, tortured, and forced to make a humiliating confession and name supposed subversives in his circle of friends, his experience had a deeply chilling affect on Cuban intellectual life. In its aftermath, the Cuban government began to exercise considerable control over the arts, and many of the intellectuals who had imagined themselves as revolutionaries during the 1960s increasingly found that there was no place for them in Cuban society.

Some chose exile. Others developed an increasingly sophisticated repertoire of strategies for critiquing the regime while remaining within the revolutionary fold. Jesús Díaz (who was only forced into exile after many years of critical work), Tómas Gutiérrez Alea and Senel Paz, the author of Document 8.2, wrote, produced plays and films, and generally skirted a fine line between art and politics in their work. The text presented here, which is an excerpt from Paz' brilliant short story, *El bosque, el lobo y el hombre nuevo* (The Forest, the Wolf, and the New Man[10]) had life both as literature and as the basis for one of the most important films in Cuban cinema history, *Fresa y chocolate* (Strawberry and Chocolate, released in 1993), which was directed by Gutiérrez Alea and Juan Carlos Tabío. Published in 1990 and set in 1979, the story considers the relationship between a young, upright revolutionary student (the archetypal New Man) who is studying at the University of Havana and his urbane homosexual friend, Diego. They embody many of the conflicts between the new, revolutionary Cuba and the bourgeois elites of the *ancien regime*, with the crux of the story focusing on whether or not Diego can remain in Cuba. Diego is a fierce nationalist, and swears loyalty to the Revolution, yet his need to express himself freely ultimately leaves him with no choice but to emigrate. The selection here is drawn from the portion of the story where Diego elects to leave.

Paz set this story in 1979 largely because this was a moment when the ideals of the Revolution remained viable to many within and outside of Cuba. The Soviet Union was still supporting Cuba then, and Fidel's charisma had not faltered much during a decade of significant transitions away from the free-for-all of 1960s era reform (and its vast dreams, as embodied in Che's work) and towards a heavily institutionalized Revolution that was more closely aligned with the Soviet model. In 1979 it seemed that the Revolution still had life, and could promise better standards of living and greater equality, even if it could not promise the political freedoms, freedom of artistic expression, and rich intellectual life that many in the island's artistic and intellectual circles desired.

Most Cubans knew that some of the Revolution's accomplishments were illusory, that beneath all the bluster Cubans continued to struggle, continued to hoard dollars and rely on the black market for many of their necessities. Given the chance, many would choose exile over life on the island, as 125,000 did when Fidel Castro briefly lifted exit restrictions in 1980 (the Mariel boat lift). Even then, few could imagine just how crucial Soviet aid was to maintaining the Revolution. They would discover the extent of their dependence after 1989, when the collapse of the Soviet Union devastated the island's economy, bringing widespread hunger and devastation. For tens of thousands of Cubans their only escape from the disaster lay in shabbily constructed flotation devices that they hoped would deliver them to the United States. By the early 1990s, over a million Cubans were living in the United States.

Writing from 1990, Paz offered 1979 as a moment in which the choice between freedom and equality still seemed possible. From 1989 forward, Cubans were faced with different challenges. They had to determine how to revive the economy, were forced to open the island to trade and private investment, to reinvigorate the hotel and restaurant sector in search of hard currencies, and to turn a blind eye while sex tourism again flourished. By the end of the 1990s a taxi driver could earn many times what a doctor was paid, and many of the vaunted accomplishments of the 1960s seemed like distant history.

Yoani Sánchez, the author of Documents 8.3, 8.4. 8.5, is a product of this "Special Period." She is also one of the most accomplished bloggers Latin America has produced since the advent of the form. Her work is featured on her own blog (Generación Y), on the Huffington Post, and elsewhere. Since beginning her blog in 2007, she has also been one of the most read critics of the Castro regime anywhere.

Except of course, in Cuba, where her blog has been repeatedly blocked, and where Cubans are often forced to learn what she is saying by hearing about it from abroad. In the past she furtively wrote her short postings on her own computer, put them on a thumb drive, and then emailed them from hotel computers and internet cafes to the friends who maintained her blog's German website. She would also use her time in cafes to download volumes of information onto flash drives and then take them home so that she could read the material she sought (she has long maintained that the thumb drive is an essential tool for social and political change in Cuba). Sánchez has been harassed and detained (at one point tweeting out her arrest even as it happened). So far she has refused to leave.

Her impact in Cuba is difficult to ascertain. In some sense she is like the critics long produced by the regime, tolerated to a point, and then forced into exile. This worked in the past in part because critics had access to relatively limited audiences, though it is not clear that this logic applies to people like Sánchez, whose work defies censorship in part because of the nature of the internet. At once funny, sad, and inspiring, and widely read on the island and off, Sánchez seems to have succeeded in offering an alternative narrative to life in Cuba to the one posited by the regime. Having stayed (she actively chose life in Cuba over life in Europe), she can authoritatively claim that she has remained staunchly loyal to the island even if she is a harsh critic of the Castros. Whether or not this points the way to an alternative future depends on her ability to continue to mobilize these new technologies, and whether or not they truly have the capacity to produce change.

Read together, Che Guevara, Senel Paz, and Yoani Sánchez offer us three dramatically different visions of the promise and possibilities envisioned in the 1960s. Each must be read for the individual proclivities of the author—the fiery idealism of the revolutionary set against the prose of the storyteller and the pointed critiques of the blogger. Each should also be read for the time in which it was created. Guevara's work could only be a product of the dreams of the 1960s. Paz hearkens back to the 1960s through his own ambivalent take on the New Man. Operating in two periods instead of one, Paz is also telling us something both about the height of the Revolutionary Man and his seeming demise in this story. Sánchez in turn gazes over the rubble of revolutionary reform with a cynicism that is very much of the new millennium.

In considering these texts chronologically, it is possible that we might create a larger narrative of the Revolution, of its birth, maturity, and decline. Then again, it is possible that these three different writers, each separated by decades from the other, are simply describing different worlds, or different places within the same world. This is the challenge we face when we try to sum up an experience as vast and contradictory as the Cuban Revolution.

Document 8.1 Letter from Major Ernesto Che Guevara to Carlos Quijano, editor of the Montevideo weekly magazine *Marcha* (March, 1965)

Source: Guevara Internet Archive (http://www.marxists.org/archive/guevara/1965/03/man-socialism-alt.htm). Copyright: © Ocean Press, www.oceanbooks.com.au. Reprinted by permission.

I am finishing these notes while travelling through Africa, moved by the desire to keep my promise, although after some delay. I should like to do so by dealing with the topic that appears in the title. I believe it might be of interest to Uruguayan readers.

It is common to hear how capitalist spokesmen use as an argument in the ideological struggle against socialism the assertion that such a social system or the period of building socialism upon which we have embarked, is characterized by the extinction of the individual for the sake of the State. I will make no attempt to refute this assertion on a merely theoretical basis, but will instead establish the facts of the Cuban experience and add commentaries of a general nature. I shall first broadly sketch the history of our revolutionary struggle both before and after the taking of power. As we know, the exact date of the beginning of the revolutionary actions which were to culminate on January 1, 1959, was July 26, 1953. A group of men led by Fidel Castro attacked the Moncada military garrison in the province of Oriente, in the early hours of the morning of that day. The attack was a failure, the failure became a disaster and the survivors were imprisoned, only to begin the revolutionary struggle all over again, once they were amnestied.

During this process, which contained only the first seeds of socialism, man was a basic factor. Man—individualized, specific, named—was trusted and the triumph or failure of the task entrusted to him depended on his capacity for action.

Then came the stage of guerrilla warfare. It was carried out in two different environments: the people, an as yet unawakened mass that had to be mobilized, and its vanguard, the guerilla, the thrusting engine of mobilization, the generator of revolutionary awareness and militant enthusiasm. This vanguard was the catalyst which created the subjective condition necessary for victory. The individual was also the basic factor in the guerilla, in the framework of the gradual proletarianization of our thinking, in the revolution taking place in our habits and in our minds. Each and every one of the Sierra Maestra fighters who achieved a high rank in the revolutionary forces has to his credit a list of noteworthy deeds. It was on the basis of such deeds that they earned their rank.

The First Heroic Stage

It was the first heroic period in which men strove to earn posts of great responsibility, of greater danger, with the fulfillment of their duty as the only satisfaction. In our revolutionary educational work, we often return to this instructive topic. The man of the future could be glimpsed in the attitude of our fighters.

At other times of our history there have been repetitions of this utter devotion to the revolutionary cause. During the October Crisis and at the time of hurricane Flora, we witnessed deeds of exceptional valour and self-sacrifice carried out by an entire people. One of our fundamental tasks from the ideological standpoint is to find the way to perpetuate such heroic attitudes in everyday life.

The Revolutionary Government was established in 1959 with the participation of several members of the "sell-out" bourgeoisie. The presence of the Rebel Army constituted the guarantee of power as the fundamental factor of strength.

Serious contradictions arose which were solved in the first instance in February, 1959, when Fidel Castro assumed the leadership of the government in the post of Prime Minister. This process culminated in July of the same year with the resignation of President Urrutia in the face of mass pressure.

With clearly defined features, there now appeared in the history of the Cuban Revolution a personage which will systematically repeat itself: the masses.

Full and Accurate Interpretation of the People's Wishes

This multifaceted being is not, as it is claimed, the sum total of elements of the same category (and moreover, reduced to the same category by the system imposed upon them) and which acts as a tame herd. It is true that the mass follows its leaders, especially Fidel Castro, without hesitation, but the degree to which he has earned such confidence is due precisely to the consummate interpretation of the people's desires and aspirations, and to the sincere struggle to keep the promises made.

The mass participated in the Agrarian Reform and in the difficult undertaking of the management of the state enterprises; it underwent the heroic experience of Playa Girón it was tempered in the struggle against the groups of bandits armed by the CIA; during the October Crisis it lived one of the most important definitions of modern times and today it continues the work to build socialism.

Looking at things from a superficial standpoint, it might seem that those who speak of the submission of the individual to the State are right; with incomparable enthusiasm and discipline, the mass carries out the tasks set by the government whatever their nature: economic, cultural, defense, sports, etc. The initiative generally comes from Fidel or the high command of the revolution; it is explained to the people, who make it their own. At times, local experiences are taken up by the party and the government and are thereby generalized, following the same procedure.

However, the State at times makes mistakes. When this occurs, the collective enthusiasm diminishes palpably as a result of a quantitative diminishing that takes place in each of the elements that make up the collective, and work becomes paralyzed until it finally shrinks to insignificant proportions; this is the time to rectify.

This was what happened in March, 1962, in the presence of the sectarian policy imposed on the Party by Anibal Escalante.

Dialectical Unity Between Fidel and the Mass

This mechanism is obviously not sufficient to ensure a sequence of sensible measures; what is missing is a more structured relationship with the mass. We must improve this connection in the years to come, but for now, in the case of the initiatives arising on the top levels of government, we are using the almost intuitive method of keeping our ears open to the general reactions in the face of the problems that are posed.

Fidel is a past master at this; his particular mode of integration with the people can only be appreciated by seeing him in action. In the big public meetings, one can observe something like the dialogue of two tuning forks whose vibrations summon forth new vibrations each in the other. Fidel and the mass begin to vibrate in a dialogue of growing intensity which reaches its culminating point in an abrupt ending crowned by our victorious battle cry.

What is hard to understand for anyone who has not lived the revolutionary experience is that close dialectical unity which exists between the individual and the mass, in which both are interrelated, and the mass, as a whole composed of individuals, is in turn interrelated with the leaders.

Under capitalism, certain phenomena of this nature can be observed with the appearance on the scene of politicians capable of mobilizing the public, but if it is not an authentic social movement, in which case it is not completely accurate to speak of capitalism, the movement will have the same life span as its promoter or until the rigors of capitalist society put an end to popular illusions. Under capitalism, man is guided by a cold ordinance which is usually beyond his comprehension. The alienated human individual is bound to society as a whole by an invisible umbilical cord: the law of value. It acts upon all facets of his life, shaping his road and his destiny.

The Invisible Laws of Capitalism

The laws of capitalism, invisible and blind for most people, act upon the individual without his awareness. He sees only the broadness of a horizon that appears infinite. Capitalist propaganda presents it in just this way, and attempts to use the Rockefeller case (true or not) as a lesson in the prospects for success. The misery that must be accumulated for such an example to arise and the sum total of baseness contributing to the formation of a fortune of such magnitude do not appear in the picture, and the popular forces are not always able to make these concepts clear. (It would be fitting at this point to study how the works of the imperialist countries gradually lose their international class spirit under the influence of a certain complicity in the exploitation of the dependent countries and how this fact at the same time wears away the militant spirit of the masses within their own national context, but this topic is outside the framework of the present note).

In any case we can see the obstacle course which may apparently be overcome by an individual with the necessary qualities to arrive at the finish line. The reward is glimpsed in the distance and the road is solitary. Furthermore, it is a race of wolves: he who arrives does so only at the expense of the failure of others.

I shall now attempt to define the individual, the actor in this strange and moving drama that is the building of socialism, in his two-fold existence as a unique being and a member of the community.

I believe that the simplest approach is to recognise his un-made quality: he is an unfinished product. The flaws of the past are translated into the present in the individual consciousness and constant efforts must be made to eradicate them. The process is two-fold: on the one hand society acts upon the individual by means of direct and indirect education, while on the other hand, the individual undergoes a conscious phase of self-education.

Compete Fiercely With the Past

The new society in process of formation has to compete very hard with the past. This makes itself felt not only in the individual consciousness, weighted down by the residues of an education and an upbringing systematically oriented towards the isolation of the individual, but also by the very nature of this transition period, with the persistence of commodity relations. The commodity is the economic cell of capitalist society; as long as it exists, its effects will make themselves felt in the organization of production and therefore in man's consciousness.

Marx's scheme conceived of the transition period as the result of the explosive transformation of the capitalist system torn apart by its inner contradictions; subsequent reality has shown how some countries, the weak limbs, detach themselves from the imperialist tree, a phenomenon foreseen by Lenin. In those countries, capitalism has developed sufficiently to make its effects felt upon the people in one way or another, but it is not its own inner contradictions that explode the system after exhausting all of its possibilities. The struggle for liberation against an external oppressor, the misery which has its origin in foreign causes, such as war whose consequences make the privileged classes fall upon the exploited, the liberation movements aimed at over-throwing neocolonial regimes, are the customary factors in this process. Conscious action does the rest.

A Rapid Change Without Sacrifices is Impossible

In these countries there still has not been achieved a complete education for the work of society, and wealth is far from being within the reach of the masses through the simple process of appropriation. Under development and the customary flight of capital to "civilized" countries make impossible a rapid change without sacrifices. There still remains a long stretch to be covered in the building of the economic base and the temptation to follow the beaten paths of material interest as the lever of speedy development, is very great.

There is a danger of not seeing the forest because of the trees. Pursuing the chimera of achieving socialism with the aid of the blunted weapons left to us by capitalism (the commodity as the economic cell, profitability and the individual material interest as levers, etc.), it is possible to come to a blind alley. And the arrival there comes about after covering a long distance where there are many crossroads and where it is difficult to realise just when the wrong turn was taken. Meanwhile, the adapted economic base has undermined the development of consciousness. To build communism, a new man must be created simultaneously with the material base.

That is why it is so important to choose correctly the instrument of mass mobilization. That instrument must be fundamentally of a moral character, without forgetting the correct use of material incentives, especially those of a social nature.

Society Must be a Huge School

As I already said, in moments of extreme danger it is easy to activate moral incentives; to maintain their effectiveness, it is necessary to develop a consciousness in which values acquire new categories. Society as a whole must become a huge school.

The broad characteristics of the phenomenon are similar to the process of formation of capitalist consciousness in the system's first stage. Capitalism resorts to force but it also educates people in the system. Direct propaganda is carried out by those who are entrusted with the task of explaining the inevitability of a class regime, whether it be of divine origin or due to the imposition of nature as a mechanical entity. This placates the masses, who see themselves oppressed by an evil against which it is not possible to struggle.

This is followed by hope, which differentiates capitalism form the previous caste regimes that offered no way out. For some, the caste formula continues in force: the obedient are rewarded by the *post mortem* arrival in other wonderful worlds where the good are requited, and the old tradition is continued. For others, innovation: the division in classes is a matter of fate, but individuals can leave the class to which they belong through work, initiative, etc. This process, and that of self-education for success, must be deeply hypocritical; it is the interested demonstration that a lie is true.

In our case, direct education acquires much greater importance. Explanations are convenient because they are genuine; subterfuges are not needed. It is carried out through the State's educational apparatus in the form of general, technical and ideological culture, by means of bodies such as the Ministry of Education and the Party's information apparatus. Education takes among the masses and the new attitude that is praised tends to become habit; the mass gradually takes it over and exerts pressure on those who have still not become educated. This is the indirect way of educating the masses, as powerful as the other, structured, one.

The Process of Individual Self-education

But the process is a conscious one; the individual receives the impact of the new social power and perceives that he is not completely adequate to it. Under the influence of the pressure implied in indirect education, he tries to adjust to a situation that he feels to be just and whose lack of development has kept him from doing so thus far. He is education himself.

We can see the new man who begins to emerge in this period of the building of socialism. His image is as yet unfinished; in fact it will never be finished, since the process advances parallel to the development of new economic forms. Discounting those whose lack of education makes them tend toward the solitary road, towards the satisfaction of their ambitions, there are others who, even within this new picture of over-all advances, tend to march in isolation from the accompanying mass. What is more important is that people become more aware every day of the need to incorporate themselves into society and of their own importance as motors of that society.

They no longer march in complete solitude along lost roads towards far-off longings. They follow their vanguard, composed of the Party, of the most advanced workers, of the advanced men who move along bound to the masses and in close communion with them. The vanguards have their eyes on the futures and its recompenses, but the latter are not envisioned as something individual; the reward is the new society where human beings will have different characteristics: the society of communist man.

A Long and Difficult Road

The road is long and full of difficulties. At times, the route strays off course and it is necessary to retreat; at times, a too rapid pace separates us from the masses and on occasions the pace is slow and we feel upon our necks the breath of those who follow upon our heels. Our ambition as revolutionaries makes us try to move forwards as far as possible, opening up the way before us, but we know that we must be reinforced by the mass, while the mass will be able to advance more rapidly if we encourage it by our example.

In spite of the importance given to moral incentives, the existence of two principal groups (excluding, of course, the minority fraction of those who do not participate for one reason or another in the building of socialism) is an indication of the relative lack of development of social consciousness. The vanguard group is ideologically more advanced than the mass; the latter is acquainted with the new values, but insufficiently. While in the former a qualitative change takes place which permits them to make sacrifices as a function of their vanguard character, the latter see only the halves and must be subjected to incentives and pressure of some intensity; it is the dictatorship of the proletariat being exercised not only upon the defeated class but also individually upon the victorious class.

To achieve total success, all of this involves the necessity of a series of mechanisms, the revolutionary institutions. The concept of institutionalization fits in with the images of the multitudes marching toward the future as that of a harmonic unit of canals, steps, well-oiled apparatuses that make the march possible that permit the natural selection of those who are destined to march in the vanguard and who dispense rewards and punishments to those who fulfill their duty or act against the society under construction.

Perfect Identification Between Government and Community

The institutionality of the Revolution has still not been achieved. We are seeking something new that will allow a perfect identification between the government and the community as a whole, adapted to the special conditions of the building of socialism and avoiding to the utmost the commonplaces of bourgeois democracy transplanted to the society in formation (such as legislative houses, for example). Some experiments have been carried out with the aim of gradually creating the institutionalization of the Revolution, but without too much hurry. We have been greatly restrained by the fear that any formal aspect might make us lose sight of the ultimate and most important revolutionary aspiration: to see man freed from alienation. Notwithstanding the lack of institutions, which must be overcome gradually, the masses now make history as a conscious aggregate of individuals who struggle for the same cause. In spite of the apparent standardization of man in socialism, he is more complete; his possibilities for expressing himself and making himself heard in the social apparatus are infinitely greater, in spite of the lack of a perfect mechanism to do so. It is still necessary to accentuate his conscious, individual and collective, participation in all the mechanism of direction and production and associate it with the idea of the need for technical and ideological education, so that the individual will realise that these processes are closely interdependent and their advances are parallel. He will thus achieve total awareness of his social being, which is equivalent to his full realisation as a human being, having broken the chains of alienation.

This will be translated concretely into the reappropriation of his nature through freed work and the expression of his own human condition in culture and art.

Work Must Acquire a New Condition

In order for it to develop in culture, work must acquire a new condition; man as commodity ceases to exist and a system is established that grants a quota for the fulfillment of social duty. The means of production belong to society and the machine is only the front line where duty is performed. Man begins to free his thought from the bothersome fact that presupposed the need to satisfy his animal needs by working. He begins to see himself portrayed in his work and to understand its human magnitude through the created object, through the work carried out. This no longer involves leaving a part of his being in the form of labour power sold, which no longer belongs to him; rather, it signifies an emanation from himself, a contribution to the life of society in which he is reflected, the fulfillment of his social duty.

We are doing everything possible to give work this new category of social duty and to join it to the development of technology, on the one hand, which will provide the conditions for greater freedom, and to voluntary work on the other, based on the Marxist concept that man truly achieves his full human condition when he produces without being compelled by the physical necessity of selling himself as a commodity. It is clear that work still has coercive aspects, even when it is voluntary; man has still not transformed all the coercion surrounding him into conditioned reflexes of a social nature, and in many cases, he still produces under the pressure of the environment (Fidel calls this moral compulsion). He is still to achieve complete spiritual recreation in the presence of his own work, without the direct pressure of the social environment but bound to it by new habits. That will be communism.

The change in consciousness does not come about automatically, just as it does not come about automatically in the economy. The variations are slow and not rhythmic; there are periods of acceleration, others are measured and some involve a retreat.

Communism's First Transition Period

We must also consider, as we have pointed out previously, that we are not before a pure transition period such as that envisioned by Marx in the "Critique of the Gotha Program", but rather a new phase not foreseen by him: the first period in the transition to communism or in the building of socialism.

Elements of capitalism are present within this process, which takes place in the midst of violent class struggle. These elements obscure the complete understanding of the essence of the process.

If to this be added the scholasticism that has held back the development of Marxist philosophy and impeded the systematic treatment of the period, whose political economy has still not been developed, we must agree that we are still in diapers. We must study all the primordial features of the period before elaborating a more far reaching economic and political theory.

The resulting theory will necessarily give preeminence to the two pillar of socialist construction: the formation of the new human being and the development of technology. We still have a great deal to accomplish in both aspects, but the delay is less justifiable as far as the conception of technology as the basis is concerned; here, it is not a matter of advancing blindly but rather of following for a sizable stretch the road opened up by the most advanced countries of the world. This is why Fidel harps so insistently on the necessity of the technological and scientific formation of all our people and especially the vanguard.

Division Between Material and Spiritual Necessity

In the field of ideas that lead to non-productive activities, it is easier to see the division between material and spiritual needs. For a long time man has been trying to free himself from alienation through culture and art. He dies daily in the eight and more hours during which he performs as a commodity to resuscitate in his spiritual creation. But this remedy itself bears the germs of the same disease: he is a solitary being who seeks communion with nature. He defends his environment-oppressed individuality and reacts to esthetic ideas as a unique being whose aspiration is to remain immaculate.

It is only an attempt at flight. The law of value is no longer a mere reflection of production relations; the monopoly capitalists have surrounded it with a complicated scaffolding which makes of it a docile servant, even when the methods used are purely empirical. The artists must be educated in the kind of art imposed by the superstructure. The rebels are overcome by the apparatus and only the exceptional talents are able to create their own work. The others become shame-faced wage-workers or they are crushed.

Artistic experimentation is taken as the definition of freedom, but this "experimentation" has limits, which cannot be perceived until they are clashed with, that is, until they confront the real problems of man and his alienated condition. Senseless anguish or vulgar pastimes are comfortable safety valves for human uneasiness; the idea of making art a weapon of denunciation and accusation is combatted.

If the rules of the game are respected, all honours are obtained—the honours that might be granted to a pirouette-creating monkey. The condition is not attempting to escape from the invisible cage.

A New Impulse for Artistic Experimentation

When the Revolution took power, the exodus of the totally domesticated took place; the others, revolutionaries or not, saw a new road. Artistic experimentation took on new force. However, the routes were more or less traced and the concept of flight was the hidden meaning behind the word freedom. This attitude, a reflection in consciousness of bourgeois idealism, was frequently maintained in the revolutionaries themselves.

In countries that have gone through a similar process, endeavours were made to combat these tendencies with an exaggerated dogmatism. General culture became something like a taboo and a formally exact representation of nature was proclaimed as the height of cultural aspiration. This later became a mechanical representation of social reality created by wishful thinking: the ideal society, almost without conflicts or contradiction, that man was seeking to create.

Socialism is young and makes mistakes. We revolutionaries often lack the knowledge and the intellectual audacity to face the tasks of the development of the new human being by methods different from the conventional ones, and the conventional methods suffer from the influence of the society that created them (once again the topic of the relation between form and content appears). Disorientation is great and the problems of material construction absorb us. There are no artists of great authority who also have great revolutionary authority.

The men of the Party must take this task upon themselves and seek the achievement of the principal aim: to educate the people.

Socialist Realism Based on the Art of the Last Century

What is then sought is simplification, what everyone understands, that is, what the functionaries understand. True artistic experimentation is obliterated and the problem of general culture is reduced to the assimilation of the socialist present and the dead (and therefore not dangerous) past. Socialist realism is thus born on the foundation of the art of the last century.

But the realistic art of the 19th century is also class art, perhaps more purely capitalist than the decadent art of the 20th century, where the anguish of alienated man shows through. In culture, capitalism has given all that it had to give and all that remains of it is the foretaste of a bad-smelling corpse; in art, its present decadence. But why endeavour to seek in the frozen forms of socialist realism the only valid recipe? "Freedom" cannot be set against socialist realism because the former does not yet exist; it will not come into being until the complete development of the new society. But let us not attempt to condemn all post-mid-19th century art forms from the pontifical throne of realism at-all-costs; that would mean committing the Proudhonian error of the return to the past, and straight jacketing the artistic expression of the man who is born and being formed today.

An ideological and cultural mechanism must be developed which will permit experimentation and clear out the weeds that shoot up so easily in the fertilized soil of state subsidization.

21st Century Man

The error of mechanical realism has not appeared (in Cuba), but rather the contrary. This is so because of the lack of understanding of the need to create a new human being who will represent neither 19th century ideas nor those of our decadent and morbid century. It is the 21st century man whom we must create, although this is still a subjective and unsystematic aspiration. This is precisely one of the basic points of our studies and work; to the extent that we make concrete achievement on a theoretical base or vice versa, that we come to broad theoretical conclusions on the basis of our concrete studies, we will have made a valuable contribution to Marxism-Leninism, to the cause of mankind. The reaction against 19th century man has brought a recurrence of the 20th century decadence. It is not a very serious error, but we must overcome it so as not to leave the doors open to revisionism.

The large multitudes of people are developing themselves, the new ideas are acquiring an adequate impetus within society, the material possibilities of the integral development of each and every one of its members make the task ever more fruitful. The present is one of struggle; the future is ours.

Intellectuals Not Authentically Revolutionary

To sum up, the fault of many of our intellectuals and artists is to be found in their "original sin": they are not authentically revolutionary. We can attempt to graft elm trees so that they bear pears, but at the same time we must plant pear trees. The new generations will arrive free of "original sin." The likelihood that exceptional artists will arise will be that much greater because of the enlargement of the cultural field and the possibilities for expression. Our job is to keep the present generation, maladjusted by its conflicts, from becoming perverted and perverting the new generations. We do not want to create salaried workers docile to official thinking nor "fellows" who live under the wing of the budget, exercising freedom in quotation marks. Revolutionaries will come to sing the song of the new man with the authentic voice of the people. It is a process that requires time.

In our society the youth and the Party play a big role. The former is particularly important because it is the malleable clay with which the new man, without any of the previous defects, can be formed.

Youth receives treatment in consonance with our aspirations. Education is increasingly integral and we do not neglect the incorporation of the students into work from the very beginning. Our scholarship students do physical work during vacation or together with their studies. In some cases work is a prize, while in others it is an educational tool; it is never a punishment. A new generation is born.

The Party: Vanguard Organisation

The Party is a vanguard organisation. The best workers are proposed by their comrades for membership. The party is a minority but the quality of its cadres gives it great authority. Our aspiration is that the party become a mass one, but only when the masses reach the level of development of the vanguard, that is, when they are educated for communism. Our work is aimed at providing that education. The party is the living example; its cadres must be full professors of assiduity and sacrifice; with their acts they must lead the masses to the end of the revolutionary task, which means years of struggle against the difficulties of construction, the class enemies, the defects of the past, imperialism . . . I should now like to explain the role played by the personality, the man as the individual who leads the masses that make history. This is our experience, and not a recipe.

Fidel gave impulse to the Revolution in its first years, he has always given it leadership and set the tone, but there is a good group of revolutionaries developing in the same direction as Fidel and a large mass that follows its leaders because it has faith in them. It has faith in them because these leaders have known how to interpret the longings of the masses.

So That the Individual Feels More Fulfilled

It is not a question of how many kilograms of meat are eaten or how many times a year someone may go on holiday to the sea shore or how many pretty imported things can be bought with present wages. It is rather that the individual feels greater fulfillment, that he has greater inner wealth and many more responsibilities. In our country the individual knows that the glorious period in which it has fallen to him to live is one of sacrifice; he is familiar with sacrifice.

The first came to know it in the Sierra Maestra and wherever there was fighting; later, we have known it in all Cuba. Cuba is the vanguard of America and must make sacrifices because it occupies the advance position, because it points out to the Latin American masses the road to full freedom.

Within the country, the leaders have to fulfil their vanguard role; and it must be said with complete sincerity that in a true revolution, to which you give yourself completely without any thought for material retribution, the task of the vanguard revolutionary is both magnificent and anguishing. Let me say, with the risk of appearing ridiculous, that the true revolutionary is guided by strong feelings of love. It is impossible to think of an authentic revolutionary without this quality. This is perhaps one of the great dramas of a leader; he must combine an impassioned spirit with a cold mind and make painful decision without flinching. Our vanguard revolutionaries must idealise their love for the people, for the most hallowed causes, and make it one and indivisible. They cannot descend, with small doses of daily affection, to the terrain where ordinary men put their love into practice.

A Large Dose of Humanity

The leaders of the revolution have children who do not learn to call their father with their first faltering words; they have wives who must be part of the general sacrifice of their lives to carry the revolution to its destination; their friends are strictly limited to their comrades in revolution. There is no life outside the revolution.

In these conditions, the revolutionary leaders must have a large dose of humanity, a large dose of a sense of justice and truth to avoid falling into dogmatic extremes, into cold scholasticism, into isolation from the masses. They must struggle every day so that their love of living humanity is transformed into concrete deeds, into acts that will serve as an example, as a mobilizing factor.

The revolutionary, ideological motor of the revolution within his party, is consumed by this uninterrupted activity that ends only with death, unless construction be achieved on a worldwide scale. If his revolutionary eagerness becomes dulled when the most urgent tasks are carried on a local scale and if he forgets about proletarian internationalism, the revolution that he leads cease to be a driving force and it sinks into a comfortable drowsiness which is taken advantage of by imperialism, our irreconcilable enemy, to gain ground. Proletarian internationalism is a duty, but it is also a revolutionary need. This is how we educate our people.

Dangers of Dogmatism and Weaknesses

It is evident that there are dangers in the present circumstances. Not only that of dogmatism, not only that of the freezing up of relations with the masses in the midst of the great task; there also exists the danger of personal weaknesses, which might threaten our task. If a man thinks that in order to devote his entire life to the revolution, he cannot be distracted by the worry that one of his children lacks a certain article, that the children's shoes are in poor condition, that his family lacks some necessary item, with this reasoning, the seeds of future corruption are allowed to filter through. In our case, we have maintained that our children must have, or lack, what the children of the ordinary citizen have or lack; our family must understand this and struggle for it. The revolution is made by man, but man must forge his revolutionary spirit from day to day.

Thus we go forward. Fidel is at the head of the immense column—we are neither ashamed nor afraid to say so—followed by the best Party cadres and right after them, so close that their great strength is felt, come the people as a whole, a solid bulk of individualities moving towards a common aim; individuals who have achieved the awareness of what must be done; men who struggle to leave the domain of necessity and enter that of freedom.

That immense multitude is ordering itself; its order responds to an awareness of the need for order; it is no longer a dispersed force, divisible in thousands of fractions shot into space like the fragments of a grenade, trying by any and all means, in a fierce struggle with their equals, to achieve a position that would give them support in the face of an uncertain future.

We know that we have sacrifices ahead of us and that we must pay a price for the heroic fact of constituting a vanguard as a nation. We the leaders know that we must pay a price for having the right to say that we are at the head of the people that is at the head of America.

Each and every one of us punctually pays his share of sacrifice, aware of being rewarded by the satisfaction of fulfilling our duty, aware of advancing with everyone towards the new human being who is to be glimpsed on the horizon.

We Are More Free Because We Are More Fulfilled

Allow me to attempt to come to some conclusions: We socialists are more free because we are more fulfilled; we are more fulfilled because we are more free.

The skeleton of our complete freedom is formed, but it lacks the protein substance and the draperies, we will create them.

Our freedom and its daily sustenance are the colour of blood and swollen with sacrifice.

Our sacrifice is a conscious one; it is in payment for the freedom we are building.

The road is long and in part unknown; we are aware of our limitations. We will make the 21st century man; we ourselves.

We will be tempered in daily actions, creating a new human being with a new technology.

The personality plays the role of mobilisation and leadership in so far as it incarnates the highest virtues and aspirations of the people and does not become detoured.

The road is opened up by the vanguard group, the best among the good, the Party.

The basic raw material of our work is the youth: in it we place our hopes and we are preparing it to take the banner from our hands.

If this faltering letter has made some things clear, it will have fulfilled my purpose in sending it.

Accept our ritual greetings, as a handshake or an "Ave María Purísima."

PATRIA O MUERTE

[Fatherland or Death]

Document 8.2 Senel Paz, "El Lobo, el Bosque, y el hombre nuevo" (Excerpt)

Translated by Robert Forstag.

The following weeks and months passed pleasantly enough until the Saturday when Diego cracked open the door when I arrived for tea and abruptly announced: "You can't come in. I have someone here who doesn't want to be seen and I'm having a wonderful time. Please come back later on."

I left, but only retreated to the sidewalk on the other side of the street so that I could see the face of the person who didn't want to be seen. Diego left the house shortly afterward—by himself. He seemed nervous, looking down the street in both directions before quickly scurrying around the corner. I rushed to catch up, and managed to see him get into a car with diplomatic plates that was partially hidden in a back alley. I had to hide behind the column of a building, because the vehicle suddenly raced away.

Diego in a car with diplomatic plates! I felt an unbearable heaviness in my chest. So it was true after all. Bruno was right, and Ismael was wrong[11] about such people needing to be analyzed on an individual basis. Not true. You can never let your guard down: Fags are natural born traitors: It's their original sin. I myself, on the other hand, am completely free of any duplicity. I could forget all about this[12] and be happy. For me, it had been nothing more than class instinct. But I couldn't manage to be happy. I felt hurt. It hurts when a friend betrays you. It gets you down deep. And it made me angry that I had once again been so stupid, that I had let myself be manipulated by another person. It really hurts when you have no choice but to recognize that the hard-liners are right, that you're just a sentimental sack of shit ready to make friends with anyone. I reached the boardwalk of Old Havana and, as is so often the case, I noticed that nature reflected my state of mind: The sky had suddenly become overcast, claps of thunder grew louder and louder, and the air was heavy with impending rain. I found myself heading directly to the university, in search of Ismael, but I realized in a moment of clarity (or whatever you want to call it, because I find it hard to credit myself with actually having clarity) that I wouldn't be able to make it through a third meeting with him—not with that clear and penetrating gaze of his. And so I stopped. My second meeting with Ismael had followed the elaborate lunch I had had with Diego that had replicated the meal described in Lezama Lima's *Paradiso*, when I needed to sort things out in order to keep my head from exploding. "I was wrong," I had told him back then. "He's a good guy, just a poor bastard really, and it doesn't make sense to go on watching him."

"Weren't you the one who said he was a counter-revolutionary?" he responded sarcastically.

"Even as far as that point goes, we have to recognize that his experience of the Revolution hasn't exactly been like ours. After all, it's hard to be around people who'll only accept you if you stop being who you are. To summarize. . . ."

But I didn't go on to summarize anything. I still didn't trust Ismael enough to say what I was really thinking: "His actions reflect who he really is, and what he's really thinking. He conducts himself with an internal freedom that I can only wish that I had myself. And I'm someone who is committed to the cause."

Ismael looked at me and smiled. The difference between the clear and penetrating gazes of Diego and Ismael (to wrap things up with you, Ismael, because this isn't your story, after all) is that Diego's only pointed out how things really were while Ismael's demanded that, if you didn't like the way things really were, that you take immediate action in order to change them. That's why he was better than either of us. He made some casual conversation with me and, when we said our goodbyes, he placed his hand on my shoulder and said he hoped we would stay in touch. To me, this signaled the release from my duties as an agent, and the beginning of our friendship.

What would he think now if I told him what I had just found out? I went back to Diego's apartment building prepared to wait for him as long as I needed to. He came back in a taxi during a driving rainstorm. I followed him into the building and entered his apartment before he could close the door.

"The boyfriend already left," he said jokingly. "What's with that face? Surely you aren't jealous. Or are you?"

"I saw you get in the car with diplomatic license plates."

He was not expecting this. He suddenly turned pale, fell like a lump in one of his chairs, and looked down at the floor. When, after some time, he finally lifted his head, his face looked ten years older.

"Let's have it. I'm waiting."

Now it was time for the confessions, the remorse, the begging for forgiveness. He would give me the name of his counterrevolutionary faction and I'd go to the police—straight to the police.

"I was going to tell you, David, but I didn't want you to know so soon. I'm leaving."

"I'm going," in the way that Diego was now saying it, is something that has dreadful implications for us. It means that you're leaving the country for good, that he will blot you forever from his memory—and that you in turn need to blot the person saying those words from your memory. It also means, whether you like it or not, that you will be seen as a traitor. You know that from the beginning, but you accept it because it is part of the price of your ticket out. Once you have that ticket in your hand, you'll never convince anyone that you weren't thrilled when you got hold of it. But this couldn't be true in your case, Diego. What would you do with yourself far away from Havana, from the heat and filth of its streets, from the raucousness of its people? What could you possibly do in another city, my dear friend—in a city that could not lay claim to Lezama Lima, or where you could see Alicia Alonso dance for the last time every single weekend? In a city that didn't have bureaucrats and party hardliners to criticize, and without a loyal friend like David at your side?

"It's not for the reasons you suspect," he said. "You know that politics really doesn't matter to me at all. It's because of what happened with Germán's exhibition. You really aren't very observant, and you don't realize what a stir it caused. And they didn't fire him. They fired me. Germán reached an understanding with them. He rented a room and started working for Havana by making crafts. I admit that I went too far in defense of the works that were exhibited, that I didn't show party discipline and that I acted selfishly, taking advantage of my position. But so what? Now, with this record in my file, the only work I'll be able to get is in agriculture or construction. Now tell me, what am I going to do with a brick in my hand? Where would I put it? It's just a reprimand at work, but who's going to hire someone that looks like me? Who's going to go out on a limb for me? I know it's not fair. The law is on my side by all rights, I should end up getting a ruling in my favor and being compensated. But what am I supposed to do? Fight? I'm weak, and the weak have no place in your world. In fact, you act as if we don't even exist, as if the only reason we're weak is to torture you and to join the cause of those who've betrayed the Revolution. Life is easy for you people. You don't suffer from Oedipus complexes. You aren't tormented by beauty. None of you ever had a cat that you loved that you saw your father cut up so that he could make a man out of you. It's possible to be a fag and be strong at the same time. There's no shortage of examples of this. I have no doubt about that at all. But this isn't true in my case. I'm weak. I'm terrified of growing old. I don't have the luxury of waiting 10 or 15 years for you to re-examine your views, even though I am fully confident that the Revolution will eventually correct its mistakes. I'm 30 years old. At most, I have another 20 good years left. I want to do things, make plans, gaze into the mirror of *Las Meninas*, give a lecture on the poetry of Flor and Dulce María Loynaz. Isn't this my right? If I were a good Catholic and I believed in the afterlife, I wouldn't care, but I've been infected with your materialism after being exposed to it for so many years. This is the only life there is—there isn't anything else. In any case, this is most likely the only life we have. Do you understand me? I'm not wanted here. What's the point of continuing to run in circles? Anyway, I like being who I am and to spread my wings every once in a while.

"I ask you, as a friend: Who is it that I'm offending by doing this. They are, after all, my own wings."

Not all of his final days here were sad. At times, he seemed euphoric, flitting about among packages and old papers. We drank rum and listened to music.

"Before they come and take inventory, make sure you take my typewriter, electric burner, and this can opener. Your mom will find it really useful. Here are my studies on architecture and urban planning—quite a few, aren't there? And they're good. If I don't have the time, send them anonymously to the City Museum. There are accounts here of Garcia Lorca's visit to Cuba. It includes a very detailed itinerary and photographs of places and persons with captions that I wrote." A black man who I didn't recognize suddenly appeared. "You can keep the anthology of poems on the Almendares River. You can supplement it with some other poems about it that I have here, even though the Almendares doesn't inspire poetry any more. Look at this photo. It's me during the Literacy Campaign. And these here are of my family. I'm going to take all of them with me. This is one of my uncles, a very handsome man who choked on a *papa rellena*.

Here I am with my mother. She was a good-looking woman, wasn't she? Let's see, what else do I want to leave with you? You took all the papers already, didn't you? Send the articles that you consider the most digestible to the magazine *Revolución y Cultura*, where there might be someone who appreciates them. Choose topics having to do with the nineteenth century. They're more likely to be published. Give the rest of them to the National Library—you know to whom. Make sure you don't lose contact with that person. Give him a cigar every once in a while, and don't be offended if he pays you some compliment—it won't go any further than that. I'll also give you the name of someone at the Ballet. And these as well, David Alvarez: the cups that we've used to drink so much tea together. I'm entrusting them to you. If you have the chance some day, send them to me. Like I told you before, they're made of porcelain from Sèvres. But not because of that—they belonged to the Loynaz del Castillo family and they were a gift. OK, I'll level with you. I actually stole them. My records and books were already taken away. You already took yours, and the ones that are left are to throw the people taking the inventory off the scent. Find me a poster of Fidel with Camilo Cienfuegos, a miniature Cuban flag, the photo of Martí in Jamaica and the one of Mella with his hat. But move fast!: I want to send these in the diplomatic pouch, along with the photos of Alicia in *Giselle* and my collection of Cuban coins and banknotes. Do you want the umbrella for your mother, or the cape?"

I generally accepted everything in silence. But at times, a certain hope surged within me and I would give him back some of the items.

"Diego, what if we write to someone? Think about who it could be. Or I could go and ask to meet with some government employee, and you can wait for me outside."

He looked at me sadly, rejecting that line of thinking.

"Don't you know some lawyer, one of those sympathizers with the exiles who are out there? Or some closeted fag who has an important position? You've done a lot of favors for a helluva lot of people. I graduate in June. By October, I'll have a job, and I can give you fifty pesos a month."

I stopped when I saw that his eyes were tearing up, but he always managed to pull himself together.

"I'm going to give you one last piece of advice: Pay attention to the clothes you wear. You're no Alain Delon, but you have a charm and a certain air of mystery that, regardless of people say, always tends to open doors."

It was me who couldn't find anything to say in response. I lowered my head and started rearranging his packages and looking them over.

"No, not that one! Don't unwrap it. Those are Lezama Lima's unedited manuscripts. Don't look at me like that. I swear that I'll never use them in an inappropriate way. Well, I also swore to you that I would never leave, and I'm leaving—but this is a different matter. I will never use them as a bargaining chip and I'll also never give them to anyone who could use them for political purposes. I swear by my mother, by that basketball player[13]—and by you. So there! If I can weather the storm ahead without using them, I'll return them. Don't look at me like that! Do you think that I don't appreciate my responsibility? But if I find myself in a tight spot, they could help get me out of it. You're making me feel bad. Pour me a drink and get out of here."

He did worse and worse as the date of his departure drew near. He had trouble sleeping and he lost weight. I was with him as much as possible, but he didn't say much. At times, I think that he didn't even know that I was there. Curled up in the big armchair[14] in his apartment with a book of poems and a crucifix in his hands—for he'd suddenly become more religious—he seemed to have lost color and vitality. He listened to the low and smooth voice of Maria Callas. One day, I noticed him looking at me with a special intensity. "I know you love me. Has being my friend helped you? Was I disrespectful toward you? Do you think that I am hurting the Revolution?"

Maria Callas was no longer singing.

"Our relationship has been appropriate, yes. And I appreciate you."

He smiled.

"Don't evade the issue. I'm not talking about appreciation, but about love between friends. Please, let's not be afraid of words any more."

This was also what I had wanted to say, I suppose. But I have that problem of mine. So in order to be sure of my affections and of the fact that, at least in some ways, I was different—that I had changed during the course of our friendship—and that I had become the person that I had always wanted to be, I added: "I'd like you to come and have lunch with me tomorrow at El Conejito. I'll go early and get in line. You just need to get there before noon. It'll be on me. Or, if you prefer, I can come and get you and we can go together."

"No David. That won't be necessary. Everything has worked out just fine."

"Diego, I insist. I really want to do this."

"OK, but not El Conejito. Once I get to Europe, I'm going to become a vegetarian."

Did I really want—did I really need—to be seen with him? Is this what had to happen for me to be at peace with myself or some such thing? Well, I suppose that's true. He arrived at the restaurant at ten minutes to twelve, when people were crowded around the door underneath a Japanese umbrella. He was dressed in a way that allowed me to identify him from two blocks away. He shouted out my complete name from the other side of the street, waving his arm, which was adorned with bracelets. When he reached me, he kissed me on the cheek and started describing to me a beautiful dress that he had just seen in a shop window, and that he said would be perfect for me. But to his surprise—and mine, and that of the other people waiting in line—I got the better of him by defending a different style of clothing. That's one thing about us shy people: If we manage to shake off our inhibitions, we can be brilliant. The lunch thus turned out to be a kind of celebration of his technique for loosening up communists.

Turning to my literary education, he added other titles to my reading list. "Don't forget the Countess of Merlin. Start finding out about her. Your encounter with that woman will be something that will have people talking."

We finished up our desserts in Coppelia, and then made our way through a bottle of Stolichnaya back at Diego's place. It was all wonderful until we stopped drinking.

> "I needed this Russian vodka in order to tell you two last things. I'll leave the most difficult for last. David, I think that you are somewhat lacking in initiative. You need to be more decisive. You shouldn't be a spectator, but an actor. I assure you that you'll do better now than you did in *A Doll's House*.[15] Don't stop being

a revolutionary. You're probably thinking, 'Who is *he* to be talking to me like this.' But I do have my own moral standards. At one point, I told you that I am a patriot and a devotee of Lezama Lima. The Revolution needs people like you, because we can't let the *yanquis* take over. But your food, your bureaucracy, the kind of propaganda that you engage in, and your arrogance might bring it all to an end, and it is only people like you who can help (Cuba) avoid such a fate. It won't be easy for you. It will take a real emotional investment on your part. The other thing that I have to tell you—let's see if I can actually do it, because my head is bowed in shame, go and pour me the few remaining drops of vodka—is this: Do you remember when we met in Coppelia? I wasn't very nice to you on that day. I was with Germán, and when we saw you, we made a bet that I'd take you back to my place and get you into bed. We made the bet in dollars. I did it as a way of motivating myself to approach you, because I always had a respect for you that tended to make me freeze up. Spilling the milk on you was part of the plan. Your shirt and the Manila tablecloth hanging on the balcony were the sign of my victory. Of course, Germán went and spread the word—and afterward even more, now that he hates me. In some places lately, because I've only been spending time with you, they call me 'the Red Queen.' Other people think that this silliness of mine is nothing more than a cover, and that I'm really being sent to Western Europe as a spy. Try not to worry about it too much. These kinds of questions about a man don't really harm him. On the contrary, they lend him an air of mystery, and many women would willingly fall into his arms with the idea of getting back on the right track. Do you forgive me?"

I remained silent, and he interpreted this as a yes, that I forgave him.

"So you see, I'm not so good after all. Would you have been capable of such a thing, behind my back?"

We sat looking at one another.

"OK, now I'm going to make our last cup of tea. After this, you'll leave and you'll never come back again. I don't want any goodbyes."

And that was it. When I was back in the street, a long line of Communist Youth Pioneers blocked my way. They wore freshly ironed uniforms and each carried a bouquet of flowers. Even though flower-carrying Pioneers had for some time been a clichéd symbol of the future, the sight made me happy—maybe for that very reason. I stood looking at one of the boys, who stuck his tongue out at me as soon as he noticed. At that point, I told him (I told him, I didn't promise him) that I would go to all lengths to defend the next Diego that crossed my path, even if no one understood what I was doing, and that I would not feel detached from my Spirit and my Conscience as a result of doing so. On the contrary. And that's because, if I understood things correctly, acting in that way would mean fighting for a better world not only for you, my young Pioneer, but for me as well.

At that point, I wanted to close this chapter of my life by thanking Diego in some way for everything he had done for me. I did this by going to Coppelia and asking for ice cream just the way he did.

And that's why, even though they had chocolate, I asked for strawberry.

Document 8.3 Yoani Sánchez, "Architecture of the Emergency," October 11, 2009

Source: Translation by Mary Jo Porter. Reprinted by permission of Mary Jo Porter and Yoani Sánchez. Originally posted at: http://lageneraciony.com/arquitectura-de-la-urgencia/.

In the early morning they removed the first bricks from the exterior wall, to sell them for three pesos each on the black market. Like an army of ants, the poorest people in the area took over the old factory—now closed—and began to dismantle it. Some kids watched from the corner in case the police approached, while their parents sifted through the residue of the debris to extract the mortar. Deft hands knocked down during the day and carried away at night these construction materials that would allow them to build their own homes. After three weeks, all that was left of the enormous building was the floor and some columns standing in the vacuum. Everything that could be used had been moved to the territory of needs, had gone to support the architecture of the emergency.

On an island where to acquire cement, blocks or steel is comparable to getting a bit of lunar dust, destroying in order to build has become common practice. There are specialists in extracting clay bricks intact after eighty years of being embedded in a wall, experts in peeling off the glazed tiles from a demolished mansion, and adroit "deconstructors" who extract the metal girders from collapsed heaps. They use the reclaimed materials to build their own habitable spaces in a country where no one can legally buy a house. Their main "quarries" are those houses that have fallen down or workplaces abandoned for many years by the apathetic State. They fall on these with an efficiency in looting that one might want to see in the dozing bricklayers who work for wages.

Among these skilled recyclers, some have been killed by a collapsing roof or falling wall, riddled by too many holes in its base. But now and again lady luck also smiles on them and they find a toilet without cracks, or an electrical socket that, in their hurry, the owners of the demolished house couldn't take with them. A few kilometers from the site of the looting a small dwelling of tin and zinc slowly begins to change. The tiled floor from a house that collapsed at Neptuno and Aguila streets has been added, along with a piece of the exterior railing from an abandoned mansion on Linea Street, and even some stained glass from a convent in Old Havana. Inside this house, fruit of the pillaging, a family—equally plundered by life—dreams of the next factory that will be dismantled and loaded onto their shoulders.

Accompanying the blog posting was the following YouTube posting: http://www.youtube.com/watch?v = bFTOJOgvtvg.

In it, the Cuban poet *Amaury Pacheco*, reads his poem "Plan económico." It goes like this:

Economy! We have fulfilled the annual plan:
1,100 street hustlers; 2,000 young prostitutes; 8,000 opportunists.
Plus, 300 non-mentally disabled and the syndrome of mediocrity.
Economy! In times of a Havana that is unrecognizable,

By sweeping the house, you cleanse the economy.
Strong legs for the rocky path,
Legs that are only for the percentages of economic shame.
Shameful economy! Economy of shame! Economy of shame!

Document 8.4 Yoani Sánchez, "The Blackout Ends," February 9, 2011

Source: Translation by Mary Jo Porter. Reprinted by permission of Mary Jo Porter and Yoani Sánchez. Originally posted at: http://lageneraciony.com/termina-el-apagon/.

Seated in an armchair in a hotel with my laptop open, I note the slow blinking of the WiFi transmitter and watch the stern faces of the guards. This could be one more day trying to enter my own blog through an anonymous proxy, jumping over the censorship with a few tricks that let me look at the forbidden. On the bottom of the screen a banner announces that I'm navigating at 41 kilobytes a second. Joking with a friend I warn her we'd better hold onto our hair so it won't get messed up from "speeding." But the narrow band doesn't matter much this February afternoon. I'm here to cheer myself up, not to get depressed all over again by the damned situation of an Internet undermined by filters. I have come to see if the long night of censorship no longer hangs over Generation Y. With just a click I manage to enter the site that, since March of 2008, has not been visible from a public place. I'm so surprised I let out a shout and the camera watching from the ceiling records the fillings in my teeth as I laugh uncontrollably.

After three years, my virtual space is again visible from inside Cuba.

I don't know the reasons for the end to this blockade, although I can speculate that the celebration of the 2011 Havana International Computer Science Fair has brought many foreign guests and it is better to show them an image of tolerance, of supposed openings in the realm of citizen expression. It is also possible that after having proved that blocking a website only makes it more attractive to internauts, the cyberpolice have chosen to exhibit the forbidden fruit they so demonized in recent months. If it's because of a technical glitch that will soon be corrected, once again throwing shadows over my virtual diary, then there will be plenty of time to loudly denounce it. But for the moment, I make plans for the platforms www.vocescubanas.com and www.desdecuba.com to enjoy a long stay with us.

This is a citizen victory over the demons of control. We have taken back what belongs to us. These virtual places are ours, and they will have to learn to live with what they can no longer deny.

Document 8.5 Yoani Sánchez, "In 2013: Reasons to Stay," January 1, 2013

Source: Translation by Mary Jo Porter. Reprinted by permission of Mary Jo Porter and Yoani Sánchez. Originally posted at: http://lageneraciony.com/en-este-2013-razones-para-quedarse/.

Someone has to be at the foot of the aircraft steps, saying goodbye and waving their handkerchief. Someone has to receive the letters, the brightly colored postcards, the long distance phone calls. Someone has to stay to look after the house that was once full of children and relatives, to water the plants they left and feed the old dog that was so faithful to them. Someone has to keep the family memories, grandmother's mahogany dresser, the wide mirror with the quicksilver peeling off in the corners. Someone has to preserve the jokes that no longer spark laughter, the negatives of the photographs never printed. Someone has to stay to stay.

This year, 2013, when so many await the implementation of Immigration and Travel Reform, could become a year when we say "goodbye" many times. While I respect the decision of each person to settle here or there, I can't help but feel sad for the constant bleeding of creativity and talent suffered by my country. It's frightening to know the number of Cubans who no longer want to live here, to raise their children on this Island, or to realize their professional careers in this country. A trend that in recent months has me saying goodbye to colleagues and friends who leave for exile, neighbors who sell their homes to pay for a flight to some other place. Acquaintances I no longer see, I learn some weeks later are now living in Singapore or Argentina. People who got tired of waiting, of postponing their dreams.

But someone has to stay to close the door, turn the lights off and on again. Many have to stay because this country has to be reborn with fresh ideas, with young people and projects for the future. At least the illusion has to stay, the regenerative capacity must remain here; the enthusiasm clings to this earth. In 2013, among the much that remains, one thing definitely must be hope.

For Further Reading

Alvarez Borland, Isabel. *Cuban-American Literature of Exile: From Person to Persona*. Charlottesville: University Press of Virginia, 1998.

Anderson, Jon Lee. *Che: A Revolutionary Life*. New York: Grove, 1997.

Del Aguila, Juan M. *Cuba: Dilemmas of a Revolution*. Boulder: Westview, 1994.

Eckstein, Susan Eva. *Back from the Future: Cuba under Castro*. New York: Routledge, 2003.

Farber, Samuel. *The Origins of the Cuban Revolution Reconsidered*. Chapel Hill: University of North Carolina Press, 2006.

Higgins, Michael. "Cuba: Living the Revolution with Oscar Lewis," *Dialectical Anthropology* 3:4 (1978), 365–372.

Miller, Nicola. "The Absolution of History: Uses of the Past in Castro's Cuba," *Journal of Contemporary History* 38:1 (2003), 147–162.

Pérez, Louis A. Jr. *Cuba: Between Reform and Revolution, 3rd ed.* New York: Oxford University Press, 2005.

Pérez-Stable, Marifeli. *The Cuban Revolution: Origins, Course, and Legacy*. New York: Oxford University Press, 1993.

Quirk, Robert. *Fidel Castro*. New York: Norton, 1995.

Sweig, Julia E. *Inside the Cuban Revolution: Fidel Castro and the Urban Underground*. Cambridge, MA: Harvard University Press, 2002.

Valdes, Zoe. *Yocandra in the Paradise of Nada*. New York: Arcade, 1999.

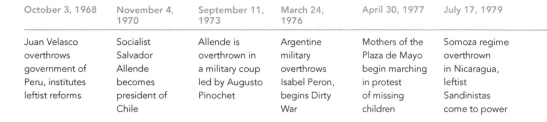

October 3, 1968	November 4, 1970	September 11, 1973	March 24, 1976	April 30, 1977	July 17, 1979
Juan Velasco overthrows government of Peru, institutes leftist reforms	Socialist Salvador Allende becomes president of Chile	Allende is overthrown in a military coup led by Augusto Pinochet	Argentine military overthrows Isabel Peron, begins Dirty War	Mothers of the Plaza de Mayo begin marching in protest of missing children	Somoza regime overthrown in Nicaragua, leftist Sandinistas come to power

June 19, 1990	April 5, 1992	September 12, 1992	October 16, 1998	November 2000	April 19, 2005	April 7, 2009
Alberto Fujimori elected president of Peru	In self-coup, Fujimori shuts down congress and judiciary, and suspends the constitution	Sendero leader Abimael Guzmán captured	Augusto Pinochet arrested in London on charges brought by Spanish Judge Balthazar Garón, although eventually released due to poor health	Fujimori flees country after re-election because of corruption scandals	Adolfo Scilingo, only Argentine Dirty Warrior to ever confess, is sentenced to 640 years in prison for crimes against humanity by a Spanish court	A Peruvian court finds Fujimori responsible for the deaths of twenty-five Peruvians and sentences him to twenty-five years in prison

The Terror

9

May 17, 1980	May 17, 1980	December 10, 1983	January 26, 1983	1987	October 5, 1988
Peru holds its first elections since military took power	Sendero Luminoso launches rebellion in Andean highlands of Peru	Raul Alfonsín becomes Argentine president, ending military rule	Peasants in Uchuraccay, Peru, kill eight journalists, who had gone to the village to investigate the murder of seven senderista guerrillas	Raul Alfonsin passes a Full Stop Law, calling for no more prosecutions of Dirty Warriors after attempted coup	Plebiscite in Chile rejects continuation of military rule

On April 5, 1992 Peruvians awoke, to the news that their president had overthrown his own government. Some were outraged, others cheered. Few were particularly surprised. At the time, in various parts of the country, at least three guerrilla armies were blowing up power stations and murdering their enemies (including feminists, human rights activists, and anyone insufficiently doctrinaire). Dogs hung from trees in the countryside, the symbolic victims of Maoist[1] trials. Except for the cocaine business, the economy was a shambles. Guerrillas, army officers, and corrupt government officials were growing rich from cocaine while Peru fell apart.

Alberto Fujumori's autogolpe,[2] the war against the guerrillas that followed, his brief tenure as the nation's savior, and his ultimate reckoning for corruption and human rights violations, are stories that have corollaries across Latin America in the last quarter of the twentieth century. Between the 1960s and the 1990s, the region went through one of the bloodiest periods since independence. Military and other authoritarian governments unleashed unprecedented levels of violence against what they represented as a communist threat. The statistics are staggering. Most governments in the region have never fully accounted for the dead, but truth commissions in Chile (the Rettig Commission) and Argentina (National Commission on the Disappearance of Persons, CONADEP) concluded that right-wing military dictatorships in those two countries murdered at least 2,279 and 8,961 persons respectively (both commissions acknowledged that the actual numbers were far higher).[3] In Guatemala, a civil war during these years took nearly 300,000 lives. In El Salvador, 75,000 lost their lives in a civil war. Peru's Truth and Reconciliation Commission concluded that 69,280 people died or disappeared between 1980 and 2000 as a result of that country's armed conflict. In all cases, these numbers do not include those who were arbitrarily imprisoned, tortured, and/or forced into exile, numbers that reach into the tens of millions for the region as a whole.

This period in Latin America's past is deceptively difficult to narrate. Sometimes called dirty wars, sometimes called guerrilla wars, sometimes labeled as "terrors" (terrorists vs. terror states), the stories of these conflicts must negotiate a series of traps. Told as tragedy, we risk becoming disturbingly caught up in the gruesome details of torture and murder, turned into voyeurs who symbolically re-enact these acts on their victims through our lurid fascination with the violence. Latin Americans become a shadowy people, unable to live by the rules of modern civility. Alternatively, we can transform certain victims (Salvador Allende's Popular Unity in Chile, Che Guevara's guerrillas in Bolivia, Mexican student protestors in 1968 and 1971, and even Peru's *Sendero Luminoso* [Shining Path]) into romantic figures, idealists who were crushed by right-wing violence. This may allow us to tell stories with definitive heroes and villains, to satisfy our desire for moral clarity. What we risk is gaining that clarity at the expense of understanding the past for all its ambiguity.

Courts of law assign guilt and punish those convicted of crimes, and it is extraordinarily tempting to throw around terms like "crimes against humanity" when describing the dirty wars. It is also appropriate in many cases. Still, if we view these events simply as horrible crimes committed by evil men, we capture only a small part of this history. The twentieth century, and in Latin America's case, the late twentieth century, was an era of holocausts, acts of violence made all the more dramatic by modern technologies of death. And authoritarian governments and men in uniform had no monopoly on the bloodlust. It could often be found on every side in every conflict. The question is: why?

First, we might start with terminology. Labels like "dirty war," "war on terror," and "war on subversives" describe conflicts that defy clean categorizations. As a whole, they speak to unconventional forms of warfare where the enemy is within, and rarely in uniform. Conventional wars, even some civil wars, play out around discrete territorial boundaries. Competing factions control specific zones, and dress in uniform fashion so as to distinguish themselves from the enemy. Dirty wars, which while newly acknowledged are nothing new, cast suspicion on a vast civilian population. States undertaking dirty wars use specific optics to divide that population into friendly and subversive, fearing enemies everywhere. In some instances, especially societies with large impoverished indigenous and African populations, it is the color of one's skin that raises the specter of the threat. Elsewhere it is the place of origin, occupation, age, and ideology. Whatever the reason to distrust them, dirty warriors tend to see anyone who is anything but assertively loyal to the regime as a threat to be controlled and perhaps eliminated. This is the problem with paranoia; when you cannot identify the enemy by the uniform they wear, you see the enemy everywhere.

In the most violent instances, these dirty overlay actual civil wars. In Chile, Uruguay, Brazil, and Mexico, guerrillas never threatened to topple the existing regimes. In some cases, like Argentina, the threat posed by the guerrillas was difficult to quantify. In still others, including Colombia, El Salvador, Guatemala, and Peru, guerrilla insurgencies took over significant portions of the national territory during their civil wars. These were also the countries in which racism weighed most heavily on the conflicts, and where the losses of life were the greatest.

Where to Begin, Which Story to Tell?

Were the dirty wars the product of a specific context, a late twentieth-century crisis that needs to be explained with very close attention to specific circumstances—the cold war, U.S. imperialism, and local conflicts—or were they the product of some essential, unchanging quality of life in the region? Those who prefer the latter explanation sometimes start this story with the sixteenth-century conquest of the Americas, establishing an unbroken chain of violence dating to the original sin.[4] Histories of torture, of extrajudicial killings take us deep into the Latin American past, and one could argue that the only thing new here is the fact that these acts are increasingly exposed. Latin America becomes a region of failed states, never quite modern, and forever destined to be second-class, unable to solve its own problems because they run so deeply through the "open veins" of the region.[5]

Those who object to this way of narrating the terror that engulfed the region between the 1960s and the 1980s point out that Latin America in 1960 was profoundly different from Latin America even a century earlier. In 1960 civilian governments ruled most countries in the region. Even if those governments had imperfect records of respecting democratic processes and human rights, most did rule with some sort of democratic mandate. The phenomena we typically associate with democratic societies, a relatively free press, opposition political parties, an independent judiciary, could be found in many countries in the region. At the very least, it did not seem in 1960 that the region as a whole was destined for a dark period of conflict and authoritarian rule. And then, in the years following the Cuban Revolution, civilian rule collapsed in country after country. By 1980 almost no government in Latin America had come to power through the ballot box. The scale of violence that accompanied this change was unprecedented.

Certain macro-level explanations for Latin America's distinct path may be in order. Economies across the region faced significant challenges during the 1960s, problems that only grew worse as time wore on. Import substitution industrialization (ISI),[6] which provided steady economic growth in the region from the 1930s to the 1950s, had also produced some serious distortions, and, by the late 1960s, these were growing increasingly difficult to ignore. ISI depended on the state's ability to support industry and fund a broad array of educational, health, and welfare programs (including transportation, housing, and food subsidies), but as GDP growth slowed during the 1960s, most governments in the region found themselves pressed by expanding debt, high rates of inflation, increased unemployment, and social unrest. They had to borrow from abroad simply to maintain their current levels of spending. Much of the money they borrowed went to propping up inefficient industries that could not compete against foreign, higher quality and lower cost imports. As the debt began to grow, it became clear that the status quo could not be sustained.

Critics used terms like *crony capitalism* (a capitalist system where the state works mainly in the interest of big business) or *clientelism* (a state where the government functions principally by doling out favors and patronage to its supporters) to describe the logics that ruled Latin American economic and political systems. When the system was capable of delivering material benefits in spite of self-dealing, the poor and relatively marginalized played along. In moments of crisis, when the state could no longer deliver the goods, many turned to violence to press their interests.

Latin Americans were also burdened by another problem. Their nations were among the central sites for the proxy battles of the cold war. Leaving aside the motives of both the United States and the Soviet Union, both superpowers intensified the volatility of already polarized nations through their struggles for hegemony in the region. American soldiers and arms flowed freely into Latin America during the cold war, accompanied (though hardly equaled) by an influx of Soviet AK-47s, munitions, and at least in one case, intercontinental ballistic missiles. Guerrilla armies could count on aid, training from Moscow, and safe haven in Cuba should their struggles fail. Their enemies could count on millions in military and economic aid from Washington.

Only rarely did the U.S. government opt for direct military intervention. American officials found it much more cost effective to cultivate, arm and train their allies in the region. Conservative and elite groups who, like their American friends, increasingly identified all political opposition with an insidious Soviet threat, were often more than willing to undertake the battle themselves. While some no doubt believed that their enemies were communist revolutionaries (and some no doubt were), in identifying the political opposition as communist they were able to justify extreme measures, and ensure a steady supply of military aid and advice from the U.S. government. Measured in constant 2010 dollars, U.S. military aid to Latin America rose from almost nothing in 1952 to nearly a billion dollars annually in the aftermath of the Cuban revolution.

The U.S. Army School of the Americas, which was established in Panama in 1945 and trained several generations of junior military officers from across the region, was a central component of this endeavor. Already focused more on internal threats than external ones, trainees were encouraged to believe that a new revolutionary threat, concocted in Moscow but carried out by their own citizens, imperiled their nations. Students at the School of the Americas learned new tactics in counter-insurgency and the latest torture techniques. They forged relationships with American counterparts who could ensure the flow of weapons and aid. And they had any pre-existing anxieties about communism firmly reinforced.

The unrest they faced could be attributed to both local and global patterns—dimming economic prospects combined with youth culture, idealism unleashed by the Cuban revolution, and cold war politics. Most of the Western democracies saw periodic outbursts of violence between the 1960s and the 1980s. Student radicals disrupted campuses and challenged conservative traditions from Paris to Berkeley. Radical movements kidnapped people from Quebec to Italy, robbed banks, set off bombs, and preached the demise of capitalism even in some of the most exclusive neighborhoods in the world. In response, governments across the West armed themselves heavily and used their repressive capacities against their perceived enemies. Incidents like the massacre at Kent State University in May 1970, in which National Guardsmen opened fire on anti-war protesters, killing four and wounding nine, were emblematic of an era in which the United States government in particular spied on, harassed, and imprisoned its own citizens without the due process of law.

Latin Americans brought their own particular traditions to these conflicts. When young idealists attacked the government, they took on political systems with dubious reputations. Latin Americans typically believed their governments were exceptionally corrupt. Their politicians were known for using their offices for illicit gains, for doling out favors to well-connected supporters, and for being relatively unresponsive to the popular will. They maintained the social peace by delivering the goods (education, healthcare, and other programs), but few people in Latin America really believed that their governments governed in the people's interest.[7]

By the mid-1960s the leftists who had long offered these critiques were increasingly joined by young people, a generation that questioned the values of their parents in novel ways. Like the counter-culture in the United States (and in fact influenced by it), Latin America's counter-cultural generation combined the alienated children of a prosperous middle class with the offspring of a newly ascendant urban working class in a series of protest movements. Some young Latin Americans were motivated by what seemed to be a closing off of economic mobility as societies that had once prospered under ISI increasingly struggled to provide upward mobility to their youth. Others were drawn to radically democratic ideas, straining against both the authoritarianism of the state and the authoritarian tendencies of their own parents. Sex, drugs, and rock and roll were certainly involved, lubricants for a generation that strained at their parents' conservatism.

Latin America's counter-culture consolidated within the high schools and universities of the region, where foreign icons like the Beatles, the Rolling Stones, and Elvis were supplemented with local heroes, figures like Che Guevara—now a martyr to most young radicals—and the Chilean folk singer Victor Jara. Che signaled the possibilities of social revolution, the need for militant struggle. Jara provided a melancholy soundtrack that reminded listeners of the everyday struggles of poor people, and of the need to make a more egalitarian future. Student protests rocked much of the region during 1968, the most notable case being the protests in Mexico that culminated in the October 2 massacre at Tlatelolco, where several hundred students were gunned down by government snipers. The most radical students in Mexico, Brazil, and Argentina committed themselves to the violent overthrow of the system, forming rural and urban guerrilla groups that would use kidnappings, assassinations, and bombing campaigns in their attempts to foment revolution.

The Mexican essayist Alma Guillermoprieto once described Che Guevara as the "harsh angel" who hovered over all this, convincing a generation of young idealists to hurtle themselves against the barricades in a futile struggle.[8] Though rejected by those who continue to lionize Che, her words act as a reminder that the revolution he promised to Latin America played out as tragedy for a generation of young idealists who stood little chance against the weapons arrayed against them. Indeed, the most radical of the revolutionaries provoked a response not just from the military, but from social conservatives and the middle class in several Latin American countries that buttressed the extreme forms of violence that followed. Conservatives recoiled at the young men in long hair, young women wearing jeans and sandals. They responded viscerally to rock and roll, drugs, and intimations that the students in the schools and universities were having sex before marriage. These things were destined to produce a backlash.

In the years after Tlatelolco, repression and radicalization became a self-reinforcing cycle across the region, perhaps most pronounced in Argentina, where during the early 1970s the military, police, and the *Alianza Anticomunista Argentina* (Argentine Anticommunist Alliance, AAA) went to war against the guerrillas of the *Ejército Revolucionario del Pueblo* (People's Revolutionary Army, ERP) and the *Movimiento Peronista Montonero* (Montoneros, MPM). The latter was the largest urban guerrilla movement in Latin America during the 1970s. The political right has long claimed that these two groups represented a grave threat, exploding more than 5,000 bombs during the 1970s and kidnapping or killing more than 3,000 people. They point to spectacular incidents that had the capacity to terrorize the civilian population, including repeated bombings of the Sheraton hotel in Buenos Aires, kidnappings of businessmen, bankers, and other "civilians," and the murder of hundreds of soldiers and police. By end of 1975, 137 soldiers had been killed by guerillas. In the weeks leading up to the 1976 coup, the Montoneros attacked the police academy in Buenos Aires and detonated a bomb next to the army headquarters, breaking windows in the Casa Rosada.

Even if we take these numbers as inflated, the impact of press reports of bombings, murders, and kidnappings (one report in the mid-1980s had the guerillas causing 6,000 casualties[9]) produced a powerful terror effect. Just as crime statistics can prompt calls for police to ignore the civil rights of presumed suspects, these statistics had the capacity to ratchet up support for a radically authoritarian response. Ultimately, the debate as to whether the guerillas killed 3,000 or fewer than 1,000 (in 1995 the Argentine Government claimed the ERP killed 700 people) is probably less significant than the fact that in the years before and during the dictatorship millions of Argentines believed that their personal safety was endangered by the seemingly random acts of violence that urban terror movements enact. If the Montoneros and ERP could be named as the reason why you were afraid, and in a corollary vein, the victims of the military could be named as the people who had caused that fear (and therefore not randomly chosen, but disappeared because they had done something wrong), then complacence while the regime systematically detained and murdered thousands could be explained as an act of self-preservation. The actual existence of the threat mattered less than the belief that the threat was real.

"Your war is clean," reads the text in the poster in Figure 9.1, an advertisement in the Buenos Aires newspaper *La Nación*, in March 1976, just days before the military overthrew the government of Isabel Perón. It is in part an allusion to the fact that critics condemned the increasing use of torture and illegal detentions by the military as a "dirty" war, somehow beneath civilized people. The advertisement challenges this view, insisting that their actions were not just clean, but cleansing, that this was a just war. Both extreme left and right spoke in ritual ways about these acts, believing that they were somehow engaged in an exercise that would purify society, eliminate a cancer. Whether it was the cancer of bourgeois capitalism or communism, of patriarchy or feminism, of tradition or rebellion, or of terrorism (this accusation was traded throughout these years) did not matter. The enemy was corrupt, impure, foreign. For the nation to survive, the enemy had to be annihilated. Dehumanization was here turned to genocide, and the perpetrators of violence made into victims who sacrificed themselves to save the world.

By the time of the coup in Argentina, the military already had over 5,000 people under detention. During the dictatorship, the military would maintain at least 340 concentration

Figure 9.1   "You are not alone . . . your people are behind you."

Source: Courtesy of *La Nacion*, March 1976; also appears in Diana Taylor, *Disappearing Acts: Spectacles of Gender and Nationalism in Argentina's "Dirty War"* (Durham: Duke University Press, 1997)

camps in the country. The government ultimately released 8,600 from detention, sending many into exile (3,000 went to the U.S.). Most of those released spent less than a year in detention, though more than 400 spent between seven and nine years in the camps. Among those never seen again were 4,000 Montoneros. Other victims included activists, trade unionists, students, people who had uncovered government corruption, and leftists in general. Young, pregnant women were also among those kidnapped. About 500 were held in prison until they gave birth. The newborns were then adopted by couples with ties to the regime, and their parents murdered.

The success of these tactics was even more pronounced in Chile, where a largely unarmed left never undertook anything like the volume of violent acts that Argentines witnessed. In 1970 Chileans narrowly elected Salvador Allende of the *Unidad Popular* (Popular Unity, UP) president. Allende was the first committed socialist to be democratically elected in Latin America, though he only won the election with 36.6 percent of the popular vote, and even before taking office he confronted sabre rattling from the military. Faced with a Congress dominated by opposition parties, Allende undertook a relatively moderate series of reforms, completing a process begun by his predecessor to nationalize Chilean copper, supporting bottom up efforts to redistribute unused lands and take over factories, and instituting price freezes and wage hikes. The relative merits of these reforms remain in dispute. Those on the right claim his economic policies were foolish, and some of the left insist that he did not have enough time to see them through. What remains undisputable however, is the fact that a broad coalition of enemies, including many middle-class and elite Chileans, the military, and the U.S. government (which placed an embargo on Chile after the nationalization of U.S. assets), came together as early as 1971 in an effort to destabilize the regime. The U.S. blockade hurt, as did coordinated efforts across the economy to withdraw goods and services, along with actual acts of sabotage. Middle-class women marched repeatedly in protests during these years, banging empty pots and claiming that Allende was making it impossible for them to feed their children. Most of these opponents hoped that in the 1973 congressional elections Chileans would return a two-thirds majority for the opposition parties, which could then impeach the president. To their surprise, Allende's UP coalition actually gained votes in the 1973 election, eliminating the legal means to overthrow him. It was then that General Augusto Pinochet decided to act. He led a coup that overthrew the government on September 11, 1973. Allende died in the assault, allegedly by his own hands.

Though there were acts of violence prior to the coup, most of those acts were undertaken by opponents on the right, while Allende resisted arming revolutionary groups like the *Movimiento de Izquierda Revolucionaria* (Movement of the Revolutionary Left, MIR), which in any event disavowed terrorism as a legitimate means of struggle. The Chilean right was then forced to conjure up a series of chimera, fears of a militant left, fears that the Allende regime would adopt more radical reforms, fears of a fifth column connected to a global communist revolution. Chileans were fully aware of the radical reforms undertaken in communist Cuba, of the capacity of Argentine guerrillas to disrupt their country through violence. They feared youths who seemed to have little regard for traditional values. Right-wing and middle-class support for a surgical strike against the Chilean left was, in this sense, over-determined.

After the coup, the government immediately banned the parties on the left. All political activity was banned. Many in the middle class were initially relieved, and then surprised when the coup was not followed by a relatively quick return to democracy. Instead, in the following weeks up to 30,000 prisoners passed through the National Stadium. Nearly 2,000 of those prisoners were executed within a matter of months, and 1,300 more are missing to this day. At least 663 MIR militants were among the disappeared, as were Victor Jara and Charles Horman, an American working in Chile who was the subject of the film *Missing*. As many as 200,000 Chileans were also driven into exile in the weeks and months after the coup. The Chilean secret police (the DINA) followed some into exile, murdering enemies in Argentina, the United States, and elsewhere through *Operación Condor* (Operation Condor), a secret pact between several Southern Cone governments. Some allege that the regime even went so far as to murder Pablo Neruda, then the greatest living Latin American poet, poisoning him in the days following the coup. Described as politicide by Steve J. Stern, Pinochet's project endeavored to eliminate the Chilean left in its entirety.

Elsewhere in Latin America the threat posed by the left was much more substantial. Colombia's *Fuerzas Armadas Revolucionarias de Colombia* (Revolutionary Armed Forces of Colombia, FARC) was able to control vast stretches of the countryside during the 1960s and 1970s. Though they lacked the capacity to overthrow the state, they contributed to a general escalation of violence in Colombian society. Together with other guerrilla groups, right wing paramilitaries, and the army, these combatants forced more than five million Colombians to flee their homes. Guatemala's *Ejército Guerrillero de los Pobres* (Guerrilla Army of the Poor, EGP), El Salvador's *Frente Farabundo Martí para la Liberación Nacional* (Farabundo Martí National Liberation Front, FMLN), and Nicaragua's *Frente Sandinista de Liberación Nacional* (Sandinista National Liberation Front, FSLN) were among the guerrilla armies that carried out long-standing rural insurgencies during the 1960s and 1970s. Each insurgency in turn became the pretext for military and paramilitary campaigns that in some cases took a genocidal turn. Entire communities, including tens of thousands of non-combatants, were wiped out by regimes that saw the threats they faced in racial terms. To be dark-skinned, rural, and poor was to be a likely subversive.

In each of these cases, those individuals with the power to mobilize the repressive apparatuses of the state used their authority to enrich themselves and pursue personal vendettas under the cover of civil war. Much of what happened at the higher levels was cynical and indefensible, carried out with impunity under the cover of a crisis. Still, the violence was as widespread as it was, and the general public as complacent as they were, because it was more than mere self-interest that was on display in these incidents. The critical question is: Why did so many people who were otherwise not well served by authoritarian and corrupt regimes side with the military during this era? Why did the call to socialist revolution not gain more adherents in one of the most unequal parts of the world?

The answer, at least for some people, was fear. They feared reprisals from the regime and paramilitaries to be sure, but their fear was stoked by the very actions of the revolutionary left. A bomb might explode in a hotel. You might get caught in the crossfire of a bank robbery, or be in a public setting when some other attack occurred. Attacks by the Montoneros and others were splashed across the pages of the major dailies throughout Latin America, reminding everyone to be afraid. Beyond this, there was the fear that, should the left take power, they might confiscate your property, attack your values (many Catholics feared that atheist Marxists would destroy the Church), forcibly indoctrinate your children into their revolutionary ideology, and take away what little freedom you enjoyed. It seemed that only a strong state, which targeted specific subversives with legitimate and lethal force, stood between a vulnerable population and their demise.

This is the way that many regimes across the region maintained a modicum of legitimacy during the 1970s even as they undertook horrific acts of violence. And this too is why the only regime to fall to a guerrilla insurgency during these years was the Somoza dynasty in Nicaragua. Reviled as one of the most corrupt dictators the region had ever seen (Anastasio Somoza's family controlled upwards of 40 percent of the wealth in the country in 1979), and broadly believed to have murdered the widely respected journalist *Pedro* Joaquín

Chamorro,[10] by 1979 the number of people in the country who would defend Somoza had dwindled to a tiny number of close associates, themselves beneficiaries of corruption. As was the case with Batista in Cuba twenty years earlier, Somoza was forced to flee because the vast majority of Nicaraguans disdained him even more than they feared the Sandinistas. He died a year later in Buenos Aires, at the hands of a hit squad that included members of the ERP.

And then there was Peru. Peru's dirty war began during the cold war, and was characterized by a struggle between a Marxist left and a free-market right in ways that were similar to struggles elsewhere in the region. Like Guatemala, El Salvador, and Colombia, the conflict in Peru also had qualities of a true civil war in which a rural insurgency took over a significant part of the national territory while demonstrating a capacity to disrupt daily life everywhere. The Peruvian state also responded in ways that were similar to states elsewhere in the region, covering egregious human rights violations and self-dealing under the mantle of a war on terror, a war in which unflinching loyalty to the state was the price to be paid for the return of peace.

Where Peru differs from most other countries in the region is in the nature of the insurgency. Unlike Chile, where the left was relatively unarmed, and Argentina, Nicaragua, El Salvador, Mexico, and Guatemala, where the atrocities committed by the guerrillas paled next to the atrocities committed by the state, in Peru there is reason to believe that the guerillas, and especially *Sendero Luminoso*, surpassed the state in the intensity of their violence (Peru's Truth and Reconciliation Commission concluded that only about one-third of those who died in the war were killed by government forces). The insurgents here were just as enamored of violence as their enemies, and were perhaps even more doctrinaire than the right. Fueled by money from the cocaine trade, Peru's insurgents were also better able to arm themselves and sustain a war against a well-armed Peruvian state than their counterparts elsewhere in Latin America. Whereas Che's guerrilla army in Bolivia, and others in Mexico, Venezuela, and elsewhere failed in part because the insurgents could not count on the support of their erstwhile peasant allies, Peru's revolutionaries could draw enough revenue from the drug trade to fund their war without much rural support. Peru's dirty war was thus both another cold-war conflict and something entirely new: an apocalyptic orgy of violence fueled by the insurgency's capacity to sustain itself through autonomous revenue streams.

These aspects of the conflict make it difficult to draw clear moral lines in Peru. This in turn offers the opportunity to focus our attention on the larger phenomenon of violence in Latin America during these years instead of getting caught up in long-standing and unresolvable debates over heroes and villains. Moving into the murk, we have the opportunity to understand just how certain forms of fear, and certain imaginings of terror and the terrorist, metastasized in the latter decades of the twentieth century. We live with those developments in our own age of terror.

Sendero's War

Peruvians were introduced to *Sendero Luminoso* on May 17, 1980, when members of the movement burned the ballot boxes for Peru's first democratic elections in more than a decade in the southern highland town of Chuschi, Ayacucho.[11] Although *Sendero*'s decision to condemn the return of democratic rule seemed odd to many foreign observers, and even to many Limeños, it made complete sense to many in the highlands. Democracy did not promise much to the poor and rural peoples of Ayacucho, who held a generally dim view of all power emanating from Lima. Neither did it appeal to Peru's extreme left, which viewed democracy as simply another bourgeois tool to oppress the masses and protect capitalism.

The particular constellation of events that explain *Sendero*'s rise from a quirky movement led by a provincial philosopher into a guerrilla army that almost toppled the Peruvian state may be best explained by beginning with another moment, twelve years earlier, when the military overthrew the civilian government of Fernando Belaúnde Terry. Belaúnde's fall was not the common story of conservative U.S.-backed soldiers toppling a left-leaning president. In fact, it was the reverse. The officers who took power in 1968 did so precisely to ensure that the state deliver on social reforms Belaúnde had promised. Elected in 1963 on the promise to ameliorate rural poverty, Belaúnde had done the opposite, resorting to the violent repression of both peasants and his critics on the left to stay in power. In the end, it was the men who were charged with carrying out his repressive policies who removed him. General Juan Velasco's regime nationalized many of the large firms that dominated the economy, and launched a major land reform, creating agricultural cooperatives out of the old estates in much of the highlands.

Some peasants benefited, but these reforms were limited in scale, and left millions bitter for having been excluded.[12] Velasco's nationalization program was also burdened by bureaucratic incompetence and mismanagement, and in the early 1970s the economy went into a tailspin. He was overthrown in a coup within the coup in 1976, and his successors did their best to undo his left-leaning policies, with few positive results. Having seen failure heaped upon failure, the military had little prestige left when it gave up power in 1980. Still, very few people outside of Lima were pleased that Belaúnde, whose heavy-handed policies in the highlands left lasting anger, won the 1980 election.

Belaúnde imposed severe austerity measures in an effort to promote exports and stem capital flight. His opponents on the left responded with a general strike in January 1981, which further crippled the already weak economy. By the end of 1982, inflation was running at 70 percent, and the foreign debt had ballooned to $11 billion. The national currency (the sol) lost 80 percent of its value during the year. It is unsurprising that in these circumstances radical solutions to Peru's problems would have found a constituency. Believing that free-market capitalism was the only solution to Peru's problems, the far right pushed to dismantle any remaining remnants of ISI, through force if necessary. The far left, dominated by *Sendero*, preached the end of bourgeois capitalism.

In Ayacucho the economic crisis simply added one more set of problems to a region already at the breaking point by the late 1970s. Peasants here benefited relatively little from Velasco's land reforms, and had no cushion to fall back on as the national economy deteriorated. Students at the *Universidad Nacional San Cristóbal de Huamanga* in the city of Ayacucho were similarly discontented, as the path that has once signaled upward mobility—a university education—seemed less and less likely to provide them with what they desired. Always pulled towards the left, university students here and elsewhere in Peru grew more and more radical.

Taking a cue from Chairman Mao, during the 1970s radical students in Ayacucho increasingly idealized the image of the disciplined, communal, and revolutionary peasant. They imagined that they would lead this peasant in a revolution that would swarm the cities, besiege hated Lima (hated both for its wealth and for their exclusion from that wealth), and destroy the capitalist state. Many were drawn to Abimael Guzmán, a professor of Philosophy and Mathematics at the university, and at his bidding left the city of Ayacucho for the surrounding countryside after graduating, where they worked for years as teachers, preparing the peasants to accept the revolution that *Sendero* promised to launch. Guzmán would lead the revolution under the nom de guerre *Presidente Gonzalo*.

After announcing itself to the world in 1980, *Sendero* won some striking victories. Their teachers-cum-revolutionaries parleyed their moral authority into swift and summary justice, gaining enormous sympathy in the countryside. Peasant women saw female *senderistas* punishing drunken husbands and wife beaters, and lent their support. What better image could there be of moral rejuvenation at a time of crisis than the image of a man punished by a woman's hand? The same could be said of *Sendero* justice against other widely hated targets. Corrupt government officials, landlords, and cattle thieves met ugly fates at the hands of *Sendero*'s cadres in the early 1980s. So too did the agrarian cooperatives, Velasco's panacea for rural poverty that in practice had become hated symbols of the ways that reform had helped some peasants but excluded others. Landless *Sendero* supporters were encouraged to invade and occupy the cooperatives, effecting a bottom-up termination of state-directed agrarian reform.

In these early years the revolution expanded rapidly through the countryside. Belaúnde indirectly contributed to its growth by first failing to take *Sendero* seriously, and then by sending in the Marines, a branch of the military mostly recruited from the coast, which had little knowledge of the culture or politics of the highlands. Baffled by the differences they encountered and fearing terrorists around every corner, the Marines adopted a scorched earth policy in Ayacucho.

Indiscriminate killings simply made their position more vulnerable, turning more and more communities against the government and pushing many directly into *Sendero*'s camp. The presence of so many violent outsiders also produced a kind of hysteria in the highlands, a sense that the world really was coming to an end. In the midst of the crisis some highlanders turned to religion (evangelical Protestantism expanded significantly during these years), seeking spiritual rescue from the carnage. Others spread rumors that linked the Marines to apocalyptic fears. They were Argentine mercenaries sent to kill all rural folk. They were *pishtacos*, ravenous whites who murdered Indians for their fat, using it to make church bells and expensive soaps that were sold to Europeans.

It is not surprising that under these circumstances *Sendero* was able to expand its influence in rural areas beyond Ayacucho. The guerrillas were particularly successful in the coca-rich upper Huallaga valley, where by the mid-1980s *Sendero* had implemented a protection racket in which growers paid *Sendero* to leave them alone and protect them from the state. This in turn fueled further expansion of the war and the purchase of a growing military arsenal. As the highlands slipped from government control, bombings, blackouts, murders and kidnappings grew more frequent across the country, and especially in Lima. By the late 1980s *Sendero* controlled the poor barrios that ringed Lima, and the government seemed incapable of stemming its spread.

Sendero never could have expanded in this fashion without a significant level of rural support, but that support was far from complete. Peasant sympathizers often saw *Sendero* as an opportunity to form a strategic alliance, and would just as easily turn on the revolutionaries when circumstances dictated. Indeed, the ties between peasant and *senderista* were always tenuous. Though *senderistas* represented themselves as participants in an organic peasant war, their revolution was shaped by the goals of university educated guerrillas. *Senderistas* considered themselves Gang of Four Maoists, painting the slogan "Death to the Traitor Deng Xiaopeng" on the walls in Andean communities, seemingly fighting simultaneous battles against the Chinese government, the Peruvian state, and civil society.

As the war drew on, *senderistas* increasingly treated peasants as if they were ignorant tools of revolution, to be called to arms when useful and destroyed when recalcitrant. In contrast to the early years of the struggle, when their successes had in part been linked to their capacity to understand the desires and values of their erstwhile supporters, over time *senderistas* demonstrated less and less tolerance for local customs, local values, local age-based hierarchies, and increasingly treated indigenous cultures with contempt. In their blindness to local life-ways, they also failed to understand the extent to which a long history of violent conflicts with outsiders had fortified highland communities with a capacity for self-defense.

Communities that might have thrown their support behind *Sendero* for killing a corrupt government official often turned just as quickly against the movement when doctrinaire *senderistas* made demands they viewed as unfair. Others never had any sympathy for the guerrillas, and fought them without prompting. Just such an incident happened when seven *senderistas* were killed by *comuneros* (peasant rebels) in the village of Huaychao, Ayacucho in January 1983. Limeños, who considered this a sign of peasant loyalty to the government, generally celebrated the incident. Their jubilance faded though, when a group of eight journalists on their way to Huaychao to write about the incident were murdered while passing through the village of Uchuraccay. This incident is the subject of Document 9.1 in this chapter.

Few of the movement's actual militants were peasants. In fact, most *senderistas* were current or former university students, drawn to the bloody path plotted by Guzmán. And it was not just students from Ayacucho, but from Lima and other cities who organized *senderista* and other revolutionary cells on their campuses during the 1980s as they prepared for the final battle against capitalism. Often drawn into the movement out of youthful idealism and a sense that Peru was facing an existential economic and political crisis, their views hardened into revolutionary anger and rage once the government subjected them to torture and long imprisonments (Figure 9.2). Indeed, most of the *senderistas* who ever made it to a jail cell were urban, middle-class students. Their rural comrades and sympathizers met more violent ends.

The very fact that these students initially decided to attend a rally or meeting of revolutionaries spoke to a cascading effect, the result of one crisis after another discrediting all forms of constituted authority. Aside from the human toll, one of most significant losses in all this was Peruvians' faith that moderate solutions might solve their problems. Both the extreme left and the extreme right obliterated all middle ground. Arbitrary arrests, detentions, and torture by the military no doubt had this effect. So too did *Sendero*'s acts. Anyone who was within *Sendero*'s reach could be singled out for spectacular executions for seemingly insignificant slights.

Figure 9.2 December 16, 1986: Peruvian police arrest a student from the state university of San Marcos during the protest organized by students and teachers of the state universities in Lima. Thousands of teachers and students marched through the streets of the capital and submitted a set of economic demands to the Economics Ministry.

Source: AP Photo/LEP

Over time, violence served as an end in and of itself. In the highlands, where their enthusiasm for blood-letting disturbed many peasants, *senderistas* came to be known as monsters (*ñakaq*, or destroyers of life). Government soldiers, known for their own orgies of violence, were viewed with similar trepidation. Caught in the middle of two armies, peasants were forced to live double lives, always hiding their true affiliations and beliefs in order to survive the depredations of murderous outsiders. Some even organized self-defense forces, known as *rondas-campesinas*. Though officially at war with *Sendero*, *ronda* members generally took a dim view of all outsiders (Figure 9.3).

Throughout the 1980s the Peruvian state proved unable to stem the escalating violence. Alan García was elected president in 1985 on the promise that he would restore respect for human rights and fix the economy. He did neither. In June 1986 he sent troops into three prisons in Lima and Callao in an effort to regain control of the institutions from rioting

Figure 9.3 An unidentified young woman holds a home-made shotgun as she forms up with other members of a government-sponsored civil defense group near Ayacucho

Source: AP Photo

Sendero inmates, killing 267. Under his administration. Peru's foreign debt grew to nearly $20 billion (U.S.), and by 1989 the inflation rate was nearing 10,000 percent. Between 1988 and 1990, per capita GDP declined by 20 percent.

These were the issues that framed the 1990 presidential elections, in which the relatively unknown Alberto Fujimori was elevated to the nation's highest office. Systemic crises often favor candidates who can claim to be political outsiders, and Fujimori seized this role by trading on the fact that he was an ethnic outsider to Peru's elite community. He cast himself as a representative of Peru's poor and disenfranchised indigenous masses. He adorned himself in local costumes as he traversed the highlands in search of votes, and promised aid to those most affected by the economic and political chaos.

It must have seemed a little like a betrayal then, when Fujimori did an almost immediate about-face once assuming the presidency. In a practice that was distressingly common during these years, he immediately adopted the free-market economic policies he had attacked during the campaign. Within months of taking office he imposed a series of austerity measures (fujishocks), drastically reducing government spending, food subsidies, and price controls. Peruvians were further put at the mercy of international markets when he significantly reduced tariff barriers, opening the economy to cheap foreign imports and further weakening domestic manufacturers.

Fujimori also took on *Sendero* (and those he defined as terrorists more generally) in dramatic fashion. He legalized the *rondas campesinas*, providing them with arms and training. He stepped up the military presence in Ayacucho and relentlessly persecuted communities suspected of supporting *Sendero*. He expanded the role of the *Servicio Nacional de Inteligencia* (National Intelligence Service, SIN) in the war, creating a secret force called the *Grupo Colina* (Colina Group) to go after the terrorists. This category itself was expanded to include not just *Sendero*, but protesters, political opponents, journalists, and the occasional bystander.

The new president was fortunate that by 1990 his predecessors had already done much of the groundwork needed to defeat *Sendero*. Alienated by the brutality and dogmatism of the *senderistas*, peasant support for the rebels had been on the wane since at least 1982. Moreover, after 1984 the government shifted the focus of its counter-insurgency program from the Marines to the Army, bringing an end to many of the most problematic aspects of the government's efforts to combat *Sendero*. Army officers often came from the highlands, spoke Quechua, and were more sensitive to community needs and interests than their Marine counterparts. They built roads, provided telephone service, and offered much needed supplies. They replaced indiscriminate killings with a more strategic approach to rooting out *Sendero* and winning popular support. "Civic Action" became a watchword for military officials aiming to win the hearts and minds of the nation's poor.

These actions were critical, but may have been less important than the simple fact that a growing number of highland communities had grown weary of *Sendero*'s violence and bloodlust, and were willing to cooperate with government efforts to defeat the revolution. After 1984 it was *Sendero*, not the Army, which was more often accused of perpetrating indiscriminate killings and showing a complete disregard for the interests of Andean peasants. In the end *Sendero* was in a war as much against the peasants and urban poor as against the state.

By 1990 *Sendero* could be found actively terrorizing not just peasants, but their rivals on the political left. The 1992 murder of community activist María Elena Moyano was a particularly powerful example of this development. Machine-gunned to death and then blown up with dynamite in front of her own children, Moyano was one of a number of urban leaders from the Lima slums who *Sendero* eliminated because they were insufficiently revolutionary (feminists were particular targets). Her death produced outrage, though it did not spark significant mobilization in the slums against the rebels. By this time those individuals who had to face *Sendero* on a daily basis in the cities mostly ducked their heads to stay out of the line of fire, and hoped the nightmare would soon come to an end. They needed a sign from the government that it was winning the war before they did anything that might put them at risk.

They received such a sign on September 12, 1992, when Fujimori announced that he had captured Presidente Gonzalo, who had been hiding in an apartment above a dance studio in Lima (he was betrayed by his psoriasis medication, which was found in the trash). With the capture of Guzmán, the tide rapidly turned against the rebels across the country, and Fujimori reached the height of his popularity. In the slums as well as the wealthy neighborhoods, he was widely admired for saving the country from chaos. For his part Fujimori claimed, with some legitimacy, that by centralizing power in the hands of the executive and clearing away of all dissent from congress and the judiciary, the autogolpe had allowed him to fight his war on the terrorists. Most seem to have agreed that the death of a few innocents was the price Peruvians had to pay to put an end to the scourge that was *Sendero*.

In succeeding years Fujimori would grow more certain that Peruvians needed his strong hand to guide them through their remaining economic and political troubles. He wrote a new constitution that allowed him to be re-elected in 1995, and then did an end-run around that constitution to have himself re-elected in 2000. By then though, Peruvians were increasingly weary of his dubious strategies for holding onto power. Caught up in a vote buying scandal in the aftermath of the election, he fled the country for exile in Japan in November 2000.

Peruvians then took a deep breath, and then began to examine their recent past. Alejandro Toledo, who assumed the presidency in 2001, named a Truth and Reconciliation Commission, which began to look into *Sendero*'s war. They concluded that around half of the nearly 70,000 people who died in the conflict were killed by *Sendero*, the rest being the responsibility of the state, *the rondas*, and other private groups. In 2002, at the closure of the public hearings of Peru's Truth and Reconciliation Commission, Chairman Salomón Lerner Febres summed up his experience.

> The stories we have attentively heard, feeling sorrow and respect, create in us Peruvians the obligation of wondering what happened to us, how we arrived to those extremes of degradation that the victims have courageously and generously shown us with their narratives. I said degradation, and although this word may sound excessive, it is actually only a pale reflection of the acts we have been hearing about these days. We have spoken about crimes committed from an absolute position of power against unarmed and inadvertent victims. And if this had not been sufficient for the executioner, they were crimes committed under the cover of darkness and with malice aforethought, as the witnesses in these Hearings have told us repeatedly. Was not that already excessive?

Apparently not. The violations had to be committed, besides, with rage and merci-lessness as if the others' suffering had become the main goal, a sick enjoyment motive for those executing these crimes, and for those who ordered them from comfortable and safe shelters or offices. The testimonies that have been presented to us coincide in pointing out this relish for cruelty, this desire to destroy the victims' dignity, start-ing with the use of language. The recurrence of insults, as if physical force were not sufficient, also reveals a disdain based on considerations of race, culture or poverty, and patently shows the devaluation of women. This vulgar language of executioners against unarmed victims reflects, in brief, the patterns of social alienation that, as we know, are still embedded in our country, and which are perhaps the greatest obstacles to achieving a fair and democratic society.[13]

Fujimori remained untouched by the findings of the commission until he attempted to return to Peru in 2006 in order to run, once more, for the presidency. Arrested in Chile and then extradited to Peru, during the following two years he faced trials for corruption, abuses of power, and for his role in the deaths of more than two dozen people killed by the Grupo Colina. He was convicted on several charges, and is currently serving a twenty-five-year prison sentence.

The Documents: Scenes from the War

How does one tell the stories of the bloodbaths that engulfed so many Latin American soci-eties between the 1960s and 1980s? For those given to Manichean visions of the world—the easy juxtapositions of good versus evil—it seems easy. You choose the good (usually an innocent victim, a student, an indigenous person, often a woman), and the evil (often some faceless but monstrous military figure), and tell how, without provocation the latter bru-talized, tortured, and perhaps killed the former. It is a powerful story, and the audience is generally left silent, moved by the story, horrified and indignant.

During the 1980s a genre of Latin American writing called *testimonio* grew increasingly popular as a means of relating these experiences. Rigoberta Menchú shocked audiences with the tales of her life, moving readers deeply while relating the terrible fates suffered by her father, mother, and several brothers. Alicia Partnoy moved readers with her account of surviving torture by the Argentine military. Even Adolfo Scilingo, a member of the Argentine Navy and a torturer himself, managed to evoke a certain amount of sympathy by speaking truth to power. These texts evoke strong emotions. They are tragedies with sympathetic victims and monstrous perpetrators.[14]

There are, of course, problems to this approach. Beyond the troubling questions raised by the voyeuristic quality of these texts,[15] the simple notions of good and evil they convey offer few explanations of how otherwise normal people (people who today wander the streets of any number of Latin American cities) engaged in the inhuman acts these texts describe. This practice also tends to obscure other, very real things, such as the fact that some of the victims (many of whom also walk the streets today) threw bombs, robbed banks, and kidnapped their erstwhile enemies. These are, to borrow a term from Christo-pher Browning, "ordinary people."[16] Even more, the Manichean nature of these texts can serve to reinforce a series of Northern stereotypes about the South (women as passive, indigenous peoples as mystical, non-political, Latin American men as violent machos).

Testimonios did help discredit the dictatorships, and as such constitute an important part of the Latin American past. That said, as military rule fades into the past, we may be well served by telling a more complex story of the era. One way to begin this task involves an effort to understand just how the political and other differences that characterized these societies metastasized into a tendency to dehumanize one's adversaries. In Peru, where the animus and cognitive failures were so widely shared, we have an exceptionally good window onto these tendencies. We have an enormous amount of evidence of the sympathies and sentiments that divided Peruvian society. These divisions were clearly rooted in the historical conflicts between coast and highlands and all the attendant cognitive failures (Limeños and Andean villagers each failed to see the other clearly). As with other countries, Peru was also riven by conflicts between left and right, and conflicts within the left. Each of these struggles seemed all the more urgent in the midst of an economic catastrophe.

We begin with an early and revealing example of the cognitive failures and deep anxieties that framed this epoch in Peruvian history. Document 9.1 is an excerpt from an essay published by the Peruvian novelist Mario Vargas Llosa in the *New York Times Magazine* in July 1983 (the entire essay can be found on the book's website, www.routledge.com/cw/dawson). Vargas Llosa was improbably named as the head of a commission sent to investigate the murder of eight journalists in the village of Uchuraccay in the southern Peruvian Highlands in early 1983. This essay was based on the commission's findings. He reveals some troubling assumptions about Andean peasants, rendering them as fundamentally primitive, unaware that they lived in a modern nation and thus unaccountable for their actions.

Vargas Llosa's observations were roundly criticized in Peru, in part because they were factually incorrect. Many peasants from the region had a great deal of experience living in coastal regions, and understood full well that Peruvian law did not allow them to execute outsiders. Later investigators would raise other questions about the massacre, insinuating that the military had been complicit in the murders, suggesting that the peasants were led to believe that the journalists were *senderistas*. Their neighbors had, after all, just killed a number of *senderistas*, and they no doubt were particularly anxious at that moment. Some even suggested that the locals may have thought the journalists were *pishtacos*. In any event, at this point the *comuneros* had good reason to fear outsiders. *Senderistas* returned to the region repeatedly in the following years to carry out murderous reprisals, and during much of the decade both Uchuraccay and Huaychao (where the original murders took place) would be left deserted.

Document 9.2 is an excerpt from President Gonzalo's "Interview of the Century," given to the *senderista* paper *El Diario* in 1988 (the entire interview can be found on the book's website). If Vargas Llosa inflicted rhetorical violence on the peasants, and perhaps justified other forms of violence indirectly, Gonzalo celebrated actual violence—a war of annihilation. The text is quite chilling to read. More chilling is the fact that his sentiments resonated so deeply with a certain segment of the Peruvian left. We must wonder what it was (or is) that underpinned such millenarian thinking, why it was that middle-class university students and leftists (but by this point, relatively few peasants) would find this so appealing, why violence was so romanticized? We should also note that Gonzalo's love of violence is remarkably similar to the sentiments expressed by the torturers in Chile, Argentina, and elsewhere. They too described it as cleansing, as ritual. The nation is reborn in the bloodbath.

One of the curious things we see in juxtaposing Documents 9.1 and 9.2 is that both Vargas Llosa and Presidente Gonzalo had a superficial view of peasant and indigenous cultures. Both imagined that rural cultures needed to be remade, that in their present form they were either useless or dangerous. Both then, ultimately make peasants into components of a larger scheme, a larger war. Neither was destined to mourn too many peasant deaths, as their lives, as they were, offered little to the cause.

We see in Document 9.3 Fujimori's rationale for dismantling the Peruvian state on April 5, 1992. Some Peruvians note that his rhetoric in 1992 had a long history, and was not so unlike that of earlier coups d'état. It was certainly similar in tone and explanation to the Argentine and Chilean cases of the recent past. Something needs to be destroyed. The state and civil society are rotten to the core. A powerful, visionary figure will save the country, but he can only do so if freed from a bankrupt series of processes. Fujimori declared that he was not overthrowing a democratic system. He claimed he was paving the way for the establishment of a democratic state.

Document 9.4 leaves us with a cautionary tale about the extremes that Fujimori went to in his war against *Sendero*. When Fujimori was ultimately held to account for his response to *Sendero*, aside from charges of abuse of authority and the misappropriation of funds, he was charged with responsibility for four specific cases of human rights violations perpetrated by the Grupo Colina. Those incidents included the kidnappings of journalist Gustavo Gorriti and businessman Samuel Dyer after the 1992 autogolpe. A third case involved the killings of fifteen people in the Lima neighborhood of Barrios Altos in 1991. The document included below concerns the fourth incident, the massacre at Valle Nacional (Cantuta) University on July 18, 1992 (Figure 9.4).

Figure 9.4 Family members of victims of the Cantuta massacre

Source: Reuters/Mariana Bazo

In the early morning hours of that day, hooded security officials entered the homes of several students and professors. The students were taken out of their dormitories and forced into the fetal position, their faces pushed to the ground. One by one, soldiers pulled their faces up by the hair, identifying students individually, and eventually separating nine from the group. They, along with one professor, were taken away, murdered, and secretly buried in mass graves on the property of the Lima water utility. Fujimori denies knowing about the killings. He denies knowing even that the Grupo Colina existed. He was nonetheless found guilty at trial for his role in the killings.

Document 9.1   Mario Vargas Llosa, "The Massacre," excerpt from "Inquest in the Andes: A Latin American Writer Explores the Political Lessons of a Peruvian Massacre," *New York Times Magazine*, July 31, 1983

Source: "Inquest in the Andes," published in the *New York Times Magazine*, July 31, 1983. Copyright © Mario Vargas Llosa, 1983.

The Massacre

How did the murder of the reporters take place? The Uchuraccayans refused to give us the details. We assumed the Indians came down the mountainsides that encircle the village and attacked suddenly, as the reporters approached, before anyone could speak. We supposed that they used sling-shots, which shoot stones so fast that they can hit a viscacha, the large, burrowing rodent of the pampas, running at full speed. (Proudly, they demonstrated that for us.) We were inclined to believe that there had been no dialogue—first, because the Iquichanos thought that the strangers were armed, and, second, because three of the journalists, Octavio Infante, Amador García and Félix Gavilán, spoke Quechua and could have tempered the hostility of their attackers.

But the facts turned out to be colder and crueler. They came to light two months later, when a patrol escorting the judge in charge of the separate judicial investigation, which is still going on, found a camera in a cave near Uchuraccay. Apparently, it had been uncovered by viscachas digging in the earth where the villagers had hidden it. It was a Minolta, serial number 4202368, that had belonged to the young photographer from *El Observador*, Willy Retto, and it contained film which, when developed, provided a horrifying document.

It seems that Willy Retto had the presence of mind to take pictures during the moments just before the massacre, perhaps when the lives of some of his friends had already been taken. There were nine photographs; all were confiscated by the investigating judge. Somehow, three of the pictures found their way onto the pages of *Ultima Hora*; they were promptly reproduced by other papers. In one of these pictures, the hulking Jorge Sedano is on his knees next to the bags and cameras that someone, possibly Octavio Infante, has placed on the ground. In another picture, Felix Gavilán, the local correspondent with his radio program for the Indian peasants, has his arms raised. In the third picture, 22-year-old Jorge Luis Mendivil, with his teen-ager's face, is gesturing, as if asking everybody to calm down. From a reliable informant, I have learned that three other pictures—the last three pictures on the roll of film—show an Iquichano advancing threateningly on Willy Retto. The pictures prove that some words had been spoken but that talk did no good—that, although the Iquichanos saw the strangers were unarmed, they attacked them anyhow, convinced they were their enemies.

The massacre had magical and religious overtones, as well as political and social implications. The hideous wounds on the corpses were ritualistic. The eight bodies were buried in pairs, face down, the form of burial used for people the Iquichanos consider "devils"—people like the dancers of the tijeras, a folk dance, who are believed to make pacts with the Devil. They were buried outside the community limits to emphasize that they were strangers. (In the Andes, the Devil merges with the image of the stranger.) The bodies were especially mutilated around the mouth and eyes, in the belief that the victim should be deprived of his sight, so he cannot recognize his killers, and of his tongue, so he cannot denounce them. Their ankles were broken, so they could not come back for revenge. The villagers stripped the bodies; they washed the clothes and burned them in a purification ceremony known as pichja.

Knowing the circumstances does not excuse the crime, but it makes what happened more comprehensible. The violence stuns us because it is an anomaly in our ordinary lives. For the Iquichanos, that violence is the atmosphere they live in from the time they are born until the time they die. After our return from Uchuraccay, new tragedies confirmed that the Iquichanos' fear of reprisals by Sendero Luminoso was justified.

On April 3, four Senderista detachments, augmented by hundreds of peasants from a rival community, attacked Lucanamarca, 120 miles from Uchuraccay, and murdered 77 people in the village square, most of them with axes, machetes and stones. There were four children among the decapitated, mutilated bodies. On July 18, the guerrillas attacked Uchuraccay at dawn, in reprisal for the slaying of the five Senderistas there on Jan. 22. General Noel's office in Ayacucho said at least eight peasants were slaughtered—again in the village square—with bullets and axes. All indications were that the war in the Andes was continuing.

When our commission's hearing in Uchuraccay was over, and, overwhelmed by what we had seen and heard—the graves of the reporters were still open—we were getting ready to return to Ayacucho, a tiny woman from the community suddenly began to dance. She was quietly singing a song whose words we could not understand. She was an Indian as tiny as a child, but she had the wrinkled face of a very old woman, and the scarred cheeks and swollen lips of those who live exposed to the cold of the uplands. She was barefoot, and wore several brightly colored skirts and a hat with ribbons, and as she sang and danced she tapped us gently on the legs with brambles. Was she saying goodbye to us in an ancient ritual? Was she cursing us because we belonged to the strangers—Senderistas, "reporters," sinchis—who had brought new reasons for anguish and fear to their lives? Was she exorcising us?

For several weeks, I had been living in a state of extraordinary tension as I interviewed soldiers, politicians, policemen, peasants and reporters and reviewed dispatches, evidence and legal testimony, trying to establish what had happened. At night, I would often stay awake, attempting to determine the truth of the testimony and the hypotheses, or I had nightmares in which the certainties of the day became enigmas again. And as the story of the eight journalists unfolded—I had known two of them, and had been with Amador García just two days before his trip to Ayacucho—it seemed that another, even more terrible story about my own country was being revealed. But at no time had I felt as much sorrow as in Uchuraccay on that late afternoon, with its threatening clouds, watching the tiny woman who danced and tapped us with brambles, and who seemed to come from a Peru different from the one I live in, an ancient, archaic Peru that has survived in these sacred mountains despite centuries of isolation and adversity.

That frail, tiny woman had undoubtedly been one of the mob who threw rocks and swung sticks, for the Iquichano women are famous for being as warlike as the men. In the photographs from Willy Retto's camera, you can see them at the front of the crowd. It wasn't difficult to imagine the community of Uchuraccay transformed by fear and rage. We had a presentiment of it at the hearing, when, after too many uncomfortable questions, the passive assembly, led by the women, suddenly began to roar "Challa, challa!" ("Enough, enough!") and the air was filled with evil omens.

If the essential facts of the journalists' death have been clarified—who killed them, how and why—there are others that remain hidden in obscurity. What happened to Juan Argumedo? Why won't the Iquichanos take responsibility for his death? It may be that, in their minds, Juan Argumedo was a "neighbor"—someone from a rival area, but an area they had to coexist with for reasons of trade and travel—and a confession that they had killed him would be tantamount to a declaration of war on the valley farmers. If so, this precaution has failed: There have been several bloody confrontations between the Indians of Uchuraccay and the peasants of Chacabamba and another valley village.

Another unresolved question is the red flag. General Noel said the reporters were murdered because they walked into Uchuraccay with a Communist flag, and the villagers made the same statement to our commission. Willy Retto's photographs show no such flag. And why would the reporters carry a flag that could only mean danger for them? In all probability, the villagers, in realizing their mistake, invented the story to give greater credibility to their claim that they thought the strangers were Senderistas. The red flag they turned over to Lieutenant Bravo Reid of the Tambo patrol was, in all likelihood, the one they alleged had been flown over Iquicha by the Government representative at that village—the flag the Indians tied around his neck after bringing him to Uchuraccay.

Even more dramatic than the blood that flows through this story is the lack of understanding that made the blood flow. The reporters believed that, in the earlier incident at Huaychao, the Senderistas had been murdered by the sinchis and not the peasants. In Uchuraccay, the peasants killed some strangers because they thought the strangers were coming to kill them. It is possible that the journalists never knew why they were attacked. A wall of disinformation, prejudice and ideology separated one group from the other and made communication impossible.

Perhaps this story helps to clarify the reason for the mind-shattering violence that characterizes guerrilla warfare in Latin America. These guerrilla movements are not "peasant movements." They are born in the cities, among intellectuals and middle-class militants who, with their dogmatism and their rhetoric, are often as foreign and incomprehensible to the peasant masses as Sendero Luminoso is to the men and women of Uchuraccay. The outrages committed by those other strangers—the Government forces of counterinsurgency—tend to win peasant support for the guerrillas.

Put simply, the peasants are coerced by those who think they are the masters of history and absolute truth. The fact is that the struggle between the guerrillas and the armed forces is really a settling of accounts between privileged sectors of society, and the peasant masses are used cynically and brutally by those who say they want to "liberate" them. The peasants always suffer the greatest number of victims: At least 750 of them have been killed in Peru since the beginning of 1983.

The story of the eight journalists reveals how vulnerable democracy is in Latin America and how easily it dies under military or Marxist–Leninist dictatorship. It is difficult for people to defend a free press, elections and representative institutions when their circumstances do not allow them to understand, much less to benefit from, the achievements of democracy. Democracy will never be strong in our Latin American countries as long as it is the privilege of one sector of society and an incomprehensible abstraction for all the others. The double threat—the model of Gen. Augusto Pinochet in Chile and the model of Fidel Castro in Cuba—will continue to haunt democratic government as long as people in our countries kill for the reasons that the peasants of Uchuraccay killed.

Document 9.2 The Interview of the Century, 1988 (Excerpt)

Source: http://www.blythe.org/peru-pcp/docs_en/interv.htm#BM4

El Diario: Chairman, let's talk about the people's war now. What does violence mean to you, Chairman Gonzalo?

Chairman Gonzalo: With regard to violence we start from the principle established by Chairman Mao Tsetung: violence, that is the need for revolutionary violence, is a universal law with no exception. Revolutionary violence is what allows us to resolve fundamental contradictions by means of an army, through people's war. Why do we start from Chairman Mao's thesis? Because we believe Mao reaffirmed Marxism on this question, establishing that there are no exceptions whatsoever to this law. What Marx held, that violence is the midwife of history, continues to be a totally valid and monumental contribution. Lenin expounded upon violence and spoke about Engels' panegyric praise of revolutionary violence, but it was the Chairman who told us that it was a universal law, without any exception. That's why we take his thesis as our starting point. This is an essential question of Marxism, because without revolutionary violence one class cannot replace another, an old order cannot be overthrown to create a new one—today a new order led by the proletariat through Communist Parties.

The problem of revolutionary violence is an issue that is more and more being put on the table for discussion, and therefore we communists and revolutionaries must reaffirm our principles. The problem of revolutionary violence is how to actually carry it out with people's war. The way we see this question is that when Chairman Mao

Tsetung established the theory of people's war and put it into practice, he provided the proletariat with its military line, with a military theory and practice that is universally valid and therefore applicable everywhere in accordance with the concrete conditions.

We see the problem of war this way: war has two aspects, destructive and constructive. Construction is the principal aspect. Not to see it this way undermines the revolution—weakens it. On the other hand, from the moment the people take up arms to overthrow the old order, from that moment, the reaction seeks to crush, destroy and annihilate the struggle, and it uses all the means at its disposal, including genocide. We have seen this in our country; we are seeing it now, and will continue to see it even more until the outmoded Peruvian State is demolished.

As for the so-called dirty war, I would like to simply point out that they claim that the reactionary armed forces learned this dirty war from us. This accusation clearly expresses a lack of understanding of revolution, and of what a people's war is. The reaction, through its armed forces and other repressive forces, seeks to carry out their objective of sweeping us away, of eliminating us. Why? Because we want to do the same to them—sweep them away and eliminate them as a class. Mariátegui said that only by destroying, demolishing the old order could a new social order be brought into being. In the final analysis, we judge these problems in light of the basic principle of war established by Chairman Mao: the principle of annihilating the enemy's forces and preserving one's own forces. We know very well that the reaction has used, is using, and will continue to use genocide. On this we are absolutely clear. And consequently this raises the problem of the price we have to pay: in order to annihilate the enemy and to preserve, and even more to develop our own forces, we have to pay a price in war, a price in blood, the need to sacrifice a part for the triumph of the people's war.

As for terrorism, they claim we're terrorists. I would like to give the following answer so that everyone can think about it: has it or has it not been Yankee imperialism and particularly Reagan who has branded all revolutionary movements as terrorists, yes or no? This is how they attempt to discredit and isolate us in order to crush us. That is their dream. And it's not only Yankee imperialism and the other imperialist powers that combat so-called terrorism. So does social-imperialism and revisionism, and today Gorbachev himself proposes to unite with the struggle against terrorism. And it isn't by chance that at the VIIIth Congress of the Party of Labor of Albania Ramiz Alia dedicated himself to combatting terrorism as well with the pioneers of the people's revolutionary army! It is no longer a plot against some detested individual, no act of vengeance or desperation, no mere "intimidation"—no, it was a well thought-out and well prepared commencement of operations by a contingent of the revolutionary army. Fortunately, the time has passed when revolution was "made" by individual terrorists, because people were not revolutionary. The bomb has ceased to be the weapon of the solitary "bomb thrower," and is becoming an essential weapon of the people.

Lenin taught us that the times had changed, that the bomb had become a weapon of combat for our class, for the people, that what we're talking about is no longer a conspiracy, an isolated individual act, but the actions of a Party, with a plan, with a system, with an army. So, where is the imputed terrorism? It's pure slander.

Finally, we always have to remember that, especially in present-day war, it is precisely the reactionaries who use terrorism as one of their means of struggle, and it is, as has been proven repeatedly, one of the forms used on a daily basis by the armed forces of the Peruvian State. Considering all this, we can conclude that those whose reasoning is colored by desperation because the earth is trembling beneath their feet wish to charge us with terrorism in order to hide the people's war. But this people's war is so earth shaking that they themselves admit that it is of national dimensions and that it has become the principal problem facing the Peruvian State. What terrorism could do that? None. And moreover, they can no longer deny that a Communist Party is leading the people's war. And at this time some of them are beginning to reconsider; we shouldn't be too hasty in writing anyone off. There are those who could come forward. Others, like Del Prado. . .

At the end of 1982, the armed forces came in. The CC had anticipated this for more than a year. It had studied the involvement of the armed forces, and concluded that it would increase until the army had substituted for the police, who would then assume a secondary role. This is how it has been, and given the situation it could not have been otherwise. We had prepared ourselves, but nevertheless, we had a second problem. The introduction of the armed forces had its consequences. They came in applying a policy of genocide from the beginning. They formed armed groups, called mesnadas, forcing the masses to join and putting them in front, using them as shields. This must be said clearly: here we see not only the policy of using masses against masses, an old reactionary policy already seen by Marx, but also a cowardly use of the masses, putting the masses in front of them. The armed forces have nothing to boast about— with good reason we have called them experts at defeat, and skilled at attacking the unarmed masses. These are the armed forces of Peru. Faced with this we convened an expanded session of the CC. It was a large meeting and it lasted a long time. It was one of the longest sessions we've ever had. That's when we established the Plan to Conquer Base Areas, and the People's Guerrilla Army was created to respond to a force that was obviously of a higher level than the police. It was there that we also raised, among other things, the problem of Front-State.

Thus arose the second problem, the problem of confronting the genocide, the genocide of 1983 and 1984. It is in the Party documents. It's not necessary to go into it a lot, but we do want to stress the fact that it was a vicious and merciless genocide. They thought that with this genocide "they would wipe us off the map." How real this was is shown by the fact that, by the end of 1984, they began to circulate among their officers documents concerning our annihilation. The struggle was intense, hard, those were complex and difficult times.

In the face of reactionary military actions and the use of mesnadas, we responded with a devastating action: Lucanamarca. Neither they nor we have forgotten it, to be sure, because they got an answer that they didn't imagine possible. More than 80 were annihilated, that is the truth. And we say openly that there were excesses, as was analyzed in 1983. But everything in life has two aspects. Our task was to deal a devastating blow in order to put them in check, to make them understand that it was not going to be so easy. On some occasions, like that one, it was the Central Leadership itself that planned the action and gave instructions. That's how it was. In that case, the principal thing is that we dealt them a devastating blow, and we checked them and they under-stood that they were dealing with a different kind of people's fighters, that we weren't the same as those they had fought before. This is what they understood. The excesses are the negative aspect. Understanding war, and basing ourselves on what Lenin said, taking Clausewitz into account, in war, the masses engaged in combat can go too far and express all their hatred, the deep feelings of class hatred, repudiation and con-demnation that they have—that was the root of it. This has been explained by Lenin very clearly. Excesses can be committed. The problem is to go to a certain point and not beyond it, because if you go past that point you go off course. It's like an angle; it can be opened up to a certain point and no further. If we were to give the masses a lot of restrictions, requirements and prohibitions, it would mean that deep down we didn't want the waters to overflow. And what we needed was for the waters to over-flow, to let the flood rage, because we know that when a river floods its banks it causes devastation, but then it returns to its riverbed. I repeat, this was explained clearly by Lenin, and this is how we understand those excesses. But, I insist, the main point was to make them understand that we were a hard nut to crack, and that we were ready for anything, anything.

Marx taught us: one does not play at insurrection, one does not play at revolution. But when one raises the banner of insurrection, when one takes up arms, there's no tak-ing down the banner, it must be held high and never lowered until victory. This is what he taught us, no matter how much it costs us! Marx has armed us then, as Lenin has, and, principally Chairman Mao Tsetung taught us about the price we have to pay—what it means to annihilate in order to preserve, what it means to hold high the banner, come what may. And we say that in this way, with this determination, we overcame the sinister, vile, cowardly and vicious genocide. And we say this because someone—he who calls himself president—makes insinuations about barbarism, without blushing, when he is an aspiring Attila the Hun playing with other people's blood.

Have we gone through difficult times? Yes. But what has reality shown us? That if we persist, keep politics in command, follow our political strategy, follow our military strategy, if we have a clear and defined plan, then we will advance, and we are capable of facing any bloodbath. (We began to prepare for the bloodbath in 1981 because it had to come. Thus we were already prepared ideologically, that is principal.) All this brought about an increase in our forces, they multiplied. This was the result. It turned out as the Chairman had said: the reaction is dreaming when it tries to drown the revo-lution in blood. They should know they are nourishing it, and this is an inexorable law. So this reaffirms for us that we have to be more and more dedicated, firm, and resolute in our principles, and always have unwavering faith in the masses.

Thus we came out of it strengthened, with a larger Army, more People's Commit-tees and Base Areas, and a larger Party, exactly the opposite of what they had imag-ined. We have already talked, I believe, of the bloody dreams of the reaction. They are nothing but that, bloody dreams that, in the final analysis, end up being nightmares. But I insist: by persisting in our principles and fighting with the support of the masses, mainly the poor peasants, we've been able to confront this situation. It is here that the heroism of which I have already spoken, the heroism of the masses, has been expressed.

Document 9.3 Fujimori's 1992 Declaration of the Autogolpe

Source: www.congreso.gob.pe/museo/mensajes/Mensaje-1992-1.pdf. Translated by Robert Forstag and Patricia Rosas.

A Message to the Nation from the President of Peru, Alberto Fujimori, Engineer
April 5, 1992
My fellow Peruvians:

For the past 20 months, my government has proposed building a genuine democracy, a democracy that would effectively guarantee equal participation for all citizens. One in which there would be no place for special privileges or sinecures and one that would truly allow us to conquer, in the medium term, the problems of underdevelopment, extreme poverty, lack of opportunity, corruption, and violence.

Like many Peruvians, I thought that this might be the last chance for Peru to fulfill its destiny. The initial phase of my administration has seen some undeniable progress, which is a result of the discipline and order with which the nation's affairs have been managed and of the Peruvian people's responsible and self-sacrificial attitude. We can thus point to the reinsertion of our country into the international financial structure, the gradual reining in of hyperinflation, and a climate of increasing confidence and stability.

But today we can sense that something is impeding our continued march toward national reconstruction and progress. And the Peruvian people know what is holding us back.

They know that it is nothing other than the rotting of our government institutions. Chaos and corruption and a failure to identify with the most vital national interests on the part of some of our most important institutions, like the legislative and judicial branches, are tying the hands of the government when it comes to achieving our goals of national reconstruction and development. To the ineffectiveness of Congress and the corruption of the judiciary, we can add the obvious obstructionism and covert scheming of the political parties' top leaders as they try to undermine the efforts of the government and its citizens. Those leaders, an expression of traditional shady political machinations, are interested solely in blocking the economic measures that could lead to a recovery from our nation's bankruptcy, which they themselves have brought upon us.

Similarly, there are groups that are interested in seeing the Pacification Strategy fail because they do not have the courage to take a clear stand against terrorism. With utter disregard for the future of our nation, people who only yesterday were the bitterest of political rivals are now joining forces for the purpose of preventing the successful functioning of the government. The reason behind this unholy alliance is a shared interest in regaining lost political ground. In the struggle against drug trafficking, the Congress has shown itself to be weak and inconsistent. This is clearly seen in its position on legislation proposed by the Executive aimed at imposing sanctions on money laundering, abolishing banking secrecy, punishing the trafficking of goods obtained as a result of the illegal drug trade, and punishing public servants and officials engaged in the concealment of drug-trafficking activities. All of these measures, proposed by the government in Legislative Decree No. 736, were repealed by Congress with no explanation whatsoever and without considering that such action would leave the country powerless to impose the kinds of tough penalties necessary against those involved in the illegal drug trade.

The irresponsible and negative attitude displayed by legislators also shows a disdain for constitutional mandates, which are knowingly violated. This is the case with the enactment of Law No. 25397, the Law on Legislative Control of the President of the Republic's Regulatory Actions, which attempts to tie the president's hands, depriving him of powers essential for governing. This affects such important matters as economic policy and the fight against terrorism, by denying the President the authority to designate which areas are in states of emergency.

Without the least regard for the powers vested in the president by our Constitution, attempts have even been made to deny him the possibility of fully or partially complying with the Annual Budget Law. This demagogic and obstructionist excess has resulted in a very significant deficit in the budget, which may result in the reoccurrence of hyperinflation if urgent corrective measures are not taken. In an act that constitutes an affront to a country that is suffering severe economic hardship, Congress has grossly expanded its budget and improperly provided an extension of the cédulas vivas[17] to former congressional representatives. This action shows lawmakers' complete disregard for the complaints asking for austerity, efficiency, and seriousness in legislative matters—a complaint repeated on numerous occasions by ordinary citizens. Numerous times, congressional sessions could not proceed due to the chamber's lack of a quorum.

The irresponsibility, carelessness, and sloth of the so-called "Fathers of the Nation" have resulted in the tabling of many bills that were critical for the functioning of this country.

The people of Peru, the vast majority, have called for efficiently run institutions, committed to our nation's supreme interest, that would channel, focus, and harness the country's energies. Consequently, they have consistently rejected their Congressional representatives' irresponsible, unfruitful, anti-historical, and anti-national conduct, which lets the agenda of groups and party leaders prevail over those of Peru. The country wants a congress that addresses our major national challenges, free from the vices of political caciquismo and clientelism.

A justice system overcome by political sectarianism, venality, and complicit irresponsibility is a scandal that irreparably discredits democracy and the rule of law. The nation has grown weary of this state of affairs and wants solutions. It desires an effective and modern justice system, which would constitute a full guarantee for civic life. It does not want to see any more corrupt fiefdoms in places where irreproachable morality should be the order of the day.

Among other examples of how justice operates in this country, let it suffice to mention the inexplicable release of drug traffickers, or the egregiously partial treatment accorded to them, or the mass release of terrorists who not only have been convicted but who have confessed to their crimes. All are a misapplication of the standard of fairness. We must contrast that with the dubious slowness that characterizes proceedings against citizens with limited resources and the unusual degree of diligence in cases involving persons with power and influence. All of this makes a mockery of justice.

Corruption and political infiltration have permeated every level and every court in the judiciary. In Peru, justice has always been a commodity sold to the highest bidder. We are not denying that there are honest and upright judges and prosecutors. We need to rescue them by once and for all removing their corrupt colleagues. Regionalization represented a great hope for the peoples of Peru, but it was infected from the very beginning by the evils of the traditional political system. Thus, instead of representing a solution, regionalism is a problem with multiple facets because it has created regional "microcentralisms" and a new source of national frustration. Bloated bureaucracies, hungry for power and for government funds, have been installed in most of the regional governments, and each mirrors all of the vices and defects of the capital's old centralism.

There is nothing new in their ideas about how to spend the treasure of the nation and its people. Instead of privileging spending on necessary public works, they give priority to profligate spending that has no constructive purpose. We cannot allow this to continue.

Nobody believes that Peru can indefinitely postpone fundamental socioeconomic changes. Thus, now more than ever, the nation needs a profound transformation, not just a band-aid of partial reform. Peru cannot continue to let terrorism, drug trafficking, and corruption weaken it. We need to strengthen our resolve by radically altering the structures of our nation's institutions. We cannot wait three more years for citizens, committed to acting in the best interests of the people, to enter the congress. We also cannot wait even one more day to completely overhaul the nation's judiciary. The fate of our nation has hung in the balance during the past twenty months, and it will continue to hang in the balance in the future, for we have only just begun the task of rebuilding. The government is aware of the historic necessity of eliminating all obstacles that stand in the way of this process of reconstruction.

If the nation does not rebuild now—if it does not lay the foundations for national development—then there is no possible guarantee for the welfare of Peruvians as a civilized collectivity, as a Nation-State.

After rebuilding, our objective is to achieve a prosperous and democratic society. The current democratic formality is deceptive and false, and its institutions often serve the interests of the privileged groups.

It is true that the Constitution contemplates mechanisms for its own modification. But it is also true that, for this to happen, two consecutive first-session ordinary legislative sessions must convene, and this would mean that we would have to wait until nearly the end of the present presidential term to have the legal instruments needed for Peru's general rebuilding.[18] And this would happen only if Congress decides to approve the necessary modifications, including those that are contrary to its members' own interests, such as, for example, a reduction in pay compensation and a no-reelection rule.

What institution or mechanism will let us undertake all the profound changes that, in turn, will propel the nation forward? There can be no doubt that neither Congress nor the judiciary are agents of change. Instead, they are standing in the way of transformation and progress.

As President of the Republic, I have directly witnessed these irregularities, and I have felt that it is my responsibility to take emergency actions in the interest of hastening the process of national reconstruction. It is for this reason that I have decided to take the following extraordinary measures:

1. Temporary disbanding of the Congress of the Republic until the approval of a new organic structure for the nation's legislative branch, which a national referendum will approve.
2. Comprehensive reorganization of the judiciary, the National Council of the Judiciary, the Court of Constitutional Guarantees, and the Public Prosecutor's Office to ensure the honest and efficient administration of justice.
3. Restructuring of the Office of the General Comptroller of the Republic to ensure proper and timely oversight of the government, which will lead to imposing drastic sanctions on those responsible for the misappropriation of the State's resources.

As a citizen elected by a large majority of our nation's voters, I reaffirm that my only motive is my desire to have the Peruvian nation achieve prosperity and greatness. This will only be possible through a profound transformation of the State and its institutions, so that the latter become true engines for development and social justice.

Therefore, governmental continuity will temporarily occur through an Emergency and National Reconstruction Government, whose principal objectives are:

a. Modification of the current Constitution in order to reflect the creation of a new structure for both Congress and the judiciary, for the purpose of converting these branches of government into effective instruments for order and development. The former is to be transformed into a modern legislature, one which reflects the interests of the nation and which is subject to periodic renewal.
b. Radically inculcate morality in the judiciary and its affiliated institutions.
c. Modernize the government administration to adapt it for purposes of development and the best and most rationalized utilization of resources.
d. Pacify the country within a legal framework that imposes severe penalties on terrorists and drug traffickers. Doing this will guarantee a climate of peace and tranquility to make national and foreign investment possible.
e. Confront drug trafficking and associated illegal activities head on, and successfully eliminate isolated instances of immorality and corruption in law enforcement agencies and other institutions.
f. Admonitory punishment of all cases of immorality and corruption that involve government officials.
g. Promote a market economy within a legal framework that provides security and encourages efficiency and competitiveness in those participating in the economy.
h. Reorganize the educational system and adapt it to our development needs, foster a patriotic consciousness, and encourage the mass construction of schools. Doing this will generate employment at the same time.

i.   Decentralize the powers of the Central Government by means of a regionalization process that would reduce both the bureaucracy as well as the number of regional deputies.

j.   In the medium term, substantially increase the standard of living for the population as a whole, creating conditions for the comprehensive development of the human being. As long as this transitional situation lasts, we will suspend those Constitutional articles that are not compatible with these governmental objectives. Thus, congressional functions will be assumed by a Council of Ministers, which will have the authority to issue decree-laws.

In addition, as quickly as possible, we will create a commission tasked with comprehensively reorganizing the judiciary.

In addition, we will quickly form another commission, consisting of renowned jurists, to draft a constitutional reform bill for the previously indicated reason: to ensure that our Magna Carta meets our needs for development, modernization, and pacification of the nation. In due course, a national referendum will be held to pass that constitutional reform. Any real social change must revolve around the nation's youth, yet these young people must be imbued with a national spirit. We are a country of young people, and it will be the nation's youth who will determine our future. Young people are the most sensitive, idealistic, and honest component of our population. We must ensure that they do not fall prey to drugs, fanaticism, or frustration. Their energy will serve as the catalyzing agent for our nation's transformation.

The youth will understand that it is a matter of planting the seeds of a new nation and leaving behind the fetid ruins of the old order of corrupt politicians, judges, and officials who stand in the way of true democracy. Doing this will let the true interests of the nation guide the destiny of the Republic, rather than the pseudo-democratic formalities that do nothing but hinder our progress.

For Peru, there is only one path forward: national reconstruction. Nothing will change unless we ensure that this rebuilding happens and that the Peruvian people's will for transformation and quest for self-renewal not be undermined by sterile legislative debates or corrupt judges and government officials.

It is essential that the nation understand that the temporary and partial suspension of the present legal system does not constitute the negation of true democracy. On the contrary, this action constitutes the beginning of a search for a genuine transformation that will guarantee a legitimate and effective democracy and that will allow all Peruvians to become the builders of a Peru that is more just, more developed, and better respected within the family of nations.

As Commander-in-Chief of the Armed Forces and the National Police, I have undertaken to ensure that these institutions immediately take the steps required to guarantee compliance with these announced measures and to safeguard civil order and citizens' safety.

Goodnight

Document 9.4 A Day in the Trial of the Century, by Carolina Huamán Oyague (Family Member of La Cantuta Victim)

Source: www.fujimoriontrial.org/?page_id = 98

It's difficult to describe the mix of feelings that overcome me today; almost 15 years and five months have passed since that morning when a premonition abruptly woke me and drove me to my sister's room. I looked for her, desperate and full of anxiety. I had never imagined all the horror that would come after. For me, the pain still feels like it is July 18, 1992. So many years have passed and today, finally, Fujimori is seated in the defendant's chair. Today, finally, the light at the end of the tunnel is no longer so faint; though hazy, I can read Justice. Some would hope that it is only a word, but it embodies a combination of actions and compromises that we decide to make.

Seated in this court room, I see the person who was principally responsible for the kidnapping, torture and murder of my sister. Today he is before a court, the time has come for him to be accountable and face justice. His mocking smile is no longer spontaneous, but feigned, in order to maintain his circus; his clowns try a thousand different scripts, but the show does not work anymore. The absence of his popular stage becomes more evident. Before the lack of arguments, the clowns remove their masks and act, like those who lack valid reasoning; they make themselves up and show themselves as they are, as they always were behind cameras ensnared by corruption. They are no longer accompanied by that false power with which, over all these years, they tried to bend us, incapable of understanding that power is not made by exercising force over others. Real power is internal; is able to create, to convert ideals into reality, and permits us to leave our Utopia because we are reality. The executioners could not destroy our ideals, despite such infamy. Even with the extreme to which they took us, we did not lose our capacity to bear fruit, to grow in the spirit. It has been our perseverance, and above all our immense love for our loved ones, that kept us from being defeated.

Day after day I listen attentively to the declarations of the defendant Fujimori, while multiple events come to my mind. With each answer, a train of images charges my memory. Today he wants us to believe that he was a neophyte, a victim of discrimination, a gift, a defender of human rights; saying that his information channels gave him mistaken facts. It sounds humorous, considering the control he exercised, that today he tries to erase our memory, but we remember the militia support for the coup d'état. We remember his famous, celebrated phrase "dissolve." We remember the climate of impunity that he incited, giving orders and promoting laws that would impede us from reaching justice. So many times I was at my mother's side before some government institution, demanding justice, but they never heard our cries, much less stopped to see our tears. I remember their response to the horror that he called only "a simple excess . . . what sister are you talking about, that person does not exist, she fled with her boyfriend." Their tanks at the head of their victorious general to intimidate Congress, their accomplices closing the path to our mothers dressed in black, the delivery my sister's remains in a cardboard box, their forbidding her to be buried, the fraudulent sentences from the military, their midnight laws, the Cantuta Law, the threats my family received, the harassment and stigmatizing by their purchased press. I remember how he discredited the Armed Forces because in his government, there were no friendly soldiers, only fear of everyone in a uniform. He never thought about the human rights of Peruvians when he sent our soldiers to fight a futile war while he trafficked arms to the enemy with his partner, Montesinos.

The defendant Fujimori tries futilely to play dumb when they remind him of statistics, names, acts of horror, the halo of barbarity that his death squadron left; and five minutes later his egocentrism betrays him. Then he reminds us that he was in everything; in every village, in every activity that determined the events, reminding us that he was omnipresent and omnipotent. It is impossible for him to conceal his pride, but history teaches us that it is this ill-fated attitude that prints black pages in the memory of humanity and carries all those self-proclaimed saviors to failure.

So many sentiments converge within me during these times; sadness and impotence left by the malevolence of mankind, the absence of that which will never be filled. But there is also happiness and solidarity found in the gestures and expressions of beings who are incapable of being indifferent with their neighbors, who could not help but feel indignant, who were in that way our strength and a sign to keep going forward in the fight for justice, no longer just for our family members, but for all of the Cantutas that today are represented in this one trial.

The visualization of Alberto Kenya Fujimori and all that he represents converts everything in a whirlpool of emotions, images, memories, affronts without a mea culpa or even a simple apology. That's how my smile comes out easily upon the ludicrousness of his arguments. I wish tears did not run down my cheeks, but sometimes they come and it is impossible to stop them; they arrive along with all the vividness and with the hurt of seeing human beings like the former dictator Fujimori, capable of restoring human misery, incapable of seeing the magnitude of their mistaken acts, of the negative impact of their acts on others, self-involved and blinded by the pure ambition for power and money.

For Further Reading

Burt, Jo-Marie. "'Quien habla es terrorista': The Political Use of Fear in Fujimori's Peru," *Latin American Research Review* 41:3 (2006), 32–62.

Carey, Elaine. *Plaza of Sacrifices: Gender, Power, and Terror in 1968 Mexico*. Albuquerque: University of New Mexico Press, 2005.

Feitlowitz, Marguerite. *A Lexicon of Terror: Argentina and the Legacies of Torture*. New York: Oxford University Press, 1999.

Gorriti, Gustavo. *The Shining Path: A History of the Millenarian War in Peru*. Chapel Hill: University of North Carolina Press, 1999.

Grandin, Greg. *The Last Colonial Massacre: Latin America in the Cold War*. Chicago: University of Chicago Press, 2004.

Mayer, Enrique. "Peru in Deep Trouble: Mario Vargas Llosa's 'Inquest in the Andes' Reexamined," *Cultural Anthropology* 6:4 (1991), 466–504.

Menchú, Rigoberta, and Elisabeth Burgos-Debray. *I, Rigoberta Menchú: An Indian Woman in Guatemala*. London: Verso, 1984.

Palmer, David Scott. "'Terror in the Name of Mao': Revolution and Response in Peru," *Perspectivas Latinoamericanas* 2 (2005), 88–109.

Partnoy, Alicia. *The Little School. Tales of Disappearance and Survival in Argentina*. San Francisco: Cleis Press, 1998; 2nd ed. 1986.

Payne, Leigh. *Unsettling Accounts: Neither Truth nor Reconciliation in Confessions of State Violence*. Durham: Duke University Press, 2007.

Poole, Deborah, and Gerardo Renique. *Peru: Time of Fear*. London: Latin America Bureau, 1992.

Smith, Gavin. "Pandora's History: Central Peruvian Peasants and the Re-covering of the Past," in Gerald Sider (ed.), *Between History and Histories: The Making of Silences and Commemorations*. Toronto, University of Toronto Press, 1997, pp. 80–97.

Starn, Orin. *Nightwatch: The Politics of Protest in the Andes*. Durham: Duke University Press, 1999.

Stern, Steve. *Shining and Other Paths: War and Society in Peru, 1980–1995*. Durham: Duke University Press, 1998.

Taylor, Diana. *Disappearing Acts: Spectacles of Gender and Nationalism in Argentina's Dirty War*. Durham: Duke University Press, 1997.

Verbitsky, Horacio. *Confessions of an Argentine Dirty Warrior: A Firsthand Account of Atrocity*. New York: The New Press, 2005.

At A Glance: Environment

Environmental factors, topography, and biodiversity have long played a role in setting the conditions for life across Latin America, yet historians struggle with the question of how we might factor the role of the environment into the Latin American past. Environmental determinism of the likes of Alfred Crosby and Jared Diamond,[1] which focuses on the ways that heat, pathogens, minerals, and something as seemingly insignificant as the wind have had a significant influence on human history, offers an attractive alternative to histories in which great men shape events to their likings. Still, environmental history sometimes leaves relatively little room for human agency or the complexities of the relationships between humans and their environments. More satisfying are the approaches taken by those scholars of Latin American environmental history who consider the ways in which environmental factors form part of a larger set of influences on historical change in the region.[2]

In any event, we are well served by understanding the critical physical features of the region, so that we might consider the ways that existing conditions and changing circumstances have impacted and will impact life here. In the figures included below, we have the opportunity to consider the ways that altitude, access to water (both fresh and saltwater), and proximity to the Equator have impacted life in the region. We might also consider other factors, including navigable rivers, rainfall, average temperatures, soil conditions, natural resources, and the locations and types of the forests that characterize different zones in Latin America.

Figure E.1 is a standard topographical map of Latin America. Certain elements, such as the Andes mountain range and the Amazon River basin (both of which have long created significant transportation and communications challenges) stand out immediately. Others should also be considered, including the river systems such as the Rio De la Plata and Orinoco, the great plains (*pampas*) of Argentina and Uruguay, the highland plateaus of the Andes (the *altiplano*), and the island chains of the Caribbean. One might also note the combined roles that elevation and proximity to the Equator play in shaping the population patterns of the region. Although much of Latin America is in the tropics, most of the major urban centers are in more temperate zones, due to a combination of altitude and latitude.

Figure E.2 is a climate map. The vast climate variations in the region, which are dependent on altitude, latitude, the nature of the land masses, and global wind and water currents, alert us to the ways that environmental diversity contributed to different histories in the region. Climate, including rainfall, average temperatures, and temperature extremes, intersects with technology to play a significant role in the types of economic activity which are possible in any setting. They also influence patterns of human settlement.

Figure E.3 introduces deforestation, which is a pressing environmental concern in much of Latin America. Human-caused environmental change poses a great number of challenges for people in the region, especially poor people living in fragile ecosystems that are vulnerable to collapse due to rising temperatures or changes in the amount of rainfall. The disappearing forests of the Americas, like the disappearing coral reefs of the Caribbean, threaten the livelihoods of millions of people, and also represent significant challenges for the planet as a whole. The issue has attracted more attention in the Amazon than in most other regions, in part because the global ecological cost of the destruction of this forest. Amazonian forests produce 20 percent of the world's oxygen. Seventeen percent of the Amazon forest has been lost in the past fifty years, most of it to logging of precious woods, ranching and farming. Millions of people have been displaced in the process, and the planet has suffered an enormous loss in biodiversity.

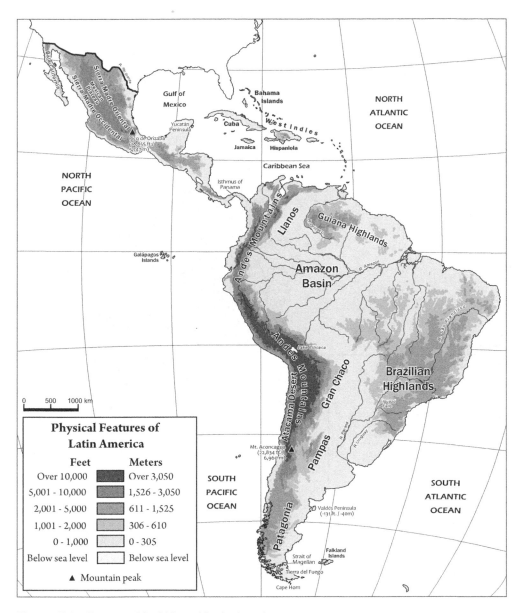

Figure E.1   Topographical Map of Latin America

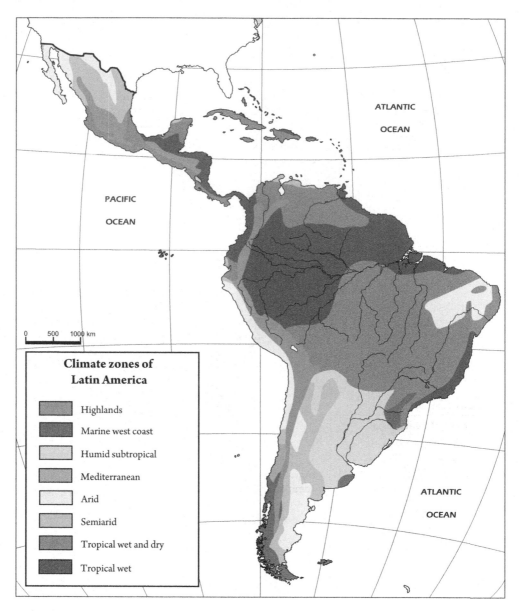

Figure E.2   Climate Zones in Latin America

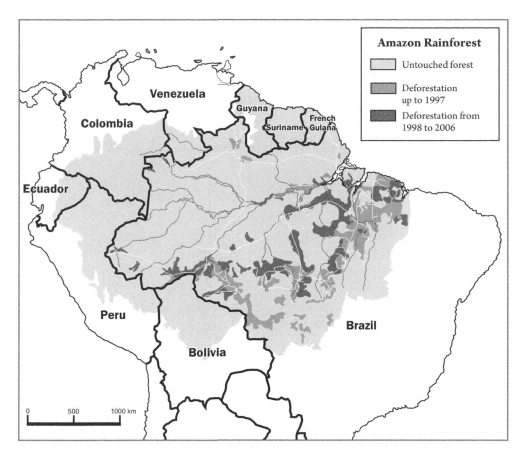

Figure E.3   Deforestation in the Amazon

April 30, 1977	May 1982	1983	October 1988	1980s	1980s
Madres de la Plaza de Mayo begin marching in Buenos Aires, Argentina	Argentina invades the Malvinas Islands	Return to democracy in Argentina	Augusto Pinochet loses referendum on the continuation of military rule	Rise of Medellín cartel in Colombia	Mexican migration to the United States expands during successive economic crises

2007	September 19, 2010	April 3, 2011	2012
Mexicans in the United States send $26 billion in remittances home	*El Diaro de Juarez* publishes open letter to the drug cartels	Javier Sicilia's open letter to the politicians and the criminals	The Caravan for Peace tours the United States

Speaking Truth to Power   **10**

1993	1995	2000	2003	July 4, 2004	2006
Women begin disappearing in Ciudad Juárez, Mexico	Aguas Blancas Massacre in Guerrero, Mexico	U.S. government launches Plan Colombia, which distributes billions in military and police aid to fight the drug cartels	Mothers of missing women of Juárez tour the United States in search of support	March Against Delinquency draws 350,000 participants in Mexico City	Felipe Calderón elected president of Mexico, immediately declares war against the cartels

As a rule, Latin American states are weak. They have always found it difficult to collect taxes, enforce their own laws, govern their territories, and command obedience and loyalty absent the threat of violence (what we might call their "hegemony"). This was never more evident than during the dirty wars, when the ideological battles of the cold war brought out a bloody-mindedness that decimated a generation of the region's youth. Fearing that they could not contain spiraling social and economic conflict, the generals tried to wipe out their enemies—an act that in the short run caused carnage across the region, and in the long run promised only lasting wounds and a thoroughly discredited state. Strong states are strong because they rely on relatively little violence and explicit deal-making to maintain order. Weak ones must buy the loyalty of their allies, and brutalize their enemies, perceived and real.

In the distant past this weakness often worked to the benefit of marginalized peoples, who could use crises to negotiate the terms under which they would consent to be ruled. Revolt, protests, and riots forced any number of governments to offer concessions, as did simple foot-dragging, absenteeism, and other tactics of resistance, because no Latin American state had the capacity to effectively dominate all its opponents. What we might call this "balance of forces" seemed to change during the dirty wars, both because of what seemed like the ideological importance of the conflict and because Latin American military leaders had new tools at their disposal. The technologies employed by the late twentieth-century state turned the tactical advantage towards militarized regimes. The capacities of the Argentine and Chilean state to inspire terror were dramatically enhanced by the surveillance and torture techniques of the cold war, as was the capacity of the Peruvian and Guatemalan states to kill indiscriminately. Those in power saw these technologies as a godsend that could guarantee peace and security. Their enemies saw a brave new world in which states ruled more through fear than consent.

Neither vision ever quite came to be, in part because of the dirty warriors' failure to understand the processes they unleashed. Inasmuch as the dirty warriors were also cold warriors, relying on their allies in the West to remake their economies and develop new modes of control, they inadvertently made themselves vulnerable to global pressures that would be part of their undoing. Their victims, powerless and often despised at home, found in international allies opportunities to bring novel types of pressure on the military regimes that ruled their societies. They likewise found a language that superseded the states that denied them rights—a language that abandoned the long-held practice of insisting that we enjoy rights as citizens (and therefore rely on the state to respect those rights) and instead insisted that they enjoyed rights as human beings, rights that could be defended on a global stage instead of a local one.

Those who challenge authoritarian but purportedly nationalist regimes invariably open themselves up to charges of treason, especially in weak states. The critic who sheds uncomfortable light on those in power threatens to ruin everything, to undermine the national project, and more than this, threatens to embarrass those who fear that embarrassment alone can represent a mortal wound. This in turn speaks to a sense of fragility, an anxiety that "we" are not robust, that "we" need to stand in line behind our leaders and be loyal, lest the social whole fail because of our individual proclivities. This tradition in Latin America is visible in the moments when the *caudillo* or the modernizing state would broach no opposition, but this anxiety represented a particularly pronounced feature of the cold war world, when the battle between communism and capitalism took on existential tones. This presumption of vulnerability has invariably put those most disaffected by existing regimes in a double-bind, because to even give voice to your experience is to threaten the nation. It is also why those who complain of missing children or arbitrary detentions and torture are often told very loudly, and by more than a few critics, to silence themselves. It is why then as now those critics are often accused of being traitors. It is also why, in the context of the dirty wars, these voices needed to work both within and beyond their nations if they were to ever gain redress for their grievances.

Victims of the dirty wars did not just tap into an increasingly global network of activists, they did so using means that promised to transform the ways that people across Latin America connected with each other and with the world. The regimes they challenged came to power in an era when relatively few people in the region had telephones (too expensive; they were mostly the preserve of the middle class and the wealthy), when the means citizens had for learning about the world—radio, television, newspapers—came in the form of a few limited outlets, largely controlled by media monopolies working under licenses from the state, and when migration rates in the region had not yet reached the point where news flowed globally and rapidly through transnational gossip networks. In 1968, the Mexican state was largely able to contain the story of the Tlatelolco massacre. It was not until three years later, when Elena Poniatowski published *la noche de Tlatelolco*, that the full story began to emerge. Similarly, in 1973 in Chile and 1976 in Argentina, the juntas could rely on a largely compliant news and television media to frame the coups according to their narratives.

A decade later, these forms of control were becoming increasingly impossible. On one level, exile and migration produced networks that made it difficult for states across the region to control the story. With a million Argentines and two hundred thousand Chileans living in exile, information about what was going on in these countries began to flow more freely than ever, filling the pages of North American and European newspapers and magazines. The same was true for the waves of Mexican, Central American, and Caribbean migrants who, during the 1970s and 1980s, created new information networks in the global north. That news in turn found its way back to their home countries, first through letters, visits, and furtive telephone conversations, and later through the fax machine, which became ubiquitous in much of the region after the mid-1980s. With their capacity to transmit reams of data in an instant, fax machines accompanied the unraveling of authoritarian rule in Latin America.

This represented just the beginning of a technological revolution that would transform the media and political landscapes of Latin America. Email, cellular telephones, and the internet more broadly provided the grease that allowed nascent networks to flourish, driven as much by the possibilities generated through this connectedness as through any particular ideological agenda. They produced a dynamic in which the Latin American state, long the arbiter of rights and the rules of the game, faced challenges to both its policies and to its very form; challenges that were exacerbated by the waves of crime and narco related violence that engulfed the region in the decades after the return to democracy. Through it all, the victims of violence would consistently search for novel forms through which to redress their wrongs, sometimes through local protest, but increasingly through the global networks that transformed international politics in the late twentieth and early twenty-first centuries.

Mothers, Sisters, Daughters

There is no better place to start the story of human rights and technological change in Latin America than with the *Madres de la Plaza de Mayo*.[1] The *Madres* were a product of the particular circumstances of Latin America's dirty wars, in which authoritarian states systematically made their enemies "disappear," and government officials actively denied any knowledge of what was going on. After coming to power in March 1976, the Argentine junta not only closed off all forms of political opposition, it also refused to release any information about the thousands of young people the military plucked from the streets and sequestered in its torture chambers. Government officials either stonewalled or ridiculed family members who came to their offices in search of information. This was why a loose assortment of mothers decided to occupy Argentina's most important public space. They confronted all physical threats stoically, never wavering from their single demand: the return of their children. This act—assuming the public face of grief and rage during a time when Argentines were largely silent—helped bring down one of the bloodiest dictatorships in Latin American history, a government that in less than a decade murdered somewhere between 9,000 and 30,000 people.

A group of fourteen women started gathering in the Plaza de Mayo on April 30, 1977. They were mostly working class (Figure 10.1). Most had never worked outside of their homes and had never before shown much interest in politics. Many had never voted in an election. We cannot say for certain, but some may have even supported the March 1976 military coup. After all, at the time of the coup Argentines from all social classes believed that the country was verging on chaos, a problem many blamed on rebellious youths, feminists, and communists. Military rule promised a re-assertion of traditional family values. It promised that order and respect for authority would be restored. Working-class mothers were not immune to this appeal.

Then their children began to disappear. As mothers do everywhere, they went to the authorities. Sitting in government offices, waiting for answers from recalcitrant government officials, they slowly realized that it was not just *their* children who were missing; hundreds, and maybe even thousands of other women shared similar fates. So, at a time when all forms of protest were prohibited, they decided to gather weekly in the Plaza de Mayo and publicly demand the return of their children. At first, they sat around the edges of the plaza, knitting and standing in small groups. Later, they moved towards the obelisk in the center of the plaza, marching in a circle for the duration of their demonstration. All

Figure 10.1 The Madres de la Plaza de Mayo, 1977
Source: AP Photo

the while they performed the role of decent folk, people who were grieving a loss and did not deserve the fate that the Argentine state had bestowed upon them.

Prior to 1976 most members of the group never imagined joining a public protest, let alone openly confronting a government official. And yet as newly assertive political actors, they openly defied the regime's ban on political organizing, and actually made themselves, the mothers of the nation, into political targets. Invariably adorned in their white headscarves, their motherly appearance belied the fact that they were one of the most openly bellicose groups in Argentine political life. Motherhood thus proved to be a flexible claim for the *Madres*, as it does for most women who enter politics. By the end of 1977, 150 mothers were regularly protesting weekly.

Their mere presence pushed the regime's human rights violations out of the shadows and onto center stage. Political prisoners, "the disappeared," were no longer simply statistics. They were somebody's child, grandchild, sister or brother, maybe even someone's mother or father. This was a brilliant tactic, especially given the fact that many of these supposedly apolitical women had very political children. Their claim to human rights somehow made a universal claim for their children (that nobody should be kidnapped by the state) and a very particular claim for themselves (that they were particularly aggrieved because they, if not their children, were apolitical mothers). In doing so, they made themselves the victims of the disappearances, rendering the state's claim that their children were terrorists void.

At first the generals allowed the *Madres* to march relatively unmolested. They could barely imagine that these women represented a political threat. Soldiers told them they could not sit in large groups in the plaza, and occasionally taunted them, though they did not drive them from the square. This arrangement did not last. Within months the junta began to fear that these women might threaten the government's efforts to portray itself as a defender of family values, and the secret police began stalking the *Madres*, even kidnapping and killing a few. Soldiers blocked off the plaza, forcing the *Madres* to the margins, hoping they could contain the public relations damage.

They were too late. Reports about body parts washing up on the beaches of Uruguay (the remains of victims tossed from airplanes over the South Atlantic) had reached the international media and, with the World Cup in Argentina approaching in 1978, a growing number of foreign journalists took interest in what was going on in the country. Members of the international press began to attend the demonstrations, writing sympathetic pieces about the *Madres* for their readers back home. With a growing national and international profile, it became impossible to eliminate the *Madres* without making the regime an international pariah, so the regime instead began to paint them as terrorist sympathizers, as the *locas* (madwomen) of the Plaza de Mayo. Foreign observers found themselves split on the label. Human rights sympathizers saw it as one more reason to condemn the regime. Cold warriors repeated it ad nauseam.

The generals' efforts to contain the damage went awry in December 1977. Somewhere between the eighth and the tenth, Argentine security forces under the command of Alfredo Astiz, a sadistic torturer with the nickname "blondie" (allegedly because of his good looks) kidnapped thirteen individuals linked to the *Madres*. Among them were two French nuns, Alice Domon and Léonie Duquet. The French embassy immediately protested, and within days the junta declared that the Montoneros (a leftist urban guerrilla group) had kidnapped the nuns. As proof, the government released a photo that showed the nuns standing in front of a Montoneros banner (the photo was in fact taken in the basement of the Naval Mechanics School, ESMA). Neither the United States nor the French governments were taken by the ruse, and both immediately ratcheted up the pressure on the Argentine government to release the nuns. President Carter also decided to send a fact-finding mission to Argentina. Foreign skepticism over the junta's story was borne out some months later when the bodies of several of the kidnapping victims (including the two nuns) washed up on an Argentine beach near Mar del Plata. This left no doubt as to who had killed the nuns, as it was the junta's practice to dispose of their victims by throwing them into the ocean from military planes.

With the Carter administration increasingly distancing itself from the Argentines, his critics on the North American right leapt to the junta's defense. Writing in the *Miami News*, on August 18, 1978, Ronald Reagan declared: "inevitably, in the process of rounding up hundreds of suspected terrorists, the Argentine authorities have no doubt locked up a few innocent people. . . The incarceration of a few innocents however, is no reason to open up the jails and let the terrorists run free so they can begin a new reign of terror." Reagan was repulsed by the fact that the U.S. ambassador to Argentina "mingles in Buenos Aires with relatives of the locked up suspected terrorists, thus seeming to legitimize all their claims to martyrdom." Reagan got at least some traction for these claims in the U.S. media, as several outlets repeated the junta's claims that most of these women did not even have children.[2]

Still, as more and more evidence emerged from Argentina, it was impossible to maintain this story. In August 1979, the Inter-American Commission on Human Rights of the Organization of American States (OAS) toured Argentina and investigated 6,000 disappearances. The junta was terrified about the OAS visit, and raided the offices of four human rights organizations in advance, reputedly executing and eliminating traces of numerous political prisoners. For their part, the *Madres* lined up around the block to testify before the panel, leaving an indelible impression on the Commission and the International Press. The Commission presented a 266-page report to the OAS at a meeting in November 1980, with members of the *Madres* in attendance. It painted a dismal picture of the regime.[3]

As had earlier been the case at the UN Human Rights Division, the Argentine government was able to use threats and bullying within the OAS to ensure that nothing concrete came of the report. Not that this mattered much, because the real power of the report lay in its capacity to act as a rallying point for the variety of non-governmental organizations (NGOs) that by 1980 had actively taken up the *Madres'* cause. By the time Ronald Reagan was elected president, Amnesty International and other human rights groups had flooded the North American media with examples of torture and forced disappearances in Argentina. In June 1981, the *Madres* were awarded the Truth and Freedom Award from the Rothko Chapel of Houston. During that summer several *Madres* toured the United States, traveling to Washington to plead their case directly to Reagan. Argentine officials complained bitterly about the tour, but were met by equally forceful statements both from the *Madres* and from exiles living in the United States.

These pressures without question played a role when in May 1982 the Reagan administration made a decision that would be instrumental in bringing an end to military rule in Argentina. It was then that the junta, in an effort to counteract flagging support at home, launched an invasion of the Malvinas Islands (known in Britain as the Falklands), betting that a weakened Britain and staunch support from the United States would guarantee success. At home this was a low point for the *Madres*, who were accused of treason and broadly reviled for failing to support this effort to assert Argentine sovereignty over a long-disputed territory. Yet Reagan, who had offered subtle signals that he would support the Argentines, instead opted to back the British. This decision in turn helped transform the invasion into a disaster, because the British understood they could respond with their full military capabilities without risk of alienating the United States. The junta's forces were routed, sparking massive protests in Argentina. The generals responded by promising a return to civilian rule, which came in 1983.

Reagan was no friend of human rights groups, and earned a well-deserved record for supporting authoritarian regimes in the region. He actively supported Operación Condor, a network that military leaders in the region used to assassinate their enemies in other countries. Reagan was not however, immune to political pressure from his critics. There were several moments during his years in power when American political activists working with relatives of "the disappeared" forced him to distance himself from authoritarian regimes. This may have been the case in 1982, but it was clearly the case in 1988, when the Reagan administration actively supported a process that would bring down another Latin American dictator. This time the challenge came in the form of a plebiscite.

When Augusto Pinochet engineered Chile's 1980 Constitution, he included provisions that in 1988 the government would hold a plebiscite to determine whether or not he should continue to rule the country for another eight year term. The plebiscite was intended as a form of sham politics, a carefully stage managed event that would give Pinochet enough semblance of legitimacy to keep human rights groups at bay and maintain Chile's good international standing. Pinochet had problems that were not entirely like the Argentine junta. Though he was widely regarded (at least internationally and among Chile's middle and upper classes) as the man who had saved the Chilean economy from the disaster of communism, he was also dogged by the claims of mothers of the Chilean disappeared (in Chile, mainly consolidated around the *arpillera* movement, which sewed tapestries depicting missing loved ones and displayed them publically). Sting, then one of the most popular musicians on the planet, included a song about these Chilean mothers that directly attacked Pinochet on his 1987 album (the song was called "They Dance Alone"). Pinochet also faced active opposition from Chilean exiles and a series of opposition parties that continued to organize and hold rallies against the regime inside the country. General strikes in 1984 and 1987 and the repression that followed revealed a persistent opposition to military rule, even as Pinochet insisted that the vast majority of Chileans unconditionally supported the regime.

As 1988 and the promise of the plebiscite loomed, Pinochet was likely surprised to learn that his friends in the Reagan administration were committed to the vote. Reagan was under a great deal of scrutiny in the United States, widely criticized both for his support of a guerrilla movement in Nicaragua made up of soldiers formally affiliated with the Somoza dictatorship (the *contras*) and mired in investigations over a botched arms for hostages deal that had involved Nicaragua and Iran. His own vice president, George H.W. Bush was then running for the presidency, and did not need the sort of news that would further tarnish his democratic credentials. This helps to explain why the Reagan administration not only demanded that the plebiscite be held; it gave active support to the No campaign. The U.S. government offered $1.6 million for voter registration, education, and computing through the National Endowment for Democracy. Privately, administration officials warned Pinochet to obey the results.

Figure 10.2 Advertising emblem of the coalition for the "No" vote in Chile, 1988

Pinochet seemed likely to win the plebiscite in any event. The economy was doing well. He had considerable political support from conservatives, and regime opponents feared either that their votes would not be counted, or that they would face retribution for going to the polls to cast a "No" vote. The latter a fear that seemed reasonable given the fact that several prominent organizers of the "No" vote were harassed and intimidated during the campaign. Still, the coalition of fourteen political parties that formed the opposition organized a brilliant campaign that took the regime by surprise. Not only did they register millions of voters (7.5 million voted), they put together a media campaign that ran circles around the government's efforts. While Pinochet's spin doctors used their allotted airtime (each campaign received fifteen minutes airtime per day in the weeks leading to the October 5 plebiscite) to inspire fear of a return to the communist past with images of steamrollers crushing televisions and other consumer goods, the No campaign put together a brilliant strategy that both reminded viewers of Pinochet's crimes and insisted that their eyes were focused on a democratic, prosperous future. The campaign was symbolized by the slogan "Chile, joy is on the way" and by a rainbow, juxtaposed against a "No" (see Figure 10.2). An astounding 97.53 percent of the electorate voted on the plebiscite, giving the No a 55.99 percent to 44.01 percent victory. Pinochet briefly considered attempting to overturn the results, but his own generals warned him against this strategy. Within days he began to implement plans for presidential elections, which would take place in 1989.

Global Motherhood

The role that indirect pressures created by the mothers of "the disappeared," both in Chile and Argentina, played in these events should not be underestimated. The visceral quality of their claims, the fact that Reagan himself felt it necessary to attack them, reminds us of the power their grief had as a foil to military rule. That their force was felt indirectly, in some ways channeled through U.S. politics, alerts us to their capacity to move beyond the traditional spaces of political struggle. It was their ability to speak to an international audience, to mobilize international networks, and to create a human face for the interconnected global phenomena (the cold war, the School of the Americas, U.S. support for dictators) that represented their power.

In transforming motherhood from a private matter into a public issue, the mothers of the disappeared blurred the distinction between feminist and feminine politics. While they gained access to the public sphere because they were "traditional," the claims they made (respect for human rights) and the way they made them (sometimes going so far as to openly provoke the soldiers sent to rein them in) transformed the category they occupied. That said, there are limits to the extent to which grief can be transformed into a larger agenda for women's rights. Movements like these often mask deep internal ideological differences, and do not tend to develop larger feminist or social justice agendas without splintering apart. Indeed, when some members of the *Madres de la Plaza de Mayo* attempted to widen their rights claims beyond finding their missing children, other members balked. After working-class *Madres*, led by Hebe de Bonafini, expanded what were originally personal demands about their children into a broad agenda for reform based on their rights as mothers, a small faction split from the movement and took the name *Línea Fundadora* (Founding Line), claiming that the increasingly radical demands of the *Madres* were a betrayal of the movement's original goals.[4] This faction spoke to the interests of middle-class mothers and those from the interior of the country, who tended to eschew larger political agendas and were much more likely to work cooperatively with the state and other human rights groups. They showed little interest in using motherhood to demand broader social change.

Larger efforts in Latin America to organize women around reproductive rights, equal pay, or the treatment of women in the home or workplace have revealed the class, religious, and cultural cleavages that characterize women's movements the world over. Grieving mothers however, continue to act as a visceral basis upon which global solidarity networks continue to find common ground. Mothers whose children have been kidnapped and murdered cannot be explained away as a necessary step towards modernization explained some how as a first generation of industrial workers who suffer in sweatshops so that later generations might prosper. It is instead something that no parent can ignore, something that all fear, and something that seems impossible to justify.

This then has been the ethos around which other, recent mothers movements have organized, seeking again to connect to powerful forces in the global North through their pain. We see this most poignantly in a series of events that took place in Northern Mexico beginning in the 1990s, when hundreds of young women in Cuidad Juárez (many of them workers in the assembly plants that serve the U.S. market) were kidnapped, sexually assaulted, murdered, and dumped in the nearby desert. The women who lost their lives in these crimes were doing what an increasingly large segment of poor Latin American women have been doing since at least the 1970s: they had taken up jobs in the growing maquila sector along the U.S. border so that their families could survive in an economy that provided few opportunities for their male counterparts. These workers were not so much part of a new tradition of female work (poor and working-class women have always labored in commerce, agriculture, service, and in factories in the region) as they reflected women's factory employment on a scale never seen before, and work that took place in a context where the state seemed to be withering away. Two generations earlier women factory workers in Medellín, Colombia, Buenos Aires, Argentina, and São Paolo, Brazil might have had paternalistic factory owners who worried about their well-being or been overseen by government bureaucracies that wished to ensure they maintained their proper comportment (and remained viable as the mothers of the next generation of citizen/workers). In the late twentieth century, these women were simply the surplus poor, dark skinned migrants from somewhere else whose only value to foreign factory owners lay in their low wages and willingness to work long hours with a minimum of complaint. They were neither potential customers (their wages could not purchase the things they made, which were destined for foreign markets anyway) nor potential mothers for a nation (which many thought too large in any event).

In the free for all that was the border zone, where hundreds of thousands of migrants passed through every year and only a few stayed, few people of influence had any interest in pressuring the state over the disappearances of a few poor women. Already under pressure because of growing crime and tightened budgets, Mexican officials first ignored the crimes because of the ethnicity, class, and reputed professions of some victims (some may have been sex workers), and then botched the investigations by torturing suspects until they confessed. Twenty years earlier this strategy might have worked, but this time the families of the victims found new ways to get around the old barriers. They did not just complain to the police; they went to the media, in both Mexico and the United States. And they did as mothers, sisters, and daughters.

In 2003 a group of mothers of the murdered women toured the United States. One of its leaders, Norma Andrade, spoke before a sub-committee of the U.S. Congress. She condemned both the perpetrators of the crimes and a state that failed in the first instance to protect her child, and in the second instance to investigate the crime. When she returned to Mexico, government agents followed her home, and warned her and other mothers to keep quiet, to stop talking to the media, to stop embarrassing them. She refused, and within days reports that the government was harassing her were published in the Mexican and U.S. media.

After Andrade's pleas and the threats she received for making them received wide notice in the press, Mexican President Vicente Fox committed new resources to the investigation. In early 2004, he appointed prominent human rights lawyer María López Urbina to examine both the crimes and official malfeasance. After a short investigation, she filed charges against eighty-one current and former state and local officials. Her prosecutions did not promise to end the killing spree, and the scope of her authority was quite limited. Nonetheless, the sheer number of charges filed against officials irrefutably exposed the Mexican state's failure to live up to a fundamental responsibility.

Thanks to the efforts of grieving mothers in Juárez, Mexicans are now familiar with the term *feminicide*, which denotes the murder of women because they are women. They are also increasingly aware that it is a national problem. And while simply naming something and exposing it to public scrutiny does little to solve the problem of violence against women, it is a critical beginning. It forces a dirty secret into the open, where it can no longer be ignored.

Other Terrors

The Human Rights groups that emerged across the region during the 1970s had a very clear target: states that systematically violated the rights of their citizens. For the most part, when we thought of violence in Latin America during this era, we imagined organized state actors and occasionally organized guerillas, a clash that we could make sense of in ideological terms. Compared to state terrorism, the other forms of violence that character-ized daily life—crime, corruption, the growing use of illicit drugs—seemed almost quaint. This is no longer the case.

By the early years of the twenty-first century, it was clear that a surge in violence was a taking hold across the region. In some places that violence was tied to persisting ideological struggles. In most places the violence, read often as the criminal in nature, seemed ideo-logically empty, nihilist. Today, a series of shadowy actors, including drug traffickers, urban gangs, paramilitary organizations, and government officials in the pay of criminals are the notable actors in a region-wide crisis in human security. They are the product of changed circumstances, in some ways linked to the return to democracy, and in others produced by profound economic and demographic shifts.

Latin American cities, already large by global standards in 1950, exploded in the latter half of the twentieth century. At first, urbanization was the product of concerted govern-ment efforts. ISI policies promoted industrial development and good factory wages, while simultaneously discouraging small-scale cultivation in favor of capital-intensive export agriculture. Small farmers in much of the region found it increasingly difficult to make a living in the countryside, and migrated in search of work. By the 1970s several urban cen-ters in Latin America had become mega-cities, enormous urban complexes characterized by the massive growth of slums on their periphery. Today, Lima, São Paulo, Rio de Janeiro, Buenos Aires, Bogotá, and Mexico City are among the largest cities in the world.[5]

In the early years of rapid urban expansion, local governments extended social services to meet some of the needs of the new arrivals, building public housing, transportation networks, and schools. Even in the best of times however, Latin American states proved unable to provide social and other government services for the growing urban populations and increasingly poor rural communities. This problem worsened significantly in the 1970s as stagnant economic growth put new demands on an already overstretched state.

Facing a government that could not deliver the goods, Latin America's urban and rural poor developed informal networks to provide water, electricity, to build roads and sewers, and relied on neighbors and friends to maintain order in their communities. The weak ties that many in these communities had to the state were further weakened by the fact that, when government officials arrived, they often threatened to disrupt carefully managed subsistence networks by reshaping the public spaces of the communities, arresting informal leaders, and dismantling the informal services the poor had constructed for themselves. The alchemy of all this—people who could not rely on the state for services but expected the state to be a hostile actor in their communities—made these misery belts rich recruiting grounds for the informal economy. It was not difficult to find people in these communities who would happily work in producing, transporting, and selling various forms of contraband, as this was a source of income and status among people effectively abandoned by the state. Some of the work was as simple as selling cigarettes without tax stamps. Informal economy vendors might also sell stolen or contraband goods, counterfeit watches, jeans, and handbags, and pirated videos. More significantly, these communities were a critical recruiting ground for the workers who would make Latin America one of the most important global players in the trade in illicit drugs, particularly cocaine, marijuana, and methamphetamines.

Beginning in earnest in the 1970s, a growing number of young men from these communities became workers in a burgeoning global trade in illicit drugs, based in places as diverse as Medellín, Colombia, Santiago, Chile, Havana, Cuba, and Culiacán, Mexico. Their bosses imagined themselves as entrepreneurs who moved merchandise to willing consumers, helping themselves and their societies in the process. At a time when the economy was worse than anyone could remember, they may have been the most important source of export revenues in the entire region.

Many of the early drug kingpins were widely admired. They were modern-day Robin Hoods, taking the money and even vitality of those who oppressed Latin America and in turn re-vitalizing their own communities by building hospitals, schools, and apartment buildings. They supported local teams, customs, and the devotion of local saints. Some even became national symbols of Latin American defiance of the United States. Colombian narco-trafficker Pablo Escobar successfully ran for the Colombian Congress in 1982 on a platform that included a provision that called for a ban on the extradition of drug traffickers to the United States. Escobar later lost much of his shine when he brought down an Avianca flight in November 1989 while attempting to assassinate César Gaviria Trujillo, killing 107 people, but narcos of his ilk remain compelling figures in parts of Latin America today. Some are loathed and feared for the violence they beget, while others maintain loyal followings when they use their wealth to contribute to their communities, acting as a state in the absence of the legally constituted state. Mexico's Familia Michoacana, which effectively ruled large parts of Western Mexico in the early 2000s, did so at least in part by claiming to be more honorable and upright than corrupt government officials.

Wars Without End

Concurrent with the rise of the drug lords, the U.S. government stepped up its own war on drugs, shifting its attention away from earlier efforts to treat addicts and towards active interdiction. Successive U.S. administrations declared that they would not approve aid or favorable trade agreements for regimes that did not take an active (some would say militarized) role in disrupting the flow of illicit drugs. It was during this period that U.S. military aid to Latin America gradually shifted its focus from the cold war to the war on drugs. Since the mid-1990s U.S. military and police aid to the region—now mostly under the auspices of counter-narcotics measures—has grown to around a billion U.S. dollars annually.

Colombia is ground zero for these developments. Beginning with the Andean Initiative, which funneled $200 million in military aid to the region and made Colombia the third largest recipient of U.S. military aid (behind Israel and Egypt), and followed by the Plan Colombia, which since 2000 has funneled $8 billion in military-police aid to Colombia, the United States has played an active role in militarizing Colombian society. A similar package in 2007 that provided U.S. $1.9 billion in aid to Mexico has had similar affects in that country, supporting (critics say pushing) a militarized approach to the drug conflict there.[6]

In the Mexican case, a majority of the money was spent purchasing military equipment, in particular Blackhawk helicopters. The Colombian government also bought a great deal of weaponry, but also funneled millions to paramilitary groups, many of which have close ties with the military. Originally created by Colombian elites to protect their interests and cultivate civilian support in opposition to the guerrillas, the paramilitaries have attacked union organizers, peasants, and anyone perceived as a threat to the established order. They have also acted as a force unto themselves, raising revenues through active participation in the drug trade, and protecting growers, laboratories, and traffickers. Not to be outdone, military units stationed in these zones have also taken a piece of the action, leaving the rural civilian population completely vulnerable, and driving millions to flee the coca zones for the urban slums of cities like Bogota and Medellín. Colombia's civil war, which pits nearly fifty-year-old guerrilla insurgency against the military, has resulted in somewhere between 50,000 and 200,000 deaths, and produced five million internally displaced people. U.S. military and police aid has exacerbated these conflicts, without having much effect on the cultivation of coca (which has remained stable since 2003).

The Mexican state has fared no better in its drug war. In 2007 President Felipe Calderón sent more than 40,000 troops to the border to regain control of Mexico's North from the cartels. He spent about U.S. $7 billion fighting the drug war, in some cases displacing entire police forces in the process. The results were both inconclusive and costly, and resulted in somewhere between 60,000 and 120,000 deaths (it is a matter of how it is counted[7]) during Calderón's term of office. Calderón faced a particularly strong challenge from the *Zetas*, a group of former Special Forces soldiers who once worked against the drug cartels and are now major players in the drug trade. Taking advantage of the tendency of the Mexican press to focus on spectacular violence, the *Zetas* earned national headlines by providing journalists with images of beheadings and other grisly murders.

Neither Latin American states nor the United States seem capable of winning the war on drugs, in part because with gross revenues of perhaps $40 billion annually, the traffickers are well positioned for the fight. Interdiction efforts have what many describe as a balloon effect. When one area is pressed (as in the Caribbean in the late 1980s and early 1990s), the trade expands to another region. Today, as interdiction efforts have increased in Mexico, more and more of the trade has shifted to the even weaker states of Central America, particularly Guatemala and Honduras. It also appears that some organizations have begun to build submarines to move the drugs into the United States. The reasons for this are relatively simple. One kilo of cocaine sells for $1,000 in Colombia's interior, $25,000 in the United States, and $60,000 in Britain.

Those who favor interdiction must cope with extraordinarily well-armed adversaries (often using weapons that made their way into Latin America through the militarization of interdiction efforts), criminal networks that can draw on a seemingly endless supply of desperately poor and alienated labor, and on states that are too weak or corrupt to sustain the effort. Government officials throughout the region, including in the United States, must regularly decide between risking their lives in the fight or working with the drug gangs for a little extra pay.

The corrosive effect that the trade has had on the state and civil society can be measured in any number of ways. Latin America's overcrowded prisons are now overflowing with persons convicted of drug crimes (80 percent of the women in Mexican prisons are there for drug crimes). Militarization has also renewed fears about police and military impunity, about the fact that in the midst of the drug wars extrajudicial killings by the police and military seem to have been on the rise. During Felipe Calderón's drug war, the Mexican *Comision Nacional de Derechos Humanos* (National Human Rights Commission, CNDH) received 4,772 complaints of human rights abuses by the military, including over 100 complaints of forced disappearances.

Serious as they are, these violations account for only a small part of the violence that has engulfed parts of Latin American in recent times. Criminal gangs, armed with money and weapons from the trade, turned to kidnappings, extortion, and a booming street-level drug trade across Latin America in order to make money. The police have proven completely inadequate to the task of dealing with the crisis, at least in part because police forces across the region are plagued with officers who either take bribes to look the other way or actively participate in these gangs. Those police officers who refuse to go along with the gangs can put their lives at risk, and generally find that the safest alternative lies in quitting their jobs. In August 2008, all twenty members of the police force in Villa Ahumada in Chihuahua (eighty miles south of El Paso, Texas) resigned after their police chief was murdered less than twenty-four hours into his tenure. Those police officers who remain committed to the battle increasingly treat their posts as war zones, going about heavily armed, covered in body armor (which they often pay for themselves), their faces hidden by masks that protect their identities. They do their best to move their families out of harm's way, often to the United States. Others will accept bribes or actively work for the cartels, as this option is often less fraught with danger than the alternative.

It is unlikely that a more secure police force would necessarily be the answer to this dilemma. Victims, bystanders, and criminal suspects generally have good reason to fear the police independent of the corrupting effect of the narcotics trade. Police agencies in Latin America have an exceptionally poor record of respecting civil rights. Even police agents who might be inclined to investigate crimes have few resources to do so, and, partly because of this, officials generally find easy targets to blame for criminal acts. For the most part, this means focusing on young, impoverished males (who often tend to have darker skin than the elites) from marginal neighborhoods. For example, residents of Brazil's *favelas* (urban slums) are commonly blamed for the country's crime problems, and extra-judicial killings by the police of young black men from these communities are commonplace. Upwards of 1,000 people in Rio alone die at the hands of the police annually, in incidents usually explained as "acts of resistance followed by death." The term is strikingly similar to the phrase "shot while trying to escape" (the *ley fuga*), used elsewhere in Latin America to describe those summarily executed by the police.

At times this problem seems overwhelming. In order to correct this, reformers must not only change the culture of policing, they must increase salaries, protect police who come forward with charges against their fellow officers, and reform a judiciary that has no tradition of punishing malfeasance on the part of agents of the state. They must do this in the face of a long history of graft and lax investigative techniques, all the while facing the simple truth that their enemies are wealthy and threatening. Crime is profitable, and the traffickers have immense resources to either buy off new police agents or successfully intimidate them into silence. The military is a poor alternative, because it too is easily corrupted. Soldiers are generally even more poorly paid than the police (something like 100,000 troops have left the Mexican military to work for the traffickers in recent years).

Given these overlapping phenomena, it should be little wonder that Latin America today has the highest homicide rate of any region in the world at 22.2 per 100,000 people. This is five times the world average, translating to 100,000 homicides in the region annually. Homicides have doubled since the 1980s. Honduras actually leads the region, with 82.1 per 100,000, followed by Venezuela, with 45.1 per 100,000. Property crimes have increased by a factor of three in recent years, and crime rates continue to rise, particularly in urban areas. Seventy-five percent of the world's kidnappings take place in Latin America. Arrests and convictions for these crimes are startlingly rare, in part because so few crimes are ever reported. Victims rarely turn to the police, as public officials are often involved in the crimes. Among the poor especially, the police are more often seen as a menace than a solution to the violence.

Journalists have been threatened for simply reporting on these phenomena. Latin America has in recent years become one of the most dangerous regions in the world to be a journalist. Some have faced arbitrary detention and arrest from governments aiming to clamp down on press freedoms; aiming in particular to limit criticism of the state. Others have been caught in the crossfire of the drug wars, unprotected by a state that does not want the story covered and attacked by narcos who see the press as a threat to their business. Between 2007 and 2012 alone, two dozen journalists were murdered in Mexico. Reeling from the deaths of two of its own reporters in 2010, the newspaper *El Diario* in Juárez was prompted to publish a front page editorial pleading with the cartels. The paper declared: "We would like you to explain what you want from us, what you want us to publish or not publish, so at least we could know what to expect." In the years since this extraordinary plea, several newspapers have publicly proclaimed that they will no longer cover the drug war. In their surrender, they join a long line of those who have opted for self-preservation in the face of enemies that can kill at will, and a state too weak to do anything about it (see Document 10.7, below).

These acts of capitulation speak to the limited strategies available to those seeking to survive the violence. In the absence of states that can guarantee a right to human security, individuals are often left to their own devices. Their cities become obstacle courses, filled with practices, places, and times deemed dangerous. Those with means can sequester themselves and their families in gated communities, such as the "countries" of greater Buenos Aires, or the high security apartment buildings of Santa Fé in Mexico City (ironically, this is also where many wealthier traffickers live). They can hire private security guards and arm themselves against kidnappings, armed robberies, and carjackings. Those with fewer means must rely on friends and neighbors to protect them from the threats posed by the narcos and the state. In extreme cases, poorer rural communities have literally shut the rest of the world out, declaring themselves self-governing entities and blockading the roads that enter their towns.

Whether it entails building barbed wire around a fortified estate or roadblocks to a poor community, extreme localism is risky. While it is a good short run strategy of self-preservation, it does little to stop a determined narco or government agency from penetrating one's community and wreaking havoc. In the long run it is more likely that those who have taken a page from the experiences of the mothers of "the disappeared" will have an impact on violence in the region. Contemporary victims rights movements have enlarged the field of struggle, building new national and international movements to combat recent

Figure 10.3 Mexico City, March against Delinquency, July 2004
Source: Photo by Alexander Dawson

waves of violence. In 1997 Josefina Ricaño created *Mexico Unido Contra la Delincuencia* (Mexicans United Against Delinquency, MUCD) and gained international headlines in July 2004 when the organization massed more than 350,000 on Mexico City's streets (see Figure 10.3). Similar efforts in other countries have made judicial reform one of the most pressing political issues in contemporary Latin America.

Like the victims groups that reached out to activists in the United States and elsewhere beginning in the 1970s, MUCD had a local and an international focus. Supporters agreed that the Mexican state was weak and corrupt, but they believed their problems were made worse by the insatiable appetite for illicit drugs in the United States. Over time this critique expanded into a larger focus on the fact that over 100,000 illegal weapons flowed into Mexico from the U.S. annually. They joined a growing chorus of international experts and government officials that has openly called for policies that would decriminalize possession of small amounts of drugs and offer treatment instead of incarceration for addicts (for example, the Report of the UN's Global Commission on Drug Policy in June 2011).

Victims of the drug war have also taken their case to the United States directly. During the summer of 2012, the Caravan for Peace crossed the country, uniting activists from both sides of the Rio Grande in an attempt to highlight the global repercussions of the war on drugs. Though supported by marijuana activists, most participants were not themselves drug users, but instead among the tens of thousands of Mexicans who have fallen victim to the violence of the drug war. Seemingly ignoring a state that seems ill equipped to deal with the crisis, the Caravan for Peace went directly to U.S. citizens with their stories of the violence that has engulfed Mexico in recent years. Caravan members asked North Americans to reform their own laws; laws which incidentally have done little to reduce the consumption of drugs and attendant criminality in the United States. Most importantly, the Caravan members called for an end to the militarization of drug control and a new era in which those with drug problems were treated instead of incarcerated.

The Caravan did not yield immediate results, nor did its organizers expect rapid solutions. It was instead important for the networks it helped to build, new connections that once again offered an opportunity for those denied their rights to advocate for themselves on a global stage. When your state is weak, when it is unwilling or unable to recognize your right to have rights, this is often your only option. The *Madres de la Plaza de Mayo* were one of the first groups to mobilize in this way, taking advantage of a changing world even as they insisted on their traditional ways. The Caravan for Peace was simply one of the latest iterations of this phenomenon.

This suggests that one of the lessons the *Madres de la Plaza de Mayo* offer to those victimized by the drug wars of the twenty-first century. The *Madres* changed their country precisely because they found a means to reconfigure the terrain of their battle. They did not simply address a recalcitrant Argentine state and a seemingly indifferent Argentine public; they addressed a global audience that could see its own complicity in their plight. To be sure, American human rights activists abhorred the atrocities committed by the dictatorships in Latin America, but it was their own government's complicity in these crimes that underscored the urgency of action. It is the hope of those who participated in the Caravan for Peace that they might have the same effect, making their own victimhood at the hands of the U.S. government visible to those who have the capacity to change that government.

The Documents: Something Old, Something New

The authoritarian regimes that once sought to narrow, even eliminate politics instead produced the opposite effect, a proliferation of political and social movements, first in opposition to military rule, and later organized around a series of "rights." Unlike the political movements of the past, which often worked under the umbrella of right- or left-wing politics, these movements have tended to be nimble and issue oriented. At the same time, emergent communications technologies have left a powerful imprint on the social movements of a democratic Latin America, not least because of their capacity to make visible and international things that just a few short decades ago might have been erased.

We see a powerful iteration of that shift in Document 10.1. Taken from a television news interview in the Plaza de Mayo during the late 1970s, it offers a brief capsule of the demands made by the *Madres de la Plaza de Mayo*. The language used is Spanish, but words represent only a small part of the impact of the video. It was the sight, sounds, and passion of these mothers—one talking about a daughter who was pregnant when kidnapped, another saying they simply need to know the fate of their children, living or dead, and another begging the foreign journalist to whom she was speaking to please, please help them, because "you are our last hope"—that had the capacity to capture global attention. The visceral quality of a real grieving mother addressing the camera terrified the generals, and prompted many Argentines to deny that it could be possibly true. It also inspired human rights activists across the global North to action.

By the 1990s, oppositional movements in Latin America commonly turned to supporters in the United States and Europe for protection and support. This invariably entailed performances that were attuned to their understandings of what constituted a sympathetic ear. This notion of performance does not necessarily indicate something false—the idea that one pretends to be something one is not in order to gain sympathy—rather it reminds us that Latin American activists crafted narratives that drew on and sometimes reframed certain experiences in order to capture an audience. The *Madres* crafted their narratives, as did Rigoberta Menchú and indigenous leaders, who often understood that North American activists were particularly drawn to a utopian version of indigeneity, the Indian who was closer to nature, more egalitarian, the primitive communist. One of the movements that mobilized these sympathies better than almost any other was the Zapatista Army of National Liberation in Mexico (the EZLN), whose Revolutionary Womens' Law is Document 10.2.

The EZLN announced its rebellion against the Mexican government through two actions on January 1, 1994. The first was a brief occupation of the city of Bartolomé de las Casas, Chiapas. The second came in the form of a series of pronouncements intended to introduce the movement to the world. The *Declarations from the Jungle* and Revolutionary Laws cast the EZLN's grievances in such a way as to perfectly align it with the international activist left. Disseminated broadly through email lists, these statements created the impression of a leaderless movement committed to social justice and women's rights that had chosen the date of the inauguration of the North American Free Trade Agreement to say "enough!"

That these claims did not perfectly reflect the practices within the movement certainly matters. The EZLN was not leaderless at all. It was dominated by figures like Subcomandante Marcos and Comandante Ramona (the author of the Women's Revolutionary Law), who pushed for the rebellion in spite of the fact that local groups in the region were deeply divided over this decision (see Figure 10.4). And it is also certainly true that many of the provisions of the EZLN's laws would never be implemented in meaningful ways. Yet if we focus on these failings, we miss the larger point of what was arguably the first rebellion of the digital age. These laws were as much about the allies the Zapatistas needed if they were to survive as they were about the facts on the ground, and the Zapatistas successfully took their war to a virtual community over which the Mexican state had no power. This in turn made it next to impossible for the Mexican army to do to these rebels what they have done for decades, which is eliminate them under the cover of darkness. The Revolutionary

Figure 10.4   Comandante Ramona of the EZLN, author of the Women's Revolutionary Law

Women's Law then, had multiple lives. It was a utopian vision for a hoped for transformation of social relations. It was also an emergency flare, an effort to call a global network to a cause in order to allow that cause to survive.

Document 10.3 offers an emergency flare of another kind. Here we have a video of a confrontation between the Guerrero (Mexico) State Police and a group of peasants in a place called Aguas Blancas. The video was shot on June 28, 1995, while police stopped and then killed seventeen members of the Southern Sierra Peasant Organization (OCSS). The victims were travelling to a demonstration in the town of Atoyac de Álvarez, where they intended to demand the release of a comrade from police custody. State officials initially claimed that members of the group had attacked the police, and that they had responded in self-defense. They released photographs in which they showed peasants with guns in their hands to back up their claims. The governor of the state, Rubén Figueroa, also presented a two minute and twenty-two second video that seemed to support their claims by revealing the bodies of peasants with arms of various calibers.

The survivors, many seriously wounded, immediately disputed these claims, but given the fact that they were members of a radical peasant group that many believed wanted to overthrow the government, their claims were immediately treated with suspicion. This probably would have been the end of the affair, except that the claims of the police began to unravel when, shortly after the incident, the newspaper *El Sol* in Acapulco published two different photos of one of the victims, which seemed to indicate that police

Figure 10.5 Original photograph of one of the victims of the massacre at Aguas Blancas

Source: *El Sol de Acapulco*

Figure 10.6 Image of the figure in 10.5, showing a gun placed in the victim's right hand

Source: *El Sol de Acapulco*

had planted a gun in his hands (see Figures 10.5 and 10.6). The photos in turn prompted a Human Rights investigation by CNDH, which in turn led to charges of misconduct against four officers.

   To this point the massacre was a local scandal, and officers on the scene seemed likely to bear the full blame for what seemed like a garden-variety police coverup. It became something else entirely when, on February 25, 1996, the journalist Fernando Rocha aired the original fourteen minute forty-eight second video of the massacre (the unedited version of the earlier tape), demonstrating both that the police had murdered unarmed peasants and that Governor Figueroa had, at the very least, covered up the crime. Mexican President Ernesto Zedillo responded by forcing Figueroa to resign on the March 12, 1996, and twenty-eight members of the police and four other mid-level government functionaries were ultimately jailed.

   Most served relatively short sentences, and Figueroa did not spend a single day in jail, in spite of the evidence that he knew that something was planned for the roadblock (he had been assured that the peasants would not reach the protests). On top of this, members of

the OCSS continued to be harassed by state officials. At least thirty-four more members of the group were assassinated in the three years following the massacre. It can therefore seem like cold comfort to insist that there is something particularly meaningful in this video's ability to lift the veil from government secrecy, using the very tools the government had used to manipulate the narrative. Yet the fact that a two-minute, highly redacted video, used to give the impression of verisimilitude became a fourteen-minute, unedited video that brought down a governor and sent more than two dozen police officers to jail, speaks to the power that new forms of media have in contemporary Latin America. Compact devices, which record on easily replicated tapes, disks, and now thumb drives, have created a universe in which it is virtually impossible for states involved in any number of conspiracies and cover-ups to remain confident that they can control the narrative. This is especially true when the data stored on that stick or tape has the explosive power of the videotape of the Aguas Blancas massacre.

There can be no question that states retain the advantage in many ways. They have more capacity to disseminate their narratives, and regularly use these technologies to spy on and target their enemies. Nonetheless, the proliferation of digital technologies, miniaturization of recording devices (today, the smart phone), and the global nature of information networks have exposed government malfeasance in unprecedented ways. Government officials videotaped at a casino in Las Vegas, spending ill-gotten gains, suddenly have to answer for something they have always done under the cover of darkness. A "citizen's television" brigade can use their cell phones to record student protests in Chile, recording incidents of police violence against peaceful protesters and documenting the circumstances under which some are arrested.[8] States across the planet have responded in varying ways to these trends, typically with a mix of efforts to control the flow of information and promises of greater transparency, yet to date they have invariably been a step or two behind their critics. As 1960s countercultural figure and author of the *Whole Earth Catalogue,* Stewart Brand once said, "information wants to be free"—freely accessed and free flowing.

Video plays a different role in Documents 10.4 and 10.5, which are music videos shot as a part of the No Campaign in the 1988 Chilean plebiscite. The No Campaign was given fifteen minutes per day on TV, starting at 10:45 p.m. on September 5, 1988, to make their case. The Yes campaign likewise had fifteen minutes of official broadcast time, along with positive reporting during the remainder of the day. Given their obvious disadvantage, the No campaign needed to communicate a great deal in a short time, and do it in ways that would inspire Chileans to support them at the polls. They also had to find a way to satisfy leaders of the fourteen different parties that made up their coalition. Relying in large part on these videos, the campaign was remarkably successful in developing a strategy that both reminded Chileans of the atrocities of the previous fifteen years, and captured the sorts of positive energy that they needed. Their success is neatly encapsulated in the songs presented here. "No" and "Chile, la alegria ya viene" (Chile, joy is coming) point to the future. They assure viewers of the happiness that will flourish in a post-dictatorship Chile. And just as important, they mock the dictator, making him into an ugly relic of the past. Although criticized by hard-liners for trivializing the issues that Chileans confronted, the cathartic quality of the videos seem to have played a role in mobilizing the "No" vote.

We see here a different capacity to mobilize, this time drawn from the media savvy authors of a long-shot effort to unseat a dictator. Those who participated faced polls that suggested Pinochet would easily win (not the least because many might stay away from the polls out of fear). They knew that they would face significant reprisals after the vote for openly mocking the dictator, and were also aware that he might simply steal the vote. All of these factors make the courageousness of their work seem all the greater, and the clever, optimistic tone of these songs seem all the more impressive as an example of using the medium to its maximum effect.

One might say the same of the individuals featured in Document 10.6, a collection of Chilean students who took their protests over tuition hikes and university governance to a global audience in a series of flash mobs which were quickly posted on YouTube in 2011. Here you see students in central Santiago dressed as zombies and dancing to Michael Jackson's *Thriller*. Zombies, the living dead, resonate everywhere in the second decade of the twenty-first century, providing Chilean students an instant connection to a global youth culture in crisis.

Much has yet to be determined about the power of virtual social networks and new media. Critics rightly point out that Facebook, Twitter, Tumblr, and other new forms of human connection often produce thin relationships, superficial friendships and fleeting personal commitments. Unlike the kinds of social associations that in the past produced long-term commitments through the mutual sacrifices made by members, these networks have yet to prove capable to doing much more than temporarily disrupting the day to day order. Discipline and cohesion in the face of real and sustained threats often requires a depth of camaraderie that movements based on social networks have not yet manifested. If they are to produce sustained pressure on their adversaries, the members of these movements need to find ways to address these shortcomings. The Chilean flash mob offers us an opportunity to contemplate what those strategies might be, and to do so in a way that offers glimpses of the potential power of these sorts of spectacles in shifting the terrain of politics in the early twenty-first century.

Although the visual is today a critically important part of the struggle for rights in Latin America, other modes remain. The written word has a lasting place in the political struggles of Latin American dissidents, and today it continues in the form of manifestos blasted to the world through email lists and blogs. Documents 10.7 and 10.8 offer us significant examples of the ways in which new media have not entirely displaced older forms. The first is the *Open Letter to the Drug Cartels* penned by the editors of *El Diario de Juárez* on September 19, 2010. The letter caused a great deal of consternation in Mexico and the United States, because its threat to capitulate revealed in the most naked way the costs of the drug war, which in the previous years had resulted in the deaths of dozens of journalists. What is more, it offered the possibility that the drug war simply could not be won, and reminded everyone that the war had placed one of the essential elements of a democratic society—a free press—in an utterly untenable situation. Some condemned the paper for its letter, but most believed that its words rang true.

Our final text is Javier Sicilia's *Open Letter to Mexico's Politicians and Criminals*, written shortly after his twenty-four-year old son Juan Francisco was killed along with seven other youths in Cuernavaca, in March 2011. Sicilia, one of Mexico's greatest contemporary poets, first responded to the death by announcing that he could no longer imagine himself as a poet. He turned his attention to organizing a series of marches in Cuernavaca calling for an end to the drug war. His letter, released on April 3, became the rallying point for further action, including his National March for Justice and Against Impunity, in which he and his

supporters marched from Cuernavaca to Mexico City, where they held a rally attended by over 200,000 people. Similar protests were held on that day in other Mexican cities and around the world. The same activists organized the Caravan for Peace, which toured the United States during the summer of 2012, reaching Washington, D.C. on September 11. The symbolism of the date was lost on no one.

Document 10.1 Madres Video Where Are Our Children?

www.youtube.com/watch?v=LAP5wlHNPZA

Document 10.2 Revolutionary Womens' Law. (Published in *El Despertador Mexicano**, January 1, 1994)

(Translation from Zapatistas! Documents of the New Mexican Revolution, Brooklyn, NY: Autonomedia, 1994)

In the just fight for the liberation of our people, the EZLN incorporates women into the revolutionary struggle, regardless of their race, creed, color or political affiliation, requiring only that they share the demands of the exploited people and that they commit to the laws and regulations of the revolution. In addition, taking into account the situation of the woman worker in Mexico, the revolution supports their just demands for equality and justice in the following Women's Revolutionary Law.

First: Women, regardless of their race, creed, color or political affiliation, have the right to participate in the revolutionary struggle in a way determined by their desire and capacity.

Second: Women have the right to work and receive a just salary.

Third: Women have the right to decide the number of children they will have and care for.

Fourth: Women have the right to participate in the affairs of the community and hold positions of authority if they are freely and democratically elected.

Fifth: Women and their children have the right to primary attention in matters of health and nutrition.

Sixth: Women have the right to an education.

Seventh: Women have the right to choose their partner, and are not to be forced into marriage.

Eighth: Women shall not be beaten or physically mistreated by their family members or by strangers. Rape and attempted rape will be severely punished.

Ninth: Women will be able to occupy positions of leadership in the organization and hold military ranks in the revolutionary armed forces.

Tenth: Women will have all the rights and obligations elaborated in the Revolutionary Laws and regulations.

[* *El Despertador Mexicano* was then published by the EZLN and distributed in San Cristóbal de las Casas on January 1, 1994.]

Document 10.3   Aguas Blancas Massacre (Warning: this is a disturbing video, in which we see the deaths of seventeen peasants at the hands of the police.)

http://www.youtube.com/watch?v=Wut8XF07CM4

Document 10.4   "No"

http://www.youtube.com/watch?v=PI9gNUoknIg

Document 10.5   La Alegria ya viene

http://www.youtube.com/watch?v=H3Jph-eMjX8

Document 10.6   Zombies for Education

http://www.youtube.com/watch?v=sVjqtxGr1nY

Document 10.7   The *Diario de Juárez* Open Letter to the Drug Cartels, September 19, 2010

Source: *El Diario de Juárez*. Translated by Robert Forstag.

WHAT DO YOU WANT FROM US?: AN OPEN LETTER FROM *EL DIARIO* (CIUDAD JUÁREZ, MEXICO)

To: The leaders of the various organizations that are fighting one another over the control of Ciudad Juárez

The loss of two reporters of this publishing company in less than two years represents an irreparable loss for not only all of us who work here but also—and most especially—for their families.

We want to make it clear to you that we are communicators, and not fortune-tellers. Therefore, as information workers, we want you to explain what it is you want from us, what it is that you would have us publish or refrain from publishing, so that we can know what the likely consequences are.

You are now the *de facto* authorities of this city. This is because the legally constituted authorities have been able to do nothing to stop our co-workers from being gunned down, despite the fact that we have repeatedly asked them to do so.

This is why, in the face of this undeniable reality, we've posed our question to you. This is because the last thing we want is for another of our colleagues to fall victim to your bullets.

Even though all those in the journalistic profession who work in the border region have suffered the consequences of this war that you and the federal government are waging, it is *El Diario* that has been the most severely affected, because it is the only outlet that has suffered the loss of two of its employees.

We don't want anyone else to die. We don't want anyone else to be injured. And we don't want any more intimidation. It is impossible to do our work in these conditions. So tell us what it is that you expect from us as a media outlet.

This is not a surrender. It also doesn't mean that we've given up on the ongoing work that we've been engaged in. What it is instead is a call for a truce with those who have imposed their own law on this city, as long as they respect the lives of those of us who dedicate ourselves to the task of informing others.

In the face of the power vacuum whose consequences the residents of the state of Chihuahua all live with, in an environment in which there are no sufficient guarantees for citizens to safely live their lives and conduct their activities, journalism has become one of the most dangerous professions. This is something that *El Diario* has come to realize through first-hand experience.

For those of us who run this publishing company, even though our goals and mission of doing a good job of informing the community remain the same as they were 34 years ago, we can now see no point in putting the safety of so many of our co-workers at risk by allowing their precious lives to be used as means to deliver coded or uncoded messages among various organizations, or by those organizations to the official authorities.

Even wars have rules. And in any clash of arms, there are protocols and guarantees among the warring parties that aim at assuring the safety of the journalists covering the conflict. For this reason, we once again ask you, the leaders of the various drug trafficking organizations, to explain what it is you want from us, so that we can cease paying tribute with the lives of our fellow workers.

From the message left by one of these groups in a blanket placed yesterday morning at the corner of Ejército Nacional and Tecnológico, it seems reasonable to infer a claim of responsibility for the death of the photographer Luis Carlos Santiago Orozco, which occurred at a shopping mall last Thursday afternoon.

The threatening message was found on a placard addressed to so-called commanders and a captain. This message warned that the same fate that befell our photographer awaited those two individuals if they did not return a specified sum of money.

Ever since such messages began to appear wrapped in blankets or painted on walls, *El Diario* has taken them very seriously indeed, because they have proven to be well founded, given that a number of them have been followed by action.

On the other hand, nearly two years after the murder of our colleague Armando Rodríguez Carreón, we are very skeptical that the supposed enforcers of justice who are about to complete their terms of office will provide any trustworthy clarification regarding these events.

There have been many indications and promises that the case would be resolved without any of these actually materializing. This is why, at this point, if someone were to actually be identified as the person supposedly responsible for the crime, our natural reaction would be one of skepticism and caution.

This newspaper is not going to unquestioningly accept the first suspect identified as being the presumed perpetrator of the attack against Rodríguez Carreón. This is because we have information that indicates that there is a search for a scapegoat to pin this crime on—a crime that, for us, is a particularly sensitive matter.

If their purpose in such an action is to relieve some of the pressure they face, it will be counterproductive, because it will only end up engendering an even greater lack of confidence than currently prevails among most of our citizens in the face of the magnitude of impunity that we have witnessed.

In any event, in order to be acceptable to *El Diario* at this point, any conclusion reached regarding this case would have to also be endorsed by international journalism and human rights organizations.

Four and a half years ago, when Felipe Calderón Hinojosa was in the middle of his presidential campaign, he visited the offices of *El Diario* in order to be interviewed regarding a variety of different subjects.

At that meeting with the communications employees of this newspaper, the man who is now president of the Republic responded to a question regarding the guarantees that would be offered by his federal administration regarding the satisfactory development of freedom of the press.

Calderón responded as follows: "When it comes to murders [i.e., of journalists] then, just as I am protected because I am a candidate, I feel that, to the extent of the danger involved in an activity conducted for the benefit of the community, there should be mechanisms that protect that activity. A journalist who has been threatened, or who carries out an investigation of organized crime, must have special protective mechanisms at his or her disposal, and it's a good thing that the Special Prosecutor's Office was created to address such circumstances."

By now, this story is well known: The president, in order to attain a legitimacy denied him at the polls, embarked—without a proper strategy—upon a war against organized crime. He also did so without appreciating the strength and scope of the enemy in this war, or the consequences of such a confrontation for the country.

The Mexican people—and especially the citizens of Ciudad Juárez—have become non-consenting participants in this conflict, and have been set adrift as a result of wrong decisions that have put them right in the middle of it, with results that everyone knows and that the majority of citizens abhor.

This was the context in which journalists were dragged into this savage conflict, without the president having reflected on the promise he made in the meeting room of *El Diario*. Because what has happened is that those working in the media have conducted investigations on organized crime, have been threatened, and have been in the middle of this war as privileged and intimidated witnesses. Despite all this, they have never received from their government the "mechanisms of special protection" that the president characterized as indispensable.

The only defensive weapons at the disposal of those of us dedicated to the profession have been the search for truth, our deployment of words, our typewriters—nowadays our computers—and our cameras.

As a protector of the rights of its citizens—and therefore, of communicators—the state has been absent during these war-torn years, even when it has seemed to act protectively in various operations that in practice turned out to be colossal failures.

Last Friday, following the murder of the photographic journalist Luis Carlos Santiago Orozco, *El Diario* published an editorial in which it drew attention to this absence by posing the following question: "From whom do we demand justice?" This question reflects the state of mind of citizens who no longer know who they can call on for help.

Just a few days ago, medical associations raised the possibility of a doctors' strike for the purpose of pressuring governments to find answers, following the kidnapping of a number of physicians—several of whom were murdered despite the fact that the requested ransom had been paid.

Others, such as merchants and business owners, have also considered actions aimed at applying pressure, such as a strike on the payment of the taxes and fees essential for the functioning of government.

Justice has been so sadly lacking, and the desolation and powerlessness so deeply felt in all sectors of society, that it would hardly be a preposterous notion to apply actions that really would hurt those who have the obligation to do more in order to preserve the safety of our city, our state, and our nation.

In contrast, those with the greatest obligation to protect our citizens have either become mired in fruitless debates over the question of whether Mexico is as bad or worse than Colombia was 20 years ago (a contention expressed by US Secretary of State Hillary Clinton and endorsed by serious media outlets such as the *Washington Post*) or have offered us a circus by means of the extravagant expenditures to celebrate the nation's Bicentennial. These resources could have been better used to bolster our country's anemic security strategy.

As if all this were not enough, our president continues to pontificate about peace in our nation as if it were something real by sending a letter to every family in Mexico in which, among other things, he rhetorically emphasizes that the white of our national flag symbolizes "the peace that we have achieved."

Such a statement is nothing more than mockery for the citizens of Ciudad Juárez, who have been drowning in a bloodbath, and who know less about peace than anything else in these troubled times.

In Ciudad Juárez, we have reached a point where adopting other kinds of measures in order to force our legally established authorities to respond more decisively has become an urgent necessity. This is because the patience of so many of our citizens has simply been exhausted.

In the meantime, *El Diario* has taken the position indicated at the beginning of this article—that of calling upon the conflicting groups to declare what it is they want from us in the communications media.

We, the victims, are thus addressing our executioners.

As if the abuses, attacks, and intimidation of the communications media weren't enough, yesterday the Secretary of Education and Culture of the state of Chihuahua, Guadalupe Chacón Monárrez, poured more salt into the wound by declaring that we in the press are guilty of causing the psychological terrorism that prevails in our city.

So now we are, in the mind of this government official, not victims, but perpetrators of terrorism—all as a result of doing nothing more than our duty of informing the community of what is happening in this border region.

It ought to be very clear to the Secretary of Education that terrorism comes from sources other than communications media, which serve as a vehicle for providing information as to what is happening in this city.

Chacón Monárrez specifically referred to the primary school and kindergarten in the northwest of our state, where not only parents but also the teachers themselves live in fear that something might happen to them as a result of threats made by a group engaged in extortion.

It was in fact mothers and fathers who approached this newspaper in order to express the fear that they felt—and that they still feel—over the safety of their children. These threats were not issued by *El Diario*. It was also not this newspaper that suggested to these parents that they report the intimidation to which they had been subjected.

In the face of such circumstances, what did the Secretary expect? That we only listen to these parents and then bid them farewell? Or that we advise them to report the threats to the Office of Prior Investigations after they themselves made it clear that they don't trust the authorities because they don't take any action?

The reporter who met with the parents did what he had to do: He wrote an article about what he had been told and delivered it to the editor, who in turn did his duty by publishing it because it dealt with an important matter that involved the safety of a lot of people—including children.

It wasn't the information reported—and which was echoed by other media outlets in the city—that constituted terrorism. In this instance, the terrorism was perpetrated by those who threatened the children, their parents, and their teachers. But those most responsible for fomenting terrorism are those who are responsible for and capable of stopping it, but who have failed to do so, whether out of omission or negligence, or even as a result of collusion.

The Secretary of Education said that she couldn't imagine anyone showing disrespect to children, and that the threats may have been a hoax. It is noteworthy that she doesn't live in this city, where adolescents, children, and even babies have been massacred. Her comments make a mockery of those parents whose children have died as a result of the violence, and are unforgivable.

Hernán Ortíz, an anthropologist and researcher at the Autonomous University of Ciudad Juárez is entirely right when he responds to Chacón Monárrez that the press should not be blamed for the terrorism that we've endured for so long, but that we should blame the incompetence of the government. This reflects the view that we expressed earlier in this article.

The secretary issued the following plea: "With all due respect, I want to urge the press not to become participants in this, because psychological terrorism is something that is achieved by means of communication."

What is she trying to tell us? To stop publishing? To only report "good" or "positive" news (as others have previously urged in this regard)? We in the media gather information and report on everything that happens in the city, and it is our readers who qualify as "good" or "bad" what they read, hear, or see.

In any event, the Secretary of Education has been invested with the great respon-sibility of assuring that children now in our schools emerge with properly educated minds, so that they don't turn into our future criminals.

What Chacón Monárrez has done is created a smokescreen for the purpose of con-cealing the incompetence of authorities who have failed to do their job.

http://www.unpuntoenelinfinito.com/analisis-denuncias/2559-carta-abierta-ciudad-juarez.html

Document 10.8   Javier Sicilia's Open Letter to Mexico's Politicians and Criminals, April 3, 2011

Source: Translated by Narco News (www.narconews.com). Reprinted by permission of Javier Sicilia.

April 4, 2011

The brutal assassination of my son, Juan Francisco, of Julio César Romero Jaime, of Luis Antonio Romero Jaime, and of Gabriel Anejo Escalera, is added to so many other boys and girls who have been assassinated just the same throughout the country, not only because of the war unleashed by the government of Calderón against organized crime, but also the rotting of the heart that has been wrought by the poorly labeled political class and the criminal class, which has broken its own codes of honor.

In this letter, I do not wish to speak with you about the virtues of my son, which were immense, nor of those of the other boys that I saw flourish at his side, studying, playing, loving, growing, to serve, like so many other boys, this country that you all have shamed. Speaking of that doesn't serve for anything more than to move what already moves the heart of the citizenry to indignation. Neither do I wish to talk about the pain of my family and the families of each one of the boys who were destroyed. There are no words for this pain. Only poetry can come close to it, and you do not know about poetry. What I do wish to say to you today, from these mutilated lives, from the pain that has no name because it is fruit of something that does not belong in nature—the death of a child is always unnatural and that's why it has no name: I don't know if it is an orphan or widow, but it is simply and painfully nothing—from these, I repeat, mutilated lives, from this suffering, from the indignation that these deaths have provoked, it is simply that we have had it up to here.

We have had it up to here with you, politicians—and when I say politicians I do not refer to any in particular, but, rather, to most of you, including those who make up the political parties—because in your fight for power you have shamed the fabric of the nation. Because in middle of this badly proposed, badly made, badly led war, of this war that has put the country in a state of emergency, you have been incapable—due to your cruelties, your fights, your miserable screaming, your struggle for power—of creating the consensus that the nation needs, the unity without which this country will not be able to escape. We have had it up to here because the corruption of our judicial institutions makes them complicit with the criminals and creates the impunity that allow them to commit crimes, because in the middle of that corruption that demonstrates the failure of the State, each citizen of this country has been reduced to what the philosopher Giorgio Agamben called, using a Greek word, "zoe": an unprotected life, an animal, a being that can be violated, kidnapped, molested and assassinated with impunity. We have had it up to here because you only have an imagination for violence, for weapons, for insults and, with that, a profound scorn for education, culture, and opportunities for honorable work, which is what good nations do. We have had it up to here because your limited imagination is allowing our kids, our children, to not only be assassinated, but then later criminalized, made falsely guilty to satisfy that imagination. We have had it up to here because others of our children, due to the absence of a good government plan, have no opportunities to educate themselves, to find dignified work. They are spit out onto the sidelines become possible recruits for organized crime and violence. We have had it up to here because the citizenry has lost confidence in its governors, its police, its Army, and is afraid and in pain. We have had it up to here because the only thing that matters to you, beyond an impotent power that only serves to administer disgrace, is money, the fomentation of rivalry, of your damn "competition," and of unmeasured consumption, all of which are other names of the violence.

As for you, the criminals, we have had it up to here with your violence, with your loss of honor, your cruelty and senselessness.

In days of old you had codes of honor. You were not so cruel in your paybacks and you did not touch the citizens nor their families. Now you do not distinguish. Your violence already can't be named because, like the pain and suffering that you provoke, it has no name nor sense. You have lost even the dignity to kill (in an honorable fashion). You have become cowards like the miserable Nazi sonderkommandos who killed children, boys, girls, women men and elders without any human sense. We have had it up to here because your violence has become infrahuman—not animal, as animals do not do what you do—but subhuman, demonic, imbecilic. We have had it up to here because in your taste for power and enrichment you humiliate our children and destroy them, producing fear and fright.

It is you, "señores" politicians, and you, "señores" criminals—in quotes because this epithet is given only to honorable people—who are with your omissions, your fights and your actions, making the nation vile. The death of my son Juan Francisco has generated solidarity and a cry of indignation—that my family and I appreciate from the depth of our hearts—from the citizenry, and from the media. Again, the phrase comes back to ring in our ears—after the thousands of known and unknown dead who we carry on our backs, so many innocents murdered and debased—this phrase ought to accompany the great citizen mobilizations that we need, in these moments of national emergency, to create an agenda that can unify the nation and create a state of actual governance. The citizen networks of the state of Morelos are calling for a national march on Wednesday, April 6, that will leave at 5 p.m. from the monument of the Dove of Peace to the Government Palace, demanding justice and peace. If the citizenry does not unite in this and reproduce it in all cities, in all towns and regions of the country, if we are not capable of obligating you, "señores" politicians, to govern with justice and dignity, and you, "señores" criminals, to again embrace your codes of honor and limit your savagery, the spiral this violence has generated will bring us on a path of horror without return. If you, "señores" politicians do not govern well and do not take seriously the fact that we live in a state of national emergency that requires your unity, and you, "señores" criminals, do not limit your actions, you will end up winning and having power but you will govern and reign over a mountain of ossuaries and of beings that are beaten and their souls destroyed, a dream that none of us envy.

There is no life, Albert Camus wrote, without persuasion and without peace, and the history of Mexico today only knows intimidation, suffering, distrust and the fear that one day another son or daughter of another family will be debased and massacred. And what do you ask of us? That the deaths that happen all around us be treated like statistics, like an administrative issue. That we get used to it.

Because we do not want that, next Wednesday we will take to the streets. Because we do not want another boy, another child, murdered, the citizen networks of Morelos are calling for national unity. We must keep unity alive in order to break the fear and isolation that infects us, body and soul, and which is the product of the inability of you "gentlemen" politicians, and cruelty of you, "master" criminals.

All of this brings to mind the words of Bertolt Brecht, who in considering the horrors of Nazism, the impact of the integration of crime into the daily life of a nation, said: "One day they came for the blacks, and I said nothing. Another day they came for the Jews, and I said nothing. One day they came for me (or for a son of mine) and I had nothing to say."

Today, after so many crimes incurred, when the mangled body of my son and his friends have mobilized the public and the media again, we talk with our bodies, with our walk, with our cry of indignation, so that Brecht's words do not become a reality in our country.

We must reclaim our dignity as a nation.

For Further Reading

Alvarez, Sonia E. *Engendering Democracy in Brazil: Women's Movements in Transition Politics*. Princeton: Princeton University Press, 1990.

Benjamin, Thomas. "A Time of Reconquest: History, the Maya Revival, and the Zapatista Rebellion in Chiapas," *American Historical Review* 105, no. 2 (April 2000): 417–450.

Branford, Su, and Jan Rocha. *Cutting the Wire: the Story of the Landless Movement in Brazil*. London: Latin American Bureau, 2002.

Campos, Isaac. *Home Grown: Marijuana and the Origins of Mexico's War on Drugs*. Chapel Hill: University of North Carolina Press, 2012.

Cardenas, Sonia. *Human Rights in Latin America: A Politics of Terror and Hope*. Philadelphia: University of Pennsylvania Press, 2011.

Chacon, Justin Akers, and Mike Davis. *No One Is Illegal: Fighting Racism and State Violence on the U.S.-Mexico Border*. Chicago: Haymarket Books, 2006.

Gootenberg, Paul. *Andean Cocaine: The Making of a Global Drug*. Chapel Hill: The University of North Carolina Press, 2009.

Guest, Iain. *Behind the Disappearances: Argentina's Dirty War against Human Rights and the United Nations*. Philadelphia, University of Pennsylvania Press, 1990.

Hammond, John. "Law and Disorder, The Brazilian Landless Farmworkers Movement," *Bulletin of Latin American Research* 18:4 (1999): 469–489.

Hanchard, Michael, ed. *Racial Politics in Contemporary Brazil.* Durham, NC: Duke University Press, 1999.

Hayner, Priscilla B. *Unspeakable Truths: Transitional Justice and the Challenge of Truth Commissions,* 2nd ed. New York: Routledge, 2010.

Kornbluh, Peter. *The Pinochet File.* New York: The New Press, 2004.

Lovell, Peggy A. "Race, Gender, and Work in São Paulo, Brazil, 1960–2000," *Latin American Research Review* 41, no. 3 (October 2006): 64–87.

Reichman, Rebecca. *Race in Contemporary Brazil: From Indifference to Inequality.* University Park, PA: Pennsylvania State University Press, 1999.

Staudt, Kathleen. *Violence and Activism at the Border: Gender, Fear, and Everyday Life in Ciudad Juarez.* Austin: University of Texas Press, 2008.

Wolford, Wendy. "The Difference Ethnography Can Make: Understanding Social Mobilization and Development in the Brazilian Northeast," *Qualitative Sociology,* June 2006, 1–18.

Wolford, Wendy, with Angus Wright. *To Inherit the Earth: The Landless Movement and the Struggle for a New Brazil.* Oakland, CA: Food First Books, 2003.

Wright, Thomas C. *State Terrorism in Latin America: Chile, Argentina, and International Human Rights.* Lahman, MD: Rowman & Littlefield, 2006.

Youngers, Coletta A., and Eileen Rosin, eds. *Drugs and Democracy in Latin America: The Impact of U.S. Policy.* Boulder: Lynne Rienner, 2004.

At A Glance: Technology

Communications technologies have long been the lynchpins of the global economy and global politics. Global trade has relied on the ability of suppliers to find their customers through technological means since the age of the telegraph, and has expanded exponentially as that connectivity has improved. Communications technologies have also been critical to systems of political repression (facilitating the movement of police and troops, aiding in the surveillance of enemies of the state) and movements that sought to topple authoritarian governments since even before Paul Revere's famous ride. Radio stations have announced revolutions and the toppling of dictators (sometimes, as happened in Cuba in 1957, prematurely), fax machines have moved clandestine news in and out of societies with no freedom of the press, and, most recently, Twitter was credited with helping to facilitate the 2011 Arab Spring.

Given the importance of these innovations in communications technology, it is significant that Latin Americans lagged behind the United States and Europe in connectivity during much of the twentieth century. Telephone landlines were expensive, as was cable. Radio, television, and newspapers tended to be relatively subservient to the state. But the advent of cellular technology dramatically changed this as on-the-scene-reporting of events were disseminated around the world by individuals. While landlines and cable broadband grew slowly or stagnated during the early years of the twenty-first century, the use of cellular telephones skyrocketed. Less than 20 percent of Latin Americans today have fixed landlines, compared to more than 50 percent of people in the United States. Cell phones, on the other hand, continue to grow in popularity. Today, Latin America has a higher per capita saturation of cell phones than does Canada.

The maps below illustrate that growth, showing cell-phone usage per capita in Latin America as compared to the rest of the world. **Figure F.1** offers a clear impression of just how important this form of communication is in the region. Having essentially leapfrogged landline technology, the region today as a whole is on par with or exceeds most of the nations of the Global North. **Figure F.2** complicates this finding by examining the frequency with which cellular phones have broadband access. This offers a strong indication that, while cell phones are affordable for many in the region, smart phones often remain out of reach. In practical terms this means that Latin Americans have much greater access to telephony than they did a generation ago, and that other communication tools, such as those enabling texting, are widely available, but that access to the internet most likely remains primarily the preserve of those with means. Poorer Latin Americans living in cities often gain access at internet cafes and a limited number of public libraries. They must often pay a prohibitive price for this access.

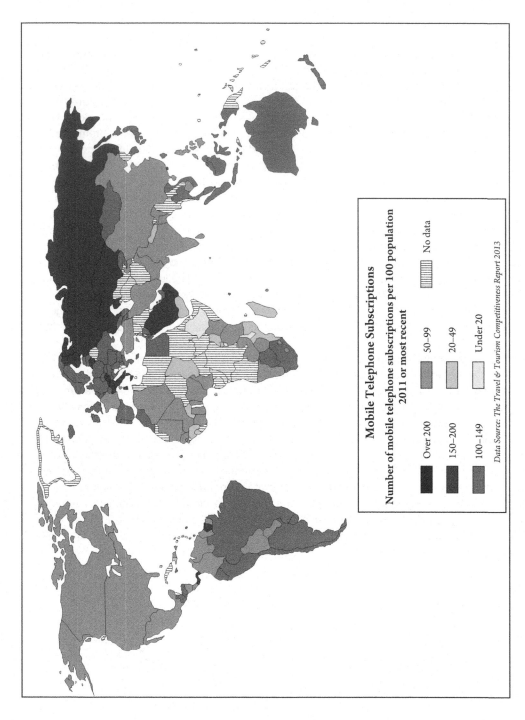

Figure F.1 Mobile Telephone Subscriptions World Map

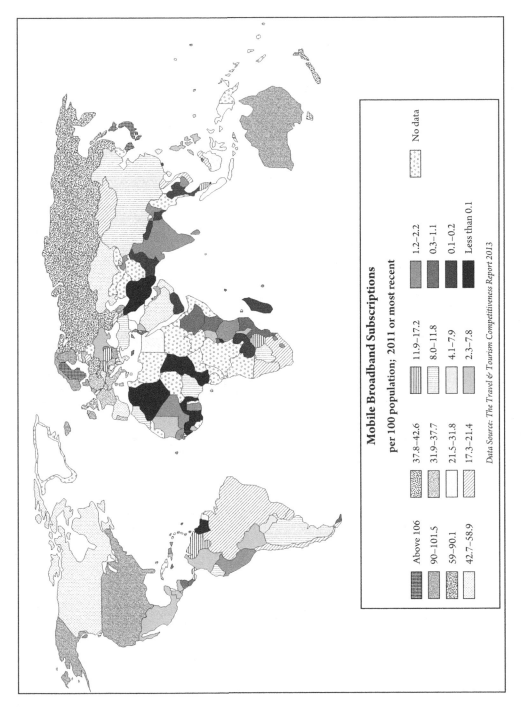

Figure F.2 Mobile Broadband Subscriptions World Map

September 19, 1985	February 1989	1993	January 1, 1994	December 6, 1998	April 2000
Earthquake reaching 8.1 on the Richter Scale hits Mexico City	Popular Rebellion known as the Caracazo engulfs Caracas	Plaintiffs in the Lago Agrio case file suit in New York	North American Free Trade Agreement comes into effect	Hugo Chávez elected president of Venezuela	Water War in Cochabamba

November 26, 2006	February 2011	March 2012
Rafael Correa elected president of Ecuador	A judge in Nueva Loja Ecuador, rules in favor of the plaintiffs in the Lago Agrio Case	Indigenous rights activists undertake "March for Water, Life and Dignity" in Ecuador

Towards an Uncertain Future

11

December 2001	September–October 2003	October 27, 2002	April 27, 2003	December 18, 2005
Riots in Argentina force President Fernando de la Rua from office	Gas War in Bolivia	Luis Ignacio Lula da Silva elected president of Brazil	Néstor Kirchner elected president of Argentina	Evo Morales elected president of Bolivia

We live in anxious times. The New World Order broke down unevenly, perhaps first in Latin America, where it was never quite a consensus but more a series of conclusions drawn in boardrooms, government offices, and at the dinner tables of middle- and upper-class families, but everywhere we look the confidence of President George H.W. Bush's End of History is fast in retreat. Caught up in its own struggles with a drawn out financial collapse and diminished global stature in the aftermath of the Iraq War, the United States has not been in much of a position to counter the growing dominance of China and the increased confidence of other nations in the Global South. This has created opportunities for political and social movements across the planet, opportunities to embrace ideas and values that strayed from the neoliberal orthodoxies of the World Bank and International Monetary Fund (IMF), yet in doing so the advocates for a new, new world order are continually reminded that the desire to ameliorate poverty and inequality, and the desire to address environmental concerns, must forever compete with the demand that our economies grow more and faster, that they be more productive and more efficient. They must contend with the seemingly universal assumption that without economic growth, we have no future at all.

These imperatives have produced distinct political constellations across the globe. In China, the voices that continue to call for redistributive economic policies, government transparency, consumer guarantees, human rights, and environmental regulation are largely silenced. The Chinese state insists that these demands are foreign to Chinese culture, and the people are told that they must abide with the great transformation lest they be traitors. In Europe, and to a lesser extent the United States, the demand for growth has produced seemingly intractable conflicts between an increasingly remote economic elite and a populace that feels largely powerless to improve their lot. In 2012 youth unemployment was at more than 50 percent in several European countries. More than one quarter of people in the United States between the ages of twenty-five and thirty-four were unemployed. No one seems to believe that this crisis generation will ever recover those things it aspired to possess—good middle-class jobs, education, benefit, and a possibility of a smooth passage to retirement.

Latin America, oddly enough, was ahead of this curve. The crises gripping the Global North today happened a generation ago in this part of the world, and the precariousness with which many in the North are newly aware has long been a defining component of middle- and working-class experiences in Latin America. Latin Americans saw in these experiences what many North Americans and Western Europeans have only just begun to learn; that even as power is often remote, held in the hands of the managers of multinational corporations and government bureaucrats whose agendas are never transparent, power can also be immediate, residing both in the police officer's billy club and the rock thrown by the protester.

As a result of the crises they have faced over the past thirty years, Latin Americans have developed a repertoire of tools that allowed them to seize power wherever they could. Many of the strategies they used have been individual. They migrated, they worked the system to the best of their advantage, they hoarded dollars when they feared economic collapse, or turned to crime and other illicit activities. Collectively, they adopted increasingly unruly forms of politics, using protests and civil disobedience to have their voices heard. And lately they have elevated new political figures on the left who spoke to their grievances in ways that created enormous anxiety among the traditional political elites of the region. During the cold war that anxiety would have been matched with violence. In the new democracies, and with the United States focused on its problems in the Middle and Far East, the story has played out quite differently.

The resurgence of the Latin American left has taken place during what has been the most sustained commodity export boom the region has seen in half a century. Buoyed by Asian demands and record prices, exports of minerals (in particular gold, platinum, lithium, silver), hydrocarbons, and agricultural commodities (particularly soybeans) boomed during the first decade of the twenty-first century. This was the critical reason that while much of the Global North cratered economically in 2008, most of the economies of Latin America continued to see robust growth. Growth however, did not bring an end to the forms of disruptive politics that became increasingly common during the worst years of economic crisis. If anything, the political unrest in Latin America is more pronounced today than it was a decade ago.

In an effort to make sense of the fact that renewed economic growth has not produced stability, the following pages will draw from the work of economist Albert Hirschman, whose 1970 book *Exit, Voice, and Loyalty* offers us a model of how members of societies in crisis behave.[1] Hirschman posited that when states fall into crisis, citizens tend to opt out or engage, depending on what they perceive their options and best interests to be. Loyalty in turn is the product of the interplay of these options. It is sometimes generated by a state's capacity for reform, and sometimes produced by the impossibility of exit. It is in understanding the interplay of these three phenomena that we have the opportunity to understand the trajectory of the recent past, and what that portends for an uncertain future.

Exit

In the early morning hours of September 19, 1985, the ground beneath Mexico City shook from an earthquake that reached 8.1 on the Richter scale.[2] Though relatively distant from the epicenter, Mexico City was particularly vulnerable because most of the city was built on a dry lakebed. Moments after the quake much of the ground beneath the city turned to the consistency of quicksand. The country was already something of a ruin—four years into a deep economic crisis with no end in sight—and the government was ill prepared to deal with this disaster. Nearly 100,000 people were left homeless, and around 10,000 were killed.[3] Entire neighborhoods were left in ruins as 412 buildings collapsed and 3,124 suffered extensive damage.

Hardest hit of all were the great modernizing accomplishments of the post-1940 Mexican state, public housing for workers and the middle class, hospitals and schools, the symbols of progress and prosperity that had been instrumental in maintaining social peace through decades of one party rule. Built by politically connected construction companies that used bribes to avoid close inspections, these buildings were almost never constructed with the appropriate quality of concrete or the amount of rebar called for in the construction codes.

More than half of the square footage destroyed in the earthquake belonged to the government, including Juárez Hospital (1,000 dead) and the General Hospital (316 dead). Though some infants in the Children's Hospital miraculously survived for days after the earthquake and were rescued, eighty infants were among the dead in the General Hospital. Another 600 people perished in the collapse of the Nuevo Leon building in the Tlatelolco apartment complex, a building that residents had long complained was unsafe. Just a week earlier government inspectors had responded to their complaints by declaring the Nuevo Leon to be one of the safest buildings in the country.[4]

If this was not enough, President Miguel de la Madrid was nowhere to be found in the early hours after the earthquake. Soldiers and police officials were seen trying to keep relatives of those trapped in collapsed buildings away from the disaster zones so that they could loot at will. The owners of factories were reputed to have secured heavy machinery to raze their buildings while employees were still trapped inside. Even as it resisted foreign offers to help in the rescue effort, the Mexican government proved utterly incapable of dealing with the crisis.

For the most part, Mexicans had given up on their government long before the earthquake. After several years of grinding unemployment and economic crisis, the earthquake merely cemented the end of the era in which Mexicans of all classes looked to the government for jobs, favors, protection. Critics on the left saw this moment as an opportunity to condemn the corruptness of the forms of crony capitalism that had long dominated the

Figure 11.1   Collapse of the Mexico City General Hospital, 1985 earthquake

Source: Wikimedia Commons / U.S. Geological Survey / photo by M. Celebi

region, and call for genuine socialist reform. Those on the right called for an entirely different solution. They demanded that Latin America embrace what would later become known as the Washington Consensus—a model that called for the gradual withering away of the state through privatization, deregulation, and global trade and investment. Inasmuch as the earthquake reinforced Mexicans' sense that the state could and would no longer act as protector, it also signaled what would gradually be the triumph of the latter perspective over the former.

Beginning with Chile in 1973, over the course of two decades almost every country in Latin America drifted to the right. The conditions that drove this shift were similar everywhere in the region. In country after country during the late 1970s and early 1980s, governments faced deep recessions linked to changing global commodity prices and interest rates. After growing at an average rate of 5.6 percent during the 1970s, during the first half of the 1980s the economies of the region shrank by 0.4 percent.[5] Poor economic management, government inefficiencies, widespread corruption, spiraling foreign debt (the region as a whole went from an external debt of about $25 billion in 1970 to more than $450 billion in 1990) deepened these problems, producing what most refer to as the "lost decade" of the 1980s. During that period. inflation at times topped 1,000 percent, and in several Latin American countries unemployment reached 40 percent. Those with the means to do so tended to send their money abroad in an effort to shield themselves from the worst of the crisis. Those who could not faced underemployment, unemployment, the loss of their life-savings, bankruptcy, and among the poor, hunger.

Believing that the skyrocketing debt represented one of the greatest obstacles to a return to growth, governments in the region repeatedly sought to reduce their debt burden through negotiations with the IMF and other financial stakeholders. In order to make any headway in these negotiations, they were forced to make a series of concessions. They had to reduce the public sector, reduce government regulation, and open their economies to trade and investment. These changes were implemented through "austerity measures" and "shock treatments," the latter an oddly psychiatric approach to the economy, in which a series of shocks were applied to the system wherein government services were abruptly cut and prices for staples allowed to increase rapidly. Foreign and finance ministers around the region protested the deleterious effects that IMF backed policies had on the region during the 1980s, noting that the demand that governments across prioritize debt repayments and embrace austerity measures made it even more difficult to recover from economic crisis. Their protests made little difference. First world bankers generally insisted on these measures as a precondition for the IMF seal of approval, which in turn made it possible for Latin American nations to trade in the global marketplace. With domestic consumption devastated by the crisis, everyone seemed to believe that access to this marketplace represented the region's only hope for the future.

The inevitability of free trade and free markets seemed even greater after 1989, when the collapse of the Soviet Union seemed to indicate that the capitalist world was invariably stronger and more dynamic than the socialist alternative. Cuba, which had long relied on Soviet subsidies, sank into an economic funk that brought hunger to the island for the first time in decades and produced a new flood of exiles produced. The drum beat of reform could be heard across the region. Struggling states everywhere were pressed to embrace shock treatments, austerity measures, reductions in the state sector, and new trade agreements.

Working-class and poor people tended to oppose these measures, largely because these policies were invariably tied (at least in the short run) to declining standards of living. Middle-class and elite Latin Americans responded in a less uniform manner. Those who had long depended on the privileges provided by a place in the bureaucracy or a cozy relationship to the state did their best to protect the old prerogatives. Those who concluded that the only way forward lay in the embrace of free trade and investment abandoned their old networks in favor of new ones that they hoped to use to become players on a larger stage. Local markets, which had long supported local workers and manufacturers by creating a captive market of consumers, would be abandoned for global markets in which Latin American goods could only compete if they were cheaper and of as high quality as all competitors. Cheap labor, ideal growing seasons for northern consumers, and a bounty of mineral and hydrocarbon wealth would be Latin America's competitive advantage.

This then, was the first sort of exit prompted by the lost decade, as members of the elites opted to exit an arrangement with the state that had persisted for decades and align themselves with a global class of producers and consumers. They purchased homes in Miami, Houston, Los Angeles, and elsewhere, and spread their assets globally as a hedge against crisis. They withdrew their children from crumbling public schools and universities, and sent them either to private educational institutions or abroad. And they withdrew from civil society, hiring private security, and wherever possible locating their homes in increasingly sequestered communities where high walls and razor wire promised a respite from the turmoil. In the early 1990s, the armored car industry (in which SUVs and other vehicles were transformed into bullet proof fortresses at a cost of tens of thousands of dollars) was one of the few growth industries in the region.

Theirs was a virtual exit. For the most part, they remained physically present even as they exited, a political arrangement that has persisted for decades. For those at the other end of the spectrum, exit would mean something else entirely. The rural poor, increasingly unable to preserve their access to land as the export economy ramped up, were first forced to exit the countryside for the cities, which created a wave of rural to urban migration that was made worse in countries like Peru and Colombia by the fact that millions of rural folk found themselves displaced by armed conflict. Once in the cities, they were forced to compete for work with already established and increasingly vulnerable poor folks in contexts where union jobs, already scarce, were drying up, where wages could not keep up with inflation, and where social and public services were largely improvised, provided not by the state but by networks of the urban poor.

Some would then exit the formal economy, with its union jobs and benefits, for the informal sector, selling contraband goods, working in unlicensed shops, or turning to illicit activities. For others, the best alternative lay in the choice to search for opportunities in another country. Today, over 20 million Latin Americans live outside their country of birth, where they often toil under harsh conditions, facing daily discrimination because of the color of their skin or their foreign origin, with no recourse to legal redress. Recent reports suggest that the 300,000 Bolivians, 70,000 Paraguayans, and 45,000 Peruvians living in the city of São Paulo, Brazil work under slave-like conditions.[6] The 1.1 million Bolivians living in Argentina confront similar challenges.

The most popular destination for international migrants is the United States. Mexicans in particular have long migrated here in search of work, a phenomenon that expanded significantly during the economic crisis of the 1980s. Currently, almost half a million Mexicans migrate to the United States every year, and about 10.6 million people born in Mexico now live permanently in the United States. Ironically, a significant number of contemporary migrants come from rural communities that suffered economic catastrophes with the introduction of the North American Free Trade Agreement in 1994. As peasant farmers, they simply did not have the means to make their plots of land viable in the new economy, and decided to sell their labor in the global market for the highest price it could fetch. Many of those migrants now travel to the United States annually to work in a series of agricultural harvests, and then return home to tend to their meager agricultural parcels and reconnect with their friends and families. They are circular migrants, tied to their communities of origin, and returning there frequently, though over time many spend considerable periods in their adult lives working abroad.

Mexican migrants in the United States are crucial to a host of industries, including hotels and restaurants, construction, migrant agricultural labor, slaughterhouses, domestic service, and landscaping. Mexicans in the United States have created significant communities in agricultural zones across the country, and in major cities like Houston, Dallas, Los Angeles, Chicago, and New York. The money they pay in taxes represents an important revenue stream for the government, in part because the Social Security Administration understands that the contributions they collect from these migrants will never be paid out as benefits. There is little credible evidence to suggest that the economic impact of these migrants has been anything but positive.

Migration has had a similarly striking impact in Mexico. Remittances (money sent home by migrants in the United States) edged over $20 billion in the early twenty-first century, peaking at $26 billion in 2007. They are the third largest source of foreign earnings in Mexico, behind only oil and manufactured goods. Today, well over a million families in Mexico survive principally on the monies sent home by their relatives in the United States, and this money has in turn fueled building booms in communities across the country, as migrants have built homes for themselves, along with churches, schools, hospitals, and other public facilities. Migrants also pay an important role in Mexican politics, contributing their votes and resources to politicians who promise to defend their interests.

Still, for all their importance to both the United States and Mexico, undocumented migrants continue to live a precarious existence. Unlike the trade agreements that created a common market in Europe, NAFTA explicitly excluded the freedom to migrate, offering that opportunity only to a limited number of professionals (a category which explicitly excluded most Mexican migrants). This means that most migrants must violate U.S. law to enter the country, even though there is plenty of otherwise legal work awaiting them. There are today around eleven million undocumented immigrants in the United States. About 57 percent of these come from Mexico, and 24 percent from other Latin American Countries. Those who come to the United States without papers are subject to an array of dangers long before they reach the U.S. border, including gangs that demand exorbitant fees for safe passage along the way, and others who will kidnap migrants and hold them for ransom. Once at the U.S. border, they face an increasingly difficult crossing.

Voice

Exit is not invariably the best option. For those who cling to the national and local loyalties they grew up with—if not to a corrupt and inefficient state, then to one's neighbors, to that feeling of belonging that characterizes local, regional, and national communities—or those who cannot move, or simply insist that they must change the world they inhabit rather than inhabit a different world, the choice is to act and to speak out. This sort of voice offers daunting challenges. How in fact do you reform police agencies with long histories of human rights abuses and corruption? How do you go up against a corrupt judiciary and criminal networks which, because of weapons smuggled in from the United States, are often better armed than state security agencies? How, indeed, do you make a more equitable, more democratic, and more stable polity out of the ruins of the 1980s? Neoliberal economists promised that market reforms would do just that, but their claims had a self-serving quality. The economists and their friends in the business sector were not going to suffer the pain. We might even say that the neoliberals abandoned any pretense of being concerned with poverty and inequality by insisting that robust economic growth was the only cure for these problems. To dissent in this moment was to go against history, to deny the fact that the socialist alternative had evaporated with the end of the cold war.

It seemed that the left was dead. And then it was not. Shock treatments, austerity measures, and economic policies that favored a comprador class of globally connected elites acted as a catalyst for a new generation of leftist politicians, some of them former guerrillas who had forsaken violence for mainstream politics. Sensing that the end of the cold war might open opportunities to ascend to positions of real power, this new generation of leftist politicians also tended to eschew their radical economic and social agendas of the past. Socialists in Chile and Uruguay, and the Worker's Party in Brazil, gained a political foothold and found themselves ready to compete for higher office largely because the parties had become much more centrist. All were now avowedly democratic. All spoke of the economy in terms that calmed the nerves of bankers and IMF officials. All promised a continued commitment to free markets, investment and trade, insisting that they would improve the delivery of social services, target the very poor, and increase social spending by tapping into the wealth created through economic growth rather than distributing existing wealth downwards. Under the new left the wealthy would not be threatened. Technocrats would improve the system rather than upending it.

Following a model that relied on careful political compromises, the occasional pay-off (evidenced by the *mensalão* scandal in Brazil), and a commitment to fiscal discipline, Ricardo Lagos in Chile, Tabaré Vázquez in Uruguay, Lula da Silva in Brazil and others made a space in Latin American societies for a reformist left in the early twenty-first century. They won election largely by tapping into voters who did not self-identify as leftists, but who saw in these leaders an opportunity to ameliorate some of the negative consequences of globalization while not undermining the potential for economic growth. And interestingly enough, these moderate leftists pursued policies that were not entirely distinct from those of the right-wing governments that came to power during the same years, notably in Colombia and Mexico. In these instances the right, like the left, sought to distance itself from the undemocratic past, and avoided the dogmatism of the past. Like the left, the right implemented programs that were designed to reduce the number of people living in extreme poverty while doing very little to address inequality.

We might consider all of these undertakings as one and the same, an indication that these reformist voices signaled the death of not just the ideological left, but also the ideological right in Latin America, in favor of regimes generally concerned with providing basic services, making goods and services broadly available at relatively low cost (one's ability to consume now being just as important to the average Latin America as political affiliation might once have been), and fostering economic growth. These regimes speak in the voice of a technocrat hoping that broad prosperity will lessen the threat of exit. They also speak in the voice of a technocrat who is terrified of the capacity of poor people to voice their demands in a particularly disruptive manner.

What they fear most is the mass insurrection, the types of seemingly leaderless eruptions that in the neoliberal era have repeatedly threatened regimes of the right and the left in Latin America. If we consider yet another form of voice, we might see in the mass insurrection a novel form of politics undertaken by those who lack the option to exit, and who can find no other means to make their grievances heard. The crowds of the mass insurrection do not offer a clear adversary with whom the state might negotiate. Their demands are often inchoate, contradictory. And yet they remind us that millions of people in Latin America have been left behind by globalization and have no means to make their needs known through the institutional channels in the new democracies. In order to speak, they must take to the streets.

Four instances of mass insurrection in recent years stand out for their role in reshaping the political landscape of the region: the Caracazo in 1989, the Argentine riots of 2001,

Figure 11.2   Latin America's new left. Former president of Paraguay, Fernando Lugo, president of Bolívia, Evo Morales, former president of Brasil, Luiz Inácio Lula da Silva, president of Ecuador, Rafael Correa, and former president of Venezuela, Hugo Chavez, at the World Social Forum.

Source: Wikimedia Commons / Fabio Rodrigues Pozzebom / Agência Brasil

and the Water and Gas Wars in Bolivia (2000 and 2003, respectively). Though each of these popular rebellions seemed to be spontaneous uprisings, as a rule they were the outcome of long histories of unresolved grievances. The specter of foreigners growing wealthy off of local suffering often played a powerful motivating factor, whether it was first world banks that were extracting their pound of flesh (anti-Semitism did play a role in some of these conflicts), or foreigners actively controlling the national wealth (water and natural gas in the case of Bolivia). And in each of these instances popular insurrections revealed the tenuousness of state power in Latin America in a new era of precariousness. The crowd, the popular coup, and the ever-present fear of mass mobilization would emerge as one of the most important forms of voice in Latin America in the early twenty-first century.

In the United States, political commentators on both the left and the right have been quick to dismiss movements like Occupy Wall Street, in part because their impact seemed ephemeral. Not so with protest movements in the last several decades in Latin America. The 1989 Caracazo had a profound impact on a young Hugo Chávez, who was deployed to crush the uprising. His experiences in this conflict inspired both his failed 1992 coup and his run for the presidency in 1998. Chávez rode the anger of those masses throughout his career, never entirely in control and forever needing to rely on them to maintain his grip on power. This was powerfully demonstrated when he was overthrown in a coup in 2002, only to return to power when the country erupted in rebellion. That rebellion was rooted in many things—popular hatred of the elites in one of the most unequal countries in the hemisphere, a sense that Venezuela's oil wealth had too long been steered towards the oligarchy, and a sense that the crowd was the only defense that Chávez had against powerful interests—but as much as anything else, it was a product of the fact that Chávez delivered the goods. Social spending increased in Venezuela from 11.3 percent of GDP in 1998 to 22.8 percent of GDP in 2011. This contributed to a significant drop in inequality. Poverty and extreme poverty, after peaking at 62.1 percent and 29.8 percent in 2003, declined steadily until his death in 2013.

In the Argentine case, the riots began when the government of President Fernando de la Rúa decided to confiscate two thirds of the value of all Argentine bank accounts (the *corralito*) in order to deal with a fiscal crisis brought on, at least in part, by a decade long practice of pegging the national currency to the dollar. Isolated in the Casa Rosada with the country spinning out of control, de la Rúa was forced to flee by helicopter in late 2001, leaving the presidency to pass through several hands until Eduardo Duhalde (who had lost the previous election to de la Rúa) took over in early 2002. Duhalde served until 2003, but his continued insistence on carrying out de la Rúa's reforms paved the way for the former leftist guerrilla Néstor Kirchner to be elected in 2003. Along with his wife (and later president) Cristina Fernández de Kirchner, President Kirchner took a much more radical path than the technocrat left trod elsewhere in the region. Like Chávez, whose financial aid was critical to the Kirchners (Chávez purchased $4.5 billion in Argentine debt, helping Argentina escape the clutches of the IMF), they won allies at home and in the international left through their willingness to challenge neoliberal orthodoxy, to limit the power of big business, and to defy the IMF.

Nowhere was the connection between popular mobilization and radical political shifts more evident than in Bolivia. Here, a series of conflicts over natural gas and water profoundly destabilized the political system between 2000 and 2005. Bolivians got their first real taste of the insurgent power of popular groups during a conflict over rate increases implemented by the foreign owned water utility Aguas de Tunari in Cochabamba in April 2000. Though protests against the rate increases were first organized by middle-class residents of the city, the protestors chose a target and developed a symbolic repertoire that struck a nerve in the surrounding valley. The image of a foreign company making excessive profits from something that was so essential to life—so impregnated with symbolic importance— provided a powerful rallying cry. Thousands from around the region joined the protest, setting up roadblocks that brought life in the valley to a standstill. Aguas de Tunari was quickly forced to capitulate.

After Cochabamba, roadblocks rapidly emerged as a key currency in Bolivian politics. Often organized by members of the *Confederación Sindical Unica de Trabajadores Campesinos de Bolivia* (Bolivian Confederation of Rural Workers—CSUTCB), roadblocks paralyzed La Paz from June to September 2001 during protests over a variety of government policies. More followed between January and April 2002 after the government outlawed the sale of coca grown in the Chapare region. In February 2003, when the government increased income and gasoline taxes at the behest of the IMF, the government faced not only renewed roadblocks, but a police mutiny and riots that left thirty-two people dead. None of this however, would compare to the Gas War of September 2003.

Bolivian natural gas production skyrocketed in the early 2000s, largely because of a government policy to privatize the country's gas fields and invite foreign investment.

During this time, many economists, government officials, and businessmen argued that Bolivia should begin to export its gas to the United States, where liquefied gas extracted in Bolivia could fetch four times the price it received in Brazil or Argentina (the country's two largest export markets). In 2001, a consortium made up of Repsol-YPF, British Gas, and BP/Bridas announced plans to export 168 million cubic meters of gas in liquid form over twenty years to North America. In 2002 President Jorge Quiroga signaled his approval of the plan, which called for private interests to build a pipeline to Mejillones in Chile at a cost of $6 billion, where gas would be liquefied and shipped. Investors argued that this was the most cost effective and thus most profitable way to ship the gas to the U.S. market. The only drawback was that in order to do this, the Bolivian gas had to be shipped to Chile.

This was a hard sell in Bolivia. Chile was the country that had stolen Bolivia's access to the sea, albeit more than a century earlier. Bolivians generally view this loss as one of the great tragedies in their history, and as a source of many of the problems that have haunted them ever since. What was more, that gas would leave the country in unprocessed form, and all the benefits associated with processing the gas into liquid form, or adding further value, would accrue to foreigners (many of whom would be Chilean). By 2003 the vast majority of Bolivians favored nationalization of the gas industry in order to ensure that its principle benefits fell into Bolivian hands.

Protesters took to the streets of Cochabamba and La Paz in September 2003, demanding that the government defend gas as a national patrimony. The following day police killed six Aymara-speaking protesters in the town of Warisata, leading to further protests and eventually a general strike on September 29. Roadblocks went up across the country.

The most important roadblocks went up in El Alto, the poor city that rises above La Paz, whose 900,000 residents makes it larger than the capital. El Alto is deeply linked to La Paz; each day 100,000 people travel between the two cities, mostly for work. It is also the home of the gas refineries that keep its sister city running, the critical highways that lead to the capital, and to the international airport, but these structural linkages betray a stratified geography. Above la Ceja (the marker between the two cities) the city is self-identified as Aymara, below lie the *criollos*, and to cross the line is to enter a world where outsiders feel unwelcome. These distinctions gave a distinctly racial tone to the protests. The Gas War, like the Water War before it, seemed to pit a long oppressed indigenous majority in Bolivia against a white and *mestizo* elite.

El Alto was able to suffocate La Paz in early October 2003, evoking long dormant fears of race war in Bolivia among residents of the capital. Facing severe fuel and food shortages in the capital, on October 12 President Gonzalo Sánchez de Lozada declared martial law in El Alto. Violent clashes in the aftermath of the decree left sixteen dead, and the government in an untenable position. On October 13 he suspended the gas project. A few days later Sánchez resigned and left the country, leaving Vice President Carlos Mesa in power. This assured a truce, but at a cost of sixty-three lives. Mesa did not fare much better, as protests and roadblocks became an everyday occurrence. Facing strikes from *cocaleros*, peasants, miners, indigenous rights activists, and others, he resigned in June 2005.

With the country in what seemed like a constant state of popular insurrection, Bolivia needed a leader who could answer popular grievances and restore some semblance of

Figure 11.3 El Alto road block
Source: Reuters/David Mercado

order. The task fell to Evo Morales, a former coca grower from the Chapare region and one of the leaders of the insurrections. Morales managed to insinuate himself at the lead of the protest movement by evoking his indigenous origins (true, Morales was reputed to speak only Spanish, but he was as close to being indigenous as any president in Bolivian history) and promising a twenty-first-century version of socialism. In December 2005 he was elected president with 53.7 percent of the popular vote. His party, the *Moviemiento al Socialismo* (Movement towards Socialism, MAS), won a majority in the congress.

Morales immediately decreed a new hydrocarbons law that substantially increased the taxes and royalties charged to foreign companies, and established Bolivian ownership over the fields. On May 1, 2006 (Labor Day in the socialist world), soldiers accompanied by Morales occupied the gas fields, while MAS operatives hung banners from refineries and gas stations around the country proclaiming the fields the "property of the Bolivian people." In December 2007, he proposed a new constitution, which granted indigenous peoples greater political, cultural, and legal autonomy. The new constitution also promised a major land reform, outlawing estates of larger than 5,000 hectares. It was passed by national referendum in January 2009, with 61.43 percent of the vote.

Figure 11.4   Marchers from El Alto

Source: AP Photo/Dado Galdieri

and Loyalty

Morales, the Kirchners, and Hugo Chávez built political machines in deeply divided societies in part by attacking their enemies (sometimes with dubious legal means) and in part by rewarding their friends. Attacks on one's foes can have the effect of generating loyalty among ones supporters, but it is rarely enough. All three needed to provide specific benefits to their supporters in the form of government programs, improved access to goods and services, and the promise of a more egalitarian society at some point in the future. In societies with long histories of authoritarian right-wing rule, it is often the case that one can deliver these things imperfectly, but at a certain point charisma and promises of a better future need to be met with concrete results, or those who helped you get into power will try to push you over the brink, as recent protests in Brazil over bus fare increases and government corruption can attest.[7] And yet even in relatively good times loyalty can be elusive. Since the late 1990s the region as a whole has seen stable economic growth, reductions in inequality, and regular democratic elections, but this has not produced the sorts of political quiescence we might have expected.

Before going further, it is worth noting a few salient details. On a rhetorical level, Latin America seems sharply divided between left and right. From the outside, it can appear that left-wing regimes (e.g., Venezuela, Bolivia, Brazil, and Ecuador) focus on poverty reduction, while right-wing regimes (e.g., Colombia, Chile, and Mexico) focus on promoting economic growth. In practice however, the differences are not so great. Across the region, governments of the left and right have devoted significant resources to reducing extreme poverty since the 1980s. In 1980, for example, 40 percent of Latin Americans were poor, while 18.6 percent were indigent poor. By 2011, however, 30.4 percent were poor, and 12.8 percent were indigent poor.[8] In 2011 the working poor earned more than they did a generation earlier, had lower fertility rates, and better access to healthcare, food, and education. At the same time inequality has narrowed, with the GINI coefficient (which measures inequality) decreasing across the region at a rate averaging 1 percent per year during the past decade (the only country where inequality increased in recent years is Guatemala). The GINI coefficient fell at approximately the same rate in Mexico (ruled by the right-wing PAN) and Venezuela.

The public sector remains significant in all countries in the region, as does the private sector. Even Cuba has recently embraced limited private sector openings, and private enterprise has in fact grown at a more rapid rate than the public sector in Chávez' (and Nicolás Maduro's) Venezuela and Morales' Bolivia. Furthermore, across the region the forces of globalization have been at work for decades. Fiscal prudence—that is, policies that are designed to maintain low rates of inflation, maintain stable currencies, and make a broad array of products available to consumers of all classes—is a high priority in every country in the region. Almost every country in Latin America today welcomes foreign investment, has opened up its markets to trade and international competition, and has privileged an export sector that seems to offer the best opportunity available for economic growth.

Latin America as a whole began a period of sustained economic growth in the late 1990s that, except for a brief dip at the beginning of the global financial crisis in 2008, continued into 2013. Even amidst continuing global economic turmoil in 2010–2011, GDP growth in the region averaged nearly 5 percent, and left-wing regimes performed no worse overall than those on the right. The simplest explanation for this growth is that the region as a whole entered a commodity boom in the early 2000s, driven largely by growing Asian demand for the minerals, hydrocarbons, and a variety of cash crops grown in the region. Proponents of mining and other extractive industries promise that, with another decade of robust growth, these economic sectors could eradicate extreme poverty in Latin America.

Politicians on the left and right understand the risks of a heavy reliance on commodity exports. They can cause inflation, distort local economies, and the results can be disastrous if global demand dries up. They pursue these policies because they see few other alternatives. This indeed is why Evo Morales, Ecuadoran President Rafael Correa (elected in 2006), and Peruvian President Ollanta Humala (elected 2011) have each pursued mining projects in spite of promises they made to their indigenous constituents. Although the Peruvian, Ecuadoran, and Bolivian states have passed laws that call for mining projects to respect the rights of indigenous peoples and of nature, each has opted to privilege economic development and its potential to lift individuals out of extreme poverty over the more abstract (if no less real) imperative to save the planet. In Peru, opposition to the U.S. owned Newmont Corporation's $5 billion Minas Conga project in Cajamarca resulted in the imposition of a state of emergency in the region, scores of deaths, and broader accusations that the local indigenous opponents of the mine are somehow primitive savages or "extremists" who stand in the way of progress. This in turn prompted the government to water down the laws that called for effective consultation with indigenous communities in the granting of mining concessions by excluding Quechua-speaking communities in the Andes from protection under the law.

In Ecuador, President Correa has issued permits for several large-scale mining projects, in some instances ignoring laws he signed. After the government signed an agreement with the Chinese-Canadian company Ecuacorriente for the Mirador Project in the El Condor mountain range in early 2012, the *Confederacion de Nacionalidades Indígenas del Ecuador* (Confederation of Indigenous Nationalities of Ecuador, CONAIE) organized a fifteen-day, 700-kilometer "March for Water, Life and Dignity." Correa, like Humala in Peru, is inclined to criminalize these protestors, and regularly reminds them that a majority of Ecuadorans stand behind his pro-mining agenda.

The nature of these mining conflicts reminds us that the landscape of political loyalties in Latin America has shifted rather dramatically in recent years. Humala and Correa were elected based upon their claim to represent a popular voice, and indigenous peoples in particular. Like Morales, who has faced his own conflicts with erstwhile indigenous allies over plans to construct a 182-mile highway through the *Isiboro Sécure National Park and Indigenous Territory (TIPNIS)*, in 2011, they have had more trouble maintaining those coalitions than they anticipated. Presidents on the left are increasingly aware that they cannot assume that they command the loyalty of their presumed constituencies. In part this reflects their need to deliver the goods (as President Dilma Rousseff of Brazil failed to do in 2013), and in part it speaks to the emergence of new constituencies whose primary loyalties lie elsewhere.

The most pronounced of those new constituencies are indigenous peoples. Indigenous forms of attachment have a history that dates back thousands of years, though the recent politicization of indigeneity in Latin America dates to the 1960s. In 1969, when the International Labor Organization signed Convention 169 in Barbados, most Latin American nations agreed in principle to the right of indigenous self-determination. At the time it was a cheap commitment, as there were very few communities in the region that openly advocated for these sorts of rights. Over the following decades however, while the rights of peasants, workers, and the poor were whittled away by states that had abandoned their commitment to social welfare, indigenous rights became one of the most salient political languages in the Americas.

In almost every country in the region, the lost decade of the 1980s saw the emergence of newly assertive indigenous rights movements, whose leaders insisted that long histories of colonialism and discrimination justified their claims to autonomy from the nation states within which they were embedded. Self-determination included the right to practice customary law (*usos y costumbres*), to choose their own leaders, to settle disputes according to their own mechanisms, to educate their children in their own languages, and to openly practice their own religions. Indigenous leaders have also demanded that their territorial rights be respected, and generally insisted that they (and not the state) owned the subsoil (the mineral, and particularly hydrocarbon wealth) of the lands they occupied.

The indigenous right to autonomy has been recognized in many countries in the region in recent years, though without specifically interrogating the legal definitions of autonomy it is difficult to know what it means.[9] In Mexico, self-determination, as codified into law in 2001, is little more than a promise of tutelage from the state. The steps taken in Bolivia and

Ecuador have been more radical. Bolivia has promised indigenous communities territorial and legal autonomy, creating the basis of a parallel judicial system, though the constitution reserves subsoil rights for the state. Ecuador's 2008 constitution also promised limited autonomy to Ecuador's indigenous peoples, granting them some territorial, cultural, and political rights, while again reserving the subsoil in their territories as the national patrimony. The constitution did however include provisions that invested nature (*Pacha Mama*) with rights of its own, and in the years since indigenous and environmental activists have repeatedly sought to use this provision to slow the growth of mining in the Ecuadoran Andes and Amazon. Part transnational environmentalist fantasy and part the product of a long history of deep engagement with the land, claims about the rights of nature (indeed, loyalty to nature) resonate broadly because of the ways that a reconceptualization of nature and its attendant claims (some activists also call for the embrace of *buen vivir*, or good living, a concept that calls for living more harmoniously with nature) speak to global concerns about climate change and the unsustainability of development models that continue to expand humanity's carbon footprint. The destruction of indigenous communities to make way for gold, silver, copper, and other mines thus reminds us of the larger destructive force of mining, which acts as the starting point in global commodity chains that leave in their wake poverty and inequality, poisoned rivers, air, and soil, and a planet that is increasingly out of balance.

Thirty years ago the suggestion that loyalty to mother nature might supersede loyalty to the state would have produced gales of laughter. Today, it does not seem quite so far-fetched. Latin American states have not been able to recapture the broad complaisance of their citizens in the aftermath of the dirty wars, economic crises, and the neoliberal era. The dreams of an earlier era—of national unity, stability, and loyalty—do not quite fit in a present where loyalties proliferate. Correa may want to remind the CONAIE that a majority of Ecuadorans want the mines. It is just not clear that the CONAIE cares what a majority of Ecuadorans want. They owe no loyalty to that polity. And if, indeed, they are loyal to mother nature, we all might be the better for it.

The Documents: The Lago Agrio Case

Conflicts over extractive industries play out in various settings over a long period of time. In the first instance, they pit governments wanting economic development and deep-pocketed multinationals against environmental activists and locals who want to slow or stop the projects. Once projects begin, the battles often focus on the division of royalties, on how best to mitigate environmental and other impacts, and on efforts to deal with the forms of violence that tend to populate the margins of these projects. In the last instance, the struggle is over what happens once the site is exhausted, and the multinational moves on. At this time, truths that were once hidden start to become more obvious. Outside experts begin to test the wells. The long-term health impacts of extraction on the local flora, fauna, and people become increasingly evident. Faced with charges that they hid the true environmental costs of their projects, some companies disappear into a labyrinth of mergers, acquisitions, and bankruptcies. Others, especially those that have longer-term plans in country, opt to negotiate some form of remediation, or produce their own expert reports that deny local claims. Lawsuits ensue; lawsuits that while once fruitless because of business friendly courts in Latin America, have in recent years become increasingly globalized. Today, plaintiffs and activists endeavor to match the reach of their adversaries with a globalized reach of their own.

The first of these global legal battles began with a lawsuit filed in New York State in 1993. In the suit, representatives of 30,000 residents of the province of Sucumbíos in Ecuador accused the Texaco Corporation of creating an environmental disaster in their region while working there between the 1960s and 1990s. They accused the company of failing to follow the most basic safety standards, of dumping toxic wastewater into unlined pits, of polluting the local water supply, of leaving the local soil poisonous and thus unsuited for agriculture, and of poisoning the local population. Texaco was also accused of fraudulent practices, of relying on a friendly government in Ecuador to falsify reports, to undertake shoddy remediation, and to simply cover up their behavior. Knowing they were unlikely to get a fair trial in Ecuador, where the government was friendly to the United States and to Texaco, they opted to take their claims to the New York, where they believed a fair trial was more likely. Here they also hoped to get support from a public that would be outraged to learn of Texaco's behavior.

The trial dragged on in New York for eight years, until in 2001 Texaco (now part of Chevron) convinced the New York judge hearing the proceedings that the case ought to be heard in Ecuador because, contrary to the plaintiff's claims, a fair trial could be had there. In the new trial in the city of Lago Agrio (the capital of Sucumbíos), Chevron again fought bitterly, delaying the trial as much as it could in order to build a case against the plaintiffs. This time however, their stalling tactics backfired. When in 2007 Rafael Correa assumed the presidency, what had once been a political and judicial environment very friendly to Chevron became a setting favorable to the plaintiffs. When the judge in the case finally ruled in February 2011, he awarded the plaintiffs $8.6 billion U.S., with the promise to more than double the award if Chevron refused to apologize for its actions.

Chevron immediately fought back, appealing the case in Ecuador. Meanwhile the plaintiffs, with the support of the Ecuadoran State, began an effort to freeze Chevron's assets in several countries, including Canada, Argentina, Brazil, and Colombia. This time it was Chevron who turned to the U.S. courts, asking Judge Lewis A. Kaplan in New York to place an injunction against Ecuador seeking these damages. Kaplan granted the injunction, which was later overturned. In the meantime, the legal wrangling on an international scale continued, and in February 2013 the United Nations Commission on International Trade Law (UNCITRAL) ruled against Ecuador in the Chevron case, concluding that the verdict violated previous agreements releasing the company from future liabilities. The court in Lago Agrio disagrees, insisting that the agreements freeing Chevron of liability concerned only future claims made by the Ecuadoran state, and not private citizens.

By late 2013, the case devolved into a series of claims and counter claims about intimidation and judicial malfeasance. In a New York courtroom Chevron leveled claims that the plaintiffs bribed two Ecuadoran judges in the case (Alberto Guerra and Nicolas Zambrano), and backed up those bribes with threats of violence should the rulings go against them. In late October 2013, Guerra offered corroborating testimony in New York supporting Chevron. He indicated that Zambrano had been promised $500,000 out of any settlement. Steven Donzinger (who Chevron accuses of racketeering) shot back, claiming that Guerra had been paid $326,000 by Chevron for his testimony. Guerra countered by insisting that while the company was paying him, it was not for his testimony.

At this point relatively few things are clear. We can be certain that Ecuador has a weak judiciary, which Chevron counted on when it applied to move the case there. Second, it seems clear that neither the plaintiffs nor the defendants have entirely clean hands; that what we see in the current litigation is the result of shifting political climates that created opportunities for the plaintiffs to wield their influence at the expense of Chevron. At the very least, it seems likely that portions of the ruling excerpted below were ghost written by individuals associated with the plaintiffs.

In the effort to measure right versus wrong, this seems not that much different from Chevron's venue shopping—a practice that has now led Chevron to shop for a favorable ruling in Judge Kaplan's court. U.S. law will favor Chevron. It will be exceptionally difficult for the plaintiffs to demonstrate to the U.S. standard that their verdict in Ecuador was just, and Kaplan has been inclined to come to the aid of Chevron in the past. Corporate power works through the law. In the U.S., through codified practices that favor the wealthy. Physical bribes are rare, and when exposed are a source of scandal. By contrast, the Ecuadoran system has been historically characterized by much more naked influence peddling. Lawyers for Chevron knew that when they first applied to move the case. And they use that now when they attempt to discredit the verdict.

That said, the courts are merely one venue in which this case is being heard, and given the way they work, perhaps not the most important venue. The Lago Agrio verdict, the content of it, and the global nature of the battle around it may result in short term victories for Chevron, and will likely never lead to a single cent being paid—except to the lawyers (Chevron has spent more than $2 billion in legal fees and hired 2,000 lawyers to work on this case). More important is the way it speaks to the shifting terrain over which environmental, indigenous, and poor peoples' rights are contested. In spite of Chevron's protests, a significant percentage, perhaps even a majority of Latin Americans (and U.S. citizens, for that matter) are more likely to believe the findings of the Lago Agrio court than the rulings by Judge Kaplan. Within the United States itself a series of rulings (e.g., Bush v. Gore, Citizens United) have undermined public faith in the judicial system to an unprecedented degree in recent times. Tens of millions of Americans have come to believe that the U.S. court system, like their political system, has been captured by corporate interests and is no longer an impartial arbiter of the social order. Latin Americans have long believed similar things about their own political systems, though the Lago Agrio case reminds us that new actors are increasingly capturing the levers of power. The new left, indigenous activists, and a global network of sympathizers have found new avenues to empowerment, and are exploiting them in ways that terrify entrenched interests.

The documents below speak to the competing claims to power that animate this conflict. Document 11.1, which is an excerpt from the summary of the judge's decision in the Lago Agrio trial prepared by the plaintiff's lawyers (the original decision ran to nearly 200 pages), details many of the bases on which the judgment was rendered. Interestingly, it does not represent a complete whitewash for the plaintiff's claims, but is instead a detailed effort to weigh various pieces of testimony and evidence against one another. Document 11.2, which is an excerpt from the injunction that Judge Kaplan granted to Chevron in March 2011, is interesting not because of his interpretation of the law which binds his decision (it would seem he was wrong) but because of the way he reads the larger issues of the trial in Ecuador. What we have here, then, are two profoundly different interpretations of the same evidence.

Court transcripts (in this case, two rulings) are one of the types of historical records from which historians must construct their stories of the past. Although most are not as diametrically opposed as these two, they invariably represent partial renderings, colored by the lenses through which their narrators experienced the events described therein. Documents like these do not really give us an opportunity to know the truth. These contradictory renderings suggest that there is more than one truth, and both sides in this conflict can be fairly accused of opting for the truth that favors their views. This provides the reader with an opportunity to think about both text and context, about the way that each document works to produce a particular version of events, and of the ways that each document speaks to the values and interests of its author. We have here an opportunity to see an Ecuadoran court that is the product of a particular history, of a political opening that was unexpected by Chevron's lawyers. We also see a U.S. court that is the product of its own particular history and values. Chevron specifically sought out Judge Kaplan for the injunction because they believed he was likely to grant it.

This reminds us that what we need to look for in these documents is not so much truth, but power. We need to see where power lies, geographically speaking, and how that power authorizes itself. Ecuadorans will not be surprised to learn that kickbacks were promised to a judge. Neither will most North Americans. Those expressing indignation, those who in turn decide that their sympathies lie with Chevron rather than the plaintiffs, will do so through their own ideological lens. Similarly, those who claim it does not matter, and that the original Lago Agrio ruling should stand because Chevron has done as much wrong as Donziger, are making their own ideological statement. On the other hand, if we instead recognize that both sides have had the power to generate spatially restricted truths (one in an Ecuadoran courtroom, and one in a New York courtroom), and that the truths generated by each side find powerful adherents in both Latin America and the United States, we begin to understand something about the changed geopolitical landscape that characterizes Latin America in the early twenty-first century. U.S. power, which was never absolute, faces more challenges from more actors in the region than it has since the "American Century" began. Some fear that the decline of U.S. influence will simply be accompanied by rising Chinese power. The Lago Agrio case suggests an alternative narrative, where the forms of influence and domination that elites and outsiders once relied on (in this case the judicial system) are being challenged and reshaped by the millions who have not shared in the bounties of globalization.

In 1993, the plaintiffs in the case faced a world where there was little or no possibility of justice in their home country, so they and their lawyers chose to take their struggle to the United States. It was something of a legal Hail Mary, an effort that was as much theater as it was legal process, and it yielded ambiguous results. As legal process, the case reinforced the power of global capital. As theater, it introduced millions across the planet to the plight of those affected by Texaco's years in Ecuador. It also mobilized a global network of activists, who have launched similar claims in other regions. The protestors who today confront mining companies in Mexico, Peru, Guatemala, Chile and elsewhere, and who have used the legal process successfully in several Latin American countries (in July 2013 the members of a Diaguita community in Chile won a major victory against the Canadian company

Barrick Gold over contamination of their water resources[10]), do so in light of the history of this conflict. Although they may never collect their award, the plaintiffs in this case have changed the landscape of environmental and indigenous protest in Latin America. Future Texaco's are well aware that they cannot act as they did in the past.

Document 11.1 Summary of Judgment & Order of Superior Court of Nueva Loja, *Aguinda v. ChevronTexaco*, No. 2003–0002, February 14, 2011 (prepared by plaintiffs' U.S. counsel detailing judicial order finding Chevron liable . . . and ordering the company to pay damages of approximately $9.5 billion, with potential punitive damages of an additional $9.5 billion)

On February 14, 2011, after approximately eight years of litigation in Ecuador, Judge Nicolas Zambrano Lozada, the Presiding Judge of the Provincial Court of Justice of Sucumbíos, rendered judgment in the form of a 188-page opinion. Judge Zambrano ultimately found Chevron liable for approximately $8.6 billion in damages (primarily for remediation of contaminated soils), awarded ten percent of that amount to the entity representing the Plaintiffs (by operation of law), and would grant an additional, punitive award amounting to 100% of the base judgment, which Chevron could avoid by publicly recognizing its misconduct in a measure of moral redress.

The majority of the opinion is devoted to identifying and analyzing the vast quantities of scientific and other evidence of damages in a court record exceeding 200,000 pages. Below, we summarize the most pertinent aspects of Judge Zambrano's opinion, including: (1) the Court's assessment of Chevron's liability for environmental contamination of the former Napo Concession area and the effects flowing therefrom; (2) the Court's observations concerning Chevron's procedural misconduct throughout the trial; (3) the Court's analysis of Chevron's legal defenses to liability; and (4) the Court's handling of the parties' mutual allegations of fraud and manipulation.

I. CHEVRON'S LIABILITY

Texaco's Substandard and Unlawful Practices. The Court observed that the essence of Texaco's conduct itself was not really in dispute—Chevron representative Rodrigo Pérez Pallares had admitted in a letter to a popular Ecuadorian magazine that Texaco dumped approximately 16 billion gallons of "production water"—water containing PTEX, TPH, and polycyclic hydrocarbons—directly into the surface waters between 1972 and 1990. (113[11]) It also was undisputed that Texaco had dumped oil waste into unlined pits that were merely shallow excavations in the ground—Chevron's experts simply argued that this was "common practice" for the times. (159) Testimony from former Texaco workers indicated that "all of the mud would come out and the pit would spill oil towards the estuary. There was no water wall, there wasn't anything; they did not put a membrane, anything." (167)

The Court assessed Chevron's fault from both an objective and a subjective perspective; the former asking whether the generic "reasonable oil company" would have acted in the same manner, the latter asking whether Texaco—with its particular knowledge set as evidenced in the record—was acting reasonably in light of that subjective knowledge. (81) The Court took note of a book entered into the record entitled "Primer on Oil and Gas Production" published by the American Oil Institute in 1962. (81–82) The Court—expressly skeptical of both parties' experts in light of their diametrically opposing interpretations of the same set of facts with respect to virtually every topic in the case—emphasized the reliability of the publication due to the source, and the fact that it was published long before the litigation ever came about. (81) As an objective matter, the Court noted that as early as 1962, the industry was aware that "[e]xtreme care should be employed to handle and disposition of the produced water not only because of the possible damage to agriculture, but also because of the possibility of contaminating lakes and rivers that hold drinking water as well as water for irrigation." (81) . . . the Court concluded that Texaco had the means, but not the will, to employ safer but perhaps more expensive methods. (162–164) With respect to the use of unlined pits, the Court found that the historical texts also undermined Chevron's assertion that this method was "common practice." (161) The Court also cited to correspondence between Texaco officials demonstrating that they were aware of the problems with unlined pits, but decided to continue using them because they were "efficient and profitable," and the alternative would be too expensive. (161–162)

In assessing the reasonableness of Texaco's practices, the Court also engaged in a detailed analysis of the laws in force during the time of Texaco's operations in Ecuador. (61–71) The Court found that Texaco violated multiple provisions of Ecuadorian law, including *inter alia:* the Health Code of 1971, the Water Law of 1972, and the Regulation of Hydrocarbon Operations Law of 1987. (62–64, 70) The Court took note of the fact that the laws applicable at the time broadly prohibited the infliction of *any* environmental harm; but at the time, there was an absence of regulations that specifically established tolerable "parameters." (66, 70) Nonetheless, the Court rejected Chevron's argument that a lack of regulations to animate the many blanket prohibitions on pollution found in the law somehow excused Texaco from the obligation to comply with the law. (71) The Court found that Chevron was well aware that its operations fell short of legal mandates—the record evidence demonstrated that Texaco had incurred several penalties over the course of its operations. (71)

In addition to the applicable laws and standards of the day, the Court also assessed Texaco's conduct in view of the requirements of its concession contract, which allowed Texaco to exploit the waters of the Napo Concession "without depriving the towns of the water volume that is indispensable for them for their domestic and irrigable necessities, neither making difficult the navigation, nor taking the drinkable and purity qualities of the waters, nor preventing fishing." (62) On a related note, the Court also rejected Chevron's argument that it could not be held liable for negligent conduct where that conduct occurred under the presumed auspices of State authority—the Court found that there was "no legal authority nor jurisprudence" to support the notion that an "administrative authorization" of some sort would defeat the rights of third-party claimants. (78) Indeed, the Court noted that where Texaco incurred administrative penalties, those penalties were doled out with the express reservation that they would not adversely affect the rights of potential third-party claimants. (79)

In sum, the Court concluded that Texaco's "system was designed to discharge waste to the environment in a cost-effective way, but did not correctly address the risks of damages." (166) The Court further opined that the damage was "not only foreseeable, but also avoidable. Thus being the case, and since the duty is legally demandable from Texpet to prevent such damage under the historic legislation in effect in the era in which it operated the Consortium, in the opinion of this Presidency the acts of the defendant are clearly a conduct amounting to gross negligence." (175) . . .

Based on the record evidence and the economic criteria largely proposed by expert Gerardo Barros, a court-appointed expert sponsored by Chevron, the Court concluded that an award of approximately $5.4 billion and $600 million would be appropriate for the remediation of soil and groundwater contamination, respectively. (177–181) While the Court rejected the majority of Plaintiffs' claim for ecological damages, with respect to the restoration of native flora and fauna, the Court awarded $200 million. The Court also found that an award of $150 million dollars would be sufficient to effect the delivery of potable water to the residents of the Concession area. (183) The Court noted that damages can be assessed not only for past and present damage, but also for damage that is reasonably foreseeable "according to the circumstances of the case and the experiences of life." (76) On the issue of the impact of Texaco's operations on human health, the Court conducted an extensive survey of the many health studies in the record evidencing a range of health problems engendered by petroleum operations. (126–234) The Court observed that Chevron's experts tended to attack these studies based on their inability to firmly establish cause-effect relationships, notwithstanding the fact that these studies explicitly disclaimed that they did not purport to conclude such a relationship existed. (135) It would be up to the Court to determine whether the "association" evidenced in the studies would amount to sufficient legal causation. (136) To reach its ultimate conclusion, the Court also relied on numerous surveys and interviews of Concession area residents conducted in the context of the judicial site inspections. (139–143) The Court recognized that such evidence certainly does not constitute "incontrovertible proof," but it was nonetheless persuasive in light of the "impressive coincidence between the facts described by all of these declarations," and the lack of any countervailing testimony. (144) The Court also assessed human health impacts by way of a risk assessment method, as suggested by Chevron's counsel. (145–146). Ultimately, the Court found that there was a "reasonable medical probability" that the health problem experienced by persons in the Concession area had been caused by oil-related contamination. (170–171) The Court awarded $1.4 billion reflective of the need to augment the healthcare system to respond to health issues—with the exception of cancer, addressed separately—engendered by exposure to oil-related contamination. (183)

Cultural Impacts. The Court recognized that conduct such as that engaged in by Texaco can have "particularly severe consequences in cases that affect the ecosystem where groups whose cultural integrity is strongly associated with the health of the territory live, as the environmental degradation can potentially threaten the very existence of the group." (147) In order to assess impacts on the affected communities' way of life, the Court reviewed, among other things, interviews taken in the context of the judicial inspections. (147–151). Ultimately, the Court rejected most of Plaintiffs' bases for cultural damages—the Court did not find that there was a valid "loss of land" claim and did not agree that Plaintiffs could recover for loss of culture engendered through contact with Texaco workers. (152, 154). The Court agreed, however, that forced displacement due to the damage to rivers and soils caused by Texaco's oil extraction operations caused real and recoverable damage to the indigenous communities' way of life. (153) The Court awarded $100 million to execute community rebuilding and ethnic reaffirmation programs within the affected communities. (183)

Cancer. The Court rejected the Plaintiffs' request for damages up to approximately $70 billion to address past and future excess cancer deaths in the affected area resulting from oil-related contamination, noting a lack of specificity in the demand as to particular cases. (184) Nonetheless, the Court found ample evidence in the record from which to conclude that cancer is a serious oil-related health problem in the Napo Concession area, warranting supplementation of the Court's general healthcare award in the amount of $800 million. (184)

Punitive Damages. The Plaintiffs sought up to $40 billion in the form of an unjust enrichment award, in order to disgorge Chevron of its ill-gotten gains and to assure that polluting and remediating only if "caught" becomes a less attractive option than simply acting as a responsible corporate citizen in the first instance. Although the Court rejected Plaintiffs' unjust enrichment claim, the Court nonetheless recognized the need to assure that Chevron and others would be dissuaded from engaging in similar misconduct—both in terms of the underlying pollution and the unethical behavior displayed by Chevron throughout the trial (see Section III, below)—in the future. (185) The Court also recognized Chevron's failure to treat the Plaintiffs with a modicum of human dignity (e.g., portraying them as scoundrels, denying their *existence*, and vowing to litigate against them until the end of time), further warranting the imposition of punitive damages. (185) Thus, in consideration of the grave and willing nature of Chevron's offenses and the shocking nature of its procedural misconduct (among other factors), the Court assessed punitive damages in the amount of 100% of the remedial damages. (185) Nonetheless, Chevron was given the option to avoid punitive damages altogether by issuing a public apology to the Plaintiffs, "a symbolic measure of moral redress" recognized by the inter-American Court of Human Rights. (186)

II. CHEVRON'S PROCEDURAL MISCONDUCT THROUGHOUT THE TRIAL

"Unresolved Issues" Raised by Chevron at the Eleventh Hour in an Effort to Delay Resolution of the Case. The Court recognized Chevron's overarching complaint that the Court incorrectly applied the principle of expeditiousness thus preventing Chevron from fully exercising its right to a defense. (35) The Court noted, however, that Chevron's attempts to portray the litigation as a railroading are not supported by the realities of a case "which has lasted almost 8 years and accumulated more than two hundred thousand folios of files." (35) Far from swift justice, the extreme protraction of the case was "not the fault of the judge but [of] the. . .parties who have debated and complicated even the most common aspects of the procedural process." (35) By way of example, the Court noted Chevron's bad faith efforts to delay resolution of the case by "reopening" issues that had been previously resolved by the Court or already abandoned by Chevron. (36)

Addressing Chevron's conduct vis à vis the judicial site inspection process and the reports prepared by the many scientific experts who participated in that process, the Court observed: "the challenges to the different reports have been taken to extremes by the defendant, who has alleged the existence of crucial errors in practically all the expert reports not presented by themselves, showing a lack of objectivity in their arguments which when examined by the judge have failed to . . . [show] . . . errors that might affect the integrity of the reports." (39–43) The Court engaged in an exhaustive analysis of Chevron's many claims of "crucial error," concluding that Chevron's objections to virtually every site inspection report not commissioned by Chevron were *legal* in nature (e.g., the expert did not account for the supposed release of liability secured by Texaco in the mid-1990s), and did not actually speak to the integrity of the inspection data. (40–43) The Court noted that challenges were raised against each and every expert, including the manner by which they were nominated and named. (36) The Court was even asked to appoint a third expert to resolve contradictions between the party experts; and Chevron accused the Court of violating a "procedural contract" to the extent the judge exercised his discretion to modify the site inspection plan to suit the practical realities of the case. (36–38) The Court observed that a third expert for each site was not necessary and would inject undue complication into an already complex process; the 56 judicial inspections with their respective expert reports constituted more than enough evidence to allow the court to render a reasoned decision. (38) The Court concluded that Chevron's many objections to the evidence-gathering process appeared to be designed to "impede the normal advance of the evidence gathering process, or even prolong it indefinitely." (36)

Chevron's Frontal Attacks on the Integrity of the Court. Judge Zambrano lamented the fact that, over the course of the trial, an inordinate amount of the Court's time has been occupied with addressing Chevron's constant attacks on the integrity of the Court. (58) The Court noted that Chevron has repeatedly accused the Court of engaging in a "judicial lynching," despite a lack of any valid basis to challenge the Court's decisions. (58–59) By way of example, the Court referred to the "unfounded and gratuitous" complaint filed by Chevron against then-presiding Judge Germán Yánez Ruiz. (58–59) Chevron accused Judge Yánez of a "lack of integrity" based on his decision to appoint an expert where the parties could not agree to one, notwithstanding that the Judge was statutorily authorized to do just that. (59) Regarding the pervasive nature of Chevron's shocking disrespect for the judicial process, Judge Zambrano observed: "This is not about isolated events . . . [It has] been constant throughout the process and ha[s] been publicly repeated by the spokespersons of the defendant company, reaching the ears of the Judge . . .[These] offences against his judicial competence . . . shall be also considered when passing ruling." (60)

A Pattern of Vexatious Conduct. In summation of Chevron's behavior throughout the course of the litigation, the Court observed that "the following constitutes a display of procedural bad faith on the defendant's part: failure to . . . [produce] . . . documents ordered coupled with a failure to submit an excuse on the date indicated; attempting to abuse the merger between Chevron Corp. and Texaco Inc. as a mechanism to evade liability; abuse of the rights granted under procedural law, such as the right to submit the motions that the law allows for [. . .]; repeated motions on issues already ruled upon, and motions that by operation of law are inadmissible within summary verbal proceedings, and that have all warranted admonishments and fines against defense counsel defendant from the various Judges who have presided over this Court; [and] delays provoked through conduct that in principle is legitimate, but . . . [which have] . . . unfair consequences for the proceedings . . . such as refusing and creating obstacles for payment of the experts who took office, thus preventing them from being able to commence their work. . . ." (184–185) As noted above at Section I, Chevron's course of conduct ultimately factored into the Court's award of punitive damages. (185)

III. CHEVRON'S LEGAL DEFENSES

"Chevron Cannot be Held Liable for the Actions of Texaco.". . . the Court found bad faith in the fact that Chevron intentionally created the impression of a merger in its presentations to the public, but in the context of litigation, denied that any merger had occurred. (12) The Court looked to United States corporate veil-piercing jurisprudence, which has become a model for Ecuadorian law on that issue, and observed that "allowing the right of the victims . . . to disappear because of mere formalities within the merger would be considered by the U.S. courts as 'manifest injustice'." (13, 16) . . .

"Plaintiffs' Claims Were Extinguished by the Release of Liability Granted to Texaco by the Ecuadorian Government in the Mid-1990s." The Court observed that the 1995 and 1998 agreements held out by Chevron as precluding the claims in this case unambiguously contemplate Texaco's release from claims brought by the Republic of Ecuador or by Petroecuador. (32, 34) Furthermore, even if the Release were not so clearly limited on its face to potential claims by the *government*, the Court noted that the release still could not correctly be construed as precluding claims by Ecuadorian citizens. (30–32) The Court found that the peoples' right to bring a claim is fundamental and inviolate, citing the Ecuadorian Constitution as well as multiple human rights conventions. (30–32, 176) The Court observed that Chevron's argument rests on a perversion of the general principle that the government acts in the name of "the people"—entering into a contract with a private company such as Texaco is not the type of fundamental, representative act that could somehow be construed as binding all citizens. (30–31) The Court observed that if the agreements between the government and Texaco actually did purport to release claims held by non-parties to the agreements (i.e., the people of Ecuador), the contracts would be illegal (and presumably unenforceable). (32–33)

"The Case is Invalid Because it is Premised on Ecuador's Environmental Management Act, Which Did Not Exist Until 1999." The Court recognized that under Ecuadorian law, retroactive application of the law—i.e., holding a party liable for conduct that would have been lawful when it occurred—is impermissible as a general rule. (27) However, *procedural* provisions of the law are the exception to the general rule of non-retroactivity—to the extent that a code provision governs process and procedure, it takes effect and supplants the former rule immediately. (27) In this case, the Plaintiffs did not rely on the LGA for a substantive cause of action—the Court observed that strict liability and negligence claims are premised upon the Ecuadorian Civil Code, and Chevron violated a host of environmental laws in existence throughout the period of its operations in Ecuador. (28, 60–70) The subsections of the Environmental Management Act implicated in this case govern: (1) the identity of the Court that will hear claims for damages that are "environmental" in nature (the law dictates that such a case will be tried before the President of the local state court in the jurisdiction where the underlying events occurred); and (2) the nature of the case as a "verbal summary proceeding." (27) The Court found both provisions to be "clearly procedural," and thus applicable notwithstanding the retro-active application of the law. (28) . . .

IV. THE PARTIES' MUTUAL ALLEGATIONS OF FRAUD AND MANIPULATION

The Alleged Falsification of the Report of Plaintiffs' Site Inspection Expert, Charles Calmbacher. The Court reviewed and recognized the deposition testimony of Plaintiffs' expert Charles Calmbacher . . . in which Calmbacher testified that the judicial site inspection reports submitted to the Court by Plaintiffs' counsel on his behalf were not authorized. (48) However, the Court also noted that Calmbacher had "personal issues with the plaintiffs' team due to labor and money issues," and, apparently prior to the rift, Calmbacher had given statements to the press condemning Chevron. (48–49) Although the Plaintiffs had not been given the opportunity to question Calmbacher regarding his apparent personal animus and contradictory public statements, on balance, in light of the seriousness of the allegations and the limited scope of the reports (they related only to two well sites, Sacha 94 and Shushufindi 48), the Court concluded that it would *not* consider the Calmbacher reports in its ruling. (49)

Plaintiffs' Involvement in the Preparation of the Global Damages Assessment Report (the "Cabrera Report"). At the outset of its discussion concerning the Cabrera report, the Court acknowledged that Chevron had filed a "huge number" of motions attacking Mr. Cabrera and the report on every conceivable basis. (49–50) The bulk of the Court's analysis in this regard focused on Chevron's complaint regarding Plaintiffs' level of involvement with the Cabrera Report. (50–51) The Court stated that it had viewed and scrutinized the documents, emails, and video clips submitted by Chevron in relation to the Cabrera Report and Mr. Cabrera's alleged contacts with the Plaintiffs' team. (50) The Court also acknowledged Plaintiffs' challenge to Chevron's video evidence on the grounds that it is deceptively edited and constitutes a fraction of the total video evidence in Chevron's possession. (50) The Court noted that Chevron's evidence regarding the Cabrera Report could not be deemed valid "proof" under Ecuadorian law (submitted, as it was, outside the proof period), and further observed the impropriety of Chevron's demands that the trial be suspended unless and until Chevron deemed its foreign evidence-gathering process complete. (50–51) Nonetheless, the Court recognized the seriousness of Chevron's allegations concerning the Cabrera Report, and—accepting as true Chevron's allegations that it needed more time to gather evidence—that it might be unfair to render a judgment based on the

Cabrera Report. (51) Accordingly, the Court *granted* Chevron's petition to disregard the Cabrera Report. (51)

Alleged Misconduct as Evidenced by Outtakes from the Documentary Film, Crude. The Court noted the tangential nature of any allegations relating to Attorney Steven Donziger—although Mr. Donziger's affiliation with the Plaintiffs' legal team seems clear based upon his public statements, there is nothing in the court record indicative of his participation in the case. (51) The Court took note of Mr. Donziger's "disrespectful statements" captured in the Crude outtakes, but found his utterances to be inconsequential. (51) Moreover, even if the Court were inclined to exercise its authority to judge the conduct of Mr. Donziger, it would not do so without giving him an opportunity to explain his statements—particularly when those statements were presented in the form of "small and limited portions of selected and edited hours of filming." (51–52) Most critically, the Court found that it would be inappropriate to punish the Plaintiffs themselves for any alleged misconduct on the part of Mr. Donziger. (51)

Plaintiffs' Alleged Attempt to "Whitewash" the Cabrera Report through the Submission of Additional Reports in September 2010. On August 2, 2010, then-presiding Judge Ordoñez invited both Chevron and Plaintiffs to file submissions in which the parties could suggest appropriate economic criteria for the assessment of damages. (57–58) Approximately 45 days later, both parties submitted briefing bolstered by reports prepared by American experts; Chevron, however, has accused Plaintiffs and their experts of attempting to deceive the Court through "ideological forgery," covertly disguising the maligned Cabrera Report as the work of another expert who has not been impugned. (57) The Court opined that Chevron's charge of ideological forgery was "reckless [and] without merit." (58) In reaching that conclusion, the Court observed: (1) no one had attempted to pass these reports off as anything more than the work of experts *hired by the Plaintiffs*; these experts were not assistants to the Court, and their reports would not even be treated as true "expert reports" under Ecuadorian law; (2) to the extent that these experts reviewed and relied on work found in the Cabrera Report, that reliance was fully disclosed to the Court; and (3) the Plaintiffs delivered to the Court precisely what it had asked for; Plaintiffs did not purport to deliver anything more than a series of economic reference points to aid the Court in its valuation of the damages evidenced elsewhere in the record—Plaintiffs never claimed that these reports were intended to prove the *existence* of environmental damage. (58)

Notwithstanding the Court's rejection of Chevron's attacks on the reports of Plaintiffs' experts submitted in September 2010, the Court appears to have had little use for these reports in the grand scheme. Of the six reports, the opinion makes *no mention at all* of the reports submitted by experts Dr. Robert Scardina (delivery of potable water), Dr. Daniel Rourke (excess cancer deaths), and Jonathan Shefftz (unjust enrichment); and the report of Carlos Picone (healthcare) is mentioned only where the Court dealt with Chevron's motion to dismiss based on "ideological forgery." In fact, the court did not award *any* damages at all with respect to excess cancer deaths and unjust enrichment. (184–185) Only the reports of Dr. Lawrence Barnthouse (natural resources damages) and Douglas Allen (soil and groundwater remediation) receive substantive mention—but the Court's use of these reports appears to be *de minimis* at best. (180–182) Soil remediation costs account for the majority of the overall damages award—approximately $5.4 billion of it—but the Court *did not rely on Douglas Allen's report to reach that figure;* instead, the court relied on the valuations proposed in the report of Gerrardo Barros, a court-appointed expert who performed work in the case at the request of Chevron. (180–181) Allen's report is mentioned only as a reference point, as the Court noted that its Barros-based valuation is consistent with Allen's general hypothesis that costs will ostensibly double when a more rigorous cleanup standard is adopted. (181) . . .

Document 11.2 UNITED STATES DISTRICT COURT SOUTHERN DISTRICT OF NEW YORK CHEVRON CORPORATION, Plaintiff, against STEVEN DONZIGER et al., Defendants. OPINION, LEWIS A. KAPLAN, District Judge.

. . . A provincial court in Ecuador has entered a multibillion dollar judgment against Chevron Corporation ("Chevron") in an action brought by indigenous peoples in the Amazonian rain forest (the "Lago Agrio Plaintiffs" or "LAPs"). The gravamen of their case is alleged pollution of the rain forest in years ending in 1992 by Texaco, Inc. ("Texaco"), the stock of which Chevron acquired at the end of 2001.

This claim originated in the United States. Three American lawyers began the original litigation in this Court many years ago. After the New York suit was dismissed in 2000 on forum non conveniens grounds, they brought a successor lawsuit on a different legal theory (the "Lago Agrio" case) in Ecuador. The judgment at issue here was entered in that case.

The LAPs' attorneys and other representatives have stated that they intend to seek to collect on that judgment in multiple jurisdictions around the world, including by ex parte attachments, asset seizures, and other means, as promptly as possible, starting before completion of the Ecuadorian appellate process. The purpose of such multiplicitous and burdensome proceedings against a company like Chevron, which would be good for the money if the judgment ultimately stands up, is plain. By their own admissions, it is to exert pressure on Chevron by means of this litigation strategy to force a quick and richer settlement. Chevron contends that the judgment is not enforceable outside Ecuador because the Ecuadorian legal system does not provide impartial tribunals or procedures compatible with the requirements of due process of law, and it was obtained by fraud led in major degree by a New York City lawyer, Steven Donziger, substantial parts of which were conducted in the United States. It brought this case for, among other relief, a declaration that the judgment is not entitled to recognition or enforcement. It now seeks a preliminary injunction principally to bar the enforcement of the judgment outside Ecuador pending the resolution of this case on the merits or, at least, the resolution of its prayer for a declaratory judgment.

This is an extraordinary case. The amount involved is large. Chevron challenges the fairness and integrity of the judicial system of Ecuador and thus implicates considerations of international comity. There are issues concerning the reach of U.S. law and questions pertaining to the conduct of the New York lawyer and others. There are other concerns.

The Court is mindful of the seriousness of each of them and does not act lightly. In the midst of the many "trees" in this vast record, however, sight should not be lost of the forest. Several points must be borne clearly in mind from the outset.

First, a great deal of the evidence of possible misconduct by Mr. Donziger and others, as well as important evidence regarding the unfairness and inadequacies of the Ecuadorian system and proceedings, consists of video recordings of the words of Donziger and others made by a New York documentary film maker, Joseph Berlinger, whom Donziger invited to film activities in relation to the Ecuadorian case and who ultimately released a documentary film about it called Crude. Still more comes from e-mails and other documents between and among Donziger and others working with him that were produced in related cases. Yet neither Donziger nor any of the other key actors has denied Chevron's allegations or attempted here to explain or justify under oath their recorded statements and written admissions. Thus, the record includes uncontradicted and unexplained statements by Donziger and some of his alleged co-conspirators including such highly pertinent comments as this:

"They're all [i.e., the Ecuadorian judges] corrupt! It's—it's their birthright to be corrupt."

Nor was this an offhand remark or a new sentiment on Donziger's part. In a brief filed in this Court in 2000 in an effort to avoid a forum non conveniens dismissal of his earlier case, Donziger stated that Ecuador could not provide an adequate forum and that its judiciary was corrupt.

Second, the submissions made by Donziger and the two LAPs who have appeared by counsel (the "LAP Representatives")—the rest have defaulted—are replete with complaints that there is no hurry here, that the judgment cannot now be enforced under Ecuadorian law, that Donziger should have been given more time to respond to the motion, that the argument of the motion should have been delayed, and the like. As will appear, none of these contentions has merit even considered in isolation. But the details of each of these points should not obscure this overriding fact.

When it heard the preliminary injunction motion, this Court noted that any urgency could be eliminated if the defendants agreed to a temporary order that they maintain the status quo—that is, that no effort would be made to enforce the judgment—for a period sufficient to permit submission of additional papers and deliberation by the Court. The LAP Representatives refused. And while Donziger offered an extension of the temporary restraining order ("TRO") as to himself alone, that offer was essentially illusory because the lack of comparable relief as to the LAPs and some of the other defendants would have left Chevron without the protection that it sought—the LAPs simply could have used lawyers other than Donziger to seek enforcement. Moreover, when Chevron sought a severance and an expedited trial of its claim for a declaration that the judgment is not entitled to recognition or enforcement, the LAP Representatives, after first agreeing, back-pedaled and objected.

Third, it must be borne in mind that this is a preliminary injunction motion. As the Supreme Court has said:

"The purpose of a preliminary injunction is merely to preserve the relative position of the parties until a trial on the merits can be held. Given this limited purpose, and given the haste that is often necessary if those positions are to be preserved, a preliminary injunction is customarily granted on the basis of procedures that are less formal and evidence that is less complete than in a trial on the merits." Moreover, where, as here, the district court concludes that the risk of harm warrants a TRO to maintain the status quo to permit appropriate consideration of whether to issue a preliminary injunction, "Rule 65," in the eloquent words of the late Judge Friendly, "demands such but only such thoroughness as a burdened federal judiciary can reasonably be expected to attain within" the limited period during which the TRO may remain in effect. Fourth, there has been a great deal of posturing on both sides. Chevron, for example, complains of the Ecuadorian legal system and judiciary while the LAPs attempt to make much of the fact that Texaco, years ago, successfully obtained a forum non conveniens dismissal of the first of these cases, arguing among other things that the courts of Ecuador would be an adequate forum. Fair enough. But before rising to the bait on either side, however, it is well to bear in mind that the positions of both sides have changed 180 degrees since the predecessor litigation in New York. Chevron then touted the adequacy of the Ecuadorian judiciary, while the plaintiffs—in briefs bearing Donziger's name as counsel—argued that Ecuador could not provide an adequate forum and that its judiciary was corrupt. Similarly, the LAP Representatives argue that the LAPs are poor, indigenous people of the rain forest who cannot properly be sued in New York. In doing so, however, they utterly ignore the fact that they previously have sued both Texaco and Chevron here, voluntarily participated in still other cases in this Court, are voluntarily litigating in other federal courts around the country, and for years used Donziger and his New York office to mount public relations, political and fund raising efforts in support of their Ecuadorian efforts. So a good deal of the rhetoric and argument in this case on these and other issues must be viewed with a critical eye. The parties here have submitted a large evidentiary record. The facts are essentially undisputed although the same perhaps cannot be said of each of the inferences to be drawn from certain of them. The Court has considered the matter carefully. This is its decision on the motion together with its findings of fact and conclusions of law. . .

While the evidence necessarily is incomplete, the record before the Court indicates the likelihood that (1) the concept of a global assessment by a court appointed expert and the selection in particular of Cabrera was accepted by the Ecuadorian court in order to forestall the filing by the LAPs of a complaint against the judge relating to a "sex for jobs" scandal, (2) Cabrera was not at all independent of the LAPs, as he had been selected, paid some money, and promised future compensation by them if they won, (3) the Cabrera report in fact was planned by Fajardo and other LAP representatives and, at least in substantial part, written by Stratus, (4) at the LAPs' request, Stratus submitted to the court comments on the purported Cabrera report without disclosing that Cabrera in at least major respects was not the author and that much of the report on which they purported to comment had been written by Stratus itself, (5) Cabrera, Fajardo, and the ADF, and others on the LAP side falsely represented to the Lago Agrio court and to the world at large that Cabrera was completely independent, and (6) when the provenance of the Cabrera report came out in the Section 1782 proceedings, the LAPs procured and submitted as new and independent analyses reports from still other consultants who had not visited Ecuador, conducted any site inspections, nor obtained any samples for this purpose, and had relied upon data in the discredited Cabrera report. For purposes of this motion, the Court so finds . . .

Political Influence to Use the Criminal Process Against Former TexPet Lawyers to Extort a Settlement

We have referred previously to the consideration and abandonment in 2006, for lack of evidence, of criminal charges against two of Texaco's (and now Chevron's) attorneys, Pérez and Veiga, who negotiated and signed the Settlement and Final Release.

The Crude outtakes include a brief interview with Donziger on his way to President Correa's January 2007 inauguration, a subject discussed below as it relates to its consequences for the Ecuadorian judiciary. For present purposes, however, it is relevant that Donziger boasted that President Correa's inauguration was a potentially "critical event" for the outcome of the Lago Agrio litigation. Soon thereafter, Donziger explained that the LAPs and the ROE had "been really helping each other" and discussed the importance of working his contacts in the new government. On January 31, 2007, Donziger met with Joseph C. Kohn of Kohn Swift & Graf, P.C., a U.S. law firm providing financial support for the Lago Agrio litigation. He explained to Kohn that the plaintiffs had been working with the Prosecutor General's office and that, although the criminal proceedings were closed, there is "no finality" in Ecuador. Approximately a week later, the LAPs, in a radio segment, asked President Correa to bring criminal charges against Chevron's attorneys, specifically mentioning Pérez.

This campaign continued. The outtakes show Donziger and others planning a press conference to pressure the Prosecutor General to bring criminal charges. On the following day, Donziger asked that posters be made of "Texaco's four accomplices," including Pérez and Veiga—posters that later were displayed at a press conference and a demonstration.

In March 2007, President Correa pledged his full support for the LAPs. He followed that pledge with a meeting with Yanza. In a telephone conversation on or about April 23, 2007, Yanza reported to Donziger and Fajardo on a conversation he had had with President Correa. To the extent that his report may be gleaned from the outtakes, Yanza told Donziger that President Correa had an interest in learning more about the alleged environmental harm and "fraud in the field." He added to Donziger that President Correa "insist[ed]" that he continued to "[think] about doing something in the Prosecutor's Office." A day or two later, Yanza again reported to Donziger and Fajardo, asserting on that occasion that Yanza had "coordinat[ed] everything" with President Correa.

Within a few days, President Correa, Yanza, Fajardo, and others boarded a government helicopter together to tour the Oriente region. In a voiceover in Crude, Donziger bragged: "We have achieved something very important in the case. We are now friends with the President." That "friendship" immediately became apparent. On the same day as his visit to the Oriente region, President Correa issued a press release "urg[ing] the Office of the Prosecutor to permit the Prosecution of the Petroecuador officials who accepted the remediation carried out by Texaco."

The fact that there was no mention of the TexPet lawyers apparently bothered Donziger. In a telephone conversation the next day that was captured by Berlinger's cameras, Donziger said that "perhaps it is time to ask for the head of Pérez Pallares—given what the President said." On the following day, President Correa broadcast a call for the criminal prosecution of "Chevron-Texaco . . . homeland-selling lawyers" in addition to the prosecution of Petroecuador officials.

Finally, in one of the outtakes, Fajardo reported: "So, the President thinks that if we put in a little effort, before getting the public involved, the Prosecutor will yield, and will re-open that investigation into the fraud of, of the contract between Texaco and the Ecuadorian Government."

On November 30, 2007, Ecuador's new Constituent Assembly, which by then was controlled by President Correa, removed the Prosecutor General, who had found no basis to support criminal charges against the Individual Petitioners and former ROE officials, and replaced him with Dr. Washington Pesántez Muñoz. Dr. Pesántez had been the District Prosecutor who had decided in March 2007 that "the report on the special audit conducted by the Comptroller General of Ecuador . . . showed that there was no evidence of civil, administrative or criminal nature liability on the part of . . . representatives of the TEXACO company, with respect to environmental damage that had allegedly been caused in the Amazon region." Several months later, however, Dr. Pesántez decided that the criminal case should be reopened. On March 31, 2008, less than a week after Cabrera reported a damages finding of $16 billion and a day before he filed his report with the court, Pérez and Veiga received notice that the new Prosecutor General had reactivated the criminal charges based on "new" evidence.

On July 31, 2008, representatives of the LAPs, including Donziger, held a press conference during which Yanza commented that the plaintiffs had presented evidence to the Prosecutor General's office to encourage an investigation. President Correa, in a radio address less than two weeks later, offered his support for the criminal prosecutions:

"But previous governments supported Texaco Chevron and betrayed our people: they signed agreements saying that everything was resolved, which has been one of the principal arguments by Texaco Chevron in its defense, when in fact nothing was resolved. Now, the Prosecutor General (Washington Pesántez), has, very properly, opened an investigation to punish those people, because it was a lie: there was nothing, nothing resolved, nothing cleaned up, all of the pollution."

In June 2009, the Prosecutor General's office ordered Cabrera, in his capacity as the expert who conducted the environmental analysis regarding Texaco's presence in Ecuador, to give testimony. A month later, it issued a statement describing Cabrera's testimony. The account included a description of the global assessment process and the fact that Cabrera had referred the Prosecutor General to his report. Pérez and Veiga now face criminal charges in Ecuador. On April 29, 2010, the Prosecutor General issued official accusations to them. They await a preliminary hearing to determine whether the prosecution will proceed. It is reasonable to conclude that the Prosecutor General has revived the prosecution at least in part on the basis of the ostensibly independent Cabrera report, which was covertly written by the LAPs' consultants, at the urging of the LAPs with the support of President Correa.

The Legal and Political Climate in Ecuador—Fair Trial Becomes Impossible and the ROE, at the LAPs' Urgings, Seeks to Prosecute Chevron Lawyers for Tactical Reasons

The Court has drawn attention already to the fact that Aguinda plaintiffs and Texaco expressed sharply differing views to Judge Rakoff in 1999 and 2000 concerning the Ecuadorian courts and legal system. Donziger, representing the former, asserted that the Ecuadorian system was inadequate and the judiciary corrupt. Texaco disputed this. But the issue here is whether the judgment rendered in 2011 at the conclusion of a lawsuit begun in 2003 is foreclosed from recognition and enforcement by virtue of the conditions during that period, not during 1999–2000. It therefore is necessary to review the situation in Ecuador during the relevant time period.

The Ecuadorian Judiciary

The Court has noted already the inauguration of President Correa, Donziger's comment that prediction that it would be a "critical event" for the Lago Agrio litigation, and President Correa's pledge of full support for the Lago Agrio plaintiffs. It is important as well to consider the already troubled state of the Ecuadorian court system and the impact of President Correa's rise to power upon it.

The Ecuadorian judiciary has been in a state of severe institutional crisis for some time. Matters have deteriorated recently.

From 1979 to 1998, judges of the Supreme Court of Justice, the highest court in Ecuador at that time, were appointed by the National Congress for six-year terms and therefore were highly susceptible to political influence. Ecuador's Nineteenth Constitution, in effect from 1998 until October 2008, overhauled the appointment system, providing that Supreme Court justices would serve life terms and that the Supreme Court en banc would appoint new justices. A brief period of stability and judicial independence followed these reforms.

The 2004 Purge of the Supreme Court

This changed dramatically when the Ecuadorian Congress in 2004 and 2005, just after the Lago Agrio litigation was filed, purged the three highest judicial tribunals in Ecuador. In December 2004, the Congress, at the instigation of then-President Gutierrez, unconstitutionally replaced 27 of the 31 justices of the Supreme Court with new justices elected by Congress. Just five months later, President Gutierrez declared a state of emergency and removed all of the Supreme Court justices, including those recently elected. As a result, Ecuador was left without a Supreme Court for most of a year during which the Lago Agrio case was pending.

Ecuador's judiciary appears never to have recovered from these events. In November 2005, following President Gutierrez's downfall, new justices selected by a new qualification committee established by Congress were appointed. In May 2006, this new Supreme Court purported to limit lower-court judges to four-year terms and arrogated to itself the power to appoint and re-appoint lower court judges. "This circumstance made stability and continuity of the appointments of lower-court judges dependent on whether their rulings demonstrated their loyalty to the positions held by the higher-court judges who appointed them." In consequence, Supreme Court justices serve at the will of Congress and lower court judges have short terms of offices and futures dependent on reappointment by the Supreme Court.

President Correa's Influence Over the Judiciary

President Correa was elected president of Ecuador in 2006. He has condemned Ecuador's oil contracts as "true entrapment for the country." Moreover, the state of the Ecuadorian judiciary only worsened with the election of President Rafael Correa in November 2006.

Shortly after assuming office, President Correa commanded the Supreme Electoral Tribunal, with threats of violence, to set a date for a plebiscite to create a Constituent Assembly to draft a new Constitution. When the Tribunal obeyed, 57 of the 100 congressional representatives challenged the constitutionality of the Tribunal's proceedings and voted to remove the President. The Tribunal, by then subservient to the President, dismissed these 57 representatives and called on 57 alternate representatives loyal to the President to fill their seats. The representatives who had been dismissed brought suit in the Constitutional Tribunal, which ruled in their favor and ordered that they be reinstated. President Correa immediately condemned that decision. That very day, the newly appointed congressional majority unconstitutionally removed all of the judges of the Constitutional Tribunal and appointed new judges. The new Constitutional Tribunal reversed its previous decision with respect to the 57 original representatives and from that day forward consistently has backed the administration's decisions. In April 2007, Ecuador voted to draft a new constitution, and a Constituent Assembly was formed. It issued "Mandate No. 1," which, among other things, eliminated Congress, the duties of which were assumed by the Constituent Assembly, and declared the Constituent Assembly's supremacy over the judiciary. When this was challenged before the Constitutional Tribunal, that body ruled that no judge could countervene the Constituent Assembly.

The new October 2008 constitution has further concentrated power in the hands of President Correa. It subjects certain decisions of the Supreme Court (renamed the National Court of Justice) to review by the Constitutional Tribunal (renamed the Constitutional Court). In addition, it terminated the appointments of 31 Supreme Court justices and subjected them to a lottery from which 21 randomly would be selected to serve on the National Court of Justice. Most of the 31 justices refused to submit to the lottery and resigned in protest, causing a gap of several months before the government was able to appoint interim justices. Since his re-election in November 2008, President Correa has continued to interfere in judicial matters of interest to the Ecuadorian government. In a number of recent cases, judges have been threatened with violence, removed, and/or prosecuted when they ruled against the government's interests. "In addition to direct government intervention in specific cases . . . the Judiciary is also frequently pressured by threats and criticism from key officials in the Correa Administration." The Justice Minister has called for the removal of an entire list of criminal judges, leading the President of the Court of Guayaquil to state that "this is only part of the government's plan to take over the country's courts of justice." In 2009, the President of the Civil and Criminal Commission of the National Assembly stated that "[o]ur system of justice has completely collapsed." And in June 2010, the Judicial Council publicly declared that currently "the Judicial Branch is not independent."

"The absence of an independent Judiciary has in many cases allowed the Government to breach contractual relationships and stipulations with impunity. . . . Such breaches occur especially when there is interest on the part of the Government or strong political pressures." The Correa administration has targeted large foreign companies in particular for such treatment. In 2009, Ecuador withdrew from the International Centre for Settlement of Investment Disputes, and President Correa soon thereafter requested that Congress terminate 13 bilateral investment treaties that prescribed fair treatment toward foreign companies.

All this has led numerous independent commentators, identified in the Alvarez Report, to conclude that the rule of law is not respected in Ecuador in cases that have become politicized. Alvarez himself concludes that "[t]he cumulative effect of the political pressure on the Judiciary cannot be overstated. . . . The situation has become so dire that, in those cases where President Correa or others in his administration express a view, the judge must either rule accordingly or face the high likelihood of public condemnation, removal from office, and even criminal prosecution. It is not possible to rely on the independence of the Judicial Branch, because it no longer acts impartially, with integrity and firmness in applying the law and administering justice. Rather, on the contrary, members of the Judiciary are subject to constant pressure, temptations and threats that influence their decisions." Reports by the World Bank and the U.S. State Department are to similar effect.

The World Bank's Worldwide Governance Indicators show that in 2009 Ecuador was ranked in the lowest eight percent of the economies studied with respect to "Rule of Law," lower than both Liberia and North Korea. Likewise, the State Department's three most recent Human Rights Reports for Ecuador have recognized that Ecuadorian judges sometimes decide cases as a result of substantial outside pressures, particularly in cases of interest to the government . . .

For Further Reading

Albro, Robert. "Bolivia's 'Evo Phenomenon': From Identity to What?", *Journal of Latin American Anthropology*, 11:2 (Nov. 2006), 408–428.

Andreas, Peter. *Border Games: Policing the U.S.-Mexico Divide*. Ithaca: Cornell University Press, 2001.

Brysk, Alison. *From Tribal Village to Global Village: Indian Rights and International Relations in Latin America*. Stanford: Stanford University Press, 2000.

Canessa, Andrew. "Todos somos indígenas: Towards a New Language of Indigeneity," *Bulletin of Latin American Research* 25:2 (2006), 241–263.

Corrales, Javier. "In Search of a Theory of Polarization: Lessons from Venezuela, 1999–2005," *European Review of Latin American and Caribbean Studies*, 79 (Oct. 2005), 105–118.

Dunkerley, James. "Evo Morales, the 'Two Bolivias,' and the Third Bolivian Revolution," *Journal of Latin American Studies*, 39:1 (Feb. 2007), 133–166.

Ellner, Steven B. "Venezuela: Defying Globalization's Logic," *NACLA Report on the Americas*, 39:2 (Sept.–Oct. 2005), 20–24.

Garfield, Seth. *Indigenous Struggle at the Heart of Brazil*. Durham, NC: Duke University Press, 2001.

Gerlach, Allen. *Indians, Oil, and Politics: A Recent History of Ecuador*. Lanham, MD: Rowman & Littlefield, 2003.

Gustafson, Bret. "Spectacles of Autonomy and Crisis: Or, What Bulls and Beauty Queens Have to Do with Regionalism in Eastern Bolivia," *Journal of Latin American Anthropology*, 11:2 (Nov. 2006), 351–379.

Haber, Stephen, et al. *Mexico Since 1980* Cambridge: Cambridge University Press, 2008.

Levitsky, Steven, and Kenneth M. Roberts, eds. *The Resurgence of the Latin American Left*. Baltimore: Johns Hopkins University Press, 2011.

Lucero, José Antonio. *Struggles of Voice: The Politics of Indigenous Representation in the Andes*. Pittsburgh: University of Pittsburgh Press, 2008.

Mallon, Florencia E. "Indian Communities, Political Cultures, and the State in Latin America, 1780–1990," *Journal of Latin American Studies* 24 (1992), 35–53.

Martínez, Rubén. *Crossing Over: A Mexican Family on the Migrant Trail*. New York: Picador, 2002.

Nevins, Joseph. *Operation Gatekeeper: The Rise of the 'Illegal Alien' and the Remaking of the U.S.-Mexico Boundary*. New York: Routledge, 2001.

Parenti, Christian. "Venezuela's Revolution and the Oil Company Inside," *NACLA Report on the Americas*, 39:4 (Jan.–Feb. 2006), 8–13.

Parker, Dick. "Chávez and the Search for an Alternative to Neoliberalism," *Latin American Perspectives*, 32:2 (March 2005), 39–50.

Rappaport, Joanne. *Cumbe Reborn: An Andean Ethnography of History*. Chicago: University of Chicago Press, 1994.

Rappaport, Joanne. *The Politics of Memory: Native Historical Interpretation in the Colombian Andes. 2nd edition*. Durham, NC: Duke University Press, 1998.

Rappaport, Joanne. *Intercultural Utopias: Public Intellectuals, Cultural Experimentation, and Ethnic Pluralism in Colombia*. Durham, NC: Duke University Press, 2005.

Roberts, Bryan R., and Alejandro Portes, "Coping with the Free Market City: Collective Action in Six Latin American Cities at the end of the Twentieth Century," *Latin American Research Review* 41, no. 2 (June 2006), 57–83.

Salman, Ton. "The Jammed Democracy: Bolivia's Troubled Political Learning Process," *Bulletin of Latin American Research*, 25:2, 2006, 163–182.

Sawyer, Suzana. *Crude Chronicles: Indigenous Politics, Multinational Oil, and Neoliberalism in Ecuador*. Durham, NC: Duke University Press, 2004.

Sieder, Rachel. "The judiciary and indigenous rights in Guatemala," *International Journal of Constitutional Law* (OUP) Vol. 5 (2), 2007, 211–241.

Steiglitz, Joseph. *Globalization and its Discontents*. New York: Norton, 2003.

Valencia Ramírez, Cristóbal. "Venezuela in the Eye of the Hurricane: Landing an Analysis of the Bolivarian Revolution," *Journal of Latin American Anthropology*, 11:1 (April 2006), 173–186.

Veltmeyer, Henry, and Petras, James F. "Bolivia and the Political Dynamics of Change," *European Review of Latin American and Caribbean Studies*, 83 (Oct. 2007), 105–119.

Wade, Peter. *Blackness and Race Mixture: The Dynamics of Racial Identity in Colombia*. Baltimore: Johns Hopkins University Press, 1995.

Wolff, Jonas. "(De-)Mobilising the Marginalised: A Comparison of the Argentine Piqueteros and Ecuador's Indigenous Movement," *Journal of Latin American Studies* 39:1 (February 2007), 1–29.

Yashar, Deborah J. *Contesting Citizenship in Latin America: The Rise of Indigenous Movements and the Postliberal Challenge*. Cambridge: Cambridge University Press, 2005.

Epilogue

The ending is critical. A good ending helps the story feel finished, helps it make sense to the reader. Histories tend to end with commonly accepted turning points, affirming to the reader that the end of the era means the end of the text. It is easier this way, it gives our stories predetermined beginnings and conclusions. Histories of the colonial period usually end with independence. Stories of specific processes (revolution, emancipation, industrialization) are likewise framed by what the author determines to be the end of that process. Even texts that bring us into the present do this, as history by definition concludes with the current day. When compelling, these endings have the power to give the past a finished quality, and to constitute a place and its people. We can describe Latin America because we have imagined a Latin American past.

It is my hope that this text has made that task difficult. Instead of a history of Latin America, the reader was introduced to eleven distinct Latin American pasts, each in some ways incommensurable with the other. We might see whispers of a common Latin American past in the way current claims about indigeneity evoke memories of earlier struggles over race and citizenship, or in the ways that economic growth and progress remain as important in the region today as they did a century ago. Nonetheless, these similarities are probably better understood as an invitation to dialogue about linkages, continuities, and discontinuities than as evidence of that elusive thing we would call Latin America.

What would that dialogue look like? We might begin by wondering why we need a concept of Latin America at all? Would the histories of this region be more compelling if they were simply local, national, or framed by some larger concept, such as the post-colonial world? Would we be better served by a frame of reference that makes the inequality between rich and poor nations the center of our narrative? Should we make the past a morality tale, or a search for the Latin American essence? Or should we do as we have done here, and tell multiple histories that rely on a variety of approaches to the past? In this last approach, Latin America does occasionally seem to come into the picture—especially in stories of colonial pasts, global politics, and common economic crises—and yet it also slips away just as often, as we find ourselves compelled to think about specific experiences and stories that don't seem to fit into the frame.

Throughout the chapters in this text, we see individuals working to shape the worlds they live in. Like people everywhere, they are invariably constrained by their pasts, their present circumstances, and the limits of what they believe to be possible. In making an effort to understand these people on their own terms and to develop a more nuanced view of the worlds they lived in, it becomes much more difficult to either insert them into a morality play or stand in judgment of their failures and shortcomings. And it is only then that we begin to appreciate the rich histories of the places we study.

Glossary

Agrarista (agrarian) Those who demand land be distributed to peasants. Term used principally in Mexico.

Altiplano A region of high mountain plateaus. Term used in the Andes.

Austerity measures Fiscal policies implemented to reduce government debt and spending relative to GDP, usually at the behest of the International Monetary Fund (IMF).

Authoritarian government System where the will of leaders tends to override civil society.

Banana republic Central American and Caribbean nations where a dependence on just a few commodity exports makes the country extremely vulnerable to external pressures.

Baroque catholicism A tradition in which elaborate symbolism and ornate decorative practices were used to project the authority of the Catholic Church.

Bourbon reforms A general term describing economic and political reforms undertaken by the House of Bourbon, which came to power in Spain after the end of Habsburg rule in 1700. Overall, changes undertaken during the course of eighty years were intended to improve defense, make administration more efficient, and generate more revenue for the crown.

Cabildo A town council.

Cariocas Residents of Rio de Janeiro.

Carnivalesque Describes moments of social inversion, when marginalized and oppressed groups symbolically place themselves on top of society, subverting the social order.

Castas Colonial term describing people of mixed racial (and cultural) origins.

Caste system Colonial system that enforced social position through caste status.

Caudillo (caudillismo) Military strongmen.

Clientelism A political system in which political networks work principally to dole out political favors to friends and allies of office holders (distributing the spoils provided by the state).

Cocalero A peasant coca grower. Term used in Bolivia.

Cold War The period from 1948 to 1989 characterized by global competition between the United States and U.S.S.R. Regions like Latin America were the settings for numerous proxy battles.

Compadrazgo   A notion of fictive kinship, in which godparents and close friends effectively become family members.

Comunero   Peasants with a strong connection to community and long history of resistance against outsiders. Term used in the Andes.

Conservatives   A nineteenth-century term describing groups that sought to maintain colonial-era political, social, and cultural hierarchies. Conservatives generally believed the end of the old order would produce chaos.

Corporatism   Systems in which one participates in political and social life as a member of a corporate group (as a member of an indigenous community, a union, or a professional association, for instance).

Coup d'état   The overthrow of a government by a small elite, usually led by members of the military.

Criollos   Persons of European origin born in the Americas.

Crony capitalism   An economic and political system where businessmen rely on close connections with the state to prosper, and where those without such connections are deeply disadvantaged.

Debt peonage   A labor practice in which workers are tied to their employer through debt, and generally cannot leave that employer until debts are paid.

Dependency theory   An economic theory that posits that poor regions remain impoverished because of asymmetrical relations with more prosperous regions.

Descamisados   Literally "shirtless ones," Eva Perón's term for her supporters.

Dirty wars   Refers to conflicts (1960s–1990s) that involved state-sponsored violence meted out against largely unarmed groups identified as "subversives." Torture, summary execution, and forced exile were relatively common strategies for silencing regime opponents.

Enganche labor   A labor contracting system, common in plantation agriculture, in which workers sign a contract (often under duress) and are forced to work until the contract ends.

Estancia (estancieros)   Large rural estates. Term used commonly in Argentina.

Favela   Urban slums. Term used in Brazil.

Feminicide   The murder of women because they are women.

Finca (finqueros)   A rural estate, sometimes a plantation. Term used in Southern Mexico, Central America, and parts of South America.

Gamonalismo   The Andean system in which large landowners exploit and dominate the indigenous and other poor peoples on their estates.

Golpe de Estado   The overthrow of a government by a small elite, usually led by members of the military.

Gross Domestic Product (GDP)   The value of all goods and services produced in a given country during a single year.

Haciendas (hacendados)   Large rural estates. Term used in Mexico.

Hegemony   The domination of one group over another. Hegemony suggests that domination is not simply a function of military influence, but of cultural and social practices as well. The concept imagines that systems of domination are contested and negotiated, and not simply coercive.

Historietas   Graphic novels (comic books).

Import Substitution Industrialization (ISI)   An economic policy, popular from the 1930s to the 1960s, that promoted industrial growth by supplanting imports with domestically produced manufactures.

Junta   A small group of military leaders (sometimes including some civilians) who dominate the state, often in the aftermath of a coup.

Kataristas   A political tendency in the Andes that emerged during the 1960s, which sought to empower a radicalized indigenous peasantry in part through the defense of indigenous cultures.

Latifundia   A system in which large agricultural estates rely on workforces that are tied to or dependent on the estates.

Ley fuga **"Shot while trying to escape"**   A policing practice in which criminal suspects are executed without first being tried and convicted.

Liberals (liberalism)   Nineteenth-century term describing those who favored some array of individual rights, free market capitalism, and limited democracy. Liberals opposed monarchy and special privileges (*fueros*) for the monarchy, the aristocracy, Indian villages, the church, and the military.

Libertos   Former slaves.

Limpieza de sangre **"Cleanliness of the Blood"**   Term used to denote the amount of European blood in any given individual, which in turn played an important role in personal prestige during the colonial and later periods.

Machista   A term used to describe contexts in which characteristics considered to be aggressively heterosexual and masculine are valued.

Manichean   Practices and belief systems that tend to divide the world into extremes of good and evil.

Manumission   The act of freeing an individual slave.

Maoists   Aficionados of Mao Zedong. Maoists advocate a revolution in which peasant guerrillas overwhelm the cities.

Marshall Plan   Plan by the U.S. government to speed the reconstruction of Europe at the end of the Second World War through aid and investment.

Mass politics   Political movements based in the widespread mobilization of popular groups through mass communication techniques.

Media luna   The eastern lowland departments of Bolivia.

Mestizo   A person with both European and indigenous ancestry. It may denote race, but is principally a cultural signifier.

Millennarianism   Popular movements that coalesce around the belief that a major transformation in the world is pending. Millennarian movements are generally informed by a deep religious sensibility that in turn spurs dramatic political acts.

Misery belts   The impoverished, often ad hoc communities of rural migrants that emerged on the fringes of Latin America's largest cities, beginning in the 1960s. Rural migrants continue to move to these communities, but they are now the home to multiple generations of the urban poor.

Monocrop economy   An economy that is dependent on the export of a very limited number of commodities.

Mulatto   A person of African and European ancestry.

Narcotraficante   Individuals who earn income in the illicit drug trade.

Neo-liberalism   Sometimes called neo-conservatism, describes the belief (increasingly popular after 1970) that governments needed to reduce spending, regulation, and taxes, and promote foreign trade and investment.

Oligarchy   Political or economic system in which power rests in the hands of a small elite.

Orientalism   The practice of representing non-Western cultures as irreconcilably different from those of Western Europe and the United States, and implying that this difference indicates inferiority.

Peninsular   An individual born in the Iberian Peninsula.

Plantations   Agricultural estates in semi-tropical and tropical environments that cultivate a limited number of high value commodities.

Populism   Political practices in which leaders appeal for support from a broad community of supporters, defined as the folk, citizens, or the people, usually with the aid of mass communication.

Porteño   A resident of Buenos Aires.

Positivism   A nineteenth-century ideology, informed by the writings of Herbert Spencer and Auguste Comte, which posited that society needed to be governed by scientific principles rather than democratic practices. "Order and Progress" was a key positivist claim.

Radionovelas   Radio soap operas.

Relics   In Catholic tradition, the physical remnants of a deceased saint, venerated as a representation of that saint.

Rentier states   A state that derives most of its incomes from rents (i.e., royalties from mineral concessions and hydrocarbons), making it less reliant on other forms of taxation. Political theorists suggest that, because they do not rely on a broad citizenry for tax revenue, rentier states tend to be less democratic.

Rondas campesinas   Peasant self-defense committees, which played a critical role in the Peruvian civil conflict of the 1980s and 1990s.

Samba   A popular Brazilian musical form, rooted in a mixture of African and European traditions.

Serrano   A person from the high desert regions of Northern Mexico. Used to describe the followers of Pancho Villa in Mexico's 1910 Revolution.

Shock treatments   The sudden imposition of economic austerity measures (i.e., cuts in government spending), meant to "shock" the economy into health.

Tango   An Argentine music and dance form, originally popular among poor residents of Buenos Aires.

Testimonio   A literary practice that emerged during the 1980s, which relies on the testimony of persons who self-identify as members of marginalized or oppressed groups (e.g., indigenous peoples, women, victims of torture).

The Two Republics   The Spanish colonial practice of attempting to divide the population into two distinct communities, *indios* and *españoles*.

Usos y costumbres **(customary law)**   A right claimed by many contemporary indigenous groups, to preserve their customary governance, judicial, and other practices.

Vanguard   A small, committed elite, which endeavors to shape a mass of followers to reflect its ideals.

Notes

Introduction: Latin America's Useable Past

1 The former is the city's largest urban park, and the latter is Mexico City's historical central square.
2 These last designations are typically reserved for persons born in the United States, but they can be found sometimes in the media as descriptions of Mexicans.
3 This is a vaguely obscene term for people from Mexico City, commonly used in other parts of the country.
4 For our purposes, Latin America comprises Mexico, Central America, the Caribbean, and South America. For an excellent in-depth discussion of this question, see Marshall Eakin, "Does Latin America Have a Common History" (a pdf is available on the book's website www.routledge.com/cw/dawson). See also Thomas Holloway, "Latin America: What's in a Name?" in *A Companion to Latin American History* (Waltham, MA: Wiley/Blackwell, 2008). Benedict Anderson's *Imagined Communities* (London: Verso, 1983) also offers an interesting way of approaching this issue.
5 The term often used to describe this phenomenon is orientalism.
6 This narrative suggests that Mexicans share a common culture built on the trauma imposed on indigenous cultures by the Spanish Conquest in 1521. It constitutes a chapter in his epic work, *The Labyrinth of Solitude* (New York: Grove, 1961). Claudio Lomnitz' *Exits from The Labyrinth* (Berkeley: California University Press, 1993) represents one of the most interesting critiques of this tradition.
7 Trouillot, Michel-Rolph. *Silencing the Past: Power and the Production of History* (Boston: Beacon, 1995).
8 For examples of this tradition, see Fernando Henrique Cardoso and Enzo Faletto, *Dependency and Development in Latin America* (Berkeley: University of California Press, 1979); Brooke Larson, *Colonialism and Agrarian Transformation in Bolivia: Cochabamba, 1550–1900* (Princeton: Princeton University Press, 1988); Stephen H. Haber, ed. *How Latin America Fell Behind: Essays on the Economic Histories of Brazil, 1800–1914* (Stanford: Stanford University Press, 1997).
9 On this, see the brilliant essay by Clifford Geertz, "History and Anthropology," *New Literary History*, Vol. 21, No. 2, (Winter, 1990), 321–335.
10 For more on the concept, see Walter Johnson, "On Agency," *Journal of Social History* 37:1 (Fall 2003). One interesting reading of this question can be found in Vincent Peloso, *Peasants on Plantations: Subaltern Strategies of Labor and Resistance in the Pisco Valley, Peru* (Durham, NC: Duke University Press, 1999).

11 This is the conclusion some read from reading Michel Foucault. See, for example, Foucault, *Discipline and Punish: the Birth of the Prison* (New York: Random House, 1975).

12 This concept figures prominently in Michael Hardt and Antonio Negri, *Empire* (Cambridge MA: Harvard University Press, 2000). Jon Beasley-Murray offers an idea of how it applies to Latin America in *Posthegemony: Political Theory and Latin America* (Minneapolis: University of Minnesota Press, 2011).

13 I draw from Bourdieu, *Outline of a Theory of Practice* (Cambridge: Cambridge University Press, 1977).

14 See, for instance, Bernard Goldberg, *Bias: A CBS Insider Exposes How the Media Distort the News* (New York: Perennial, 2003).

1 Independence Narratives, Past and Present

1 "Shot Heard Round the World," by Bob Dorough, *Schoolhouse Rock*, 1976. See http://www.youtube.com/watch?v = Y6ikO6LMxF4.

2 A good place to start on Sáenz is Sarah Chambers, "Republican Friendship: Manuela Saenz Writes Women into the Nation, 1835–1856," *Hispanic American Historical Review* 81: 2, 2001, 225–257.

3 A free womb law declared that children born to slaves would be free.

4 The full letter was nearly 8,000 words long, and can be found in Spanish on the website.

5 See it here: http://vimeo.com/29701339.

2 *Caudillos* Versus the Nation State

1 "[T]hey do things differently there." From Poles Hartley, *The Go-Between* (London: H. Hamilton, 1953).

2 This is a system of government where power is controlled by a small number of elites.

3 *Mestizo* is a common term in Latin America, indicating a person with both European and indigenous ancestry. It is often used as a racial category, but is also used as a cultural category, with no reference to physical ancestry.

4 Latin American liberals followed the dictates of intellectuals like Adam Smith and John Stuart Mill, and believed in maximizing economic and political freedom in the interest of progress.

5 The term for the owners of large estates varies from region to region. They and their estates are variously known by the terms *hacendados/haciendas*, *finqueros/fincas*, *estancieros/estancias*, *latifundistas/latifundia*.

6 *Protecturia de indígenas.*

7 Facundo was a real *caudillo*, but the text was indirectly aimed at Rosas.

8 Shumway, *The Invention of Argentina*, 206.

9 This term describes persons from Buenos Aires.

10 These are owners of large estates, or *estancias*.

11 Florencia Mallon's *Peasant and Nation* is fascinating on this point.

12 The term denotes people of mixed racial origins.

13 Translator's note: The political party that opposed Rosas.

14 Translator's note: In 1820, Juan Manuel de Rosas, leader of the Federalist Party, was given the title of "Restorer of the Laws" by the legislature when he reestablished the Federalists' legal government.

15 Translator's note: Refers to the British and other fair-haired, light-skinned foreigners, with a pejorative connotation.

16 Translator's note: Crested *caracara* (Polyborus plancus), a bird of prey common to Argentina and belonging to the falcon family.

17 Translator's note: The Day of Sorrows was the Friday before Good Friday. Vatican Council II decided to remove it from the liturgical calendar since it duplicated the feast day of Our Lady of Sorrows, September 15.

18 Translator's note: Reference to the 1833 Revolution of the Restorers, which defeated the governor, Juan Ramón Balcarce, and established Juan Manuel de Rosas' dominion over the province of Buenos Aires.

19 Translator's note: A rectangular piece of fabric or leather wrapped around the back and front of the waist, passed between the legs over the trousers, worn for warmth and protection by farmhands, gauchos, and, in general, by the humbler elements of society, the prosperous preferring to wear the traditional short Spanish trousers called *calzón corto español*.

20 Translator's note: Azul was located south of the province of Buenos Aires.

21 Translator's note: Matasiete = Killed seven. In Lunfardo, *matahambre* means "a dead man"; "*matahambre*" or "*matambre*" is also a typical Argentine dish that translates as "rolled flank steak."

22 Translator's note: "Franciscan Saint and Patron of the Blacks and Mulattos of Buenos Aires," in Evelyn Picon Garfield and Iván A. Schulman, *Las literaturas hispánicas: introducción a su estudio* (Detroit: Wayne State University Press, 1991, 146).

23 Spanish: "verga." According to literary critics Burgos and Salessi, *El Matadero*, the term refers to the use of sodomy as a form of torture employed by the Federalists. In the story, the "verga" is clearly a whip, specifically an *arreador*, used by cowboys, herders, and carters, also called "verga de toro" because the skin of a bull's penis was used to cover its wooden handle (Diccionario Argentino,1910). In English: "pizzle": a whip made from a bull's penis.

3   Citizenship and Rights in the New Republics

1 Debt peonage tied workers to agricultural estates because the workers were extended a loan (sometimes involuntarily) and then required to work for a specific employer until the loan was paid off. They would often accrue more debt while working, and thus become caught in a cycle of debt.

2 People with African and European ancestry.

3 At the time Africans made up 40 percent of the island's population.

4 Partly due to these pressures, Britain would proclaim emancipation in 1834 for its 668,000 slaves. A system of forced apprenticeships would be abandoned amidst strikes and protests four years later.

5 A resident of São Paulo.

6 A resident of the northeast.

7 *Capoeira* is an Afro-Brazilian form of dance that invokes self-defense as a part of its form.

8 The entire exchange can be found at Maria Eugenia Echenique, Josefina Pelliza de Sagasta, The Emancipation of Women: Argentina 1876, translated by the Palouse Translation Project. *Journal of Women's History*, Volume 7, Number 3, Fall 1995, 102–126.

4   The Export Boom as Modernity

1 Friedman was the Nobel Prize-winning University of Chicago economist who became one of the most important advocates of free market capitalism for Latin America during the 1960s–1980s.

2 Clorinda Matto de Turner believed that the largely vegetarian diet consumed by Indians caused their brains to swell, and urged that more meat be introduced into their diets. She was not alone in describing what others called the "tragedy of meat," and in trying to introduce miracle cures to Indian backwardness (Manuel Gamio, the father of Mexican anthropology, later tried to introduce a tortilla made in part from soybeans).

3 Over time, raw materials have consistently lost value relative to manufactured goods.
4 The larger issue of women workers has received a great deal of attention in recent years. See, for example, Ann Farnsworth-Alvear, "Talking, Fighting, Flirting: Workers Sociability in Medellin Textile Mills, 1935–1950," in *The Gendered Worlds of Latin American Women Workers*. See also Elizabeth Quay Hutchinson, *Labors Appropriate to their Sex.*
5 GDP measures the value of all goods and services produced in the national economy in a single year.
6 This analysis is drawn from Victor Bulmer Thomas.
7 In Mexico a series of domestic measures, including the privatization of land (which put land and labor on the market), and the suppression of *alcabalas* (taxes that placed barriers to internal trade), produced a growth rate of 2.3 percent per year 1877–1910, doubling per capita income.
8 An excellent example of this can be found in Greg Grandin, "Can the Subaltern Be Seen? Photography and the Affects of Nationalism," *Hispanic American Historical Review* 84:1 (2004), 83–111.
9 In this, they were unlike about one-third of the students in the school, who fled.

5   Signs of Crisis in a Gilded Age

1 See his book, *Hybrid Cultures: Strategies for Entering and Leaving Modernity* (Minneapolis: University of Minnesota Press, 1995).
2 Millennial movements generally mix deep religious devotion, a sense that the end of the world as we know it is at hand, and rebellion. Mexico had its own millennial movements, including Tomochic in 1892.
3 This concept alerts us to the ways that economic systems based on private property and free markets have the capacity to transform social relations that had previously operated by different logics.
4 I draw here from William Roseberry's concept of hegemony. William Roseberry, "Hegemony and the Language of Contention," in Gilbert Joseph and Daniel Nugent (eds.), *Everyday Forms of State Formation: Revolution and the Negotiating of Rule in Modern Mexico* (Durham, NC: Duke University Press, 1994), 355–366.
5 Consider the role that the raising of the U.S. flag at Iwo Jima in 1945, and Chief Nguyễn Ngọc Loan's execution of a Việt Cộng officer in 1968, have had in in encapsulating World War Two and the Vietnam War.
6 Miners were, of course, a distinct part of this group, and in some regions factories were built in rural areas. Plantation agriculture, which tended to be highly mechanized and specialized, could also be included. Miners and rural workers did take part in various labor movements. Several important strikes during this era took place at mines (e.g., Cananea, Mexico, 1906).
7 In all, two million immigrants came to Argentina between 1870 and 1910, mostly from Spain and Italy. The rural working class remained largely Argentine born, while the urban proletariat was largely foreign born.
8 In 1914 there were only 110,000 Jews in Argentina, out of a total national population of 7.9 million.
9 At the time, British investment in Latin America was still greater, at $5.8 billion, but the United States was clearly on its way to overtaking the British.

6   Commerce, Coercion, and America's Empire

1 We use the term "American" here to describe the United States. There has been considerable debate among scholars about its merit in recent years. Some have substituted North American or some other term because they find the very term imperialistic (we leave aside how Mexicans and Canadians feel about the use of North American in this context). I use the term for two reasons.

First, it is how citizens of the United States call themselves. Second, Latin Americans generally know what it means, and very few of them use the term to refer to themselves.

2 See Eric Williams, *Capitalism and Slavery* (Chapel Hill: University of North Carolina Press, 1944).

3 Alan M. Taylor, "Foreign Capital in Latin America in the Nineteenth and Twentieth Centuries," Working Paper 9580 *National Bureau of Economic Research*, March 2003, http://www.nber.org/papers/w9580.

4 The plantations they left in their wakes suffered from reduced biodiversity and were not easily turned to other forms of agriculture.

5 Víctor Raúl Haya de la Torre famously identified Central America as the critical testing ground for U.S. imperialism in Latin America (see an excerpt from 1929's *A donde va indoamericana* on the website (2nd ed., Santiago de Chile: Ercilla, 1935). Others in this camp included Augusto Sandino, C. L. R. James (author of *The Black Jacobins*), and Fidel Castro.

6 The plan also empowered local peasant committees to oversee their lands, shifting power from the central government to marginalized groups.

7 The domino theory, which proposed that weak regimes would fall to communism when influenced by communist neighbors, eventually seriously weakening the United States, was first articulated by George Kennan in a 1947 article in *Foreign Affairs*. It was a guiding theory of U.S. cold war politics, and part of the rationale behind both U.S. policy in Latin America and the Vietnam War.

8 Allen Dulles once served on the Board of Trustees of the UFCO, and John Foster Dulles served as legal counsel to the Firm before joining the administration. Both held UFCO stock.

9 In the aftermath, UFCO agreed to new taxes on profits of 30 percent (up from 10 percent in 1953). A total of 250,000 acres of land were returned to the company, but the UFCO did agree to give up 100,000 for a land reform, and the United States gave $80 million in aid. After PBSUCCESS, the Eisenhower administration allowed an anti-trust suit against UFCO to proceed that weakened the company, which ultimately rebranded itself as Chiquita Bananas.

10 Bartenders at the Hotel Nacional in Cuba even invented a drink named after movie star Mary Pickford.

11 The conglomerate was founded in 1902, as a joint venture between the Imperial Tobacco Company and James Duke's American Tobacco Company.

12 The film debuted in Mexico City in December 1944, and in the United States in 1945.

13 The film debuted in Rio de Janeiro in 1942, and was released in the United States in 1943.

14 Sandino wrote a notable letter to Hipólito Yrigoyen in 1929, called his "Plan for Realizing Bolívar's Dream."

15 Sandino was killed in 1934, but the movement that overthrew the U.S.-backed Somoza regime in 1979 was named for him.

7   Power to the People

1 Daryle Williams, *Culture Wars in Brazil*, p. 87.

2 Rádio Nacional began as a commercial station and was taken over by the government in 1940, but continued as a commercial venture, featuring music and *radionovelas*.

3 There is some question as to the authenticity of the note. Quoted in Levine, *Father of the Poor: Vargas and His Era*, 150–152.

4 Levine, *Father of the Poor*, p. 138.

5 The Cristero revolt centered on the defense of Catholic traditions in the face of anti-clerical government programs. It was also very much a defense of local practices and autonomies against a state that was viewed with a great deal of distrust.

6 Much of the material for this section is drawn from Joy Elizabeth Hayes, *Radio Nation*.

7 By the late 1930s Emilio Azcárraga would control two national networks, one affiliated with NBC and the other with CBS. He would ultimately command 80 percent of the radio and TV audience in the country.

8 Socialist Education combined John Dewey's "action school" with left-wing principles.
9 Hayes, p. 58.
10 Listen to Cárdenas' oil expropriation announcement at http://www.youtube.com/watch?v=8GlFYQfgSK8.
11 Literally, "A Peronist Day." The phrase was used among Perón's supporters for decades to describe a good day.
12 See Chapter 5.
13 As with translations of slang generally, in order to maintain the form and meaning, this translation is not literal. For the Spanish version, see the book's website www.routledge.com/cw/dawson, or www.todotango.com.
14 Clientelism involves politicians acting as personal agents for their constituents, providing favors and benefits in return for support. The Radical Party used this strategy to gain votes in working-class neighborhoods consistently during the 1910s and 1920s.
15 This is the term used in Latin America to describe military governments characterized by a committee of officers rather than one dominant leader.
16 Ten thousand people died in the earthquake, which remains the greatest national disaster in Argentine history.
17 It was originally called the *Fundación Maria Eva Duarte de Perón*.

8   A Decade of Revolution in Cuba

1 For a recent example of this, see Sean Penn, "Conversations with Chávez and Castro," in the *Nation*, November 25, 2008, and Roger Cohen "The End of the Cuban Revolution," in *New York Times*, December 5, 2008.
2 Thirty years later doves again landed on Castro during a speech commemorating the Revolution, causing a similar debate.
3 *"Hasta la victoria, siempre"* is perhaps the most important revolutionary slogan.
4 This is the measure economists use for describing inequality. Zero would be perfect equality. Most Western European nations have Gini coefficients of around 0.3; Latin American nations, where we see some of the greatest inequality on the planet, average around 0.5.
5 In the fifteen years after Kennedy announced that all Cuban exiles would be granted immediate asylum in the United States, 700,000 Cubans took advantage of this offer. Dentists, doctors, and technicians fled (20,000 out of 85,000 professionals), leaving the island's schools, hospitals, factories, and administration without expertise, but also open to control from revolutionary cadres.
6 Pilar López Gonzales was a protagonist in Oscar Lewis and his research team's study of life in revolutionary Cuba, the three-volume *Living the Revolution*. See Oscar Lewis, Ruth M. Lewis, and Susan M. Rigdon, *Four Women: Living the Revolution: An Oral History of Contemporary Cuba*, Champaign: University of Illinois Press, 1977.
7 Small farms also generally provided little tax revenue, as small farmers were good at avoiding taxes.
8 Junta Central de Planificación.
9 See, for example, Lino Novás Calvo's *Manera de Contar* (New York: Las Americas Publishing Co., 1970).
10 It received the Premio Internacional de Cuentos Juan Rulfo in 1990, and the Premio de la Crítica Literaria in 1992. It has been published in twenty countries, eleven languages, and staged as a play on over fifteen occasions.
11 Fellow students of David's at the university, who debated the threat that Diego posed to the Revolution because of his homosexuality.
12 David refers here to the fact that he had earlier spied on his friend Diego, which he had fears was a form of betrayal.

13 Translator's note: Earlier in the story, Diego related the story of his discovery that he was gay, as a result of an unexpected sexual encounter with a basketball player at the Catholic school that he attended as a boy.

14 Translator's note: The armchair is referred to as the "la butaca de John Donne" in the Spanish original.

15 Translator's note: The story opens with Diego watching David in a performance of Ibsen's *A Doll's House* by a university theatre group of which David is a part, and in which he spectacularly bombs.

9 The Terror

1 Maoists are communists who pattern their idea of revolution after the Chinese Revolution and Chairman Mao Zedong. They tend to be exceptionally doctrinaire and vanguardist, and follow a strategy of fomenting a rural revolution among peasants that is intended to surround and ultimately choke off the cities.

2 He overthrew himself. The term *golpe de estado* is the Spanish equivalent of the French coup d'état.

3 The 1984 report for the CONADEP can be found in English at: http://web.archive.org/web/20031004074316/nuncamas.org/english/library/nevagain/nevagain_001.htm. The Rettig commission report can be found at: http://www.usip.org/ library/tc/doc/reports/chile/chile_1993_toc.html.

4 Look no further than Werner Herzog's 1972 film, *Aguirre: Wrath of God*, to understand how this narrative can explain all types of modern holocausts.

5 One version of this narrative can be seen in Eduardo Galeano's *The Open Veins of Latin America: Five Centuries of the Pillage of a Continent* (Monthly Review Press, 1997). It was originally published in 1971.

6 ISI relied on high tariffs, subsidized inputs to industry (in several countries government monopolies in oil, steel, electricity, and transportation reduced production costs), and a labor force made compliant by a mix of wages and social spending (free education through university, health care, pensions, subsidized transport), along with occasional repression.

7 A classic example of this complaint can be seen in Carolina Maria de Jesus' *Child of the Dark* (New York: Penguin, 1962) which is based on diaries she wrote between 1955 and 1960.

8 See her book *Looking for History: Dispatches from Latin America* (New York: Vintage, 2002), 73–87.

9 *National Geographic*, Volume 170, 1986, p. 247.

10 Chamorro had published a story impling that Somoza had taken blood donated by Nicaraguans to help victims of the 1972 Managua earthquake and sold it on the U.S. blood market.

11 It was named for a phrase used by José Carlos Mariátegui to describe the prospects of a Marxist revolution.

12 Some beneficiaries also chafed under the seemingly arbitrary and overly bureaucratic nature of the government's programs.

13 See www.cverdad.org.pe/ingles/informacion/discursos/en_apublicas08.php.

14 In Scilingo's case, he generated sympathy through his tale of following orders, of remorse, and of unfair treatment at the hands of civilian authorities. See Menchú's *I, Rigoberta Menchú*, Partnoy's *The Little School*, and Verbitstky's *Confessions of an Argentine Dirty Warrior*.

15 Diana Taylor argues this persuasively in *Disappearing Acts,* 1997.

16 I draw this concept from Christopher R. Browning, *Ordinary Men: Reserve Police Battalion 101 and the Final Solution in Poland*. New York: HarperCollins, 1992.

17 Translator's note: Pensions paid to former congressional members at the level of current congressional pay.

18 Translator's note: The first session of the Peruvian legislature is between July and December, so the text (*para que ello suceda se necesitan dos primeras legislaturas ordinarias consecutivas*) means that

the reforms would have to be approved during two consecutive July–December sessions, in other words, as much as a year and a half could pass before the reforms would be approved (April 1992 to December 1993).

10 Speaking Truth to Power

1 *Mothers of the Plaza de Mayo*. This is the plaza that faces the Casa Rosada, Argentina's Presidential Palace.
2 See David Vidal, "Relatives of Missing Latins Press Drive for Accounting; 30,000 Reported Missing," *New York Times*, January 5, 1979; "Latin America's 'Disappeared' victims," *Christian Science Monitor*, January 23, 1979; "Latin American bishops debating church's role," *Christian Science Monitor*, February 8, 1979. See also "A Voice of 'the Disappeared'," *Los Angeles Times*, October 21, 1979; "Political Prisoners' Plight in Latin America Told," *Los Angeles Times*, November 5, 1979.
3 See the link to the 1980 Interamerican Commission Report on Human Rights in Argentina, which details many specific stories of forced disappearances brought to the commission: http://www.cidh.org/countryrep/Argentina80eng/toc.htm.
4 This happened in 1986.
5 Today, Mexico City has around 18 million residents. São Paulo has 17.7 million, Buenos Aires 12.4 million, Rio 10.5 million, Lima 7.5 million, and Bogotá 6.8 million.
6 Since 1996 Colombia has received $7,413,585,638 in military and police aid. Mexico has received $2,409,441,555. During that same period, Mexico has purchased $4,755,313,431 worth of U.S. arms and equipment, and Colombia $3,264,534,327.
7 See http://truth-out.org/news/item/13001-calderon-reign-ends-with-six-year-mexican-death-toll-near-120000.
8 See Vladimir Hernández, "Chile: ¿quiénes son los que filman las protestas estudiantiles?" *BBC Mundo a Santiago*, June 14, 2013. http://www.bbc.co.uk/mundo/noticias/2013/06/121127_chile_marchas_estudiantes_abogados_defensores_vh.shtml.

11 Towards an Uncertain Future

1 Albert Hirschman, *Exit, Voice, and Loyalty: Responses to Decline in Firms, Organizations, and States* (Cambridge, MA: Harvard University Press, 1970).
2 The epicenter of the earthquake lay off the coast of Oaxaca.
3 Some believe that number to be as high as 40,000.
4 The government claimed 289 dead, but tenants put it at 600.
5 A good analysis of the larger causes of the crisis can be found in Jeffrey D. Sachs and John Williamson, "External Debt and Macroeconomic Performance in Latin America and East Asia," *Brookings Papers on Economic Activity*, Vol. 1985 (No. 2) 1985, 523–573.
6 See http://www.bbc.co.uk/mundo/noticias/2013/05/130514_brasil_esclavitud_bolivianos_haitianos_lav.shtml.
7 The protests were also informed by a general unease with the amount of government money being spent on sports facilities in anticipation of the 2014 World Cup and 2016 Rio Olympics.
8 Figures on the decreases in poverty from *Social Panorama of Latin America* United Nations, ECLAC—2011. That nonetheless represents an increase in the numbers of poor and indigent poor, from 136 million poor (and 82 million indigent) in 1980 to 174 million poor and 73 million indigent in 2011.
9 Various indigenous rights became law during these years in Nicaragua, Colombia, Ecuador, Guatemala, Peru, Brazil, Mexico, Chile, Bolivia, and Venezuela.

10 "Chile court rules for Indians against Barrick Gold," Yahoo News, July 13, 2013. http://news.
yahoo.com/chile-court-rules-indians-against-barrick-gold-184917213.html.
11 These numbers indicate the page on which this information can be found in the ruling.

At A Glance

People

1 Mariana Campos Horta, "Afro-descendent and Indigenous Population in Latin America," November 18, 2011, http://perla.princeton.edu/category/blog.

Economy

1 This includes most European Nations, along with the United States, Canada, Mexico, Chile, South Korea, Australia, Japan, and Israel.

Environment

1 See Crosby's *Ecological Imperialism: The Biological Expansion of Europe, 900–1900, 2nd ed.* (Cambridge: Cambridge University Press, 2004), Diamond's *Guns, Germs and Steel: The Fates of Human Societies* (New York: Norton, 1999).
2 See, for example, Warren Dean, *With Broadax and Firebrand: The Destruction of the Brazilian Atlantic Forest* (Berkeley: University of California Press,1997), Stuart George McCook, *States of Nature: Science, Agriculture, and Environment in the Spanish Caribbean, 1760–1940* (Austin: University of Texas Press, 2002), John Soluri, *Banana Cultures: Agriculture, Consumption, and Environmental Change in Honduras and the United States* (Austin: University of Texas Press, 2006), Shawn William Miller, *An Environmental History of Latin America* (Cambridge: Cambridge University Press 2007), and J.R. McNeill, *Mosquito Empires: Ecology and War in the Greater Caribbean, 1620–1914* (Cambridge: Cambridge University Press, 2010).

Index

Page numbers in *italics* refers to a table/figure